GEOGRAPHIES FOR ADVANCED STUDY

EDITED BY EMERITUS PROFESSOR S. H. BEAVER M.A. F.R.G.S.

Human Geography

2nd Edition

Geographies for Advanced Study
Edited by Emeritus Professor Stanley H. Beaver, M.A., F.R.G.S.

Human Geography

2nd Edition

Aimé Vincent Perpillou

PROFESSOR OF ECONOMIC AND POLITICAL
GEOGRAPHY AT THE SORBONNE

*Translated by the late E. D. Laborde,
sometime assistant master, Harrow School,
and S. H. Beaver.*

LONGMAN

Longman Group Limited London

Associated companies, branches and representatives throughout the world

Published in the United States of America by Longman inc., New York

First published 1966
Second edition and first appearance in paperback 1977

Library of Congress Cataloging in Publication Data
Perpillou, Aimé Vincent, 1902–
  Human Geography.

  (Geographies for advanced study)
  Bibliography: p.
  Includes index.
  1. Geography, Economic. I. Title. [DNLM:
1. Geography. 2. Ecology. GF51 P43h]
HF1025. P4313 1977 330.9 76–55302
ISBN 0–582–48571–1
ISBN 0–582–48572–X pbk.

Set in Monotype Times
and printed in Great Britain by
Richard Clay (The Chaucer Press) Ltd,
Bungay

CONTENTS

Part III Technical Factors and Stages in Human Emancipation

Part IV   Human Settlement

LIST OF PLATES

viii

ACKNOWLEDGMENTS

The photographs are reproduced by permission of the following:
Aerofilms Library Ltd: Plates 14, 21, 22, 29, 30, 34; S. H. Beaver:
Plates 10, 12, 19; Gabrielle Bertrand: Plate 26; Camera Press: Plates
2, 20; The National Film Board of Canada: Plate 18; J. Allan Cash:
Plates 16, 32; Fairchild Aerial Surveys, Inc: Plates 8, 33; Ewing
Galloway: Plate 5 and back of jacket; The Photographic Survey Corporation Ltd, Toronto, Canada: Plates 3, 11, 17 and front of jacket;
Paul Popper Ltd: Plates 1, 15, 23, 25; *Radio Times* Hulton Picture
Library: Plates 6, 7, 13, 35, 36, 37; Plates 4, 9, 24, 27, 28 and 31 are from
photographs by the author.

MAPS AND DIAGRAMS

EDITOR'S PREFACE

This book was specially written for this Series in the late 1950s. Unfortunately its translator, Dr. E. D. Laborde, died in 1962 before his task was accomplished; the first sixteen chapters are Dr. Laborde's work, and the remaining chapters were translated by Mrs. Laborde and the Editor. The lapse of time between the writing and the final printing of the book has naturally made necessary many textual modifications, and these have been effected by the Editor and Professor Perpillou, to whom the apologies of the Editor and the Publishers are due for the many delays which have occurred.

S. H. BEAVER

University of Keele
July 1965

PREFACE TO THE SECOND EDITION

The decade that has elapsed since the first edition of this book has seen many changes of methodology and emphasis within Geography. But the basic concern of the geographer remains the interpretation, in time and space, of man's relationship to his environment, both the physical environment and the social, economic and political environment that he himself has created. Professor Perpillou's volume, enriched by a new concluding chapter, many textual alterations and additions, and a re-cast bibliography, continues to uphold the French tradition of 'géographie humaine'. I trust that the translation of all the new material, for which I am responsible, maintains the high standard of Dr. Laborde's original version.

S. H. BEAVER

Eccleshall, Staffordshire
March 1976

INTRODUCTION

It is only proper for human geography to submit to a kind of self-examination if it is to justify its place among the sciences which study the earth and man. Even in the last century the aim and scope of this field of enquiry was already causing heated controversy, the echoes of which still resound in the vigorous language of Lucien Febvre ; [1] and today there is still in human geography no real unity of method and indeed no real homogeneity of content. This is one of the peculiarly distinctive features of this branch of knowledge, which is related to both the natural and social sciences without ever completely identifying itself or its aims or methods with either the former or the latter.

However intertwined may be the bounds of the field of study of the various sciences, and whatever may be the complexity of their mutual borrowings, there are well-recognised spheres of mathematics, of physics, or of biology, and so on. Each of these sciences has its own aim and peculiar method ; but both aim and method are universal. Nothing of this sort occurs in the domain of human geography, in which the mode of conception and classification of facts does not depend on strict rules, but mainly on habits of thought, on the spirit and even on the system of teaching which, from country to country, and even from one university to another, places geography in different faculties. Today, these problems of definition and method, which might be thought out of date, still haunt the minds of young geographers and even international conferences of scholars.

Some lay special emphasis on the close relation between human geography and the natural sciences. 'Is human geography not mainly the ecology of man ?' they ask. The study of the physical and biological background is a necessary introduction to anthropology and so to human geography. Some brilliant investigation in medical geography and the recent works to which it has given rise show that the study of man cannot do without either the discipline or the evidence of the natural sciences. Another school of thought gives 'political man' priority over the individual and sees human geography mainly as the science of societies. The essential problem

---

[1] L. Febvre, *La Terre et l'évolution humaine*, 1922 ; English translation, *A geographical introduction to history*, 1925.

of human geography is, therefore, to recognise how far this branch of knowledge differs from others whose field of enquiry is more or less the same.

In the last edition of his *Principles of Human Geography* (1934) Huntington enlightens us about his own notion of the aims and methods of human geography. His main thesis is to explain by means of the various natural factors of relief, distance from the sea, soil, and climate, man's economic life and the state of civilisation reached by different communities. For this purpose he describes a number of large areas in which the return for human toil and application have not had the same degree of success. He reviews in turn hot lands, monsoon lands, deserts, cold countries, and countries with a temperate maritime climate, the last mentioned being in his opinion the most favoured by nature and the most suitable for supporting the higher forms of civilisation. In this account existing facts are connected with other existing facts that depend on quite a different chain of facts, and this is done without any apparent necessity to look to the past for an explanation of the present. Everything seems to go on in a world without a past. For that reason, of course, settlement and the changing forms of dwellings have but an insignificant place in a human geography which takes no account of the freedom of choice between the opportunities afforded by the physical environment, a freedom which has always been had by even the most primitive communities.

These American notions are opposed by those of a German geographer, Otto Maull, who in the 'thirties had published a kind of manual of human geography. In this work on *Anthropogeography* there was a remarkable and significant omission of economic geography. There were two important chapters, one on the races of man, with amplified passages on acclimatisation and diseases (*Rassengeographie*) ; the other on political geography and particularly on the state. Its ideas reflect those of pre-war German *Geopolitik*, a study of the functions of the state, intended to base German imperialism on what were bogus scientific principles rather than to set out methods of investigation proper to a true science. An enquiry into the nature of states, the extent of their territory, their possible expansion, their forces of expansion, and their destiny, may certainly come within the scope of human geography ; but the study of such topics should be analytical, since they are clearly relative. The moment they aspire to scientific dogmatism they cease to fall within the scope of human geography. Way back in the nineteenth century, in Germany, F. Ratzel had defined the basis of a 'political geography' as the study of the structure and evolution of States and of human societies in relation to their geographical space and their cultural background; but the methods and objectives of this new geographic discipline were subsequently diverted and ossified into a body of non-scientific doctrine, that had nothing in common with Ratzel's work, by the disciples of *Geopolitik* during the first third of the twentieth century.

In France, human geography has rejected both American materialism and German ideology. Albert Demangeon, one of the leading French scholars, insisted again and again on the widening of the horizons of the field of study and on the exclusion of dogmatism from it ; and he emphasised its connexion with history and the social sciences rather than with the natural sciences, since these are more prone to bow to determinism. He tried to make his students familiar with works which were most suitable to the topics of human geography and would lead them to reflect on its many-sided problems. During a course of study he would suggest a discussion of the works of a sociologist such as Maunier, an ethnographer like Mauss, an economist like Siegfried, or a medieval historian like Marc Bloch. In the same year he would make them examine *London Life and Labour*, the report of an enquiry on London by a group of economists, town-planners, and sociologists. Only at the end of such an approach did Demangeon define the aims and methods of human geography, in doing which he referred to the teachings of Vidal de la Blache. His conclusions, set out at the beginning of his *Problèmes de géographie humaine*, define the geographer's aim and specify the three governing principles of his method.

Human geography cannot be reduced to mere ecology, in spite of the attractiveness of the works of Humboldt and Berghaus, for too much of the relation between man and the physical environment is outside the competence of the geographer. For example, Demangeon considers that it is not the geographer's business to study the races of man, even though certain human races seem to belong to a clearly defined domain. Environmental influence does not in fact prevail in certain hereditary features whose effect is visible on the anatomy, physiology, and even pathology of some human groups. Among these hereditary features which are independent of environment the colour of the skin is the most readily noticed, but physiologists have demonstrated, notably in connexion with malaria, an unequal capacity for resistance in various racial groups ; for example, taken all round, the Melanesians and Polynesians seem to be the least susceptible of men to malaria. Demangeon also emphasised that the short stature and flat faces of the Bigudens of Pont l'Abbé could be explained by the selective strengthening of certain features by long evolution away from the main streams of migration, and by the persistence of archaic types owing to inbreeding as well as by Uralo-Altaic hereditary influence due to a very remote migration. It is not the geographer's business to decide the point, for human geography is above all the study of human communities in their relation to the environment in so far as they are societies and groups working together.

Human geography should begin its investigations with communities and not individuals, because the idea of aggregation is essential in mankind. Three fields of research lie open to the geographer :

1. The study of the human race, that living force which makes use of natural resources. Its numbers, distribution, and varieties lie within the scope of demographic geography, which is an important branch of human geography.

2. The study of the occupation of the land of human communities, from the most modest hamlet to the complex which forms the state.

3. The study of the utilisation of natural resources ; the exploitation of the major climatic belts of the globe, each with its concomitants of cultivated plants and domestic animals ; the exploitation of sea and mountain ; the description of the main areas of production and directions of trade : all these incorporate in the field of human geography the whole content of economic geography.

When the aims of human geography are understood and its scope defined, there is still a need for a definition of its methods and the means which it uses. In human geography there exists no constant force of determinism arising from natural factors. This cannot be too often repeated, for the illusion of determinism is persistent.[1] Causality acts only in an uncertain, local, and temporary manner in contradiction to the philosophic notion of it. Owing to the untrammelled freedom of his will, man is himself a cause of decisive disturbances in the mechanical development of physical factors as well as in the more subtle control of biological agents. It is unnecessary to repeat that islands are not always foredoomed to a maritime life, since such a life comes about mainly owing to contact with civilisation (though Polynesia may provide examples to the contrary). Nor need it be recalled that the English took to the sea only through contacts with Scandinavian, Venetian, and Hanseatic traders. In the same way, agriculture is more than a function of the quality of the soil, for there are fertile lands which remain untilled and poor lands which are intensively cultivated. The full use of natural advantages, the response to the suggestions of nature,

[1] See, for example, A. F. Martin, 'The necessity for determinism', Trans. Inst. Brit. Geog., 1951, 1-11.

depends essentially on the technical skill and degree of civilisation of the human groups living in the region. By means of irrigation and the scientific use of fertilisers man very often masters the productivity of the soil wherever the climate and lack of balance in the region do not impose absolute limitations.

On the environment studied by the geographer the most distant reactions from elsewhere converge and are amalgamated by the daily increasing complexity of trade and communication. The setting up of American synthetic rubber factories on one side of the world may ruin the *heveas* on the other side, though the trees have every advantage of sun, climate, and even quality.

Nowhere does nature offer anything but possibilities, the use of which depends on human initiative. This fundamental principle allows one to avoid many over-simple explanations. After the work of such men as Davis and Bowman it is surprising at the present time to see some North American schools spreading a neodeterminism as childish as it is useless. How can one hold nowadays that Germany, with its politically bracing climate, would infallibly subjugate the little states of central Europe which were politically weaker! In emphasising Huntington's or Griffith Taylor's exaggerations we cannot avoid condemning their fallacious arguments in matters of human geography. Such arguments lead inevitably to the surrender of the principle of observation to that of system and induce those who abandon themselves to such fallacies to present exploded theories of a bygone age as original discoveries, for it was by Montesquieu that the geographical determinism dear to Huntington was first expressed in its most over-simplified form. But Montesquieu had the excuse of not being a geographer and had no pretence to being one.

The revival of these fallacies is possible only because human geography is so easily likened to sociology or, more generally, to social science anxious to elaborate general theories rather than to grasp what is peculiar and perhaps unique in phenomena. Geography is not a science of abstractions. Its generalisations are valid only on condition of being constantly faced with reality, that is, with a territorial basis. In the most primitive communities such as hunting tribes the use of the same hunting grounds according to precise and often very complex rules creates a solidarity which is independent and often stronger than the ties of blood. Rural communities more than any others demonstrate the strength of their attachment to the soil in, for instance, the grouping of dwellings, the organisation of the ownership of cultivated land, the common use of material, wells, and irrigation works. This attachment, the study of which falls to the geographer, does not exclude other social bonds of a psychological kind, such as kinship or religion ;

but these lie within the scope of the sociologist or ethnologist. Human geography ought above all to preserve a territorial basis. It studies a human complex not in isolation, *in abstracto*, but in a geographical unit characterised as much by its purely physical features as by its material relation with other areas, whether adjacent or remote. In such an exactly defined field of study geography is able to seize on the unquestionable relation between man and the earth, but care should be taken not to widen its scope. Extrapolation, hasty generalisation, and baseless comparisons should be avoided in every serious study in human geography.

Furthermore, as Demangeon used to say, a geographical fact does not acquire a precise, concrete meaning until its place on the map is exactly indicated with proper clearness and, if possible, in connexion with other geographical phenomena. By keeping strictly to the rule of placing on the map the results of research human geography preserves the positional basis fundamental to its character.

Finally, human geography, unlike other social sciences, cannot be satisfied with the study of facts that are actually visible, but must turn to history to discover the original appearance and past evolution of the facts. Diving into archives is as indispensable for the geographer as for the historian. The notion of evolution faces us every time the reason for what we see escapes us or seems to contradict the logic of the existing environment, using this word in its widest sense. Nothing worth while can be written on a topic of rural or urban geography without constant appeal to history and its sources. The geography of an old country with a European civilisation cannot be understood without a knowledge of the history of the deforestation and clearing of its land, the draining of its valleys, the control of water, and, lastly, of the partition of its soil. Now, this slow mastery of the land, pursued under different social systems, by means of techniques and agricultural systems which have changed again and again in the course of ages, by different social classes and at times even by different racial stocks, has left in archives and customs clearer traces of these episodes than exist on the soil itself.

In so far as it is above all the definition and explanation of a kind of contract between Land and Man, human geography presupposes an awareness of the notion of 'humanised space', which can only be defined by the close interdependence of the physical environment and human societies, quantitatively and qualitatively assessed; some of these relationships will be inherited from the past, others will be active at the present time, whilst yet others will be oriented towards the future by the complex interplay of politico-economic and sociopsychological factors. This precise definition of geographic space, subtler and more synthetic than the former more general notion of 'environment', is now one of the major and most fundamental problems confronting human geographers. As the twentieth century draws towards its close, the problem has taken on new dimensions, because of the extraordinary acceleration in the exchange of ideas, the shrinking of distance and the sharp interpenetration of forms of civilisation and modes of life that characterise the modern world.

When seen in this light, human geography is a science of patient research rather than one of spectacular generalisations. It leads neither to laws nor to definitions. It regroups its facts and arranges them in series which it then compares with other series from other parts of the earth or found in the more or less distant past. It arrives at partial and cautious syntheses which are suggested by the facts themselves and not deduced *a priori*. A deep sense of relativity should be the cardinal virtue of true human geography.

FIG. 1.—MODES OF LIFE AND TYPES OF ECONOMY
(Pages xix–xxii)

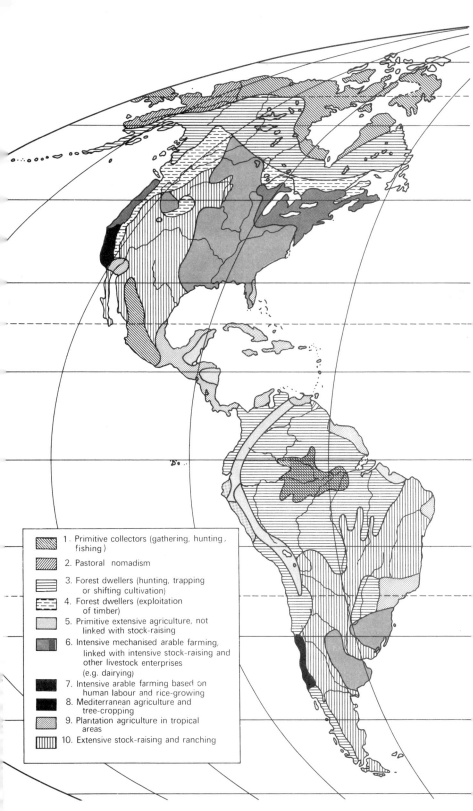

1. Primitive collectors (gathering, hunting, fishing)

2. Pastoral nomadism

3. Forest dwellers (hunting, trapping or shifting cultivation)

4. Forest dwellers (exploitation of timber)

5. Primitive extensive agriculture, not linked with stock-raising

6. Intensive mechanised arable farming, linked with intensive stock-raising and other livestock enterprises (e.g. dairying)

7. Intensive arable farming based on human labour and rice-growing

8. Mediterranean agriculture and tree-cropping

9. Plantation agriculture in tropical areas

10. Extensive stock-raising and ranching

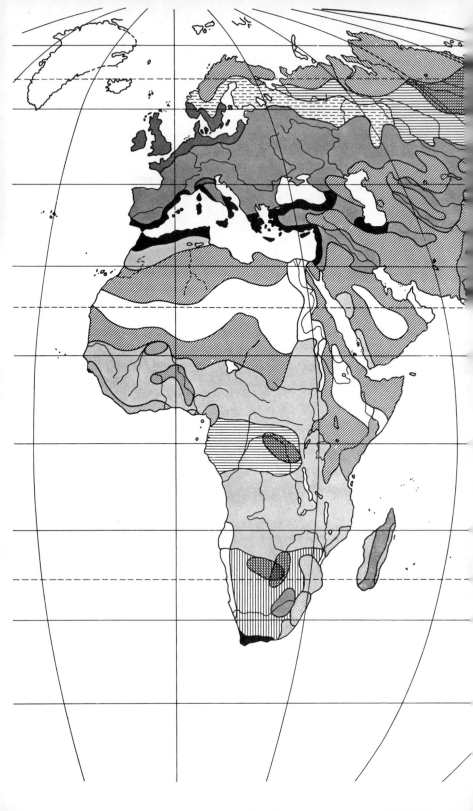

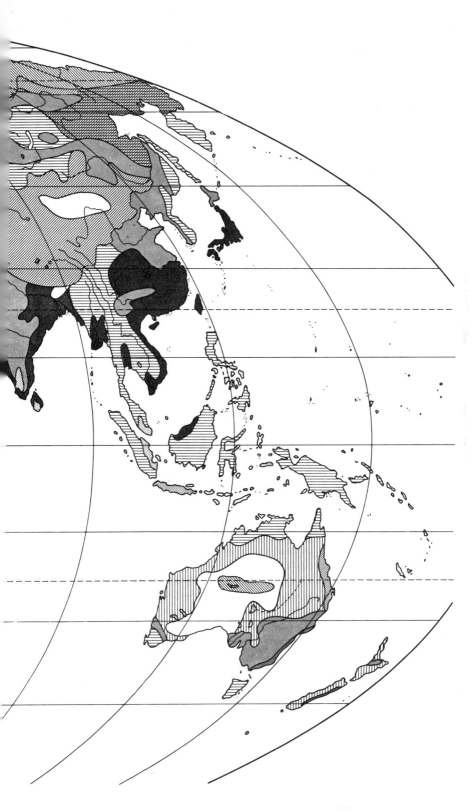

PART I

MAN AND THE FACTORS OF
HUMAN EVOLUTION

CHAPTER 1

MAN AND THE NATURAL ENVIRONMENT

In all the natural conditions that help to determine the development of human life climate plays a predominant part, for it is the chief factor in the formation of the botanical environment and it decides the vegetable and animal associations. Hence, the main climatic belts of the earth form the basic framework within which human activity takes place. Although many communities have moulded and mastered nature, they are nonetheless bound to submit to certain of her laws. The more primitive the community and the more rudimentary its techniques, the more heavily do these laws weigh on them. But in view of the achievements of the great modern industrial states, which seem to laugh at physical conditions and completely dominate nature by their technical powers, it is right to enquire into the price paid for this artificial ascendancy over the environment.

INFLUENCE OF CLIMATIC FACTORS

The character of the vegetation is strictly dependent on the conditions of temperature. Botanists and scientific agriculturalists have proved that every plant has a specific zero below which it cannot live. There is also an optimum temperature in which the plant is at its greatest vigour. For each of the functions of vegetable life, whether germination, foliation, blossoming, or fructification a specific zero and optimum can be observed in the temperature.

During the last twenty years or so these ideas of limitation have probably seemed to lose their strictness. The selection carried out by Soviet agriculturalists, together with the process of 'vernalisation', has effectively pushed up the polar limit of several cultivated plants and brought under cultivation areas hitherto barren. But to achieve cultivation in the Arctic the natural limits of the plants have been modified only by the artificial creation of veritable biological monsters which are the offspring of man's ingenuity and would certainly not survive his disappearance. Such achievements merely prove that human techniques can in favourable conditions modify the limitations imposed by nature. It should not be concluded that this power of modification is complete, for in many plants the limit of cultivation still coincides with the belts of optimum temperature observed by botanists. Thus, the northern limit of the regions in which the date palm bears ripe fruit coincides almost exactly with the mean annual isotherm for 19° C. The essential factor in the limit of the vine seems to be the temperature in summer, for the grape ripens only in those countries in which the mean temperature from April to October exceeds 15° C. Similarly, it has been calculated that maize ripens at the period of the year when the sum of the daily maximum temperatures, counting only those days with a maximum of 13·5° C or over, has reached 2,500°C. Plants are affected by temperature far more than animals are, and, in spite of partial successes, it would still be impossible today to acclimatise a plant in places where the temperature régime is utterly different from that of the original environment. Cultivation has been undertaken in the Arctic only with cereals, fodder, roots, and fruit trees which have been accustomed to grow in continental climates where the winters are harsh or even severe.

The succession of the seasons regulates the cycle of plant life, and, consequently, man's periodical occupations or movements. Agricultural work is arranged according to the times of plant growth and rest. Seasonal displacements of shepherds to and fro between mountain and plain obey the cycle of changes in the vegetable cover. Even the herring, cod, and sardine fisheries are affected by the rhythm of the seasons.

Since temperature is the vital factor in the distribution of plants, it is evident that their growth is essentially dependent on the total amount of insolation during the year; that is, on the number of warm days. Hence, botanically speaking, Köppen's cold, temperate, and hot belts have a precise geographical significance.

The conditions due to sunlight and the luminosity of the atmosphere are as important as those due to warmth. Now, the distribution of light varies with latitude. The maximum duration of sunshine in any one day increases towards the Poles, being 14 hours 34 minutes in lat. 40°, 15 hr. 45 min. in lat. 50°, 17 hr. 44 min. in lat. 60°. In lat. 68° 30′ it reaches 24 hours in summer. In cold countries the action of light hastens growth. For instance, spring barley ripens in 107 days in southern Sweden, but in only 89 days in Lapland in spite of the far lower temperature, this being compensated for by a far longer period of insolation. The figures for spring wheat show that in lat. 48° 30′ in Alsace there is an interval of 145 days between sowing and ripening. This contrasts with the 114 days at Skibotten in lat. 69° 30′. But the 145 days in Alsace have only 1,795 hours of daylight against 2,486 hours during the 114 days in Lapland. Thus, in polar regions the intensity of light partly compensates for the shortness of the warm season and explains the rapidity of the vegetative process in plants. In the Soviet Union as in the Canadian North and Alaska farmers have skilfully taken advantage of this compensation.

All plants need water. For them water is not only a constituent element that must be renewed, but also the vehicle which carries their food into them. Yet they are more tolerant of irregularities in the rainfall régime than of a disturbance in their optimum temperature system. Xerophilous plants differ from hygrophytes, the former being adapted to drought, the latter to damp. Hence in dry regions the vegetable world presents a floristic mixture, an outward appearance, and a woody character that make the plants peculiar and so indirectly affect human life. The means of livelihood which a country can give to man depends in large measure on the quantity of water that can be supplied to the plants. This accounts for the fact that besides the three great belts of temperature there is ecologically a dry zone which encroaches on the other three and is characterised by a lack of water and man's efforts to adapt his mode of life to this deficiency.

All things considered, the division of the earth's surface into major climatic zones, each providing a unique geographic space for plant and animal life and for human enterprise, retains its value in contemporary geography. At the present time, 'zonal geography', more synthetic than the 'regional geography' of the early twentieth century, bases its teaching and research, without being too constrained by mathematical definitions, on the character of the great ·and fundamental zones defined by Köppen in 1884.

THE ESSENTIAL PART PLAYED BY VEGETATION

Plants have the property of being able to take in the elements of air and soil and to change them into food for man. To become food inorganic matter must pass through a plant. 'In drawing from the air nutritive elements which plants alone can break down', wrote Vidal de la Blache, 'the vegetation is like a living food-factory.'

The vegetable kingdom supplies food for the animal kingdom. This it does directly to herbivores and indirectly to carnivores. The vegetation of a country is always in harmony with the types of animals in it. If, for example, one should wonder why the great pachyderms disappeared from Europe before the historical era, or why the horse, which lived in America during the Quaternary epoch, had completely disappeared before man came on the scene, the answer would seem to be that these radical upheavals in the animal kingdom merely reflected changes in the plant cover, forests having replaced steppes, and steppes forests.

Thus by the operation of both the plant and animal worlds the chief modes of life, especially among primitive man, are placed in natural settings determined by climate and vegetation. The belts of vegetation, covering more of the earth's surface than is covered by bare rock, snow, and ice, correspond broadly to particular modes of life. These main natural units are therefore plainly 'human regions'. In each of them man's life is subject to the power of the natural environment as represented by the climatic régime and the plant and animal associations. Over this environment man has a control which is more or less effective according to the efficiency of his tools and the ingenuity of the techniques he has invented. Different human groups may adapt themselves differently to similar environments, but whatever their efforts, they can none of them free themselves wholly from it. The instance of pre-Columbian America, taken from a thousand others, may be used to point to the close correspondence between natural regions and modes of life among peoples with more or less primitive techniques. On either side of the equator there was a symmetrical repetition of types of civilisation closely related to the climatic conditions. In the fjords of Patagonia and British Columbia there were fishing communities; buffalo hunters in the prairies and guanaco hunters in the pampas; maize cultivators in the tropical and subtropical regions; and cassava growers in the equatorial region.

Taken all round, the earth's surface presents four types of regions to man for his activities. These are cold, temperate, warm, and dry. They have existed ever since the present climate has prevailed; that is, since Neolithic times. This period in man's history succeeded the Palaeolithic Age, from which it differed profoundly in climate, mode of life, and techniques. The Palaeolithic Age is known to have ended at a time when the climate was cold. It was marked in Europe by an extension of the ice-cap and in the deserts of the Old World by conditions of humidity which enabled steppes abounding in game to spread over areas now dry and bare. For mankind this period meant the dissemination of the hunting mode of life over which climate exercised a strong and rigid influence.

With the Neolithic Age the face of the earth changed, and the evolution which resulted in the present conditions of human life was already beginning in Europe. Finds of this age prove that from its beginning human life was lived with the same scenery, the same plants, the same animals, and, with some slight variations, the same climate as today. Among the finds are the bones of our chief domestic animals (ox, sheep, goat, pig, and dog) and the seeds and other traces of our principal cultivated plants.

Although the Neolithic Age does not mark the farthest point in the past to which research in human geography may go, since it is possible to study the distribution and life of the palaeolithic hunters, it must at least be recognised that the safest starting point for the study of an agricultural community is to be found in the people of this new age, possessing as they did the very elements of our civilisation. Neolithic man was in fact in possession of all the techniques of the cultivator and the craftsman by means of which the country-folk of Europe have lived almost up to our times, though they are not yet all known to some of the primitive and backward peoples of today. Cultivation of the soil, domestication of animals, pottery-making, and weaving were the main inventions of neolithic man. He built villages, made clearings, and organised his fields; and apparently he worshipped the seasons and Mother Earth. Some undoubtedly practised human sacrifice to maintain the fertility of their fields.

This soil-based civilisation was not established everywhere at the same time throughout the world. It appeared late in high latitudes, in Scandinavia, for instance, where the retreat of the ice-cap was slow in taking place. If de Morgan is to be believed, bronze was probably known to the Egyptians about 5000 B.C., at which time there flourished in Picardy the earliest neolithic civilisation, known as the Campignian. The Bronze Age did not begin in Sweden, however, until the eighteenth or seventeenth century B.C. Among the peoples of eastern Siberia the beginning of the Bronze Age does not go back farther than the first year of the Christian era.

As a rule, progress was slow in other aspects of this civilisation. The use of iron dates only from the fifth or third century B.C. in Sweden, whilst Italy had been familiar with it since the twelfth century B.C. But once formed and uniformly spread, the civilisation moulded in the Neolithic Age has undergone no changes but those due to human intelligence, for there have been no further major climatic oscillations, and conditions generally have constantly remained more or less as they are today.

Huntington accepts the occurrence of important climatic variations within historical times. He quotes in proof of them the disappearance of cities in Asia Minor, like Palmyra, which though flourishing at the beginning of the Christian era has left only a few ruins in the desert. Other Roman towns, precariously built on the fringe of the African desert, probably succumbed to a progressive desiccation of the country. Lastly, changes of level in inland seas like the Caspian have revealed climatic cycles corresponding to an alternation of rainy and dry periods. Huntington even attributes the agrarian revolution which took place in Italy about 200 B.C. to a decrease in rainfall, with the result that the yield of corn was less, the peasants were so impoverished as to be forced to sell their holdings, the system of large farms (*latifundia*) was started, and there was an exodus of peasants to the towns. He carries his paradox to the point of connecting the changes in climate with important historical events like the revolt of the slaves, the agrarian troubles at the time of the Gracchi, and the barbarian invasion, which according to him were all provoked by the desiccation of pasture lands in Asia and the consequent migration of the starving people towards less arid lands. None of these conclusions stand examination of the facts. Diggings in Palmyra, for instance, have shown that the growth of the city as a great trade-route town, together with the multiplication of cisterns and *foggaras*, was the cause of the fertility of the surrounding district. It was to Palmyra that in the days of Rome the district owed the existence of villages set in well-watered fields and gardens as well as the use of the pastures in the nearby mountains. The destruction of the city by Aurelian, and no hypothetical change of climate, was alone responsible for the abandonment of the hydraulic installations and, consequently, for the desiccation of the district. Today, the climate of Palmyra is no drier than in the third century of our era. The *fellahin* sow and reap corn in the beds of the wadis and on the mountain slopes. They are more afraid of the passage of Bedawin sheep than of the lack of water. Rational planning carried out with capital accumulated at Palmyra from the caravan traffic had succeeded in bringing cultivation and fruitfulness to a region in which agricultural possibilities are latent and which could still flourish again today. Contrary to Huntington's views, the desert has not advanced into the Palmyra district during the last five centuries; the truth is that in the hundred years between the Antonines and Aurelian there existed a human society sufficiently knowledgeable and with the means to transform into a rich oasis an arid strip inhabited before and depopulated after the fall of the city.

Although it may be granted that periodic variations in existing climatic conditions, during which long sequences of dry years are in fact experienced in regions of climatic extremes, these are really only cyclic episodes of short duration. There is no proof that within historical times permanent, increasing variations have occurred in the climatic complex of the globe. At most can it be accepted, as Emm. de Martonne suggests, that certain local modifications in the organic environment or superficial physical phenomena within the border regions of the polar and warm climates, are delayed sequels of the great climatic upheavals which accompanied the end of the last ice age. But, on the whole, there is no evidence for thinking that our climate, with its four basic aspects, differs from the one that prevailed at the dawn of the Neolithic Age.

THE MAIN ANTHROPOGEOGRAPHICAL REGIONS

In each of the earth's bioclimatic zones the nature of the climate, flora, and fauna gives rise to general conditions which may or may not favour the formation of human communities and the development of their activities. As a rule, cold countries comprise regions with long winters, with mean temperatures below 0°C for at least three months in the year and a mean above 10° C during five months at most. Nearly all these lands are in North America or the Soviet Union and they extend northwards from lat. 50°. In Scandinavia they do not really begin south of lat. 60°. The increasing severity of winter northwards in these land areas makes it necessary to distinguish between polar lands and the countries more righly called cold.

Whether the climate is oceanic, as in Norway, or continental, as in Canada or Siberia, cold regions enjoy summers that are at times fairly warm and last, depending on latitude and geographical situation, between two and four months, thus permitting the growth of forest and the practice of agriculture. Here stretches the great forest of conifers and birch, almost encircling the earth, a forest that is still intact in the *tayga* of Siberia. Thanks to the abundance of berries and nuts, it is the home of large numbers of land animals that retire into holes in winter. Besides these, there are squirrels and martens as well as many wolves, bears, and various species of deer. Owing to the shortness of the vegetative period, agriculture is possible in only a few sheltered spots and at the cost of much effort. Furthermore, in this forest region the soil, which is termed *podzol* in the Soviet Union, is of slight fertility. In the long, damp winters of the climate the soil has been leached and drained of all its mineral elements. Added to this, not far below the surface there have formed impermeable layers rather like hard-pan (*alios*), and this makes the mediocre conditions far worse. These factors all limit the chances of agriculture and stock-rearing, but on the other hand, the existence of the vast forest makes the country a hunting ground for fur-bearing animals and a source of forest products. Hence the forests of the North are the world's chief source of timber and the greatest producers of cellulose and wood pulp for the world market.

Polar lands are marked by very long winters and very short summers. The temperature rises above 0° C for hardly as long as two months in the year. In Spitzbergen, for instance, the mean for February is −21·8° C, that for July 3° C. At Verkhoyansk the January mean is −48° C and the July mean 16° C. At Danmarkshaven in Greenland in lat. 76° 46′ N. the mean for February is −28° C and for July 4° C. In these latitudes all life is dominated by the fact that the soil remains permanently frozen, often to a great depth, so that the only vegetation possible is tundra, consisting of mosses in the swampy areas and of lichens in the drier parts. Trees, of which the dwarf birch is typical, are rare, small, and shrub-like, and there is no wood for man's uses; hence the economic importance of driftwood brought down by the Siberian rivers during the break-up of the ice and scattered by the currents along the shores of the Arctic Sea.

The animals living on the tundra are herbivorous mammals like the reindeer and musk-ox, rodents, and carnivores like the glutton, Arctic fox, wolf, and sable, which prey on the rodents. Ice-capped lands, including most of Greenland, afford little space for herbivores and carnivores, and animals like the polar bear, seal, walrus, and penguin live in the sea, the mammals having their skin lined with a thick layer of blubber which serves both as a protection from cold and a reserve of nourishment. In winter reindeer have thick coats of long hair. They migrate according to season from one feeding ground to the next. The caribou is a forest animal, but other species of reindeer move regularly to and fro between the Arctic coast and the edge of the forest. In summer they range along the shores which are then carpeted with lichen, and they cross in herds from island to island. In winter they often collect in huge numbers, pressing so closely together that the condensation of their breath in the still, cold air forms a bank of fog that conceals them from their pursuers. Life is difficult and almost impossible for man, unless he can make a small shelter to protect himself from the cold air. The outposts of civilisation—meteorological stations or strategic bases in both the American and Asiatic Arctic—in which a handful of men live cannot be regarded as adapted to the polar environment, since they are maintained by a steady supply of specially prepared food and by a scientifically devised outfit together with a large stock of fuel and power from other regions. Existence in a country without a knowledge of its difficulties and detailed resources is not adaptation. Life cannot really be supported by agriculture in the polar regions. Since the vegetable kingdom provides no food, man must live on meat and fat alone. He depends wholly on hunting or in some places on certain species of reindeer which he has domesticated, which furnish him with food, clothes, and fuel, and whose migrations he is bound to follow. Human life is a constant struggle leaving little time for the satisfaction of the higher needs and for progress towards the refinements of civilisation.

Temperate regions are peculiar in having a climate with four seasons. These are due to differences in temperature, which interpose two intermediate seasons, spring and autumn, between the two basic seasons of winter and summer. Owing to these transitional seasons, there are no sudden changes from warmth to cold and vice versa, as there are in cold regions. This explains the lengthening of the vegetative period, which makes possible the ripening of fruit and grain. Nor are there sharp contrasts between wet and dry seasons, as there are in hot countries, for the rainfall is distributed more or less evenly through the months. The yearly occurrence of a winter, which though short prevents man from sowing or harvesting and forces him to live all the year round on the yield of the summer harvest, inculcates forethought and thrift as chief among the vital duties of civilised society.

The temperate regions are far less extensive than the cold, warm, or dry regions. On the continent of Eurasia they occupy central and western Europe and, at the opposite end of the continent, northern China. In America they include the eastern United States, most of the Mississippi valley, and British Columbia. In the southern hemisphere their area is small and restricted to the southeast of Australia, all of New Zealand, and the country around the River Plate, together with a few mountain-ringed islands in southern Chile. In the southern hemisphere the climate is marked by greater uniformity and less clear-cut seasons than in the northern hemisphere, whose vast populations are mainly of the white race and have outstripped the peoples of other regions in reaching a high degree of technical civilisation.

What natural conditions has the climate of the temperate regions afforded for human settlement? Mountains apart, two vegetation-types are found: forest, consisting mainly of broad-leaved trees, and steppe, which is now chiefly grassland, but originally had more trees than are on it today. Forest used to prevail wherever rain fell at all seasons; that is, in districts farthest north or nearest the sea. Steppe prevailed in inland districts where conditions were less favourable to the growth of trees; that is, where the summers were drier and the winters colder. Such conditions existed in the treeless parts of Hungary, around the lower Danube, in southern Russia, northern China, and the prairies of North America.

Broad-leaved forest and steppe afforded space whose soil could be used where cultivated plants and domestic animals existed. In the forest areas in these latitudes 'grey soil' has developed in milder and fairly damp climate in the shade of broad-leaved trees. It is a moderately strong retainer of humus, with plenty of acid organic matter, fairly well exposed to evaporation in summer, of fine texture, and free from hard-pan. It may also be yellow, sandy on the surface, fairly rich too in organic matter, and mixed with a more or less brown clay. In the steppe regions the presence of rich herbaceous vegetation together with the absence of trees has permitted the formation of another kind of soil known in southern Russia as *chernoziom*. It covers a region whose annual rainfall is scarcely more than 200 to 500 mm. The lower layers are of silt covered with a thick mantle of humus resulting from the secular decomposition of vegetable matter and having a mean thickness of 1 metre. This soil is black, includes in its composition calcareous or mineral concretions, and has proved of great fertility on being tilled.

It is characteristic of temperate lands that in neither climate nor vegetation do they place any insurmountable obstacle in the way of human settlement and that plants and animals associated with the earliest human communities grow readily in them. It seems that most of these plants and animals come from the steppe after first finding a footing in those outposts of the steppe, the forest glades. They then invaded the forest area after man had removed the trees. On the fertile soil of the former forest grasses like wheat, oats, and rye have found it easy to grow in the favourable climate, in whose long vegetative periods they have time to ripen. The cereals were joined by plants which flourished originally as weeds of the field before being selected and cultivated by man. Such was the case with flax, the oldest textile fibre. Wheat is typical of the plants that man has adapted and cultivated to meet his needs. After infiltrating with the help of irrigation into countries with a low rainfall, it has passed through the adjacent temperate regions, where improved methods of breeding have enabled it to penetrate into the cold regions beyond. Its yield and food value have caused it to be regarded everywhere as the basis of the diet.

In hot lands the divisions of the year are governed not by temperature, but by rainfall. There is neither winter nor summer in them, and the annual range of temperature is small. On the other hand, there are usually clearly marked wet and dry seasons. Europeans who live in the tropics call the wet season 'winter', but that is because it keeps them indoors, just as winter does in cold countries. It makes the bush impossible for travel and closes the highways constructed at great cost by governments. The dry season, which in general is pleasant for Europeans and allows easy movement about the country, owes its name of 'summer' merely to the activity which it permits in cultivation and transport.

Hot countries cover an immense area of the globe, occupying a good third of the continents, especially in the Amazon basin in South America, the Congo basin in Africa, and in India, Indo-China, southern China, and the East Indies in Asia. The regions with almost continuous rain must be distinguished from those with periodic rains. The former correspond more or less to the equatorial belt, which is marked by short, heavy showers, a damp, exhausting climate, permanently high temperature, a small annual range, and great diurnal heat, which has given rise to the saying that night is the winter of the tropics. This type of climate prevails in the basin of the Congo and around the lower Niger, where the temperature seldom falls below 20° C and where the annual range scarcely exceeds 2° C, but where four days out of seven are rainy. In the basin of the Amazon 245 days of rain and a temperature range of less than 2° C have been recorded at Pará.

In regions with periodic rains there is a sharp difference between the wet and dry seasons. The latter lasts nine months at St Louis in

Mali, three months at Libreville, six months at Majunga, four months at Caracas, five months at Vera Cruz in Mexico; seven months at Bombay, five months in Madras, four months at Hanoi, and three months at Saigon; whilst at Shanghai only the month of December is really dry.

These two types of hot climate are reflected in the character of the vegetation and, consequently, in the conditions they afford to human life. In the equatorial belt the climate favours long-lived plants, like trees, and plants with slow vegetation, like those that put out leaves and fruit only every eighteen or twenty months. Hence, in the wettest regions there is a growth of perennial vegetation, chiefly dense rain forest. The vegetation is so luxuriant, so tangled, that man can neither penetrate it nor clear it away. Even when he has succeeded in clearing a corner of the forest, trees tend to cover lost ground again. In this region the forest is far more hostile to man than in the temperate lands. It often forms an invincible obstacle. Even the plantations of *heveas* in Malaysia, Sumatra, Amazonia or on the coast of Liberia are but outposts of a powerful civilisation which keeps its hold over its conquests at great expense. Animal life is scarce in the forest, except on the tops of the trees and on the edges of the mass of vegetation, where it is plentiful. The rivers contain a proliferating fauna, in which even the small fry are apt to be dangerous. Mammals and birds are so few that the pygmies of the Congo have to travel far to find game.

The regions with a long dry season cover large, more or less open spaces. In one place they are savannas, that is, vast areas of tall grass dotted here and there with lone trees; in other places they are scrub with widely spaced little trees; in others, again, they are parkland with open forest in which large glades occur here and there. These grasslands still support the greatest reserves of game in the world in the shape of herds of herbivores which can move about easily in the grass   Nowhere else is animal iife more plentiful. It includes antelopes, buffaloes, rhinoceroses, zebus, elephants, and zebras, not to mention the lions, tigers, panthers, wolves, jackals, hyænas, etc., which hunt and eat them. They are all swift-footed animals, but cannot penetrate into the depths of the forest.

The same contrast is seen once again in the opportunities which each of these regions offers to man. In the equatorial belt the forest is a repellent environment in which man can gain ground only with difficulty and but for a short time. Much of the soil is lateritic and has almost wholly lost its lime, potash, and magnesia, keeping only its aluminium and iron. Hence, its yields are mainly forest products. It is thought too that the rain forest has been the principal factor in the development of lateritic soil. When the land has been cleared of trees and cultivated, it produces only roots and tubers, which are easily planted, grow quickly, and demand more from the atmosphere than from the soil. A few trees, like the banana, coconut, and some varieties of palm yield fruit in plenty almost without any form of cultivation. In these regions man is dominated by nature, but supplied with his primitive needs; so he remains improvident and restricted to a vegetable diet, which is poor in nitrogenous matter and food value.

On the other hand, the part played by the dry season is vital in regions with a periodic rainfall, for it has led to the development of a form of agriculture based on the cultivation of food plants like rice and millet. It calls for regular work and forethought, and sometimes it has led to highly advanced agricultural civilisations like those in the monsoon region of Asia. But even in this kind of civilisation the diet is essentially based on grain, which is rich in starch but poor in nitrogenous matter. This leads to a search for nitrogen, often with great ingenuity, in fish-rearing, fishing, or the growing of special crops.

Dry regions are found in every latitude, in the warm belt as well as in the temperate zone. Apart from the areas that have scarcely any rain in the course of the year, it can be said that the dry regions are essentially those in which the season of warmth is the dry season. Maps showing aridity are often valuable for marking the boundaries of dry regions, for the simple reason that they establish a local connexion between the temperature, on which depends the plant's need for water, and the amount of rain which heaven sends at the same time. In this way it will be seen that in the three summer months there is only a tiny fraction of the annual precipitation. This fraction is only 13 per cent at Marseille, 9 per cent in Athens, 3 per cent in Algiers, 2 per cent at Teheran, 4 per cent at Perth in Western Australia, 3 per cent at Lima, and 3 per cent at Santiago de Chile. At Jerusalem and Cairo the rainfall recorded during the three summer months is nil.

This unfavourable type of rainfall is due to many causes: for instance, distance from the sea or situation in a high pressure belt under a stagnating mass of dry air. In any case the amount of precipitation is not enough to ensure the growth of plants and, consequently, the settlement of human communities engaged in normal forms of agriculture. Three belts differing greatly in vegetation and rainfall régime suffer from this unfavourable climate. They are the Mediterranean coast lands, the steppe belt, and the desert belt.

In the middle latitudes between lat. 30° N. and lat. 45° N. there stretches, mainly on the continent of Africa, a long narrow region which includes the Mediterranean coast lands. Owing to the high pressure system which centres round the Azores, it has a period of summer drought lasting for several months. This dry period is the controlling factor in the type of vegetation. To it are due the characteristic features of trees and shrubs like the olive, vine, and fig, whose long roots draw moisture from deep down below the surface. Sugar and oil become concentrated in their fruit in summer, at which time nearly all the annual plants die. Thus, the climate is reflected in the arrangement of food crops. To this type of region belong not only the European Mediterranean, but also southern California and the southwest of the Cape of Good Hope Province and of Australia.

Around the dry regions that occupy nearly all the continental interiors there runs a semi-desert fringe which does not lend itself to tree growth, but is covered with a huge carpet of temporary grass. It begins in south Russia and continues across central Asia to Mongolia, where it bears the significant name of 'land of grasses'. It is found also in Africa on the outskirts of the Sahara and all over the Kalahari. In the Americas it covers much of western United States and western Argentina.

This belt of steppes turns green periodically. It is a frontier between the desert on the one hand and the open areas of the temperate lands on the other, and it is the habitat of herbivorous mammals, among which are the horse, gazelle, and antelope in the Old World and the bison in North America. On the steppes these animals range in vast herds from one feeding-ground to the next according to season. Pastoral life still exists in many of these steppe lands, and flocks continue to be the chief form of wealth and the mainstay of life. As the steppes become gradually drier, they change little by little into desert. In the temperate belt there are deserts like the Great Basin of the United States, the Atacama in South America, and those stretching from Mesopotamia to Manchuria. In the warm belt there are deserts like the Sahara, the Namib, and the interior of Australia. These are areas in which drought is at times complete. They have very hot summers and are sometimes the hottest places on earth. Their great range of temperature, diurnal and seasonal, and the enormous rate of evaporation explain the extreme poverty of plant life and, consequently the impossibility of any human settlement, except where a spring occurs.

These dry lands all present common characteristics which may be profitably studied and related to the needs of human communities. First, their treeless nature has made them suitable areas for the early development of civilisation. There are no forests and no swamps to be got rid of, and there are wide open spaces for movement. Adaptation to drought has placed at man's disposal a whole world of plants with peculiar aerial and underground parts, which makes them grow quickly even in a dry climate. Thus, we have the grasses that carpet the steppes and the shrubs and scrub that live in the Mediterranean and in the desert. Secondly, the soil is especially fertile in dry lands, for the low rainfall does not leach it and remove its mineral elements. If water is given to these apparently dead lands and the sand cleared from their surface, plant life can spring up in plenty. Such a miracle is performed' by irrigation, that techique of high civilisations, which is wonderfully effective, but delicate to handle, for when it is badly managed it may ruin naturally rich soils after having temporarily fertilised them.

PHYSIOGRAPHIC FACTORS

Although climate carves out on the surface of the earth the main regions in which are included the basic types of human life, it should be recognised that within each climatic belt physical factors cause differentiation and tend to produce variations which many a time have been taken advantage of by man in so far as he has been intelligent enough to detect them or, having detected them, to have been able to make use of them.

The soil, that mantle of superficial matter which covers the solid rock below, is a basic element in the differentiation and evolution of modes of life, but man has only gradually understood its structure and properties. There are two kinds of soil: those formed *in situ* by autogenous decomposition, and those which have been transported from elsewhere.

Autogenous residual soil derives its character from the parent rock and the changes it has undergone; but, other things being equal, it is sandy and poor and quickly leached when derived from granite. When its parent rock is basaltic lava or limestone, it is physically clayey and heavy, but fairly rich in the elements of fertility. In hot countries laterite forms from all kinds of parent rock and is everywhere the cause of the poverty of much of the soil, owing to its inability to fix the colloidal solutions of mineral salts and to encourage the work of bacteria. There is still much discussion about the nature and classification of laterite. It is certain, however, that this kind of formation, whether in the form of true laterite or of more or less lateritised soil, covers nearly a quarter of the continents.

Soil laid down by running water, ice, or wind and soil which has been formed by the action of frost and moved by solifluction towards lower ground, are often composed of a mixture of rock-waste. They are generally richer and better than residual soil. Apart from alluvial fans and deposits on flood plains, the kinds of transported soil which have played the greatest part in the history of human settlement are loam and glacial drift, both of which contain an equal proportion of sand and clay. In the American State of Wisconsin it has been possible to compare the yield from drift soil with that from the driftless area without a covering of glacial deposits. On drift soil the yield of maize is 17 per cent higher, that of rye 14 per cent, and that of potatoes 30 per cent. The alluvial soil areas on the deltas in India and Indo-China are centres of prosperous cultivation and the same is true of the Nile valley.

On the whole the area which can be used by man varies greatly according to the nature of the soil. An approximate estimate has been made of the proportion of the world's soil that is fit for cultivation at the present day. In Europe it is 50 per cent of the land surface, in South America 25 per cent, in Asia 25 per cent, in North America and Africa each 20 per cent, and in Australia 10 per cent. But this estimate is provisional, and the proportions can certainly be raised, for good soil still remains to be discovered and used on the steppes and in the forests of the various continents. Besides, modern scientific agriculture is learning how to modify the physico-chemical structure of the soil and to impart a degree of fertility where sterility or exhaustion is reported. It is none the less true also that at the present day a great deal of soil is being destroyed through erosion which has become active owing to human imprudence. In the United States vast areas of soil have been ruined by extensive cultivation and crazy exploitation. In Brazil the *fazendas* have exhausted immense areas by coffee-planting and have reduced them to sterility. In Africa bush fires hasten the formation of laterite and so cause complete sterility. Today it is clear to both geographers and scientific agriculturalists that the destruction of good soil in many areas constitutes one of the most serious and irremediable evils in our present state of knowledge, since it strikes at the common, fundamental heritage of mankind. The degradation of the soil has frequently been blamed for the disappearance of flourishing civilisations like that of the Mayas in Central America and possibly like more than one Indo-Malay civilisation in the Far East. Hence, pedological problems have special importance in human geography.

Mountains form special regions whose particular climates modify the conditions of plant and human life. Similar modes of life are practised on mountain masses situated far from each other and inhabited by peoples with no racial connexion. In fact, mountains constitute environments in which the influence of relief and climate acts with a force unusual in such relatively small areas, and they therefore direct human reactions more insistently.

In Western Europe the temperature has been found to fall 0·5° C for every 102 metres of ascent. Hence, zones of vegetation rise one above the other up the mountain sides. The lowest zone, which is an extension of the lowland at the foot of the slopes ends between 800 and 900 metres above the sea. In central Switzerland barley cultivation stops above the 800 metre contour. Above these heights begin the mountain belts. First, half-way up the slope where precipitation is greatest there is a forest belt which ends at various heights according to the degree of exposure. The upper limit is at 1,600 metres in the Pre-Alps in Dauphiné, 2,100 metres in the High Alps in Tarentaise, 1,200 metres in the Vosges, and 2,300 metres in the eastern Pyrenees. The forest belt is succeeded by 'alpine' pasture, where conditions are dry and cold, but sunny. The ground is covered with tufts of grass and in spring is brightly coloured with flowers. On this zone are the upland summer pastures which are used by flocks and herds brought up from the lowland below. Lastly, right on top there is eternal snow, whose lower limit, that is, the mean height above which the snow does not melt, varies from mountain range to mountain range. This snowline is at a height of 2,700 metres on the northern slopes of the Pyrenees and at 3,000 metres on Mont Blanc. Thus, by climbing mountains in Europe one sees the same belts of scenery at appropriate heights as are seen in a journey to the polar regions. In each belt there are special conditions of life for plants and man. It should be added that in the lowest belt there are difficulties inherent in upland cultivation, such as the washing of loose soil downhill, frequent outcrops of rock which must be cleared away, and absence of level ground leading to terrace construction. Hence, the natural environment on a mountain range demands special modes of life.

Islands may be regarded as little regions held as in a matrix and remarkable for the uniformity of their natural conditions. Isolation has caused survivals of endemic, archaic forms of life. Up to the arrival of Europeans in Australia the native mammals had kept their Mesozoic character with their marsupials and ornithorhynchi. In New Zealand mammals are represented in the native fauna only by one species of rat and one species of bat. Out of the twenty-six species of land birds described by Darwin in the Galápagos Islands all but one are peculiar to these islands. Owing to their restricted size islands are unfavourable to the development of certain species, as is illustrated by the size of Shetland ponies. Isolation on islands induces differentiations which have been recorded by historians and scientific observers. For instance, there is the survival of French in the Channel Islands, the continued use in Sardinia of the Roman wooden plough and in Ireland of ancient instruments, and the backward state of the Caroline islanders, who are still almost in the stone age. On the other hand, islands afford refuge for hard-pressed peoples and incidentally become veritable melting-pots in which the most incongruous specimens of humanity are amalgamated to form united little communities. The best example of such melting-pots at the present time is Tristan da Cunha, a tiny islet in the South Atlantic, where a handful of people, 200 strong, have succeeded in creating a peculiar set of local traditions which quickly assimilate new comers. Islands often shelter the last traces of dying civilisations. For instance, Anglesey was the refuge of the druids who fled from the Romans. Formosa had been a refuge for the Ming dynasty during the political troubles of the seventeenth century before becoming the final bastion of Chinese nationalism against Communism. Ceylon (Sri Lanka) became a refuge for Buddhists driven out of India.

Being the home of peoples safely protected by the sea, islands afford to human communities peace and an opportunity to prosper through the exploitation of the resources of the land as well as those of the sea. Thus, it is stated that in many Pacific islands an advanced type of agriculture is necessarily practised to supply food for the inhabitants. Such is the case in Tonga and Samoa, and it was true of Fiji even before the development of sugar plantation and the introduction of Indian labour.

The sea, which surrounds all the continents and penetrates deeply into them, forms another natural environment. It is wild and difficult to cope with, but gives rise to peculiar modes of life. It represents a storehouse of food from which man has drawn supplies since early times, and it is also a highway which he learnt to use in the dim past. There was coastwise traffic in the Ægean as early as the third millennium B.C., and the knowledge of many inventions during the Stone and Bronze Ages was spread to other shores, starting from the Ægean and reaching as far as Britain. The epic voyage of the argonauts and the travels of Odysseus are proofs of very ancient sea enterprises. They were doubtless the forbears of these strings of boats which have ploughed the seas of the Levant right up to our own times. Along the coasts of tidal seas the beaches which are uncovered at the ebb form a huge stretch of aquatic life that has been exploited by the coastal folk since primitive times. In the ocean, in the North Sea, in the waters around Japan, and on the Newfoundland Banks there are fishing grounds that have fed men for centuries. Consequently, the exploitation of the sea has given rise to occupations that reflect peculiar natural conditions which are found on coasts.

Whether these natural conditions stem from climate or landforms, they all exert constant influence on man's life, leaving a deep and often indelible impression. They introduce into modes of life a rigidity that is astonishing at times when one calculates the chances of instability and change demanded by human intelligence. It is often true that owing to this social structure, communities have made rigid and lasting the suggestions of the environment, by rendering impossible changes that the environment would not have resisted. Probably some environments have fostered in human communities which have chosen to live in them an inertia and indolence so strong that, despite the contacts of civilisation and intercourse with other peoples, they have perpetuated a rigid form of structure and material civilisation. But the speed with which during the last few decades communities that had remained very primitive and ossified in their environment have been able to progress shows that these adaptations are never indestructible and that the environment has not been alone responsible for their conditions or their rigidity.

Nevertheless, the natural environment helps to maintain between different groups of mankind fundamental differences which are observed by human geography, and which show up the contrast between hunters on the one hand and pastoralists on the other, or between wheat growers and rice cultivators. Even in the political structure of modern states, and especially in those newly formed, which are only slightly urbanised and have far more primitive techniques than European or North American peoples, the traditional opposition between the *fellah* who tills the soil and the nomadic herdsman is clearly manifest. In the world of today these fundamental contrasts have lost none of their force. To be convinced of this one need only think of a comparison between the Chinese peasant, the African cultivator, the European farmer, and his counterpart in the New World.

CHAPTER 2

MAN AND CIVILISATION

Whilst plants and animals are relatively passive in their relations with the natural environment, man is an active agent. Hence, it is useless to try to base the whole of human geography on the influence of natural environments. Man comes into the world more helpless than all other animals. Weaker in body, slower in being able to walk, less agile, and with less efficient senses, he is nevertheless their superior owing to his intelligence, by means of which he has been able to gain control over nature, and by his own ingenuity to ensure his means of subsistence. For instance, he has ceased to use his bare hands as weapons and has produced mechanical devices and tools that have increased his power. Similarly, his faculty of speech has enabled him to concert action with his fellows and consciously to adapt his life to fit natural conditions. Again, his forethought has gradually led him to make plans for the future. Generally speaking, man has been able to get out of nature by his own efforts more than she would have given him of her own accord. He has been able to modify his surroundings to suit his own plans and interests. The search for means to master nature constitutes civilisation in the true sense. Whilst animal life is wholly subject to the conditions of the natural environment and is incapable of modifying them, man's peculiarity lies in his ability to react to the conditions, to control them and adapt them to his needs. The standard of civilisation is measured by man's power to control nature. Hence, man has become a peculiarly powerful agent, a source of creative energy, in the conditions in which he lives. For a full understanding of man's various modes of life and customs, the mind must grasp everything that human intelligence can invent to increase mankind's means of existence and determination to survive; his tools, modifications of plants, domestication of animals, preservation of experience by means of language and writing, and his organisation of individuals into communities, large or small.

The power of man's mind seems to have increased especially at certain periods of ferment. During the whole Palaeolithic age the first steps forward in civilisation were very slow. At that time man had only very simple modes of life based on hunting, fishing, and collecting; but with the Neolithic Age progress was speeded up. When we realise them, we are amazed at the immense changes introduced by neolithic man into human life by the host of inventions of lasting usefulness due to him. These compare more than favourably with the meagre contribution brought to the common heritage by all succeeding civilisations.   To neolithic man we owe the invention of all the techniques on which every great civilisation has been based. With him the wretched animal who was in turns hunter and hunted became the organiser of nature.   Neolithic man cultivated plants, reared animals, and was the first to live a settled life.   He invented pottery-making and weaving, and fashioned various objects, the most important of which was the wheel, for without it none of our inventions would have been realised.   Furthermore, he built villages, codified the law, and connected funeral rites with religion.   Thus, he gave a vast heritage of traditions and beliefs, the knowledge of which preceded that of the use of metals and made man's subsequent progress possible.

The ability to use metals was another gigantic step forward.   It is still the foundation stone of our civilisation.   No other discovery in man's history can be compared with it before the coming of the modern machine age, which is only a remote application of it and, up to the atomic age, did no more than follow up the inventions of prehistoric man.

THE TECHNIQUES

The degree of perfection in techniques has always been highly revealing evidence of the intelligence and creative imagination of a civilisation.   Weber has rightly said that the intelligence shown in techniques that demand a great deal of material ingenuity and positive judgment is a far better means of appreciating the intellectual level of a human community than are ideas of religion and superstition.   Some peoples whom otherwise one would be tempted to regard as underdeveloped have produced inventions which bear witness to an astonishing degree of inventiveness.   Among them are the aborigines of Australia, who invented the boomerang; the South American Indians, who invented the blowpipe; and the tribes of central Africa, several of which perfected methods of extracting salt contained in plants.   Ethnologists rightly consider that skill in using the properties of solid matter is one of the most essential characteristics of human intelligence.

History shows that stone was the first material that man used for his tools.   This was probably due to its being found loose and ready for use in the alluvium of streams.   The study of the development of stone techniques has had surprisingly accurate results, and, in consequence, a remarkable uniformity of character has been observed in certain tools everywhere, and this uniformity has been seen to pass through the successive stages of stone-working.   The first stage, which was by far the longest, covers the whole Palaeolithic Age, when stone (usually flint) was merely split or cut, and artifacts at first roughly shaped though later delicately dressed with the help of chisels also cut from flint. The second stage was the Neolithic, during which the stone was worked on polishers of hard rock and the artifacts were delicately shaped.

During the Palaeolithic Age Chellean man's only tool was the hand-axe, sometimes called a knuckle-duster, which was shaped by splintering. Acheulean man used the same kind of axe, though it was smaller, less rough, sharper, and with a better edge. He also had in his tool chest dressed splinters which he used as awls and scrapers, possibly for the purpose of removing from pelts all bits of flesh and fat which might putrefy. Mousterian man greatly improved his set of tools by adding more awls, cutting edges, and scrapers which he made from broad splinters knocked off from flint nodules. But with Aurignacian, Solutrean, and Magdalenian man, who lived in the Reindeer age, there arose in the Stone Age with the appearance of reindeer hunters a civilisation so remarkable as to be regarded as the beginning of a new period, the Upper Palaeolithic. To flint were added other hard materials, like reindeer horn, bone, and ivory, out of which were made weapons and tools from the pickaxe for digging flints from alluvium to fine needles for sewing pelts with tendons and dried sinews. The purpose of these new objects is clearly something more than mere use, for they display a sense of artistry which makes them little works of art that in some cases are expressive and living. 'In archaeology the appearance of these first works of art', writes Déchelette, 'is as it were the first smile of the infant man.'

This outburst of delicate, artistic modelling and carving is sought in vain in the Neolithic Age. Possibly in the Reindeer age when game seems to have been plentiful, man had leisure and happy, carefree hours favourable to a flowing expression of artistic feeling. Perhaps the hardworking man of the Neolithic Age, who was engaged in the rude labour of digging the soil and was possibly strained at times by agricultural routine, did not have the same amount of leisure. This would be but an early example of the fact many a time noticed in the course of later centuries, that man often pays for added security with the loss of some of his freedom and for progress in wellbeing with a reduction of his periods of leisure. It has been shown (by D. Faucher) that the great revolution in the countryside due to the spread of the practice of weeding crops had brought in greater wealth, but also caused a strain on the workers and an overloading of the calendar. In fact, neolithic art took refuge in tombs, to build which man learnt to collect and balance enormous blocks of stone. Craftsmanship and utilitarian work gained all that was lost by artistic achievement. Stone-cutters acquired such skill that their solid material seemed to become plastic in their hands, and from it they made sharp daggers, tiny arrowheads with rows of barbs, knives, awls, and saws. Their polishing-stone enabled them to give axes an edge unequalled before, to shape handy tomahawks, to turn out special tools, chisels or gouges for carving bone. It is not surprising that these skilful craftsmen, who carried their inherited techniques to the peak of perfection, should themselves have invented the new operations of weaving, ceramics, and plant and animal selection, all of which tended to increase and improve the means of existence.

Many scholars see in the invention of fire man's first step towards civilisation, but the invention occurred so early that no one knows when man learnt to produce fire at will and to keep it going. Though primitive peoples far removed from each other use the same methods of producing it, the general diversity of method seems to favour invention in many places. Some make a groove in a piece of hard wood and then, surrounding it with easily inflammable stuff like tinder, they vigorously push another bit of hard wood backwards and forwards along the groove. Others make a hole in a piece of wood and, putting a pointed stick into the hole, spin it round rapidly either with their palms or with a bow which accelerates the rotation. Whatever the method, the invention of fire conspicuously widened the possibilities of the diet, for man was thenceforth able to roast his meat and parch his corn.

The working of metals brought man new weapons and more effective tools, and these were probably more easily renewable. With the use of bronze the sword became a fearful weapon in the hands of those who first forged them. Shield and breastplate were soon associated with it. The use of iron brought more reliable weapons, and other tools like the plough were added to the material heritage of civilisation. This upset the relative power of different peoples. But in truth the practice of metallurgy has been one long series of inventions. It demands first of all the production of high temperatures, so that it is only achieved with the help of bellows. The more primitive goatskin bellows seems to have been known very early, perhaps from the end of the third millennium B.C. in middle-eastern Asia and northeast Africa. The improved piston bellows were used in India and China during the first half of the first millennium B.C. Unlike other inventions, working in metals was not common to all mankind. We know that Australia, the Pacific islands, and the greater part of America were ignorant of it until the arrival of Europeans. On the other hand, one of the busiest metallurgical centres came into being very early in northern Mesopotamia and Asia Minor, where the beginning of the age of metals is known to have taken place in the third millennium B.C., with the working of copper, bronze, and gold. Copper was possibly the first metal to be worked, for the earliest copper axes were smelted and then hammered to look like stone axes. Though the working of iron was cradled in the same region, it certainly spread into central Europe during the first millennium B.C., and it was one of the essential factors of the power and spread of Celtic civilisation, first in the Hallstatt period about the ninth century and later in the La Tène period beginning with the fifth century.

Progress was also made in ceramics, that is, in the making of hollow vessels from clay and hardening them by baking. The potter's art, which was unknown to palaeolithic man, seems to have been discovered independently in several places; but it is almost always associated with settled agricultural communities, a type of settlement which multiplied in neolithic times. In Alsace archaeologists have shown that whilst axes and arrowheads are found in plenty in forest settlements, which were doubtless the homes of hunters and herdsmen, pottery and millstones for grinding corn are plentiful in the settlements on loess, where dwelt agricultural people.

CULTIVATION OF PLANTS AND DOMESTICATION OF ANIMALS

By selection of plants and animals human intelligence upset the natural environment whilst developing civilisation. To make sure of his daily bread as well as to have stocks of food which could be made use of at any time, man collected around him a whole association of plants and animals as allies and dependants. This was a long and exacting task which demanded a world of patient observation. Current opinion in ancient times attributed superhuman wisdom to the originators of the chief crops and the domestication of animals.

All the plants and animals which have become man's partners have literally been shaped by human effort. Plants have been improved by grafting and pruning, animals by crossing and selection. Hundreds of varieties of wheat, maize, and rice have enabled these cereals to be adapted to many shades of climate. The potato and beet which were originally poor tubers and small roots, have through cultivation become rich storehouses of nutritive substances. Naturally thin and fibrous, the root of *Raphanus raphranistrum* has developed through cultivation into four kinds of radish, five kinds of kale, and four kinds of horseradish. In its natural home of the Atlantic coasts the leaves of the uncultivated cabbage are few and inedible, but cultivation has modified the various parts of the plant in turn. Thus, by modifying the growth of leaves it has produced six different varieties of savoy, ten varieties of green cabbage, and seventeen varieties of headed cabbages; by modifying the root it has produced three kinds of kohlrabi; and by modifying the flowers it has made eleven varieties of cauliflower.

Similarly, in domesticating animals man has brought about morphological and physiological transformations, and the properties of height, fleece, colour of the coat, fatty secretions, etc., which these animals have acquired have been passed on to their offspring. During the eighteenth century English farmers bred different strains of cattle, some to give milk, others to give beef. The poultry yard is itself a product of innumerable experiments whose early successes are lost in the mists of time. Whilst the *Gallus bankiva* of southeast Asia lays only six or eight eggs a year, our domestic hen, which is derived from it, continues to lay almost daily and may lay as many as several hundred eggs.

By associating themselves with these plants and animals men have created lasting modes of life. Harvests from cultivated plants have the advantage over collection that they afford a permanent or periodic and not a precarious supply. In stock-rearing the domestication of the horse and camel brought into being powerful help in war and transport. Besides, by adding to man's supplies these new techniques enabled a great increase to take place in the world's population, and this brought on another factor of progress.

It is not known for certain what plants were first chosen for systematic cultivation. Possibly at the beginning man cultivated only certain varieties, relying on gathering to get the fruits of others. In the stomach of the Tollund man, who had lain fossilised in peat for two thousand years, there were found seeds of cultivated plants (beans, flax, lentils) and a whole assortment of the seeds of six or seven wild plants. It seems established that in Europe the cultivation of cereals goes back nearly everywhere to neolithic times. In pile-dwellings in northern Italy there have been found seeds of wheat, oats, barley, and rye, together with beans, peas, and flax seeds and fibres. Wheat and barley appear to be the earliest, for the most ancient prehistoric finds sometimes reveal the presence of several varieties of wheat, which proves that the crop was no new one. Wheat was cultivated in China about 2800 B.C., in Egypt in 3000 B.C., and in neolithic beds in Denmark and Sweden wheat and various seeds are found, dating from before 3000 B.C.

What gave man the idea of sowing and planting in order to reap later? Probably the choice of plants was made almost haphazardly after a vast deal of observation, for within his gathering ground man learnt to know every useful tree, shrub, and grass, together with their economic properties. He learnt how to handle them carefully, to shelter, and even to tend certain plants which seemed valuable; but all these efforts fade away into the mists of time. All that can be said is that today certain backward tribes of cultivators do not go beyond the food plants in the natural vegetation of their district, whilst they destroy the other plants so as to have only those that are useful to them. This type of cultivation acting by elimination and selection and favouring the spread of only useful species by removing their rivals, appears to have been practised by all the original tillers of the soil.

In this way nearly the whole collection of cultivated plants had become known in the earliest times, and there are few recent acquisitions. With astonishing ingenuity and curiosity early man recognised all the uses to which he could put his various crops. Food was provided by some plants, among which were grasses (wheat, barley, rice, maize), legumes (peas, beans, lentils), tubers or roots (turnips, carrots, onions, potatoes), and fruit (nuts, apples, olives, figs, oranges, dates). Plants like flax, hemp, and cotton provided clothing, whilst others like the vine, tea, coffee, cocoa, opium, tobacco, and many more were grown as luxuries. Oppel reckons that out of the total number of cultivated plants 68 per cent yielded food, 16 per cent luxuries, and 15 per cent were used for industry. In a more exhaustive survey A. de Condolle counted 247 basic species of cultivated plants, 199 of which belonged to the Old World and 45 to the New. America is remarkable for its poverty in useful plants. Out of 28 species of cereal 26 come from the Old World, and 21 tubers out of 29; 35 industrial plants out of 38; and 75 fruit trees out of 95, not to mention 28 species, or nearly all of the legumes. Most of the important cultivated plants go back several thousand years, and species like the cinchona and the rubber tree are the only newcomers to have been cultivated in modern times.

The contingent from the Old World comprises two groups of plants belonging to two different climates. On the one hand are the main food plants of temperate countries, such as wheat, barley, rye, and oats; on the other are the main food plants of hot lands, such as rice, millet, and sugarcane. All probability and every shred of evidence point to the plants of the temperate belt having an origin to the south of that belt, and more particularly in the dry fringes of the belt which extends along the Mediterranean region as far as southwest Asia. This provenance is confirmed by the presence of certain plants that grow with the cereals; for instance, the cornflower which grows wild in Sicily has migrated northwards with the cereals. Traces of it are found in the pile-dwellings at Robenhausen. These facts argue in a general way that all neolithic civilisations came from the south. Movement from south to north is also attested by the fact that the countries of northern Europe still cultivated only the cereals in the Bronze Age, and that peas, beans, and lentils did not reach them till later.

The original home of the food plants in hot countries seems to have been monsoon Asia. From that region rice, millet, sugarcane, and tea spread through the tropics. It is thought that millet, a plant very sensitive to frost, came originally from India. It figured among Chinese cereals, which from the third millenium B.C. were ceremoniously sown by the Emperor every year. Adaptable in its numerous varieties to many different climatic types, it is found in an immense area stretching from north China through central Asia to south Russia. It once spread further to become one of the essential crops of western Yugoslavia, a position it held for a long period which has only just ended. In Africa it has spread over wide areas, where it is cultivated by the savanna Negroes. Even in countries where it has been supplanted by rice, it still covers much territory, as it does in the interior of Taiwan, and above all all in the Deccan.

From prehistoric times the Old World has been in possession of its ancient heritage of cultivated plants, to which no further addition has ever been made; but real upheaval took place in the distribution of cultivated plants when suddenly American introductions came to claim a place in the Old World, whilst from the Old World plants were carried over to America. From the New World came maize, the potato, the common bean, tomato, cocoa, tobacco, coca, quinine, and cassava, not to mention almost useless plants like the aloe and the cactus. America had developed its own set of cultivated plants from the earliest times. Maize seems to have been the first, coming even before cassava and the potato. Its extraordinary spread, which probably started from Central America and Mexico, is explained by the ease with which it is grown. It is sufficient without any preparation to bury a grain of maize in a little hole dug with the aid of a stick. Many American plants now form part of the agricultural wealth of the whole world. Amerindians drank cocoa before Europeans discovered the continent. From Peru comes cinchona, whose leaves the natives chewed, as Asiatics chew betel nut. Of Peruvian origin too, the tomato became known in Europe as early as the sixteenth century. The pineapple is also of American provenance and was carried by slave ships to Africa and Asia. With the gift of cassava America provided Africa with a high-yielding food plant. The potato and Jerusalem artichoke have the same origin. At the discovery of America the practice of smoking and chewing tobacco and of taking snuff existed nearly throughout the New World. The greatest change of all in international agriculture, however, was due to the introduction of maize and the potato into the rotation of crops.

The origin of the domestication of animals, like that of cultivated plants, is lost in the mists of time. No animal has been domesticated since the beginning of history, and our domestic species retain no traces of the country in which they first became associated with man and his life. The earliest definite evidence of domestication dates from the Neolithic Age. Swiss pile dwellings have furnished huge quantities of the bones of dogs, pigs, horses, oxen, sheep, and goats. These bones can be clearly distinguished from those of wild animals, especially from those of the stag, which was the chief game animal of neolithic man.   It seems that the dog was the earliest of man's companions, after which, it is thought, came the ox, sheep, pig, and goat.   The horse, whose remains are not found in the earliest pile dwellings, is probably the last comer.   Hence, a long time elapsed between the domestication of the dog and that of the horse.   It is even thought that the domestication of the dog had already been achieved long before the beginning of cultivation, and that bands of emigrants who came at a very distant date from Asia to America took the dog with them.   Close study has indeed shown that in every case the American dog is descended from the Asiatic wolf.   Apparently dogs followed the tracks of parties of hunters and collectors and ate the remains of their meals, and in this way they are supposed to have acquired the habit of accompanying and becoming parasites of man.   This association is thought to have reached such a stage that the dog undertook the defence of man against intruders and that man gradually became interested in the breeding of such a precious ally.   This primitive relation between man and dog was achieved long ago when man was still a wanderer.   Crossing with wolves, jackals, and coyotes gave rise in course of time to various breeds of dogs.   That man has been followed by the dog in all his wanderings is proved by the fact that the remains of dogs are found in the earliest human dwelling-places before man had a fixed abode.

It is clear that domestication of other animals was effected only after the development of cultivation, that is, when sedentary life became possible.   At the very beginning of historical times an ample set of domestic animals existed: in the Near East at the end of the fourth millennium, B.C., at the end of the second millennium in China, in the first millennium in Persia and Aryan India.   The earliest drawings of domestic cattle are in Tell-el-Obeid and date from the fourth millennium.   At Ur there are monuments showing wheeled carts about 3200 B.C.

Domestication of animals is the outcome of a long series of incidents, some deliberate and others spontaneous, about the course of which we know almost nothing.   All we know is that our domestic breeds are due to repeated crossing of wild species with domestic or newly domesticated species.   It is possible that the first domestic ox was a fat-humped zebu, *Bos sondaicus*, of southeast Asia.   Its tame descendants were taken to Africa and Europe by neolithic man.   He also tamed a European species, *Bos primigenius*, which was crossed with the first.   Today the prototypes of our horned cattle are either disappearing or completely gone.   Attempts at domestication were probably made once more in comparatively recent times, since, for instance, drawings in the Egyptian pharaohs' monuments of the fourth millenium show slaves in charge of antelopes, gazelles, and hyænas which they were probably trying to tame.

It is even more difficult in cases other than that of the dog to know how the methods of domestication were thought out and the stages passed. Perhaps man attracted the animals by giving them food, perhaps drought drew man and animal round the same water-hole. In the opinion of other geographers the liking many people show for keeping tame animals opened the way to domestication. Certain customs have been described as existing in pre-Columbian America, which seem to have led animals towards domestication. In the Inca empire the Indians carried out immense drives every two or three years in order to trap in huge pens herds of wild vicuñas, guanacos, and deer. After shearing them they released the females and the finest males. The *rodeos*, in which in later years colonists in Argentina rounded up their herds of cattle that were at other times left in a wild state on the pampa, have only continued a very old tradition of techniques in South America. Even today in the state of Mysore wild elephants are still caught by means of great drives, and are afterwards tamed and trained to work. In pre-Columbian America one portion of the animals kept in the pen was used as a stock of fresh meat for the princes and nobles. Young animals taken thus were successfully reared, and so the herd of domesticated llamas and alpacas was formed.

Probably in the course of man's history experiments in domestication were made on hundreds and hundreds of animals, but in the whole vast world of animals less than forty species have really been domesticated. These are: *Mammals*: horse, ass, buffalo, yak, zebra, ox, pig, sheep, goat, camel, llama, alpaca, reindeer, cat, dog, rabbit; *Birds*: swan, goose, duck, hen, pigeon, peacock, pheasant, guinea-hen, turkey, and ostrich; *Insects*: bee and silkworm.

These animals are reared mainly to provide food. Birds give eggs, mammals milk, bees honey; oxen, pigs, sheep, and poultry yield meat; the supply of these foodstuffs is kept up by the offspring of the animals consumed. The pig is the only animal reared for its flesh alone. Man makes his clothing from furs or skins, according to the region. He gets wool from the sheep and llama, hair from the camel and goat, silk from the silkworm, and feathers from the ostrich. Woollen garments have been discovered in Scandinavia in Bronze Age deposits. To help him in his work man has used the ox, ass, horse, buffalo, camel, reindeer, llama, and even the dog; and he also rears animals to protect him from other animals, to watch over his safety, and for warlike purposes.

Asia has supplied the largest number of domestic animals, and the most valuable, the majority of which have come from the vast expanse of steppes separating the temperate and hot countries. From this region come the horse, ox, camel, pig, goat, and hen. Africa has contributed the cat, guinea-hen, and ostrich. But there are immense regions which, so to speak, have known no domestic animals, or have used only one or two species. Before the arrival of Europeans in Australia there was no cereal and no mammal suitable for domestication. North America had its bison which might have been domesticated by the Indians, but which in fact remained wild. Only the turkey has been domesticated there. Peru gave us the guinea-pig, and the Andes the llama and the alpaca. Like the camel the llama might have given milk; but apart from its use as a beast of burden, it has been used only for its wool and, when dead, for its flesh. With their docile, swift, and strong domestic animals the Euroasiatic civilisations had at their disposal a form of power incomparably greater than American civilisations, which had to depend on man's strength alone.

The present distribution of domestic animals is worldwide, for most of them have accompanied man everywhere. There are, however, limits to their distribution. These are sometimes due to religious ordinances, as in the case of the Jews and Muslims, who regard the pig as unclean. At other times the limitations are due to climate, for some domestic animals avoid extremes of temperature or rainfall. Thus, the ass, a typical African creature, cannot stand severe winters; the pig, the goat, and even the ox, do not live in very cold countries. European and Asiatic animals have been repelled from east and west Africa by flies whose bites are deadly. Other domestic animals are confined to definite countries: the llama and yak to mountain regions, the camel to steppes and desert, and the reindeer to the Arctic.

An idea of the ingenuity expended by man in domesticating animals may be given from the examples of a few beasts. Thus, the number of breeds of dogs scattered about the world may be reckoned at least at two hundred. Besides its duty as a sheep-dog, it is used for its sense of smell and its ability to track down game or wild animals. In Polynesia and throughout central Africa certain varieties of dogs are bred for eating. Lastly, in polar regions dogs draw sledges, and but for this many polar expeditions would have been impossible. It renders similar service in some civilised countries by drawing little carts, which in Belgium and Austria carry round milk cans. Formerly, dogs turned the wheels of churns and worked the bellows in forges.

The ox plays a double rôle in human economy, and this makes it one of the pillars of civilisation in Europe and Asia. As a beast of burden among agricultural peoples it has had to learn to draw the plough. Now, the plough is what has raised man from the stage of the hoe and spade to the higher plane of more effective and more productive agriculture. As a source of milk it was certainly not amenable at first; indeed, the development of lactation has been the work of long efforts at adaptation and skilful selection, for, like the yield of wool, that of milk is a quality that has been slowly worked up. Curiously enough, the use of milk itself is not known to all cattle rearers, for neither the Chinese, the Indo-Chinese, nor the Indonesians drink milk.

These great achievements of mankind are not the only ones due to the exercise of intelligence. The most striking, most complex, and most peculiar is man's domestication of his own species, a most important step forward, to which mankind owes its richest experiences, its best pledges of progress and duration, but which may also contain the worst of dangers and the germs of the most implacable destruction.

Today, indeed, mankind is confronted with a grave problem. Has not that spiritual energy, which has not ceased to grow and to increase in vigour and efficiency over the millennia, enabling man to control natural forces and to mould the surface of the globe, now more than ever before over-reached itself? The modern scientist, and particularly the geographer, can discern an undeniable impoverishment resulting from these transformations of geographic space: animal species rendered extinct or rapidly disappearing; the catastrophic destruction of the world's forest cover and the irreversible degradation of the natural vegetative mantle; the erosion, also irreversible, of fertile soils; the total destruction of the natural environment by the uncontrolled extension of biologically sterile areas, covered with buildings and routeways, the consequence of world-wide urbanisation; the exhaustion of energy sources and non-renewable raw materials . . . and so on.

These are the destructive results—now universally termed 'pollution'—of man's occupation of the earth, of which he has only recently become acutely aware. Is the human race, having mastered forces far greater than its own physical powers, now in process of destroying itself by inconsiderately ruining the very physico–biological mechanisms that have controlled the world from its origin and continue to do so, without a thought for its own survival? And does not civilisation carry within itself the germs of self-destruction, ever more harmful as man's power increases and his polluting numbers rise?

CHAPTER 3

HUMAN SOCIETIES

From the earliest times prehistoric man appears as a social animal bent on organising his activities in company with others, not in couples or in crowds, but in groups in which duties are shared as well as advantages. Few animals live in communities, and they nearly always do so for the purpose of mating or rearing young. The desire for a life in common led prehistoric man to form communities, invent means of keeping together, and making cohesion permanent. Hence, even in the material conditions of primitive life, there were family groups in which the family was the kernel of a wider group. Frequency of intercourse between such groups which were in some cases separated by great distances; use of language, which makes it easier for man to carry out concerted action; and elaboration of common religious beliefs, which are attempts to understand and interpret the phenomena of life—all these factors of social life play as important a part as do the factors of material life both in the character of the mode of life, the formation of human settlements, and the evolution of mankind.

FAMILIES AND GROUPS

Very soon a host of groups were formed next to each other, some being tributary to others. Complications due to intercourse gave rise to very varied types of community not all of which were equally fitted to follow in the path of evolution and to achieve progress materially and socially. Little is known of the social life of palaeolithic man. The evidence all points to the belief that he lived in family groups *sensu stricto*, but that families would join forces for a season for hunting or gathering, as is still done at the present day by peoples who have kept to a primitive mode of life.

The restlessness shown throughout neolithic civilisation is displayed in this way too. The megalithic remains, whatever was their significance or use, could only have been built by the toil of many communities able to supply abundant labour. The *dolmens, menhirs,* and *tumuli* were so solidly built that many are still found intact in Great Britain, Armorica, Spain, and Portugal as well as in other countries in Asia and America.

The family made its appearance very early, with its own ceremonies and customs. Reindeer hunters, who buried their dead in caves near their dwellings, had funeral rites as far back as the

33

Quaternary. Many types of civilisation would be incomprehensible but for family obligations which often had a stronger influence than material conditions. Thus a matriarchal system obtains in the Bismarck Archipelago. When a man dies, his inheritance goes not to his son, but first to his sister's son and eventually to his brother by the same mother. The basis of this practice seems to be that no account is taken of blood relation between mother and child or between maternal relatives. When a marriage breaks up, the mother keeps the children.

In Negro families the right of ownership belongs to the *paterfamilias* alone, for to him alone belongs the real wealth of the family; that is, his wife and his slaves. Hence the necessity to transmit wealth collaterally, for, if the male children succeeded to the property, they would in fact inherit the right of the deceased over the property, that is, over the women; and this would lead to incest and would be absolutely repugnant to the moral sense of the Negro.

In Muslim families the *paterfamilias* has absolute authority based on force. He is his wife's master and he withdraws her from the sight of strangers. For this reason the Arab house is a real fortress whose only opening is a single strong door and whose rooms look out on to an interior courtyard. As the wife is isolated in this way, she can play only a small part in the economy, whilst in other types of civilisation nearly all the life of the family depends on her work. In many communities at the present day the family is still a basic element. Up to the Communist revolution in China it represented the unit of production within which the members gave each other help, and the moment a man left his family, he became isolated and lost.

TRADE

Among the conditions in which primitive folk lived none was so fruitful as the differences between the resources of one group and another, a fact which led to trade, borrowing of ideas, movement and travel. Primitive communities were not fixed to one spot. They had dealings with each other, sometimes at distances so great as still to cause surprise. There is proof of direct intercourse between peoples in western Europe during the Neolithic Age, when at Grand Pressigny in the French *département* of Indre-et-Loire there were factories making large quantities of flint tools. As these are easily recognised owing to their colour and texture, it is accepted that there was a great trade in them, since their remains are found as far as Brittany, northern France, and western Switzerland. In a cave in Chaleux in Belgium there have been finds of fossil shells which came from deposits near Rheims, Versailles, and the Ardennes. At a Reindeer period settlement near Issoire in the French *départe-*

ment of Puy de Dôme other fossil shells have been found, derived from the *faluns* of Touraine. Other finds show that even in the Reindeer period there was intercourse between the Mediterranean and the Atlantic.

Students of prehistoric times have proved that neolithic civilisation had centres in various parts of the world and that between these centres there was communication, carriage of goods, and migration. Remains of a neolithic civilsation which was rich in pottery have been found in China and particularly in the provinces of Honan and Kansu. Remarkable likenesses exist between stone hoes found in China and North America, between pottery from China and Central America, between ornaments of the Chinese Bronze Age and articles collected in New Guinea, New Zealand, and the Marquesas. Astonishing likenesses have been noticed between Oriental clubs and neolithic clubs found in Italy. Hence, it is clear that during the whole prehistoric period human groups did not live in isolation, but passed on material progress from one to the other. The civilisation based on the use of iron seems to have been carried from central Europe through Illyria into Greece and perhaps into the Peloponnesus by the Dorian invasion. In the Bronze Age strings of beasts of burden transported tin from Cornwall along the Pilgrims' Way to ports on the Straits of Dover and then through the valleys of the Loire and Garonne towards the Spanish coast. As early as the second Bronze Age Phoenicians were seeking the metal in Tartessus. Ore from Galicia and Britain was collected at a port on an island in the Guadalquivir. At the end of the Bronze Age trade in metals enriched Sardinia and the Balearic Isles.

Active and adaptable, man has carried from country to country customs and new modes of life which the natural conditions of the environment might not have brought out. In this way the action of peoples with initiative has often helped others to advance whole stages along the path of progress. American Indians passed abruptly from the Stone and Copper Ages to the Iron Age. Similarly, the Polynesians jumped over both the Copper and Bronze Ages. The Magyar pastoralists who settled in Hungary became agriculturalists through contact with the Slavs. In less than a generation Japan adopted a foreign civilisation. All these examples of assimilation and borrowing reveal the remarkable malleability of some human communities. But this should not make us forget the age-long unchangeableness that fixes others.

LANGUAGE

During the course of the prehistoric period man became, according to Pierre Janet a 'chattering animal' who 'speaks his actions and acts his words'. In the absence of documents we do not know the stages of this revolutionary advance without which no human community would have attained the kinds of organisation which today are studied by geography. With the help of sounds made by the voice language has enabled man to give a sensory and perceptible existence to recollections recorded by his memory and to thoughts which have been suggested by his intelligence. At first oral, then much later written, language strengthens man's response to the world outside him. It acts as a social cement by giving man the faculty of concerted action and of transmitting to his descendants all the knowledge that his mind has acquired. It may be said that language is a faithful record of the ideas of a people and the product of its civilisation. Some peoples who have disappeared survive in their language and in the graphic traces that they have left. Today scholars unite in reviving old tongues that have been dead for thousands of years, but whose written monuments make it possible to rediscover the systems on which they were formed and which attest the intelligence of those who formed and spoke them.

The chief feature in the life of a language during the historical period is indeed its record in writing, an innovation fraught with immense consequences. At first, writing was based on pictographs, that is, it represented sounds by pictures expressing a sequence of ideas. In Mesopotamia they were drawn on clay tablets. In Egypt at the beginning of the Memphite empire the idea took shape that papyrus reeds should be crushed and made into sheets. On these a reed dipped in ink was used for writing. But the decisive step was taken when writing became alphabetical. Some think that the alphabet took its rise in Phoenicia, for on the sarcophagus of the Phoenician king Hahiran (1245 B.C.) are seen characters from which are derived the Aramaic, Hebrew, European, Persian, and Indian alphabets. Others, including Sir Arthur Evans, place the origin of the first alphabet in Crete, and hold that Cretan writing preceded Phoenician, passing to Cyprus and then to Asia Minor at the time of the great Ægean thalassocracy. The pre-Columbian civilisations of America knew nothing of writing. Now, writing confers greater value on the language of the people who speak it. The Lithuanians, who between the eleventh and fourteenth centuries extended their empire as far as beyond Kiev, had remained pagan and had no knowledge of Western culture. They asked their Russian neighbours for writing-masters; and so these conquerors borrowed from Russian many refined ways of expression which they had lacked before. Vilna, the Lithuanian capital, was situated in a district in which White Russian was spoken and where the city was beyond the limits of the Lithuanian tongue. This change in original forms and traditions by a human community seems to have occurred in a similar manner among the Bulgars, for whom the Russian alphabet was the vehicle of ideas and linguistic matter foreign to old Bulgarians.

Today there is a great number of different languages, and the number is continually increasing. As new nations are formed, they set up previously unimportant dialects as literary and official tongues; scholars revive dead languages; attempts are made to create universal languages, among which Esperanto has had the greatest following; and lastly, greater intercourse between peoples by the simultaneous use of several tongues to commercial languages, two clear examples being the *lingua franca* of the Levant and the pidgin English of the Far East.

An examination of the morphological structure of languages places them in three main categories. First, monosyllabic languages, in which all the words are invariable roots, and their relation in a sentence depends on the place they occupy in it. To this category belong Chinese, Annamite, Siamese, and Tibetan. Secondly, agglutinative languages, in which words are formed of several elements joined together, only one having its full meaning, the others being merely prefixes or suffixes. To this category belong Japanese, Ethiopian, Coptic, Basque, Malayo-Polynesian dialects, the language of Australian aborigines and those of the primitive folk in central Africa and America, and Dravidian tongues. Thirdly, inflexional languages, in which the roots of words can be modified in form to express their relation to other roots in the same sentence. To this category belong Indo-European and Semitic languages.

By a strange paradox which has perhaps weighed heavily on mankind and will weigh still more heavily in the future, languages tend to remain distinct and more and more irreconcilable, whilst in other spheres of human civilisation there is a tendency towards unity in the realms of science, industrial technique, and the means of transport and communication. In Europe all the Slav nations have their own tongues, the vitality of which never ceases to increase, and each of the Scandinavian countries has its particular language. This divergent evolution is one of the tragedies of the day.

In the course of history some language groups have lost ground or completely disappeared, whilst others have increased in vigour and have spread. Such changes are of interest to the geographer because they imply developments in human groups and their state of civilisation. Before the arrival of the Celts the peoples of western Europe were Iberians and Ligurians, who spoke languages that have now been lost, though their memory is kept in many place names. The Celtic tongues were in their turn pushed back by the Romance and Germanic languages westwards into Wales, Scotland, Ireland, and Armorica. The languages of other great civilisations, like Babylonian and Egyptian, disappeared in the same way and were replaced by Greek and Arabic. On the other hand there are examples of progressive languages which have gained ground in the past and are still gaining more. At the dawn of history, about the middle of the second millennium, B.C., the Old World witnessed the astonishing growth of Indo-European languages, which became established without the aid of writing over a vast domain stretching from the Atlantic to India and from Scandinavia to Greece. In the first centuries of the Christian era an Indonesian dialect spread over the whole of the island of Madagascar. At a date certainly more recent the Bantu languages became established throughout South Africa. In days gone by Arabic spread over the whole of North Africa from Egypt to Morocco and right up to the present time it has been forcing back Berber, the language of the former inhabitants of the country, but in which there was no writing or literature.

English, the most flexible and simplest of the Germanic languages, has spread over nearly the whole of North America, plays the part of a common language amidst the innumerable tongues in India, and forms the basis of pidgin English. The possession of an easy language that is widely used is an advantage to a people, for it acts as a cement to their moral unity and fosters a common set of manners sentiments, and ideas. Acting apart from the natural and economic conditions, and even at times in spite of them, language gives a people cohesion in their relation with other communities. But this advantage is not without danger, for by persisting in the use of a language not of worldwide use, by refusing to employ in business and to teach children a language that is more widespread than the mother tongue, a people severs valuable contacts with civilisation and quickly improverishes its patrimony. By cementing a too exclusive nationalism the language of a people can also be the best means of keeping it in a state of cultural and material mediocrity.

At the present time, it is estimated that there are some 2,800 living languages or dialects spoken by groups of varying size within the 3,900 million inhabitants of the world. In terms of distribution and usage they may be divided into three groups:

(i) The 'national' official languages used in various countries for diplomacy, government and administration. They are relatively few in number, and some of them have been adopted outside their country of origin by other states as an auxiliary or 'vehicular' language. Thus some countries have two or more official languages, like Afghanistan (Pashtu and Persian), Belgium (French and Flemish), Canada (French and English), and Switzerland (French, German, Italian and Romansch).

English and French function as official languages in most of the African states that came into existence with decolonisation after

1945, and also in several states that became independent earlier. Such countries have often also adopted another official 'national' language in addition to the main vehicle of communication; this is usually a tongue common to several of them, such as Hausa in West Africa and Swahili in East Africa, and it is used in local administration. English remains an auxiliary language for the various states of India, in which the national language is officially Hindi; but, disregarding the numerous dialects, there are also fifteen other languages, spoken by more than 200 millions of the Indian population.

(ii) Official regional languages spoken by large minorities and even, as an auxiliary tongue, by majorities; they are written, and have a literature and a current press; they are used in advertising and in local business transactions, in local and even in national government. The U.S.S.R. is a good example, a veritable linguistic museum indeed, in which 120 languages are recognised officially and used bilingually with Russian, which is the official language of the whole Union.

(iii) In the third category are languages that are really only dialects or variations from a prototype, but are more or less widespread. Their multiplicity is often explained by their lack of a written literature. Such are most of the Polynesian, African and Amerindian tongues. Many of these languages are used locally and by only small minorities; they nevertheless constitute the only means of expression for human groups that may be small in relation to the majority but quite numerous in themselves—such as the Temachek language of the Tuaregs, spoken by less than a quarter of a million people.

All in all, at the present time the languages in the first group represent a little under 7 per cent of the total number of spoken languages, but twelve of them, used as 'national' or 'vehicular' languages, are understood and used by 2,800 million people, or 68 per cent of the world's population:

	million
Chinese	950
English	350
Russian	206
Hindi	200
Spanish	192
German	120
Bengali	108
Portuguese	107
Arabic	104
French	83
Italian	66

THE PART PLAYED BY RELIGION

The intellectual achievement of a people is profoundly different from its material progress and is often quite independent of it. Material progress is due to the techniques and operations which have been invented to produce and transform things needed to support life. Intellectual achievement is effected by beliefs and institutions that have given man his interpretation of life and the physical world. It often happens that materially backward peoples show themselves endowed with a wonderful gift of intelligence. A hundred years ago the Polynesians were certainly more backward than the African Negroes, since they were ignorant of pottery and metallurgy, but they were far superior in general intelligence and mythological wealth. In fact, there exists a whole world of the intellect which lies outside both geography and the natural sciences, but should not be ignored, since religious beliefs exercise a powerful influence on human communities and are at times in violent opposition to other influences arising from natural factors.

The basic fact in religion is to be found in a belief in the existence of invisible powers that accompany man and intervene in all life's activities. These 'spirits' are lodged within man or in the world outside, in forests, streams, or mountains. At first they are more or less vague, then they are given a personality, and religion is the worship paid to them.

Quite early in human history a cult of the dead appears: the most ancient burials go back more than 80,000 years. The Neanderthal people (*Homo sapiens neanderthalensis*), Middle Palaeolithic precursors of the Upper Palaeolithic *Homo sapiens sapiens* with their Mousterian culture, were already burying their dead. Funeral monuments stress the intention to honour the dead and render them inoffensive, even at the cost of human sacrifice. Later, the practice of burning the dead gives proof of a change of idea. The 'spirit' or 'double' is conceived as separated from its bodily trappings and pursuing an independent existence in a world beyond perception. From these primitive beliefs came the great religions that were cradled in Egypt, Mesopotamia, Persia, and India and were all idealistic conceptions that have taken a firm hold on man's intelligence and material life.

The fundamental influence that religion exercises on human society is its demand for restraint of a kind different from that imposed by the physical environment. It prescribes prohibitions and regulations. The worship of plants and animals is found among primitive peoples. The Hidahu Indians of North America never felled a living tree, but used only dead ones. The Ainus of Hokkaido, who live by hunting bears, go through a ceremony of atonement when they have killed one. Furthermore, every year they celebrate a Bear Feast and piously reserve a place of honour for the skulls of the bears killed. Ethnologists tell of similar customs among the Eskimos, who hunt the caribou. These people make long incantations invoking *tuctu*, the magic name for the caribou, and after each kill ceremoniously bury the entrails of a young animal sacrificed for this purpose. Religion forbids Jews and Muslims to eat pork, and in consequence they do not keep pigs. Similarly, Muslims are forbidden wine and they therefore grow the vine solely for the purpose of getting grapes for making into raisins. Among Christians fasting causes a great consumption of fish, and this has caused a remarkable growth of fishing in northwestern Europe, and its development into an important modern industry in countries in which essential foods are supplied by agriculture and the rearing of cattle.

In India the social and moral framework of the country is based on the Hindu caste system. A caste includes only such persons as may join in marriage and have meals together. It represents a collection of prohibitions and duties and is the expression of a system founded on beliefs that establish the principle of authority and order in the community. It was perhaps introduced into India by the Aryan conquerors for the purpose of preventing themselves from being absorbed by the natives. Buddhism developed as a reaction against Hinduism. It was willing to receive the unfortunate and the outcast, and inspired meditation and a taste for solitary life. In central Asia one-fourth of the men at least are monks vowed to celibacy, a moral restriction which deeply influences demography and manpower.

Religious feelings are a force that causes movements and displacements in human communities and at times dictates their projects and their political systems. Journeys are undertaken by men who aim at neither the search for nor the exchange of wealth, but merely at satisfying a religious feeling. In early times devotees could have been seen heading for the holy places of ancient Greece, and later for those of Celtic Gaul. There are Muslim pilgrims to Mecca and Kairuan. In the Middle Ages Christian pilgrimages increased along routes dotted with monasteries, houses of refuge, and hospices. There were long journeys to the holy cities of Rome, Jerusalem, and Santiago de Compostella, and within each Christian country innumerable shorter journeys were made to places sanctified by martyrs and apostles, like the shrine of St Thomas-à-Becket at Canterbury. Great adventures like the Crusades, which had such important effects on international trade, were inspired by religious faith, the Christian desire to wrest the Holy Sepulchre from the Infidel. Even in the sphere of political government and moral civilisation Christian ideas planted the spiritual unity of the West on a wide basis of tradition and Greco-Latin culture within the framework of the Church. Within the states themselves wars of religion have demonstrated the part which religious thought can play in the organisation of human groups. Taking Islam as an example, we can estimate the influence exercised on the life of communities by a religion whose simplicity holds 380 million people within its faith. The Koran is not only the holy book, the basis of religious life, as the Gospels are for the Christian, for it does not confine itself within the spiritual sphere but regulates a whole series of material practices, so that religion at times dominates the most trivial activities of life. Muslim faith is maintained by prayers offered up five times a day, by the annual fast of Ramadan which lasts twenty-eight days and during which the faithful must neither eat, drink, nor smoke from sunrise to sunset, by pilgrimage to Mecca, the dream of their whole life and undertaken as soon as circumstances warrant. The Muslim drinks no alcohol and eats no pork; he does not lend at interest, which in Muslim countries leaves banking to Greeks, Armenians, and Jews. Furthermore, Islam is a religion of power and authority. The Koran is a code, a political handbook, a basis of government. Islam is a theocracy in which political power rests on religious sentiment. This is an ancient conception in the East. 'In all times the Oriental has been a man for whom religion is the great, the only reality, the dominant passion. . . . Alexander realised that the only lasting hold on oriental minds lay in their religion: he therefore became a divine monarch, a god. Islam has all its roots in this oriental past.' (Gautier.) Besides, it is an attractive religion for simple souls, and its devotees do not willingly give up its doctrines. In Africa and India it wins converts every day. Crook has said that in India the rapid progress made by Islam is explained by the attraction exercised on converts by its freedom from the caste system, its humanitarian attitude towards widows and orphans, its lesser rigidity in religious restrictions, Islam permitting the eating of meat, and its repugnance to child marriages, which cause illness and inferiority in Indian traditionalist society.

The number of different religions is far from equalling that of languages. Towards the middle of the twentieth century the denominations were as follows (figures in millions):

Roman Catholics	416
Protestants	230
Other Christians	176
Total Christians	822
Hindus	258
Buddhists	213
Confucians	358
Shintoists	17
Muslims	380
Jews	16
Miscellaneous religions	127

In the eyes of the human geographer these religious denominations fall into two main categories:

1. Those which admit to their faith only persons of a certain race and which tend in this way to stress the isolation or perhaps just the peculiarity of a human community. To this type belong most primitive religions and especially those that are totemic; ancestor worship, of which Confucianism and Shintoism are varieties; and even Judaism, in that Jehovah is above all the god of a chosen and predestined people.

2. Those which try on the contrary to group together persons of different races for the worship of the same god without distinction of race, caste, or social standing. To this type belong especially Christianity, Islam, Buddhism, and several modern philosophical religions. These great unifying faiths have clearly played the greatest part in the evolution of civilisation and the concord of mankind.

TYPES OF CIVILISATION

The proper geographical idea of civilisation stems from the fact that there are as many civilisations as there are human communities, each of which has been formed by the action of its intelligence, by the natural setting in which it lives, and by intellectual and material imports which may have come to it from neighbouring communities. However far back history is traced, human communities are seen to have differences not only in activities, but also in physical environment. Consequently, there are on the earth's surface geographical regions which are territorial areas of civilisation.

This is the proper geographical manner of studying civilisation. It leaves to other disciplines, and particularly to philosophy, the task of examining the general idea of a single civilisation, an idea not to be separated from the notion of unbroken progress, the notion of a human ideal which would bring increasing gains to all nations and would be adopted by all the underdeveloped peoples one after the other. This was a hope dear to French philosophers in the eighteenth century. Before their time Vico had already expressed it, and it is found in German writers of the classical period, such as Herder, Kant, and Goethe. It rests on a conception of human progress which baffles the judgment of all geographical science that pays due regard to facts. Human geography cannot decide, as some would wish it to do, that civilisation is a constant and continuing state of superiority. Let us not wrangle whether it is a steady act of faith in the future or man's need to seek consolation in illusions. Such consolation remains platonic and cannot in any case avail itself of the backing of science. For human geography every civilisation has its own character and must be judged by itself rather than as a function of an arbitrarily imagined human evolution. To define and explain it recourse must be had to methods and processes of analysis which would apply equally to the Eskimo and the Fuegian, the Kirghiz and the Targui, the Chinese peasant and the Negro cultivator, the desert nomad and the dweller in a large town, without troubling to discover whether the gulfs that separate them can and ought to be filled.

It is agreed that from mankind's earliest days there have existed centres of civilisation that have been more advanced than others owing to their mastery of nature. It is clear that these centres must have appeared simultaneously, or sometimes perhaps in succession, in several different environments, quite independently. Quite early, however, men, endowed with some mobility and a memory, must have exchanged ideas and techniques; from the remotest periods of prehistory, an astonishing diffusion of tools and techniques between far-distant human groups has been revealed by specialist studies.

The latest prehistoric discoveries in East Africa, on the borders of Lakes Rudolf and Bavingo, in northern Kenya and southern Ethiopia, have pushed back our knowledge of the origin of man and of civilisation by about 10–12 million years. The finding of human bones and the remains of animals show that this area of eastern Africa was one of the earliest cradles of humanity. Provisional conclusions from these recent finds tend to suggest that between 40 and 35 million years ago—and long before the advent of the first glaciations about 1·6 million years ago—there dwelt in the dense equatorial forests a variety of placental primates from which the first human stocks sprang. It was between 20 and 10 million years ago that certain of these animals, already gifted with the first glimmerings of intelligence, emerged from the forests, where for 15 to 20 million years they had lived essentially by the gathering of vegetable materials, to inhabit the more open treed savanas. For the millions of years they must have retained, in the savanas, their mode of life and feeding, for it was only about 2·5 million years ago that they appear to have crossed the threshold of 'humanity'. For 18 million years they were slowly but surely making the conquests that led progressively to this threshold.

The first conquest was the discovery of the use of hard materials, chosen for their natural shapes and without any fashioning, as implements. The remotest human ancestor had already become 'Homo habilis', the most ancient tool-user. The last million years of this long period had witnessed the assumption of a two-legged stance, that gave the creatures an upright stature and left the arms available for all sorts of complex actions, psychologically coordinated and planned through memory; *Australopithecus habilis* had become a two-handed animal, and this encouraged the development of intelligence because of the immense possibilities that the use of hands invited. Aristotle could well say, in the fourth century B.C. and two thousand years before our current prehistorians, that 'man is intelligent because he has hands'.

There was another major change in the life of this sub-human creature: instead of vegetarian, he became carnivorous and a hunter. But another million years were to elapse before *Homo habilis et erectus* discovered the making and control of fire. This took place during the Mindel glaciation between 700,000 and 300,000 years ago. Then, following these conquests and discoveries, came the more complex elements of civilisation, including an increasing mastery of the art of fashioning stone pebbles, first of flint chips for cutting, then of two-faced implements. Further, the archaeologists have discovered, in Ethiopia, especially in the Omo deposits, traces of planned dwellings, and notably places for cutting up slaughtered game— teeming with teeth and bones of *Dinotherium*, *Stylohypparion*, elephant, hippopotamus and horse, flint implements and innumerable relics of a life already organised into small groups, maybe no more than one family, but observing certain customs.

From about 50,000 years B.P. further progress is evidenced by the successive cultures known as Acheulean and Mousterian, up to the beginning of the last or 'Würm' glaciation. These people had already spread over vast areas beyond Africa; they are found in Europe, the Middle East, and in the steppes of the Far East. Stone tool-making had made great strides, and the techniques already varied from one region to another. Man's mental evolution is evidenced in the appearance of the first burials, which multiply continuously during the Stone Age, down to 10,000 years ago. Spiritual enrichment grows between the fiftieth and tenth millenia, when art appears in the form of cave-paintings.

From this time man seems to possess all the physical and mental qualities that characterise his present-day counterparts. Neanderthal man progressed into *Homo sapiens sapiens*, who ceased to make stone implements at the end of the Upper Pleistocene. From the tenth millennium, with the age of polished stone (the Neolithic) and of metals, the deglaciation opened up new areas biologically favourable for the expansion of the human species, that now colonised the Americas for the first time. In the Holocene period, the Mesolithic marks the end of the Old Stone Age, and the Neolithic coincides with a human upheaval and an era of enormous and rapid progress. In a few thousand years, man became sedentary; he transformed his temporary shelter into a permanent dwelling and a village; he became a cultivator and stock raiser; he created artificial biological environments by deforestation and the selection of useful plants; he invented spinning and weaving, the art of modelling clay and baking pottery, and later the smelting and fabrication of metals. His inventions multiplied—first the wheel, then the waggon, then the bellows for forges; many new cultures arose, and at the same time in all probability the elements of spoken languages. Finally, between the eighth and fifth millennia appeared the first states, hearths of an active civilisation—of which history traces the origins and the progress.

In the northern hemisphere these states are isolated from each other and are rather difficult to reach, yet they are in the same belt of the globe, a belt that is neither temperate nor tropical, but one of treeless steppes with a warm, dry climate. It stretches from the Sahara right to the steppes of central Asia and the loess plain of China between lat. 25° N. and lat. 40° N., and it comprises Egypt, Iraq, the Punjab, and the Hwang Ho plain. Historical documents inform us that the people of the lower valley of the Nile, Mesopotamia, and northern China had a well organised civilisation, some by 3000 B.C. and others by 2000 B.C., and this supposes even earlier beginnings. Vast regions of the earth have remained incapable of a similar effort to control nature. These include the hot, wet tropics, isolated lands beyond the Tropic of Capricorn, and the forests of northern Eurasia. On the other hand, the favoured regions, which have made great advances on their own and then have been helped by borrowings from each other, have much in common. Such common features include a position on the banks of a great river like the Nile, Tigris-Euphrates, Indus, Ganges, and Hwang Ho, whose flood waters and silt make for fertility; a knowledge of methods of using the water for irrigation in hot, dry climates; the cultivation of important food crops like wheat and rice, which has led to a great increase in population; the early development of metallurgical and artistic techniques; the use of improved languages and means of expression, such as writing; and the rise of great religions. Emphasis has been laid by Gautier on the fact that the seeds of all our dogmas, Christian, Jewish, and Muslim were sown in the East between the Pamirs and the Nile.

Outside these centres of ancient Oriental civilisation there are more recent ones which differ greatly in origin and especially in dissemination. First, there is Europe, whose civilisation has spread over the whole world; then, on the other hand, the isolated high tablelands of Central and South America, whose civilisation scarcely passed beyond the bounds of its original home.

In Iraq tradition and ruins bear witness to a civilisation due to man's success in his struggle with water, a civilisation that was the achievement of a community numerous owing to the soil having been fertilised and properly organised for common toil. The work of separating land and water is a Sumerian tradition. At Eresh, El-Ubaid, and Ur the floors of ancient dwellings have been found. They are like artificial islands constructed with alternate layers of straw matting and reeds embedded in earth, dung, or bitumen. Thus man's first work in these regions was really an effort to drain and raise the level of the soil. The extent of the floods on these low plains is attested by the traditions relating to the Deluge. The rivers, with their fertilising waters and silt, determined the whole technique of the use of clay, since no other materials were available. Hence, walls were of clay, buildings of brick, and an immense number of vases and other articles were of earthenware. These sedentary peoples who had mastered the water could dominate the world outside. They observed the heavenly bodies, grouped them into constellations, and distinguished the planets from the stars. They invented the duodecimal notation, which was applied first to the divisions of the year and the day. They introduced square measure and measures of volume and weight. All these steps in progress spread out round their homeland, and gave rise to the civilisation of the Ægean in the west and that of India in the east.

In Egypt progress was due to the same cause as in Mesopotamia. There was the need to protect the land from floods; the reclamation of land by organising drainage and irrigation; a dense population due to the fruitfulness of the soil; and collective skill in the direction and execution of constructing canals, dykes, and gigantic buildings. Here as in Mesopotamia other successes due to man's intelligence also led to the mastery of nature's laws. The first regular division of time had been based on the movements of the moon. This was the month, that is, the time taken between two occurrences of the same phase of the moon. The lunar calendar was replaced in Egypt by the solar calendar because attention had been drawn to the sun by a phenomenon which was periodic in that country. This was the flooding of the Nile, which takes place every year at the summer solstice. The solar year was introduced by Julius Cæsar into Rome, which passed it on to the Christian Church.

Connected with these mainland centres of civilisation and directly descended from them was the special type of insular and maritime culture which arose in Crete. It appeared at the beginning of the second millennium B.C. and had novel features which distinguished it from the civilisation of agricultural plains around great rivers. In the world of islands and coastal settlements in the Mediterranean it reigned supreme on account of its industrial superiority, the skill of its craftsmen, and its mastery of bronze metallurgy. In the second place, the whole civilisation depended on shipping and on the expansion of its trade. It exerted a supremacy of a previously unknown type based on the exploitation of the sea, and about 1750 B.C. it extended right round the shores of the Mediterranean. Its traditions and customs have come down to us from the Greeks.

Other civilisations burgeoned about the same time on the banks of the Indus in northwestern India. Material prosperity there had the same causes as on the banks of the Nile, Tigris, and Euphrates. There too a great river, the Indus, watered a fertile land, but over a far larger area than that of Sumer. Excavations carried out on the sites of the two large towns of Mohenjo-Daro and Harappa have revealed the existence of a vigorous centre of Indian civilisation as far back as the third millennium B.C. Though these towns were destroyed in the second half of this millennium, they nevertheless handed on their civilisation to the Indo-Europeans who occupied the country at that time and whose arrival probably marked the downfall of proto-Indian culture. Then there began the formation of a second Indian civilisation which grew up between the fourth and fifth centuries B.C., a period which extends between the composition of the Veddas and the elaboration of the laws of Manu. The caste system, which was unknown to the Veddas, had taken shape by the date of the laws of Manu.

In far eastern Asia right away from the regions described above Chinese civilisation developed on the plain of the Hwang Ho. The natural conditions were like those of the Nile valley and the river plains of western Asia, though the winters were more severe. Yet the people who settled on the edge of the steppes learnt, as did those mentioned above, to apply the art of controlling water and using it for irrigation. The treatment of metals was skilfully practised, and the plastic arts were carried to a high degree of achievement. The Chinese were ahead of other people in many technical inventions, such as the use of coal, the contrivance of the yoke for draught animals, and of the wheelbarrow, and the art of making lacquer and paper (second century B.C.). Paper was later introduced by the Arabs into India and the Near East, whence it passed to Europe. The Chinese had brought printing into use in the seventh century of our era and by the twelfth century had had movable types. They had discovered and perfected the weaving of silk and the making of porcelain by the tenth century. From the very beginning of our era their chemists had discovered the formula for making gunpowder, a formula which became known in England through the Arabs and Byzantines.

European civilisation is a protracted creation cradled in Mediterranean countries and inherited from civilisations in the Near East. It has grown up and enriched itself in the west and centre of the continent, but in its most peculiar features it has in modern times blossomed in Western Europe, from which it crossed the Atlantic into the New World and in fact reached every part of the globe. Originally, it did not receive its impulse essentially from agriculture, as it had done in the Near East, but from overseas commerce, a liking for trade, and the conquest of distance, matters that imply a wish to draw human communities together for a common interest. This civilisation has displayed a whole galaxy of maritime cultures: Greek, Carthaginian, Venetian, Norman, the Hansa, and, one after another, all the peoples of Western Europe. For this development Europe seemed preordained by its tapering forms, peninsulas, and islands, and by the deep penetration of the seas which reach the very heart of the continent. But it is really the initiative and perseverance of its peripheral peoples that has gradually mastered the sea and reaped the benefit of the close contact between continent and ocean.

The personality of Europe began to show itself in history when from the third millennium B.C., and especially during the whole of the second millennium, the continent was gradually occupied by Indo-European peoples. They were nomadic herdsmen who brought Europe into touch with the old civilisations of the East. As far back as the second millennium (1900–1150 B.C.) there took place in central Asia Minor the great confederation of the Hittites, which contributed notably to the spread of Mesopotamian civilisation towards the Ægean. Between the twelfth and eighth centuries B.C., others settled in western Asia Minor and the south of the Balkan peninsula, where they picked up the heritage of Eastern civilisations, drew instruction from Crete, and themselves became the initiators of a great civilisation which they spread throughout the Mediterranean from the Black Sea to the Straits of Gibraltar. These were the Hellenes.

Hellenic civilisation, the first stage in truly European culture, made vital contributions to the intellectual and material aspects of life. Its characteristics were, on the one hand, an orderly, clear, and inquisitive mind which excluded from its thoughts nothing of the world outside, and, on the other hand, a technical ingenuity which contrived inventions capable of increasing man's control of nature. These included improvements in the casting of bronze and the welding of iron, devices for lifting, new types of boats, the construction of breakwaters and harbours, the endless screw, the paddle wheel, the watermill, transmission gear, the hydraulic clock, the pump both suction and force, the siphon, and the principle of the windmill. Roman technique added scarcely anything to Greek technique, except in architecture and road construction.

A second stage in European civilisation is seen in the Middle Ages, beginning in the eleventh century. This stage was remarkable for its practical inventions, which were the most effective since Hellenic times. In transport we owe to it the modern methods of harnessing, the use of the properties of the magnetic needle, the vertical rudder for ships, and the two-doored river lock. In industry it perfected the windmill and applied the watermill to grinding corn, sawing wood, fulling cloth, and working hammers and bellows in smithies.

In several other branches of the material world it greatly improved the techniques of the ancients.

A third and last stage in European civilisation embraces modern times from the seventeenth century, and especially since the middle of the eighteenth. Primed by technical inventions such as the microscope, thermometer, barometer, and air-pump, it burst out into the Industrial Revolution, that English offspring of coal and steam, which caused an upheaval in industry and transport that affected the whole of man's life. Its effects were so rapid, so profound, and so universal, that the concept of civilisation has long been restricted by some to the elements of European culture.

In the history of civilisation pre-Columbian America represents a world which was isolated for centuries and neither received nor gave anything to other continents. Two native centres of civilisation grew up, one in Mexico, Guatemala, and Yucatan, the other in Columbia and Peru. Both were situated in the tropics, but were on high tablelands where altitude modified the heat of summer. They have one feature in common with the centres of civilisation in the Old World, namely, a dry climate which led to the control of streams by means of irrigation works. Their formation took place far later than those in the Old World. This was because human settlement in America is comparatively recent. No certain proofs have been found of palaeolithic man's existence in America, and the continent was empty of mankind until, after the retreat of the Quaternary ice-cap, immigrants reached it from Asia and Oceania across Bering Strait and the Aleutian Islands or in the extreme south along the sub-Antarctic lands.

In these distant times migrants from Asia brought with them a very early form of civilisation. They took with them neither cereals nor domestic animals, except the dog, nor any of the techniques known in Europe and Asia since the Neolithic Age. American civilisation was wholly developed in that continent independently of Western civilisation, and reached its highest peak in Mexico and Peru, where it attained its zenith in Central America among the Mayas, Toltecs and Aztecs, and in South America among the Chibchas and even more among the Quechuas. Among the last named the Incas built up between the twelfth and fifteenth centuries a vast empire stretching for more than 4,000 kilometres from lat. 2° N. to lat. 35° S., and having an area fifteen times as large as that of Britain. Common characteristics have made these communities a distinct form of civilisation. On their arrival the Spaniards were surprised to find peoples who had built towns and temples, constructed roads and bridges, and cultivated maize, tobacco, and cassava, knew how to smelt and alloy copper and precious metals, and carved objets d'art, but were almost entirely ignorant of the use of domestic animals, of iron, the wheel, glass, and the tools of the Western world, and were without writing. If the Spaniards had not arrested the development of this civilisation, it would have achieved a very efficient adaptation of the American environment. In fact, as it appeared too late, remained in isolation, and disappeared too soon, it failed to spread and has made only slight contributions to the progress of mankind in general.

So, in proportion to a community's ability to control or master nature, it has evolved a form of civilisation peculiar to itself. Though natural factors may bestow elements of stability and permanence on man's mode of life, the same is not true of the factors of civilisation which on the contrary impart a changeable and whimsical character. Where two countries have the same natural potential, it may so happen that one will remain static whilst the other will make great progress in civilisation. The same country and the same group of people may pass through several stages of civilisation. Some countries have times of progress and expansion in civilisation, whilst others undergo periods of retreat and regression. Striking contrasts may occur in the same mode of life owing to a difference in the stage of civilisation.

Mesopotamia, Egypt, India, and China have given birth to great civilisations; and certain periods have witnessed great expansions of human communities. The Upper Palaeolithic culture spread over a vast area and was homogeneous from Siberia to Western Europe; the Neolithic Age marked the dispersion throughout the world of a form of civilisation dependent upon agriculture and stock-rearing, and characterised by pottery-making and the worship of the dead. But progress does not move in a constant direction. Years of mediocrity and quiescence succeeded the civilisation of the Pharaohs. Art was less animated, less powerful in the Neolithic Age than in the Reindeer era. The Veddas of Ceylon lost the skill of working stone and making clothes of bark cloth; their social discipline weakened, and they tended gradually to disappear. In some countries several forms of civilisation have succeeded each other. The most astonishing example of progress of this kind comes from America, where the majority of the population was still in the Stone Age when the Europeans arrived. Suddenly at one stroke they got the use of iron tools and weapons, cultivated plants, and domestic animals from the Old World. Among the latter were the ox, that complement of the plough; the sheep, which multiplied into immense flocks; and the horse, which turned the pedestrians of the prairie and the pampa into excellent riders. At the same time America also got all the material civilisation of Europe with its various types of buildings and its crafts, together with its moral culture and the Christian religion. Other countries, like Tunisia, have had several forms of civilisation

superimposed on or replacing each other. Punic civilisation, introduced by the Phoenicians whose cultivation of cereals and planting
of trees improved the land, was replaced by Roman civilisation
under which agriculture was improved still further and the number
of towns increased. Roman culture was superseded by Arab
civilisation, which had discarded a sedentary urban life in favour of
a nomadic career, and was in its turn supplanted by European civilisation, which again improved agriculture, introduced mining, and
revived town life. Nearer our times another instance of rapid
change in the type of civilisation comes from Japan, where in three-
quarters of a century there has been a development that took more
than seven centuries to achieve in Europe. An old agricultural
nation, isolated and artificially withdrawn from intercourse with
foreigners, Japan has become in three-quarters of a century an industrial country with a merchant navy and a share in world commerce. At the present moment China is trying before our very eyes
to change no less radically, and to establish an industrial state.

Differences in the stage of civilisation, and unequal means of
acting on and reacting to nature, lead to the development and continuance of extraordinary contrasts in the mode of life. Gathering
involves on the one hand the collection of fruit from forest and scrub,
as is done by the Bushmen, Australian aborigines, and the hillmen
of Indo-China; and on the other hand the search for and tapping of
rubber trees in the basin of the Amazon or the Congo, an operation
which would be impossible but for modern means of transport, and
which is carried out for commercial purposes. What a difference
there is between the primitive methods of hunting practised by the
prairie Indians, the pygmies of African forests, the Samoyedes and
Tungus of the tundra on the one hand, and on the other the methods
of trapping fur-bearing animals with the traps and fire-arms of the
trappers around Hudson Bay or in present-day Siberia. What a
contrast there is between the Eskimo method of fishing with its out-
of-date devices, and trawling from big motorised cod-boats on the
Grand Banks.

In hot lands we see side by side the native cultivation of roots and
trees: bananas, cassava, and yams; and the large-scale plantations
of coffee, sugarcane, and rubber of European enterprises. In dry
countries we see the contrast between settled stock-rearing on the
grasslands of the United States and nomadic pastoralism on the
steppes of Asia; or between the nomadic Boers with their ox waggons and the nomadic Bedawins with their saddle and pack animals;
between careful irrigation in Egypt and India, and a ruined irrigation
system in Iraq. In temperate lands agriculture is carried out by a
great labour force in some parts of Europe, but by machines in the
United States and Great Britain; in one place the plough is used, in

another the hoe; here cattle are reared for beef, there for milk; here sheep are bred for wool, there for mutton. Looking at mountain regions we see that in Switzerland and Savoy the grass is used from the valley bottoms right up the mountain slopes, whilst in Japan and the United States there is no economic connexion between the lowland and the upland. In Europe domestic animals supply milk and meat, but in monsoon Asia they are used only as pack or draught animals. In industry huge factories in England contrast with domestic crafts in India and China. Finally, commerce had its great centres at first in the eastern Mediterranean, then in the course of time in the western Mediterranean, and at length on the shores of the Atlantic. Shipbuilding, which was centred in the United States at the beginning of the nineteenth century, moved to England at the end of the same century. Underlying all these migrations and changes, all these contrasts, and all this diversity in ways of life under similar conditions, there are essential differences, accentuated to a greater or lesser degree, in the nature of civilisation.

PART II

FORMS OF ADAPTATION TO THE ENVIRONMENT

CHAPTER 4

HUMAN LIFE IN COLD REGIONS

The cold regions of the earth cannot be regarded as bounded by the
Arctic and Antarctic Circles, which are mathematical lines drawn
round latitude 66½ N. and S. and do not coincide with any particular
condition of life; or the mean annual isotherm for 0° C, since
this indeed includes some very different climates; or by the treeline, on the score that tree growth extends over a large part of
the region. The northern limit of cereals would seem to suit the
facts in the northern hemisphere, since it marks a fundamental
change in man's way of life. In spite of the recent achievements of
scientific cultivation in the Arctic, this line marks the end of agriculture and the beginning of a region inhabited by stock-rearers,
fishermen, and hunters. Thus delimited, the cold belts include vast
areas stretching far beyond the Arctic and Antarctic Circles. But it
is indeed scarcely necessary to discuss the Antarctic region, for, in
spite of its vast extent—it has been estimated to cover about 13
million square km—it is without permanent human settlement.
In the southern hemisphere only the southern tip of South America
and its most southerly islands comprising Tierra del Fuego, Staten
Island, southern Patagonia, and some of the mountains in Chile
fall within an inhabited part of the world.

The Arctic region forms a more varied and more instructive area
for the human geographer. Excluding the Arctic Sea, it extends over
nearly 11·6 million square km. Greenland alone covers some
2·2 million square km and Banks and Melville Islands and Baffin and
Victoria Lands together have an area of more than 500,000 square km.
Alaska measures more than 1·3 million square km, the Canadian
North nearly 3·9 million and the Soviet Arctic taken altogether nearly
as much. The region is therefore a vast part of the *oecumene* (inhabited land), in which man's activities take on very varied aspects.

NATURAL CONDITIONS

The features of the climate generally impose special conditions on
the life of men, animals, and plants. The essential facts seem to be
the long severe winter together with the absence of a summer of
reasonable length. Winter is the season in which the sun does not

57

appear above the horizon. Continuous night reigns for several months, and the length of this period explains the low temperature of the mass of air in immediate contact with the Poles. The fall in temperature is all the more pronounced because, during the period of insolation in summer, the obliquity of the sun's rays reduces the amount of heat absorbed by the soil and the surrounding air. Apart from its effect on climate, the polar night itself is a principal factor which powerfully affects the life of both animals and man. Explorers who have wintered among the Eskimos testify to the depressing influence of the long night, which gradually undermines the temperament and morale of even those most adapted to the conditions. The darkness and close confinement which it entails frequently bring on mental disorders, fits of madness, or suicide due to neurasthenia. These ills are to be imputed far more to isolation in the darkness of winter than to the inevitable privations which the conditions involve.

The cold is incredibly severe. In the Jana valley in which Verkhoyansk is situated as well as in the upper valley of the Lena and near Oymekon the mean temperature is known to be –51° C during the whole of January, and every winter the temperature falls below −59° C. It has even been known to reach −70° C, and yet this district is inhabited and is now colonised by Russians, for the complete stillness of the air enables man to bear these low temperatures. Apart from the danger which high winds and storms cause by burying shelters under snowdrifts, these gales are a serious threat to the nervous and thermic balance of the body. Men who have successfully endured the lower temperatures in calm weather have been known to die as a result of 'windchill' during violent storms. Travellers say that a temperature of −51° C in calm weather is borne more easily than one of −34° C in tempestuous winds. Man's most terrible enemy is the blizzard, the *purga* of Siberia, which envelops the traveller in whirling snow and makes it impossible for him to find his way. On such occasions even the dogs' scent is often at fault, and the animals refuse to obey. The wisest course is to stop and await the end of the storm. It is impossible to light a fire, for a match is extinguished at once by gusts and the fuel blown away. Sledges are set up as a windbreak, and the men shelter in their fur-lined sleeping bags. If the storm does not last too long, they may by this means escape being frozen to death.

Another feature of the climate is the abruptness of its great changes of temperature. They occur on the reverse slopes of mountains facing the sea, where winds blowing from the ocean towards the interior of the land are warmed by a process similar to that of the *foehn* as they pass across the mountains. Thus, in Scoresby Sound a sudden rise of temperature has been observed in winter from −20° C to 4° C. The disturbance in the human system caused by such changes accompanied by furious winds may well be imagined.

Since the temperature remains below 0° C for ten months, the ground is frozen so deeply that summer cannot bring about a complete thaw. This permanent freezing of the ground has incalculable results. The relief of the land, which is overlaid with mud caused by the thaw and not always cleared off, gives rise to the special type of morphological landscape that has been described at length by Russian geographers. The mantle of detritus, whose transformation into soil is controlled by the permanently deep layer of hard, impermeable, frozen rock, assumes a reticulated polygonal structure and clutters up the surface with a layer of pebbles.

The frozen layer, known as *tjäle* in Scandinavia, *merzlota* in the Soviet Union, and *permafrost* in Canada, is equally inconvenient everywhere. Owing to the seasonal thaw it helps to make the growth of trees impossible, since the roots would encounter the frozen rock when they penetrated the liquefied soil. It has set the Russians serious problems in the construction of their Arctic airfields and forced them to make the runways of earth brought from the south; and further difficulty is caused in building houses at Magadan, Bereliak, and Seymshan, where a pile foundation brought on a local thaw of the *merzlota* and thus the weakening of the structure. The instability of the ground has prevented the construction of railways in the Arctic, and modern roads, like those in Alaska and the Canadian North as well as in eastern Siberia, have had to be protected against frost by a careful system of drainage. Even in northern Sweden the ground freezes in winter down to a certain depth; but the phenomenon reaches its greatest development in North America and Siberia. Under the Siberian tundra the *merzlota* appears only 60 cm below the surface layer which is melted in summer. Vast stretches are turned into swamps. Trenches dug in the bottoms of valleys have proved the *merzlota* may go down more than 90 metres below the surface. The thickness of the frozen layer depends greatly on the geological composition of the rock. In the soft rock of the Siberian plains, for instance, the *merzlota* goes deeper than in the granite of North America. At Irkutsk a sounding proved the rock frozen to a depth of 217 metres. Furthermore, there are often several layers of frozen rock one below the other alternating with unfrozen layers. It was in this 'fossil ice', much of which dates back to the Quaternary, that there occurred the discovery of the frozen mammoths which during the last century attracted ivory hunters to these icy regions.

So harsh are conditions in winter that they impose an immense effort at adaptation on living things. Few woody plants are found in polar vegetation. On the Taymyr peninsula only a small number of shrubs have been counted. The Arctic willow (*Salix polaris*) lifts its head scarcely 15 mm above the lichens and mosses. At the southern end of Greenland in the latitude of Oslo there are forests of birch trees 3 or 4 metres high, but with gnarled and twisted boles. Rowans, alders, and junipers are also 3 or 4 metres high, but their growth-rings sometimes show the undersized trees to be four hundred years old. Moreover, these plants are seen only in sunny places, in the southern part of the region. Some low growing plants growing in a fairly rich assortment are often found arranged in characteristic cushion shape. They include the crow-berry with its black fruit, the swamp whortleberry, the myrtle, the osier whose pliant boughs may reach up some 2 metres in damp, sheltered soil.

One of the characteristic features of all Arctic vegetation is that the plants are all dwarfs. In the Siberian Arctic it has been observed (Middendorf) that one-third of the shrubs are between 15 and 40 cm tall. The grass is sometimes higher than these dwarf shrubs. As for the mosses, they are often only a few mm in height. This dwarf flora has, however, large underground parts, which is a means of escaping the fatal effect of radiation and ensuring their continued life. The similarities in structural alteration caused to the plants by cold and lack of moisture have been emphasised (Emm. de Martonne). Many of the features of Arctic flora are plainly xerophilous, and the plant associations in the region present the sparse appearance that they do in arid countries.

Like the flora the fauna adapts itself to the cold. Warm-blooded animals do not practise hibernation owing to the very low temperatures, but their bodies are covered with thick fur of closely set, very fine hair, as in the case of the ermine and Arctic hare, or with a coarser coat like that of the reindeer or musk-ox. To this protective covering is added a thick layer of fat, which in the seal may be as much as 10 cm. In the herbivorous animals this reserve of fatty matter forms during the summer. Chief among the mammals are the carnivores and consequently defensive camouflage covers the ermine, Arctic hare, Arctic fox, the ptarmigan, and the snowy owl with a white coat that makes them difficult to see against the snow.

The outstanding features of both the flora and the fauna of the cold regions is their poverty. The vegetable and animal worlds alike comprise a considerable number of individuals, but these belong to a very few species.

In contrast with the tropical flora, Arctic flora shows great uniformity in the circumpolar belts. The more severe the cold, the fewer the species. In Iceland the flora is fairly varied, but it grows gradually poorer in Greenland, Spitzbergen, and the Taymyr peninsula and is utterly impoverished in Melville Island, where there are only sixty species of plants. Research has established that polar flora does not comprise more than 800 species, whilst Mediterranean flora comprises more than 7,000. There is the same contrast in the animal kingdom. In the tropics there are sixty-nine families of mammals compared with a mere eight in the polar belts. Birds are better represented, but 114 out of 160 species are marine, and, as in the animals, there is a progressive impoverishment of continental species. South of latitude 68° N. there are still twenty species of sparrows, but north of lat. 74° no more than two remain. In the insect world the species scarcely amount to twenty, about ten of which are beetles and there are some lepidoptera (butterflies and moths) and diptera (mosquitoes).

The coming of summer in these cold regions has been likened to an explosion. In the north of Siberia the temperature rises abruptly in the month of May. At Golskikha on the estuary of the Yenisey in lat. 71° 45′ N. everything is still under snow in mid-June, but a few weeks later the ground is carpeted with flowers. Near Yakutsk the snow melts in a few hours. Half a day is enough to thaw a river like the Angara, i.e. to melt away a sheet of ice nearly 1 metre thick. Two days later the grass literally shoots up, and before this the ground is covered with daisies and anemones. In the polar regions as a whole the sharp rise in temperature occurs in May, and this causes the vegetation to grow rapidly. As soon as the air temperature reaches 3° or 4° C plants begin to blossom. This happens right from the month of May in southern Greenland and all along the forest border of the New and Old Worlds. It is later near the sea, where fog sometimes makes insolation less effective. In Spitzbergen, for instance, the blossoming period occurs between 21 June and 20 July. This extraordinary vigour of the vegetation explains Russian success in high latitudes with the cultivation of cereals like barley, rye, and oats and some kinds of summer wheat able to ripen completely in fourteen weeks. This is due to the fact that air and soil store up solar calories, for from July night is reduced to a mere twilight and the period of insolation extends, at least in theory, to twenty-four hours a day. The sun's small angle of inclination above the horizon gives great advantage to slopes facing south. The snow melts on them first, the melt-water drains off them easily, and there first the grass springs up green right up to the remaining patches of snow. There too game collects and man's best hunting grounds are to be found.

In the middle of Arctic Siberia it is not uncommon to see the thermometer rise in summer to 36° C. The earth is hot enough for bare feet not to be able to endure direct contact with the soil. Throughout the cold regions the surface of the ground rises to much higher temperatures in summer than the air over it. In

Spitzbergen at the head of a south-facing fjord the following records were taken about midday in July:

	C
Air temperature 1 metre from the ground	4
on a plant tuft	15
on the ground	10
75 mm below the surface	9

The rock is frozen at a depth of between 24 and 30 metres

On the average when in summer the air temperature near the ground reaches 3° C, the layer of soil in which the roots of the plants spread out reaches between 10° and 15° C, so that the roots are contained in a warm medium in which the temperature is nearly constant owing to the slight diurnal range. Between lat. 70° and 78° N. the diurnal range in June is 4·5° C, in July 3·4° C, and in August 2°9· C. Hence the extreme importance of microclimates in the Arctic. The great success in cultivation in these difficult regions could most often be explained as due to the judicious use of slight advantages in soil and aspect, which though negligible in less harsh climates, assume here an essential discriminative value in the choice of sites for human settlement and cultivation.

Summer is a clearly marked interval between two very severe winters and enables living beings to penetrate into the cold regions right up to astonishingly high latitudes. In the hard climate of Verkhoyansk, in which the mean annual temperature does not rise above −16° C, there is a forest of larches. These trees are able to bear very low temperatures, and besides for the three months of June, July, and August they enjoy a mean of 11° C and in July one of 15° C. This summer warmth allows the forest to advance northwards along the valleys of Siberia to more than a degree of latitude beyond the limit reached in Europe. It also allows the growth of a large variety of phanerogams, of which Melville Island has sixty species and New Siberia thirty-six.

The extraordinary swarm of mosquitoes that exist in the tundra and on the borders of the great northern forest has become a commonplace story. The insects were a frightful handicap to the construction of the Alaska Highway, they are a scourge in the salt and gold mines in the Soviet Arctic, and they help to hasten the northward migration of reindeer at the beginning of summer. But surprisingly enough, the number of mammals increases in very high latitudes. Thus, the large ice-free areas on the north coast of Greenland and the nearby islands harbour herds of musk-oxen and crowds of hares and lemmings. Traces of Eskimo encampments have been discovered as high as in lat. 81° N.

Climatic conditions become progressively more severe from south to north and thus cause a zonal distribution of the chief forms of plant and animal life. It is scarcely possible to speak of a belt of cultivation, for these regions are beyond the limit of cereal cultivation and the zones of normal agriculture. Only by persistent effort is it possible to succeed in making sporadic centres of cultivation which appear as veritable oases in the midst of deserts that repel attempts at agriculture. On the whole, in the northern hemisphere, where sub-polar nature presents some contrasts, there are three types of clearly distinct physical environments whose resources are very often blended by human communities. They are forest lands, tundras, and the sea, the last of which forms another vital region that is by far the best endowed by nature.

Until recently there was no cultivation in the Arctic. The indigenous flora affords man only berries, lichens, roots, and several kinds of sorrel; but the cultivation of cereals has been deemed impossible. A few favourable districts, which have the advantage of both good insolation and a supply of melt-water in spring, could be used for cultivation, but their combined areas are small. In Iceland, where the natural vegetation allows the rearing of sheep and goats and in addition today a few horses and cows, the inhabitants have succeeded in cultivating patches of vegetables and potatoes on a total area of not quite 1,000 hectares in the whole island, which measures 105,000 square km. In northern Scandinavia the Lapps sow barley, but the harvest is exposed to the risk of either a late spring or frost in an early autumn. Modern scientific farming and technique have, however, made possible the cultivation of small areas in the Arctic wherever exceptional mineral wealth or imperative strategic necessity has caused the establishment of permanent centres of population.

One of the most important of these today is situated on the Kola peninsula. Near the fishing centres on the Murmansk coast polymetallic mines and industrial plants which refine aluminium or produce chemicals have given rise to settlements of several thousand persons. There the Soviet Government has started an original kind of cultivation. In the Khibini tundra in lat. 67° 44′ N. it has introduced the cultivation of European forage crops to feed the domestic reindeer which supply meat to their Arctic 'towns'. Then, in drained swamps crammed with artificial fertiliser the 'Industria' sovkhoz sows corn in an area of about 5,000 hectares. The sowing is done with seeds that have germinated under frames. As the frames are heated by electricity, they also enable the cultivation of a great variety of vegetables, not to mention tomatoes, which ripen during the Arctic summer. At the mouth of the Yenisey another centre of cultivation near Igarka has succeeded in producing the forage needed for a little herd of milch cows and in growing oats and beans on some 100 hectares. The vegetables are grown in underground chambers which are heated and lit by electricity generated by windmills driven by Arctic winds assisted by petrol engines. In the upper Kolyma valley and on the shores of the Sea of Okhotsk around Bereliak cultivation under frames enables cabbages, cucumbers, tomatoes, and melons to be grown. Sown under heated frames at the beginning of March three months before the thaw, these vegetables are put into the open air in summer, when they are ripened by the heat of the sun. Stranger still are the results obtained in Yakutia, where the first attempts at cultivating cereals took place about forty years ago. The earliest Russian colonists thought wheat cultivation impossible and copied the Yakuts in eating roots and the juicy part of pine bark. When attempts at cultivation were made, the cereals were killed by frost, but after a few good seasons successful crops were grown, and from the seeds were obtained varieties that proved to be acclimatised. Today, besides growing barley, oats, wheat, rye, and potatoes, the Yakutsk district has apple orchards. To achieve this the Soviet scientific farmers took advantage of the astonishing accumulation of heat induced in the surface soil in summer. The apple trees are trimmed down to a height of 60 cm, and their spread is limited to three metres in circumference. In winter they are covered over with fir branches piled up so as to form several beds, which are then over-laid with a thick covering of earth. Buried in this way the trees escape the killing frost. In spring the earth is cleared away and the fir branches removed. The trees are whitewashed to prevent the burning rays of the sun from scorching the bark and to help the diffusion of calories all round the plants. The ingenious and minute use of the smallest favours of climate enable one to realise the real hostility of the environment to man's crops. What treasures of science, what expenditure of energy it takes to get a few kg of apples from a tree which in another climate would yield 50 kg without any trouble. In the New World around Fairbanks, White-horse, and Yellowknife 'civilised' man has surrounded himself with familiar plants in the same artificial conditions. Northern Greenland, which is little favoured by its climate, is about to see the beginning of one of these oases in the American base at Thule. These are only feelers, and frankly speaking, very risky ones of our civilisation reaching out into the Arctic solitudes. What are a few thousand hectares of cultivation scattered over millions of square km of forest and tundra?

In the cold regions there is a continuous spread of forest which forms the southern boundary of the north polar environment. In the New World it covers 270 million hectares, and in the Old World 700 million hectares. The migration of man and of animals is nearly every-where subject to a seasonal rhythm in which they make the forest their refuge in winter and the treeless tundra their haunt in summer.

In the Arctic the treeline coincides fairly well with the isotherm for 10° C, but not with any parallel of latitude. In Alaska and the basin of the Mackenzie forest stretches for more than 500 km north of the Arctic Circle, but in eastern Canada it ends at lat. 57° N. on Richmond Gulf owing to the low summer temperature caused by large expanses of ice in Hudson Bay. It moves north again in the Old World as far as the northern tip of Scandinavia and the Kola peninsula and reaches lat. 72° 50′ in Siberia at the mouth of the Khatanga, 1,600 km farther north than Richmond Gulf. It retreats slightly southwards again between the Lena and Bering Strait, where it does not pass north of lat. 64° N. Here the trees are broken or killed by dry, violent winter storms that in north-east Siberia cause an enormous fall in temperature. Nowhere, however, is the treeline a real line, for as one goes northwards the trees become smaller and smaller and less and less densely spaced, and the forest breaks up into clumps of little trees and, leaving the high ground bare, grows in the valleys and in the sheltered lower slopes. Then, creeping along at ground level it leaves its last representatives in the tundra in the shape of dwarf shrubs, birches, and junipers, whose branches do not grow upwards, but tend to stretch out parallel with the ground so as to rest on the warmest layers of air. In the Yukon valley and that of the Khatanga the advantage of having deep, sheltered valleys enables the forest to advance northwards.

Birches form the border of the forest in southern Greenland, Iceland, northern Scandinavia, and the Kola peninsula, but in all other parts of the region conifers form the rearguard. These are *Pinus nigra* and *Pinus alba* in North America, *Picea obovota* on the east coast of the White Sea, and *Larix sibirica, Pinus sibiricus, Pinus sylvestris*, and *Pinus cembra* (Siberian cedar) throughout the Siberian tayga. Along with the conifers are also found massive stands of poplars, alders, and willows. The undergrowth is formed by a thick carpet of red whortleberries, bilberries (*Vaccinium oxycoccus*), and strawberry plants. In clearings in Siberia *Heracleum sibiricum* grows into tall grass. The forest harbours a fauna consisting of various ruminants and carnivores, swamp birds, grouse, and hazel hens. The streams swarm with fish, the choicest of which is the sterlet (*Acipenser ruthenus*), which may reach a weight of 3 kg. The plentiful game supports hunting and fishing peoples, the most typical of these being the Tunguses of the tayga, who number 40,000 and are scattered over the region between the Yenisey and the Pacific. In Canada as in Siberia the forest border of the cold belt contains the finest species of fur-bearing animals, including the black or silver fox, black bears, ermine, and sable.

Another peculiar country is the tundra. This name is given in the

Soviet Union to cold expanses stretching from the edge of the forest to the shores of the Arctic Sea. In Canada they are called 'barren lands' or 'barren grounds'. The environment is hostile to tree growth, and phanerogams, of which there are more than 120 varieties, do not always succeed in flowering and bearing seeds; but from the end of June compact masses of anemones are found to the south of Hudson Bay, where there are also six varieties of edible berries, which are picked by the Eskimos in mid-July.

The tundra is a paradise of mosses and lichens over the greater part of its surface. Two genera of mosses are dominant, namely, *Polytrichum*, which has a short stem and greenish-brown leaves packed together like a fir bud and covers nearly all of Arctic Siberia; *Sphagnum*, which grows in swamps and damp valley bottoms, forming peat bogs wherever water does not run off. The slightest feature in the surface of the ground brings on a difference in grasses, and phanerogams cluster on humps where the soil is drier and better warmed by the sun. As this kind of feature often occurs on the borders of the tundra, it forms a fairly continuous belt of good pasture, as the Siberian Samoyedes well know. In the New World, and at any rate on the shores of Hudson Bay, the edge of the forest advances far too near to the sea to give room enough for such pastures. Perhaps this explains the absence of pastoralists in high latitudes in the New World.

Farther north the humps form the habitat of lichens and, especially in Siberia, of the variety known as *Cladonia*, or 'reindeer moss', which is the favourite food of Samoyede reindeer. The tundra is alive in summer only, for then a whole fauna of large and small herbivorous animals, rodents, and carnivores ranges about. Summer is the only season in which the tundra affords man a living either by hunting, fishing, or stock-rearing.

The last belt of the Arctic region is the maritime fringe near the Pole. It is a world apart, without plant life, but swarming with animal life. This exuberance, for which the sea alone is responsible, is found to be as great off the shores of Antarctica as within the compass of the Arctic Sea. The disappearance of land fauna is accompanied by an astonishing proliferation of marine fauna, which explains the swarm of annelida, echinoderms, molluscs, crustacea, and the host of planktonic elements found in the region. Being well supplied with food, the coastal waters serve as assembly grounds for schools of fish, which themselves attract innumerable species of fish-eating birds and mammals as far north as lat. 82° N.

Among the birds the dominant species are those that fish, swim, and dive in the sea. Some are only occasional visitors to the region. The eider duck (*Somateria mollissima*) finds shelter for its nest as far north as lat. 80° N. Seamews, gulls, and cormorants, which haunt polar shores in flocks, are ubiquitous species attracted to high latitudes by the abundance of fish. Others, such as penguins, guillemots, and loons, live permanently in the region. Auks (*Alcidæ*), which are found on Arctic shores, have a limited power of flight. On the other hand, penguins, which live in the southern hemisphere, have atrophied wings that are practically changed into fins. Their countless flocks cover the ice cliffs and shores of Antarctic lands, the coasts of Tierra del Fuego, Patagonia, and the Falkland Islands. Currents of the Southern Ocean have carried them to Tristan da Cunha, Kerguelen, St Paul, and Amsterdam Islands, to New Zealand, South Africa, and the Galápagos Islands.

The most remarkable sea mammals are the walrus and seal. There are two species of walrus, one of which is confined to the North Atlantic, where it is found in the fringing seas of the Arctic and on the northern coasts of Newfoundland and Labrador. The other, which is remarkable for its much longer tusks, is confined to the North Pacific, where it is found in Bering Sea, especially around the Pribilof Islands, and in the archipelago off the western coasts of Arctic America (Banks Land). Seals live in the same waters. Every year in the breeding season they gather in enormous herds on the sloping beaches of Arctic islands. In these 'rookeries', the ground of which they literally carpet with their outspread bodies, sealers kill them in thousands. In the Antarctic seas mammals are represented by the sea-lion, or eared seal, which abounded at the beginning of the century all around Antarctica, but thoughtless massacre has made them scarce in some of the more accessible rookeries. The big cetaceans, like the right whale, being deep-sea animals, have only incidental interest for coastal life, and their exploitation calls for different techniques than those which the northern peoples have painfully elaborated. On the other hand, the polar bear (*Ursus maritimus*) is the king of Arctic beasts. It feeds mainly on fish and seals and does not hunt land animals except when the ice is too thick for it to fish. On those occasions it eats anything, including the bodies of stranded whales and birds with their young. When intense cold deprives it of all sources of food, it makes a nest in the snow and hibernates for several months.

Throughout the cold regions the environment is one of marked difference in the seasons. In the three basic parts—forest, tundra, and coast—winter is a dead season during which shelter is necessary; but summer is a season of life and exuberance. In winter all animals that do not hibernate leave the tundra for the forest, and birds fly to countries farther from the pole. In summer the whole region is astir with the movement of living creatures. There are bird migrations, the passage of schools of fish along the coasts and in the rivers, and long journeys of herds of grass-eating animals. These differences and this periodicity impress themselves strongly on human life even in the heart of the most modern Arctic 'towns'.

The scarcity of provisions afforded to man naturally by the plant world increases the seriousness of the occasions when food plants cannot be grown. Besides, few of the plants yield food for the gatherer. As a result the animal world has to be drawn on throughout to provide a means of livelihood, whether by hunting, fishing, or stock-rearing; and as a rule there is a more or less successful combination of all three activities. In fact, a single means of earning a livelihood is seldom adequate for the subsistence of a human community, and therefore peoples who are restricted to one activity only, like the Indians and Eskimos who hunt caribou in the Canadian North or the Onas who hunt guanacos in Tierra del Fuego, are counted amongst the most wretched and insecure of men. Taken all round, the peoples of the cold regions are clearly divided into two groups differing in mode of life. On the one hand, there are the fishermen and hunters who live by killing and eating wild animals; and on the other hand, the stock-rearers who live mainly on domesticated reindeer.

Hunters and Fishermen.—There are two spheres of hunting and fishing the land and the sea. These are equally full of game, but are in fact exploited by different types of men. The sea with its more varied resources has produced the most original types. Both in the Old and New Worlds hunters in the Arctic pursue two kinds of game today. In summer they hunt for subsistence and in winter for the fur trade. The animals which supply food are the reindeer and the American caribou, which is a smaller variety. The whole life of the Yakuts of Siberia and of the Eskimos in Canada is organised to suit reindeer hunting. In May just when the reindeer, which have been harassed by mosquitoes and gadflies, leave the forest for the ice-free pastures of the north, they are thin and often covered with sores. Those killed are scarcely fit for dogs' food. In August and September, when the beasts return to the forest after having been fattened in summer, the real hunt begins. In some years herds of several thousand animals are seen moving in columns thirty to sixty miles long. The Yakuts prefer to attack them as they pass across a stream. As soon as the herd has followed its leader into the water, the hunters shoot forward in boats to delay the crossing, whilst the most skilful, armed with short spears, penetrate into the mass of swimming beasts and slaughter them. Good hunters have been seen to kill a hundred reindeer in less than half-an-hour. When killed, the beasts are pulled up on to the banks and cut up. The meat is dried, smoked, or frozen if the temperature is suitable, and forms a stock of winter food.

In Canada also caribou hunting takes place in summer. As soon as spring begins, the Eskimos move away from the coast where they had hunted seals all the winter and go to find the caribous, which are then starting on their summer migration. On the hunting grounds they used often to come into collision in former times with the Denes and Algonquin Indians, who had left the forest in pursuit of the caribous. The traditional method of hunting consisted of driving the animals towards natural or artificially constructed narrow passages at which the hunters lay in ambush and attacked the herd with arrows and spears. Sometimes, too, the herds were driven into deep water, where they were at the mercy of the hunters. All through the summer the men followed the caribou, moving day after day, to set more ambushes. The game killed in the day was quickly prepared, dried, and placed in a 'cache', that is, in an underground hiding-place dug down to the frozen rock, carefully marked—and the chase was resumed. Every clan has a certain number of store-houses of this kind to which it has recourse in winter.

The method of hunting has scarcely changed. But the introduction of fire-arms, which at first caused greater slaughter, had the effect of making the game dangerously scarce. Besides, frightened by the noise of the guns the caribou deserted some of the hunting grounds to use other routes less accessible to man, so that the Eskimos gave up using guns when hunting for food and when it was necessary to remain as long as possible in touch with a big herd. They keep the guns for hunting in winter, when they shoot single beasts.

In winter hunting takes place in the forest. The peoples of northeastern Siberia, like those of Alaska and Labrador, are actively engaged in it. The Eskimos are mainly busy with trapping foxes, but the Tunguses and natives of Kamchatka chiefly hunt sables. This is a difficult business, for the sable is very shy. The hunter must face hardships that put a strain on his constitution, for he cannot light a fire since the scent of it would be enough to drive away the game. Winter hunting is carried on only for the cash return it brings. With the money got from the sale of furs the natives, both American and Asiatic, are able to buy tea, flour, arms, and ammunition as well as little things whose use was formerly unknown, but was learnt on their contact with civilisation.

Fishing in lakes and at river mouths is the natural and often indispensable complement of hunting. On the coast of the Anadyr and the Sea of Okhotsk it is more important than hunting for procuring a stock of provisions for the winter. Among the Tunguses and Koriaks, who are both hunters and stockmen, it plays a great part in procuring food, especially among the forest families who have no domestic reindeer. It is carried on in both spring and summer.

Spring fishing brings in a valuable food supply just when the winter stocks become exhausted. From the beginning of May plaice and haddock make their way up the river mouths. Then herrings arrive off the coast, followed sometimes by cod, nearly at the same time as salmon move down the river. The consequent swarm of fish attracts Tungus clans to the coast, where men and dogs give themselves up to feasts of fresh fish, nobody giving a thought to laying up stocks for the winter. This need occurs to them only during the summer fishing, which takes place at the end of June. At that time the fishermen build dams and set traps in the streams so as to catch the schools of salmon-trout which for three months move to and fro between the sea and the upper valleys of the rivers. The fish caught are threaded on to sticks and put in the air to dry. In the bright, dry weather this is an easy operation, but fog often necessitates its completion by smoking the fish in a fire of rotten birch logs.

Fishing is the chief business carried on along the coasts, but it is combined with hunting sea animals. The abundance of animal life explains why the whole of the Arctic coast is peopled with fishermen, including the Norwegians of Finnmark, the Tunguses, Chukchis, and Aleutians; but nowhere in the Old World does one find a people so well adapted as the American Eskimo to make a living from the sea. They are a typical coastal people who have been able to take advantage of whatever Nature gives for man's use. Thanks to them the Arctic archipelagoes of the New World are inhabited, whilst the islands off the coast of Siberia have never had permanent native settlements. Today, the territory occupied by Eskimos extends from lat. 79° N. on the coast of Greenland to lat. 53° 4′ south of Hudson Bay. From east to west it stretches from the coast of Greenland to the coast of Alaska. In this vast expanse which covers 22 degrees of latitude and 60 degrees of longitude Eskimos occupy only the coastal strips, for only a few tribes in Alaska and Labrador live far from the sea. As a coastal people they depend wholly on the sea for their food. In 1819 Parry noticed that the Eskimos on the west coast of Baffin Bay had nothing in their summer tents but what came from the sea: food was fish or seal meat; clothes and boots of sealskin; the framework of the tents, the uprights of the doors, the fastenings, the frames of the boats, and the sledge-runners were made of whalebone, and their knives were sharpened walrus teeth.

The caribou, musk-ox, lemming, and other land game are for the Eskimo merely a windfall or a seasonal contribution to the larder. His prey is usually the seal, which is harpooned just as it comes out of its air-hole in the ice to breathe on the surface. The Eskimo knows all the seal's tricks and can outwit it in a thousand ways. However, the *Delphinidæ*, grampuses, and right whales are as popular with him. In Disköfjord, lat. 69° N., it sometimes happens that ice from the open sea closes the mouth of an inlet before the whales in it can get out, and the animals are slowly driven towards the inner end of the fjord. Such a windfall, known by the Eskimos as *savssat* (bottling up), attracts to the neighbourhood tribes that come from afar to profit by it. Thus, it may be that in one season several hundred narwhals and whales may be killed, and these supply an enormous quantity of meat, fat, leather, and bone. The tools, dwellings, and even the customary laws of the Eskimos are strictly adapted to making a living from the sea and to its hardships.

Stock-rearers.—In the cold regions there are no cereals, but the climate allows the use of the pastures that spring up in summer. Domestic animals like the ox, horse, sheep, and even the pig have penetrated very far today into the cold regions, but none of them has been able really to endure a pastoral mode of life. The artificial conditions in which beasts are kept makes them merely extras. Only in Iceland has the sheep become the basis of a rural economy. Since the thirteenth century the rearing of the animal has been strictly regulated by legislation. The law fixes the time of fecundation, and a lamb born out of season involves a heavy fine on the owner. Every spring the flocks in a district are all collected and taken in a body to the summer pastures, or *affretur*. The return of the flocks at Michaelmas is followed by the slaughter of many of the animals, for, as the stocks of forage are small, only a few beasts can be kept through the winter. The dried, smoked, or frozen carcasses form the meat supply for the winter. Icelanders have for long lived almost exclusively off their sheep, which at the present time number half a million head. The wool provides the cloth for their clothes; the membranes got from lambing have long served to replace panes of glass in the farm windows.

Except in Iceland, however, there are no sheep in the Arctic. The flocks introduced by the Danes into the district of Julianehaab where southern Greenland is free from ice are there only as an experiment. Although in summer they graze on the meagre crop of willow, dwarf birch, daisies, and rhododendrons, they have to spend the winter under cover, and for more than six months they must have their food eked out with dried fish. So, in fact, the experiment is a skilful exercise in zootechnique rather than a genuine case of acclimatisation.

To the same kind of successful experiment belongs the rearing of an English breed of pigs in some of the settlements in the Soviet Arctic.

To feed the pigs locally grown oats and barley plants are cut when green, and ensilaged; but the grain and fish meal which are indispensable for fattening the animals come from Vladivostok by lorry or aircraft.

Oxen and horses have a less artificial life. In Iceland cattle are small and usually hornless. Fed in winter with fish waste, they yield little meat, but give a fair amount of milk, from which a sort of cheese called *skyr* is made and stored in casks in summer when milk is plentiful and is eaten during the winter. The horse was introduced into Iceland about a thousand years ago, and in the eighteenth century its breeding became an important industry. In the nineteenth century Icelandic horses were sought after owing to their small size to draw waggons in coal mines in Scotland and Belgium. Yet for the Icelander cattle- and horse-rearing are not regarded as important.

Cattle and horses are perhaps more necessary to the Yakuts and other nomads in eastern Siberia. In Yakutia the ox can be kept without difficulty as far north as lat. 62°. There is grass enough in summer for a supply of good hay to be cut for the winter. Unfortunately, the hay-making season coincides with the fishing season. There is not time for the men to store up the hay, and the beasts have to be satisfied in winter with dried fish and birch-twigs. The cows give so little milk that a dozen are needed to satisfy the wants of a single family; and it is rare for so many to be kept; hence, milk is a mere extra and in any case has only recently been introduced into the diet. Formerly, indeed, the Yakuts regarded horned cattle as unclean. The difficulty of food supply has alone gradually led them to replace the horse by the cow not only, as a draught animal, but also for its yield of milk and beef. Before cows came to be kept, all these functions were performed by the horse. Small and shaggy, robust and quiet, the Yakut horse can, like reindeer, smell out patches of grass under the snow, uncover them with its hoof, and graze on them. But this is often only an unimportant and precarious adaptation. In Gothhaab in western Greenland the keeping of cattle has had to be given up owing to the harshness of the winters. The little herd which has been acclimatised at Julianehaab is fed in winter with nothing but imported provender.

The only animal which is really adapted to life in the Arctic is the reindeer. Whenever European settlement has tried to overcome Nature in the polar regions, it has used the reindeer instead of its traditional set of domestic animals. Thus, in Canada a large herd of domestic reindeer was imported from Lapland and introduced by stages as far west as Alaska. The New World now contains nearly 600,000 domestic reindeer. Similarly, the Soviet Government has set up some thirty *sovkhozy* and veterinary posts to improve the breed of reindeer. Murman alone has two, and these supply more than 2,000 tonnes of fresh meat a year. Closely related to *Cervus tarandus*, the reindeer has been domesticated throughout the north of the Old World from the Chukchee peninsula to Norway. It reaches its southern limit near the source of the Amur and the Sayansk Mountains, where it is restricted to the snowclad slopes on the eastern flank of the range. The other slope, which faces the deserts of central Asia, is in fact within the camel's domain. Indifferent to cold, the reindeer feeds in summer on grass and soapwort, and in winter it eats lichen, which it tears from the rocks after having removed the snow with its hoofs and horns. When tamed, it continues to lead a wandering and very free life, keeping its wild and unprepossessing character. Its training begins as soon as it is three years old and continues for five years. It therefore remains intractable for nearly one-third of its life. So true is this that to milk the females it is necessary to lasso and hobble them. Though it has a moderate appetite, the reindeer causes its owners some difficulty over its food. Large herds, amounting perhaps to 18,000 head, quickly use up the moss and lichen on their feeding ground, thus forcing pastoral tribes to be constantly on the lookout for new pastures. An unremitting watch must be kept to hold the herd together, for reindeer tend to scatter and wander off in search of food. During snowstorms the Chukchees force themselves to make regular rounds of the herd so as to keep it together. An attack by wolves may also disperse a herd and cause a third of its number to be lost.

In winter reindeer easily find their food under the snow when this is still soft; but when it has become hard, they can no longer clear it away. They must then be driven into the forest to feed on bark and twigs. Sometimes the herdsman fells trees to put lichen and upper branches within reach of the animals. With such a diet the reindeer grow thin and at times die of exhaustion and inanition. In summer mosquitoes and gadflies drive the beasts mad, inflicting stings that sometimes develop into sores, and not infrequently some epizootic disease ravages the herds. There are memories of an anthrax epidemic which killed more than 100,000 reindeer in the Russian Arctic.

The reindeer is invaluable. But for it movement in the tundra would be very restricted. Strong and enduring, it is used almost everywhere as a draught animal, even by the people who harness dogs to their sledges for fast travel. The Tunguses and Koriaks even use them for riding. Its skin is worked into leather for making boots and clothes; its coat is woven into coarse cloth; its sinews and guts when drawn out are used as string and sewing thread; its bones are fashioned into harpoons, fishhooks, and other gadgets. But above all it supplies the daily food without fail in winter or summer. The people of the Arctic in Asia are big eaters of reindeer meat, but scarcely drink the milk. They preserve the meat by cutting it up into thin strips and drying them in the air. Among the Lapps, on the other hand, the milk is the chief food throughout the summer, and meat is eaten in winter only. Reindeer milk is very thick and nourishing. It contains four or five times as much fat as cow's milk. In summer the Lapps use only some of the milk, storing away the rest in the shape of cheese for eating in winter, or in the form of chilled cream at the end of the summer and as soon as the temperature is right for it.

Necessary for man's very life, the reindeer is also the criterion of wealth and social status. With four or five hundred reindeer a Lapp or Chukchee family is safe from famine and can lead an independent life. With fifty or a hundred reindeer the Lapp must find additional income, as, for instance, by watching and milking the herd of a big owner whose livestock usually averages 1,500 or 2,000 beasts. When some accident or other reduces a Lapp's herd to just a few beasts, he entrusts them to a neighbouring stockrearer and looks for some other means of making a living. He may become a fisherman on the coast, or he may hire out his labour to a Norwegian farmer. Among the reindeer-breeding Chukchees wealthy owners had before collectivisation as many as 10,000 beasts which were divided into several herds and grazed separately under the eye of a member of the family. Clans that had only a few hundred reindeer used to join together to live in common and form a single pastoral unit before the start of the kolkhoz system. Among all the peoples of the Arctic in Asia, as also among the Lapps, the loss of reindeer brings poverty and failure. The ravages of yellow anthrax among the herds were as much the cause of the rapid decay of the Ostiaks of the Yenisey and of the Voguls in the last century as was contact with the Russians. Among the Samoyedes, Tunguses, and Chukchees a clan which loses its reindeer is condemned to a wretched settled state and is forced to live wholly on fish. The term 'fisherman' means beggar. It seems indeed that most of the fishing tribes which are now settled between the Khatanga and the Anadyr or on the shores of the Sea of Okhotsk were formerly reindeer breeders. Some families still have a few. In the Arctic region of Asia it is so necessary to have a reindeer that people who are almost wholly hunters (like some Yakut tribes or like the Karagasses in their former condition in the Uda basin) used to ensure a margin of security by keeping a herd of about a hundred reindeer.

Hence, passing from the nomadic life of a reindeer owner to the sedentary life of a fisherman is tantamount to bankruptcy and social downfall. To be unable to take advantage of the possibilities spread

over vast areas and necessarily out of reach of sedentary peoples is
to be poor and reduced both economically and socially. In these
cold regions life cannot be ample and easy without mobility and
nomadism.

Nomadism in the Arctic.—The means of livelihood of peoples in cold
regions all assume continual movement, for man's life depends on
the fauna, which forces him to constant migration. So man is more
or less nomadic throughout the regions: hunters and fishermen, because their game moves about or because they must cover wide areas
in order to find and kill it; stockmen, because the reindeer changes
his pasture according to the season. People who travel great distances with ease are best able to live in this environment. The degree
of mobility is the measure of civilisation.

The seasonal movements of hunters and fishermen follow local
exigencies. The Tunguses of the Lena move down at the end of
June to the islands on the delta, where wild geese alight to build
their nests. They live at this time on eggs and birds, at the same
time catching plenty of fish in the distributaries. In September just
as the reindeer, now fattened, are making their way southwards,
they are pursued for some weeks; then as soon as the streams are
frozen over, the hunters go back to their villages, which are situated
near parts of the coast where fishing is possible during the whole
winter. The Yukaghirs lead an even more restless life. In June
they follow the river downstream at the same time as the salmon,
sterlet, and *tashyrs*; then shortly afterwards they retrace their steps
just when the big fish begin their migration upstream from the sea
and clouds of birds of passage (swans, ducks, and wild geese) alight
in the swamps inland. Their wanderings are arranged so that at
the end of August they reach the fords of the Andzhuga just as the
reindeer are crossing. Then in September they hasten back to the
estuaries to find enormous schools of herrings. Lastly, at the beginning of winter a series of expeditions enables them to slaughter
more reindeer just when the herds are crossing the Kolyma from
west to east. There are innumerable variations of this nomadic
hunting life, for any local chance of securing game may change its
rhythm. Thus, the Dolgans of the east coast of Khatanga Bay go to
the Taymyr peninsula in summer to collect fossil ivory, and they
leave the peninsula only to fall on the herds of reindeer which at the
beginning of autumn are winding their way southwards.

No calendar, however, is more firmly fixed than that of the coastal
Eskimos. In winter, when walrus and seal collect at certain points
along the coast, the Eskimos place their winter dwellings nearby,
fifty or sixty persons of the same tribe living sometimes in a single
hut, as is done at Angmagssalik. In summer, on the other hand,

seals scatter on the high seas just when other sources of supply appear on the land, for salmon swim up the streams and into the lakes, caribou and deer are seen on upland feeding grounds, and the tundra becomes a practically unlimited field of activity for the hunter and fisherman. The variety and scattered condition of the game involves the dispersal of the Eskimo tribes, who leave their winter dwellings and enter on a nomadic life, which is symbolised by the movable tent, the summer shelter. In this way the people of Angmagssalik camp at fifty different places in the course of a summer. The hunter's life is therefore made up of alternate assembly and dispersal closely following the habits of their game.

The stock-rearers too are subject to migration. From one end of Eurasia to the other Arctic reindeer breeders travel from north to south and back again every year. In northern Scandinavia and Russia the Lapps spend the winter in villages situated in the forests of Finmark or the Kola peninsula. They begin migrating at the beginning of June and make for their summer haunts some 4–500 km from their winter settlements. The Samoyedes live in the summer on the shores of the Arctic Sea at the mouths of streams then full of fish and around the lakes on the Taymyr peninsula. In September they move back into the country of the meanders of the Ob and Taz, where reindeer still find a few leaves on the shrubs. There they wait until the rivers and swamps are frozen over before making safely for the forests in the south, where they spend the winter. Farther east the Tungus herdsmen travel more than 1,500 km in 10 to 20 km stages, facing many changes of fortune on the way to the coast and back. The Chukchees, who are not interested in winning a livelihood from the sea, travel alternately from the forest country to the treeless upland feeding grounds, where the tributaries of the Anadyr are full of fish.

To accomplish these journeys the Hyperboreans have had to invent means of travelling, and they have invented some that are wonderfully adapted to the natural conditions. The fishing peoples have communal boats like the umiak of the Eskimos, which holds several families and is at the disposal of the community; and one-man boats like the Eskimo *kayak* or Aleutian *baidakan*, which is used for fishing and hunting. Almost indestructible, easy to right or to manœuvre, the kayak enables a skilful paddler to keep up an average speed of 15 km an hour for a whole day. Being light enough to be carried on a man's head, it enables repeated portages to be quickly made. The Eskimos, who are extraordinarily skilful and hardy boatmen, have learnt to use bladders filled with air to float ashore the heavy animals which they have killed out to sea. They are such good sailors that whalers used at one time to engage them as pilots. Their sense of direction and their powers of observation enable them to travel by sea to distant lands with the help of outline maps and sketches.

To move about on land the Hyperboreans have found in the sledge the most suitable means of passing over the slippery surface of ice and snow. The draught animal alone differs from tribe to tribe. Some, like the Ostiaks, Ghiliaks, and Eskimos, have dog teams, whilst the Tunguses, Koriaks, and Lapps prefer the reindeer. Dogs travel faster and are priceless whenever speed is a matter of life and death. Arctic dogs, or huskies, are like wolves with their short pointed ears and their long, black, brown, grey, yellowish, or rust-coloured coats. The normal team for a sledge consists of twelve dogs. They are very carefully trained, and a good leader can find his way on dark nights and in snowstorms along a route which he has already followed to a food depôt or a camping site. Feeding dogs presents great difficulty, for they eat meat and fish, as men do, without yielding any article of food, as reindeer do, except in cases of emergency when the dogs may be sacrificed to save men's lives.

The reindeer, which requires no food of man, supplies him with milk, but is slower. A pair of reindeer will draw a sledge laden with up to 40 kg. at a rate of 4 km an hour and the animals must be un-harnessed three times a day so that they may graze. The reindeer is suitable for long journeys and slow migrations, whilst the dog is suitable for hunting trips.

These various means of transport all enable man to use the greatest possible number of ways of earning a livelihood and to face what a traveller has called by the expressive name of 'round of hunger'.

EVOLUTION OF COMMUNITIES

Man's existence in the Arctic furnishes a remarkable instance of ingenious adaptation to the resources of an animal environment. Animals are far less reliable as a means of livelihood than are the resources afforded by other climates, nor do they offer the security due to regular renewal. Hence the precarious nature and wholly artificial character of all life in the cold regions. Food, clothing, and even the dwelling depend almost exclusively on the animal world. Various kinds of game, fish, and reindeer meat and milk make up the diet of the Lapps, Yakuts, Tunguses, and Ostiaks. For them the only vegetable food, apart from tea and flour obtained by some communities who are in contact with civilisation, consists of seasonal berries or lichen recovered from the entrails of reindeer that have been killed by the hunter or else slaughtered. The raw material of clothing comes from the skins of bears, dogs, domestic reindeer, or seals. The garments are so warm that the Hyperboreans are not afraid to sleep in the open air, and European explorers have found no better clothing, nor have present day settlers in the Arctic discovered any more suitable.

The whole social organisation has received the impress of the environment, which makes itself felt even in religion. In summer when families are scattered, the hunter brings back his prey to the tent of his own family; in winter, on the other hand, strict collectivism is in force among all the members of the same community. The occasional bit of game is shared among them all, as is the food brought from distant caches. Furthermore, the winter dwellings and the ground they stand on are the common property of the tribe. Differences between life in winter and summer impose certain daily observances. For instance, it is forbidden to wear reindeer skin, which comes from a summer animal, at the same time as sealskin, since this is a winter animal. It is also forbidden to eat reindeer meat and fish at the same meal. In summer the only religious practices are rites connected with birth and death; in winter communities practise great collective ceremonies, services of supplication for success in hunting or for deliverance from famine. The group feeling is so strong that individual breaches of tabus are regarded as the cause of public disaster in the shape of destructive storms or the disappearance of game.

On the whole life is precarious. The incidence of natural factors leaves but a slight margin for the play of man's initiative. This probably helps to explain the rigidity of the social institutions and also the difficulties encountered by attempts at progress. Ethnologists and geographers have been astonished at the complexity and strength of social organisation among the Hyperboreans. Some have thought that the various forms of Arctic civilisation must have been developed in a less unfavourable environment, and that either the climate has worsened or else that the Hyperboreans formerly dwelt in countries farther to the south, where they had already developed efficient techniques which enabled them to adapt themselves to Arctic conditions after having been driven away from their original habitat by other forms of civilisation.

It seems indeed that well before the arrival of Europeans and contacts with civilisation (which is always a terrible business for underdeveloped peoples) many of the Hyperboreans were already on the way to disappearance. As early as 1850 only the ruins of former Eskimo settlements were found between Point Barrow and Bering Strait, though previously they had been numerous. The equipment of many of the hunting tribes both on the Coppermine coast and in the inland parts of the Lena and Yenisey valleys had become less efficient, and in consequence life had become more difficult. Yet contact with civilisation has not always been fatal to the Arctic peoples. Certainly, it has often made their hunting grounds poorer or brought a train of terrible diseases, including measles, tuberculosis, and venereal diseases, the effects of which have been all the more dreadful because they attacked biologically defenceless peoples who were ignorant of the most elementary hygiene. But often too the equipment and complementary resources brought by civilisation enabled the Arctic peoples to renew their vigour and increase their means. Trade with Russian and with Hudson's Bay Company trappers has provided the Hyperboreans with utensils and iron tools which have replaced their old equipment. Today, instead of reindeer horn harpoons and bone arrowheads they have axes, saws, chisels, knives, and firearms of European or American manufacture. The whale-oil lamp has given place to the Primus stove, and even the sewing machine has been introduced into Greenland. But above all the Hyperboreans have adopted the use of new kinds of food in the shape of tea, sugar, and flour, and they have begun to drink alcohol and to smoke. These new needs have unfortunately helped to upset the precarious equilibrium of Arctic economy, to make men less adapted to the environment, and to destroy at a blow their autonomy and the bonds of their social life.

Nowhere else in the world has civilisation tried harder to preserve the natives from becoming less adapted to the environment and to protect them from deadly contacts. In Alaska the Americans have sought to give back to the Eskimos their economic independence by acclimatising for this purpose a herd of reindeer. The experiment has been successful in proportion as these inveterate hunters have consented to become pastoralists. Today, there are 30,000 reindeer owned by Eskimos, who are organised in cooperative societies that differ little from Soviet *kolkhozy*. In Greenland the Danes have long protected the Eskimos from undesirable contacts. It needed the second world war to teach the latter the use of money. In spite of these precautions it seems indeed that the approach of civilisation has brought on a considerable fall in population. Ratzel's estimate of the numbers of the Hyperboreans as 400,000 persons in the last century was probably exaggerated, but in any case it would seem that present figures limiting the number of Hyperboreans in Eurasia to 50,000 and that of the natives of the American North to 45,000, represents a great decrease.

It is agreed, however, that the total population of the Arctic today exceeds 700,000 persons, a figure that had probably never been reached before. But this population consists of immigrants, European or American, whose mode of life has nothing in common with that of the natives. The cold regions have long since attracted settlement on their fringes owing to the wealth they contain, but this wealth would appear desirable only to trading and industrial nations. It has been discovered gradually, so that the penetration of the Arctic by higher forms of civilisation has been made in successive stages. The first stage was probably begun by fur trappers. The abundance of fur-bearing animals in Siberia has indeed been known since the Middle Ages, yet it was not until the seventeenth century that the Russians organised the fur trade. A great fair established in 1643 made Irbit the market for sable, fox, and marten from Tartary and beaver from Kamchatka. About the same time, in 1670, the Hudson's Bay Company was formed and for two hundred years was destined to control the trade in furs from an area in Canada as large as Europe. In Siberia as in the Canadian North stage posts and trappers' camps were the beginnings of effective colonisation by civilised men.

The second stage was reached later when there was an extraordinary increase in the use of fat in industrial countries. Even as far back as the eighteenth century Dutch whalers, more than 14,000 in number, were slaughtering large numbers of whales, and the end of the nineteenth century was marked by hecatombs of whales and seals. The slaughter was rounded off at the beginning of the present century by Scandinavian, British, and American factory-ships. There is no doubt that the growing scarcity of this useful marine mammal has greatly contributed to the decadence of the Aleutian islanders and of some Eskimo tribes. In the end the whalers themselves suffered from the decrease in the number of animals in their hunting grounds, and international conventions instituted measures of protection for the whales and seals. Today the seal population of the Pribilof Islands has recovered its numbers and is now subject to reasonable exploitation under the control of the Land Office. Every year it supplies 70,000 skins, 200 tonnes of oil, and 35 tonnes of meat. Still greater production comes from the Soviet Arctic, where the sealing *kolkhozy* at Archangel and Murmansk account for most of the 750,000 seals slaughtered every year.

This destructive kind of exploitation has been followed by a rational assessment of marine wealth, which has also helped to settle in the Arctic other forms of colonisation. Fishing centres for catching cod, halibut, herring, and freshwater fish line the whole coast of Siberia. The *kolkhozy* at Murmansk have a large fleet of motor trawlers which in the fishing season land more than 2,000 tonnes of various kinds of fish every day. Farther east the fishing centres in Taymyr and on the Yenisey have given rise to canning factories at Ust-Port, Ribnoye, and Dudinsk. Every year they can 400,000 tonnes of fish caught in the sea, in Lake Taymyr, and in the Khatanga. Lastly, all along the coast of Bering Sea, Kamchatka, and the Sea of Okhotsk are fishing ports and canneries, the busiest of which are at Magadan.

The waters of the American Arctic are exploited in the same way.

The Edmonton company which has a whole flotilla of fishing boats on the Great Slave Lake actually uses a good part of the catch to feed its litters of mink and other fur-bearing animals, but to the north of Prince Rupert fishing for cod, herring, and salmon ensures the seasonal activity of a host of canneries, whose output is eaten all over the world. More than 200,000 tonnes of fish are caught every year in the sea and rivers, 150 tonnes being of salmon alone.

The final stage was reached, however, when it was discovered that on both continents the Arctic contained sources of power and valuable minerals. Modern means of transport wove a thin, but strong network of routes around it, and towns have arisen from the ice-bound solitudes. Coal and mineral oil abound in the Arctic. The first coalfield to be worked was in Spitzbergen. It was known as far back as the eighteenth century, but its first real use was to refuel whalers at the beginning of the present century. Exploited in turn by the English, Americans, Scandinavians, and Russians, the coalfield produced more than 700,000 tonnes of coal in 1939, half of which was raised by Arktik Ugol, a Soviet concession holder. A large number of coalfields have been found scattered about the Soviet portion of the Arctic. Those on the Pechora and Vorkuta have greater reserves than the Donbass and have an annual output of six million tonnes. Another field is worked at Norilsk in the lower Yenisey valley and another on the lower Khatanga, the belt continuing to the lower Lena and Kolyma valleys. Oil has gushed up in the same regions. In the estuaries of the Khatanga and Lena there are deposits that are still imperfectly known. In the upper basin of the Pechora two oilfields feed a refinery at Ukhta, which supplies petrol to the airfield at Ust Kozhva.

In the New World there are similar sources of power. Thirty-two coalfields have been discovered in the Canadian North, notably in Ellesmere, Banks, and Melville Islands. Two coalfields are worked: one near Dawson in the Yukon valley, and the other near Carmak in the Lewes valley. The largest, however, are in Alaska and yield nearly 400,000 tonnes a year. The busiest mining centres are in the Matanuska valley, but reserves have been found as far as Cook Inlet and Kotsebur Sound. Oil has become the target for organised exploitation. During the 1939-45 war Canadian oilfields on the Mackenzie and at Norman Wells poured out oil at the rate of 47,000 tonnes a year into the Canol pipeline, which led to the refinery at Whitehorse. The end of the war involved the dismantling of the pipeline, but the fields are being worked at a lower rate of production to supply local needs. Other deposits have been found in Alaska all along the coast of Beaufort Sea and at Uniat in the Colville valley. These are promising enough to cause the construction of another pipeline being envisaged from Uniat to Fairbanks.

The presence of fuel has rendered possible on-the-spot working of innumerable metals and minerals hidden in the rocks under the tundra. Around Murmansk the Kola peninsula has become a polymorphous industrial region. An ingenious hydro-electric plant uses water from Lake Imandra and the Neva. Part of the current is used in winter to keep the temperature of the lake above freezing-point and so to enable the turbines to work continuously. The plant, which produces a million kilowatts, is connected with the hydro-electric power-stations on the Svir and Volkhov farther south. This current is wholly used to feed aluminium refineries which treat bauxite from Kandalaska, the chemical *kombinat* at Kirovsk, which produces phosphatic manure derived from the Khibini Mountains, and the nickel *kombinat* which employs 50,000 hands. Although coal from Spitzbergen, which is imported through Murmansk, is unsuitable for use in coke ovens, the Soviets have begun to work the iron mines at Lake Imandra. Altogether the Kola industrial region has found work for between 200,000 and 250,000 persons.

The smaller industrial centres gravitate round the coalfields on the Pechora, which supply the forest *kombinaty* and round those in the lower Yenisey valley, where the three settlements of Norilsk, Dudinsk, and Igarka contain the workshops of another polymetallic *kombinat* which treats copper, nickel, cobalt, and gold. Away in the east the deposits of tin, silver, and pitchblende and the goldfields in the upper Kolyma basin, which have an annual yield of 500 tonnes of pure metal, have given rise to settlements at Verkne Kolymsk, Seimshan, and Magadan, where there are now 50,000 Russians.

Gold, rare metals, and radioactive pitchblende have caused mining towns to spring up in the Canadian Far North. Two companies armed with very modern equipment extract gold from the sands of the Yukon and the quartz veins at Yellowknife. Since 1930 the pitchblende on the Great Slave Lake has been worked by a chartered company which extracts annually as much as 1,000 tonnes of salts of uranium, an output little inferior to that of Zaire. At Port Radium an oil wharf and sheds for ore are the reason for the existence of the settlement, which has built itself a hospital and a chapel. Similar settlements are now growing up on the radium and uranium ore fields in Ungava and Labrador, where the River Hamilton will work a hydro-electric plant producing 500,000 tonnes a day.

Alluvial gold, together with copper and platinum mines have made Fairbanks with its population of 7,000 persons into the chief town in Alaska. Sulphur, rare metals, and iron lodes occur and await the arrival of labour and equipment to be mined. The exploitation of this wealth has brought home the need for faster and more efficient means of communication than those afforded by the environment. Motor roads and railways have advanced towards these mining districts. In the Soviet Union a good road system connects the three main centres in the lower Yenisey valley, but the longest motor road joins Magadan to Verkne Kolymsk, the mining centre in the Kolyma valley. A fleet of lorries ensures the transport of the valuable ores to Magadan throughout the summer. The system in Alaska is better connected. Its backbone is Alcan, the Alaska Highway which runs over tundras and swamps and through virgin forest.from Edmonton *via* Whitehorse to Fairbanks. Three roads connect it with Anchorage, Valdez, and Skagway.

The pioneers of Arctic railways were Scandinavians who, to work the iron mines in Lapland constructed one after the other the lines from Gellivare to Kiruna and from Gellivare to Narvik, which goes as far north as lat. 68° 30'. But with the development of the Arctic the railways have gone even farther north. Although the line from Moscow to Archangel stops in lat. 64° 30' N., the one from Leningrad to Murmansk which was constructed in 1916 reaches the 69th parallel. More recently, the one from Kotlas has gone beyond Vorkuta to reach even farther north. In Canada the Hudson Bay Railroad has its terminus at Churchill about lat. 58° N., the line from Skagway to Whitehorse reaches 61° N., and in Alaska the line from Cordoba to Kennicott goes as far north as lat. 63°; but the longest and most ramified joins Seward to Fairbanks (65° N.) through the valleys of the Matanuska and the Tanana, a feeder of the Yukon. This line, which is the most modern in the New World, is fit for traffic at all seasons. These railway tentacles, which have been constructed in difficult technical conditions, symbolise the penetration of the industrial way of life into the Arctic and the attempt to draw off the wealth of the region.

Together with the navigable rivers the roads and railways are but bits of equipment and means of exploitation. But the place of the Arctic in world communications has long been foreseen. As far back as the end of the sixteenth century a shorter seaway to the Indies than the one round the Cape of Good Hope had been sought, first in the northeast and then in the northwest. The Northeast Passage was the first to be traversed, but only modern equipment and organisation makes the use of the Northern Sea Route possible. This is in the hands of the Russians. Today, convoys of cargo boats sail between Murmansk, Archangel, and Vladivostok preceded by ice-breakers, assisted by aircraft observation, and guided by wireless and radar stations. The traffic which is twenty times greater than before the war, now carries about five million tons of cargo. A great administrative organisation, *Glavsevmorput*, controls development. About a hundred wireless telegraph and meteorological stations are manned by specialist crews who hibernate for eight months amidst ice and darkness. During the four months when there is traffic the ships have to struggle against time, for any delay entails the risk of being imprisoned in the ice for eight months. Hence, the equipment of the Arctic ports is growing more and more efficient so as to expedite the handling of goods. Anderma, Novi Port, Igarka, Dudinsk, Dikson, Tiksi, and Ambarshik have been equipped with cranes less powerful, but more up-to-date and easy to handle than those at Murmansk and Archangel.

In the New World there has been no similar effort. The Northwest Passage is more tortuous, difficult, and longer obstructed by ice. The only far-reaching success has been the construction of a railway to Hudson Bay, the establishment of a grain port at Churchill, and, in consequence, the use of a direct route from Winnipeg to Liverpool for Canadian wheat by shortening the haul *via* Montreal by 1,700 km. Although it has not fulfilled all expectations, the Winnipeg-Churchill railway carries on an average 100,000 tonnes of wheat a year.

However, at the present time, towards the end of the twentieth century, one may glimpse in the American northland, in which numerous important mineral resources, recently exploited both by Canada and the United States, lie concealed beneath the ice-cap, the vast possibilities of development and peopling made available by modern technology. In these inhospitable solitudes powerful equipment is being installed, and the feasibility is being seriously considered of using the Arctic north-west passage, even as the Russians are doing along the coast of Siberia.

Since 1950, indeed, the oil companies of Canada and the United States, and the great international consortia that have explored and exploited the submarine oilfields of the North Sea, have discovered beneath the polar ice, off the Alaskan and Canadian coasts, oil reserves estimated at 5,000 million tonnes. The first wells were drilled on the coasts of Alaska and Yukon, at Prudhoe Bay, and then at Banks Island and Ellef Ringnes, in the Canadian arctic archipelago; these occurrences of oil and gas are believed to be as great as those of Texas. By 1980, the American arctic could be yielding 100 million tonnes of crude oil a year, or as much as Lybia or Nigeria.

These deposits have encouraged an 'oil rush' in the Far North by the great international petroleum companies, attracting colossal investments of multi-national capital to finance the submarine explorations, the difficult and costly installation of large drilling platforms in seas exposed to ice-floes, and the construction of long crude-oil pipelines from Prudhoe, on the Arctic Ocean, to Valdez, on the Pacific coast of Alaska, 1,350 km distant. Furthermore, the maritime transport of this oil is also envisaged, using 250,000-ton tankers and the north-west passage to reach eastern Canada and Europe. Thus the Far North will become an industrial territory dominated by the great combines of modern industrial economy. This evolution, accelerated at the moment by the feverish search for new sources of energy, will completely upset the life of the Arctic lands, totally destroying the old adaptations and traditional modes of life of the native peoples even more profoundly than has been the case in the equally inhospitable arid lands of the Middle East and the Sahara.

It needed the second world war and the unforeseeable progress in air communications to reveal the potential crossroads for the main airlines of the world. The direct line from Moscow to San Francisco passes over the Pole. The Soviet Union has established on a sector of the Arctic an airway running between Moscow, Archangel, Vorkuta, Igarka, Tiksi, and Anadyr. These places are so many air bases with runways protected against frost, with heated hangars, and supplies of petrol. In America there are three large active airports at Whitehorse, Fairbanks, and Anchorage. Whitehorse is used by three large aircraft companies, among them Pan-American Airways, Canadian Pacific Airways, and Northwest Airlines. The last of these runs a long-distance service from New York to Tokyo; touching at Anchorage and at Shemya in the Aleutians, the aircraft covers the distance in forty hours. Around these large airfields gravitate an imposing number of secondary ones which serve local traffic. In this roadless country the aircraft replaces the lorry and car. Between the 'towns' and isolated centres of production the aircraft is made use of by miners, trappers, fishermen, and farmers. The Canadian Yukon Air Transport Company serves the Mackenzie valley, Yellowknife, Port Radium, and Coppermine in this way. American companies carry 10,000 tonnes of freight a year on the runs Fairbanks-Nome, Fairbanks-Whitehorse, Fairbanks-Barrow.

This invasion of industry and its technical equipment into the Far North explains the attempts to introduce systems of agriculture and stockrearing proper to the region. Between Archangel and Kamchatka there are 3,000 agricultural establishments of European type. In Canada similar farms have been started in the Mackenzie valley surrounded by fields of vegetables covering a total area of 300 hectares In Alaska three settlements have sprung up, one at Anchorage, the second in the Tanana valley, and the third in the Matanuska valley; and in these the railway had led to an increase in the number of units of cultivation. Around Palmer 7,500 acres are cultivated, and in the Tanana valley forty farms share 10,000 acres.

Finally, the Arctic has witnessed the growth of large towns, those delicate plants of industrial civilisation. There are Archangel with a population of 300,000, Murmansk with 150,000, Kirovsk and Magadan each with 40,000, Norilsk and Igarka with 20,000 each, Whitehorse with 11,200, Fairbanks with 7,000, and Yellowknife with 6,000. These are for the most part modern towns, or else recently modernised, and have hospitals, cinemas, schools, clubs, banks, and miniature sky-scrapers with foundations of concrete pillars. Lit by electricity and with bus or at least taxi services, they are connected with the rest of the world by their airfields and wireless masts. Whether Canadian, American or Soviet, they are all equally foreign to their surroundings. Far from having sprung from it, they have conquered it after a great struggle. Their supply lines run afar right into the very heart of the temperate regions. Out of 700,000 persons who live in the cold sub-polar regions today, there are not 100,000 who are really adapted to the conditions of the environment and would be able to live out their lives if some unthought-of disaster chanced to destroy the slender connexions with modern civilisation which have been taken at some risk into the midst of these inhospitable lands. In the last quarter of the twentieth century, the great northern lands of America and Asia represent the ultimate stage in the conquest of the globe by modern man.

CHAPTER 5

HUMAN LIFE IN TEMPERATE REGIONS

The temperate regions cover only a tenth of the surface of the earth's dry land; yet they play a decisive part in human life. In some respects they seem to be the most favourable areas for the complete development of mankind, areas in which technique has reached its highest efficiency and civilisation its highest form. These favoured regions are distributed over the earth in two unequal belts. In the southern hemisphere the temperate belt is very broken, and the small blocks into which they are divided by vast expanses of ocean have practically lost the geographical unity which the stability of the climatic conditions would tend to produce. It is represented by the southern tip of South America, southeastern Australia, and New Zealand. Discontinuity and isolation explain the backwardness of these areas as compared with similar regions in the northern hemisphere. Caught up late in the general progress, they afford neither the variety nor the strength of human reactions in the northern belt.

In North America the northern temperate belt covers the south of Canada and the greater part of the United States. In Eurasia it stretches from eastern Siberia to the west coast of Ireland. Spreading widely as it faces the Atlantic, it becomes narrower towards the east, where in 14° of latitude Japanese territory reaches into both the cold regions and the tropics.

Considering only the most general features and without taking account of the innumerable shades of climate which appear in consequence of climate and position relative to the sea, it is agreed that over the whole of these regions the climate is marked by extreme variability of the atmosphere, all movement being governed by the west–east passage of low pressure centres and by the seasonal shifts of vast masses of air. As a result precipitation is distributed over the whole year, whilst the length of winter and summer is evenly balanced. The climate favours a vegetation-type rich in species and has made systematic cultivation easy, especially in the selection of food plants that have a high yield and whose produce is easily kept in store. It has likewise favoured selection in domestic animals which had long been accustomed to find their own food in the plants of the region.

The climatic and biological environment suits man, whose body need exert only moderate effort in it. The very variability of the climate eases exertion temporarily. But the periodical return of a season in which food is difficult to get and crops cannot be grown has had vital consequences for human societies, which have been forced to develop forethought and thrift and to draw up a calendar of seasonal activity. To use the enforced idleness of winter he postponed the manufacture of tools and clothes till that season. In this way industrial occupation became inseparable from agriculture, and the textile industry became established in the countryside between the sixteenth and the eighteenth centuries. The child of leisure and need, industry led to the exploitation of forests and mines and to the working of looms, which were originally winter activities. It also brought on the control of motive power, the construction of roads, and the maintenance of trade relations.

In fact, those parts of the earth in which nature's gifts are most minutely utilised lie in the temperate belt. They are the chief regions in which agriculture and stock-rearing are carried on, and they contain great industrial countries between which there is an intricate maze of routes, and in some parts of which there are vast swarms of humanity. More than 1,600 million persons, or two-fifths of the population of the world, are there assembled.

This fraction of the human race produces 80 per cent of the world's yield of wheat and more than 60 per cent of all cultivated cereals. It produces 98 per cent of the potato crop and 98 per cent of the world's meat and dairy produce. It raises 97 per cent of the world's coal, produces 88 per cent of the steel used, and 88 per cent of the electric power. It launches 95 per cent of the world's ships and manufactures 90 per cent of its motor cars. For once Huntington did not carry his optimism too far when he estimated that each inhabitant of the temperate belt produced on an average five or six times more than any inhabitant in any other part of the world. We shall now try to explain this accumulation of wealth and activity.

VEGETATION IN TEMPERATE REGIONS

In the temperate belt there are two basic types of vegetation, and these are closely connected with conditions of soil and humidity. They are the forest region and the steppes.

A broad belt of continuous forest separates the Arctic, which is treeless owing to the cold, from the arid steppes, which are treeless owing to drought. In the southern hemisphere the temperate belt is more disconnected, as was said above. Probably, the belts afford the most favourable conditions for treelife. The vegetative period nowhere lasts less than three months, and the summer temperature is everywhere high enough for plant growth. Nor is drought anywhere serious enough to stop the annual growth and development of trees. In the regions farthest inland, where precipitation is less than ten inches, the rainfall maximum occurs in the summer months.

This happens, for instance, in eastern Siberia and in the north of Canada and Alaska.

The temperate forest consists of conifers or deciduous trees according to latitude and altitude, but in each of these types there is great homogeneity, and vast areas are covered with trees of a single species or a very small number of related species, so that there are stands of fir, oak, beech, or chestnut according to circumstances. Not many epiphytes grow on them, and the undergrowth is poor and consists mainly of mosses, lichens, and cryptogams. The acid soil under fir woods is covered with dry needles and is often without any vegetation at all. Oak forests, on the other hand, favour an undergrowth of bushes, ferns, and grass and have in the past been used as reserve feeding-grounds for livestock.

On the continent of North America coniferous forest covers a wide area and is found in fairly low latitudes. In the northeast the dominant species is white pine. On the coasts of British Columbia and California, which are milder and wetter, there are numerous varieties, including fine timber trees like the sequoias. The belt of deciduous forest is less remarkable. Oak forests occur in the mountainous parts of the west, and deciduous forest also covers part of the Atlantic coast as far south as Chesapeake Bay and the slopes of the Appalachians as far as southern Kentucky.

In the Old World the forest reflects in its gradual modifications the transition from the maritime climatic areas with their mild, wet winters to the continental climatic areas with their cold, drier winters. The Atlantic coast of Europe is particularly favourable to deciduous forest which needs a long period of vegetative growth. It is pre-eminently the home of the oak in association with the birch, ash, willow, and walnut. In Great Britain it is found growing at a height of 300 metres and as far north as lat. 58° N. It penetrates some distance into central and eastern Europe, where its stands are commoner than those of the beech and chestnut.

The polar limit of the two last-mentioned trees runs from northwest to southeast. The beech covers whole sections of the Chilterns, Downs, and Cotswolds, the plateaus in the Pays de Caux, the sandy soil of the Ile-de-France, and the Burgundy ridge. The chestnut is more restricted. Southwest of a line from the south of England to Lake Constance it bears fruit which ripens. Farther north beyond a line passing through the Harz Mountains, Dresden, and Budapest the chestnut is merely a forest tree and does not normally bear fruit. With these trees are associated in the undergrowth shrubs and bushes that demand either a mild winter or a prolonged vegetative period. Among them are the reed (*Ulex*), holly (*Ilex*), box, camellia, magnolia, rhododendron, and certain varieties of heather. In central and eastern Europe these plants grow only in favourable spots, but along the Atlantic coast they are common everywhere. This wealth of plant association explains the extraordinary variety of the local flora.

Present-day climatic conditions are not, however, sufficient to explain the European vegetation types. By examining pollen from peat bogs botanists have found that the distribution of flora in Europe has been due to successive modifications of the plant cover owing to alternations of Ice Ages with interglacial periods. At the beginning of the Pleistocene era Tertiary vegetation was pushed southwards towards the Danube valley and southwestwards towards France and the Mediterranean, where it replaced the Eocene tropical vegetation. At that time north Germany and southern England were covered with tundra on which grew the arctic willow (*Salix polaris*), mountain avens (*Dryas octopetala*), and dwarf birch (*Betula nana*). On the retreat of the ice the plants of the former Tertiary flora reinforced by Mediterranean and Asiatic species reconquered their old domain. However, various species had different fates in this reconquest. *Pinus excelsa*, which had been widespread before the Ice Ages and had been pushed back beyond Finland, did not succeed in advancing to the west of the Central Highlands of France. *Abies alba* recovered nearly all its former area, but the beech did not go beyond southern Scandinavia. This return of central European plants towards the northern countries kept pace with the steady increase in temperature during the whole period of Lake Ancylus and the Littorina Sea. It occurred, it is thought, in three stages, each of which was marked by peculiar forest scenery, first with Scots pine and birch, then oak, then beech.

In Denmark and southern Sweden Arctic vegetation gave way to forest composed of a mixture of birch, aspen, and pine (*Pinus sylvestris*), the first of which occupied swampy areas, whilst the others grew in drier soil. The frost-resisting Scots pine spreads today as far north as the birch. It seems to have formed the chief element in the great forest which spread over the whole of central and northern Europe immediately after the retreat of the ice; and with the pine, birch, and aspen there appeared in the undergrowth shrubs like the juniper (*Juniperus communis*), rowan (*Sorbus*), plum (*Prunus Padus*), lianas (*Viburnum*), and ferns (*Pterix aquilina*).

In the northern countries the predominance of the Scots pine was overthrown by the oak, which according to the evidence of peat bogs pushed back and then completely took the place of the pine in Jutland. The invasion of the oak had already begun in Sweden at the Lake Ancylus period, but it did not go beyond central Sweden and southern Norway. With the oak came the sycamore (*Acer platanoides*), ash (*Fraxinus excelsior*), ivy (*Hedera helix*), and a whole train of plants of the undergrowth, among which were holly and the foxglove. In its turn the oak was supplanted by the beech over a wide extent of its domain, especially in southern Sweden and in Denmark. The expulsion of the oak was so complete in places that its undergrowth disappeared with it. These movements to and fro of plant associations, which have left sparse stands as relics and testimony amid different botanical surroundings, combine with a thousand shades of climate to make the forest regions of the Old World a domain of infinite variety.

Forests do not now form, and seem never to have formed, a continuous mantle in the temperate regions. Sometimes there is a break in them filled with other vegetation types, like the moor or the steppe; at other times they thin out and give way to vast continuous grass plains as soon as the falling off of the oceanic climate eastwards increases the lack of moisture beyond the limits tolerated by trees.

Treeless spaces in the midst of the forest are occupied by an association of xerophilous plants, the commonest constituents of which are heather, reed, and broom. Such a place is a moor or common. In western Europe it covers damp and peaty soils. It is found on uplands of old rock in Britain, Brittany, and the Vosges; and it forms large clearings in the Ardennes, the slate uplands along the Rhine, and the Hercynian *massifs* in central Germany. It is due to the thinning out of the forest or to a peculiar, original formation just like the forest. Pedologists have shown that in some kinds of climate the forest is an unstable type. Even before the process of soil evolution was known, it had been suggested (Passerat) that the extensive moors on the western parts of the Central Highlands of France had sprung up after the spontaneous destruction of the virgin forest as the result of a kind of auto-intoxication or of soil exhaustion. We know today that the leaching of the soil, podsolisation, the formation of hard-pan in the sub-soil layers, or the formation of peat on the surface are all processes of natural evolution causing the disappearance of the forest cover.

But there are also districts that do not take kindly to tree growth. In them the soil is poor in phosphates or lime and either saturated with humic acids or exposed to strong winds. In fact, areas that are unfavourable to tree-growth and must always have had clearings in the forest cover are easily spotted on the map. There are first of all peat bogs due to the wet periods in the Ice Ages and found in valley bottoms as well as on sandy slopes or on ill-drained heights on peneplains. The names *moor*, *fen*, *venn*, and *fagnes* are applied to this type. Then there are moors associated with dry, silicious, sandy soils like those on the Campine or on the North German Geest. Lastly, there are 'islands' of grass whose appearance coincides with that of soils that are naturally dry or too friable to allow trees to take root firmly, as, for instance, the *savarts* of Champagne, the

English Downs, the French Causses, or the loam terrains of Beauce and Cambrésis.

As one goes away from the sea and penetrates into the heart of Eurasia, the rainfall decreases and, owing to the summer heat, is soon not enough to allow the growth of trees. Grass then becomes the basis of the vegetation type. These treeless regions are called *steppes* in Europe and Asia, *prairies* in North America, and *pampas* in the Argentine. They form vast continuous expanses in the *puszta* in Hungary, the Black Earth country in Russia and southern Siberia, and the prairies of Illinois, Missouri, Manitoba, and Saskatchewan. On studying the Russian steppes Krasnov proved long ago that they constituted a vegetation type adapted to the physical environment and not an impoverished formation. In fact, he pointed out that in southern Russia horizontal plains were covered with steppe, whilst clumps of trees grew on the more broken areas. Indeed, gullies afford trees some protection from winds and *burany* (blizzards) which damage trees in the open. Slopes prevent the stagnation of water and the formation of salts harmful to trees. Wherever there are not these slight physical advantages, the tree gives way to grass.

The origin of the steppes presents a problem that has been debated for more than a century and has been kept going in all its fullness today by agricultural experts. Many hesitate to regard them as original vegetation types due solely to natural conditions. In the prairies and mountain pastures of the Old World and in the uncultivated moorlands in poor districts many geographers and botanists see the result of human action. Certain it is that many of these moors have been artificially caused on the site of former forests, as is shown by clumps of willows, alders, ash, poplar, and even oaks that survive in their flora, Sheep pastures, which were so numerous in south Germany in the last century covered ground formerly clad in woods, and it has been shown by Krause that most of the moorland in north Germany had originally been wooded.

The existence of natural glades in virgin forests cannot be reasonably doubted either. Apart from mountain pastures, where the length of time during which they are covered by winter snows precludes tree growth, wet areas like the *Märschen* have certainly never been wooded. The same is true of loess clearings, for they almost always coincide with regions that show the greatest traces of occupation by man in the past, as, for instance, the great loess terraces in the valleys of the Elbe and Saale, or on the eastern sides of the Harz Mountains, the lowlands of the Rhine, the Alpine Foreland from Switzerland to Lower Austria, the plateaus of the Swabian and Franconian Alb, the basins of the Main and Neckar, and northern Bohemia. It is now thought that settlement in these steppe areas in

Europe took place at a time when they had not yet been invaded by trees. Cultivation and continual cropping by animals sufficed to keep the trees beyond the limits of the natural clearings, which were, therefore, preserved, not made, by man. The destruction of the virgin forest in the New World was formerly attributed to pre-Columbian stock-rearers, but the damage done is now considered to be of less importance, and the steppes are now regarded as belonging to an original vegetation type.

The difference between the forested areas and the treeless regions in the temperate belts may therefore be accepted as a basic feature in human geography. Clearings formed man's first attempt at modifying his environment. From them begin the changes that have made the natural landscape unrecognisable. The clearings have now become filled with swarms of human beings, and both forest and steppe have been transformed into arable fields, meadows, orchards, and woodland.

CULTIVATED AREAS AND THEIR ARRANGEMENT

In modern times the modes of life in the temperate regions stem from the same origins and are of the same kind. No other instance of such general likeness occurs anywhere else in the world. Of course, the tropics support more numerous swarms of people, but they are far from showing in their modes of life the same general uniformity or the same degree of kinship as the temperate regions do. In the tropics the forms of civilisation differ from continent to continent and exist in large, relatively isolated geographical units, each of which is based on a heritage of plants and techniques belonging to the unit. On the other hand the type of agricultural mode of life that has developed in Europe has gained quasi-universal expansion. Europeans have carried it with them not only to the other side of the Atlantic, but also to the other hemisphere, to South America, South Africa, and Australia.

This mode of life stems from a form of agriculture which clearly associates the cultivation of crops with the keeping of domestic animals. Of course, the initial stages of this life did not begin in the very heart of the temperate belt, but rather on its dry borders on the Mediterranean and the steppes of Asia; but they became firmly rooted in the temperate forests and there had their finest development. This was a seemingly paradoxical destiny for agriculture in the forest region.

To begin an agricultural life in a temperate forest assumes a whole long development and a great accumulation of capital. The forest must be cleared, food plants cultivated, and animals needed for labour must be bred, ingenious schemes devised for satisfying a variety of needs, and man himself adapted to the local exigencies of different regions. In this way has been formed a robust and prosperous agricultural system capable for feeding multitudes of people endued with sufficient flexibility to emigrate and win prosperity in all the overseas lands in the temperate belt. Wherever it has taken root, the system has spread by taking possession of the wooded areas and by the rapid settlement of the treeless expanses where the tree formed no obstacle to grain cultivation. The forest has retreated in all directions, and forest life exists now only on the very borders of the temperate belt or in localised regions, like mountain masses, which are favourable to tree growth.

This view of life in the temperate regions assumes, therefore, that man's efforts determine the modification of the natural environment. This process of modification is not understood without a knowledge of man's conquest of the forest. This is an agelong phenomenon in the course of which our whole system of agricultural life has been gradually strengthened and enriched.

In Europe, apart from small isolated glades, the areas of steppe which have remained hostile to forest run in two big tracts across the centre of the continent to join the steppes on the Black Sea. The first tract starts from the valley of the middle Rhine and follows the basin of the Neckar, the Swabian Jura, Switzerland and south Germany, Moravia, and the Danube. The other begins in northern France and passes through Belgium, northwest Germany, the basin of the Saale, and the northern border of the Carpathians. The choice of these steppes by prehistoric settlers is explained less by the fertility of the soil than by the readiness of the environment to accept plants and animals from treeless regions. Men settled and dwelt there for long without touching the forest otherwise than for the immediate defence of their fields against the trees. In fact, from the Neolithic age to the time of the Romans the virgin forest was very little cut into. Roman writers all describe the forests of Germany as impassable, and for centuries these virgin forests formed an impenetrable barrier between the Germans and the Celts. It was only when the Chatti and the Marcomanni had broken through the obstacle that the German tribes were able to advance southwards.

In settling in treeless areas man did not altogether turn away from the forest, which played an important part in primitive economy. Its fringes, where tree growth is less dense, formed indeed a penetrable zone which was open to the air, grassy, full of game, and attractive to domestic animals, since they afforded plenty of food in the shape of acorns and beechmast for the swine and grass for the larger beasts. From early times the importance of the rights and use of pasturage has stressed the vital part played by the forest border. The list of place names due to the Middle Ages has emphasised the value attached to broad-leaved trees, which were cared for and maintained. In Germanic countries more than six thousand place names were derived from the names of deciduous trees. Thus, in England we find names like Aldershot, Appleton, Beechburn, Oakhurst, Willoughton, and Yewdale. In Latin countries names derived from the leaves, trunks, and undergrowth and from trees like the lime, which is found on the edge of the forest, are also innumerable. On these forest borders, where the resources of the woodland and treeless areas were associated, many settlements were made in early times, and the use of forest pastures for feeding animals and of the adjacent arable for growing grain was effected by means of common labour.

It was only later on that arable land was won from the forest border, which was pushed back towards the heart of the woodland; but even in Roman times the forests in Gaul were dense enough to serve as frontiers between the various tribes, and in England Andredesweald separated Sussex from the adjacent kingdoms of the Saxon Heptarchy. In France the destruction of the forests was mainly due to the monks and to wars in the Middle Ages. In Germany the chief periods of destruction extended from the eleventh to the thirteenth century inclusive. Place names in -*reutte* or *rüte* correspond to the English -*ley* or -*leigh* (as in Calverley or Wheatley), and to the French *sarts* and *essarts*. A whole book might be written on the destruction of the forest in the central zone in Russia, the Balkan peninsula, where Shumadia in Serbia affords a typical instance of the destruction of trees on the edge of the forest, and even in the British Isles, where the once widespread virgin forests have completely disappeared. Further examples can be given from the eastern United States, where the history of settlement was the story of a long struggle between the pioneers and the forest, which lasted till the time when the great treeless prairies in the centre were reached, and the civilisation of the plough was established in a few decades on a vast stretch of territory.

Out of this long struggle with the tree has come a complete transformation of the landscape. The destruction of the forest has often been complete. When it has not been complete or final and trees have grown over the ground again, the traces of man's handiwork have not been effaced, for the new growth is secondary, degenerate, and less dense, since it has occupied the area with but few species and those of little value. Often too the degenerate forms have created another vegetation-type, the dense thicket, as in the *touya* of bracken at the foot of the Pyrenees and as in the moor, *lande*, or *garrigue*. When the tree has disappeared, other plants take its place, and a wholly artificial landscape springs up in accord with the rural economy. We must now consider how man planned to combine cultivation and stock-rearing in increasingly profitable cooperation; how these plants and animals are distributed geographically; and how amid the infinite variety of both mankind and regions this distribution has produced the enormous differences that exist between the varieties of the agricultural mode of life throughout the temperate belts.

THE BASIS OF THE AGRICULTURAL MODE OF LIFE

The aim of the cultivator in the temperate region is to produce from the soil food for himself and his domestic animals. The first plants to be selected were mainly grasses that bore nourishing grain. Being strictly dependent on definite natural conditions, the plants very soon moulded man's activities to fit in with their needs. They are all annuals with a vegetation cycle of a few months. Some of them cannot ripen in short summers. The work of cultivating and reaping must therefore be done quickly. The process, which comprises ploughing, sowing, weeding, reaping, and threshing, requires a great command of energy. Besides, the soil is quickly exhausted, for to the removal of soil elements by the harvest is added the solvent action of rainwater, which, however, does not affect dry countries. Furthermore the chemical reactions to which the formation of fertilising elements is due are less active in temperate climates than in the tropics. To make up for this less degree of fertility in the soil, the earth must be ploughed and manured, and the indispensable help of domestic animals must be called on to till the large areas which are needed to produce a sufficiency of food.

Thus, cereals play a fundamental part among cultivated plants, and their importance has increased with progress in rural economy. Some, like wheat and rye, are autumn cereals; others, like barley and oats, are spring cereals. The latter have made great progress owing to the substitution of triennial for biennial rotation in the more advanced countries, where a rotation of wheat, oats, and fallow has systematically replaced the wheat-fallow series. This ready adaptability explains why the part played by cereals as human food crops has continued to increase. Commercial influence has alone been able to restrict cultivation. Thus, the cultivation of cereals decreased by 40 per cent in the United Kingdom between 1876 and 1906. But this decrease was only possible owing to the effect of modern means of transport which have enabled the cereals of the temperate region to be carried throughout the world.

The distribution of cereal cultivation is determined by conditions of temperature. Within the temperate belt it stops in mountainous regions, but every mountain district imposes different limits of cultivation according to the climatic peculiarities. For instance, in the constantly damp climate of Scotland and Norway the limit is very low, being in eastern Scotland the contour for 380 metres (much lower in the wetter west) and in Norway about 340 metres. In dry climates insolation enables corn to ripen even on very high mountains: in the Engadine cereals are grown 290 metres higher up than in the upper valley of the Rhine. The brightness of the air explains the harvesting of grain at a height of nearly 3,600 metres in the Himalayas and at a height of 4,200 metres in the Andes of Peru.

In latitude the cereals ordinarily stop short of regions where the summer temperatures are too low. They reach lat. 70° N. on the mild coasts of Norway, but on the continent of Asia they fall back to below 50° N. on the Pacific coast, and they always stand away a long distance from the southern edge of the Siberian forest.

Towards the tropics temperate cereals disappear as soon as the warm season, which is also the wet season, causes the development of leaves at the expense of grain formation, and they then give way to millet and rice. But the disappearance does not take place everywhere in the same way. Sometimes, as in parts of the Old World, there is a transitional dry belt into which temperate cereals do not penetrate except where the climate is wet enough; at other times, as in the New World, the passage from temperate to tropical cereals is gradual, and this dovetailing is one of the essential features of agriculture in the United States and the Argentine, as it is also is China and Japan.

Owing to the wide distribution of cereals the type of agriculture and mode of life in temperate lands affect vast expanses of the globe. In this immense area the various parts are interdependent, and the big producers supply those that do not produce enough food for themselves. So great a domain in which both the mode of life and the diet are the same, explains the necessity for a colossal amount of trade. Wheat, rye, barley, and oats are found in the earliest traces of the European mode of life. Other plants came later as adjuncts, but without destroying the general harmony of the system of cultivation. The late comers were, firstly, two food plants of American provenance, maize and the potato. Then, later still, clover, lucerne, and forage roots were used to replace the old fallow and to add to the fodder for the livestock.

These plants are found throughout the temperate belt. In certain favourable regions they can be seen all together sharing the soil in different proportions according to man's arrangement of them. But because of their individual constitutions each of them has its definite distribution and favourite areas:

The Older cereals.—*Wheat.* With rye, wheat is the only cereal which is easily stored up and transported, and from which good bread can be made. It has a food value far above that of the various gruels made from other cereals. It is particularly the white man's food and so it is used everywhere. Of western Asiatic provenance it has won its way into the New World and the southern hemisphere.

To ripen, wheat (an annual from sunny, treeless regions) needs a fairly great amount of heat and drought to allow an accumulation of gluten and starch in the grain. It gets both in eastern and Mediterranean countries, which were its original habitat. There the corn is the best, most nourishing, and richest in gluten, whilst in damp, temperate lands the plant yields a greater quantity of less good grain. With its southern provenance it remains by far the dominant cereal as far as about lat. 45° N., that is in Europe, to the south of a line drawn through the south of France, northern Italy, and the lower Danube valley. The same favourable climatic conditions are found in some countries with a continental climate, where the summer temperature is certain to be high and there is a good deal of insolation. Thus, in Soviet central Asia the crop may enjoy 135 days of sunshine. In western Canada diurnal insolation is longer in June and July by an hour or two than in Iowa. Wheat cannot stand great cold, but thrives in mild winters which promote tillering and allow profitable cultivation of winter varieties. It seldom grows in northern regions in which the thermometer falls below −15° C. In Dakota as in Soviet Asia the crop has failed many a time through cold. Only a thick layer of snow enables it to bear low winter temperatures.

Wheat does not require much water. Yet at certain periods of its growth it needs a moderate quantity, viz. after sowing is complete, during growth and florescence, and as the ear is budding. Favourable conditions of moisture are found in the original habitat, as also in most countries with rain in spring and those with snowy winters in which the melting snow deeply saturates the soil. On the other hand, wheat cannot stand climates which are too damp or rainy in summer, whether in maritime temperate regions like Ireland or in warm wet tropical lands or those with monsoonal rains. Of the two extremes it prefers drought, because if the worst comes to the worst it can be cultivated by irrigation, as it is in the Punjab and south Arizona.

Being full of nourishment, wheat gives good yields only in rich soil. Lime is needed to produce fine quality grain; phosphate is indispensable for the development of many grains in the ear. The soil must be consistent without being compact, and it should be deep and permeable. These requirements explain the success of the crop on plains rather than on uplands. Plateaus and plains with more or less unbroken surfaces on which the soil remains deep are favourable to ploughing, which breaks up the earth. The best wheatlands in the Old and New Worlds are found wherever silt occurs on plains. They include the belts of loess which stretch from central Europe into France; the Black Earth of southern Russia; the prairies of North America; and the Argentine Pampa.

The spread of wheat over the world was, however, due especially to its astonishing ease of adaptation. It is found in countless varieties corresponding to very different natural conditions. In a great producer like France several species are cultivated: white wheat giving high yields and square-eared wheat in the northern *départements*; red, frost-resisting wheat in the centre and east; *touzelles* and *saisettes*, which are not easily shrivelled by the sun, in the south. Soft varieties are suitable to moist, temperate lands, and hard wheat, which is in demand for milling, suits dry temperate countries like Hungary, Roumania, and south Russia. Together with winter wheat there exist several varieties of spring wheat which are sown in countries where winters are too severe and the snow cover too thin to protect the seed that is sown. The Canadian Prairies, the states of Minnesota, North and South Dakota, and the steppes of Russia are examples of this. These varieties have enabled wheat cultivation to be carried almost to the limit. In Eurasia it reaches beyond lat. 64° N. along the coast of Norway, and the southern limit lies in India on lat. 21° N. In North America its farthest limits are lat. 60° and 30° N. on the prairies and Great Plains, but along the Atlantic coast they close to lat. 45° and 35° N. In the southern hemisphere wheat is grown in corresponding, but slightly lower latitudes. Thus, owing to the difference in incidence of the seasons in the two hemispheres, there is no month in the year but has a wheat harvest somewhere in the world. No other crop is so widespread and so continuously produced.

In the vast area of wheat production Eurasia has kept the leading place. There are, however, in that continent two groups of countries in each of which wheat cultivation plays an entirely different part. The west and northwest of Europe, which are probably the least favoured parts climatically, are none the less great producers, because in them wheat cultivation takes on an intensive form with the highest yields in the world. Wheat is planted in little fields and rotated with potatoes, beet, maize, and fodder plants. In some countries like the United Kingdom, Belgium, the Netherlands, and Denmark economic crops or pasture have ousted wheat over wide stretches of arable, since these countries reckon on overseas wheat to make bread. France, however has stuck to tradition, tries to maintain a high wheat production, and thus occupies one of the leading places among world producers.

Countries in the south and east of Europe, like those in Asia from the Urals to north China have the great advantage of a dry climate, but nonetheless they are far from attaining to the yields in northwestern Europe. Whether they remain faithful to the old methods, as in Mediterranean lands or China, whether they use powerful modern machinery, as they do in the Soviet Union, their system of agriculture is still dependent on extensive cultivation with a low yield. Mediterranean lands, including southeast France, southern Italy, Greece, Algeria, Spain, and southern Portugal, produce excellent wheat, but their lowland areas are few and small, their cattle too few in number to give plenty of manure, and drought places great uncertainty on the harvests. In spite of efforts made before the second world war by Italy and Portugal to raise their wheat production to the level of their needs, Mediterranean Europe plays but a poor part in world production.

The steppe lands of eastern Europe from Hungary to the Volga have enormously increased their production during all the last years of the nineteenth century and in the twentieth century. In this area wheat assumes the guise of an economic crop and sometimes of even single-crop cultivation. In some *comitats* in the Alfold in Hungary wheat used to cover as much as 80 per cent of the arable. Industrialisation and drift towards the towns of a large fraction of the population have caused an unheard-of increase in the demand for bread cereals in eastern Europe. In the Soviet Union wheat production has increased continuously, more by sowing a greater area than by raising the yield. It is likely that under the influence of this demand Hungary, Roumania, and Bulgaria have been trying to increase their production. The loess plains in the northern Chinese provinces are certainly the greatest wheat producers in the Old World. Its harvest amounts to more than 38 million tons. China is still in the grip of an agricultural system that is without great technical means, but with mechanical equipment like that of the Soviet Union her agriculture might have a long lead in world wheat production.

North America is another of mankind's great wheat granaries. The summer warmth and a good rainfall in spring together with plenty of glacial clay have been favourable to the spread of wheat all over the continent. In this new home wheat has no exactly defined place in the agricultural system, for it is still being adjusted to the natural and economic conditions. Up to the beginning of the nineteenth century the wheat lands of the United States were in the region between Virginia and the south shore of Lake Erie, and Rochester was the chief milling centre. The opening of routes to the West resulted in the invasion of the prairies by wheatfields and the planting of the old European corn crops on the desert borders of the American West. This migration westwards was easily followed by the displacement of the milling centres, which were now set up in various places, first on a line from Cleveland to Cincinnati, then thirty years later on a line through Milwaukee, Chicago, and St

Louis, and, lastly, on the line St Paul and Minneapolis, Omaha City, and Denver. In 1838 Ohio was the U.S.A.'s greatest producer, but its place was taken one after the other by Illinois (1859), Minnesota (1889), and Dakota (1915). Today more than two-thirds of the wheat harvest comes from the two Dakotas, Kansas, Minnesota, Nebraska, and Montana. The same migration from east to west is seen in Canada to the prairies of Manitoba, Alberta, and Saskatchewan, which are continuations northwards of the wheat lands of the United States. This movement of wheat was largely the work of the Canadian Pacific Railway, the wheat fields moving westwards in step with the railway.

In the new countries in North America wheat has long been a cash crop, whose expansion has been helped by the presence of virgin land, means of transport, and, above all, the use of farm machinery to make good the lack of manpower. Few crops indeed lend themselves better than wheat to mechanical cultivation, for there are few processes, and these can be carried out on huge areas without a break. At the present time when Americans have to see to the conservation of the soil and to introduce systems of rotation, wheat cultivation is gradually being done on systems which, at any rate in the central and eastern United States, are tending to make agriculture more like the intensive system long employed in western Europe.

In the southern hemisphere wheat has found physical and economic conditions comparable with those in North America only on the plains around the Río de la Plata in the Argentine and Uruguay. On these wide plains with their virgin soil and dry climate wheat was not, however, a pioneer crop as it was in Canada. At first the plains were used as pastureland, and in the present economic conditions pasturage is ousting wheat and the land going back to stock-rearing around Buenos Aires, Montevideo, and the big towns which are surrounded by dairy farms. Since 1880 the Argentine has been a great exporter of wheat. In Chile the grain finds good climatic conditions north of lat 35° S. but the small area available for the crop together with distance from world markets has restricted the space devoted to corn and the efforts to improve the yield. Australia has devoted to wheat cultivation the grasslands with their dry climate, which form an arable halo on the edge of the sheep runs; but the harvests are uncertain. Besides, since the war Australia has tended towards a policy of producing food to be consumed in the country itself. For this reason the area devoted to wheat is decreasing, and for the same reason there is less production of wheat on the plains on the east side of New Zealand. Thus, the change from a production of corn for the market abroad to an agricultural system tending to the satisfaction of the demands of the home market now results in a diversification of crops and a corresponding decrease in wheat production in those countries where hitherto it had been kept at an abnormally excessive level.

Rye, Barley, and Oats.—None of the other old European corn crops have spread so universally or produced so many slightly different varieties. In most of maritime Europe the spread of wheat crops has taken place at the expense of rye. Since this plant adapts itself better than wheat to cold, damp, and poor soil, it is grown nowadays much farther north and far higher up mountain sides, and it is essentially suitable for the countries of central and eastern Europe to the north of the ancient Hercynian Mountains and of the northern edge of the Black Earth region. It is little cultivated in Asia, and in the New World and other 'new' countries it covers an insignificant acreage, because its low commercial value has prevented its being a rival cash crop to wheat.

Barley and oats have remained less strictly European. Owing to its rapid growth barley has spread enormously in both latitude and altitude. In Europe it is easily grown along with oats in cold countries and with wheat in Mediterranean or semi-arid lands. Between these two extremes of latitude it occurs in 'islands' of cultivation as an industrial crop supplying the raw material for brewers. Out of Europe it is grown with wheat on the west of the United States and the Argentine, in which latter the provinces of Córdoba and San Luís are the main producers, and in southern Australia, where it covers large areas in Victoria.

Oats was closely associated with wheat in Europe in the old system of three-year rotation. It likes cool, moist summers, but shuns drought and great heat; hence, it is the corn crop of maritime Europe, northeast America, and southeastern Australia. Its distribution was to a great extent linked with the use of the horse as a farm animal. In Europe it covered its greatest acreage from the beginning of the eighteenth century onwards, which was the time when the horse replaced the ox in great agricultural countries. Similarly, in the United States it spread over the prairies alongside maize chiefly in the second half of the nineteenth century, which was when the development of farm machinery caused a great use of horses before the introduction of tractors. Nowadays, world production of oats is decreasing in step with the decline of horse breeding.

Nearly all these secondary corn crops, though they are as old as wheat, have lost much of their importance for the very reason that wheat has risen in the ascendant. But to this ancient heritage of food crops there have been added as the years have gone by a number of new plants which have increased the variety of European agriculture. Some have made a veritable revolution in methods necessary, and this has been reflected in the social structure of rural society. Some of the plants are corn crops, like buckwheat and maize; others, like the potato, are tubers or roots, like beet; others again give fodder for the cattle.

The Later Acquisitions.—Buckwheat has only an incidental and limited importance. Introduced into western Europe about the sixteenth century, it is relatively delicate, liking damp, but shunning drought and frost. Its optimum climate is that of maritime Europe, but nevertheless its yield remains moderate. Its temporary success is explained merely by the chance it affords of a catch-crop after the main harvest. With its help the first attempts at intensive cultivation and at reducing the amount of fallow were carried out successfully. It owes its steady decline during the last two centuries, even in poor districts which are now cultivating wheat and artificial fodder, to the introduction of more modern systems of rotation and to crops that need weeding. Buckwheat is still grown in three areas in Europe, and is also found in the northeastern United States and sporadically in Asia. Its fortune has been less brilliant than that of maize or the potato.

Maize.—This tall, fine plant, whose wide, bright leaves bear witness to its tropical affinity, adapts itself to various kinds of soil. Certainly it prefers fertile valley soil and light silt like that found in the central States of the U.S.A., but the conditions in which it is cultivated are determined mainly by climatic factors. It requires great summer heat together with a fairly large amount of moisture. Its rapid growth requires three or four months without frost. It is essentially a spring crop and is sown at the beginning of summer. Unlike wheat it does not have deep roots; hence, maize avoids countries with cool summers, like Britain, Scandinavia, and New England to the north of lat. 44°. It likes open, airy country with plenty of bright sunshine. In this respect it is like the vine, and its distribution sometimes corresponds to that of the vineyard, notably in southern Europe. Maize also avoids the tropics with their continuous warmth and plentiful rainfall; and also arid regions, though less perhaps on account of their drought than for the low night temperatures following days of blazing heat. Hence, maize does not grow either in Nevada or North Africa. In southern Russia, as in the West of the United States, it is nowhere found beyond the mean annual isohyet for 200 to 280 mm.

Economically, maize also affords advantages which explain its widespread cultivation. Its rapid growth makes it a useful plant for hasty cultivation like that of pre-Columbian Indians or that of the first settlers in New England. In fresh settlements it was most often the pioneer crop, which ensured a food supply for the men who were clearing away the forest. As a food it has the drawback of being poor in gluten and of being difficult to make into bread; but it makes up for this drawback by being eatable without great preparation, for its cob, which still remains moist at the end of seven or eight weeks, may be just boiled in water or roasted. Less rich than wheat in nitrogenous elements, it contains on the other hand more sugar and carbohydrates. Lastly, maize gives large yields in return for a small quantity of seed. It is easily cultivated and lends itself to cultivation by hand. As its broad leaves spread apart, secondary crops can be planted between its rows, as beans and pumpkins are in the United States, gourds, tomatoes, and haricot beans in southern Europe (Portugal, Italy, and Croatia), and wheat, vegetables, and vines in southwestern France. It is typical of a crop that requires to be tended and weeded with a great deal of labour and with little help from machines; and so it is the favourite crop of the small-holder.

Maize has found its most favourable conditions in North America and especially within the bounds of the United States. The short time it requires for growth enables it to thrive as far north as lat. 55° N. along the Red River. It admirably suited the needs of semi-nomadic hunting peoples who were without agricultural implements. Sowing was done with a digging-stick, and the cobs were gathered without a sickle. It is Candolle's opinion, moreover, that the original distribution of maize must have been very limited, since without man's help its heavy and not easily detachable grains would spread the plant with great difficulty. The origins of the crop in America are lost in the mists of time. Today, maize is nowhere found in a wild state, and the great number of varieties testifies to the antiquity of its cultivation. Its grains are found in ancient Peruvian tombs and in the 'mounds' in the Mississippi valley. The whole life of the former Aymara, Maya, Toltec, and Nahual civilisations depended on maize as the main crop. For it the sun was prayed to and the rain god worshipped. The crop and its method of cultivation was made known to Europeans by the Amerindians.

Production figures show that today the United States are by far the greatest producers in the world. The crop covers all the States bordering on the Gulf of Mexico and most of those on the Atlantic coast. It is cultivated only incidentally to the west of the Rockies. In the northern States maize is associated with oats, but in the southern States with cotton. The enormous production, which is one of the bases of agricultural prosperity in the United States, is no longer due to subsistence planting, it is true, but on the contrary marks a stage in the development and characteristic specialisation of intensive cash crop cultivation. With maize cultivation is in fact associated a whole system of stock-rearing which extends far to-wards the north of the United States. The five States of Illinois, Iowa, Nebraska, Missouri, and Indiana together produce half of the North American crop. The countryside bears the marks of it in the shape of cattle pens, concrete or steel silos 15 to 18 metres high, and large slaughter-houses in the suburbs of the towns.

Nearly all the North American maize crop is converted into meat. A tiny part of the harvest (2 to 6 per cent) is sent out of the production area. Thoughtful farmers are, however, worried today by such exclusive cultivation, which sometimes looks like true monoculture, in which maize follows maize in the same soil for several years in succession. In this system of cultivation the crop is not one in a rotation, as it is in the Old World. It has, therefore, been greatly blamed for the deterioration of the soil in the prairies and the southern States. Organisations like the Tennessee Valley Authority have made the reduction of the areas devoted to maize one of the essential parts of their programmes for restoring the soil in and at the foot of the Appalachians.

The part played by maize in Latin America has always been quite different. In Mexico, where it was the main crop of the Toltecs and Mayas, it still forms the chief food of the Indians and half-castes. As it does not grow high up in mountains or in deserts, its distribution coincides with the *tierra templada* and *tierra fría* (1,000 to 2,000 metres), which are also the most densely peopled parts. It is cultivated in countless plots of land in Anahuac, especially in those districts where little estates and small-holdings are prevalent. In Brazil it is widely cultivated and sometimes yields two harvests. It is rare in the plains which have an equatorial climate, but on the contrary it is widespread in the coastal States of the centre and south, and it is still the first crop that settlers plant on newly cleared land. Then, again, its cultivation is associated with that of sugarcane and coffee. In the Argentine, as in the United States, maize has become a cash crop, but the harvest is exported directly. It is mainly cultivated on the Pampa, where fields of maize cover 3 million hectares, 2 million of which are in the Province of Buenos Aires, and 700,000 in the provinca of Santa Fe.

Maize did not find a footing in the Old World until after the discovery of America, but its botanical characteristics have enabled it to join in the old European system of cultivation and to add to the plant heritage without harming the traditional crops. As early as 1551 there was reference to it on the Rhineland. The Spaniards had introduced it into the countries on the Rhine and Danube. On their side the Portuguese took it from Brazil to Africa, India, and Malacca. Today the area in Europe covered by maize extends from the Bay of Biscay to the Caucasus, though there are gaps in the lower Rhine valley and on the Riviera. It forms the main crop in Spanish Galicia, northern Portugal, and the Basque country, in southwestern France, North Italy, Vorarlberg, the valleys of the Drava and Sava, the plains of Pannonia and Hungary, the Transylvanian basin, the lowlands of Moldavia and Wallachia, and the Ukraine. With the 43rd parallel as its axis from the Atlantic to the Black Sea, it spreads northwards beyond lat. 45° N. in Italy and the Danube basin and thus broadly coincides with the distribution of wheat and the vine.

However, within the last two decades maize has shown a considerable expansion of area in the Old World and especially in Europe. Thanks to seed selection and hybridisation by agronomists, the plant has succeeded in acclimatising itself outside its optimum areas, and with very high yields. In the Ukraine and in the southern U.S.S.R., as a result of irrigation, the area under maize has increased and production has trebled in fifteen years. Even in France, where maize was seldom grown north of the Loire, it has extended into Beauce, Brie, and even Normandy and Picardy, right up to the Channel coast. In twenty years, whilst the production of wheat in France has only doubled, that of maize has multiplied twenty times, so that France is now the fourth maize producer in the world, an unforeseen example in modern times of the sudden expansion, in response to world economic conditions, of this erstwhile American cereal in the Old World.

In Africa maize has won an important place among the tropical crops. In some places its success has been helped by irrigation. Today, with cotton it is one of the summer crops in Egypt and is necessary for feeding the *fellahin*. In other places it has become associated with the semi-nomadic cultivation of the pastoral tribes of East Africa. In other places again it has become the complement of millet, but in some parts it has ousted millet from tropical regions with a good summer rainfall. For this reason eastern South Africa and Madagascar are important centres of maize cultivation.

In Asia the spread of maize has been checked by the competition of wheat and rice. Yet the crop grows in regions with a wet tropical climate: southern China, Indo-China, and northern India. Maize originated in temperate regions and has spread to these hot countries owing wholly to the influence of European settlers. Curiously enough, on the other hand, maize has played only an insignificant part in Australia and New Zealand. Even now only the northern coast of the North Island has fields of maize, and that merely along a narrow fringe. Perhaps its absence is to be explained by the fact that the settlers in these far-off lands came from Great Britain, where the crop heritage did not include maize, and the colonists, therefore, took with them only plants of the old European stock.

On the whole, maize is very different from wheat. In the present system, indeed, it is used for food less for men than for animals. Of course, cornflour, which is made from maize, is used to make pancakes and a pap which in Italy is known as *polenta* and in the Balkans as *mamaliga*. These occupy a high place in the list of foods eaten by countryfolk, but they are not eaten everywhere, for maize is not as universal a food as wheat.

Potatoes.—The potato comes from the Andes of Chile, and yet it has become an essential crop in the Old World, which is now by far the greatest producer. Like maize it was introduced among the traditional crops without upsetting the essentials of the Old World scheme. It has increased the quantity of food produced from a given area and it helps to conserve the soil and restore its fertility by a simple and effective rotation of crops. This explains its success away from its country of origin and away from the agricultural system in which it had first been cultivated. There is much uncertainty as to the date of its introduction into Europe, but it is said to have been known in Spain between 1580 and 1585, and in fact right up to the eighteenth century it was cultivated sporadically in the Spanish territories of Galicia, Italy, Flanders, and Germany. In England it was not widely cultivated till the eighteenth century, and it was only in the latter half of that century that it became widely cultivated in Germany, France, Austria, and Hungary.

The spread of the potato is justified by the part it has played in supplying food, first for man and then for animals. Though less rich in nitrogenous matter than corn, it is richer in starch. Its yield is enormous, so that it has enabled great densities of population to be maintained in country districts. Even in dry years its harvest, though less, is never nil. It was very soon used for feeding animals, and it has enabled pig-rearing to be developed outside countries where maize is grown. Today, the map showing the distribution of pigs in Europe coincides almost exactly with one showing the main producers of potatoes. Ireland, Germany, and France stand out clearly.

In the traditional system of crops the potato has been introduced as one element in polyculture and enters the rotation with corn crops. In two-year as well as three-year systems it has brought on the disappearance of fallow and has led to the simultaneous cultivation of all the arable. Thanks to it European agriculture has finally become an extensive form of cultivation without fallow. Hence, the potato may be said to have been responsible for the great nineteenth century revolution in agriculture.

Since the potato is a storehouse of starch and alcohol, it later became an industrial crop. As in the case of the cereals, cultivation and selection gave rise to numerous varieties whose tubers supplied various demands of industry. In Germany special varieties were adapted to sandy plains, and these supplied three-fourths of the country's industrial alcohol. For these new uses potato cultivation changed its character. Instead of being a mere element in polyculture, it became the exclusive object of a monoculture over vast expanses. To plant it fresh lands were cleared in the sands and peat-bogs of North Germany and the Netherlands. In this way the land used for potato cultivation in the Old World has continued to increase.

Furthermore, the plant lends itself readily to this spread of its cultivation for it is not over-particular as to soil or climate. It certainly prefers cool countries without great heat and guaranteed against drought; but in fact it is cultivated from the cold borders of the temperate belt (Klondyke and Kamchatka) to its arid borders (Egypt). It can flourish at great heights. In the Andes, its original home, it is cultivated on the *puña* and in the high valleys of Bolivia above 2,500 metres. In the south of India it is the vital resource of the hillmen in the Nilgiris and southern Mysore, who cultivate it above 2,000 metres. It is equally at home in poor sandy soils, in granitic sands and in coarse alluvia.

The hardy character of the potato explains why the tuber has become the characteristic plant of European agriculture. Perhaps it should be added that in the Old World the potato was free from parasites which attacked the crops in the New World. A disease in the potato crop caused a famine in Ireland in 1845–46, but the Colorado beetle was not introduced into Europe until 1917, that is, more than three hundred years after the potato. The main belt of potato cultivation now stretches across the north, centre, and west of Europe. Germany, the Soviet Union, Scandinavia, the British Isles, the Netherlands, and France are the world's greatest producers.

In the New World the areas of greatest production are mainly eastern Canada and New England, which are countries with a harsh climate and poor soil. Contrary to what one sees in Europe, where the potato is grown in association with corn crops, the tuber is not cultivated in the great corn-growing regions of North America, where intensive agriculture and rotation of crops have not yet come into general use. Elsewhere on the continent, in the north as well as in the south, the potato is largely cultivated only in the mountains, and this applies to the Andes and the Rockies alike.

On the whole the potato is a food plant with great possibilities. It is now planted both on a large scale or in garden plots, and it is of prime importance in the kitchen garden. The production of 'early potatoes' has led certain districts with a favourable climate to use them as a cash crop. It was as an early vegetable that the potato was introduced into Mediterranean lands (Algeria, Provence, Roussillon). In Europe districts with a maritime climate and mild winters have been tempted to enter this kind of business. Cornwall and the Channel Islands together with the coastal areas of Cotentin and Brittany grow early potatoes to be sold in large towns. The growing of early potatoes is also carried on in whole districts of Florida and South Carolina, where the early potato takes a place beside the tomato and celery in the produce intended for distant towns.

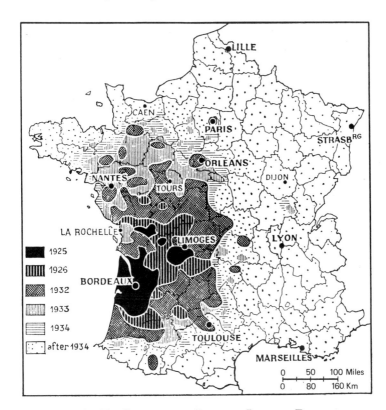

FIG. 2.—THE SPREAD OF THE COLORADO BEETLE IN FRANCE.

Sugarbeet.—Other new crops are now grown in temperate regions. Among these are fodder roots and cultivated grasses, which when used in modern crop rotation have finally abolished the practice of fallow in large scale farming and in places where crop rotation is used in mixed cultivation. Their introduction dates from the time when it was necessary at all costs to find fodder for the farm animals. The increase of cultivation at the expense of moorland, forest, and fallow—all areas given up to supporting animals—imposed the problem right from the end of the sixteenth century. The matter was one of vital importance to an agricultural civilisation based wholly on the association of stock-rearing with cultivation. How were the animals to be fed without risking a reduction in the amount of food for the human population?

The solution of the problem was found and fully applied in England about the middle of the eighteenth century. The area which under the system of three-year rotation was fallow one year in three was given up to feeding the animals. This was an ingenious solution, for it did not impoverish the soil, but on the contrary fertilised it. By feeding more animals indeed more manure was obtained, and later it was seen that the crops adopted to occupy the fallow improved the land for growing corn crops. Hence, the crops destined to feed the animals scored a huge success. Some of them were so modified by selection as to become large scale industrial crops. The outstanding case is that of sugarbeet, thanks to which countries in the temperate belt have become large producers of sugar and have wrested the monopoly of producing this commodity from the tropical regions. Previously, the hot countries alone had in the sugarcane a plant with a high yield of sugar.

The important place held by root cultivation has been the characteristic feature of English farming since the nineteenth century. Swedes play a great part in agriculture in Scotland and the North of England. Similarly, they occupy an important place in farming in New Zealand, whither they were taken by Scottish settlers. On the continent of Europe fodder roots appear in mixed cultivation only in poor districts which have large numbers of animals. But of these roots the beet has had an incredible success and at the same time has undergone a radical change in its character as a crop.

The beet, *Beta vulgaris*, grows wild by the sea especially in the Mediterranean; but in its natural state its roots are thin and fibrous. Cultivation has made them fleshy and capable of swelling out with carbohydrate. The ancients had used the plant as an ordinary vegetable, and it was only in the eighteenth century that, thanks to Margraff (1747) and Achard (1801), the presence of sugar was recognised in the threadlike roots of the beet. The Berlin Decrees, which stopped imports of cane sugar into Europe from the colonies, led to the extraction of sugar from the indigenous plant. By 1810 beet cultivation, encouraged by Government protection, was undertaken on a large scale in France.

The success of sugarbeet was due to the efficiency of theoretical science and the industrial equipment needed to crush the roots and extract the sugar from their juice. The plant was easily improved by selection and within a hundred years it was transformed, particularly in Germany, into a real source of sugar. In less than fifty years its sugar content rose from 5 to 14 per cent. At the same time the use of artificial manure and improvement in cultivation progressively increased the yield per acre. France, which had long been the chief producer of sugarbeet up to about 1870, was gradually outdistanced by Germany and did not resume a leading place until after the introduction of improved varieties of the plant and the adoption of modern machinery. Thus, the modest beetroot became in less than a hundred years a large scale crop owing to the growing demands of large urban populations and the application of modern scientific and engineering methods to the industry.

As a plant the sugarbeet needs a great deal of water especially from May to August, when its broad leaves are growing and making the carbohydrate to fill the root. A prolonged summer drought is fatal to the harvest. Later, from August to September the plant requires a bright, sunny spell to encourage the formation of carbohydrate and to make it seep into the roots. These two conditions are more important than the total amount of summer warmth. The beet does not require a great quantity of calories: hence its growing in the temperate belt and its spread into central and eastern Europe and the West of the United States, where autumn is dry and bright. It likes deep, homogeneous soil such as alluvial silt or loess. It must be tended often and carefully. Ploughing should be deep, and the sowing properly aligned. After the seed has sprouted, the seedlings must be thinned out and the plants separated. The field must be hoed several times until the broad leaves of the plants are large enough to stifle the weeds. Most of this work, which is carried out in spring and the beginning of summer, demands plenty of labour, for it needs care and discrimination and does not lend itself to mechanical aids. Furthermore, the same is true of the harvest, when the removal of the leaves should precede the taking up of the roots. As a rule the labour needed cannot be found on the spot, and districts producing sugarbeet call at least twice a year for seasonal workers. Hence, it is only possible to undertake sugarbeet cultivation near densely peopled centres with good means of communication which provide an efficient shuttle service for the workers.

The expensive machinery and artificial fertiliser required, together with the great amount of labour needed, explain why, unlike the potato, sugarbeet has failed to find a place in the rotation of crops and in small holdings, but is cultivated only on a large scale. Great capital expenditure in land and the means of production is needed, and, in return, the crop has encouraged the establishment of large units of cultivation wherever it has become the main product.

At the present time the world distribution of sugarbeet does not therefore reflect only the influence of physical factors, but even more that of economic or human actions. Its requirements in labour help to explain why it long remained absent from Great Britain and the United States. In the former the interests of canesugar in her West Indian colonies were for long a major obstacle to the introduction of the industry, but early in the twentieth century small-scale experiments were carried out, and after the war in 1918 further efforts to establish beet sugar production with the help of a Government subsidy proved successful. Another variety of the beet known as the mangold, or mangel-wurzel, is cultivated in the south and east of England, where the climate is warm and dry enough for the plant. The mangold is used as cattle food. In the United States, where sugarbeet cultivation began in 1862, progress was slow. In California and the West, where there was an idea of making sugarbeet plantations on recently irrigated land, scarcity of labour caused the plan to be quickly abandoned in favour of fruit and early vegetables. It is only of late that regions of moderate density of population have included sugarbeet in their crop rotation. They are mainly in Michigan and Wisconsin in the east and in Utah and some irrigated areas in Colorado and the West.

Central Europe remains the chief centre of sugarbeet cultivation. In Germany, where large-scale cultivation began about 1830, beet is associated with wheat in fertile, loam districts in Hanover and Brunswick and in Borde in Saxony. It is widespread in similar conditions in Bohemia, Moravia, Silesia, and even East Prussia, where imported fertiliser has enabled beet to be grown on the sandy soil. Today, Poland and Czechoslovakia are among the largest producers of beet sugar. In eastern Europe beet is largely grown in the fertile soil of Podolia, Volhynia, and the Black Earth region of the Ukraine, and Soviet agriculturalists have spread its cultivation to the irrigated parts of Turkistan.

In western Europe Belgium and the Netherlands, which with their old skill in agriculture have long tended towards industrial crops and have a labour force both numerous and skilful, are large producers of beet. In the Netherlands loam areas in Brabant and Hesbaye, the fertile soil in Hainaut, and the polders use a scientific rotation of wheat, sugarbeet, and various minor crops. France is also a large producer. About 1834 beet was cultivated in fifty-five *départements*, but foreign competition, the sugar slump in 1840 and 1875, and the demands of the crop have caused production to be concentrated around big refineries in Cambrésis, Artois, Picardy, and the Paris region with its large scale cultivation.

Southern Europe long resisted the introduction of beet owing to the summer drought. But improved irrigation has enabled some Mediterranean countries with plenty of labour to cultivate it as a cash crop, and today there are fields of beet in Granada and Córdoba, in the lower valley of the Po, and around Ferrara and Bologna. In France too beet has been introduced along the lower Rhone valley and into the irrigated parts of Provence near the Rhone.

Altogether, sugarbeet remains the characteristic crop of scientific agriculture at the peak of its technique. It has helped to transform the horizons of work in the countryside. As it yields a heavy raw material with a high proportion of waste, the crushing mills and refineries have had to be built near the fields where the root is grown, and the roots are conveyed to the mills on narrow-gauge railways. Besides agricultural labourers, there are workers employed at various stages of the manufacture of the sugar to carry fuel and chemicals (limestone and chalk) which are used in the refining. The leading crop in the rotation and requiring plenty of fertiliser, the beet leaves in the soil a good deal of manure for the benefit of the cereal that follows it. For this reason it is an essential element in high yielding intensive cultivation. The pulp and other waste matter from refineries have moreover ensured the increase of livestock rearing in districts in which intensive cultivation used previously to avoid growing fodder. The pulp is used as cattle food in winter. The advantages accruing to a nation's economy from beet cultivation are so great that it is not surprising that most countries in Europe have introduced protectionist legislation either to help their own producers or to create an economic climate favourable to establishing the crop within their own borders.

Artificial fodder has played a less spectacular, though no less effective, part in the agricultural revolution. Lucerne, sainfoin, and clover act as green pasture and, as they are planted in fields once left fallow, they have taken the place of meadows and natural grassland which in any case do not exist in some districts. With this fodder herds and flocks have greatly increased in every country in Europe. When stored like hay, it enables a large number of beasts to be kept through the winter. Lastly, the creation of artificial meadow land in the bottoms of once marshy mountain valleys has enabled the stockmen to give up the long droves due to *transhumance* and to keep their milch cows nearly all the year round within reach of the factories which prepare the milk and milk products for sale outside the valley.

In this way these crops which have been acquired one after the other by the agricultural peoples of the temperate belt and which by their adoption have transformed and enriched the traditional system of cultivation, now form a kind of botanical association whose members have all become more or less dependent on each other. They follow and help each other in the rotation into which some have attracted others, and they produce astonishing quantities of food. Some yield bread, others are used as food for man and animal. Man and his animals claim the same field in turn so that the interdependence which exists between man and his domestic animals in work on the land is everywhere demonstrated as the fundamental trait of agricultural life in temperate regions.

The Association of Stock-rearing with Agriculture.—No doubt animals were first regarded as affording produce that could not be had from agriculture. This consisted of milk and meat for use as food and also hair, fleece, leather, and skins for use in making clothes. But very soon domestic animals became docile aids to cultivation in temperate regions. The application to cultivation of their physical strength was achieved by means of the plough. That most ancient and widespread of agricultural implements, the primitive wooden plough, consisting of ploughshare, coulter, and wheels, though made more efficient by successive improvements, is still found in the most up-to-date farm machinery. At the beginning the plough was drawn by an ox or cow. In the reliefs of classical antiquity oxen are seen ploughing, and throughout medieval Europe they formed the working animals of the peasantry. It was only later that, owing to progressive requirements, the horse took the place of the ox in countries with large-scale agriculture or of the mule in southern Europe and more recently in the Southern States of America.

Although widespread throughout the temperate belt, domestic animals like cereals do not find equally favourable conditions everywhere. In any given region they do not do as well as they might unless they have climatic and agricultural conditions suitable to their use. Our domestic animals are not part and parcel of the natural environment of temperate regions to the same extent as are the cultivated plants. The ox, horse, pig, and sheep flourish further within the hot belt than do the cultivated plants associated with them in our countrysides. The special feature of their life in the temperate belt is that they are far more closely bound up with agriculture, whilst in most of the warm regions cultivation is carried out by hand.

The Ox.—The ox has played a greater part than any other animal in the history of civilisation. Its distribution at the present day bears witness to this, for the animal has achieved a remarkable ubiquity. The Old World has used the ox since prehistoric times. It is found in the heart of Africa, where it forms the wealth of the pastoral tribes of the Sudan; and it is one of the pillars of agricultural civilisation in India. It did not reach the New World before the arrival of the Europeans, for it first set its foot in the western hemisphere during Columbus's second voyage to the West Indies. From those islands it was taken to Mexico, Columbia, and Venezuela. Only in 1546 did it reach Brazil, from which country it was taken to the Pampa in 1580. From Mexico the animal travelled slowly northwards towards the wide grass plains of Texas and the West. The movement along the Texas cattle trail was to take the ox right on to the ranges in the Dakotas and Montana. But in fact another current of migration took the ox during the seventeenth century into the heart of the prairies in the middle of the continent. Spread over the

1. Eskimo igloo in the Canadian north-west; built on sea-ice 25 km offshore in Minto Inlet

THE ARCTIC ENVIRONMENT

2. Eskimo dog-team on melted ice surface in spring

3. The Canadian prairies; mechanised large-scale wheat-farming near Portage la Prairie, Manitoba

TEMPERATE ENVIRONMENTS

4. Polyculture in small fields in Auvergne, in central France

Atlantic coast between 1608 and 1630 as the servant of the European cultivation which had been introduced into those districts by the colonists, it advanced westwards in step with the several stages of agricultural settlement. Thus, the spread of the ox in the New World shows us the animal in its twofold character, first as a denizen of wide grass plains suitable for maintaining a special form of pastoral life, and, secondly, as a stall animal, the faithful companion of the sedentary agriculturalist.

Within the vast area in which it is now found the ox is used in various ways. It lends itself to heavy work such as grubbing or drawing carts. Moderate in its food, it eats far more green fodder than corn. In southern and central France, in Italy, Bavaria, and the Danubian lands it is still used in the fields. It was formerly used nearly everywhere in the United States, but it lost ground to the horse at a comparatively recent date because modern economic factors changed the old systems of cultivation. Wherever crops have spread at the expanse of fallow, wherever secondary cereals like oats have increased, and wherever scarcity or dearness of agricultural labour has at different periods of history called in the use of a faster animal, the ox has given place to the horse for ploughing and draught.

But the essential parts played by the ox and cow have not diminished in the agricultural system of the temperate regions, for they are reared especially for their meat and milk, since no other animal can equal their yield of either. For long years the ox was not reared for its meat, for the farmer would not easily sacrifice a working beast and, besides, the quantity of beef it gave far exceeded the ordinary needs of a family. During the whole of the Middle Ages and long after—in fact, until the beginning of the eighteenth century—the pig sufficed for the supply of meat to countryfolk. Increased consumption of meat in towns and more rapid transport, together with progress in the art of meat preservation were needed in some countries before the rearing of horned cattle was undertaken to supply butcher's meat. Today the production of meat follows a geographical distribution which depends mainly on the development of agriculture, but which could only be realised in temperate lands which derived their cattle from countries with the system of agriculture introduced from Europe. In fact, the great grass plains have no monopoly in the production of meat, since most of this commodity comes from areas where there is large scale cultivation producing great quantities of provender for the animals. Throughout Great Britain, France, and central Europe calves and oxen are fattened with artificial fodder, tubers, roots, pulp, and by oilcake and other by-products of milling. In the Argentine and the United States the maize-growing States are the chief producers of meat.

In old agricultural countries there is division of labour between regions with different aptitudes. Some produce store cattle, others fatten them for the butcher. This interdependence connects the grassy parts of western Britain with those in the centre and east which grow more cereals and tubers. In France grass-growing districts like Limousin are associated with areas of fertile soil where there is large scale cultivation. In these days more specialisation tends to separate districts producing meat from those producing milk and milk products. In many countries in the vast area in the temperate belt in which horned cattle are found, milk is one of the most valuable of farm products. In districts where the countryfolk keep to the old, traditional forms of cultivation, the cow is the most precious possession. Many petty graziers in Normandy who own no land have cows. Yet the importance of milk and dairying is of recent date. Apparently, butter was not eaten in France in the Gallo-Roman period. Though it is true that the popularity of milk and butter goes back to the Germans of old, it should be noted, however, that milk still came a long way behind meat in the diet of the Merovingians and even of the Carlovingians. Probably, the milch cattle were of merely a poor breed, and the cows gave milk only for a short time in the year according to the the quantity of fodder available.

It was only from the seventeenth century that the milk yield increased owing to the improvement in the breeds by selective breeding which took place in western Europe and especially in Great Britain, where the Jersey, Ayrshire, Devon and Shorthorn breeds were reared. These breeds of milkers, which were really an artificial creation of zootechny, were later to occupy the pastures and byres of the New World and New Zealand. Many of the breeds of milkers reflect today the natural conditions of the countries in which they were bred. The heavy breeds of the damp plains in northwestern Europe (Denmark, Friesland and Holland) are in contrast to the light, economical beasts in the Alps. Today the milk producing countries are essentially cool in climate, produce green fodder, and give no check to lactation owing to the heat of summer. They include Denmark, southwestern Scandinavia, the Netherlands, the British Isles, the west of France, and across the Atlantic the United States from Maine to Wisconsin along the shores of the Great Lakes. But to these regions which are naturally favoured should be added countries with large scale agriculture able to supply the cows with plenty of good feed, such as the Franco-Belgian plain of Flanders. The neighbourhood of large towns should also be added, for there a large centre of demand nearby gives rise to dairy farms just outside the built-up area. On the whole, industries connected with milk have undergone great expansion especially since the second half of the nineteenth century and, in consequence, the breeding of milch cows has been specialised to the extent that we see today achieving a scientific, technical, and commercial development. This is the state of things in Great Britain, where 70 per cent of the amount produced is used in this way, and therefore large quantities of butter and cheese are imported. Other countries, such as Denmark, New Zealand, and eastern Wisconsin, concentrate on making butter; whilst others, including Switzerland, Italy, and the Netherlands, prefer to make cheese, in which form they export their milk.

Thus, milk products have had the same fortune as beef. After being long used on the spot or near their place of origin, they have become a commodity of world trade. The expansion of the European peoples has carried the production of milk into all the new countries in the temperate belts of both hemispheres. Today, Canada, Australia, the Argentine, and, more especially, the United States and New Zealand have entered into competition with the countries of Europe. During the last decades the production of milk and meat, both of expanding consumption, have not suffered from the crises that have hit agriculture. That is why many countries have curtailed their cereal crops to concentrate their efforts on the expansion of cattle-rearing and even more on the breeding of milch cows. This change of purpose is perhaps the most prominent feature in the agricultural geography of the United States at the present time.

The Horse.—For different reasons the horse like the ox is inseparable from rural life in the temperate regions. There is little doubt of its original habitat, for it certainly comes by direct domestication from wild *equidæ* that were still found pretty widely in Europe within historical times. It seems to have been domesticated in central Asia, and it was from the East that the Babylonians and Egyptians got the animal, Man's success in domesticating it dates from ancient times, if we are to judge by the many types found in the temperate belt. Western Europe has heavy breeds used for ploughing and drawing carts. Dry countries have lighter, faster horses, of which the arab is typical. Lastly, in the islands off the northwest of Europe there are small breeds commonly known as ponies and found in Shetland, Orkney, Ireland, and Scandinavia.

Even more than the ox, the horse is an animal of the steppes and forest glades. It came into use for work on the land later than the ox, for it is suitable for long, rapid journeys rather than for patient toil. It preceded the ox as a pioneer in occupying the grasslands of America. On the Pampa as well as on the prairies of North America and in Texas it has enabled the grasslands to be used for extensive stock-rearing. It was by means of this special element in their domestic heritage that Europeans were able to cope with nature in America more effectively than were the Amerindians, who were without strong, fast-moving animals. Today the horse is found throughout the temperate belt and the bordering grasslands, but it is not found in hot countries. In the Mediterranean lands of Europe the horse gives way to the ass and mule, and in the United States the mule is used for work in all the cotton States of the South. Within its own domain the horse has become the chief animal only in districts which have a high yield of cereals, where its strength and spirit enables work in the fields to be carried on very rapidly and where it is sure to find plenty of food in the shape of oats.

The total number of horses in the world amounts to 64 million head, 16 million of which are in Europe and the Soviet Union. In spite of the mechanisation of its agriculture, the United States still has 8 million horses, the greater number of which are in the States of Illinois, Indiana, and Ohio. The Argentine, Australia, and New Zealand have 4 million, so that altogether the temperate belt alone has 40 per cent of the world's total. This distribution of the species is due to man. The first horses were taken to Iceland by the Norsemen in the ninth century, North America got its horses in the sixteenth century only, and South America still later. Hence, there is an unquestionable coincidence between the distribution of the horse and of European civilisation. The horse is used in some countries for riding, in others as a pack animal, in others again as a draught animal or for drawing the plough. In fact, the use made of the horse has varied from time to time, but unlike the ox the animal is very little used for food, a fact that explains the development of the world's horse population.

The progress of mechanisation first in transport and then in agriculture has had the effect of lessening the need for animal power. Horses are particularly numerous in regions where they are used for work, and they are less numerous in regions where the work is done to a greater extent by horned cattle or machinery. In western Europe horses are used for ploughing in Upper Bavaria, Westphalia, Zealand and Groningen in the Netherlands, all countries in which the soil is heavy. In France horses are most numerous north of a line drawn from the mouth of the Loire to the south of the *département* of Meurthe-et-Moselle. Where crops of wheat and beet prevail on alluvial plains, there too are the chief centres of horse-breeding, that is, in Brittany, Perche, Normandy, the Boulonnais, and the Ardennes. The same relation is found in Great Britain between corn-growing areas and those well supplied with horses, like Suffolk, Cambridgeshire, Essex, and Norfolk.

In central and eastern Europe the area in which horses are bred and used runs from the southern Urals between lat. 51° N. and lat. 56° N., across the Dnepr, and through Ruthenia and Hungary into the 'Saxon' districts of Transylvania which lie within a country inhabited by Romanian peasants who are still faithful to the yoke of oxen. In these eastern and Danubian lands the use of the horse is particularly justified by the necessity for speed in agriculture owing to the shortness of the period available and to the decrease in the vegetative cycle of cultivated plants. Hence the extraordinary abundance of horses in the plain of Hungary and in the interior of Russia, where before 1928 there were twice as many horses as cattle in the belt of chestnut coloured soil and podzol, especially in the provinces of Tula, Orel, Kursk, and Ufa.

Cereal crops and large numbers of horses go together in the new countries. The highest total in Australia is found in the wheat-growing plains in Victoria and New South Wales, where in the Murray valley there are 40 horses to every 100 horned cattle. On the other hand, there are few on the south coast where there is no extensive cultivation of wheat. In New Zealand many more horses are found on the cultivated plains on the eastern slopes, than on the western slopes where cereal cultivation is handicapped by the high rainfall. In the United States there are dense horse populations in the corn belt States, where maize crops alternate with oats. Further-more, not only are horses used in the prairies, but they are also bred there to supply the animals to eastern States and mules to the southern.

However, at the present day the use of the horse is restricted by mechanisation. Their number has continued to decrease in the United States as the number of tractors has increased. About the year 1900 there were 25 million in the United States, but in 1952 the number had fallen to 6½ million, the number of tractors having risen to 5 million; and it is estimated that the increase in the use of motor vehicles will further cause the disappearance of more than 300,000 horses. American economists have calculated that this development would permit the conversion of over a million hectares in which oats are grown for horses into an area for growing food crops for human consumption. They further estimate that during the past fifty years the substitution of motor vehicles for horses has enabled more than 16 million hectares, or 11 per cent of the area now under cultivation in the United States, to be returned to food production. These con-siderations enable us to understand the reasons for the decrease in the number of horses in most of the new countries.

The economic crisis which followed the Russian revolution and the collectivising of rural districts in 1928 brought on a catastrophic fall in the number of horses in the Soviet Union. In 1955 a census showed a decrease of 15 million head on the prewar figures. The total in 1939 was 22 million against 32 million in 1914. The decrease is explained by the importance of machinery in the new system of Soviet agriculture. Today there are more than 9,000 motor tractor stations with some 600,000 tractors which do 92 per cent of the ploughing in the *kolkhozy*. In actual fact, since 1933 when 250,000 tractors were available the Soviet Union has replaced the mechanical power which it had lost owing to the disappearance or slaughter of 15 million horses in consequence of the troubles brought on by frustration due to the New Economic Policy. It seems, however, that contrary to what is happening in the United States, horse breeding has still made some progress in the Soviet Union since the *kolkhozniky* have been allowed to own more private property. The truth is that since 1939 horses have ceased to be regarded as a means of production in collective farms and have been allowed to be privately owned by the peasants. This has induced a noticeable increase in the number of horses. But in the Soviet Union, as in the United States, the great advantage of the tractor is that it enables the farm calendar to be shortened. It is a most suitable machine for countries with short summers, where vast expanses must be sown shortly after the end of the harvest. These economic factors explain the decrease in the horse population over the greater part of the temperate belt.

Following an ancient practice, the use of the animal has in every country undergone a development parallel with that of the ox. It encourages a division of labour. Even today some districts still rear young animals, whilst others merely use full grown beasts. Hence the importance of the trade in adult horses and of the horse markets in most districts where the animals are bred. In France, for example, horses from the Boulonnais spend their lives in three different areas: first, in the Boulonnais, where foals and young horses are reared; then in Vimeu and the district of Caux, where they begin work as farm animals; and, lastly, in the wide cultivated plains in the Paris basin and the east, where they become heavier and stronger and are used to draw carts and the plough. This connexion between economic regions exists also in the States of Iowa, Illinois, and Kansas, where the seasonal distribution of work gives long periods of rest for the mares. This period of unemployment is used for the production of foals, which are later used on the farms in the central prairies. These practices are survivals of a skilful tradition to which the growing use of the motor vehicle will soon deal an irreparable blow.

The Pig.—The pig is reared for its meat and is the only domestic animal reared exclusively for the butcher. Agriculture has succeeded in making it an inseparable part of the diet in every country home and in this respect it may be regarded as symbolical of settled farming. The prohibitions placed on it in every land in which there prevails a pastoral life based on the use of a wide-ranging animal like the sheep, merely reflect perhaps the nomad's scorn of a sedentary life, of agriculture, and of the animal that ties man to his cultivated land. Jews and Muslims have drawn up a whole code of religious prohibitions directed against an animal that threatened the very principles of their mode of life. Though it yields a great deal of meat, the pig is a heavy feeder and must have a quantity of nourishing food such as he cannot find on pastures, as the sheep does. It therefore thrives in places where the economic conditions enable it either to feed on acorns, beechmast, or chestnuts in the forests or to be fed on waste matter from intensive cultivation, that is, on surplus corn or tubers, on kitchen swill, or waste from a dairy, flour mill, or other food factory. These conditions place pig breeding in the temperate belt and particularly in districts of highly developed intensive cultivation. In fact, pig-breeding plays a vital economic part in two regions. They are, first of all, Europe and the countries in the West that have a European tradition; and, secondly, Far Eastern countries on the Pacific coast, such as China and the islands of the Pacific.

The domestic pig is derived from the wild hog, which is similar to the wild boar. As it is only superficially domesticated, it very easily reverts to a wild state, especially in the eastern group of countries mentioned above. European breeds seem to have been crossed very early with Chinese breeds; and it was only in the eighteenth century that careful selective breeding succeeded in producing varieties that were wholly artificial, were veritable factories of meat and lard, and were restricted from that time forward to regions where there was extensive breeding of the animal.

An examination of present-day distribution of pigs clearly shows four main areas, all of which are situated in the temperate belt. One coincides with wooded districts where there are acorns, chestnuts, or beechmast. Among them are districts in the Mediterranean, parts of Spain, Italy, and, above all, Greece and Serbia. In those countries there still continues the old method of pig-rearing which existed in the forests of ancient Gaul and, nearer our own times, in medieval Europe. Agriculture is still backward and yields but a meagre surplus. Consequently, waste land is brought into use for keeping pigs, which have only a short journey to reach the woods. A whole code of rural legislation defining the conditions of pannage and the use of woodland pasture formed at one time the framework of country life in western Europe.

Side by side with these survivals of an archaic method of pig-rearing are found rich agricultural districts with a great variety of food plants and dairy waste. To this category belong Great Britain, where barley is the basis of pig food; Finland, Sweden, and Denmark; and the wide clay plains in the north of France and in Hesbaye, where large pig farms feed their animals on tubers and roots. But pig-rearing is not confined to areas of large scale cultivation, for, since the pig is prolific, omnivorous, and by no means selective in the quality of its food, it is also kept on small holdings and forms the wealth of the little peasant. Hence, it is found in mixed farming, where there is a large variety of secondary produce in the shape of potatoes, buckwheat, various roots, and fodder crops. For this reason pigs are numerous wherever cultivation is on a small scale, as in the sandy parts of the Netherlands and Germany between the Weser and Elbe, the plateau of Lorraine in eastern France, the uplands of ancient rock formation and their surroundings in the centre and west of France, and, lastly, Ireland, which produces a large surplus of potatoes.

Other high density pig-rearing coincides on the map with maize cultivation. This is illustrated nowhere better than in the United States, where the 'hog belt' coincides nearly everywhere with the 'corn belt'. Half the pigs in the country are found in the seven States of Iowa (14·8 per cent), Illinois (7 per cent), Missouri (6·9 per cent), Nebraska (6·6 per cent), Kansas (6·3 per cent), Indiana (6·1 per cent), and Ohio (5·5 per cent). Iowa has as many pigs as the States on the Pacific coast and on the Atlantic coast south of Georgia put together. One third of the maize grown in the prairies reaches the market in the shape of pork. Farther north dairy waste replaces maize. Thus, Wisconsin contains 3 per cent of the total number of pigs in the United States. In the West, on the other hand, where the pig cannot adapt itself to the pasture lands on which graze cattle and sheep and where the extensive kind of cereal cultivation does not suit pig-rearing, the animal is found only very locally on irrigated soil with crops of grass and lucerne.

Since 1850 pig-rearing has not spread far beyond the fringes of the corn belt. It has gained ground only in Tennessee, Kentucky, North Carolina, and Alabama, but it should be noted that the coincidence between the corn belt and the hog belt is less exact today than it was formerly. The greatest producer of maize at the present day is in fact Illinois, which rears far fewer pigs than Iowa. The proximity of Chicago, where maize is treated industrially for the production of glucose, ensures the local wheat crop high prices in an important market, which districts farther from the industrial centres cannot use.

Altogether, the United States contains 9 per cent of the world's pigs. The organisation of their slaughter-houses is on a world scale. In seven of the prairie towns the curing of bacon and ham and the canning of meat of various sorts has been raised to the level of a great factory industry. Giant slaughter-houses serving tailorised factories in Chicago, Kansas City, Omaha, St Louis, St Joseph, St Paul, and Oklahoma City cut up and prepare every year an average of 20 million pigs as against 10 million cattle and 14 million sheep. In these towns the number of pigs slaughtered every year is equal to 40 per cent of all the swine in Europe.

Of a world total of 687 million pigs the temperate belt contains 275 million, 139 million of which are in Europe, 67 million in the Soviet Union, and 69 million in North America. In these belts countries with dense populations consume most of the pigs they rear. This is so in China, and it is becoming so more and more in the United States. New countries, especially Canada and New Zealand, which are still sparsely populated and have inherited a European outlook, are now exporters of pork. The greatest centres of consumption of this meat in Europe are said to be Germany, the Netherlands, and Great Britain, which together use every year more than 400,000 tonnes of pork. The supplies come mainly from the adjacent agricultural countries and especially south Sweden, Denmark. central Europe, Belgium, and Ireland. Though pig-rearing is an important industry in France, imports of pork exceed the exports every year. It is a curious fact that, in spite of the ubiquity of the animal, pork should have become a high-priced industrial commodity and an article of trade between distant countries and should be allied with the most modern forms of industry in the temperate belt.

Sheep.—The sheep, which provides part of man's diet, has spread far and wide, but flourishes best in the temperate belt and has multiplied greatly there. Yet nowadays it is tending to diminish in number owing to new fashions in food. Although it is able to adapt itself to various climates from Greenland and Iceland on the one hand to the scorching tablelands of Arabia and the Deccan on the other, the sheep is best off in countries with mild winters: the Mediterranean lands, which are the oldest centre of sheep-rearing; the moorlands of northwest Europe with their maritime climate; and the countries in the southern hemisphere. Hardy and quiet, the sheep likes wide, open ranges on the grasslands, where it grazes on the grass and bushes. Hence its importance in all dry countries and its amazing spread in Australia and South America. Hence too the part it plays in dry lands on the borders of temperate regions and the tendency it manifests to retreat before the introduction of cultivated crops. Sheep-rearing seems to represent a long essential stage in the development of the European system of agriculture, which has now been completed.

The distribution of sheep is less regular today than it was in the past, when every village had a flock from which it got its wool. Nowadays this need is less urgent, and the sheep tends to be distributed according to its natural requirements. If we consider its present-day distribution on a map of the world, we see that it is found mainly in an ill-defined zone situated at the limit of cultivation and grassland along the southern boundary of the north temperate regions. This boundary strip is found both in the American Far West, in Australia, Syria, Palestine, and on the high tablelands of Algeria. True sheep country is found in areas where aridity precludes cultivation and where population is still too sparse to demand strict appropriation of the land for the production of food crops. This is so on the grasslands of South America, South Africa, and Australia, where the land used as pasture could be put under cultivation in other economic and demographic circumstances. The only countries in Europe in which sheep still hold an important place are those with wide expanses of moorland, grassland, or fallow, like the Scottish moors and the Welsh mountains, the garrigues in southern France, the Hungarian grasslands, the limestone plateaus in the Balkan peninsula, and the arid parts of Italy and southern Spain.

Among the regions in which the sheep thrives best the first place is taken today by the new countries where there are wide open spaces. Thus, Australia with about 150 million head contains more sheep than any other country in the world; New Zealand has 55 million, and the dry tableland of South Africa and the southeast of the Argentine pampa together contain over 70 million, whilst the U.S.S.R. has 140 million.

In fact, sheep-rearing cannot exist together with a system of intensive cultivation, since this uses the whole area for its crops and takes in the pastureland around. It has been said (by Thomas Moore) that sheep drive away both man and corn owing to the large area of pasture which they need. Up to the nineteenth century the great wool producers in Europe had been England, France, and Germany. They have ceased to be so today because the progress of agricultural methods has done away with grass-covered fallow and large areas of moorland, and because sheep-breeding has been directed towards the production of mutton, which requires far fewer animals than does wool production.

Indeed sheep-breeders in the temperate belt have differentiated between varieties giving finer and finer wool and those giving mainly mutton. The wool-bearing sheep spread in ancient times throughout the eastern Mediterranean lands and seems to have been introduced into Spain by the Moors about the end of the eighth century; but it was only in the fourteenth century that they took the merino to that country. Now, from time to time specialisation in wool-bearing breeds has been related to the geographical spread of the merino at the expense of local varieties. Of the world's wool-bearing sheep today probably 40 per cent are merinos. This vast increase dates mainly from the eighteenth and nineteenth centuries.

The first attempt to cross imported rams with native ewes was made in Sweden in 1723, but throughout the eighteenth century these attempts were paralysed by Spanish economic regulations, which forbade the export of merinos. Only between 1760 and 1840 could cross-breeding be systematically undertaken in most European countries. One of the clauses in the Treaty of Basle in 1795 stipulated that there should be a periodical delivery of merino rams to France. The idea of inuring merinos to the French countryside was due to Daubenton.[1] In 1776 some rams were imported from Spain into France by the orders of Turgot,[2] and ten years later a whole herd was taken from Segovia to Rambouillet, where it was intended to form a sort of nursery. By the end of the eighteenth century the sheep in Beauce, Brie, and Soissonnais had been crossed with merinos, after which Roussillon, Provence, Burgundy, and Champagne in turn had merinos. The same method of crossing took into England, Prussia, Saxony, Bohemia, Italy, Hungary, and southern Russia breeds of wool-bearing sheep which in some cases surpassed the original Spanish merino in quality of wool. Merino rams were introduced from Europe into La Plata about 1800, and a little later others were taken to Australia, South Africa, and finally to the United States. The sheep reared in the flocks throughout Australia is the merino, which is a descendant of some of the famous breed which were presented to King George IV by the Spanish Government after the Peninsular War. The stock has been greatly improved by careful and scientific breeding, which has produced a number of varieties suitable to local conditions in different parts of the country. Wool from abroad was reaching Europe as early as 1840 just when European breeders were beginning to lose interest in fleeces and to attend mainly to the production of mutton.

As a meat producer the merino was a poor animal. But Robert Bakewell (1723–95) had bred at his farm, Dishley Grange, in Leicestershire, a variety of sheep which had broad backs and short, fat hindquarters. This he had achieved by selecting native beasts and developing through heredity a certain number of fixed individual characteristics. The Leicester, or Dishley, breed was the first mutton sheep worthy of the name. Since then the production of wool-bearing and mutton sheep has gone on side by side in England and throughout western Europe. But everywhere sheep-breeding has changed. Instead of putting large flocks to graze on huge uncultivated areas, small flocks are fattened on good pasture and are ready for slaughter in a single season. A similar development has already taken place in several new countries, notably the Argentine, where cross-breds of English origin preponderate over the merinos. This

---

[1] Louis-Jean-Marie Daubenton (1746–99), a French naturalist who collaborated with Buffon.
[2] Anne-Robert-Jacques Turgot, Baron de L'Aulne (1727–81), a French economist who was Finance Minister in the reign of Louis XVI.

breed has transformed New Zealand into a great exporter of 'lamb', which is sent in the shape of chilled carcasses mainly to England. The development seems fatal today, if one may judge from what has happened in Europe, where the splitting up of landed property, the increase in population, the spread of intensive cultivation, and even the reafforestation which has gone hand in hand with progress in agriculture have made the sheep an undesirable prodigal of land. It should be added that higher prices for mutton in relation to those for wool have naturally turned investment towards the former. Now, good pasture and the results of cross-breeding have lowered the age for slaughter more and more, an effect pleasing to the farmer, who thus has to keep his animals for a shorter time. By a kind of paradox the sheep, which was formerly a symbol of extensive cultivation and the survival of fallow, has become inseparable from intensive cultivation and stall-rearing, the denizen of the luscious paddock. This development began in England, where the cultivation of turnip and rape in the east of the country first provided food for sheep on rich pastureland. Thus ends a cycle of the story of the sheep, in the course of which the animal has kept its place in agricultural systems that have always associated it with cereal crops in conditions very different from those adopted for the ox.

THE DEVELOPMENT OF THE AGRICULTURAL MODE OF LIFE

The life of the farmer, which is very complex and has been slowly moulded in the course of centuries, does not owe its characteristics merely to the influence of the natural environment, for associations of cultivated plants as well as those of domestic animals result also from man's own activities. In many a region the spontaneous vegetation has disappeared before man's crops. Domestic animals that have been bred to suit man's needs, have bent to his will in an astonishing variety of ways. Plants previously unknown or neglected have joined successfully in the rotation cycles. These facts have given intensive agriculture in temperate regions a peculiar appearance. The system has become one of the most supple, progressive, and richly varied stages in the progress of civilisation. The development is due to a series of general facts that have modified human life, but have affected Europe particularly and especially those parts that are best placed to be touched by it. The most effective of these facts springs from the rise of trade relations, for these by creating urban and industrial life have given rise to new centres of population which must be fed, and later by facilitating trade have directed agriculture towards the cultivation of economic crops. The development has ended in the paradox that these countries do not produce enough food for themselves, but strive to produce commodities that sell well, sometimes at the other end of the world.

In developing thus the countries and indeed some districts within the countries have not all advanced at the same pace. Over the whole area of the temperate belt and especially in Europe an astonishing variety of forms of country life has been observed. These reflect regional differences in soil, climate, and the effect of communications with other lands far and near. Though industrial development tends to make modes of life uniform throughout the world, agricultural development does not do the same, for it is more dependent on local conditions. The main differences stem from the variety of rural life and the infinite complexity of their associations. Intensive agriculture represents an astonishing power of production and quickly enables population to increase greatly. As men become more numerous, they naturally need more land to till, and for hundreds and hundreds of years the needs of the increasing population have been met by the occupation of new territory.

The extension of land available for cultivation began essentially with the destruction of the great temperate forests. This step marks the heroic period of the spread of agriculture through Europe, and the same procedure also began the opening up of the New World. The clearing of woodland was accompanied by a lessening of the part played by animals in supplying food. It seems agreed that at the beginning the art of cultivation was required to supply a portion of the food, whilst the mode of life was mainly pastoral. Thus, the ancient German tribes, who lived chiefly on meat and milk products grew occasional corn crops in clearings in the forest. The destruction of the forest made such crops more important and food for animals scarcer. Probably it was because cattle became more and more difficult to feed that cultivation took to a system in which rotation and fallow allowed untilled land to be used as pasture. Later, they succeeded in growing fodder crops, which enabled them to feed larger flocks. The slow and persistent struggle against the tree lasted three centuries and was the silent work of generations. The struggle with water and drainage of the marshes which has struck the imagination still more, had at times made a dramatic advance. To control the drainage needed the work of strongly organised and highly civilised communities.

Marshes and peat bogs form part of the natural landscape in regions with a rainy summer. They cover vast spaces in districts where drainage remained imperfect after the retreat of the Ice Cap. Others stretch out along great river valleys, and others again fringe low coasts where the boundary between land and sea is ill-defined. In central and northern Europe swamps and peat bogs cover more than 200,000 square km. Reclamation of peat bogs began in the

Netherlands in the sixteenth century. By cutting the peat and burning it on the spot thousands of acres have been reclaimed in north-western Europe. But many swamps are still to be reclaimed in Polesje in western Russia, in central Ireland, and on the whole of the Atlantic coast of the United States. The North Sea coast from Jutland to French Flanders forms a single geographical unit where the same strenuous toil is necessary. Marine diluvium joined to the land by dykes has been made into new land, which though devoted at first to essential food crops, has in the changing system of the world today been reserved for the production of early vegetables, flowers, and fine dairy produce. The technique of successful land reclamation has gone beyond its original home, for it was the Dutch who empoldered the marshes in Brittany and Poitou. The English Fens are a further instance of land won from the sea. One of the most imposing achievements of modern technique has been the reclamation of the Zuider Zee, the plan for which dates from 1914 and is now advanced in execution. By combining the closure of the Wieringen dyke with the skilful drainage of the continental water into the natural basin of Lake Ijssel, the soil of the huge gulf has been recovered from the North Sea, whose invasion of the basin of Lake Flevo in the Middle Ages was the origin of the Zuider Zee.

The moment came when the agricultural nations of Europe could no longer continue to extend the cultivable land, and many people were landless. By emigrating these people found new land to cultivate. This phase of agricultural development in the temperate belt, which began in fact a hundred and fifty years ago, is still in progress. In a relatively short time it has converted to the European system of cultivation vast areas which have been developed with the help of the old agricultural tradition. The reason for the spread of the European system is that on the virgin lands of the New World and of the southern hemisphere our traditional system did not meet the obstacles which it has taken centuries to overcome in its original home. It established itself best in treeless regions that were naturally unforested or in damp regions that were naturally well drained. In the United States the first settlers were pioneers in forest lands until they passed the Appalachians. But once they had crossed the mountains and were out of the woods, they had before them only the open expanses of the prairies. It was the same in the Argentine Pampa, the South African veldt, and the Australian Downs. To the south of the great forest Russian settlers had in front of them in south Russia or Siberia nothing but grass plains frequented by nomadic Asiatic herdsmen.

Yet the mastery of area, now finally ensured, would not be enough to satisfy an agricultural people continually on the increase. In the course of expansion it has occurred more than once that supply has been forced to meet demand not by increasing the area under cultivation, but by increasing the yield. The idea of cultivating plants that not only yield large crops, but also help to fertilise the soil is certainly an essential feature in the progress of civilisation based on agriculture. Yet, surprisingly enough, the idea is so recent that it has not yet penetrated into some forms of agriculture which are nevertheless already mechanised and furnished with up-to-date implements. Though the American and Soviet agricultural systems employ a great deal of machinery, they retain the use of extensive methods and are not sufficiently alive to the advantages of crop rotation and the need for the continual fertilisation of the soil.

Crop Rotation and Fertilisation.—Long before the dawn of history cultivators recognised that to crop the same soil continuously was to exhaust it. So after a few years vegetable patches were abandoned and others cleared for cultivation. This shifting, wandering form of cultivation, which still existed in Croatia in the eighteenth century and is still to be seen among the hillmen in Indo-China and among various Negro tribes in Africa, involved long journeys to and fro between plot and dwelling. It also required large areas to be available for changing from one piece of ground to another. Such a technique was in use at the beginning of history in western Europe among some peoples, including the Germans and the Celtic cultivators of moorland in Britain. It came into favour again among the early European settlers in the United States and continued as long as vast areas were left available. Its last survivals exist in the dry farming area in the West and the satellite farms on the Great Plains. It has long survived in the form of *essartage* (grubbing up) and *écobuage* (burning off) in districts of poor soil in the Ardennes, the Central Highlands of France, and the hilly parts of the Mediterranean region; but shifting cultivation gave way to a crop rotation system very early in Europe.

Another law of cultivation was discovered long before the beginning of historic times. This was that not only does continual cropping exhaust the soil, but that a period of rest revives its fertility and after a fairly short interval allows it to be used again. The realisation of this principle led to the use of the two-field system, but as this leaves half of the available land empty, it required a much greater area. The remedy was found in another discovery, namely, that a succession of different crops does not exhaust the soil as quickly as the constant repetition of the same crop even when this is interrupted by fallow. This discovery gave rise to the practice of cultivating a field two years in succession with different crops and then leaving it fallow for the third year, when used for pasturing livestock. The arable was thus divided to three parts. Each field was sown with a winter cereal the first year and with spring cereal in the second year, the third year being devoted to fallow pasture. Such was the three-field system characteristic of the most skilful and profitable European agriculture.

The system spread throughout western Europe between the seventh and tenth centuries, and it continued in use there almost unchanged for eight hundred years. But it depended on rotations of crops that could not thrive everywhere. Thus, some infertile countries and, speaking generally, the countries in southern Europe did not adopt it, at least not in its classical three-field form. For better for worse, they remained faithful to the two-field system throughout. The flexible three-field system, which permitted a harvest of cereals for bread and for gruel, and of forage crops, and in which the fallow not only rested the soil but at the same time fed the live-stock, remained in use until the middle of the eighteenth century. Only then, under pressure of certain economic facts, was the loss represented by the year of fallow realised and new systems of rotation thought of. The three-field system, being in fact essentially one of corn crops, was not of sufficient use in the development of stock-rearing.

Throughout the Middle Ages, indeed, livestock were fed on stubble, waste, rough pasture, and in woods. Agriculture could not do without animals, and the animals were kept on the common land. Now, from the end of the seventeenth century the commons began to be enclosed and cultivated. In England and France alike the peasantry as a whole suffered greatly from the progressive disappearance of the common land, from the formation of large farms by local landowners, for the enclosure for the use of the large farms of land which till then had periodically returned to public use. It then became necessary to use the fallow in some other way than as untilled grazing.

The new technique began in England and in the Märschen in western Germany. In the eighteenth century England was at a stage in civilisation favourable to such a development in agriculture. The expansion of her town population demanded the production of increasing amounts of meat, milk, and butter without decreasing the supply of corn, and there had to be food on the spot for a working population that was already producing for the world market. Hence the introduction of root crops and artificial grazing on the fallow. This brought about a revolution, for now the necessary fodder was obtained by cultivation, and an ample supply of food for the animals was ensured for the winter. The disappearance of untilled fallow and the continuous alternation of crops in the rotation enabled the soil to yield a harvest unrested without lessening its fertility. The kind of rotation and the crops used varied according to the climate, soil, and character of the market.

It is possible to have two-yearly rotation where industrial crops are grown and the soil exceptionally well fertilised. Thus, in northern France hemp, flax, tobacco, or beetroot are grown in the first year and corn in the second. In lowlands where cereal cultivation is an economic necessity, a three-field system is retained consisting in the first year of a weeded crop or artificial fodder, in the second year wheat, and in the third year oats. In parts of the United States where crop rotation is spreading, a three-field system is now commonly established consisting of clover, maize, and oats. More complicated systems often occur. When soil and climate are suitable to the cultivation of fodder crops and when the rearing of animals is in favour, a four year rotation is often used, consisting of a weeded crop, cereals, clover, and spring corn. This is the famous Norfolk system in which two out of every four crops are eaten by livestock. In French Flanders there are even five-year rotations consisting of sugar-beet, barley, green fodder, wheat, and oats. In more advanced districts many different combinations nowadays induce a variable rotation in which the farmer guided mainly by market trends replaces one plant by another and arrives at the most profitable combination. Carried to an extreme, agriculture controls Nature instead of following her directives, and the farm is a veritable factory, freed from the old ideas which, however, led to the ascendancy of agriculture over the environment.

This development all assumes a regular supply of manure for the restoration of the soil, which at every harvest is robbed of mineral and nitrogenous substances. One of the chief duties of rural economy in France has long been the collection of stable manure, and this kind of manure has remained until today the principal fertiliser. In Lorraine the dunghill stands in front of the house and along the village street. In big farmyards in northern France it occupies the whole centre of the yard. Its size is a measure of the peasant's wealth. The transport and spreading of the dung has long been one of the heaviest tasks in spring and autumn and one which calls for the heaviest carts. In the three-field system the dung is spread in summer in the fallow field. When there is a long crop rotation, the dung is spread in winter for the benefit of the weeded crops and in spring for the summer fodder crops. Peasants have always shown ingenuity in adding to the available quantity of manure including the use of moor and swamp vegetation, marine plants in the form of seaweed and kelp, the droppings of poultry, and especially the precious pigeon dung from the dovecots, not to mention the direct manuring of the soil by the animals. The droppings of sheep and cattle in the fields to be manured is a device for fertilising that goes back no further than the eighteenth century.

By the beginning of the nineteenth century the important part played by minerals in the growth of cultivated plants was recognised and agriculture gradually became dependent on industry for its supplies of fertiliser. From then on agriculture became the achievement of a whole civilisation which had its foundation not only in the soil which it had created, but also in its cities and factories. The new fertilisers for Europe's fields came thenceforth from abroad, including nitrates from Peru and Chile and phosphates from Algeria, Tunisia, and Morocco. Other fertilisers (superphosphates, synthetic nitrates) are manufactured in chemical works, whilst others (sulphate of ammonia) are by-products of gas and sugar production and basic slag from blast furnaces.

There is now so great a variety of fertilisers and their effects are so well known that it is possible to determine by which fertiliser and in what amount each crop is suited. In the most advanced parts of Europe the field has become a veritable laboratory. It has also become connected with distant enterprises that function to supply it with fertiliser. This is a very artificial state of affairs and presents great danger. Europe realised this to the full when war deprived the fields of the indispensable fertilisers, and the fertility of the land collapsed. Up to 1947 some essential crops in central Europe and Italy were still 40 or 50 per cent below their prewar rate of yield. Insecurity is the normal price paid for a technique which to increase the yield departs dangerously from the biological conditions of the local environment.

Use of Machines and Motor Vehicles.—In Europe from the earliest times man has striven to free himself from heavy physical toil in agriculture by using domestic animals to work the appliances used in cultivation. The use of animal power for tilling the land is practised nearly everywhere. This is different from both the hoe cultivation common to Asia and Africa and the mechanical cultivation in use in Great Britain, the United States, and the Soviet Union. For hundreds of years animals have been the main agents used in preparing the soil, in ploughing, that is, and harrowing and rolling. Yet a good number of operations used to be carried out without the help of animals. Sowing by hand, weeding with a hoe, harvesting with sickle or scythe, and threshing with a flail were still practised recently in many parts of France. At best, in some countries the separation of the corn from the chaff was done by animals treading the sheaves under foot. The use of manpower was enough so long as agriculture kept its old methods, its system, and its traditional crops; but it could no longer suffice when agricultural production was adapted to the new economic conditions. This was, first, the cultivation of the fallow with crops that were all more or less needing care. Then there was the cultivation of vast areas of virgin soil in America by scarce and expensive labour. This led to the extension of the use of animals by setting them to perform operations previously done by man, such as sowing, weeding, harvesting, and above all, threshing.

The use of machinery for intensive cultivation began in England. In 1731 Jethro Tull urged that sowing should be done in lines and that a horse-drawn hoe should be used for weeding. A little later the first threshing-machine and the first harvesters were made in England. As soon as the flood of settlement began in the United States, the use of machinery became necessary, and machines were adopted from the old European tradition of cultivation, just as the crops and animals had been. In 1831, the first mechanical reaper was put into service in New Jersey, and by 1866 all the heavy work in farms throughout the Union was done by machines drawn by troops of horses. These animals were imported from Europe, especially from Boulonnais and Perche. The necessity for replacing human labour made the United States the chosen land of agricultural machinery. It actually came into use there more quickly than in the old, densely populated countries of Europe, in which the countryside overflowed with labour.

A century of development ended in the replacement of men by animals and machinery in farm work, but more recent changes have seen the gradual disuse of animals to work the machinery, especially since the internal combustion engine became a handy, powerful, and economical source of power. Little by little the tractor has replaced the draught animal, whilst the equipment of farms has been improved by the introduction of a host of machines driven by electricity or by liquid-fuel motors.

On the whole, these developments, which have made agriculture in the temperate belt more and more intensive owing to the application to the soil of more labour and energy, have not brought to our old agricultural system yields comparable with those of the hoe cultivation of the Far East, but as it is put into practice over vast areas, it succeeds in producing enormous quantities of foodstuffs.

The struggle to get the greatest possible yield from crops has had as a corollary a clear tendency to specialise in crops in certain places owing to the improvements in the means of transport and of the widening of trade relations. For long ages all cultivation was forced to produce every commodity needed for local consumption. So it was, for instance, during the Middle Ages in the English manor and the *villae* of Carolingian France. Without means of rapid transport wheat and rye for making bread had to be grown locally, as had oats for the horses. Sheep had to be reared for their wool, and hemp or flax had to be grown for making linen. Yet there were instances of local crops and agricultural experiments that depended less on the

*These two maps show three degrees of variation from the mean,
showing the dominant types of land-use, calculated with relation to
the whole of France. The land-use type called 'polyculture' (N)
comprises the following : 26% ploughland, 15% meadows, 4% vines,
3% orchards, 2% horticulture, 20% woods, and 20% grazing or*

FIG. 3.—SAMPLE OF INTENSIVE AGRICULTURAL LAND USE ;
WESTERN PART OF AQUITAINE BASIN, FRANCE.

fallow. Each type of land-use becomes dominant when its variation from the normal for type N is 100, 200, or 300 per cent.

The mean variations calculated for the whole of France vary from one land-use type to another: ploughland (T) 20%, meadows (P) 10%, vines (V) 9%, orchards (F) 12%, horticulture (M) 5%, woods (B) 10%, grazings (L) 16%.

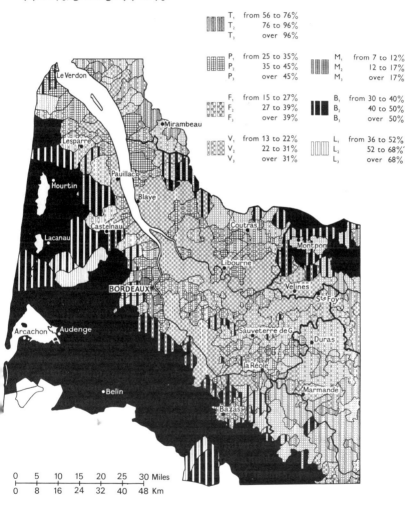

needs of local consumption than on the demands of a wider market. So it was with the vine, the wine from which was destined to be sent to countries that did not produce it; with English wool, which was exported to Flanders; and dyestuffs like woad. In the nineteenth century, owing to progress in the means of transport, conditions in the world market influenced local production. Some crops disappeared owing to competition from other countries, and regions specialised in the crops for which they were best suited. In this way external influence has greatly upset rural life in places that had long remained unchanged in their traditions. Within the sphere of cultivation these modifications are reflected in the decrease in food crops, like wheat, in face of the competition of new countries; in the oil-yielding poppy, rape-seed, and colza in the face of tropical products; of hemp and flax in the face of cotton; of dye-stuffs like woad and madder in the face of tropical products or chemical dyes; and in the vine in the face of the competition of great wine-producing lands. Crops have been replaced by others, as rye was by wheat in central and western France and as barley has replaced wheat in many English shires.

In the sphere of stock-rearing there has been an expansion wherever agriculture yielded only meagre profits. This has happened in Great Britain, Norway, Finland, Denmark, and in general throughout western Europe. It is happening even in the United States, where the rearing of milch cows is gaining ground in the cotton lands of the South after having ousted cultivation throughout New England. The change is seen too in great modifications in composition of herds and flocks, for some species have replaced others. Thus, in lands where beet is grown sheep have given place to store cattle. Elsewhere milch cows have taken the place of working animals. Today stockrearing is organised mainly in cash operations. Dairy regions specialising in the production of milk, butter, and cheese are rivals of those producing meat. The latter in turn undergo stricter specialisation and make a division of labour between breeders, rearers of young beasts, and those who fatten animals for slaughter.

Today no part of Europe can withdraw wholly from international trade. Yet an astonishing variety of modes of life that has been made possible by the immense heritage of agriculture in the temperate belt can be seen to result from many combinations of resources. Some slower and more conservative districts have kept their traditional mode of agriculture for a longer time owing to difficult communications. But today they all feel the changes which in the course of a century have modified the conditions of agricultural work in the Old World and its place in man's techniques.

Expansion of Cereals and Associated Crops of Temperate Regions

Crop	(million tonnes) 1934	1974	Growth, per cent
Wheat	168,000	377,000	90
Secondary cereals (oats, barley, rye)	143,500	216,000	90
Maize	110,400	312,700	181
Potatoes	175,000	256,000	46
Sugarbeet	67,590	75,700	12

CHAPTER 6

HUMAN LIFE IN THE TROPICS

The regions lying between the Tropics and the Equator afford human life very different conditions from those with which we are familiar in temperate latitudes. On the one hand, there are the ancient civilisations in India and China, in which the toil of generations has brought the land under man's control; on the other, there are the primitive civilisations in the interior of Africa and South America, where nature controls man and in some cases makes him helpless. Hence there are striking contrasts in the development of civilisation from continent to continent in the intertropical belt.

Compared with other parts of the world, hot lands owe some of their physical peculiarity to the existence of a rainy season which coincides with the hottest period of the year. The combination of great humidity with high temperature causes conditions eminently favourable to the growth of vegetation. All life depends on the coming of the rains, which control vegetation, work in the fields, and man's occupations.

Compared with each other tropical lands may differ profoundly merely owing to the amount of their rainfall, which makes some forested and others grass clad, with all that this difference entails in the character of the natural vegetation cover, the choice of plants to be cultivated, the animal population, and the articles of trade.

THE EFFECTS OF CLIMATE

The coincidence of the rainfall maximum with the period of high temperature depends either on the passage of the sun at the zenith or on monsoons, but in either case the phyto-climatic conditions are identical. To them must be added certain elements of soil fertility due to the influence of tropical rain. First, rapid decomposition of the mineral and vegetable elements which are made assimilable by the action of the damp heat; secondly, a high content of nitrogenous elements in tropical rains. Hence the luxuriance of the wild vegetation which places great obstacles in the way of the expansion of the means of livelihood, for the fields and roads are constantly being overrun by the forest or the savanna grasses and cannot be cleared except by burning; and the effects of this on the soil and its covering give rise to other troubles.

The advantage of such a climate to cultivated plants is that there is no check on the cycle of growth. This makes it possible to reap

138

several crops in one year and in some regions to ensure a continuous harvest throughout the year and even from year to year until the soil is exhausted. Besides, the plants cultivated are such as yield the greatest returns for the lowest cost, namely, rice, maize, bananas, and cassava.

The copious yield has certainly helped to make tropical lands almost exclusively agricultural, just as it has made the people tend to adopt simple unchanging methods of work and to adopt a system of agriculture that in some cases seems scrupulously careful, but always somewhat unprogressive. On the other hand, it has required a relentless struggle against vegetation and predatory animals, which at times get the better of proper cultivation.

The difference in the seasons is due to the rainfall régime. The beginning of the rainy season is awaited everywhere as the renewal of life. Among the Banyankoles in Uganda the year begins with the first hard showers. In Brazil most of the interior of the country lies within the region of summer rains. When the first showers fall in September or October the dormant vegetation suddenly springs to life, the whole land becomes green again, and pasture springs up for the cattle. In the Sudan the rainy season lasts five months, from June to October. In Senegal it begins only towards the end of July. In the Ganges valley the grass comes to life again and the trees recover their green under the influence of the monsoon rains. Ploughing and the sowing of rice and millet rouse the peasant from the torpor of the hot season. During the course of long weeks of rain the rivers overflow and the country is transformed into a marsh. This is the season of fever and cholera.

Nearly everywhere the dry season occurs in the months when the sun is lowest on the horizon. At São Paulo in Brazil it is a cool season with frost at times in the early morning. In Gabon the fall in temperature from May to September coincides with epidemics of pleurisy among the Negroes. In the Ganges plain this cool season sometimes brings morning breezes. In Gabon in equatorial Africa the dry season marks the return of birds. At this season too the Africans go on trips into the interior, trees are felled, and the ground cleared for crops. In Senegal it is the time of the groundnut harvest; in India of rice, millet, and cotton; in Indo-China fruit is gathered in the forest, streams are fished, and the arable fields (*rays*) are prepared. But as the midday sun rises higher above the horizon, the temperature increases. At Manila dry, dusty winds prevail from February to May, and everything gasps and withers. In the Doab between the Ganges and the Jumna the dry season ends with a furnace-like temperature. Under a copper-coloured sky the landscape looks dusty and parched. The whole countryside burns with thirst, and the first rains are a relief.

The contrast between the two seasons is not everywhere so clearly marked. It is not as strong in Ogowe, where the rainy season lasts seven months, as in the Sudan, where it lasts five months, or in Senegal, where it lasts only three months. Consequently, it does not have the same effect on the appearance of the landscape, on the vegetation, and on human life.

Heat helps to form men's habits in the tropics, especially by making less demand for shelter and clothing. In hot lands, indeed, the problem of building and fitting up a house is far less important than in temperate environments. The house is merely a store-room for food and utensils. In India, for example, the peasant spends nearly all his time in the fields, the craftsman works out-of-doors, and everyone sleeps in the streets during the stifling summer nights. Hence, large houses are useless, since they would be lived in for only a few hours. Hot countries are lands of huts, of temporary shanties built of light material; and this lightness of construction is the rule amongst all peoples living in hot countries, whatever their degree of civilisation, and it is as characteristic of the Negro's hut as of the Japanese house.

Clothing is also greatly simplified. In many tropical countries the warm, damp atmosphere allows men to do without clothes. In Papua New Guinea, until only a few years ago, and away from the coasts and from the settlements of Europeans and Australians, the natives went entirely naked, only rarely making use of a loincloth. Indian tribes in the Amazon basin and Negroes in central Africa live in a state of complete nakedness. This is true of the people around the upper Shari and the Ubanghi, the Bobos of the Sudan to the east of Sikasso, the Banyoros of Uganda, and the Fans of the Ubanghi and Gabon. All the clothes they wear is a covering of bark strips or vegetable fibres, which is more or less wide and runs more or less continuously round the hips. Though clothing is rudimentary, great care is taken over the decoration of the body, and ornamentation is an important matter. Hence the necklaces, bracelets, ear and nose pendants, the rubbing of oil or fat on the skin, painting of the skin, tatooing, and mutilation.

Many other peoples of the hot belt adopt a light, but less exiguous garment. The peasants in Madagascar, India, Annam, China, and Japan wear a simple dress, the making of which costs little. It has been calculated that in the Northwestern Provinces of India a family of five spends no more on dress than £2 a year. In Madras State only 5 or 6 per cent of the family budget is spent on clothing. Hence, the climate frees the inhabitant of a hot country from part of the cost of dress that is imposed on one who dwells in a cold country. The pauper does not suffer from lack of clothing in India so much as the poor man in Europe. The same is true of footwear. The absence of shoes, which is a mark of poverty in Europe, is in a hot country merely a simplification of the costume permitted by the climate. Hot countries are the homes of barefooted, ragged people. These simplifications are not without inconvenience. It may seem paradoxical to a European that one should feel cold in the tropics, but in fact the nights are cold, especially in the dry season. In New Guinea and equatorial Africa the natives spend the early morning warming themselves in the sun. Even in their huts they do not always succeed in keeping warm at night, though the occupants all huddle together. In Fiji they make fires in the huts. In the day the sun's heat restricts the hours of work. The morning may be devoted to heavy toil, but in the heat of the day a siesta is necessary to all. Besides, the relatively equal length of day and night prevents work before 6 a.m. and after 6 p.m. There is nothing comparable with the long day's work done in summer by the European peasant.

In the interior of hot countries the amount of rainfall is the chief factor influencing the mode of life and the form of civilisation. Now, great differences may be found in the same continent, as the table shows:

Senegal (Gorée)	421 mm
Cameroon	4156 mm
Lahore	536 mm
Colombo	2836 mm

Similarly, striking contrasts are observed in the length of the rainy season. At Lahore the rains last for three months, at Bombay four and a half, at Madras seven, and at Colombo eleven.

The best watered countries are found first in equatorial regions in the Amazon basin, Congo, and East Indies; and also in every area exposed to the full force of winds from the sea, monsoons or trades, such as the coast of Brazil and the slopes of the Sierra do Mar, the Guinea coast, the high ground in Cameroon, the eastern coast of Madagascar, the west coast of India, in Bengal, on the hills of Assam, and in Burma and the Malay Peninsula.

The seasons are not clear cut in these countries. The sky is unobscured less often and for much less long in them. They are vast expanses of forest unfavourable to the life of large animals useful to man, but swarming with little animals, insects, mosquitoes, and ants, that prey on man and his companions. The climate is unhealthy for the natives and terrible for European settlers, as those in the *tierras calientes* in Central America have found to their cost. In the Amazon basin, New Guinea, and the Bismarck archipelago the forest and the mountains which it covers inspire hopeless terror in the natives.

But, on the other hand, wherever cultivation can find a footing, whether in natural or man-made clearings, it gives astonishing yields at low cost. Owing to the short duration of the dry season, it is possible to sow and harvest throughout the year crops of tubers and roots like cassava, yam, sweet potato, and *taro* (*ndalo*), which grow from mere slips or pieces of tuber. Other crops like maize, rice, groundnuts, tobacco, and sugarcane are seasonal. There are also fruit-producing trees, which grow almost spontaneously and afford a continuous supply of fruit and nuts. There are the banana, sago, kola, and coconut trees, with various other kinds of palm.

All the high-yielding food crops require less work than do the annual cereals. The limits of their cultivation mark a definite region in which cassava replaces grain for making flour, cultivation from slips succeeds ploughing, and animals are not used as aids to cultivation. In Africa the great civilisations based on pasturage and millet cultivation end at this limit.

Less humid regions with a clearly marked dry season are characterised by great grass plains. Trees are still numerous, but they do not grow in close formation. More or less dense according to the abundance of the rainfall, they may be sparse, undersized, or thorny on the borders of the semi-desert or else standing in clumps which give the landscape the appearance of a park. Such clumps often grow in valley bottoms, in which they form strips of green foliage closely following the watercourses. To this type of scenery, which differs from country to country, but always keeps the same general characteristics, different names are given. In Guyana and the Sudan they are called *savannas*, in Brazil *campos*, in Venezuela *llanos*, in New Guinea, Chad, and Ceará the *bush*, around the upper Volta *park*, and on the Deccan *jungle*. The vegetation, being less tyrannical, leaves room for large animals. Around Lake Chad and on the Ubanghi plateau swarm birds, herbivorous animals, big game, and carnivores. Nothing prevents these countries from keeping domestic animals and undertaking stock-rearing and even some modern forms of pastoral life. The ox has gained a place in vast areas in the *campos* of Brazil, and in Africa it has advanced from the country round the upper Nile westwards into Senegal and southwards to the Cape.

In the list of food crops tubers and roots give way to grain which is sown and reaped at fixed periods and needs a dry season in which to ripen. The nature of these crops leads to a better agricultural system, periodical operations, and forethought in storing the grain and seed. This explains the greatly civilising character of the long dry season which rescues man and his heritage from the tyranny of the tree and forest.

THE FOUNDATIONS OF AGRICULTURAL LIFE

Differences in suitability for agriculture and in the array of crops cultivated are not enough to explain the differences in appearance

5. Irrigated rice-fields on steep terraced slopes in Luzon, Philippines

THE TROPICAL ENVIRONMENT

6. Ploughing rice-field

7. Transplanting rice

8. Hoover Dam and hydro-electric station on the Colorado river, with Lake Mead behind the dam; complete absence of vegetation

ARID ENVIRONMENTS

9. Making sun-dried mud bricks, Egypt

and development in various countries in the hot belt. Some are due
to difference in geographical position in relation to other lands and
to the sea. In the world distribution of hot countries there are
several large areas separated from each other by the sea or kept apart
by deserts from temperate lands. The result has been that man in
hot countries has usually developed independently of the rest of
mankind and evinces wide differences from his fellows in the rate of
civilised development.

Hot countries in America and Africa, which long remained isolated and restricted to their own natural area, must be distinguished
from the rest. In the past there was little intercourse between
tropical America and the islands of the Pacific. In spite of the later
influence of the West, its development has been slow and personal.
There was on the lofty tablelands of the Andes an advanced agricultural civilisation based on maize and cassava, but in which iron
was unknown, and there were no domestic animals except for the
llama, which was not used in agriculture but only as a beast of
burden. Everywhere else on the continent the mode of life of the
nomadic hunter prevailed. Only after the arrival of Europeans was
there any pastoral activity or any settled agriculture, except on the
high tablelands, where cultivation became based on new crops.

Tropical Africa also forms a world apart with nearly all its agricultural development resting on cereals of the millet and sorghum
family, but it has benefited from more extended relations than has
tropical America. A handful of pastoral peoples from Asia introduced stock-rearing in early times right into the heart of the continent. A little later rice, cotton, and the coconut reached it from
the same source.

As for tropical Asia, it has peculiar conditions which have for long
made it densely populated and gave it a high civilisation. Its
position in the monsoon system enabled the development of sea-
borne intercourse not only in the fringing seas of the continent, but
also across the Indian and Pacific Oceans. China, Japan, and the
islands of southeast Asia have long been open to trade and migration.
It is to this general condition of affairs that the hot countries of Asia
owe their part in the formation of highly civilised modes of life, the
influence of which was spread afar.

The effect of these general conditions is that man finds astonishing
wealth in the vegetation of the hot lands. Whether of spontaneous
growth or cultivated, plants have throughout the region water and
heat to ripen their fruit. It is therefore not surprising that the mode
of life that was the earliest to spread there and the most faithfully
adhered to was agricultural. In temperate lands the pastoral mode
of life still plays a leading part in some places and mingles closely
with the agricultural mode, but in hot lands it counts for little; and

when it does exist, it affects ignorance of agriculture. So far as forest life is concerned, it lacks the fullness that the vast expanse of the forests would lead one to suppose. Man does not owe them much of his living, for in them he finds unfavourable surroundings that are in contrast with the hospitable environment afforded by the ancient European woodland.

In hot countries man is essentially a cultivator. This is as true of the Negroes in the Sudan as of the Papuans in New Guinea, of Indians as of Chinese and Japanese. Everywhere cultivation of the soil prevails, everywhere man lives on vegetable matter. But in this great agricultural community there are a number of distinct groups, just as there exists a fundamental distinction between the two massive continents of Africa and America on the one hand and the world of peninsulas, islands, and deltas on the other to which we restrict the name Far East. On the continents the absence of any universal connexion favoured the survival of rudimentary methods of slight productive value and checked the appearance of commerce and industry before the arrival of Europeans. In the Far East the circulation of ideas and people favoured the possession of the treasures of civilisation, ensured the dissemination of rice cultivation and the adoption of intensive methods of planting the crop, and developed industry and commerce through the search for outlets. In vast areas in Africa and South America the system of extensive cultivation still prevails with rare enclaves of an intensive system. The Far East is the real home of intensive cultivation with a few islets of an extensive system.

A common feature of all these agricultural communities is that their subsistence depends very closely on crops that they cultivate without expecting any help from the animal world. In none of them is found the close collaboration between man and beast in working the land. Tropical agriculture is essentially cultivation by hand. The only exceptions occur in certain parts of the Far East. A fairly large part of India uses a plough drawn by zebus, and other countries in the Far East use the buffalo for the same purpose. But these are countries which have since early times been in communication with centres of Aryan civilisation.

Elsewhere only hand implements are used. The simple digging-stick hardened in the fire is still in use among the Melanesians and Polynesians, but the hoe which enables the centrifugal power of the arms to be used, is a more modern and effective implement. Sometimes it is made wholly of wood. In Africa it is formed of a broad iron blade fixed to a wooden handle. This simple implement is used as much by Amerindians to cultivate cassava as by African Negroes to grow millet, or by Chinese rice cultivators in monsoon Asia. It is the implement of primitive cultivators who change their patches every year as of the hardworking rice cultivators on the deltas in Asia and the maize growers in the old Inca empire. Throughout Africa south of the Sahara the Negroes have remained faithful to hand cultivation, which extends all over the continent. The plough is used only in Egypt under influence from Asia, and in South Africa, where European settlement has taken place. But in Senegal and the Sudan the plough is rarely used by either Fans,or Cafres. In hoe cultivation the Negro has preserved a collective method and a skill that bear witness to ancient provenance. In America hoe cultivation enabled the growth of the fine native civilisation that sprang up on the tablelands in the Andes and Mexico. At the present time the implement is also used by many Amerindians in the Amazon basin, the Guianas, and Ceará.

Though most of India falls within the domain of the ox-drawn plough, hand cultivation still extended, in the mid-twentieth century, over a wide area in China, Korea, and Japan. On the island of Honshu a three-pronged, long-handled hoe or a little spade served to turn up the soil, and ploughs were seen only on the lowlands around Osaka, Tokyo, Nagasaki, and Mino. Similarly, in cultivating his land the Chinese peasant used a broad, heavy hoe with iron prongs, and it was only in north China that the plough was used with domestic animals that nowadays are being very slowly replaced by tractors. It must still be emphasised that the mechanisation of agriculture has only been possible in rural communities that have already attained a fair level of technology and are within a modernised State that is already partly or very largely industrialised, such as Japan, China, and India.

Hot countries have taken but little advantage of the domestic animals of the temperate belt. As one travels from the regions with a long dry season in Africa, the sheep disappears. It is scarcely seen in Adamawa district, Cameroon, western Congo, Angola or the lakes region. Towards the south the Tropic must be passed before it is found in the drier lands of South Africa where there has been the influence of European settlement.

In tropical Brazil the sheep degenerates. Its woolly fleece changes into long hair, and there is no point in keeping the animal except in the more temperate climate of Rio Grande do Sul. The great humidity of the air and the heavy summer rains, together with the general system of cultivation, keep the sheep away from Indo-China, Indonesia, south China, and Japan. Before the Chinese came into touch with Europeans they were ignorant of the use of woollen cloth. India alone boasts of a fairly large number of little horned sheep with black or golden coats, whose flesh is the only meat Indians are allowed to eat.

The goat is better adapted to the system of hand cultivation, and consequently it is an animal of the first importance for the Negro. The little black creature is valuable owing to its small appetite and its prolific nature. The Negro gives it little attention. In equatorial Africa, where no other animal exists, it almost represents wealth in the village, a gift that only a powerful chief can give. On the other hand, the goat is almost unknown in the Far East and the islands of the Pacific.

In communities in which labour concentrates on cultivation, poultry forms a convenient source of fresh meat, though the birds are left to run free and find their own food. It is unusual not to see a few hens around the dwellings of African Negroes. In all the Far Eastern countries hens are numerous and big flocks of ducks live near the rice-fields, lakes, and watercourses. In New Guinea hens are reared mainly for the feathers they yield for women's adornment.

Dogs are found to some extent everywhere, but they do not play the same part as among our farmers and shepherds. In central Africa the dog is a feeble, sickly beast and howls instead of barking. The Negro keeps it for use as butcher's meat. The same is true of the Papuans, some tribes of whom are particularly skilful at fattening choice animals, which then constitute a luxury.

The pig, which is one of man's greatest sources of meat and fat and which makes the best of very wretched conditions, is very rare in some hot countries, but very numerous in others. It is seldom found among Negroes, and the growing influence of Islam succeeds in excluding it from a large part of tropical Africa. Only the Hovas of Madagascar, who are of Malay origin, give it an important place in their economy. On the other hand, the Far East is one of the chief areas of pig rearing. India has many breeds, and perhaps it was from that country that the pig reached eastern Asia and its islands. It is widespread in Japan and plays an important part among the non-Muslim population of Indonesia. But in none of these is the attention paid to pigs as great as in China; so much so indeed that pork figures in the daily food of the Chinese of every class.

The horse does not thrive in the tropics. In Africa it is scarcely seen except on the borders of deserts and semi-deserts, where it is the saddle horse of Hausa nobles. Even in these dry regions, however, it suffers from insect bites, and so its place in hot countries is usually taken by the hybrid mule, which is used for both transport and work in the fields. In Japan, Korea, the Philippines, Sumatra, and Burma some breeds of ponies are used by the peasants for carrying light loads, but not for field work.

Of all domestic animals the ox is perhaps the most widespread in different conditions in the tropics. It does not flourish in wet countries, and in Africa it is found neither on the coasts of Guinea, in the forest area stretching from Gabon to the Welle, nor along the banks of the Zambezi. On the other hand, it is well adapted to conditions afforded by countries with a well-marked dry season; yet tropical man does not take advantage of the benefit which the strength, meat, and milk of the cow have for farmers in the temperate belt. Herds of cattle form great wealth in the Sudan and on the tablelands in East Africa, where they constitute the basis of a pastoral life; but the animals are never used for work in cultivation, and they are only sometimes employed for transport. Beef is seldom eaten by pastoralists. Though the use of milk is fairly widespread, there are tribes that use butter merely as an ointment, and cheese-making is often unknown.

More varied use is made of cattle in India, but the animal is not fully exploited. The zebu draws the plough and carries loads, and cows yield a poor supply of milk. But beyond the borders of India the part played by the ox becomes less. From Indo-China to Korea it is a mere intermittent auxiliary. Hence, in hot lands it is extremely rare to see the close relation established between the cultivator and the pastoralist which prevails in the form of civilisation that has arisen in temperate lands. Even when a cultivator owns a few animals, he does not take the trouble to set aside a piece of land on which to feed them. Huge areas, like those in the *hara* among the mountains of Japan, remain unused, though fodder is plentiful in them. The close connexion that exists in the Alps between grazing in the valleys and on the mountains is nowhere to be found. In hot lands human progress is largely independent of the animal world, and consequently, the tropics as a whole is characterised by an elaboration of the vegetable world.

The natural advantages that food crops have in hot lands ended in the acceptance of diets in which vegetables predominate. Bread is unknown, for the cereals that yield flour will not make bread, so these are the lands of gruel and biscuits. Sweet cassava is roasted in ashes or boiled and is eaten like potato. Bitter cassava is ground into meal and made into flat cakes. Bananas are eaten raw or boiled or fried, according to the different species. Sweet potatoes can be cooked in ashes or boiled. Millet and maize are ground into flour and used to make messes with various seasonings. Lastly, boiled rice is the basic food of millions of people. The foregoing are the main products of cultivation in hot lands.

Owing to the nature of the climate, meat is little used as food; but as its elements are necessary to man's constitution, substitutes are eagerly sought after. In equatorial Africa, where there is little animal life and game is scarce, fish is eaten, and snakes, termites, caterpillars, and beetles figure in the diet when other things fail. Forest people show no repugnance to high meat. In east Africa even among the pastoral tribes meat is often regarded as a luxury.

In the Far East fish takes the place of meat nearly everywhere.

The scarcity of meat probably helps to explain the practice of cannibalism in some backward communities, and there is no doubt that it has existed in regions that suffered from a lack of meat, though Europeans have been able to observe the practice chiefly among the peoples of central Africa. The last remains of the practice seem to exist in the Congo basin among the Batekes, Balobos, Bangales, Monbuttas, and Manyemas; but it continued for long in the interior of Cameroon, and cases have recently been observed in the southern Sudan (Monteil). It would be wrong to believe that the cannibal is a depraved or degenerate brute, for cannibalism is but an extension of the eating of the meat of animals. It even seems more inveterate among the tribes that show some social progress.

Gruel, paste, corn, and tubers form a heavy and insipid diet. Consequently, efforts are made to improve the taste by means of condiments. Capsicum and curry play an important part in tropical cooking, in Africa as well as in Asia. High meat is often included in the diet to give some taste to the gruels. In Indo-China fish sauce, of which the *nuoc mam* of Annam is but a variety, is used to season boiled rice. In the most humid regions salt is scarce and is to be had with difficulty, so in Africa it has become the commodity of a whole caravan trade. It has given rise to an extractive industry in the Mauritanian desert. Blocks of salt still pass as money in trade between the nomads in dry areas and sedentary populations on the forest borders. Tribes outside the radius of this trade obtain low grade salt by the lixiviation of the ashes of certain plants culled on dry ground. With this imperative need to stir up the digestion is connected the search for other stimulants, and these are found in the shape of alcohol made from matter that varies according to what each region can offer. Bananas, millet, rice, sugarcane, and the tops of certain palms are used for this purpose. There are also special crops which, following more or less long preparation, yield matter capable of being used after infusion either for smoking or chewing. Tobacco, betel, liamba, and opium are got from plants, some of which are delicate. The simple-minded cultivators of tropical lands have introduced these stimulants to the peoples of the temperate belt, who had no real need of them, but yet consume daily vast quantities of some of them, tobacco being the chief. As they are the basis of a vast industry and a commercial organisation comparable with those required by luxurious foods, they in fact play in our industrial communities a social part unconnected with their original purpose.

EXTENSIVE SYSTEMS OF CULTIVATION

Agricultural progress has been particularly slow wherever the luxuriance of the vegetation or the absence of crop rotation has prevented a systematic use of the land, and in fact a large proportion of the area of tropical countries is still given up to extensive cultivation. The system still prevails in South America whenever it has not been replaced by the European system, and in Africa on either side of the Equator up to the point where it comes into contact with white influence in the south and that of oasis cultivation in the north. It is also the common practice in hill country in the Far East and in Australasia. It is marked by a whole set of features which point out in various ways the feeble hold man has on nature in these areas.

First of all, it requires a continued repetition of the clearing of the soil, for the same patch cannot be permanently under cultivation. The appearance of the natural vegetation has led to an exaggerated idea of the fertility of tropical soils. Some parts are irretrievably barren; others have been exhausted by leaching or by over-cultivation. As soon as the impoverishment of the soil is indicated by the falling off of the crop, a new patch is prepared on virgin land after the natural vegetation has first been removed. The felling of trees is a fundamental operation in cultivation at this level of civilisation and is seen in practice in Asia, Africa, South America, and Australasia. In all these places advantage is taken of the dry season to burn the branches and trees on the spot. In the hill country in southern India, in North and South Vietnam and in south-western Kalimantan burnt patch cultivation has lasted till our own times. It is still practised by the Negroes in equatorial Africa from Gabon to Cameroon and Zaire, and by the natives of New Guinea, in spite of the tremendous labour required there in the preparatory felling of trees by men whose only tools are stone axes, and by the Amerindians of Rio Branco and the *moradores* in Ceará.

Burning the grass in the scrub and on the savannas is less laborious and can be done year after year, but it impoverishes the soil, destroys the natural vegetation cover by causing the disappearance of the best species and so preventing the spontaneous recovery of the land during years of fallow after temporary cultivation.

The inferiority of extensive cultivation in the tropics is due to the weakness of the means of carrying it out. In agricultural communities in the Far East men play a large part in tilling the soil. They do the rougher work, leaving to the women the tasks that take a long time and require more patience or care. The low efficiency of the cultivation is therefore due less to the debility of the labour than to the inferiority of the system.

On the other hand, in the tropical parts of America, Africa, or

Australasia all cultivation, except the felling of trees, is in the hands of the women or slaves. Such a division of work which leaves the burden of cultivation on women condemns native agriculture in central and east Africa to a state of irretrievable weakness. Woman's position as a slave of the land is reflected by her social status. A veritable beast of burden, she is a form of wealth necessary to man's subsistence. Hence marriage is a bargain, a productive investment, and from this arises the tendency to multiply the number of women in the household. Polygamy is a mark of wealth, but it is also one of the conditions of prosperity.

In taking slaves into his family the Negro has no other object than to make sure of some ever ready labour. Once the slave enters the household, his lot is inhuman. Like the wife, he represents capital and in some cases exchange value, whose purchasing power the owner tries to maintain. This human capital produces interest in the shape of work. It has even been said that some African tribes, like the Fans, who do not practise slavery, 'are ignorant of one of the first steps in economic progress'. That is an over-simple view, for in reality since cultivation lacks man's strength and is left to the weak hands of women or the carelessness of slaves, it loses the advantage of more efficient work.

The same crops have not been adopted everywhere, for the climate often offers a choice. In wetter regions preference is given to food-producing trees and to tubers. This choice which conforms with natural conditions is seen to be due also to the low degree of agricultural skill in the men who make it. The crops selected yield a harvest all through the year. Food is gathered in the patch as needed, for the produce is perishable and, since it cannot be stored, barns are useless. The work shows neither care nor foresight, and crops are liable to be insufficient owing to the whims of the elements or the ravages of animals.

In the drier regions sowing and gathering take place at fixed times. Produce capable of being stored is dealt with. It must be protected, barns must be built—sometimes big clay urns, at others baskets, silos on stilts and covered with straw. Cultivation here calls for foresight, because it produces a durable reserve whose mass forms wealth.

Tubers and roots form a series of crops that are easily grown. Cassava is the edible root of an Euphorbiacea and is planted by inserting a slip in a damp hole. It needs little weeding, and at the end of six months its roots can be dug up for use. The plant is prolific, for each stock has five or six roots which continue to grow bigger for three years and may weigh 2 or 3 kg at the end of eighteen months. So each stock may yield about 30 kg of root, and 100 square metres under cultivation can feed four or five people for a whole year. The preparation of the root is less easy than the cultivation of the plant, for the root contains a poisonous juice that must be washed out. The 'farine' that is then got by grating the root is made into little white cakes called *cassavas* by the Amerindians. Manioc or cassava (*Manihot utilissima*) is of South American provenance, but is now cultivated in all tropical countries.

The yam (*Dioscorea sativa*), which is cultivated especially in West Africa, is planted in April and harvested in November. It yields enormous tubers some 30 to 35 cm long and weighing between 5 and 10 kg. The sweet potato is more widespread in Zaire and central Africa generally. It is less easily kept and cannot be cooked in so many ways. It also yields large tubers at the end of six months.

Fruit trees require less care still. The banana 'tree', which is really a giant herb, is characteristic of hot, wet lands. Its original home was Indo-China and Southeast Asia, but it spread through the whole of tropical Africa in very early times. It is planted from a sucker that grows out of the root, and it bears fruit in less than a year after the sucker has been planted. The coconut palm is just as valuable on account of its enormous yield of nuts as well as on account of the many uses to which its parts can be put. Its trunk is used for building, its leaves serve for thatching huts or when plaited for making walls and partitions. There is no hot country in existence without some specially useful tree. The kola tree is the standby in Guinea, the butter-and-tallow tree (*Butyrospermum Parkii*) in the Sudan, and the mango tree in Southeast Asia.

Tropical cereals form the basis of agricultural production wherever cultivation is on the extensive system and the climate favourable. Sorghum (*Sorghum vulgare*, durra, Kaffir corn), millet (*Penicellaria spicata*), and eleusine (*Eleusine corocano*) are the most characteristic. They do not grow in wet regions and in central Africa they disappear south of lat. 7° N., but are found in some fringing areas in Welle, Tanzania and Katanga. Similarly, they disappear as drought increases. In South Africa, for instance, they do not go west of the Great Fish River. Wherever sorghum and millet can grow in Africa, they are the mainstay of the diet and are cultivated with great care. The landscape presents the same scene of cultivation from the Sudan to Uganda with its patchwork of fields, its collection of straw huts used for storing millet, and its scaffoldings with scarecrows for frightening predatory birds from the fields.

Maize, which is wonderfully adapted to hand cultivation, has had extraordinary success in making its way into the relatively conservative systems of tropical cultivation. It originated in America, where it was the chief crop of the high tablelands of the Andes and later in the warm plains in the United States. It is still cultivated along with cassava throughout the South American continent. In Africa it is found nearly everywhere together with sorghum, for, like the latter, it is suitable for making gruel. It even grows in clearings in equatorial Africa. In the Far East it is one of the crops cultivated by the hillmen in south China and in Indo-China. Like hill rice, it is grown in the *rays*, where rain is the only source of water.

These crops are all associated in various tropical lands, where they take part in peculiar local systems of cultivation. Most of the large-scale crops move from continent to continent and have taken a place alongside those that had previously formed the mainstay of the native diet. Hence a whole series of different combinations that give a special look to the economy. In the wettest regions tubers, roots, and fruit hold first place together with green crops or cereals. Thus, in New Guinea cultivation comprises mainly coconut and sago palms, patches with sweet potatoes and yams, fields of maize, gourds, and pimento. In the Ogowe region of Gabon there are banana trees and patches with cassava, gourds, sweet potatoes, sugar-cane, and groundnuts. To these Uganda adds sorghum and sesame. In the Cameroon are banana trees with patches of yams, taro, sweet potatoes, beans, maize, and groundnuts. In the less wet regions cereals dominate the scene, though the crops grown in moister lands are not wholly excluded, for they continue to be cultivated in gardens around the huts. From the Sudan to Uganda millet, sesame, maize, and groundnuts are everywhere to be seen, but to them are added in suitable places cotton, cassava, sweet potatoes, or beans. Among the hill folk in Taiwan, Indo-China, and the Philippines rice, millet, and maize crops form the chief features of the landscape, which is varied here and there by crops of sweet potatoes, gourds, banana trees, and, now and then, even buckwheat.

In spite of the variety of produce yielded by this type of extensive cultivation, the subsistence of the people is not always ensured. Whole communities are often found in a state of half-starvation and on the point of famine. At times they try to eke out their supplies by gathering or hunting. These auxiliary activities, which take place mainly in the dry season, are an inseparable feature of extensive cultivation, and gathering in the bush, fishing, hunting, and subsidiary pastoralism are part of the agricultural life of the tribes in Africa, the Amazon basin, and the hill folk in the Philippines, Borneo, and Indo-China.

The extensive cultivation practised in hot lands does not firmly fix man to the soil. Movement from one piece of ground to another takes place at various intervals, sometimes every year, as in New Guinea; sometimes at the end of two or three years, as in Indo-China; sometimes every four or five years, as in Borneo. In this way the cultivated patches become situated farther and farther away from the villages and involve long journeys to them, unless the village itself is moved. These removals are frequent and normal among the Fans, the natives of New Guinea, the Amerindians in the valley of the Rio Negro, the Korkus in central India, and the Mois in the mountains in Indo-China. When local displacements become general, they end by affecting a fairly large number of people and are veritable migrations. At times they take place within fairly well-defined boundaries, and the tribes return after long intervals to re-occupy land that they had previously cultivated and abandoned. But it also happens that displacements gradually remove the tribe far from its original territory. This was perhaps the case with the ancient Germanic tribes, and in Africa with the Fans, who by gradually moving west and southwestwards approached the coast by slow degrees.

INTENSIVE SYSTEMS OF CULTIVATION

Besides the countries that are still given to various forms of extensive cultivation there are in the tropics some splendid centres of intensive cultivation which have been for thousands of years the densest areas of human population. In them are used the best methods of ploughing, a systematic application of fertilisers, and a choice of especially productive and nourishing crops. This success has been achieved owing to two series of causes, some of which stem directly from the soil and differentiate hill districts from plains in the same region, whilst others raise the general standard of civilisation and have placed the countries of monsoon Asia in the first rank of agricultural peoples.

The development of intensive cultivation depends on the presence of fertile and regularly watered soil, and this is generally found only in valleys or on plains. Thus, intensive cultivation is already appearing in little gardens belonging to African Negroes, whose crops are particularly well tended along the valleys in the Sudan. But this use of the land is general and systematic in tropical Asia. In fact, however, the essential difference is everywhere evident between the extensive cultivation of the *rays* in the hill country and the intensive cultivation of irrigated ricefields in the valleys and little plains. These different types of agriculture are sometimes carried on by peoples of different stock. For instance, the Thais live in the valleys, the Meos in the hills. A similar difference is seen in Java between the *ladang* in the hills and the *sawah* on the plains. In south China and Japan intensive cultivation of irrigated paddy fields is concentrated on the deltas, plains, and valleys. Finally, in India there is the same contrast between the hill country which is given up to millet and the lowlands which are reserved for rice. The predilection of intensive cultivation for lowlands is due to the thickness of the alluvia and the abundance of water in the lowlands, facts that make up for the shortcomings and irregularities of the rains.

The plains and valleys have been put to use more thoroughly and on a far greater scale in Asia than in Africa. This is because the tradition of the agricultural mode of life took shape sooner and progressed at a greater rate in Asia. On the whole tropical lands in Asia are farther from the Equator, and the alternation of wet and dry seasons is clearly marked in them. Besides, India had very early contact with the western temperate region which used the plough and domestic animals. Then, China was in direct touch with the great desert oases, where not only were cereals cultivated, but also the most exiguous supplies of water were skilfully used. From them probably came along with the Chinese themselves traditions of irrigation and hand cultivation.

Intensive cultivation depends essentially on the use of fertiliser and a minute preparation of the soil. These two techniques have not everywhere attained to the same degree of knowledge and efficiency. In India the soil is not all manured, and the amount of manure given to it is always small. Indians are ignorant of the use of human excreta as manure and have little knowledge of the use of green manure. They do not know how to preserve their manure heaps and they destroy a large part of it by using it as fuel. Hence, they have to leave part of the fields fallow, and nearly everywhere there are three concentric belts of land round the villages, the most distant being little more than poor pasture. In China and Japan the knowledge of fertilisation has reached an unequalled degree of perfection, as much by the ingenuity with which the fertiliser is obtained as by the care used in applying it to the crops metre by metre and in spreading it through the whole period of growth.

The sum total of work on the land is on the whole far more considerable in China than in India. In the latter the basic unit comprises the peasant, the yoke of oxen or buffaloes and the plough. Two animals are used for ploughing: the humped ox, or zebu, in the dry areas, and the buffalo in wet districts. The zebu is used in the Deccan and the Gangetic plain. The buffalo, which is less delicate, likes water, and is nearly amphibious, is used in the paddy fields in Bengal, Burma, Indonesia, and Indo-China. This system of cultivation which makes use of the strength of animals is incomparably more effective than the extensive system, but it cannot be compared with European systems, for its means are restricted by the poor work of ill-fed animals, the low efficiency of the agricultural implements, and the rigidity of the systems in which improvement seems impossible so long as Indians are without good supplies of manure.

In China ploughing is done by man's muscles with a three-pronged hoe, and very often the earth is crumbled with bare hands. The corollary of such horticulture is the practice of planting in lines, for this allows better results in sowing, facilities for weeding, irrigation, and applications of manure, as well as opportunities for the insertion of secondary crops of vegetables or shrubs.

When performed with or without the help of an animal, the work of intensive cultivation established a distinction between man and woman. The man undertakes the heavy work out-of-doors, the woman's particular work is house-keeping and only at certain moments does she join in the cultivation. This family cooperation and the better balance of effort are in themselves causes of high yields.

The same piece of land can in the course of a year bear two crops. The climate makes this possible wherever the soil has adequate preparation and water. Nearly everywhere a basic crop covers a field at the beginning of the rains and completes its cycle rapidly under the influence of the warmth and water it receives from heaven or from man's work. Once the crop has been reaped, others are planted on the best land during the whole dry, or cool, season.

In Sechwan, for instance, the first rice crop is reaped in September. Then wheat is sown in October or November. As it benefits by the lesser rains in February, this is reaped in May. On the balks round the paddy fields grow mulberry trees. Lastly, in the beds that remain too damp to be sown with wheat a depth of water is placed, and this is used for pisciculture. In Japan the first and fundamental crop is rice. Then on the best parts of the paddy fields there is raised a second crop of barley, wheat, beans, or colza (*Brassica rapa*). In Indo-China rice of the tenth month is reaped in November after crops of maize, sweet potatoes, and yams. In Indonesia the rice crop is followed by tubers or fodder crops. In northwest India, which is drier, the multiplicity of produce is due to other crops. According to the place the first crop grown is millet, rice, maize, or cotton, and the second crop wheat, barley, or peas. Some parts of Oudh succeed in raising double crops on 40 per cent of their area.

In Far Eastern countries, where there is often a threat of dearth, success in producing more food evidently depends on taking advantage of a possible double crop. The landscape in the cultivated area has been shaped by man. The natural vegetation has gone, trees grow only round the houses, where they generally provide a useful crop of fruit. Among the trees are bamboos, which flourish throughout the Far East, and there are coconut palms in Indonesia and southern India. However, in spite of the great variety of cultivated plants and in spite of the diversity of cereals, intensive tropical agriculture rests especially on the growing of rice.

It seems that the earliest centre of rice cultivation was in India, from which the crop spread to both China and the lower valley of the Euphrates. Throughout its history rice cultivation has spread into hot, wet regions without going far outside the tropics. It prefers a mean temperature of not less than 20° C and soil saturated with water at least at the beginning of its growth. These biological features fix it, therefore, in wet tropical regions, in general in plains where irrigation is possible when the rainfall is not adequate. Rice is a swamp plant. It has been found growing in a wild state in pools left behind after the subsidence of river floods in monsoon Asia and containing fish, which are collected by the natives. The practice is certainly very ancient. The name 'rice' must be derived from the Sanscrit *vrihi*. This became *brizi* in Iranian, and from it came the Latin *oryza*. Today there are more than 200 varieties of rice distinguished by the appearance of their inflorescence, their more or less early character, and their adaptation to certain soils.

Upland rice (*Oryza montana*) has a short stem and small grains which are sometimes coloured red. It is hardier than plains rice and is satisfied with rain water. It will grow at a height of 2,000 metres in the Himalayas, where it ripens in four months. It is cultivated in all the rice countries: in Japan under the name of *okato* and in Indo-China on the borders of the mountain forests as *cai trang*.

There is an infinite variety of plains rice, modifications occurring almost from place to place. In Java there are three varieties; *guja*, which is reaped in 90 days; *dalam*, ripening in 120 days; and *tangahan*, or *mean*, whose vegetative cycle is completed in 100 days. Similarly, in Japan there is an early rice called *wase*, reaped in mid-September, and a late variety called *oku*, reaped at the end of October. On the Tongking delta 'tenth month' rice is reaped in November and gives the heaviest yields. 'Fifth month' rice, reaped in May or June, is grown on the uplands in wet years. In southern India they also have a late rice, *samba*, and an early rice, *kuruve*.

All these varieties, which mark a great antiquity for the crop, allow rice to be adapted to a great diversity of natural conditions. In fact, every country cultivates in summer its early and late varieties which are adapted to the local climate. For instance, in Demak in Java, where there is a relatively short rainy season, early rice is planted so as to be reaped in 135 days. In regions where the water supply is less regular, a late variety is grown with a cycle of 180 days. For the same reason Bengal is assured of two main crops a year, one in September and the other in November-December. In some countries special circumstances have led to the selection of varieties of winter rice. This is the case in southern India and above all in Tongking. In the Carnatic, indeed, where the rainfall maximum occurs in November and December and the reservoirs dug along beside the rivers enable floodwater to be stored up for several weeks, a first crop of *samba* is grown by irrigation and reaped in January, and a crop of *kuruve* is grown in the same paddy field and reaped in June. In Tongking 'fifth month' is grown during the gentle winter rains in certain areas which are so lowlying as to remain flooded during the summer. In central Annam, on the contrary, the double rainy season leads to a crop of winter rice reaped in the third month (April-May) and another of summer rice reaped in the eighth month (August-September) Thus, rice shows an astonishing flexibility due to man's skill and hundreds of years of cultivation, and thus it enables a surprising proliferation of mankind to exist in the areas where it grows.

Throughout its growth rice demands great attention, and this calls for a great deal of labour, an incredible amount of toil. Fortunately, its enormous yields make extraordinarily large concentrations of labour possible. Rice must first be sown in a seed bed, which always consists of previously cultivated, rich, and mellow soil and is used for the same crop every year. It is most carefully tended, and, in countries where manure is scarce, it is given most of the quantity available. Between Bombay and Poona seedbeds show up distinctly on the landscape, forming little black squares arranged around the villages. Their colour testifies to their great richness of humus and is in contrast with the grey soils of the paddy fields. In Indo-China, where the peasants cultivate a newly cleared patch on which they wish to make paddy fields, they take care to rent a corner in an old paddy field to make a nursery that may be as much as one or two hours' walk away from the fields in which the rice will eventually be planted out.

The preparation of the seedbed is a thoroughly detailed business. The ground must be ploughed twice and harrowed several times, an operation always performed under a layer of water so as to secure a perfect levelling of the bed. When the seed is sown, the soil is left under water for twenty days, the water being renewed from time to time, for it should never be allowed to become stagnant. When the young plants reach a height of 20 to 25 cm, they are planted out in the paddy field. This field in the meanwhile has had much treatment in the shape of ploughing and harrowing carried out under water. When the paddy field has been transformed into a lake of mud, the planting out is proceeded with. It is a long, painful operation requiring many hands. As a rule the plants are taken from the seedbed by men, but the planting out is done by women, who scatter about the field, putting in some ten plants in one place, the places being about a pace apart. It is reckoned that in China, Indonesia, and southern India a team of six people is needed to plant out 200 square metres of paddy field in a day.

While the plants are growing, they must be given a second dressing and weeded so as to ensure that the water enters the soil well and to get rid of parasites. Above all, it is essential to maintain control of the water, for up to ten or fifteen days before the harvest the soil should be alternately flooded and left to dry. Rice is reaped with a hand implement: a sickle in Japan and Indo-China, but just a knife in southern India. When cut, the blades of rice are tied in little sheaves, which are then fastened to the two ends of a bamboo rod and carried to the village. The straw is used to feed animals, to thatch the peasants' houses, and sometimes as fuel.

Rice is threshed in several primitive ways. Sometimes it is trodden under foot, as it is in Tongking; sometimes it is trodden on by buffaloes; elsewhere gins or flails are used. The most essential and most wearisome of these operations is the levelling of the soil for irrigation. The need to achieve a perfectly horizontal surface makes it necessary for slopes in broken countries like Sri Lanka, Java, and south China to be terraced, and the terraces separated from each other by low banks of earth 40 or 50 cm high and able to retain the water for eight or ten days in succession. In the countries where fertiliser is scarce, the manure spread over the paddy field often contains a high proportion of inassimilable elements which form rubbish under the little fields and gradually exhaust them to such a degree that they can no longer hold an adequate layer of water. A layer of earth 40 to 80 cm thick must then be removed with a hoe from the whole surface of the paddy field. This is a tremendous task which demands the whole labour force of the village.

Water is indispensable for ground so prepared. In some countries like Indo-China water is supplied only by the rain. As long as the rains last, it is only necessary to control the drainage from the fields. Elsewhere there must be arrangements to meet a lack of water. Thus, in Tongking and in some parts of India rainwater and flood water are kept in *tanks*, or artificial lakes, dug beside the watercourses and in their alluvium. In hilly country water from brooks and springs in the mountains is channelled down on to the fields. In Java, Japan, and even south China these perennial supplies of water ensure great regularity in the harvests. On the plain of the Carnatic along the shores of the Indian Ocean water is taken from artesian wells and from water-bearing horizons imprisoned in alternating layers of Pliocene clays and sands. Between Madras and Pondicherry some of these wells are 80 metres deep. Artesian pressure forces the water up to more than 5 metres above the surface of the ground. It then has to be pumped on to the paddy fields.

The distribution of the water sets other problems. When the supply comes from above, as in Japan, Sechwan, and Java, an ingenious system of aqueducts is used, in which the water is moved by gravity into the fields. But when the fields are at a higher level, recourse must be had to special apparatus. These are *norias*, overshot scoops, which are sometimes worked by men's feet. They are found in China, Japan, and often too in Indo-China. In India simple balancing scoops are at times used to raise water from wells when the water-table is not lower than ten or twelve feet below the surface. The balances are mounted on a primitive machine, a picot, which needs the attention of two men, who by moving from one end to the other of a scaffolding alternately raise and lower the scoop. When the water-table is too low for this method, yokes of oxen are used to raise a bucket from the well by going down an inclined plane. A system of ropes and pulleys causes the bucket to scoop up water and empty it at the head of a ditch. This construction is called an *suttukaval*.

Thus it is seen that in the lands where rice was first cultivated, it demands at every stage of its growth a steady application of labour and the concentration of a great deal of human effort on small areas. Rice is indeed the cereal of small holdings, and throughout monsoon Asia paddy fields are restricted in area to some 40 square metres. Rice cultivation is adapted to a parcelling out of the land and to a certain extent calls for this development. The sight of so much toil and meticulous care used by Far Eastern rice growers indicates the importance of the cereal for them. It is included in the diet of half mankind, among whom it is far more essential than wheat or potatoes are to the dwellers in temperate lands. Almost by itself it forms the chief meal of the day for the Indian, Indonesian, and Chinese, who eat an average of 1 kg a day. Statistics show that at the present time monsoon Asia produces 93 per cent of the world crop of the grain.

Intensive cultivation, which has such important results, has another great virtue in that it attaches man to the soil and lessens the area needed to feed a human community. Though the soil does not provide all man's needs, these are seldom supplemented by occupations that remove the peasant from his land, but as a rule by home industry applied to the produce of his soil. Thus, there is spinning and weaving of silk, the preparation of tea, the extraction of vegetable oil, and the making or repairing of pottery and agricultural implements. This stability of occupation explains both the sedentary character of the community and the cohesion of agricultural villages, which are real social units in some Far Eastern lands.

It may happen, however, that intensive cultivation may go beyond its optimum. In that case the dense population which it feeds ends by exceeding both the capacity of the land to produce food and the possibility of employing the overabundant labour. The tiny plots no longer suffice to feed the families, and high rents prevent the culti-

vator from increasing his holding. The search for part-time occupation, which sometimes leads him into factories in the towns, is
harmful to the maintenance of intensive cultivation. It has been
noticed that in Japan the peasants, who have to devote too great a
proportion of their time to more remunerative industrial work, get
from their land smaller returns than before. One of the conditions
of maintaining this system of cultivation is that it should be carried
out in plots of reasonable size. Cutting up the plots does not favour
their better use. Maximum yields are obtained when the area of the
field is sufficient to occupy the peasant's time completely and to give
him a sufficient return. Hence, in Japan as in many hot countries
where intensive cultivation is practised, it is thought today that
agricultural yields cannot be maintained and increased except after
a reconstitution into large holdings of the properties now cut up
into small areas. The larger units of cultivation so obtained will,
through the reabsorption of surplus labour in urban industry, involve a considerable fall in the density of population which at the
present time paralyses intensive cultivation in tropical lands. Here
we find one of the many instances of agriculture, which, becoming
unable to make any progress itself, receives fresh impetus from a new
activity that has been developed apart from it. Industrialisation
seems to be the condition by which hot countries will resume the
improvement of an agricultural system that had reached its peak of
ingenuity and efficiency.

EVOLUTION OF AGRICULTURAL SYSTEMS

In the history of economic development in the hot countries which
remained so long unknown to Europeans, we notice several important changes that modified the mode of life owing to the adoption of
new plants, some of which were food crops, others industrial crops.
More than once in the past these countries have admitted, sometimes on a large scale, foreign methods of cultivation and kinds of
food, just as in our time they support the system of large scale
plantations producing crops for the market.

Throughout the Far East the spread of rice cultivation has caused
a vast change. Rice was taken to Korea by the Chinese before
1000 B.C., when millet had been the only cereal previously cultivated.
In Java and the Philippines rice cultivation replaced millet and
eleusine in the same way owing to Chinese influence. Thus, the
conquest of the Asiatic domain was a slow process and is still incomplete. Though there is indeed no possible further spread in
Tongking, Java, or central China, there remains in Cochin China (the
Mekong delta) much swampy land which can be improved. The
Thais, who came from China, introduced rice cultivation into other

parts of Indo-China. They are still spreading it among the Mans and Mois, their neighbours in the mountain valleys.

The crop was first introduced into East Africa from Asia by Arabs, to whom, therefore, tropical Africa owes its rice and sugarcane. Europeans were responsible for taking maize and cassava from America to Africa. These crops have caused in the systems of cultivation of native Africans changes comparable with those due to the introduction of the potato into our civilisation. Just as the potato conquered the whole temperate belt, so cassava and maize spread through the whole African continent. Cultivation in the tropics which may seem today unchangeable and in some places locked in rigid systems incapable of improvement, has in fact shown itself capable of great changes even in the traditional economy. Ever since Europeans have sailed the seas, they have been carriers of a new form of agricultural mode of life, although their influence has been very localised and has reached but a small proportion of the large number of cultivators in Asia, Africa, and America.

The tropics have always been for the people of temperate regions a source of valuable commodities. Spices were an incentive to European sailors, and it was through the merchandise from tropical lands that our merchants became rich. Not content with seeking valuable cargoes of spices, cotton, sago, coffee, tea, cocoa, sugar-cane, and silk, Europeans energetically developed plantations to produce them. Hence, throughout the tropics there has grown up the comparatively recent production of commercial crops destined for the world market and not for local consumption. The plantation system began in the West Indies with sugarcane and tobacco, which were the origins of the wealth of the slavers in Liverpool, Glasgow, and Nantes. Later, it reached the East Indies and more recently South America and tropical Africa. These commercial crops are by no means equally spread everywhere. Restricted to mere points on the coasts of Africa, they covered whole islands, causing deforestation in them. Of this Mauritius, Réunion, São Tome, Sri Lanka, and Java are examples. They even penetrated into the interior of continents, where as in Ghana and even in the southern United States and southern Brazil vast areas of original vegetation have been cleared away.

Sometimes commercial crops have flourished side by side with the traditional food crops without causing any great disturbance and have taken their place among the old crops without killing them. So it was in China and India. But at other times they have ended by monopolising almost the whole area and creating the artificial conditions of monoculture by causing the abandonment of food crops and the destruction of subsistence cultivation. This happened in

Indonesia, where food had to be imported in consequence; and it happened also in the coffee-growing parts of Brazil.

In countries still peopled by their natives commercial crops have introduced a fuller life less dependent on local food harvests and having a certain surplus of wealth. This has been seen especially in the Philippines, where the crops have led to an increase in comfort. The people of Ghana owe to their cocoa plantations their higher standard of living; and the Javanese have had their lives transformed by their rubber plantations.

Tropical plantations have introduced a new system of agriculture, for they are capitalist enterprises meant to produce commodities for sale abroad, and they are often concerned with crops that the natives do not grow. In Indonesia, for example, native cultivation supplied 75 per cent of the food, but only 20 per cent of the commercial crops. Except rubber, a good portion of which comes from native small holdings, commercial raw materials are derived from plantations of a foreign type.

One of the characteristics of plantations is that they integrate industrial and agricultural activities by treating their raw material themselves. Rubber plantations have sheds and laboratories which enable them to coagulate the latex into gum and to keep it as a liquid in cans for special industrial purposes; every sisal plantation has a factory for stripping the fibres; and there is no sugarcane plantation without its sugar mill served by narrow-gauge railways. They all require large supplies of capital to clear virgin land, plant the trees or bushes, and pay a big labour force. Their attraction of labour has caused important displacements of population, either temporary or permanent, in some tropical regions. Thus, Indonesia owes to the spread of various kinds of plantations the influx of coolies and settlers from China, who today form a mass of transplanted population of more than five million persons. Sugar plantations were responsible in the same way for the settlement of Indians in Fiji, Guyana, Natal, and Mauritius; and the coffee plantations in Kenya have attracted further Indian settlers from India to Africa.

In spite of the power with which plantations establish themselves on the ground and in spite of the skilful technique devoted to production, they cannot avoid instability. Many tropical regions have at various times in their history had changes in the nature of their crops. In Sri Lanka, for example, sugar, coffee, tea, and rubber have all taken their turn as chief crop. Brazil has seen a succession of crops of sugarcane, coffee, and cocoa and now is concerned besides with cotton. Turn by turn the West Indies have sold sugar, cotton, and coffee. Some products that are especially sought after in world markets have undergone strange migrations in the tropics. Thus coffee was taken from Arabia to the East Indies and thence to the West Indies,, whence at the beginning of the present century it reached Brazil, which was the greatest producer of the commodity before it had to face the competition of new plantations in Asia and Africa. Again, rubber plantations, which have been strictly localised in southeast Asia, have recently appeared tentatively in the Amazon basin and Africa at the instance of the Ford Motor Corporation and Firestone.

Naturally, the produce of the plantation system does not consist of the main foodstuffs, rice, millet, or cassava, since these have little value in world trade. Temperate lands are fed with the traditional produce of their own system. What they demand of hot countries are luxury goods which are really unnecessary, but by the consumption of which the rise in standard of living has increased. A feature of this development is that it is always on the increase and that to the original species have been added other products which have become recognised as useful and have been spread through the world by trade. Spices, which were among the earliest of such products, have kept their commercial importance. Cinnamon, nutmeg, cloves, and pepper still come chiefly from the East Indies. Cocoa, tobacco, cotton, coffee, and sugarcane later assumed even greater importance. Today, new products hold the attention of planters; for example, fruit, and especially bananas, which fast transport enables to reach temperate countries in good condition; copra, which since 1870 has taken commercial operations into the South Seas; groundnuts, which were introduced into Senegal in 1820 and which are now mainly grown in India and West Africa; lastly, rubber, jute, manila hemp, and sisal, which are all raw materials of great importance.

Thus, civilisation is gradually working its way into tropical lands, where it brings difficulties to some native peoples, but also introduces a great variety of means of livelihood and raises the standard of living by acquiring something more than subsistence level and by enabling the peoples to see beyond the narrow limits of their homeland.

Agricultural Production of Tropical and Sub-tropical Countries

Crop	World (mn. tonnes) 1934	1974	Africa (%) 1934	1974	Americas (%) 1934	1974	Asia (%) 1934	1974
Rice	151	321	0·8	1·4	0·8	4·7	97·4	93·3
Sugarcane	11·7	38·6	9	9	60·4	59·2	30·5	31·7
Groundnuts	9	18	10	17	7·7	16·4	82·4	66·7
Citrus fruit	9	43·2	3·6	9	66	57·7	6·3	15·6
Coffee	2·4	3·8	8	29	86	63·7	6	7·7
Tea	0·4	1·4	1·6	7·4	—	—	97	92·6
Cocoa	0·9	1·4	76	83	24	17	—	—
Rubber	0·9	3·5	0·7	5·2	1·6	0·7	97·7	94·1

CHAPTER 7

HUMAN LIFE IN DRY REGIONS

Arid regions do not lie in well-defined belts as do the temperate and hot regions. In fact, they are found in different climates. Some like the Mediterranean lands have mild winters that allow the growth of plants sensitive to frost. Others like Turkistan have severe winters that kill delicate plants. Whilst some touch the tropics, others lie within the cold belt. Some have rain chiefly in winter, as do the Mediterranean lands, California, and parts of the south coasts of Australia and South Africa, but others benefit by summer rainfall maxima, as do the Great Plains in the United States, the fringe between the Sahara and the Sudan, and the countries on the borders of monsoon Asia.

Such dry regions embrace particularly extensive areas in continental interiors, that is, those parts far removed from sea influence. Hence the greatest dry expanses form a wide band across the Old World from the shores of the Atlantic in North Africa to the Pacific coast in Manchuria. There for thousands of years have been crystallised the most peculiar and complex modes of life found in dry regions. The belt consists of a vast area of natural regions in which, of whatever race the inhabitants may be, the influence of the environment has caused fundamental likenesses in the mode of life. Other dry regions that are more isolated and remote exhibit the same physical conditions in smaller areas whether in South Africa or the heart of Australia or the United States.

The feature common to all these regions is inadequacy of rainfall and scarcity of water which in deserts may reach complete aridity. Whatever the local climate may be, the conditions of life are determined by the incidence of a dry season of more or less great length. All development of life is subject to the water supply. Even when the temperature might ensure for plants a sufficiently long period in which growth might take place, the lack of moisture imposes strict limitations.

Drought precludes the existence of forests, which is one of the basic features of dry regions in connexion with the development of a mode of life. To get food man does not have to remove them from the land. On the contrary, in some cases his work has consisted of planting trees and keeping them alive by dint of great care. As a rule the soil is open to his enterprise, and he has only to make use of the water supply. From the distribution of water result two basic appearances of the landscape, two kinds of supply corresponding to

164

two different modes of life. When the rainfall is enough to make cereals germinate, grow, and ripen, the agricultural mode of life is developed. But when the rainfall is only enough for the growth of grass, the pastoral mode of life prevails. A sedentary versus a nomadic life, an agricultural versus a pastoral life—those are the opposing modes to be seen throughout the dry regions.

So uncertain and precarious is the supply of water that all human life is of an unstable character. The yield from crops is irregular and poor, and the whole crop is at the mercy of a capricious rainfall. To feed his cattle the cultivator has to move them about so as to get good pasture. In some cases the cultivators themselves move away in order to till fields situated outside the dry region. Pastoralism, of course, assumes nomadism, and its pastures are often at the mercy of drought too. Man's resources cannot be secure so long as he is unable to control the water needed for his crops and his sustenance. Hence the rise of irrigation and hence the development of large sedentary agricultural communities wherever there exists an abundant supply of water. By acquiring control of the water and thus by gaining security in a sedentary life, man gets the opportunity of advancing to a high degree of civilisation.

THE BASIS OF THE AGRICULTURAL MODE OF LIFE

Agricultural life in dry regions depends on the cultivation of certain grains and on the keeping of certain animals that are adapted to drought. In contrast with what happens in temperate regions it never succeeds in completely occupying and continuously tilling the soil, but leaves large areas untilled and causes the type of migration known as *transhumance*. It always keeps to an extensive system of cultivation, but on the other hand, it makes up for the scarcity of water by cultivating certain plants which can get water from the soil by means of long roots. The vine and more especially the olive have become symbols of cultivation in the dry lands along the shores of the Mediterranean. Unlike conditions in temperate lands, the abundance of fruit in the diet and the part it plays in material civilisation form one of the great peculiarities of dry regions.

The shortness of the rainy season as well as the constant danger of drought has led to a choice of hardy cereals like wheat and barley. The absence of grassland and the resulting scarcity of fodder accounts for the lack of domestic animals that eat a large quantity of grass. Though the ox and ass are kept for work in the fields, meat and milk are mainly supplied by sheep and goats. Cereals can take advantage of a short rainy season better than all other crops by avoiding the terrible drought of summer when everything is scorched and severe winters that kill the seeds. Thus, in the interior of Asia wheat is sown in spring; on the shores of the Mediterranean with its mild winters wheat and barley are sown in autumn after the rains have begun and are reaped at the beginning of the dry season. Winter wheat is an astonishingly early crop in all Mediterranean lands. Its cycle of growth lasts 164 days in Malta, where it is reaped in mid-May, and 171 days at Palermo, where the harvest is always complete by 1 June. Wheat, which is the main bread cereal, is a very old crop in all countries in the Old World. Its yield is often poor, but the corn is rich in starch and is of excellent quality. In this grassless type of country barley is mainly given as food to the cattle. Hence, it is widely cultivated right across the Old World and even in dry lands in the New World. Maize, which is a more recent crop, makes use of the short rainy season that follows winter and ripens quickly in the warm spring. When the harvest is complete and the grain has all been taken from the fields, the countryside looks burnt and dead, whilst in temperate regions the grassland, woods, and verdure testify to the continuity of vegetable life and agriculture.

Domestic animals help man in tilling the soil for the production of cereals. In dry lands the ox is the main draught animal. It is found throughout the Mediterranean region and in the East, where it still plays its old part. Then come the ass and mule, which are beasts of burden and are spread today all through the dry lands. They have been introduced into Latin America, but have not reached Australia, this being a country settled by the English. Though agricultural life depends, as it does also in temperate regions, on the cooperation of human and animal effort, this cooperation does not work in so many ways nor does it have such great results. The basic cause is to be found in the lack of fodder and in the consequent difficulty in feeding many animals. In dry regions there is neither forest nor permanent grass. When the dry season comes, only a very limited number of animals can be fed on the farm, that is, those whose presence is indispensable for the work, like the oxen and asses. It is impossible to feed those that give milk, meat, and wool on local resources, and steps must be taken to get supplies from distant countries. Hence the great effects that permeate the whole organisation of the agricultural mode of life. First, there is the primitive and extensive character of the system which cannot be as progressive as that in temperate lands; secondly, its characteristic instability and mobility which are shown in one of the great phenomena of human geography, *transhumance*.

Lack of grass, scarcity of cattle, and *transhumance* of the smaller animals involves poverty of manure, which seems to be the greatest obstacle to progress in agriculture. Besides, the lack of humus due to the dry climate and the effect of surface drainage on soil that is not protected by grass and trees explain the scarcity of good land with deep soil. Hence the small size of the cultivated areas.

The geographical aspect of dry countries is one of discontinuous features. Cultivation is patchy and covers but a small fraction of the area in sight, namely, 35 to 39 per cent at most in the best parts of the Tell, in Shawya, or in the whole of the Iberian peninsula; but only 18 per cent in Greece and less still in Asia Minor. In contrast with the cultivated patches there are vast stretches of waste space like the barren grounds dotted with brushwood and *maquis* in Attica and the Peloponnesus, the *parameras* near Soria and Ávila in Spain, and the sagebrush expanses in the west of the United States.

On ploughland fallow is indispensable one year in two or three. In some places it even makes rotation unnecessary. The fields are changed round every year, and every year fresh soil is cultivated. These primitive proceedings are carried out with rudimentary implements. The soil is scratched rather than turned over, big stones are not removed by the plough, but are worked round, as are also bushes. The wheelless plough which is sometimes without an iron share makes a furrow only 10 cm deep. Even in countries like the United States, where the technique is up-to-date, long periods of fallow are needed.

The low yield from cereals and the uncertainty of the harvests due to irregularities in the rainfall make it necessary to seek out further supplies. Sometimes the cultivators move between two lots of patches on which the work is done at different times. For instance, in South Africa cultivation is shared by the High and Low Veld, and in Lycia it is shared by the coast and the mountains. In the neighbourhood of wooded hills the thousand and one resources of the forest are exploited. For instance, in Greece and Bosnia swine are taken into the oak groves, and acorns are collected; in south Italy swine are fed on beechmast, and beechwood is used for making charcoal; in Rousillon and Albères in the Pyrenees cork is cut from the cork-oak trees. In Tunisia there is seasonal movement to gather Barbary figs. Lastly, when the cultivated land is quite insufficient, it is abandoned and used for pasturing herds. In this way there is a gradual passage to a nomadic life. Indeed, the agricultural mode of life is very insecure in areas which are much threatened by drought, and the belt of cultivation undergoes a flux and reflux according to the year. This has been observed in North Africa as well as in Syria.

When the land is unable to feed the animals, both sheep and goats must leave the cultivated area and seek pasture elsewhere. Periodical movement of flocks to and from the cultivated areas and pasture has long created interdependence between plain and mountain. The plain is occupied during the rainy season on account of its natural pasture, like the *xerovuni* in Greece, and of the stubble in fields in which flocks leave precious manure. The mountains are occupied in the hot season because they keep fresh pasture all the summer. Even today *transhumance* controls the economy of the Balkan peninsula in Greece, Macedonia, and Thrace, which countries keep the ethnic peculiarity of a pastoral people, the Vlachs. It plays a very important part in southern Italy, in most of the Iberian penin- sula, and in North Africa. It has greatly reduced its radius of action in France, but it still exists in Crau, Rousillon, and all along the Pyrenees, though it is becoming less vigorous every day there.

Man has been obliged to adopt the cultivation of perennials so as to have a type of agriculture that ensures his food supply. Trees are the only plants that can grow on ridges and dry soil, because their long roots find water deep down when the surface is dry. Under the action of the sun's rays they yield in their fruit a precious accumulation of sugar (vine, fig, date) or oil (olive). However, fruit trees do not grow in all arid regions. In the coldest of them, as in the driest, the tree cannot survive. Hence, shrub cultivation has spread especially in countries with a temperate climate, which, on account of the mildness of their winters and of a less severe dry season, affords a fairly long vegetative period; for example, the Mediterranean lands or the parts of South Africa, California, and southern Australia that are like them in climate. This type of cultivation, which is now fairly widespread in dry lands, took its rise in the Mediterranean region of Europe and is there deeply entrenched, with the vine, olive, and fig as its main trees. In some regions arboriculture is the sole basis of production; for example, in the islands of the Ægean, where cereals are relegated to second place by the olive tree, vine, and fig tree and by a whole set of fruit trees and shrubs like those in which Chios and Mitylene are clad.

IRRIGATION TECHNIQUES

Man's control of nature in dry lands is not achieved until he is able to make sure of a supply of water and use it for irrigation. In temperate lands agriculture has reached this advanced stage, but yet it often depends on the vicissitudes of the rainfall. Rain indeed sometimes does as much damage as good, and man cannot regulate it. On the other hand, in dry lands when there is a perennial supply of water man can direct and distribute it as he likes. The result is a perfect type of agriculture which has been carried on in western and central Asia since ancient times.

Water is had from the rock underground or from streams. Great efforts are expended in catching, diverting, and storing it. Consider- able differences may arise in the means and sources according to the amount to be used, the season when the supply is available, and the relief of the places where the water is used. In dry lands differences in the possible effectiveness of irrigation determine as many shades of fertility as do pedological differences in temperate lands. Hence, the centres of cultivation are far more localised, far smaller, far poorer when only ground water is available from springs, ordinary wells, and artesian wells; but they are richer and better supplied by running water and reach their greatest vigour when the running water comes from big rivers that are fed from outside the dry region.

Springs nearly always rise along valleys, for the more or less deep bottoms of these features are close to the water table. Most of the oases in the Sahara are to be found in the beds of wadis; but valleys seldom form continuous oases, for these are spaced out along the *thalweg*, as in Wadi Dra (Tinsit), Wadi Jedi (Laghwat), and Wadi Dermal (Bou Saâda), in which the poor supply of water allows irrigation to take place only every twelve days. When the land to be irrigated is far from the source of supply, the water must be sheltered from evaporation during the whole of its run in. Hence, the underground aqueducts, or *foggara*, which are found under various names around Marrakesh in Morocco, in Conca d'Oro in Sicily, and in Iran, Afghanistan, and Turkistan.

When water does not gush up naturally from the rock, it must be drawn up at a cost of hard work. In some places there is little digging to be done, but in others the boring of a well and bringing water to the surface demand great effort. In Mzab water is reached through limestone at a depth of 55 metres; at Jerba between 10 and 20 metres; and at Fezzan and Khangeh at about the same depth. Water held in deep rock strata may be made to gush up to the surface and as if by magic transform the conditions of life. Thus, artesian wells have been bored in the western United States and in South Africa; in the Sahara the French have increased the number of bores especially in Hodna and Wadi Rir; and in Australia systematic boring has been carried out in the Great Basin in northern New South Wales and southern Queensland. In spite of the wonderful success achieved by some of artesian wells, ground water is not an inexhaustible source of supply. An increase in the number of wells tends to use up the water in the upper strata where the renewal of the supply takes place. It has been established nearly everywhere that as the number of bores and gushers increases, the output of the wells previously in use falls off appreciably, then dwindles disquietingly, foreboding final drying up.

These limitations explain why ground water has scarcely ever developed strong, vigorous, and wealthy agricultural communities. Taking the Sahara as an example of countries with a mean and peddling water supply for irrigation, we see a type of organisation that with difficulty keeps alive small, scattered oases which as a rule cannot support the younger generation. Thus, Mzab, like Suf, is a district from which people move away to seek a better living by trade. Most of the oases are inhabited by communities that are weak, unable to defend themselves, and fallen under the protection or political dependence of nomads. Running water naturally ensures the greatest quantity for irrigation. It is not controlled by man and may be of two kinds: streams that rise right inside the arid region and feel the effect of the dry climate, and those that rise out of the dry region and escape that effect in their headwaters. The former display all the degrees of poverty and plenty, from the wadis of the Sahara with their occasional flow on the one hand to large rivers like the Tigris-Euphrates which have their sources in mountains. The latter draw their water from distant sources and bring to dry regions the plentiful water of the tropics, in the case of the Nile, or else of glaciers in lofty mountains, as in the Oxus.

Travelling through dry countries, one encounters a whole hierarchy of streams, from the tiniest threads of water in the deserts to the powerful streams coming down from the mountains. The régime of these streams is one of excess, violence, and irregularity which makes the use of their water more or less precarious, and in all cases demands great effort to adapt it for use. Hence, there are contrasts between various dry regions and between different rivers in the same dry region. They result from the variety of hydrographic features and the degree of control over nature acquired by the people who use the streams.

In the circumstances of the Old World deserts rivers often lack the strength to make their way to the sea and end in inland basins. Not one of the oases in the Sahara is watered by wadis from its valley. Wadi Dra loses its last drop of water immediately on issuing from the Anti Atlas; and Wadi Ziz is permanent only upstream of Tafilelt, and only in spring when the snow melts does it form a big floodwater lake.

In southern Turkmenistan the Murgab and Tejen flow from less-elevated mountains than do those that feed the Oxus. In April and May they have plenty of water, but they shrink from the beginning of June. Hence the need to build dams upstream so as to check the flow of the water. The Karry Bend dam on the Tejen and the Sultan Bend on the Murgab go back to the Middle Ages. They have been repaired several times, but they are considered inadequate by modern settlers owing to the requirements of cotton growing. The idea of diverting towards these southern oases a portion of the waters of the Oxus has long been considered, for a quantity could be withdrawn without harm to the oases in the lower valley. Dams are used throughout Iran in order to store up melt-water. The countryside round Isfahan, Hamadan, and Shiraz owes its fertility to such constructions. In Iraq the rivers have not been controlled to as great a degree. The Tigris and Euphrates flow above the plain between levées and have a network of lateral arms, mort lakes and marshes which make it necessary to build dykes along the banks, and these are great obstacles to future irrigation. Only in April and May is there plenty of water following the melting of the snow in Armenia. Unfortunately, from the very beginning of the burning summer in the desert at the very moment when water is precious, the rivers are in their period of low water. Only a host of weirs placed at intervals along the whole length of the upper valley could prolong the period of high water, and their construction would present difficulties. Compared with the Nile, whose régime has adapted itself to the needs of agriculture in its valley, the rivers of Iraq have never been sources of fertility for their plain.

AGRICULTURE AND IRRIGATION

The Mediterranean Lands of the Old World.—Around the Mediterranean irrigation is not as necessary as it is in the desert, for the rainfall enables an extensive system of agriculture to be carried on over large areas. When water is available for irrigation, an intensive system based on the cultivation of crops of high market value is superimposed on or substituted for the extensive system. For this reason the development of irrigation depends very largely on the degree of progress in agricultural communities.

In North Africa the natives have long been irrigating the high plains that lie among the mountains, including Tlemcen, Bel Abbès, and Mascara in western Algeria, the valleys of Wadi Sahel and Bu Merzug upstream from Constantine. Similarly, some streams in Tunisia, like Wadi Zerud and Wadi Sbiba have been dammed. But the natives had omitted to build where streams flow from the mountain passes—just where the water is difficult to control—into the plains of Mitija, Hebra, and Bône. These torrential and spasmodic streams, whose water is not available in summer, have nevertheless been controlled by the skill of European settlers. Expensive dams involve great inconvenience, however, the worst feature being the process of silting up. The dam on the Sig and the weir on the Shelif are the only constructions that have proved profitable. Furthermore, none of the constructions have inspired North Africa with an agricultural tradition comparable with that in Spain.

Indeed, besides great expanses of *terrenos de seccano*, Spain contains irrigated land in the *vegas* of Valencia, Murcia, Almeria, and Málaga, which are all fertile regions situated on the periphery of the Meseta. They are watered by streams from the mountains through canyons that lend themselves to damming. Apart from the coastal lowland, there is irrigation only here and there in the plains inland. On the tableland of Old Castile and in the province of Zamora irrigation is scarcely to be found anywhere, and old distributory ditches have even been abandoned. In the upper valley of the Tagus lateral ditches along the Jaroma, Henares, and Tajuna change the valley bottoms into oases, but the parks at Aranjuez and the gardens irrigated from the Sierra de Altamira are surrounded only by dry fields of cereals, vines, and olive trees. Even the plain of Andalucía contains more fallow and waterless land than irrigated soil, and most of the waters of the Guadalquivir run off unproductively to the sea. Only around the towns is there irrigation, by means of simple, horse-worked *norias* which have been set up on private land. The very dry Ebro valley is more fortunate in having at its disposal the considerable volume of streams from the Pyrenees. Its valley has two irrigated districts: first, one between Logroño and Saragossa in which water is distributed both by *norias* and by two distributory canals that leave the Ebro at Tudela; secondly, the Tortosa district beyond the gorges of the Ebro, where distribution is difficult owing to the shallow canyons in which the streams flow.

Some of the high inland plains are better endowed, for they get water from winter rains and from melt-water, especially in the Sierra Nevada (3,500 m). The most famous is that of Granada, which is watered by the Genil, Darro, Monachil, and Dilar and has an area of 19,000 hectares. The distribution of the water is carried out by extremely complex and archaic rules whose aim is as much to establish the ownership of the water as the right to a supply. But this peculiarity results from the abundance of water. During most of the year everyone takes what he needs, and it is only in August and September that it is felt necessary to take turns at getting water as laid down by the ancient compilation of customs made in 1571 by Loaysa. The plain of Granada, which is known as La Vega, or *the* valley, comprises three parts. In the *carmen* zone, consisting of small-holdings around the town, only luxury fruit is grown; in the *vega* zone vines and olive trees are grown, or the land is given up to rotations of wheat-hemp-wheat or wheat-flax-wheat; lastly, the *huerta* zone has water enough for two crops a year and grows sugar-beet, maize, broadbeans, and wheat, lettuce, haricot beans, and pimento, with hemp. Wheat is irrigated two or three times and so are the vines. Throughout the Vega of Granada the soil never rests.

The Mediterranean lowlands from the Pyrenees to the Straits of Gibraltar form one of the finest irrigated areas in the Old World. Between the Pyrenees and Cape Nao the many streams have plenty of water. Large stone or brick constructions are of no use, and mere weirs and canals supply a series of oases at the point where the streams reach the lowland. In Roussillon there is a contrast be tween the *aspres*, which are barren hills that cannot be irrigated, and the *regatiu*, which is fretted with canals that date from the ninth century. They were increased in number in the thirteenth and fifteenth centuries during the period of Aragonese domination and now they form three groups at Vallespir, around the Tech, at Conflent, around the Tet, and at Salanque. The lowlands are given up to vegetables and early produce, and this has been especially so since the development of the railways which opened the way for the local products to markets in Paris and England, and since the growth at Perpignan of a large centre for exporting vegetables and fruit.

In Spain Ampurdan, which is watered by the Ter, has also been irrigated for a long time. Cereals are watered from 1 May to 31 October, and the meadows from 1 November to 30 April. Without fast transport and distribution Ampurdan has stuck to its traditional crops and has now developed into a source of early vegetables. During the last fifty years or so, however, a desire for modernisation has been shown by the introduction of rice cultivation into the irrigated area.

Farther south, Cataluña has at its disposal a fairly good supply of water, which is drawn from underground sources or from streams. This has required only very simple arrangements. The Llobregat Canal, twenty-two miles long, waters the crops around Manresa, and the Moncada Canal, which issues from the River Besos, irrigates vineyards and plantations of olive trees as well as crops of wheat, maize, hemp, and vegetables. In the *huerta* near Tarragona the water of the Francal and Gaya is led from the hills on to terraces to make a fertile oasis with various crops. The *huerta* at Sagunto, which is irrigated from the Canales, and the *huerta* at Castellón, irrigated with water from the Mijares, produce the same mixture of fruit, cereals, and vegetables.

Besides these, there is the unrivalled *huerta* at Valencia. The big coastal plain has been formed of alluvium from the Turia, Palancia, and Jucar and covers 270,000 hectares. As soon as the streams reach the lowland, they are robbed of some of their water. The Turia has a remarkably regular volume, even in summer. Eight ordinary ditches feed four canals on either bank. The constructions date from the Moorish period, but their use was not regulated till the eighteenth century. Each of the canals branches out into a host of little gutters which distribute water over an area of more than 106,000 hectares around Valencia. Apart from orchards that were planted at a fairly recent date, the irrigated land is used for a traditional two-year crop rotation of hemp, maize, wheat, and beans.

Water from the Jucar is distributed twenty miles farther south and relays supplies from the Turia. A dam and a canal ensure a large quantity of water to 12,500 hectares. The construction of dam and canal dates from the reign of don Jaime of Aragon, but the area covered was extended in the eighteenth century. Today rice is produced on two-thirds of the lowland, and on the rest are distributed the various crops of *huerta* polyculture. Since the end of the last century the irrigation system has been improved by drawing on underground water which has to be raised by mechanical pumps some 50 to 60 metres to the surface. These expensive appliances could not have been had without the cash obtained from the export of oranges grown locally.

South of Cape Nao the irrigated areas are smaller and more scattered. The dry climate causes enormous differences in the volumes of the streams, and it has been necessary to build big dams to hold water for the plains around Alicante, Murcia, Elche, Lorca, Nijar, Almeria, Motril, and Málaga. They are colossal works in masonry, and their construction goes back to the days of material prosperity, especially the end of the sixteenth century. Most of them were due to private associations, but in some cases the work was financed by the State. The Segura, which waters Murcia, was the only stream that did not have a reservoir. Two were built twenty-five years ago on the Mundo and the Quipar, which are feeders of the Segura.

In Murcia 11,000 hectares are irrigated. Two big outlet canals work three *norias* to irrigate the higher ground. In this way the water of the Segura is entirely used up in Murcia during the summer, but the return to the surface of water which had sunk into the ground, together with supplies from wells and cisterns, irrigate the soil in Orihuela, which is at a lower level. Cultivation aims at producing vegetables and fruit, and this has now given rise to a large canning industry for the export market.

The Tibi reservoir at Alicante, which was built on the Monegre, dates from Philip II, who had previously greatly improved the supply of water from a very old system, which drew its water from the Muchamiel. But today the Sociedad de los riegos de Levante has equipped pumping stations to raise water from the Segura and run it on to Alicante and Elche. In this way 400 million cubic metres of additional supplies have been given to cultivators in Alicante. The cost is unfortunately very high, and this makes the farmers in Alicante and Elche tend to produce fruit. At one time the vine was the chief crop in Alicante, whilst in Elche there was a peculiar landscape due to plantations of date palms. Raisins and dates, which find strong competition in foreign markets, are giving way now to other fruit crops, especially almonds, and these are ousting the old crops more and more.

Farther south the abundance of water from the snow-clad mountain range leads to a strange mixture of temperate and tropical crops in the little lowland areas around Almeria, Motril, and Málaga. Several of these lowlands remind one of Africa or the West Indies with their fields of cotton or sugarcanes, their banana trees, and bamboos. Almeria produces cereals and fruit, especially fresh grapes. Motril and Málaga have sugarcane fields with large refineries attached.

The Western Parts of the Americas.—The dry regions of the New World have benefited by similar treatment and have suffered from the same difficulties in very different economic circumstances. Irrigated areas are relatively few in South America. In Chile some have been constructed in the Great Valley and the secondary valleys that run into it, such as that of the River Petorca to the north of Santiago. The whole valley bottom is a ribbon of green enclosed by bare mountains, and wheat, lucerne, and early vegetables are grown side by side. The capital cost explains why only large enterprises have been able to take advantage of an area that is still sparsely peopled. The irrigated areas belong to big *haciendas* of 200 hectares in which only a small portion is artificially watered.

In northwestern Argentina irrigation is practised on the few oases centring round Jujuy, Salta, Tucumán, Santiago del Estero, Córdoba, and Mendoza. As they issue from the mountains perennial streams whose water can be dammed without great construction works are made use of by all these centres. In Jujuy and Tucumán they are used to irrigate fields of sugarcane, but Santiago and Córdoba have mixed crops, including tobacco, vines, and lucerne growing side by side, whilst orchards of apricots, peaches, and plums spread into the distance. Mendoza and the oases around it specialise in viticulture and wine production. The crops, whether sugarcane, fruit, or grapes, all belong to large estates on which a large capital outlay has been made, the prototypes of which are found in the western United States.

On the banks of the Río Grande del Norte and its feeders irrigation had once been practised by the Pueblo Indians, but even before the arrival of the Spaniards the upkeep of the canals had been given up, and the whole irrigation system had gone to ruin. In any case the natural conditions were unfavourable, since the lofty mountains to the south have no glaciers, and in summer the streams decrease greatly in volume. To start with it was only possible for the European settlers to divert water from the streams, as there were no adequate technical means of dam construction. The first step was taken by the Mormons of Utah, who merely drew water from the streams as they issued from the mountains on to their alluvial fans. Thus, the distribution of water by gravity on to the lower parts of the fans was very easy. Soon this system plainly became inadequate, and the Mormons sought water up in the mountains at the sources and sometimes even over the waterparting, as they did when they dammed the Bear River. They even set up *norias* and, later, mechanical pumps to draw fresh water from Lake Utah. Finally, in 1913 a new feeder canal was made to bring water from the heart of the Wasatch Mountains, a distance of 60 kilometres. The Salt Lake oasis is now a district of big orchards of apricots and peaches as well as of large market gardens which supply ordinary vegetables like cabbages and celery, and also tomatoes, not to mention melons intended for despatch to the New York market. At Ogden and Logan irrigation has for the past twenty years enabled sugarbeet to be profitably cultivated.

The initiative of individuals or of little groups of settlers was no longer enough to control large streams. Help was sought either from bodies with large capital or from Federal organisations like the Reclamation Service. The first dam on the Colorado was built at Fort Yuma. Then one after another the feeders of the Colorado and Río Grande were dammed. The Roosevelt Dam on the Salt River was for long one of the biggest in the world. After this, construction was usually extended to combine the formation of reserves of water for irrigation with supplies for working hydro-electric plants. On the Río Grande and the Pecos a series of dams send water to the lowlands in western Texas. Upstream from El Paso Elephant Butte Dam enables the whole valley of the Río Grande below to be irrigated. On the Missouri in eastern Montana a dam was first built at Fort Peck; then a series of dams on the Grand River in South Dakota as far as the confluence with the Missouri irrigate land on much of which sugarbeet is cultivated. In Idaho the most important dams are on the Snake River and are used to supply water for irrigating fields of lucerne, the fodder from which is sent to the dairy farms on the Great Plains. The Grand Coulee Dam on the Colorado irrigates nearly half a million hectares. The Roosevelt Dam on the Salt River has transformed the valley of that river and the Gila into a long fertile strip centring on Phoenix. Hoover Dam controls the flow of the lower Colorado and so enables water to be diverted to irrigate Imperial Valley, 480 km away, and the barren depression of Lake Salton, which is 74 metres below sea level. The Missouri Valley Authority is now still carrying out the construction of eighty dams on the Missouri and its tributaries.

In producing crops by irrigation all systems work in the same way. The irrigated land around Phoenix may be taken as an example. It is watered by a canal 63 km long, which brings water from Roosevelt dam, an immense reservoir with a surface area of more than 6,200 hectares. The land irrigated spreads over 76,000 hectares.

On it grow poplars and date palms, fields of lucerne and orchards containing an unusual mixture of fruit trees. Phoenix produces large olives with better looks than taste, oranges, dates, and various kinds of grapes. Long-stapled cotton is grown, and fields of lucerne enable a big herd of dairy cows to be kept. Imperial Valley displays the same mixture of early vegetables, fruit, and vines producing dessert grapes.

In all the 'oases' in the West fruit forms the chief crop, and it has been the chief reason for the establishment of lasting and prosperous 'islands' of settlers. The discovery of a good system of cultivation was a difficult matter. Experience showed that, if water was allowed to evaporate on the surface of the ground, crusts of salt tended to form, and the lower layers became decomposed into an infertile brown clay. Such changes in the soil due to excessive watering are a constant and dangerous threat. As this took time to discover, there were serious mistakes and irreparable losses at the beginning. Stagnant water is often due to the relief of the land. Basin-shaped areas are apt to be gradually impregnated by seepage which insidiously chokes the soil with salt. Hence, the ground should be perfectly level, and the water should flow to the foot of each tree in a concrete gutter so as to avoid both useless percolation and excessive watering.

Other precautions are also needed, for in these dry climates the sky is never overcast, and radiation at night lowers the temperature almost to freezing point. Between the trees rows of braziers are placed, and it is the duty of observatories to announce in advance night temperatures that require special precautions.

A crop needing such detailed attention cannot be grown on large plantations. In Arizona the holding of a settler averages 4 hectares. The largest farms do not exceed 40 hectares, and then only one-third will be irrigated. In California, however, irrigation has given rise to completely different social surroundings. Between 1872, when the first attempts at irrigation were made in the State, and 1885, when the number of important irrigation works greatly increased, there were several attempts to make use of water for raising crops. One of the most important came with the introduction of sugarbeet, but this had the drawback of needing a great deal of labour at a time when the country was still sparsely populated. The result was that the cultivation of fruit and vegetables was taken up instead. About 1880 these crops still represented only 4 per cent of the return from agriculture in California, whilst today they represent 80 per cent. The most important irrigated district is the double valley of the San Joaquín and Sacramento, which contains two-thirds of California's irrigated land, some 11 million hectares. The most grandiose constructions are those in the San Joaquín valley, where water from the lower Sacramento is pumped up at the downstream end of the river over the terraces on the left bank and led upstream by a lateral canal (the Delta-Mendota canal).

Grapes (for making fruit-juice, wine and raisins), oranges, peaches, hops, and asparagus are the main products, but lucerne and long-stapled cotton also hold an important place, especially in the southern or Bakersfield section of the Great Valley. Orchards are scattered and very specialised. Fruit is the most important crop in the south and centre and every year forms two-fifths of world production. Plum trees predominate around San Francisco and San José, apples around Stockton and Oakland, peaches between Sacramento and Maryville, figs around Kadota, and raisin-grapes around Fresno. The coastal valleys are just as specialised. Salinas, south of San José, produces lettuces, the hillsides at Napa and Sonoma are covered with vineyards that are cultivated by Italian settlers, the slopes of the Tehachapi Mountains carry vines, lemon trees, and cotton fields, and, lastly, green vegetables, small fruit, shrubs, and long-stapled cotton are grown in Imperial Valley.

Large mechanised industrial concerns predominate nearly everywhere. Machines are used not only in the preparation of produce for the market, but also in cultivation. Thus, to pick hops there are mechanical pickers needing only one tender, whereas formerly four hands were necessary. Similarly, cotton is picked by machines after it has been sprayed with cyanamide. There is nothing, down to the gathering of lettuces, that is not done today by ingenious machinery. Nevertheless, out of all the States of the U.S.A. it is California that attracts the greatest amount of seasonal labour on the farms. At harvest time more than 200,000 are employed on fruit farms and market gardens. The labour is cosmopolitan and consists of Chinese and Japanese, Indians and Filipinos, Mexicans and un-employed persons from other States as far away as Oklahoma, Texas, and Arkansas. One of the concerns in the San Joaquín valley, which cultivates more than 3,000 hectares, employs 2,500 hands at busy times, but in the slack season it keeps only 600 permanent workers. During the harvest 450 hands are employed in handling and packing plums, 300 in preparing grapes for the market. The concern owns a score of large irrigating pumps, about fifteen tractors, some fifty lorries; and for packing fruit its carpenters' shop makes 300,000 crates in a season.

At busy times the farmers are unable to house the seasonal labour, which is lodged in temporary camps, where the workers' families live in tents or shacks. Some of the camps hold thousands of people, men, women, and children, and remind one of encampments of nomadic tribes in the Old World. Indeed, the seasonal worker is a nomad, for he is always on the move, always in search of work.

Some groups of workers travel as much as 16,000 km a year. Their migration is on the whole from south to north, with a return south by a different route. Beginning in southern California in the region of Imperial Valley and Los Angeles it moves north as far as beyond Marysville and returns southwards in stages. In both directions the stages are settled by opportunities for work at construction or in harvesting, the latter spreading over several months owing to the variety of trees and vegetables cultivated.

This system of life based on cultivation of irrigated soil is therefore very different from what we have seen in other dry lands. Large farms are needed for this type of mechanical cultivation, which in spite of everything needs a great deal of labour to be profitable. The industrial organisation necessary for the sale and despatch of the fruit, together with the high price of land and the expense of irrigation, has precluded little men from the ownership of the soil and placed it in the hands of powerful capitalist firms, private persons, banks, or cooperative societies, which are alone capable of making available the technical means of developing such dry country in the absence of sufficiently large settled populations.

The Taming of Big Rivers.—Rivers that escape the effects of drought in their headwaters and can take enormous quantities of water right along their courses, have faced man with other problems. The most typical of those fed by glaciers in lofty mountains are the Indus, Oxus, and Syr Darya. The melt-water from snow and glaciers reaches the lower valley right in the middle of the warm season just when water is particularly precious. The Oxus, which has a rate of flow of 866 cubic metres per second in February, sees its rate rise to 4,640 cubic metres in July, 3,120 in August, and keeps it above 1,300 cubic metres until October. The régime of the Syr Darya and Zeravshan is similar. The water contains a high proportion of matter held in suspension consisting of elements that naturally fertilise and restore the soil. The Oxus contains about 1,800 kilogrammes of such matter in every 1,000 cubic metres, or three times as much as the Mississippi.

This abundance of water in midsummer has made large dams unnecessary. From early times water has been used by being led from the rivers in ditches, and this is done so enthusiastically that the Zeravshan is emptied by the time it reaches Bukhara. The flatness of the country lends itself to digging these ditches, and the operation together with the maintanance of the ditches is easy in soil that consists of alluvium and loess. In consequence, distributory ditches in Kirghizstan, Tadzhikistan, and Usbekistan are veritable rivers scores of kilometres long and more than 36 metres wide. Dating as a rule from the earliest times, they use up the water of the Zeravshan,

Kara Darya, and Churchik. Altogether they form a remarkable achievement for the time when they were dug. They were made entirely by the native people, though modern technique has added appreciable improvements. The primitive weirs made of beams, planks, and branches, some of which are very like the *korambus* of southern India, have been replaced by solid dykes.

The water from the ditches is given to the soil either by flooding, as is done in the rice fields at Bukhara, or by means of gutters, as in the cotton fields in Fergana. Sometimes, as at Khiva, the water in the canals is below the level of the land to be irrigated and must be raised by *norias* worked by camels. This simple method of irrigation, which ensures plenty of water at little cost, has sufficed for centuries to make the oases in Turkistan the finest and most fertile in the world. But modern organisation and in particular the aim of the Russians to enlarge the irrigated cotton-growing area have increased the efficiency of the old techniques by means of big engineering constructions. The scarcity of water in spring and after the beginning of September proved dangerous to the cotton and lucerne crops, and consequently, recourse was had to building dams in the mountains even on the largest streams. The first to be built were on the Zeravshan and on the Kara Darya at Kampyr Ravat in Fergana. Other constructions have more grandiose aims than the old native civilisations could have thought of. The Russians have begun construction on the River Chu in order to increase irrigation in Dzhety Su and in the south of the Betpak Dala; and they have started to divert the fast-flowing Naryn so as to distribute its water on the left bank of the Syr Darya by means of huge pipelines across the valley of the Kara Darya. This will supply water to 250,000 hectares which are still barren or inadequately watered. Another plan aims at diverting the Oxus from the head of its delta towards the Caspian Sea in such a way as to irrigate the north Kara Kum and the backland of Krasnovodsk over the whole length of the projected Turkmen canal. More grandiose still was the Davydov plan which aimed at diverting the Ob and Yenisey from losing themselves uselessly in the Arctic Sea and at making them fertilise the barren steppes in Kazakstan and Usbekistan. Two great dams, one at the confluence of the Ob and Irtysh and the other at the confluence of the Yenisey and Podkamenaya Tunguska, were to raise the water level 60 to 80 metres to form a reservoir 250 square kilometres in area, from which water would flow over the Tungay ridge to the Aral Sea at a rate of more than 400 cubic metres per second. In this way 25 million hectares of arable and 30 million hectares of pastureland would be irrigated. But it would seem that such gigantic undertakings, which completely upset vast regions of the earth, are not yet within the capacity of human engineering, even in a great industrial power. In fact, Davydov's plan and the construction of the Turkmen canal have both been given up, at least for the time being. The retention of water in mountain valleys near the sources of streams so as to divert it from its natural course and making it cross ridges by means of canals or conduits has been achieved only locally in Brazil, Chile, and southern India. In the Travancore mountains there is a dam which at an altitude of 1,000 metres holds up the waters of the Periyar, which instead of flowing down towards the Gulf of Oman, is diverted into the upper valley of the Vaigai through a tunnel a mile and a quarter long.

The Nile is an instance of another type of food-giving river in a desert region. The valley, which from Aswan downstream has a broad and almost horizontal bottom, makes the manipulation of water an easy matter. Furthermore, the Nile is regularly flooded year by year. At the end of June the flood-water, which has a greenish tinge, reaches Cairo and takes twenty days to run past. In July comes red and yellow silt-laden water, and the flood increases till September, subsidence not beginning till mid-October. This regular gift of water and fertilising silt has enabled skilful agriculture to make clever use of the Nile. Yet the floods are not perfectly regular, but vary in duration and intensity from year to year. In fact, in the three flood months the volume may be twice as great in one year as in another. From very early times two methods have been used to take advantage of the water, viz. flooding the fields directly, and watering with water drawn from irrigation ditches.

In the first case the soil gets no water except during the flood, and cultivation is the slave of the river. As the waters cover the ground from August to October, only winter crops can be grown, and seed is sown as soon as the water subsides. The crops are suited to the prevailing temperature in autumn and winter and are restricted to cereals, beans, lentils, and fodder like *bersim*, or Alexandrian clover. Hence, the Nile water very early began to be used in summer and was not allowed to run off uselessly during the times when the volume was small. After that it was possible to cultivate crops needing the heat of summer to ripen, like cotton, rice, and sugarcane. Out of this came a whole system of irrigation which made cultivation independent of the state of the river, but required big constructions either to bring water from upstream to the land farther down or else to raise water directly from the river on to the banks. Although the two systems of irrigation, by flooding and diversion, have always been in use in Egypt, hydraulic construction has been able to develop considerably, especially since engineering skill has made such great advance.

Flooding of fields from the river is achieved by making hollows enclosed by a double system of dykes, some parallel, others perpendicular to the course of the river, and meant to hold the silt-laden water long enough on the spot. Each hollow has an inflow and outflow ditch whose size is carefully regulated, since every hollow depends on its neighbour for good water circulation, The ditches remain open from mid-August till the end of October, drawing for the good of the soil eight or nine per cent of the total volume of the river. Over 600,000 hectares are irrigated in this way. The method calls for a minimum of work from the *fellahin*, and allows only one cycle of cultivation.

The irrigation works that have ensured the use of water for crops in summer consist of a series of dams, canals, and pumps. The ages have bequeathed a whole set of pumping devices that are still used by the *fellah*. The storage of water was even achieved in the Fayum (Lake Moeris) for use in irrigating the delta, but big dams and their distributory canals are of recent date. In Middle Egypt the distribution of water is regulated by dams at Asyut, Aswan, and Gebel Aulia. The dam at Asyut, 833 metres long, was built between 1898 and 1902. The water, which is carried 300 km through the Ibrahimieh Canal, irrigates 100,000 hectares. The Aswan Dam, built in 1903 and twice since made higher, had its water storage improved by the additions in 1934. Its dam wall, 1,966 metres long, raises the water surface more than 20 metres. Since 1964, a second dam, built with financial help from the U.S.S.R., has raised the water level still further, completely drowning the island of Philae and its famous temples as well as other ancient monuments along the river banks. The water level in the lake has been raised from 121 metres to 175 metres above the level of the Mediterranean, and its storage volume from 5,000 million cubic metres to 164,000 million cubic metres. At the cost of this loss, some 1·2 million hectares of irrigable land will have been gained, thus raising the total Egyptian irrigated area to nearly four million hectares. In the Fayum the Bahr Yussef waters more than 130,000 hectares, most of which are more than 45 metres below sea level.

Since the beginning of the nineteenth century the delta has been planned wholly with a view to artificial irrigation. Construction began in 1825, but the main work—the Delta Dam above Cairo—was started in 1843 and was not completed until 1900. Today the channels leading water from the river above the dam radiate westwards, eastwards, and towards the middle of the delta to water nearly 1·5 million hectares with a length of more than 10,000 km. Along the whole length of this network of channels which have made flooding in hollows unnecessary, are a host of pumping devices, some primitive like the *nataleh* or the *shaduf*, others more complicated like the *sakijeh*, an overshot wheel worked by a yoke of buffaloes or camels, not to mention the more up-to-date apparatus such as steam, motor, diesel, or electric pumps. Now dam building has spread to the Sudan, where the work will enable the barren soil to be cultivated and to give a steady flow to the dams lower down in Egypt.

The building of large reservoirs to ensure a perennial supply of water seems, however, to conflict with nature's restrictions. First, by preventing natural flooding dams retain behind their walls silt that would restore the fertility of the soil year by year. Even with the help of chemical fertiliser the soil in Egypt, which in ancient times remained ever fresh, is rapidly losing its fertility. Furthermore, the water held up by the dam percolates deep down and returns to the surface of the soil downstream carrying a slight accumulation of salts that are harmful to plants. This slow poisoning of the soil, which is a danger faced by all intensely irrigated districts, calls man's attention once more to the precarious nature of tropical soils and to the limits of the most skilful engineering which may be too ambitious in its aim to free itself wholly from Nature's trammels and to make her submit to its machinery.

Effects on Society.—Agriculture in irrigated districts is distinguished from ordinary agriculture both by the variety of its produce, their high market value, and the organisation and management of the work. A common feature in all irrigation is the independence of the crops in respect to rainfall and, consequently, the possibility of making up an astonishing association of plants from temperate regions, where they are grown in winter, and tropical plants, which flourish in summer. This strange mixture is found in the lowlands of Mediterranean Spain as well as in Thessaly and Macedonia; and in the dry parts of Africa as well as in those of Asia. The half-natural, half-artificial climate makes a double harvest possible every year by accelerating the growth of plants. In Turkistan wheat is followed by beans. In some oases in the Sahara four crops of durra (*murzuk*) are sometimes reaped in a year. But this fecundity is best seen in Egypt, where harvesting goes on throughout the year.

There are three kinds of crops in Egypt. Winter crops, or *shetui*, comprise cereals (wheat or barley), beans, onions, and fodder (*bersim*). They are grown from October to May throughout Egypt. Summer crops, or *seifi*, consist mainly of rice, sugarcane, and cotton. They are grown from April to October and are found mainly in Lower and Middle Egypt. Intermediate crops, or *nili*, are grown during the Nile floods on higher ground not reached by the water. Maize, millet, and sorghum, which all ripen quickly, are the chief crops. To these three types of crops should be added others that can be grown by using well water between the months of May and August. Thus, much of the soil in Egypt yields two harvests a year. On the best soil on the delta ingenious systems of cultivation enable at least five harvests to be reaped in three years. Such a yield from crops is possible only at the price of hard work. Every region depending on irrigation is necessarily a country of advanced civilisation. It implies the incorporation in the soil of a vast sum of toil, often too of technical knowledge, and a developed political sense, and these features of high civilisation are reflected in the regulations for the use of water.

In history, law, and religion the importance assumed in men's minds by water is everywhere seen. In Arabia a historical era dates from the bursting of a dam. In Muslim lands the transformation of a barren piece of land into a productive plantation ensures its undisputed enjoyment by the pioneer and his descendants. Real wealth and, indeed, sometimes the very foundation of political power depends not on land, but on water. This vital element of wealth, which is difficult to get and to keep, can hardly be left at the free disposal of individuals. Its use implies cooperation and understanding. It is an established fact that nearly everywhere there is a tendency to the collectivisation of water owing to its connexion with the soil. This is true, for instance, of some parts of Spain. In Valencia no one can sell land without at the same time selling his rights to water in it. The prohibition applies even to the gift or exchange of a position in the irrigation rota. When one does not use one's water, the right to it passes to the community. At times of drought the authorities have discretionary powers to ration water. Nearly identical regulations are found also in North Africa and Egypt. Even in the state of Wyoming water and land cannot be sold separately.

There are, however, cases in which the system is less strict, only part of the water belonging to the community. This is the case in Alicante, where the water used for irrigation has a twofold origin. 'Old water', which comes from the natural bed of a stream and has been used for centuries, can be transferred independently of land. On the other hand, 'new water', which comes from a reservoir and represents half the total amount available, cannot be transferred independently of the land with which it is connected. It may happen too that the ownership of water is distinct from that of land. Such is the case in several 'oases' in the United States, and it is also the case in the *huertas* at Elche and Lorca. Water is bought in such cases just as if it were fertiliser. At Elche every morning a Water Exchange is held, at which users buy a turn for watering. This system, which often creates a water aristocracy as against a lower order of landowners, is almost always prejudicial to the development of agricultural communities, for the sellers of water have no interest in increasing the hydraulic constructions, though these are necessary for economic progress in agriculture.

Nowadays, the use of water is no longer left to individual initiative. A cooperative or official organisation is needed, capable in all circumstances of subordinating private interests to the general good. In Spain organisation of this kind goes back to the Moors. The administrative bodies of the *acequias* are elected by universal suffrage, and water tribunals are entrusted with summary jurisdiction to safeguard the rights of the individual. The tribunal at Valencia meets every Thursday at eleven o'clock in front of the cathedral, and its decisions are final. In Algeria there is no social body strong enough to take in hand the organisation of the irrigation system; but in Egypt the ruler has for centuries regulated the distribution of water, and this official arrangement was confirmed by the institution during the British occupation of an Irrigation Service under the Minister of Works (1881–94) to supervise the distribution of water and to make decisions in emergency. In the United States the Reclamation Service is a similar central authority symbolical of the taking into federal keeping of a resource that is vital to a large part of the nation as a whole.

This surveillance is justified by the precariousness of an economy based on irrigated crops, an artificial and insecure situation which can only be maintained by a steady, watchful human effort. Historical maps show that many centres of high civilisation based on irrigation have ceased to exist in central Asia, Iran, Iraq as well as in North Africa, Arizona, and New Mexico. This failure should not, it seems, be imputed to climatic cataclysms, but rather to the decay of civilisation that had created these 'oases' and become incapable of maintaining either the discipline indispensable to their continuance or the technique that had made it possible to set up the irrigation systems. At the present time wherever Europeans have gone, they have sought to spread cultivation over dry regions, founding their efforts on the conviction that the deserts did not constitute an unsurmountable obstacle where water could be had. The optimism that led to the view that immense regions of the earth could be made productive is more restrained today, since cultivation by means of irrigation is known to be an intensive form of agriculture, in which an excess of zeal may in a few years ruin the soil it temporarily fertilised.

THE PASTORAL ECONOMY

In many dry countries the climate does not allow agriculture to develop, and no reserve of water can make irrigated oases blossom. These regions form extensive areas of grassland on the borders of the deserts in the vast expanse of steppe, or on a small scale among the scrub and *maquis* of the Mediterranean. They are natural open spaces, treeless, but sheltering herbivorous animals—bison, antelopes, sheep, and horses—that live in herds and at times number thousands. The herds migrate periodically in search of pasture that becomes green again after rain. Immense areas of steppe run through central Asia from Manchuria to the Volga; in Africa they occupy the desert borders and the high plateaus that stretch from Ethiopia right to the Cape; and they form large expanses in North and South America and in Australia. From early times they have been centres of modes of life depending on stock-rearing. Yet there is a fundamental difference between pastoralism in the Old World and the New. In the former pastoralism is of ancient date. It developed in the course of many centuries, the first of which were before historical times. It was contemporary with the original efforts at cultivation and was based on nomadism from its very beginning. In the New World pastoralism is of recent origin. It was unknown before the arrival of the Europeans and was started by the settlers, who brought with their domestic animals the customs of a sedentary civilisation.

The Pastoral Regions of the Old World.—The pastoral regions of the Old World stretch continuously across Asia and Africa. In them man rears and makes use of animals which he has domesticated, viz. the ox, sheep, goat, ass, horse, and camel. Almost up to the present time his whole existence still rested on these animals, which gave him not only food and implements, but also the means of trade. To feed his animals, which in their wild state had been migratory, he had to seek large areas of grassland within which he arranged the movements of his herds according as the pastures became exhausted. Furthermore, as the distribution of grassland depends on the season, he had to move his animals along periodically, and this involved him in the same movement. It was in this very area of grassland that man found in a wild state the animals which were to become associated with him. These were grass-eaters adapted to travelling and accustomed to migration.

Horned cattle and smaller animals afford man a livelihood in different degrees, for they supply him with food and clothes. The sheep belongs to the steppes and avoids cold countries, regions with wet summers, and large areas of forest. Its world distribution as well as the number of its varieties prove that it was domesticated in ancient times. It continues to play an important part in central Asia, northern China, and Persia, but monsoon lands with their high summer rainfall are repellent to it. The use made of it depends on its yield of wool, meat, and milk. Wool is an essential substance in the life of pastoral peoples, for it is used to make clothes as well as the carpets that form the nomads' chief commodity of trade. Besides meat, sheep supply fat, which is indispensable to pastoralists who have neither butter nor oil. Lastly, ewe's milk is the raw material of various milk products which, when mixed with flour, form the nomad's main diet.

The ox is less important to pastoralists in Asia, but on the contrary it holds a great place in pastoral life in Africa. The long-horned zebu reared there is found from the region of the upper Nile to the South African tableland on the one hand and to Senegal on the other. The African tablelands are vast expanses of grassland, on which in the dry season there rise bush fires lit by the pastoral peoples, especially in Usambara, Unyamuesi, and Ruanda. The ox is essentially the animal of the Hottentots and the negroes in Damaraland and Namaqualand. As far as the Sakalave clans in Madagascar, southern Africa is mainly peopled by Bantu cattlemen. In western Africa, if the ancient rock sculptures of long-horned cattle are to be believed, there has been since very early times a belt of pastoral life from the upper Nile to Senegambia, with the Fulani cattlemen as the most important.

In the whole of this part of Africa cattle supply both food and clothes. Many tribes use the skins to cover their tents and to make articles of clothing, so much so that ethnologists have been able to distinguish leather Africa, that is, Africa of the pastoralists, from vegetable-fibre Africa, that is, Africa of the sedentary cultivators. The importance of cattle in the diet does not depend on the meat that they can supply. A head of cattle is indeed too precious a treasure to be lost by being eaten. Only old or injured animals are slaughtered, and if food is short, blood is taken from the cattle without their being killed. On the other hand, milk is the usual food. Africans make very little cheese, and their rancid butter is used mainly as ointment or cosmetic and not as food. Thus, milk is the chief article of diet among the Hausas and Fulani of West Africa, the Gallas and Somalis of East Africa, and the Bechuanas and Hottentots of South Africa. Among the Banyoros of Uganda milk is the food of the upper classes, on whom it is incumbent to guard and look after the herds. Flour and other vegetable foods remain the lot of the servile classes, on whom devolves the tilling of the soil. Among the Banyankoles the routine of life conforms with the needs of the cattle. The seasonal calendar, like the timetable for the day, is divided according to the minor details of the animals' lives, such as milking, driving out to pasture, and returning them to the drinking-trough.

In fact, cattle hold a major place in the material life of these African herdsmen. They have even greater social importance than their economic function would seem to warrant. Throughout the region indeed material life rests on the produce of extensive agriculture, but the primitive methods used do not confer any lasting benefits on the soil, since the fields are abandoned at the end of a certain number of years. Cattle form the true permanent wealth which can be increased indefinitely. Among these tribes ambition turns wholly on the ownership and acquisition of cattle. Cattle are the tangible form of wealth. They are cared for lovingly; their owners are devotedly attached to them; and everything connected with them is noble. Cattle form the yardstick of a man's wealth, and by them the power of chiefs is estimated. To get them wars and raids are undertaken. With them bride-money is paid, prisoners ransomed, and subventions for war contributed. In fact, they take the place of money.

To the cattle, which means wealth, is given every honour, every consideration. It is noticeable that in these pastoral peoples certain classes own the herds and reserve to themselves all the honour and profit arising from them. Agriculture marks an inferior status. To till the soil is dangerous or unhealthy, whilst everything connected with cattle is beneficent. Often women are not allowed to milk the cows: it is enough for them to wash the utensils and churn the butter. Among the Zulus all the young men and warriors tend the cattle. It is only later that men cease to look after the cattle and return from the warrior class in order to marry and live on their lands.

Lastly, power goes with cattle, Pastoralism detaches man from the land, makes him mobile and strong. Hence, herdsmen are politically dominant in pastoral countries and in Africa as a whole. Yet as the ox is less mobile and heavier than the horse, it has not been able to give African herdsmen mobility comparable with that of the powerful nomadic peoples on the steppes of Asia.

Whether a pastoral life rests on the rearing of sheep or cattle, it requires the help of beasts of burden on account of its continual movement, and these beasts are of a different species from the animals that provide food. The ox is used as a beast of burden in Africa only. It carries loads and is even ridden. Vasco de Gama saw oxen with packs and saddles in South Africa. Today the Hottentots still use oxen to carry the tents and utensils of the tribe when they move from place to place. In Damaraland the oxen that carry loads travel fast and can go for three days without fodder or water. During the winter in Senegal, when camels must move northwards, oxen are also used as beasts of burden for the season. But the most valuable auxiliaries for the herdsmen are horses and camels.

The horse is essentially the animal of the grass plains in Asia and Europe, where huge ranges developed in it qualities that were later improved in domestication. Wild horses still existed quite recently in central Asia. The animal shows great ease of adaptation, and this has enabled it to spread over vast regions from Yakutia to tropical

Africa. In Asia it is used as a beast of burden by the Kirghiz and also by the Bedawin of Arabia, among whom it spread only in the centuries preceding the rise of Islam. In Africa it is found in all the grass lands right up to the borders of the tropical forest. Introduced by Europeans into the prairies and pampas of America, it became one of the instruments of the Spanish conquest and latterly one of the best means of extensive rearing of cattle and sheep.

At the present time it still remains indispensable to the nomadic herdsmen in central Asia, who ride from childhood. The horse is needed to move round and watch over the herds and flocks and is needed too for carrying men and things during migration or transhumance. Not long ago the Kirghiz regarded the horse as a mark of wealth. Their animals grazed freely on the steppes. The economic importance of the beasts was not limited to serving as saddle horses or pack animals, for they also provided meat, and their milk, when fermented, made *kumiss*. Among the Turkmen, Bedawin, and the Mongols the horse had the same importance.

The ass and mule are more suitable than the horse for hotter and more barren lands. The ass is thought to have originated in the grasslands between the Sahara and the Sudan. It spread thence northwards through the Atlas lands and the Nile valley, where it seems to have been a domestic animal of the ancient Egyptians. The mule, which is a hybrid produced by crossing an ass with a mare, was known to the Assyrians of old. Both ass and mule are found among all pastoral peoples. The ass, which can carry loads of between 60 and 80 kg, is the commonest beast of burden in dry Mediterranean lands, and it is found in every caravan in the Sudan and among nearly all the nomadic African tribes. The mule, being stronger, carries loads of between 130 and 175 kg, and it can travel about 60 kilometres a day. It is especially useful in mountainous countries on account of its surefootedness.

Nomads and herdsmen in high mountain regions find other local means of transport. Thus, in Asia from the Himalayas to the Bryansk mountains the yak is the beast of burden of the pastoral tribes. This animal is still near its original wild state and is stubborn and unruly. It needs no attention, lives in the open air without a shelter, and is at its best in lofty regions provided that they are not covered with snow. Its chosen home is Tibet, whence it has spread into the Tarim basin. It is also found in Mongolia, the Pamirs, and the mountains bordering on Turkistan. The yak easily carries loads of 90 to 120 kg up steep slopes. It is very surefooted, an excellent climber, and typical of mountain life. It supplies Tibetan herdsmen with milk, meat, hair, and fuel in the form of dry dung.

In another dry mountain area, the punas of the Andes, there is the llama, which is the only beast of burden domesticated by the old

American peoples. It neither gives milk nor works in the fields, but it can carry loads of 30 to 50 kg at a rate of from 16 to 20 kilometres a day. Its habitat is the same as that of *ichu* grass, which it eats. Steady and docile, it was used at the silver mines in Potosí, Cerro de Pasco, and Quito. It is also the typical animal of one kind of mountain life. Its wool is used to make felt, and its droppings serve as fuel.

Neither of these animals, however, has attained an economic importance comparable with that of the camel, the beast of burden characteristic of the belt of desert stretching from the Sahara to Mongolia. As it is able to stand both great heat and great cold, the camel is physically well adapted to the climate of this immense area. On the other hand, it is very sensitive to great humidity and will not bear a rainy season such as that in western Sudan. By structure and temperament the camel is not a fast animal, for its body is massive and stiff, its hindquarters thin, and its legs slender. In practice it moves at a walk and seldom gallops. The vast majority of African camels cover between two and two and a half miles an hour. The *mehari*, or riding camel, which is specially trained, can move faster, but fast journeys require long weeks of rest and recuperation. Camels can carry loads of 200 kg and travel ten hours at a stretch. Some Syrian camels can carry 330 kg, but on the other hand, Somali camels can carry hardly more than 150 kg.

The camel has wrongly been given a reputation for abstemiousness. In reality, its existence depends on peculiar natural fodder found in the desert, consisting of hard, thorny, and sometimes salty camel-thorn, of which it eats enormous quantities. It is valuable for two reasons: first, because its food grows out in the desert, and because fodder need not be carried for it, as it must be for the horse. Secondly, it can endure extreme irregularity in times and days of feeding. In addition, it can store up a great deal of water; indeed it is a veritable water tank, swallowing 100 litres at a time; and it can then go without a drink in winter for ten days and in summer for at least three days. It is, however, a delicate creature, for it needs at least six months' pasturage a year, it often dies of mange or fly bites, and excessive fatigue or privation kills it.

It is agreed that the homeland of the camel lies in the deserts of central Asia from Persia to Mongolia. Wild camels have been met between the Tarim and Koko Nor. From there the animal reaches the country around Lake Baykal, stopping short at the humid, wooded mountains. It has also reached northwest India, but is not found in parts where the monsoon rains are heavy. Thus its range in Asia stretches over Mongolia, Manchuria, northern China, and eastern Siberia.

The Asiatic camel has two humps. The African camel, a dromedary, has a single hump and was bred from the Asiatic animal by selection. The line of demarcation between the two varieties runs through Syria and Asia Minor.

In western Asia a number of countries suit the camel admirably owing to their natural conditions. These are Asia Minor and Armenia, where the camel is the pack animal of the Kurds; Iraq and Iran, especially in Khorassan, except the wooded districts of Ghilan and Mazanderan; Afghanistan and Baluchistan; Kirghizia and Arabia, which is renowned for its camel drivers; and, lastly, Anatolia, where the introduction of the camel coincided with the retreat of Mediterranean civilisation before the advance of peoples from the eastern steppes.

The presence of the camel in Africa is of comparatively recent date. It was imported into Egypt in 525 B.C. by the Persian conquerors. It is admirably adapted to the country, and at the present day Egypt certainly has the best pack camels. For a long time it formed the limit of the western spread of the animal. In the Sahara of ancient times, the Sahara of Carthage and even of Rome, the elephant was found all along the Atlas lands. On the tracks in the desert the ox was used. When the Greeks colonised Cyrenaica, there were many horses in the country, but no camels. It was towards the fall of the Roman Empire that the camel penetrated into the western Sahara. It is known that in the reign of Justinian the camel took part in the wars with the Vandals and that the animal had reached Maghreb by then. It advanced southwards during the Middle Ages with the Zenete Berbers, who were great camel-riding nomads from Maghreb. The movement coincided with a push southwards by the white race, which pressed the Negroes back out of the Sahara and took with it a wholly new civilisation that included the cultivation of the date palm by irrigation, the use of the camel, and the presence of warrior nomads who had a wide radius of action. The influence of these movements, which were previous to the Arab invasions, were later strengthened by the Arabs themselves. In the western Sahara camels are most numerous in Sous, Arawan, Kanem, and Tibesti. The animal is also very common among the Gallas and Somalis.

In all these dry countries the camel is used essentially for transport. There it is inseparable from nomadic life, and scarcely any pastoral tribes are without the animal, even when sheep are essential for food. The camel is indeed the necessary agent of all trading. The chief means of this activity is the caravan, which has, however, been fading away in recent years in face of rail and road construction and the use of money. But some journeys are still in full swing; for instance, the salt caravans travelling between Air and Bilma, or between Zinder and Kano, not to mention the Mongol caravans making for north China.

The Nomadic System.—The pastoral mode of life, which depends on a herd or flock to provide food and on other animals necessary to a life of movement, is essentially characterised by its mobility. Life consists of continual movement to find food for the animals. The times and stages of migrations are determined by the distribution of pasture and places for watering. Hence, the pace of migrations, their length, their duration, and their periodicity vary enormously according to whether the nomads are Asiatic Mongols, Kirghiz, Kalmuks, or Bedawin, whose movements are fixed between the desert lowlands and the peripheral mountains, or else African nomads from Maghreb and South Africa, for whom nomadism does not play so important a part.

The whole life of these people bears the mark of mobility. The dwelling is portable and is carried about. In nomadic life the home is a tent. The proportion of fixed abodes decreases as soon as the climate becomes drier and makes cultivation problematical. Baggage is reduced to a minimum, and therefore the tent furniture is of primitive simplicity, consisting of a chest, straw mats, rugs, and jars. Thus, pastoral tribes are able to enjoy great ease of movement. Their communities are mobile and scattered, for the pastures afford only limited resources. The tribal settlement is a little isolated group of tents temporarily pitched, easily struck and packed up. Such an organisation enables only a small human community to find its food. Until a short while ago the country around Lob Nor had only 300 inhabitants, and these were scattered in half a score of camps.

In every region nomadic migration is regular and orderly in character. Nothing is left to someone's discretion or to chance. The traditional ranges are fixed according to a series of watering-points and pasture. In spite of the absence of all visible boundary lines, these ranges are the common, but exclusive, property of certain communities. Violation of these rights led formerly to war and nowadays to unending lawsuits accompanied by feuds. The same rules govern the use of the pastures, to which certain tribes in successive waves during their migration take their horses and transport animals, their oxen, and, lastly, their sheep and goats, and are content with what has been left by those who went before. This discipline, which is due to the need for adaptation to the environment, explains why nomadic communities are strongly hierarchical and both in Asia and Africa have been able to form nuclei of political activity.

Sometimes the herdsmen's resources are so precarious and so monotonous that they are forced to look for means of livelihood in occupations other than stock-rearing. Uncertainty is due, first, to the severity of winters or to droughts that kill off whole herds or flocks. Then the animals can no longer be counted on for food or for trading. But the resources are always incomplete, and vegetables must be added to animal food. Hence, although nomadic herdsmen turn up their noses at agriculture, they often try to combine a primitive kind of extensive cultivation with their wandering life. Several Asiatic communities sow corn in spring, leave the field in summer when they take their animals up to the hills, and return for the harvest in autumn on coming down to the plains. But this type of cultivation yields little and remains precarious. Accordingly, the nomad, being always afraid of famine, is led at times to take by force from his neighbours what nature does not make sure of giving him. The result is raiding and war. But as a rule the herdsman tries to get complementary supplies by trade or by earning wages for the carriage of goods.

Marauding and raiding have always been one of the features of nomadic life. In Asia herdsmen have in every age been tempted by the barley fields in oases. The raids by Turkmen into Persia and those of the Mongols into northern China in many ways resembled those of the Kirghiz, whose very name means 'marauder'. In Africa all the Saharan tribes have practised marauding. Hence the agelong hostility of the peasant towards the nomad, which is one of the most widespread of human feelings.

Furthermore, the practice of violence is not only due to immediate necessity. It has often been the aim of a knowledgeable and efficient organisation and in the course of history has ended in the domination of sedentary people by nomads and to the formation of states. The nomad is a soldier ever ready to defend his pastures or his herds. His system of life and movement contains a principle of political coordination. In Asia the Mongols under Gengis Khan and Timur, the Manchus, Arabs, and, later, the Turks have formed great empires which were politically very strong. In Africa the Hycsos, Gallas, and Fulani have also formed temporary aristocratic military States.

In all ages the need to trade has bound herdsmen to cultivators. There are plenty of examples of such a symbiosis. Bedawin have always exchanged their stuffs for cereals. In the same way the Mongols have traded with the Chinese, getting tea and millet in exchange for hides and wool. In Africa the Saharan tribes used to barter salt and cloth with cultivators in the Tell for cereals and dates. The nomad would retain some valuable commodities like salt, gum, resin, balm, and incense, which he collected in the course of his peregrinations.

Local trade often brought on transactions on a greater scale. The large number of transport animals in the nomad's possession favoured the development, and the position of the belt of dry, pastoral lands between the temperate and wet tropical regions caused it very early to become an area of general intercourse and endowed it with a civilising function which it could not have had from its own poor resources. Thus, in Africa trade between the Sudan and the Mediterranean across the Sahara was able to follow long routes from Timbuktu on the one side to Tripoli or Benghazi on the other, where the trail passed through date-growing oases over which Saharan nomads had established domination, especially in Tuat and Fezzan. The goods carried in this trade have varied through the ages, cotton, guns, salt, ivory, and gold dust being its most constant articles. Trade in slaves, ostrich feathers, and kola nuts were added from time to time. Similarly, in Asia an ancient caravan trade went on between Russia and Bukhara, between China and the West, and between India and the Mediterranean. These trade routes ran through prosperous towns like Bagdad, Samarkand, Tashkent, and Damascus, all of which were big markets in touch with the desert and owing their prosperity to the political domination of the pastoral peoples. It was the control of these main arteries of universal trade and their skilful use that ensured the power and lasting character of the great empires founded by the pastoral peoples.

A glance at the pastoralists in Asia and Africa shows that the ox has not given rise to a mode of life exactly similar to that due to sheep. Whilst in northern Africa, where Asiatic influence is strongly marked, the agriculture and nomadic modes of life have been traditionally separate from each other, no such specialisation exists in the rest of the continent. In fact the pastoral mode of life of cattlemen involves only movements necessary for finding pasture, and these are therefore not displacements of the whole population with all the people and all the goods belonging to the tribe. Rather than true nomadism, it is mainly a kind of transhumance with only the herdsmen of the tribe moving away with the herds and their camp, or *kraal*; and there is almost always a centre in which live cultivators and where the chiefs have their residences. For instance, the Masai move only within defined districts and then only when the state of the pasture requires it. The perimeter of the area depends on circumstances, or the resources, and the season. The same thing happens among the Bechuanas. Only at the edges of dry scrub, as for instance in the Hottentot country, can movements anything like migrations be seen and described as true nomadism.

Development of the Pastoral Mode of Life.—The pastoral mode of life is therefore a definitely constituted type that has arisen out of precise geographical conditions and was formed in very early times. In some respects it gives the impression of being rigidly unchangeable, and yet it is seen to be everywhere in some slight association with the agricultural mode of life. Like all human matters, the pastoral mode has been unable to remain in isolation or to escape change under influences from without. It should not be regarded as a stage in the development of civilisation, but as a peculiar mode of life due to geographical conditions in dry lands and formed and developed in contact with nature by a special process.

The pastoral mode of life spread gradually over vast regions where it found favourable conditions. It seems to have begun in central Asia and eastern Europe, where it has been found to have been established at a very early period among the nomadic Semites, the terror of Babylonian kings, the Hycsos who conquered Egypt, and the Scythians who were described by Herodotus. History records invasions eastwards by nomads, beyond the Great Wall by Mongols surging westwards, and from the fourth to the fifteenth century by Turks, Hungarians, and Bulgars. There has also been an advance southwards in Africa by various waves of Arabs. But it would seem that these movements did not go deeply into east and central Africa, no doubt because there already existed in those countries a pastoral mode of life that was less mobile, more deeply rooted, and based on the use of cattle. In most of the vast regions the pastoral mode of life has remained unchanged for thousands of years, but today many signs indicate that the old framework is cracking and that a new type of life is trying to awaken those barren lands. The herdsman's zone is in contact all round with agricultural countries, which have long exercised no influence; but since the West has become a promoting centre of high and progressive civilisation armed with improved methods and implements meant to increase the productivity of the soil, it tends to push back the pastoral mode wherever it comes into contract with it and more particularly on the edges where the climate enables agriculture to gain a footing in place of pasturage. In this border zone where the two modes are face to face the better equipped, the more productive, and more diligent gets the better of the traditional, hidebound mode.

In Europe pastoral nomadism has been replaced by agriculture in the steppes of Russia as well as in the plains of Hungary. In Asia it has been thrust back by two great agricultural civilisations working from two different directions, the Chinese and Russians, which have gradually converted the Buryats, Turkmen, Kirghiz from the pastoral mode of life. In Africa retreat is on the whole less noticeable. Yet it is very evident in North Africa, where the progress in civilisation resulting from colonisation and the increase in population have caused a rapid decrease in the number of sheep. Horse and camel breeding is also on the downward trend. The cultivated area has spread on to the borders of the steppes and around artesian wells. At the same time the population is becoming more settled, for the *gourbi* (mud hut) and the resettlement village are taking the place of the nomad's tent, whilst the coastal towns are attracting the survivors of the old nomadic tribes to other occupations.

However, it does not seem as if the pastoral mode of life is on the way to complete eclipse, for the expansion of the cultivated area is limited by the need of water. Grazing is the only resource in certain regions in which the steppe is still intact. The herdsman's life is rough, but improvements can be made in the conditions in which animals exist, and consequently in their economic value. Though the pastoral mode of life is a climatic necessity, nomadism on the other hand is not an inescapable consequence at a stage in civilisation that affords man a stronger hold on nature. In these days, the grass-lands in the New World and the southern hemisphere contain a pastoral mode of life that is adapting itself to a settled life.

In these new countries the modern type of pastoralism also depends on cattle and sheep rearing. The sheep has been the means of developing wide empty spaces in Australia, New Zealand, South Africa, and America. The Argentine affords a very typical instance of the character and development of one of these great pastoral lands. Sheep-rearing has spread over the south and southeast of the Pampa in the Provinces of Buenos Aires, Pampa Central, and Río Negro. The importance of sheep, however, remained less than that of cattle so long as cultivation did not come to the help of grazing. In its natural state the country was one of virgin grass land, with tough, perennial grass and scrubby appearance forming *pasto duro*. Gradually, after being grazed by horses and especially by cattle *pasto tierno* was formed, composed of fine, soft, annual grasses. Then it was that sheep came in and in their turn influenced the cultivation of fields of lucerne, which gave enormous quantities of fodder. These provinces, however, were given up more and more to cultivation, and on account of this the number of sheep declined. But this development provoked an increase in the number of sheep farther south, right into Patagonia and Tierra del Fuego, where sheep easily endure the harsh conditions of the climate.

Like sheep, cattle have given rise in South America and Queensland to a peculiar type of pastoral life. On the eastern side of the Mexican tableland, on the *llanos* of Venezuela, and on the *campos* of Ceará there prevails as in Africa a hot climate and an alternation of hot and dry seasons, the latter of which brings on occasional crises of drought. In these regions cattle have become the means of a pastoral mode of life. The herds belong to large landowners who have their residences on the *estancias* or *fazendas* from which they derive their wealth. Sometimes too these *estancieros* live in a town, paying only seasonal visits to the ranch after the fashion of big land-owners in the days of the Merovingians in mediaeval Europe.

The care of the ranch then falls to a steward, a *vaqueiro*, whose life is spent on horseback going round the estate and inspecting the animals. Unlike the pastoral system in the Old World, the system in the New World was established with very precise commercial aims. In Brazil the cattle were reared to supply the fresh meat needed for the labourers on the sugarcane or coffee plantations. Stock-rearing therefore arose from an indispensable economic interdependence between the coast and the scrub inland. The first roads joining the coast to its backland were tracks followed by the animals moving from their native scrub to the plantations. Today pastoral life is falling off here too as cultivation and plantations advance. In the State of São Paulo, as in that of Minas Geraes, every *fazenda* keeps a herd consisting of beasts of burden and milch cows. The old form of pastoral life survives only in the interior of Ceará, where the climate is particularly dry and where the proximity of coastal towns and plantation centres in Amazonia, all great consumers of meat, has maintained pastoral conditions right up to our own times.

Distribution and Growth of Animal Populations

| | World (millions) | | Growth | Distribution in 1974 (%) | | |
	1913	1974	(%)	Africa	N. America	S. America
Cattle	259	1,182	330	10·9	12·2	22·6
Sheep	419	1,053	152	12·1	2·6	12·0
Pigs	167	687	312	0·6	10·4	15·0
Horses	*	64	—	5·3	14·0	36·8
Donkeys and Mules	*	51	—	22	—	32

CHAPTER 8

LIFE IN MOUNTAIN AND COASTAL REGIONS

In every climate, in every region in the world, mountains and seas present to man's activities areas with advantages and drawbacks that appreciably modify the general conditions of the surroundings, and thus form little worlds whose life is organised in relative independence and in which occur nuclei of peculiar civilisations. All over the world there are peoples on whom life among mountains has imposed economic straitjackets and a whole social organisation. Mountains have cradled states and kept them independent. In the Andes, as in the Alps, mountain states have attained a degree of political strength and at certain periods have even been able to extend their dominion over the plains below. But mountains have always given rise to closed societies, self-centred, and preserving old customs. They have often served as a refuge for people driven back from the lowlands by conquerors who have had better developed techniques.

On the other hand, the sea has witnessed the birth of communities whose characteristic function has been to increase intercourse between various peoples. Thalassocracies, whose institutions and power have been based on the exploitation of the sea and the domination of ocean routes, have never known the isolation which mountain regions have imposed on their people. Phoenicians and Greeks swarmed over the whole periphery of the Mediterranean, and the English have established centres of Anglo-Saxon culture on the shores of every ocean in the world. The civilisation of maritime peoples is essentially one that spreads universally.

MOUNTAIN REGIONS IN THE TEMPERATE BELT

Conditions favourable to human life fall away and disappear with height above the sea. This general rule has scarcely any exception in temperate lands, where by definition mountains form a cold region. But it in no way applies to mountain regions in the tropics, for there the highlands are more favourable than the surrounding lowlands; nor does it apply to mountain regions in an arid country, for there the highlands are well watered and are often sources of supply for the lowlands. Such an advantage implies an increase in resources at least at certain heights.

In temperate lands the dominant feature of the mountain way of life is that a livelihood can no longer be had from corn cultivation, but is got from grass that enables animals to be reared. The climate does not allow cereals to ripen. In the French Alps there are more than a hundred *communes* in which corn takes thirteen months to mature. Seed is sown in July or August, and the harvest is reaped in September of the following year. At times, before sowing his seed the farmer is obliged to melt the snow artificially by spreading over it soot, oats waste, or earth. The cultivable soil is poor, for it is constantly being eroded owing to the steepness of the gradients. Besides, scarcity of soil imposes especially difficult conditions, for it may happen that the mountaineer has to carry back by himself or with the help of a mule the soil that has slipped downhill or been swept to the foot of the slope by the run-off of water. The need to protect soil from erosion is greatest at the bottoms of the artificial terraces on which walls built at intervals hold up tiny plots, as in Valais and the Italian Alps as well as in the Himalayas, Tibet, and Yemen. These precious plots are kept free from man's dwellings, which are built off the flat ground on rocky slopes in the Alps, the Crimea, and the Himalayas, as well as in the mountains of south China. So, whenever they can, mountain people give up this difficult and disappointing form of agriculture. Long without roads, these countries had to be self-sufficient. As mountain communities can expect nothing from without, they have to grow rye and oats for bread, hemp for making underclothing, and they have to rear sheep so as to have wool for making warm clothes. Such was the old way of life in the Alps of Savoy. But with the opening up of road systems and the penetration into the mountains of the means of transport, this ancient autarkic mode of life became disorganised, and the mountain region became able to specialise in stockrearing and the forms of pastoral life for which the luxuriant grass is favourable. The active competition of the lowlands, which produce corn more cheaply, led to the progressive abandonment of the old crops, since starvation was no longer to be feared. The highest plots were abandoned first; but the bottoms were changed into lucerne fields and used for fodder crops, and corn cultivation retreated before the advance of grass.

Mountain regions in temperate lands are essentially grass-producing. Supplies of grass are got in two ways. First, grass grows in the valley bottoms and on the lower slopes near the villages on land formerly cultivated. This has solved the serious problem of the mountaineer by supplying winter fodder for his animals from 1 November to 15 May. The production of hay for this requires great care. In some districts within the Alps in which summer is warm and dry, irrigation is necessary. Hence the careful construction of irrigation dykes to lead water from springs across gullies on wooden scaffolding. Moreover, it is sometimes difficult to dry hay and to store it without loss. Hence the construction of driers on the sunny *adret* slopes. It may even happen that to get more ample supplies of hay, hill pastures far from the villages on the very border of the forest are scythed. To carry the hay to the villages would be too much trouble, so it is piled up in ricks or stored in huts. In winter when snow covers the ground, gangs of peasants take it down to the village byres on sledges.

The second type of grassy area is the hill pastures, which are extensive stretches of turf above the forest belt. They are known as 'alps' in the original meaning of the word, or else as 'the mountain'. In the French Alps these natural pastures in the mountains cover more than 300,000 hectares. In Oisans they form 34 per cent of the land surface. In high valleys in the Pyrenees two-thirds, and in some cases three-quarters, of the area of the cantons consist of mountain pastures, here known as *estives* or *estibères*, which are to be found especially between altitudes of 1,800 and 2,000 metres. These mountain pastures have short grass dotted with beautiful mountain flowers: anemones, gentians, and rhododendrons. The aromatic grass gives an excellent flavour to the milk, and it is to these pastures that herds that have spent the winter in the village are taken every summer.

In both the Swiss and French Alps the herds usually go up to the mountain pastures about the middle of June and stay there until the end of September or at times even the end of October, according to the locality. In some districts the herds are taken twenty or thirty kilometres from their villages, which is indeed a long journey. Between 15 and 24 June, according to the village and year, the animals pass through the village streets to the merry tinkle of their bells. Cows from the villages near the mountains go straight up to the *alps*, those coming from distant villages are sometimes rested at the foot of the mountains. Sheep also take part in the movement. Those from hillfoot villages are often joined by those from a distance, sometimes from low ground in Provence or other Mediterranean districts. Once the animals have all reached the alps, they are not put together indiscriminately or no matter where. The cows are given the best pastures, which are found in hollows and on level ground where the grass is richer and softer. The steeper parts, where the grass is less luscious, are reserved for calves and heifers that are destined ultimately to be slaughtered. Lastly, the sheep, which are often left untended, spend the summer on the steep slopes of cirques and rocky parts near the mountain tops.

Most of the inhabitants stay at home to make hay and do not leave the permanent villages in the valleys. Only a few skilled men go up to the mountains to watch over the herds, milk the cows, and make cheese and butter. In Tarentaise there are not more than eight such men, including the *fruitier*, who makes butter and cheese and is the highest paid; the *pachonnier*, who moves the pegs to which the cows are tied at night and spreads over the ground the dung they have left; the *boitier*, who looks after the mules used for carrying food; the *maitre berger*, who with the help of a few youngsters controls the movements of the herd; and, lastly, a *ménagère*, who attends to the cooking and feeding of the party.

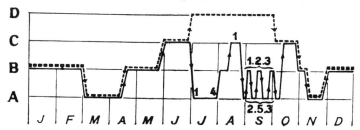

FIG. 4.—TRANSHUMANCE IN AN ALPINE VALLEY (VAL D'ANNIVIERS, SWITZERLAND).

Continuous lines indicate residence and migrations of the whole family; broken lines those of the flock and shepherd (a thin line for the time spent by the flock in the open, a thick line for the time spent in stables). **1.** Hay harvest. **2.** Ploughing. **3.** Sowing. **4.** Cereal harvest. **5.** Grape harvest. **A.** Valley dwelling. **B.** House on alpine shelf. **C.** Hill. **D.** Mountain.

These mountaineers lead a busy life. Between 2 and 3 a.m. they are all up to milk the cows, an operation that lasts till 4 a.m. Then they loose the animals so as to allow them to graze in such a way that a different, but clearly defined, area is grazed every day. About 9 a.m. they tie up the cows to stakes near the spot where they spent the night. At 4 p.m. there is a second milking. About 5 p.m. the cows are untied and put out to graze till about 6.30 p.m., when they are tied up again for the night.

The summer is not wholly spent in the same place, for the pastures must all be used, and these stretch out very far in some cases. So the party moves with its animals, some times going up, at other times going down, so that all the grass is grazed on every part of the mountain. Each successive centre of grazing is called a *remue*. In this way moves are made from *remue* to *remue* until September, when the alpine season ends, and men and animals move down to their homes. At the beginning of September some animals are sent to market and sold. The others stay on the alps until Michaelmas (29 September), after which the high valleys go to sleep till June in the next year.

Thus, the life of the mountain party is a kind of periodical shifting from winter quarters, where the animals live in byres and eat stored fodder, to the summer pastures, where the beasts live in the open on the alps. This simple shuttle movement assumes that the men have two separate dwellings, a permanent one in the village below and one in a hut above. Often, however, the simple movement is disturbed and its routine complicated, for there are intermediate stages planned to make use of all the resources spread out on the mountain sides, so that between the villages and mountains there are often areas that are temporarily occupied and in which, whether going up or down, the party stops with its animals. This kind of routine is peculiar to mountain life in temperate regions in Europe and in Asia, except the Far East, where pastoral life has not developed on the *hara* in the mountains of Japan.

To make use of the abundant grass peculiar to lofty mountains in the temperate belt rules and usages of a communal nature have come into practice. In the Alps and Pyrenees the high mountain areas are in most cases the common property of rural communities. Such commons form 51 per cent of the pastures in the high Alps and 42 per cent in the Alps of Savoy. In the western Pyrenees commons sometimes occupy two-thirds and even three-fourths of the area. In some places the *estives* are common to all the *communes* in the same valley, the documents that confirm their rights dating from the thirteenth and fourteenth century.

The system of common rights involves the use of the mountain pastures by everyone in proportion to the size of the area cultivated by land owners. The principle is that no one should pasture more animals than he can feed through the winter; but he is entitled to give away or let out his customary rights. Hence, communal use takes on various forms. Sometimes the administration is directly undertaken by the *communes*, which fix the dates at which animals are to be taken to the mountain pastures, maintain the roads, engage and pay the herdsmen, and distribute the profit from the animals among the owners. In other cases the use of the pastures is entrusted to a man known as a *montagnard*, who unites under his management a certain area of pasture, to part of which he has a right of user and part of which he rents, and on the pasture he puts animals of his own, others that he hires, and others that belong to the *communes* interested. In other cases, again, the use of the pasture is undertaken directly by each man with rights on the common land, and he takes his animals to the mountain pastures himself.

This careful organisation, which is the one used in the Alps, has had neither the time nor the means to establish itself in all the mountain regions in the Old World. Yet it represents a mode of life like that of the pastoralists. The necessity to move a herd so as to use the resources of a district completely has made it vulnerable to industrialisation as well as to economic developments that have taken modern techniques right into the mountains. The transhumance of sheep from the Scottish Lowlands to the Highlands ended long ago. Large streams of migration have also ceased between the Carpathians and the neighbouring lowlands, and they have greatly reduced their radius between the Pyrenees and the lowlands of Aquitaine, between the Alps and Provence, and between the Turanian plains and its peripheral mountains.

But though mountain regions are losing a little of their pastoral function, they are keeping their specialisation in intensive stock-rearing in Europe. With the old system of seasonal movement to and fro between lowland and mountain becoming less active and extensive than formerly; with the more modern system of developing the cultivation of artificial fodder crops on the lowlands and in the lower valleys, commerce is certainly gaining the upper hand in the farms. The sale of animals and milk products to consumers in big towns and large industrial centres has enriched once poor districts, which have given up cereal cultivation and deliberately turned to dairy produce.

Owing to this modern way of pastoral life and to this use of animals, the mountain regions in Europe look like country districts devoted to their fields, pastures, and animals. And yet this impression is not wholly true at the present time. In less than a hundred years a new mode of life has broken the traditional framework of patriarchal life in some of the mountain regions and has penetrated right to the bottoms of the most remote valleys which now resound to the hum of machines and factories. In the Alps this change has been wrought by hydro-electricity.

It was in this area in Europe that mountain industry first began. As early as 1869 a man named Berges had the idea of replacing the old mill wheel in his paper factory by a turbine worked by water power. The power was had by using a high waterfall run in an artificial channel. In 1884 after Marcel Deprez had found the way to convey electric current generated by water power over a considerable distance, the Alps (in France, Switzerland, Germany, Austria, and Italy) acquired a new industry. In this mountain region, whose life was still isolated, this new form of power created the most-up-to-date activity based on electro-metallurgy together with electro-chemistry. The northern Alps became the main source of refined metals and chemical products.

The old mountain industries due to the long periods of leisure enforced by winter were now invigorated. Weaving and the manufacture of paper and cardboard passed from the stage of domestic industry to that of the factory. Electric power was now set to work sewing machines in glove factories, pulverisers in cement works, and sawmills. Food factories, farms, and cooperative dairies were able to work their separators and churns by means of an adaptable, powerful, and cheap form of power. New industries have, moreover, turned some Alpine valleys into veritable laboratories using high temperatures from electric arcs or the reactions of an electrolytic tank. Aluminium, fine steel, sodium, and nitric acid, calcium carbide, cyanamide, and chlorine are now used in synthetic industries which complete and perfect the industrial equipment in the mountains.

From the mountain districts electricity was soon carried to the lowlands. Current from the French Alps works all the factories in Lower Dauphiny, Lyon, and Saint Etienne and lights the towns in Provence and the Riviera. Power houses in the Swiss and Austrian Alps supply current to 99 per cent of the railways. Thus, in modern times the European mountain region exports power as well as food products to the surrounding lowlands. This once poor, wild region has become one of the most useful and active portions of civilised countries.

The increasingly complete occupation of mountain regions is the result of long adaptation and integration in scientifically used areas. Settlement in the mountains assumes therefore a high standard of civilisation, energy, and time. Indeed the Alps and Jura were settled only at a fairly recent time, and the Vosges were systematically settled as late as the thirteenth century. In the United States and Australia the mountains are still condemned to solitude. The fact is that in these climates mountain regions are rough and unattractive to man, imposing on settlement hardships and restrictions.

The first of these restrictions stems from the decrease in resources with height above the sea. Hence, in a general way the limit of permanent human habitation coincides with that of the growth of cereals. On it are found the last permanent villages, the villages in which the mountaineers live in winter, the *Kirchdörfer* or *Winterdörfer* of the Germanic countries. But pastoral occupations involve temporary settlements. In the Val d'Anniviers there are *chalets* as high as 2,485 metres above the sea; the *casere* in the Venetian Alps reach up to 1,500 and even 1,800 metres. Higher up exceptional circumstances unconnected with rural life are needed for human settlement to take place. In the Erzgebirge, Carinthia, Scotland, and the Rocky Mountains, settlement has been due to mining above the zone of optimum resources. In the French Pyrenees talc and iron mines stop work in winter. Higher still there are only observatories or the hospices that accompany the ways across the mountains.

Other conditions are no less restrictive. First, there are spots to be avoided. These are often valley bottoms that are marshy or flooded by torrents in spate or that suffer from inversions of temperature causing hard frost and the stagnation of layers of frozen fog. The paths of avalanches must also be avoided, for these movements of masses of snow tend to follow the same valleys, which are accordingly shunned by villages and houses.

On the other hand, some places are sought after; for instance, alluvial fans, which consist of masses of alluvium laid down by torrents where lateral valleys enter big valleys. In them the surface is raised and looks over the bottom of the main valley, so that villages are not afraid of floods. But the chief virtue is the soil which is friable and fertile and in which the peasant sows his seed, grows his vegetables, and makes good hay. Other good spots are terraces, the flat spaces that occur on the valley slopes as natural tiers, making level stretches with a gentle slope and good soil. They are all occupied by groups of houses placed one above the other on the slopes right up in some cases to the upper limit of the terrace.

Open sunny places are most sought after. In the whole of the temperate belt there is a great difference between south-facing slopes, which have sunshine in winter, and those facing north, which do not see the sun in winter and are colder. The former are known as *adrets* in the Alps and *soulanes* in the Pyrenees, whilst the latter are termed *ubacs* in the Alps. In consequence of the difference the *ubacs* are often wooded, but, on the contrary, the sunfacing *adrets* are veritable espaliers on which snow melts soonest, and the slopes are climbed by houses spaced out so as not to screen each other.

Owing to these influences habitation is sparse and well separated. There are no big villages, but only hamlets and little clusters of houses near the land cultivated by their occupants. But complete isolation is not favoured by the very nature of mountain regions, for it is necessary to live near the precious cultivable soil, and there must not be too much dispersion since the animals must often be collected and taken to pasture by a communal herdsman. In former days in order to economise fuel in high Alpine villages there was a common oven in which each household took its turn to bake bread. Besides, from November to April men must cooperate to keep roads open and to make paths through the snow.

The mountain dwellers here, although closely packed, occupy but a small proportion of the area and form a sparse population. To-day, industrialisation and progress in stock-rearing in stalls to supply the demands of the dairy industry have emphasised the contrast between the fairly densely peopled lower valleys and the higher areas which are now nearly empty and are being further emptied owing to progressive discontinuance of large scale transhumance.

During the second half of the twentieth century, however, the traditional economy of mountain areas in the northern hemisphere temperate zone, and especially in Europe, has been upset by new economic elements having their origin in the extraordinary growth in the size and population of towns and industrial agglomerations, that in turn has necessitated the provision of holiday, tourist, and sports areas and centres in hitherto sparsely populated regions. The mountains have thus become devoted to tourism and winter sports. The Canadian and American Rockies and the Alps in Europe are the best examples of these transformations that have made the mountains, at least seasonally and particularly in winter, the scene of a considerable influx of people and economic activity. To perform these functions, the mountains have had to be properly equipped with hotels, chalets, prepared ski-runs, chair-lifts, and cable-cars. Hitherto abandoned during the winter months, the high mountains now attract tourists by the thousand, and these activities have often arrested the tendency for de-population and emigration. Here is an admirable example of remote effects in the temperate zone produced by the growth of population in the densely-peopled areas and the expansion of industry and the tertiary sector.

MOUNTAIN REGIONS IN HOT LANDS

Life in mountain regions is quite different in hot lands, where highlands form the main habitable areas. In Ethiopia, Peru, Mexico, East Africa, and southern Arabia the uplands form a specially favoured area. The only exceptions to this rule are the rice lands, in which the cultivation of a particular cereal has moulded a special type of civilisation hostile to stock-rearing and to the mountain environment. Natural factors that make mountain regions unfavourable in the temperate belt give advantages in similar regions in hot or dry countries, where altitude causes physical conditions favourable to human settlement.

As one goes upwards, the lower temperature gradually moderates tropical heat, as can be seen from the figures for Anahuac:

	Height in metres	Jan. temp. °C	July temp. °C	Mean annual temp. °C
Ulua	12	21·5	27·4	24·7
Jalapa	1,400	13·0	19·0	17·3
Mexico City	2,260	11·0	17·7	15·4

The figures for East Africa are similar. Whilst the mean annual temperature at Mombasa is 27·2° C, at Tabora, 1,230 metres above the sea, it is only 22·6° C.

Another major factor is the rapid rate at which the soil absorbs and radiates the sun's heat in a dry and rarified atmosphere. As in mountain regions in the temperate belt, inversion of temperature takes place in the valleys, which makes the local climate still healthier in some enclosed basins and narrow valleys, especially in Peru.

In the tropics, moreover, highlands escape from the main body of tropical air, however little they reach or rise above the contour for

1,000 metres. They are cooled by the trade winds just when breezes blowing alternately from high tablelands to deep depressions and vice versa stress the difference between the mountains and their surroundings.

There exists nearly everywhere a zone of maximum precipitation at varying heights. Recorded at 800 metres in Java, it rises to 1,300 metres in the Himalayas, and reaches a mean of 1,000 metres in the tropics. Above this the air becomes drier and drier, thus favouring a more direct influence of radiation on the soil and the vegetation above the cloud ceiling.

The distribution of temperature and rainfall explains the classic zoning of the belts of vegetation on tropical mountain sides. On most of the lofty mountains in East Africa there is parkland up to 1,000 metres, after which follows dense tropical forest between 2,000 and 3,000 metres, and higher up a zone of heather falling off gradually into cold, patchy grassland. Cultivation, which finds favourable areas on the upper belt, has very high limits. Maize, barley, and the potato, and in some places rice and cassava, not to mention useful plants like coffee and tea bushes, grow high up between the edge of the great forest and the coldest or driest ground near the summits. In mountain regions in Central America and on the slopes of the tropical Andes the *tierras frías* and *tierras templadas* form a zone of far denser population compared with that of the *tierras calientes* on the lower slopes, where the vegetation is luxuriant.

These conditions explain quite naturally the restriction of permanent human dwellings to the uplands, where the greatest advantage is to be found. Every extensive mountain range in Asia, Africa, or America may present a scene of its own, but they all show the common characteristic of having on their highlands groups of agropastoral peoples who have attained on the spot to a high degree of material and politico-social civilisation, formed dense settlements, built up large collections of persons with urban functions and behaviour, and often even exercised political or feudal ascendancy over the peoples in the lower valleys, whom harsher local conditions have kept in an inferior state of development. Thus, the highlands of Cameroon, Kenya, Tanzania, Madagascar, Ethiopia, and Yemen form fertile, densely peopled islands in the midst of a wilder kind of country over which man has gained little control. Such wild country may take the form of luxuriant tropical forests in the Kolla district of Ethiopia or in the valleys in eastern Madagascar; it may be dry scrub in East Africa, and bare and rocky desert in lowland Yemen.

Thus in tropical mountain regions there is a real inversion of the diagram of settlements and human activity as it exists in temperate mountain regions. Some of those that have served as refuges for defeated peoples or have been more attractive than the inhospitable lowlands to the greed of foreign invaders have been able to reach abnormal density of population and to be overpopulated at the present time. Surrounded by arid lands which were for long the ranges of pastoral nomads, the mountains in Kabylia and Lebanon still contain densities of 100 persons to the square kilometre. The same density is found in the high valleys on Mount Kilimanjaro.

These isolated highland communities, however, restrict their activities to agriculture and to keeping animals nearby. Though they afford refuge and offer promising areas for settlement, mountain regions in hot countries have remained impermeable to industry. Cut off from the life of the world by regions of thick scrub or deserts that are difficult to cross and which keep away newcomers, they still form closed worlds away from modern economic development, and they seem never to have attempted the progressive adaptation and specialisation that characterises the history of temperate mountain ranges.

MAN AND THE SEA

The sea is naturally an inhospitable and hostile element to man. On the coasts there are dangerous tides and storms, and the coastline itself is the continental frontier beyond which there is only the vast, barren, inaccessible, and fatal ocean. But the sea is also a fishpond swarming with animal life and affording inexhaustible supplies of food. To take advantage of these man merely explores the waters in order to catch his prey. In this way a whole mode of life has developed from contact with the sea. It is all the more strongly marked and efficient because it has overcome the dangers of the sea and freed man from his ties with the land.

The forms of human modes of life based on the use of the wealth of the sea fall into three groups or zones differing essentially from one another by their degree of dependence on the land, and consequently by the development of their ties with the sea. The most humble and most dependent on the land consists of collecting what the sea leaves or throws up on to the shore. Others more advanced tap the riches of coastal waters without trusting to the sea out of sight of land and always avoiding the dangers of the open ocean. Lastly, others venture afar across the waves, as they have more or less perfected their engines and boats for the mastery of the ocean. Hence, the utilisation of the wealth of the sea should be seen from two view-points: as a source of food through fishing and as a pathway along which run the great routes of commerce and world trade.

Gathering.—To some extent everywhere the seashore is a field of valuable crops that man may gather without danger and almost without trouble. In every climate throughout the world human communities live on matter collected from the sea. From very early in the history of man's evolution people living by the seaside have fed exclusively on animals left on the beaches by the tide. Neolithic man has left traces in kitchen middens found, for instance, on the Jutland peninsula and even more on the Danish islands. He probably lived only on jetsam, for he seems in fact not to have known how to cultivate the land, rear animals, or work metals. Similar heaps of shells on the coast of Brazil (*sambaquis*) indicate the same primitive diet in contemporary people.

Along the coast where the range of the tide is great enough to lay bare wide strips at ebb, the sea leaves behind large numbers of creatures. The phenomenon occurs on the greatest scale on the shores of the Narrow Seas in northwestern Europe, where the rise and fall of the tides has a range in some places of more than 10 metres. On the wide stretch left bare by the ebb, and deluged with heat and light there is a swarm of living things.

On the rocky coasts of the English Channel and the Atlantic there are viscous masses of sea-wrack on the beaches, where long sea-whipcord lies tangled. Sheltered by such plants, hiding in cracks in the rocks, and in pools swarming with food of many kinds live innumerable colonies of molluscs, crustacea, and fish. There too in holes in the rocks just below low water mark are found lobsters, crayfish, and large edible crabs. Somewhat higher up there are swarms of shellfish, crabs, and shrimps. In this zone the fishing that feeds so many poor persons is done on foot. There too are found oysters and mussels, which, whether gathered or cultivated, have given rise to real industries. The cultivation of shellfish is a triumph of ingenious acclimatisation, for in their natural state oysters and mussels live in very clear water. For cultivation they are moved into beds where the water is brackish near river mouths and where there are the best conditions for fattening. The mussels and oysters are collected from their natural water and carried to prepared beds. In the Bay of Morbihan alone there are 261 mussel beds with an area of 154 hectares. They are supplied from banks of mussels at the mouth of the Vilaine, where the water, which is greatly stirred by the waves, suits these molluscs. Similarly, on the coast of Saintonge the waters off Angoulins, Chatellaillon, and Fouras supply oysters for the beds on the Isles of Oléron and Marennes. On the shores of the Atlantic between the Loire and the Gironde there are enormous banks of 'Portuguese' oysters that are collected by the boatload.

On sandy shores the stretch between high and low water marks also swarms with molluscs. In the Bay of Mont Saint-Michel millions of cockles are gathered, there are hosts of crabs, and, when the sand is slightly muddy, there are swarms of lobworms which crowds of youngsters dig up and sell to fishermen for bait. In the deeper water off the coast of the Somme *département*, the Baie de la

Seine, and Vendée, swarms of shrimps are caught in little dragnets or bownets by fishermen's wives or children. The lower parts of beaches are often covered with veritable submarine meadows consisting of tangles of long-bladed seaweed, which shelters a whole world of crustacea, molluscs, and fish, and these are gathered by longshoremen.

This marine vegetation is itself the object of organised utilisation. Everywhere on the coast of the English Channel and the Atlantic dwellers by the shore go down to the beach to gather seaweed. Sometimes this is sea-wrack torn up by storms and deposited by the waves in long blackish trails. At other times it is shore-weed, which is cut under water and brought ashore. Everywhere man has learnt the value of these weeds as manure, which by prolonged use transforms fields on the coasts into fertile gardens.

These coastal resources are found all along the shores even when the tidal range is not very great, for the narrow intertidal zone is often compensated for by its wealth of fauna. The warm Mediterranean waters teem with an astonishing quantity of animals. A walk through a fish market in Italy astounds one by the vast quantity and variety of the crustacea, molluscs, sea-urchins, spiders, worms, and shellfish that are offered for sale and are called in Italian *frutti di mare*. Among the innumerable molluscs eaten by the Romans the oyster was the most sought after. The first oyster bed seems to have been started at the beginning of the last century B.C., and today crayfish, cuttlefish, and a hundred other creatures form an important part in the diet of the poorer people in seaside towns in Italy. On the shores of the Etang de Berre, in southern France, a great crop of mussels is gathered by dredging or raking.

In tropical seas invertebrates surpass in numbers, size, and splendid appearance everything that can be produced by temperate waters. The fauna of lagoons in atolls and round the coasts of tropical coral islands is unequalled in its abundance. During his travels in the East Indies, A. R. Wallace went into ecstasies over the vast natural fishponds. If the lagoons separating barrier reefs from the land or those within the rings of atolls are explored, an enormous quantity of life is seen; and, in fact, the existence of the islanders depends very largely on the yield from these calm and relatively shallow waters. In some of the lagoons in atolls there is pearl fishing, and in all types of lagoon the natives collect mother-of-pearl for export to Europe and Japan, where it is made into buttons. In other places annelids are picked up. Known by the native name of *palolo*, they live hidden in holes in the coral. They come out only twice a year at a time known beforehand to the coastal folk, who catch them in vast masses to eat and to turn into oil. In Samoa a favourite dish is a kind of prawn called *valo*, which is dug up from the sand in lagoons. Lastly, on the reefs at low tide the natives collect sea-slugs, which they dry and smoke for export as *trepang* to China, where it is used for making soup.

All these articles, whether cultivated or merely gathered, play an important part in the life of coastal folk. But some are rare and are much sought after among inland people. Hence, they become commodities of trade and assume general importance. Among these none plays a greater part than salt, a commodity of the greatest necessity. In all ages man has sought it eagerly. Few seas lend themselves more to the extraction of salt than the Mediterranean owing to its high salinity and its long, hot, dry summers, when crusts of salt can be seen forming in holes in the rocks. Hence, from the earliest times salt has been artificially made. Flat basins are hollowed out on low coasts and surrounded by little walls of earth. In spring seawater is allowed to enter, in summer the water evaporates, and in autumn the salt is collected.

The salt trade was one of the oldest in the Mediterranean world. Among the most ancient roads in Italy is the Via Salaria, along which the Sabines imported their salt from Rome. Just as the possession of salt mines provoked wars between continental peoples, so one of the earliest kings of Rome wrested the salt marshes at the mouth of the Tiber from the Etruscans. The coasts of the Mediterranean have always been a favourite place for salt marshes, which are found from the Gulf of Izmir to the coasts of France and Spain. Countries farther north exploit salt marshes, the importance of which has long been described by history. Thus, those in Aunis long supplied France and north-western Europe whenever difficulties of communication precluded the competition of Languedoc. In the Middle Ages the busiest roads were those from Poitiers and Limousin to the salt marshes on the coast. A charter dated 1100 mentions the Via Salinaria, which ran from Aunis to Availles-Limousine and later got the name of Chemin des Saulniers. The commercial importance of salt is found even among primitive peoples. Salt, which was a valuable product from the sea was not only used in cooking, for very early its invaluable use in preserving fish was recognised, and, in consequence, it became an article of distant trade. The ancients themselves carried the art of salting very far. It was through this that a flow of trade developed between the countries of the north and those around the Mediterranean. By going in search of salt in the Bay of Biscay the men who fished on the Grand Banks learnt the way to Bordeaux, and the town became one of the greatest centres of salting cod. But the utilisation of the resources of the sea by gathering and cultivation is achieved from the land, and the men who earn their living from it are not sailors. The mode of life of those who leave the land to plough the waves in ships is quite different.

Offshore Fishing.—In waters whose horizon is familiar to daily life the mode of life connected with fishing develops within sight of land. Some coasts are particularly favourable to this kind of fishing; that is, those where boats can move about in calm, sheltered water, protected from the dangers of the open sea by natural breakwaters, islands, rocks, or offshore reefs. They fall into two classes which throughout the world have formed the cradle of fishing communities.

First, there are the fjord coasts, which occur wherever land carved by former glaciers has subsequently been submerged by the sea, e.g. Alaska, British Columbia, Newfoundland, Labrador, Tierra del Fuego, and Norway. The fishing peoples on these coasts show astonishing contrasts between those that have not developed beyond the stage of primitive life, like the Fuegians, and those belonging to the most advanced communities, like the Norwegians. In fishing communities the natural environment is not the only factor in social organisation; it merely interacts with the stage of civilisation reached in the country as a whole to fashion local human groups.

Among some primitive peoples in high latitudes, in which barren soil or severe climates preclude all cultivation, fishing supplies the very basis of life. Besides the Eskimos, for whom fishing is a seasonal complement of hunting, the Tlinkit and Haida Indians on the coasts of Alaska have long lived by fishing in the sea and rivers, just as is done by the primitive peoples on the coasts of Siberia. The Aleuts also were a hunting and fishing people up to a few decades ago. At the extreme south of the Americas the Fuegians live by fishing in the winding channels of their archipelago. They live literally on the water, often sleeping in their bark canoes, the occupants of which form a social cell and often a clan.

Among more advanced peoples man's life no longer depends so strictly on fishing for the means of subsistence do not all come from the products of the sea. But fishing is carried on with improved boats and tackle, and the more plentiful catch nourishes a whole trade. Though prime necessities are not derived from fishing, yet it may be said that the acquisition of those necessities depends strictly on it.

In Newfoundland the inhabitants engage in offshore fishing and are always in sight of the coast or under shelter of the bays. Herrings, which spend the winter off the south coast of the island, migrate in spring towards the Gulf of St Lawrence and then in summer to the coasts of Labrador. There the fish, which are caught in floating nets, are salted, packed in barrels, or kept in ice. The salt fish is sold in the West Indies and to some extent in Europe. Fresh fish is sent to market in Boston. In the bays off Newfoundland lobsters are caught in fish-pots which are lowered to the bottom and their position marked by floats. Packing stations on the shores can the lobster meat, which is then sold the world over.

But the main wealth of the Newfoundland waters lies in cod fishing. It is carried on all round the island, off the coasts of Labrador, and nowadays even in Baffin Bay off the coasts of Greenland. In these areas it is essentially offshore fishing, whose incidents occur before the very eyes of the villages nestling in the bays. The little communities have all settled at the backs of bays, where the boats can be beached safely. When the cod come near the coast between June and September, they are caught in seines, which are nets held up in the water by floats and fastened to the shore. At other times when the cod move away from the coast, they are caught by baited lines cast from light dories. Fish not eaten locally are salted and dried. Near the fishing villages are scaffoldings formed of fir trunks and planks on which, after being cut open and gutted, the fish are hung up to dry. Salt cod is exported to countries in tropical America and to the Mediterranean lands in Europe. Thus, the livelihood of Newfoundland fishermen depends on a market that covers the whole world.

The same is true of the swarms of fishermen who lie in wait for migrating salmon as these pass along the estuaries of the North American coast. Salmon go up the rivers in Newfoundland at the beginning of summer and return to the sea at the approach of winter. These months are the fishing season, when fish are also caught in vast quantities in British Columbia, Oregon, and Washington. The fishing is often carried out by Japanese, Chinese, or Indian crews. Canneries pack the salmon in tins, which are then sold in distant Europe. On the other side of the Pacific on the coast of Hokkaido just as many salmon swim up the lower courses of the streams in autumn, and fishing for them gives work and food directly to thousands of men.

Probably the oldest and most active centre of the world's offshore fishing is to be found in Norway. The coastline is deeply inletted and offers a host of sheltered ports to quite small boats. The soil is barren, and only a narrow fringe of shore is inhabited at the foot of massive, inhospitable mountains facing a sea full of fish. Along the coast fairly shallow banks are periodically visited by migrating fish such as cod. Though herring are capricious in their appearances, the same is not true of cod, which in the last thousand years have never failed to come into the neighbourhood of the Lofoten Islands and to the north of Cape Stad.[1] This explains the worldwide importance of the Norwegian fisheries, which are the classic instance of a prosperous civilisation based on the sea and on the skilful

---

[1] Cape Stad marks the change of direction of the Norwegian coast, between Bergen and Trondheim; it also marks the northern end of the coast bordered by deep water and the beginning of the coast fringed by a continental shelf, and is thus an important hydrological limit.

specialisation of a people in the utilisation of marine resources.

Another type of coast, which is characterised by lagoons and is found all over the world from the *étangs* along the Mediterranean and the *haffs* of the Baltic to the lagoons of the coral isles of the Pacific, contains many centres of offshore fishing that have developed independently according to local natural conditions.

The greatest area of lagoon fishing occurs in the tropics. It corresponds to the distribution of the kind of coast proper to coral formations and found in an immense zone from East Africa to Central America passing through the East Indies and Oceania, the Indian and Pacific Oceans. Other lagoons in other parts of the world have given rise to a fishing mode of life, as can be seen along the Mediterranean and Baltic coasts. But though quite peculiar, these centres of maritime life occupy but a small area compared with the vast oceans in which coral reefs on the fringes of continents or islands greatly enlarge the inland water surface that fosters the fishing way of life.

Barrier reefs, whether on the borders of a continent or round an island, mark out long stretches of inland waters which encourage the presence of little boats. Thus the Great Barrier Reef of Australia, about 2,500 kilometres long and at an average distance of 100 kilometres from the coast, marks out a long basin, as do the sea-reefs of New Caledonia, which run at a distance of between two and twelve kilometres from the shore, and the Great Sea Reef, 80 kilometres long, that runs on an average 16 kilometres from the north coast of Vanua Levu in Fiji. Throughout the tropical Pacific this feature of coasts has encouraged fishing within the reefs. In the southwest fishing is of prime importance to livelihood and the standard of living in all the islands, and in some groups in Tuamotu and Tokelau the inhabitants owe nearly all their subsistence to the ocean.

Their methods of fishing are directly connected with the conditions of the environment. Little use is made of spears, and not much of line and hook, which, however, are skilfully fashioned. Bow-nets, fish-fences, and, above all, vegetable poisons are used. Nets are scarcely employed, except in lagoons to surround and catch schools of fish. A boat is needed to move about in the lagoon. Among primitive peoples boats are difficult to build, for planks cannot be cut from logs with stone tools. Canoes are made by hollowing out tree trunks, and to ensure its stability it is sometimes made double, but more often it is fitted with an ingeniously devised outrigger. Outrigger canoes and catamarans have proved ocean-going, and in them the Polynesians have become excellent seamen able to navigate across wide spaces of ocean.

Outside Oceania lagoon fishing is often found where the water is calm and shallow, as it is in the Philippines, East Indies, and the coast of Honduras. The inhabitants of these coasts were, together with the Polynesians and Malays, formerly the nuclei of navigating peoples, but today they are in course of disappearance. Hence, their influence has not been general, as was that of the fishermen in seas in the temperate belt.

The Baltic lagoons, known as *haffs*, formed a fishing ground in the old days and were the most important in Germany until fishing in the open sea had developed. Most of the little fishing smacks used in the Baltic, are in the haffs where most of the fishing is done. Certain parts of the coast where there are *nehrungs* and offshore islands are favourite spots for fisherfolk.

The sheltered lagoons in the Mediterranean are well supplied with fauna, and fishermen have always crowded near them. The entry and exit of migratory fish was early noticed, and weirs were built in the *graus* to catch them as they passed. In this way each group of lagoons acquired its own settlement of fisherfolk. This is what happened at the Etang de Berre and the Etang de Thau in southern France, the lagoons at Venice and Commachio in Italy, and those at Tunis, Bizerta, and Porto Farina in Tunisia. This type of fishing is carried on not far from land in light, frail boats that could not endure the open sea. But the temptation to pass beyond coastal waters and venture out to sea was very great, and the lead was taken by experienced men who gradually gave up coastal fishing for voyages on the open seas.

Fishing on the High Seas.—The chance of a successful voyage, the desire to extend the field of operations so as to increase the catch, the search for the mysterious places in which schools of fish hid when not making one of their fleeting appearances, were all motives that gradually led fishermen on the coast to set out to find more and more attractive fishing grounds. In spite of distance and danger these fishing grounds have attracted men owing to the great fortunes to be gained from the quantity of fish on them.

The geographical distribution of these fishing grounds depends closely on the natural conditions of their waters. They are found mainly in the north temperate belt and comprise three areas situated near the dividing line between the temperate belt and the cold belt. One of them is off the northwest coast of Europe, the second off the coasts of Newfoundland and New England, and the third off the north coast of Japan. Their similarity is remarkable both in hydrology and relief. The teeming waters contain vast masses of microscopic creatures which form fish food. They cover a continental shelf never more than 200 metres deep, so that the sun's light and heat reach the bottom. Into it rivers from the land nearby pour large quantities of organic waste.

The waters teem with life. Three great families of fish hold the first place, namely, herrings which are found mainly in the North Sea; cod, caught chiefly off Newfoundland; and mackerel, mainly off the north coast of Japan. Huge flotillas make their way to these chosen grounds; men leave their native land to dwell on the sea, and their boats become their floating homes for weeks and months on end.

Nowhere else in the world is there such active fishing on the high seas. Tropical seas are richer in species than are the colder seas, but they are poorer in numbers of fish, and they therefore do not have such important centres of high seas fishing. But they have their own kinds of fishing, developed in fringing seas with densely peopled coasts. One of these is in the Mediterranean, and the other the seas round China and Japan.

The Yellow Sea is a considerable stretch of fringing waters of no great depth and with regular currents, inhabited by a fauna of tropical and subtropical species which extend as far as the limit of the warm Kuro Siwo drift. The most important species are sea bream, sardines, sharks, tunny, and bonitos. Big flotillas of fishing smacks operate from all the large Chinese coast towns.

The Mediterranean does not contain such vast swarms of fish as the northern seas do, for it lacks the wide expanses of continental shelf, and off some coasts great depths are quickly reached. Nevertheless, certain varieties of fish, caught in large quantities, form an essential source of food. Among them are the tunny, which migrates regularly, the sardine, anchovy, and mackerel. Fishermen in the Gulf of Lion do not stay in the open sea for long, since they have only little boats, called *bateaux-boeufs* or *tartanes*. On the other hand, Greek and Italian fishermen do not restrict themselves to their own waters, but go in great numbers to the coast of Tunis and even settle on the coast of Languedoc. But fishing in the Mediterranean has everywhere kept its archaic character and uses very small boats. Usually it does not supply fish enough for the local population, which eats a great deal of the commodity. The deficit must be made up from the north, where fish is more plentiful and where fishing has become a regular industry.

Of the two great oceans that reach the Arctic and contain the most productive fishing grounds, the Pacific is still the less important. But a great deal of fishing has developed in its western portion on the continental shelf covered by the fringing seas of eastern Asia at places where the warm waters of the Kuro Siwo and the cold Oya Siwo current meet off the coast of Hokkaido. North of lat. 37° N. northern species (herring, cod, salmon) become more and more numerous. But the grounds, which are fished by crowds of Japanese boats, are of mere local importance, for little of the catch is exported, and most of it is eaten in Japan. Besides, fishing methods remain primitive.

This Pacific fishing ground does not bear comparison with those in the North Atlantic, where there are very large fishing communities endued with astonishing powers of expansion. The English, Scots, French, Dutch, Germans, and Scandinavians have all helped to make the waters of their continental shelf into a vast and continuously used fishing ground supplying enormous quantities of food for home consumption and export. They have also annexed to their own area not only the American grounds, where they continue to fish, but also the Arctic Sea, which they have gradually explored and used for fishing. They have built such improved boats and invented such efficient tackle that they catch far more fish than they can use, and with the surplus they trade all over the world.

The North and Norwegian Seas, which teem with fish and for hundreds of years have been crowded with fishermen from the adjacent coasts, witness the practice of two kinds of fishing. The old, traditional kind is based on the herring and mackerel, which are caught in drift nets, and on the cod, which is caught with lines. The other kind is modern and free from the influence of the seasons and works by catching in trawls fish chiefly meant to reach the market in a fresh condition.

The extraordinary success of North Sea fishing originated with the herring, which appears periodically during the summer months right along the east coast of Britain. Fishing takes place in summer, moving from north to south and becoming later and later towards the south. Smoking and salting herring is the chief occupation of a number of ports, such as Aberdeen, Hull, Grimsby, Yarmouth, and Lowestoft. Fishing and the preparation of fish for market form a main occupation of large ports in Germany, like Geestmünde; in the Netherlands, like Ijmuiden, Rotterdam, and Vlaardingen; and in Norway, like Bergen, Stavanger, and Kristiansand.

Modern fishing is mainly interested in bottom fish, which are flat and were once scornfully termed 'sham fish' because they could not be preserved by the usual methods of salting and smoking. Since refrigerators have come into use and cold storage installed, these fish have gained a considerable place on the market, where they are choice articles of trade. Hence the increased trawling on the northern banks of the North Sea and off the coast of Denmark. The modern motor-driven trawler, fitted with efficient equipment for storage and preserving the catch, lands enormous quantities of fresh fish, which are despatched at once to large towns by special fish trains. The industrial nature of modern fishing demands abundant and rapid means of communication, and so have been able to develop only in countries of high mechanical progress. Only a few ports have the required equipment to ensure the distribution within a few hours of fish caught perhaps at a distance of three to five hundred kilometres away. The chief are Hull and Grimsby in England, Boulogne, Kéroman, and La Rochelle in France, Ostend in Belgium, IJmuiden in the Netherlands, Esbjerg in Denmark, and Geestmünde in Germany.

Improved equipment with a consequent increase in the catch easily explains why North Sea fishermen were not satisfied with the fishing grounds off their shores. They have in fact fished other distant grounds reached by voyages that were formerly long and hazardous. Some grounds, for example those of Newfoundland, have given rise to colonies which for long found their livelihood in the sea. Others, like those in Arctic waters, are situated in dangerous areas that are uninhabitable for much of the year and in which fishing looks like a real adventure.

Like European waters, those of Newfoundland are a meeting place of warm and cold currents, which is favourable to the development of swarms of plankton. Besides, the presence of 'banks', or submarine plateaus grooved by ice erosion and littered with moraines, locates one of the most productive fishing grounds in the Atlantic. It is divided into two parts by a trench 475 metres deep, whilst the soundings on the plateau itself are not more than 90 metres: hence the presence of an extremely abundant fish fauna. Some of the fish, like the halibut, live on the bottom and grow to a huge size; others, like the cod, appear periodically, for whilst in winter it appears off the Norwegian coast, in summer it moves into the waters of the Grand Banks. At this time the fishing really begins, and the sea off Newfoundland is invaded by thousands of boats, among which are still seen old sailing smacks, steamers, and some of the most modern trawlers, fitted with echo-sounding apparatus and radar. For the people of Newfoundland, who fish in sight of their villages, fishing is almost a coastwise operation; for the fishermen from New England, who take home large catches, the voyage is somewhat longer; but for fishermen from Europe it is indeed a long distance expedition that makes them into permanent dwellers on the sea.

The first ships known to history as sailing to *Terre-neuve* came from Portugal and the Azores. But soon boats from northwestern Europe took the lead, first the French and then the English. The latter enjoyed a period of prosperity towards the end of the eighteenth century and the beginning of the nineteenth. In 1815 some 17,000 ships set out from Bristol, Exmouth, Teignmouth, and Dartmouth. But from that date the fishing passed into the hands of the settlers in Newfoundland. Of all European fishermen the French alone remained faithful to the distant grounds in spite of the distance and the hostility of the Newfoundlanders.

The first French fishermen to be seen on the Banks were Normans from Dieppe, who were there about 1506. Others from Saint-Malo and La Rochelle and some Basques followed them. At the end of the seventeenth century some 20,000 men from La Rochelle, Paimpol, Saint-Malo, Honfleur, and Dieppe in three hundred sailing ships set out for Newfoundland in February and returned in December. This great period has passed. Nevertheless, until about 1930 there were still *terre-neuvas* at Saint-Malo and Fécamp, Saint-Brieuc, Cancale, and Binic, manning stout schooners and other ships able to manoeuvre easily in the dangerous seas, where there was a risk of collision owing to poor visibility. Before the 'bankers' sailed, fishermen went off in liners to help the people of Saint-Pierre to catch cod around the coast. Then at the beginning of March the bankers, about a hundred in number, left their ports to sail across the Atlantic, the voyage lasting a month. As soon as they arrived, they spread over the Banks, spending the first days in fishing for bait. After that cod fishing began.

This job was done from rowing boats called 'dories', which each ship carried. Every evening the dories carried out baited lines and, casting them overboard, tied them to a buoy. They then returned to their ships which were moving under shortened sail in the open sea. At dawn next morning the dories went out to pick up the lines, and the day was spent in gutting, washing and slightly salting the cod. The whole cruise took place without touching land and ended in October. The ships then went back to France, not always directly to their home ports, but often to a port like Nantes, La Rochelle, or Bordeaux, where drying establishments finished the preparation of the fish for the market. Only then did the boats return home.

Today a new development has taken place in the working of the deep sea fishing through the introduction of steam trawlers in the fishing fleets, in which they have completely replaced sailing ships. These big vessels are not only used for fishing, but are also factories capable of salting the cod, extracting oil from the livers, and turning the waste into powder, whilst the roe is carefully made into bait much sought after by sardine fishermen. Only a few big ports fit out these large boats whose cruises last only a few weeks, but may be repeated several times in the same season on different fishing grounds off Newfoundland, Labrador, Greenland, the Murmansk coast, or Iceland. Today, many of these large trawlers have deep-freeze equipment; they can thus preserve the fish and deliver it to the market several weeks later in the same condition as if it had been caught but yesterday.

Nearly three-quarters of the cod brought back to French ports still come from Newfoundland and Greenland. Two-fifths are re-exported to Mediterranean countries. The industry, which for centuries was very profitable to France, has now become of secondary importance, in spite of the efficiency of the new equipment, for economic conditions in the modern world have increased the difficulty of competing with rivals who are better situated for fishing and marketing; and every day sees an increase in the share of American fishermen in the annual catch of between 165,000 and 220,000 tonnes of cod.

Northwestern European fishermen, as they sailed the seas off their own coasts, discovered in Arctic waters animals valuable for their blubber. A species of whale, the 'Biscay whale', was commonly found during the seventeenth century in the Bay of Biscay, where it was hunted by Basques. Whales are profitable prey. Their skin is lined with a layer of oily blubber from eight to twenty inches thick, which weighs nearly half of the 110 tonnes attained by some whales. A fine whale may give 33 tonnes of oil, the value of which is doubled by that of the baleen, or whalebone. It may well be imagined that bold seamen trained in the deep-water fishing school in the rough, foggy waters of northern Europe did not hesitate to venture into Arctic solitudes; and the fierceness of their hunt ended in almost complete extermination of the whale in each successive hunting-ground.

Spitzbergen, which was discovered in 1596, became almost at once the goal of the whalers. The first to arrive were English, who were there in 1608. By 1613 in addition to seven English ships there were four Dutch, four French, and one Spanish. Bitter fighting took place for the best anchorages. In the end the hunting-grounds were shared by agreement, the English keeping the bays on the west, where whalers from Hull made a station on Axel Island. The Dutch held the bays on the northwest and north, with a station at Sneerenborg, from which their ships brought back year by year to Amsterdam enormous quantities of oil. But by 1650 the whalers had to abandon the banks and fjords of the islands, and move farther west.

Then began the wholesale exploitation of the seas around Greenland, where seamen of the Hansa had been to fish in 1640. The Dutch soon visited every headland along the coast and in 1719 ventured into Davis Strait. But the English were soon there in greater numbers and held the area throughout the eighteenth century. Between 1790 and 1820 about a hundred whaling vessels set out every year from London, Hull, Aberdeen, Leith, Peterhead, and Dundee. But there too the whales became rarer and rarer, and mineral and vegetable oil began to compete with whale oil. In 1868 Hull withdrew from the Arctic. Dundee was one of the last ports to fit out as many as thirty ships for whaling in the Arctic. Commercial risks and danger soon checked whaling ventures, and

Norway alone kept a fine fleet of whalers which were gradually brought up-to-date, fitted with modern gear, and made into factory ships whose field of operations was transferred to the Antarctic.

The same near-extinction occurred in American waters after a few years of devastating hunting. Up to the mid-nineteenth century the whale brought great profit to Newfoundlanders; then in consequence of the improvements made in equipment by the Norwegians, there followed a period of greater prosperity, which began in 1897 and ended with the extermination of the whale. To find other game the whalers had to move on to the waters off Greenland.

In Bering Sea whaling began in 1848, when three hundred ships left New Bedford and San Francisco and made their way to the waters off the west coast of Alaska. In the course of the nineteenth century American shipowners made fabulous fortunes from whaling, but eventually the whales left Alaskan waters to move farther east beyond Point Barrow, Banks Island, and Fitzwilliam Strait. The whole coast of Alaska is strewn with jetsam from the many whaling ships crushed by ice. There too, however, the game grew scarcer, and Arctic whaling ceased.

The industry is now almost wholly concentrated in the hands of Scandinavians, together with a few Americans, Australians, and Japanese. The Norwegians have kept alive this peculiar occupation by constantly improving their equipment and by extending their operations over the whole world. Their ships are still to be found in the Shetlands, Hebrides, Faroes, and Spitzbergen, but they are especially active in the southern hemisphere, which is today the world's main source of whales. South Georgia, South Shetland, the Falkland Islands, Kerguelen, and the south coasts of Chile and Africa are used for whaling by big companies looking to the main chance. Their ships operate off the coasts of Gaboon and Angola, off East Africa, in the waters round Mozambique, Natal, and Madagascar, and also in the tropical seas off Peru and Panama and round the Galápagos Islands. In this business Norwegian companies are met with everywhere, and, when the companies are not Norwegian, they always include in their crews Norwegian seamen experienced in whaling.

The sea is an inestimable source of wealth for those who exploit it, from the humble longshoreman, who gathers and gleans between high and low water mark, to the deep sea fisherman who lives for several months in the year between sky and sea. But except for a few backward peoples, it is not the only source of livelihood, for it does not meet the needs of fishermen in food, clothes, or permanent dwelling. To be sure of all his means of subsistence he is obliged to exchange his fish for prime necessities, and in this way fishing leads to trade and international relations.

On the other hand, the fisherman is really a nomad. Of course, on land he has a home, a settled home, in which his family dwells. But his life is one of continual movement, for he is always on the way to or from his fishing grounds. In his boat he has a means of transport which he knows how to build, rig, and handle, suiting his course to the currents and banks. Like the steppe nomad he does not remain constantly in one place, for his pursuit of fish takes him to other lands, thus encouraging intercourse and trade. The germ of life on the sea is to be found in every fisherman. Consequently, the fisherman's life leads to foreign trade and overseas expansion History has many examples in proof of this. Phoenician expansion along the shores of the Mediterranean owed some of its success to the search for the purple needed by the dyers of Tyre and Sidon. By following the tunny the Hellenes advanced gradually into the Ægean and Black Seas, where their colonies ultimately achieved great success. The Malays, who are a race of fishermen, have spread throughout southeastern Asia as traders, and as pirates too, for piracy seems very often to be the final stage in the development of a maritime temperament. In Polynesia, where so much is owed to fishing, there was a period of expansion across the seas which spread their people and their civilisation all over the Pacific. In Europe a whole nation of fishermen developed at the inner ends of the Norwegian fjords, a nation that has become essentially a nation of seamen. They were the Vikings and Normans of the Middle Ages, who were not long in seeking other lands and spreading over the seas. They settled in Scotland, penetrated the estuaries in England and France, colonised Iceland and Greenland, probably discovered America, sailed right into the Mediterranean, where they conquered Sicily, and then took possession of the Canary Islands. They established intercourse with the East through the Baltic and Russia. In our own times the same activity continues in the same country and among the same people, and Norway is a land of seamen, a land of porters of the sea. Similarly, Amsterdam owed its prosperity to barrels of herrings, and it was by trade in fish that the Netherlands began their brilliant commercial career.

The Opening of Seaways.—All along the immense sea front formed by the shores of the continents there are favoured spots in which contact with the sea is easier than elsewhere and in which the elements allow themselves to be mastered. These places have contributed to the progress of navigation and from early times have guided the coast dwellers to use the opportunities afforded by the sea. The presence of many inlets increases the points of contact with the sea and, consequently, the accessibility of the coasts. Some types of coast make settlement difficult for man; for instance, coasts formed by vertical, inaccessible cliffs and those with dunes and bars off the shore, such as are found in North Carolina, Texas, Languedoc, southern Russia, and southwest Africa. Such too are coasts fringed with forest screens, like those in British Columbia, the Niger delta, and the Guinea coast; desert coasts, like those in Baluchistan, the Hadramaut, and northern Chile; and those, lastly, that are edged by frozen plains, like those in Siberia to the east of the Lena. These are all repellent shores on which maritime activity has been able to begin only at isolated points and on the initiative of sailors from across the sea.

Attractive coasts are essentially those with peninsulas embracing relatively small areas of sea. Norway, with its one mile of coastline for every ten square miles of surface, is fringed with such inlets. Estuaries enable ships to penetrate far into the interior of continents, and the rivers entering them may lead even farther inland. In practice, up to modern times when ships have been built that are too large to go up rivers, estuaries have enabled ocean-going vessels to move very far inland. In our times too they afford sites for a continuous line of seaports in the Baltic, North Sea, and English Channel, all of which are situated between sixty and a hundred kilometres from the sea and are what Ellen Semple has called 'river seaports'. The same is true of all the big Atlantic ports in America from New England and the Hudson to the drowned estuaries of the Delaware and Chesapeake farther south.

Of all these favourable geographical positions none afford greater advantages than those arising from a situation in narrow seas. A map of the world shows straits as attractive sites for ports, for example, the Straits of Dover, the Bosporus, the Sound, and the Straits of Gibraltar, the importance of which is twofold. The most obvious advantage is the communication they establish between two nearby seas whose trade they dominate. But they also form part of the crossroads between the seaway and the land routes that reach their shores. Narrowness of the strait lessens its importance as an obstacle. The same factors connected with narrow seas apply, moreover, to fairly small enclosed waters where the attraction of the coasts facing each other has been enough to maintain trade and vigorous maritime activity.

Similarly, islands have served as centres of many maritime settlements and as ports of call for maritime nations. Like outposts of the land, islands afford those crossing the sea a first stage in reaching the mainland. Such islands have often been pirate strongholds, but they have also afforded sailors safe and easily defended refuges where business between merchants from over the sea has been transacted in full security with those on the mainland. This explains the fortunes of Zanzibar and Hongkong, of Singapore and the Japanese islands as a whole.

Furthermore, islands have played an important part as stages in large seas, where they act as isolated ports of call. The islands in the western Mediterranean (Corsica, Sardinia, and the Balearics) were from prehistoric times centres of advanced civilisation, as is witnessed by numerous stone monuments. They served especially as rallying points for all the maritime peoples who used the Mediterranean: Etruscans, Carthaginians, Greeks, Romans, Vandals, Saracens, Catalans, and medieval Italians. The islands in the eastern Mediterranean, especially Cyprus and Crete, were similarly used as stages, as was also Gotland in the Baltic.

One should, however, guard against too strict a determinism, for in truth there are many islands that have no sea-going people and the late settlement on which is connected with the development of skills originating in other lands. Many small islands lost in the ocean have not been valued for their position until the days of steam navigation, when they became coaling stations or relay points for transoceanic telegraph cables. Such have been Thursday Island in Torres Strait, Guam, Ascension Island, Saint Helena, and Tristan da Cunha, which is now after the recent volcanic eruption, once again inhabited by small cultivators with tiny holdings, who get their subsistence from their potato fields rather than from the sea. The people on many of these island stopping-places are there merely because of maritime business with which they have no connexion: for example, the Azores, which became inhabited when the Portuguese discovered them in 1427, and Bermuda, which, uninhabited when discovered by the Spaniards in 1510, have both been settled more by landsmen and colonists than by fishermen or sailors.

Of course, some islanders, who like the Malays and Polynesians were cramped for room in their islands, have tended to migrate across the seas in search of better times. But apart from these instances, there are islanders who have never attempted to sail the seas: for example, the Corsicans, who are mountain shepherds, and the Irish, who are cultivators and herdsmen. Others have forgotten or neglected their maritime traditions for long periods in their history, whilst others have given up making a living from the sea in the same surroundings as those in which they had formerly made it: for example, the people of the Cyclades no longer think today of making a living except by growing wheat, looking after their vines, and grazing their goats.

Nor has nearness to a sea with plenty of fish always had a determining influence. The Grand Banks did not awaken any local maritime occupation before the arrival of European sailors. Similarly, though Iceland is encircled by fishing-grounds, the island remained a land of poor shepherds until the end of the last century. Without wood to enable them to build boats, without salt to enable them conveniently to preserve the fish they caught, without fuel, except peat which burns without flame and for that reason is scarcely suitable for drying fish, Icelanders for three hundred years saw the fishing fleets of Europe carry off before their eyes tons of cod and herring. Fishing began in the island on the day when some old trawlers were bought in England in return for sales of wool to industrialists in Manchester. At the present time the catch around Iceland is greater in weight than that in Danish waters. But though the Icelanders were descendants of a people with an immemorial tradition of seafaring, an economic revolution, brought about by foreign trade and the consequent improvement in their standard of civilisation, was needed before they thought to assert their marine rights and take advantage of the proximity of fishing banks which had been known to and fished by others for many years.

Physical advantages play an essential part only when ports have to be established and kept in use, but they have far less direct influence on the development of maritime activity properly so-called. The Phoenicians, for example, who founded one of the first great thalassocracies in history, dwelt on a coast with few irregularities. Today the same coast still shelters vigorous maritime activity due both to a now modernised trawler fishing fleet and to trade in the Levant, the home ports of which are Ruad, Lattaquia, Tripoli, Beirut, Haifa, and Saida. On the other hand, how many broken coasts have remained inactive! In contrast with Greece, which swarms with little ports, is Chalcidice, which is equally indented but has taken no part in maritime activity. Physical geography cannot alone explain the contrast that exists between the English coast with its large modern ports crowded with shipping, and the nearby coasts of western Ireland and northwestern Scotland, which are without shipping in spite of their countless inlets suitable for modern harbours[1].

It has also been pointed out that sandy coasts without shelter for ships have from early times had ports. Putting aside the classic and oft quoted case of Dunkirk, which is the work of modern engineering and is due to the needs of France's industrial north, it is possible to mention the northeast coast of Africa, which is flat, sandy, and unfavourable in every way, yet has a series of very active ports between Cape Gardafui and Mombasa, although the backland is an arid and practically desert region. The Arabs call it Barr el Benadir, that is, 'the coast of ports'. The existence of ports on this sunscorched coast is to be explained only by the trade brought by Somali

---

[1] Note, however, the recent development of Bantry Bay, a ria in southwestern Ireland, as a major oil terminal for 300,000-ton tankers. [*Editor's note*]

caravans from southern Ethiopia and continued across the sea to India.

The Stages in Maritime Development.—The mastery of the sea has been the result of long effort in the course of which several nations have succeeded each other in the task, and the most technical and often the most theoretical discoveries of pure science have been brought into play. These discoveries, which have one after the other all become the common property of mankind, whether they involved the use of the stern rudder, steam engine, or mathematical processes of nautical calculation, have ended in man's mastery of the oceans, a mastery which alone could make possible the occupation of the whole earth by the human species.

Consideration of the result of this vast achievement shows the main stages in development. First, there was the period of separate localities. In Europe this extended through ancient times and a good part of the Middle Ages. Secondly, there was the panoceanic period, which began after the great Renaissance discoveries with the mastery of the Atlantic and the rapid spread of trade to all shores of the Atlantic and Indian Oceans. In the former was achieved the decisive progress which during the second half of the nineteenth century included the Pacific and even the Arctic Sea in the networks of world traffic. The occupation of the whole world was made more effective still by the development of airways which have been super-imposed on the main lines of seaways over the greater part of the globe.

Each stage in the mastery of the seas has corresponded to a new conception of international relations, to a reorganisation of trade, as well as to progress in nautical technique, and these developments have reflected the standard of civilisation reached. The need for trade between human groups was in its origin the strongest factor in maritime development. No attraction seems to have been more compelling than that which from earliest times drew western peoples towards the Far East. The diversity of the two types of civilisation and of trade goods soon led to commercial relations between these two to some extent complementary parts of the world. Trade was encouraged from the beginning by the existence of a narrow zone of gaps and slender links that naturally joined Europe and southern Asia. Between Eurasia and the Indo-African landmass an area of subsidence separates the two great continental blocks. It is marked by the Red Sea, Mesopotamia, and the Persian Gulf, and farther on by groups of islands, seas, and straits in southeast Asia. This collection of passageways, isthmuses, straits, and narrows has played an immense part in man's history on the sea, one of the chief reasons being that it is shut in by deserts along its whole length.

Hence commerce in ancient times was canalised in this narrow zone. On account of this North Africa from Cyrenaica westwards belongs rather to Europe than to the African continent. It is indeed only the southern fringe of the great zone of international traffic which runs through the Mediterranean and the seas connected with it.

But even in these areas, in which man was attracted by the sea through the exigencies of international trade, he was able to master the element only very gradually. Long experience in restricted areas, in which man made discovery after discovery and thus solved all the technical problems of local navigation, enabled him gradually to spread to wider areas in which further experiments had to be made based on the scientific knowledge already acquired.

The Period of Local Navigation.—Man quickly learnt to make use of the physical advantages of enclosed seas and the wind systems on them. The use of alternating winds, which enabled a boat to sail out to sea and later to return to the shore was soon reduced to principles by the maritime peoples. These were the land and sea breezes of the eastern Mediterranean, the monsoons of the Indian Ocean and especially the *hippal*, the southeast trades in western Polynesia, and the northeast trades in the Caribbean.

The eastern Mediterranean, the Indian Ocean, the southwest Pacific, and the Caribbean were all areas in which peculiar implements and methods of navigation were elaborated, without any being capable of being spread over the whole globe. The outrigger canoe of the Pacific enabled Polynesians and Malays to cover vast expanses of the ocean. The ancestors of the Hovas crossed the whole width of the Indian Ocean to land in Madagascar. Ethnologists have shown that intercourse by sea may have been frequent along unknown routes between the American shores of the Pacific and the islands farther west. Sailing in rudimentary boats whose sailing qualities were better than might be supposed from their construction, these primitive mariners may have been able to pass from the coast of Peru to the islands of the Pacific. Each of the areas mentioned above had no intercourse with each other before the rise of pan-oceanic navigation, but each had its own type of boat. There was the *balsa* (= Span. 'raft') of the Peruvian coast, the Malay *prau*, the Norman *drakkar*, the Mediterranean *trière*, and later, in a still poorly organised society, the Hanseatic *kogge*.

On the whole, it was in the Mediterranean that some of the most important, most lasting, and most universally adopted technical improvements were devised. First, there was the substitution of the big triangular lateen sail for the primitive square sail made of a cloth sheet which was bellied out by the wind. Later, under Andrea Doria, the Genoese brought about another revolution by adding rigging to the sail to enable manoeuvres to be carried out and so to achieve a more complete use of the wind. But each of the navigational areas developed separately, and between them the sea long formed an impassable obstacle.

Beyond the familiar area, where the sailor was sure of being able to return to land and to forecast fairly closely the time of return, there stretched dangerous expanses forbidden by ignorance of the wind systems that prevailed in them and by dangers exaggerated in the imagination of sailors. Thus, to the south of the seas frequented by Arab sailors there was the dreaded Mozambique current which swept southwards furiously beyond the path of the monsoons so that return was impossible or thought to be so. Hence the northern limit of the current marked the end of the known world.

Similarly, on issuing from the Mediterranean into the Atlantic sailors of the ancient world imposed on themselves exiguous tentative bounds. Ships from Carthage and Gades went far along the coasts of Africa, and with favourable northeast trades reached as far as Sierra Leone, but in spite of the most favourable interpretations of the periplus of Hanno, they did not usually pass beyond that point. Indeed, easy navigation stopped there, for other irregular winds prevailed which delayed progress and could only be used by seamen experienced in the art of trimming sails.

Among sailors of the ancient world it was almost an absolute rule to sail in sight of the coast. Pilots headed from cape to cape or steered towards a nearby island. In the Mediterranean there are many promontories with high rocky brows that can be seen from afar; for instance, those in Cyprus, rising to 2,000 metres, are theoretically visible 170 kilometres away, and in the clear air of the Levant the actual visibility is not far off the theoretical. Hence the Mediterranean coasts were all well known to the pilots, who recognised the outline of all the capes. Navigation depended mainly on piloting. It required close observation of the coast, which was left regretfully and as little as possible. So as not to lose sight of the capes and known islands sailors did not hesitate to double the normal length of their voyages and to increase their duration enormously. In sailing from Rome to Tarragona they sailed along the shores of Etruria, Liguria, Gaul, and Spain. In these days the principles of navigation have changed. For us danger comes from the land, and, when a ship is threatened by a storm, she seeks safety by moving away from the coast and reaching the open sea. Sailors of the ancient world, when threatened by a storm, rowed for the shore. Up to the time of the Hellenes ships were beached at each stage of the voyage. For this reason an open, sandy beach was sought on which to land, and this increased the dependence on the land of all navigation. The Phoenicians and Phocians alone were able to sail out of sight of land and head across the open sea on the way to Spain.

This was one feature of their commercial superiority, and one of the secrets so jealously guarded by the sailors of Tyre that they preferred scuttling their ships to betraying it.

The practice of navigation had inculcated in the ancients a knowledge of sailing, many features of which have been lost, though many others have come into the common heritage without their origin being always known. Their caution and empiricism was still to be found in the instructions issued to Mediterranean navigators in the sixteenth century. Throughout the maritime hegemony of Genoa and Venice there continued the practice of keeping ships off the sea during the four winter months. These rules, surviving ancient times, show that the Mediterranean was, as a maritime region, one of the centres in which navigational skill made decisive progress.

The Panoceanic Period.—By facing sailors with problems unknown to the Mediterranean, entry into the Atlantic forced European seamanship into new techniques and obliged the maritime peoples to give up the routine in which Mediterranean navigation had been crystallised. The Ocean did indeed present new problems. First, the existence of tides struck sailors' imagination, and their mechanism remained a mystery to Aristotle and to the whole of the Middle Ages. Secondly, the familiar landmarks were absent, and sailors had to learn to make use of the stars. The history of this technical progress revolves round the astronomical problem of position on the sea and the meteorological problem of the scientific use of the winds.

At the start sailors tried to solve both problems in the Atlantic as they had done in the Mediterranean by sailing along coastwise. This practice was persistently used by the Portuguese and the Academy at Cape St Vincent when from the time of Henry the Navigator they undertook to find the seaway to India by sailing round Africa. Each expedition was given the task of going beyond the farthest point reached by its predecessors. Thus the Portuguese took fifteen years to reach Cape Bogador. In 1460, after a struggle lasting forty years, they had still not repeated the voyage achieved by Hanno the Carthaginian. Not until 1484 did Diego Cam reach the mouth of the Congo and push on farther south to lat. 20° S. This slow advance was due to the fact that, as they went along the coast of Africa, they came to the belt of calms, from which it sometimes took twenty days to escape. Beyond that they were sailing in the teeth of the southeast trade, which forced them to sail into the wind and to tack. On the whole, in the fifteenth century it was held impossible to sail along the coast of Africa, and the Portuguese would have been discouraged by this fruitless effort had not Bartholomew Diaz expressed the problem in wholly new terms. He made the important discovery that by sailing out of sight of land so as to cross the Equator between long. 25° and 30° W. he avoided sailing in the teeth of the southeast trade wind, which was then on his port quarter. The true Atlantic seaway, therefore, passed out to sea, and Vasco de Gama proved it shortly after by sailing from Cape Verde to St Helena Bay in seventy-eight days.

From this time on sailing across the seas was to become current practice, especially so because the voyages of Christopher Columbus had discovered farther west in the Atlantic than the Portuguese seaway a new world that could even then be mistaken for the most western islands of the East Indies. But to trust oneself to either of these transatlantic crossings one's position at sea had to be determined without the help of landmarks, and this meant that the latitude and longitude of the ship's position had to be calculated. It was, however, three hundred years before the problem was completely solved. This was done by the invention of precise instruments like the sextant, and of trustworthy chronometers which measured time correctly.

Not until the time of the voyages of the tea clippers was the technique of using planetary winds fully recorded with as great accuracy as had been formerly with the winds in the Mediterranean. Between 1845 and 1855 an American hydrographer named Maury undertook the formidable task of compiling nautical records which he translated into maps, 'Wind and Current Charts' accompanied by notes, 'Sailing Directions'. Their use was proved when the American ship *Wright* sailed from Baltimore to Río de Janeiro by the route advised by Maury and reached the Equator in twenty-four days instead of forty-one. Maury had demanded that the sailing ships, whose motive power involves no expense, need take no account of the route followed, but only of the speed with which it was covered. Successive improvements of the course of the seaways placed the Pacific within reach of ships from Europe. Buache's map still showed a *Mer de l'Ouest* on the position of Alberta, but exploration at the end of the eighteenth century and the beginning of the nineteenth brought the Pacific finally within the range of voyages from Europe.

Thus, by the end of the sixteenth century the whole of the Atlantic had been explored from north to south, as had the Indian Ocean as far south as lat. 40° S., the equatorial portion of the Pacific, and the Arctic Sea as far as Novaya Zemlya and Spitzbergen.

The area explored was only slightly increased in the seventeenth century, except in Australian waters, Baffin Bay, and Hudson Bay. The rest of the world was explored after the second half of the nineteenth century, and this important fact in the history of civilisation has caused a revolution in commercial and political ideas. After the discovery of the seaways, indeed, international trade ceased to take place overland by caravan, and the great overland routes were abandoned and forgotten. It is significant that large parts of Asia were better known to Europeans before the great voyages of discovery than they were in the seventeenth and even in the nineteenth centuries.

The discovery of open sea routes, the solution of the mathematical problem of finding position at sea, through the invention of the chronometer, and the better understanding of the meteorology of oceanic areas and of wind directions, made possible the great exploratory voyages of the eighteenth and nineteenth centuries, notably those of Laperouse, Cook and Dumont d'Urville in the Pacific Ocean.

The crossing of the seas spread the knowledge of commodities that were once unknown, rare, and dear, such as tobacco, sugar, coffee, tea, cocoa, silk, and rubber, which came one by one into European purview. Their fall in price due to the cheapness of sea transport encouraged the demand for them and stimulated their production, so that overseas trade was the chief factor in plantation development. It has also enabled colossal cargoes of foodstuffs, raw materials, and, later, manufactured goods to pass between industrial and non-industrial countries. Great crowds of people amounting to hundreds of millions of persons, who were formerly confined to their surroundings have entered the circle of world trade either as sellers or as buyers. The spread of trade to the ends of the civilised world was due to traffic across the seas. To it is also due the widening of the civilised world through the ferrying of crowds of emigrants over the seas from the days of the slave trade until the cessation of the vast white transoceanic migrations on the morrow of the first world war.

At the same time a change has taken place in the political view of the sea. Up to the sixteenth century each region of the sea was accepted as a world apart, and its shores were the objects of political domination. But from the beginnings of modern times the dream of world hegemony has not seemed a chimæra, though realisation always conflicted with it owing to the exiguity of the continents and the limits of geographical configuration. It seems possible for a nation to gain command of the sea: 'He who holds the sea has by that very fact great power on land.' The idea of unconditional control of the high seas had not occurred to Roman law, so the ancient world left modern man wholly unprepared to face the new problems, and fresh juridical conceptions were to appear. It is easier for us today to realise changes of view in international law, for we have witnessed the codification of new jurisprudence in air navigation, whose regulations are very different and to some extent opposed to those of maritime law.

In 1494 Spain and Portugal tried to secure to themselves the control of the oceans by dividing their domains along a meridian. But the Roman conception, which was opposed to the appropriation of the sea, won the day with the triumph of the principle of the 'freedom of the seas'. Though the command of the sea cannot be exercised as a right, it belongs in fact to those nations whose sailors are best

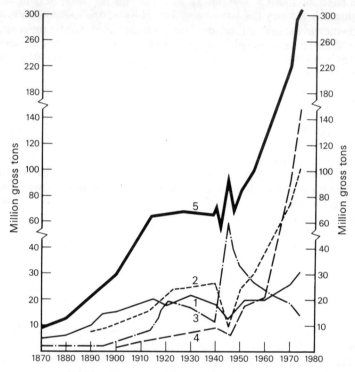

FIG. 5.—GROWTH OF WORLD MERCHANT FLEETS.

1. Great Britain. **2**. Remainder of Europe. **3**. United States. **4**. Remainder of world. **5**. World growth.
The breaks in the vertical scales indicate a change of scale.

equipped, most energetic, and most fitted to bring world trade under their flags. Sea power is but a reflection of a nation's general strength and the extent of its international relations, which means, of course, its general level of civilisation. Mastered by the progress of man's knowledge and acting as a universal bond between men, the sea belongs to those who can place their most efficient skill and most disinterested knowledge at the service of all mankind. Such an attitude excludes all autarky, all totalitarianism, and everything that restricts the area of trade and man's cultural horizons.

If the distribution of the main centres of maritime civilisation is examined on a world map without taking into account the period when each of them was particularly outstanding or their present decadence, it will be seen that some regions, and even whole continents, have always been backward in maritime enterprise. Among the latter was ranged the American continents up to the end of the eighteenth century. Except for a few restricted districts in which activity was local, namely, the Aleutian Islands, the Californian coast, the West Indies, and Tierra del Fuego, the Amerindian lived a landsman's life. Though it must be admitted that in the fifteenth century the Quechuas in the time of the Inca Yupanqui were able to sail from the coast of Peru to the Pacific islands, this effort was an isolated expedition manned by bold warriors on rafts (*balsas*).

It was only in the eighteenth century that American shipping appeared, and it fell into decay when iron replaced wood in ship construction and the steam engine replaced sails as a means of propulsion. Only since 1917 has it been possible to speak once more of United States shipping and for the first time of Canadian shipping on the high seas. Hence it was the transplantation of European civilisation into America that opened the coasts of the continent to maritime activity. This feature of our civilisation is the last gift that the Old World has given to the New. It was not given until after the New World had adopted the kind of agriculture practised in Europe and based on European crops. Later, it adopted manufacturing industry based on the use of coal and so took on another European practice.

Furthermore, every nation which has aspired at some moment in its history to worldwide relations has tried to reach the sea, to control its approaches, or to ally itself with maritime peoples. There are few land-locked States nowadays, viz. Austria, Hungary, Paraguay, Switzerland, Czechoslovakia, and the late French colony, now the Republic of the Congo. Several of these countries have secured rights of passage by arrangement with their coastal neighbours. The institution of free zones in big commercial ports for the benefit of certain users is in answer to a need imperatively felt by inland nations to have access to the sea. The need is so vital that the right of access to the sea even for nations which do not occupy part of the coast has been recognised by international law. This right of access is in process of becoming one of the fundamental principles of the body of international law, just as is the principle of the freedom of the seas.

On the morrow of the 1914–18 war reserved areas and special facilities in the German port of Hamburg were allotted to Czechoslovakia, which is connected to the sea by the international waters of the Elbe. But the most typical example at the present time is

Switzerland, which has a mercantile marine with a tonnage that reaches two-thirds of that of Portugal. As far back as the first world war Switzerland had rights in the two ports of Sète and Genoa. In 1921 the Barcelona Conference recognised the right of every country, even those without a coastline, to have an ocean-going merchant fleet, provided that it had on its own territory a port of registry as the headquarters of shipping companies flying its flag. Swiss ships frequently seen at Antwerp, Rotterdam, Genoa, and Marseilles are registered at Basle. This unexpected creation of a merchant fleet by a mountain state landlocked in central Europe illustrates better than any other example the need felt by all great modern states to have transport across the sea.

A thrust towards the sea has been a motive of diplomacy, an object of many empires, and the origin of latent rivalries that have added venom to diplomatic struggles of another kind. Some of these thrusts towards the sea have remained classic; for instance, that of Austro-Hungary towards the Mediterranean in 1914; that of Russia towards the Pacific, Baltic, Black Sea, and even the Mediterranean; that of Yugoslavia towards the Adriatic and the Ægean; and, lastly, that of the United States towards the Pacific and to strategic control of Central America, which enabled it to take full advantage of its position on two oceans. In this plan for exclusive control are included the efforts of the United States to prevent Japan from getting a footing in Central America and their precautions to ensure their monopoly of the Panama Canal and of all the canals that might be made across the isthmus.

Some countries with wide outlets to the sea have, on the other hand, tried to extend their rule to the coasts opposite. For a time Sweden succeeded in making the Baltic into a 'Swedish lake'; England had for long years encircled the Indian Ocean with British ports of call; and the United States is trying to make an 'American Mediterranean' of the Gulf of Mexico and the Caribbean Sea. The freedom of the high seas is a corollary of the desire to take possession of coastal areas.

Coastal waters to a breadth of three sea miles alone come under the control of the coastal nation. This figure, which was formerly uniform throughout the world, was based on the distance that a cannon could fire; in recent times it has been extended in many areas to 4 or 6 miles, or even, as in the case of the Sea of Okhotsk, to 10 miles, and no longer for military reasons, but rather to protect national rights over fisheries and over possible oilfields on the continental shelf. This principle of the freedom of the seas, which since the nineteenth century has been universally considered as a necessity, shows better than any other criterion the vital importance of the sea for maritime nations.

However, with the increasing power that modern technology has given to human activities, it is apparent that only the most advanced nations are capable of reaping the benefits, and then often at the expense of others, and to the extent of totally exhausting the resources of the open seas. The disappearance of whales from the northern hemisphere, the slaughter of seals in high latitudes, the continued reduction in the stocks of herring and cod in the North Atlantic and European waters, now well documented by biological specialists, have shown the dangers of this 'free-for-all'. The worldwide catch of fish, which stood at a level of 19 million tonnes in 1938, has reached 60 to 70 million tonnes a year since 1965. Such an excessive exploitation can only lead to the progressive depopulation of the seas.

In the case of fishing, it is recognised that there must be some limitation. Several maritime countries, such as Iceland, Newfoundland, Canada, Brazil, and Peru, are very disturbed to find their coastal fisheries plundered and brought near to devastation by the trawlers and factory ships of certain western European nations, the Soviet Union, and Japan. A first means of protection is the extension of territorial waters; at international conferences held in Geneva and in Caracas, there was a majority in favour of a 12-mile limit; but Canada, Brazil, Peru, and Iceland considered this insufficient and agreed to the creation, beyond territorial waters, of an 'economic zone' extending for 200 nautical miles (370 km). Save under particular agreements, this zone would be forbidden to foreign fishermen and industrial prospectors. Antarctic fisheries have also been the subject of restrictive measures, designed to fix each season's maximum catch of whales.

The discovery of immense submarine mineral resources, however, makes necessary a new definition of maritime law and of the freedom of the seas, which in future will doubtless be limited to freedom of passage and navigation. Rich oilfields have been located on the continental shelves and their adjacent slopes, so that riparian countries are now demanding that national frontiers should be extended to depths of 200 or 300 metres. Thus the discovery of oil and natural gas beneath the North Sea has resulted in the parcelling out of the sea bed between the chief bordering countries, United Kingdom, Norway, Denmark, Germany, and Netherlands, each reserving within its own sector the right of exploitation or the leasing of concessions to outsiders. Over the whole world, around Canada and the United States, Atlantic Africa, South America, and the Asiatic countries of the Middle East and the China Sea, the continental shelves are denied to free enterprise as far as prospecting and exploiting petroleum is concerned.

Furthermore, even the great oceanic depths seem likely similarly to be denied complete freedom of exploitation, for it is known that they contain enormous reserves of metallic wealth on the submarine plains at depths of 4,000–5,000 metres. In the central part of the Pacific Ocean the bottom is literally paved with manganese nodules, together with rarer metals such as cobalt and vanadium. Such resources are estimated at thousands of millions of tonnes, and modern technology may well soon be capable of extracting them from these great depths. But if this were done, it would make manganese, now relatively rare and costly, a common metal, and would ruin the present producing countries who, excluding the U.S.S.R., produce 96 per cent of the world's output and often rely on its export as their principal economic resource. This is why countries with no maritime activity, such as the African producers of manganese, are calling for some kind of internationalization of submarine resources and a severe limitation of the rights to exploit the oceanic depths. It is thus not sufficient, at the end of the twentieth century, simply to extend territorial waters to a greater distance from the land, or to limit fishing rights; the whole world economy is now concerned in the possibility of exploiting the depths of the oceans.

PART III

TECHNICAL FACTORS AND STAGES IN HUMAN EMANCIPATION

.

CHAPTER 9

DEVELOPMENT OF TECHNIQUES

The character of the physical environment and man's reaction to it do not adequately account for the differences in the modes of life that occur in the world, for man himself is a natural force that can make itself independent of the surroundings in a way impossible for plants and animals. The nature and effectiveness of human effort and the possibility of transplanting modes of life and complex activities into other parts of the globe far from where they were first developed certainly bring technology into the scope of human geography. Thus it is possible to observe in similar natural environments striking differences between various human groups. These are essentially due to differences in the degree to which techniques have been developed, that is, the degree to which the means of acting and reacting on Nature so as to elude its influence have been acquired. Within the same climatic region differences in techniques may destroy the basic uniformity of nature's influence.

FROM A PREDATORY LIFE TO INTENSIVE AGRICULTURE

The spread of techniques is seen even in the earliest stages of civilisation. Strictly speaking, primitive peoples, the *Naturvölker* of German geographers, are in a state of nature and still quite without any techniques. In fact, such people do not exist or, at any rate, exist no longer.

From our knowledge of prehistory we know that the rudiments of civilisation contain elements of techniques and that these go back to distant times when the distribution of climate over the globe was quite different from what it is now. Even among the most primitive, most isolated peoples who are not sheltered from the influence of higher civilisations man is very far from being in the state of nature described by eighteenth-century philosophers. On material foundations, some of which were very restricted, there was often built a very complex social organisation with a psychological treatment of the environment marked by totemic practices and tabus at least as much as by utilitarian considerations.

Thus, palaeolithic and neolithic clans one after another learnt the use of fire, the manufacture of tools, clay modelling, the making of rope and yarn, and, lastly, the art of weaving. Yet it is certain that with prehistoric man as with the last primitive peoples of today the techniques were still too crude to be able to save man from the tyranny of nature, especially in his efforts to find means of existence: food, clothes, and shelter.

For primitive man nature herself provides food on the shore, in plants, and in animals; but as a rule these supplies are not directly available, for to be used they require man to have tools or weapons, to observe, to take coordinated measures, to be disciplined, and to have a tactical plan. Consequently, the palaeolithic peoples, like primitive folk in the world today, adopted three elementary modes of life: gathering, hunting, and fishing.

It is to be noted that in most cases these three activities are found together and are combined in the modes of life of backward and underdeveloped peoples. The example quoted above of the Eskimos and the aborigines of central Australia and East Africa bear witness to this. They also show that these embryonic primitive techniques are observed to continue among peoples who are of very different race, but who have all undergone complete, lengthy isolation away from mankind's general movement.

A feature common to such civilisations is the weak connexion between man and the soil. He is continually moving in search of food; he is a nomad whose track is not marked on the land over which he roams. He wanders over huge areas to satisfy his immediate wants. Among his companions social structure is ill-defined. There is no division of labour except the sharing of tasks of men and women in the clan on the basis of the difficulty of the work. Now, division of labour is a necessary condition of the growth of techniques and the development of civilisation. It assumes settlement in a fixed place and as a result the new conception of a personal right to own the soil. With cultivated plants, domestic animals, and a piece of land, regular work, and thought for the future there appears the whole complex of pastoral, agricultural, or agro-pastoral civilisation whose innumerable aspects have been included above in the description of the world's various regions.

Of all man's steps taken to rise above the condition of a purely predatory animal still quite near to the brute creation and its hazards, agriculture has by far the greatest amount of geographical evidence of success, for even in the world of today it is the occupation of the majority of mankind. It produces an enormous mass of raw material and foodstuffs for consumption or trade, and it has profoundly changed the face of the globe. Original vegetation has been destroyed, forests cleared away, and a wholly artificial landscape of cultivation substituted for the natural vegetation-types. This is a phenomenon that affects area and results in the greatest variety of geographical shades of difference.

We have seen that agriculture involved first of all a choice of plants intended for systematic cultivation. These were taken from their wild condition and in some way adapted by man. The cultivation of plants creates more or less close ties between man and the land. These are looser when techniques are still undeveloped or when material conditions are particularly unfavourable; but closer when man is in possession of a number of implements and has evolved methods capable of mastering the soil. In the former case agriculture is extensive and in the latter it is intensive.

Between these two systems there is a fundamental difference. With the extensive system man has no permanent ties with the field he cultivates, and the work is of a nomadic, itinerant, and superficial character. In the intensive system man dwells permanently on the same spot and clings to his land tenaciously. The first of these systems is generally found among underdeveloped peoples, whilst the second characterises peoples who have reached a high degree of technical civilisation.

The basic feature of the extensive system is that cultivated areas are continually being changed. The natural vegetation is destroyed, usually by fire; and when there is no longer any yield from the soil, another piece of ground is used. This procedure is followed by the Korkus in central India, the Mois in Indo-China, and the Fang in Gabon. The system reflects the backward state of the peoples who use it. The digging-stick and hoe are its essential implements, and no domestic animals are used in cultivation, which is restricted to crops that are easily grown and easily reproduced. These consist of a few grain crops, some fruit trees, and, more particularly, tubers. This sort of cultivation is, therefore, especially in favour in tropical Africa and South America, and in the Pacific Islands within the hot belt.

Survivals of the system are found in certain features of rural law. It is incompatible with private property and generally calls for a scheme of communal land tenure. It sometimes requires a redistribution of land at fixed periods and regulates the common use of certain rights to the area left undistributed. Even in countries with advanced techniques that characterise the intensive system of agriculture in temperate regions, the right to common pasture land and the use of fallow by the herds and flocks of the village was a survival in the nineteenth century of the stage of extensive agriculture through which most of the agricultural peoples of Europe and other temperate lands have had to pass.

Owing to the steady work which it involves and to the need to fertilise the crops and supplement nature's parsimonious supply of water, intensive agriculture has given rise to innumerable complex techniques which constitute just so many systems of cultivation. Methods as well as implements vary from place to place. It is possible, however, by ignoring differences of detail to consider that there exist today two main areas in which cultivation is intensive.

One of them, the Eastern, seems to be ossified. It has developed little and has scarcely spread during the past centuries. Bound up with rice cultivation, its agricultural techniques attained to a high degree of perfection at a very remote period. The other, the Western, is of more recent origin and is due to the development of the extensive system of cultivation which was widespread in Europe up to the end of the nineteenth century. Indeed, it has not ceased to spread, for European colonisation has taken it to America, South Africa, Australia, and Siberia. At the present day its unequal development appears to depend on the region and the age of its introduction.

The intensive system now found in the West is based mainly on the association of ploughing and stock-rearing, which is the fundamental difference between the extensive system practised by underdeveloped peoples and the intensive hand cultivation of the peoples of the Far East. It represents a constant effort to improve the soil, struggle with the climate, arrange and distribute useful plants, and increase the strength of men and animals by the use of suitable machinery. Without doubt, the technical revolution on which it was based was the spread of plough cultivation, a development that was inconceivable without strict symbiosis between cultivation and the rearing of draught animals. The plough seems to have been invented in the Old World and to have been introduced recently into America and Australia in a form that will be difficult to improve. Whilst as early as the middle of the Neolithic period hoe cultivation took root simultaneously in agricultural communities very distant from each other, the use of the plough seems, on the contrary, to have had its beginnings on the grasslands of western Asia and southeastern Europe. The primitive plough was just a hook-shaped tree branch which was dragged along by slaves or animals. This important technical revolution took place on the steppes of the temperate region, from which indeed man got both his food plants and his draught animals. In the end it spread not only towards western Europe, but also towards the East, to China, Indo-China, and India, where the use of the plough now exists together with hoe cultivation.

Later, the primitive plough was shod with flint and still later with an iron share. Gradually, it was fitted with the now familiar accessories. In classical Greece it had wheels; the Romans added the mould-board. But even today a sort of spade or hoe dragged along by men is used for ploughing in remote parts of China and Korea.

The invention of the plough was not a case of mere technical progress from cultivation by hand or hoe, but a revolution with many divergent consequences entailing a break from the old agricultural tradition. It was in fact to end in specialisation and the training of certain animals to draw carts and the plough as well as in a different arrangement of the arable. Instead of a plot of land with ill-defined, irregular, brushwood-surrounded outlines which satisfied hoe cultivation, the work of the plough demanded a big, long field with a regular geometrical shape.

Up to the eighteenth century the implements used in intensive cultivation in Europe had scarcely been improved. Added to the plough was the harrow, which was made of iron pegs strongly imbedded in an iron frame; then the roller, consisting of a massive trunk of oak or beech and used for pressing the earth on to the seed. The implements used for reaping long remained rudimentary. For the bronze sickle of the neolithic cultivators was substituted a longer, lighter iron blade. From the Middle Ages up to the eighteenth century the implements used by the labourer were restricted to spades, hoes, rakes, axes, forks, flails, and wooden shovels, osier winnowing baskets, and sieves. At the end of the nineteenth century the reaper-and-binder machine brought about a revolution like that of the plough, for, except in regions like the semi-arid plains of the American West, where summer is dry and reaping can be prolonged, the harvest was always a critical time for grain cultivators. The peasant was less concerned about the sowing and growth of his wheat than about the hazards that might interfere with the course of the harvest. He restricted the amount of seed to the acreage which he could harvest. Machinery has upset the *data* of the problem. Applied at first to reaping, mechanisation and, later, the use of the motor engine have permitted a theoretically boundless expansion of various crops and the tilling of the whole of the cultivable soil. In these days a crop has all the more chance of increasing if the ways of dealing with it are suitable for mechanisation.

LAND-USE PLANNING AND THE IMPROVEMENT OF THE SOIL

The planning of land use is another aspect of the improvement in the methods of the intensive system. Gradually, certain crops have been linked by man and his dependants with problems of production and consumption. Quite early the cultivable land included not only the arable, but also gardens, plantations of trees and shrubs, and fodder crops. Wooded areas and heaths covered with residual or spontaneous vegetation have been added to the productive land, for heaths yield cuttings of heather, bracken, or gorse for stable litter or for making compost; and land temporarily out of cultivation together with heath and undergrowth have always been used for grazing animals.

In contrast with these carefully tilled areas are the unstable patches cleared by fire in the scrub or the forest, for intensive cultivation allows perfect and continuous use of the soil, a continuity unknown in extensive cultivation. Planning, then, is not confined to the removal of spontaneous vegetation, but often demands important constructive work, like the draining of polders and swamps. In such areas the cultivated land is protected from invasion by the sea by lines of dykes arranged in successive rows or in zigzag fashion. In some vineyards in the Iberian peninsula it has been necessary to remove barren sand so as to reach the soil below, which is capable of sustaining plant life. To check excessive damp and assist drainage on some islands off the Atlantic coast of Europe farmers collect earth and pile it up in long ridges to form strips of fertility on the barren heath. Of like character are the terraced hillsides in Mediterranean lands, western Asia, and North Africa. On slopes in the Douro valley and in Madeira such terraces form huge tiers held up by walls having an area far greater than that of the parcels of land which they support on the hillsides. These tiny parcels are vitally precious, it is true, on account of the rich crops they carry, the quantity of human toil which they represent and reward, and the great market value of the produce they infallibly yield.

The appearance of land depends therefore on the system of cultivation applied to it. Bare and open in large-scale cereal cultivation, with little pasture, and for long used as poor grazing during fallow, the rural landscape is cut up into a disorderly patchwork with ill-assorted crops, and enclosed by quickset hedges, spinneys, banks of earth, or low walls whose stones come from the ground enclosed, by fences, or some other means of enclosure. In districts where there is mixed farming, there is plenty of grass and a good supply of animals. Thus the arrangement of the crops usually determines the look of the various kinds of country.

Nowadays some of these districts, like vineyards or cereal country, are specialised. Others contain different kinds of crops, five or six being found together. Of these different land uses, *fields* are essentially ploughland, regularly used for crops of cereals, tubers, or plants that need weeding, in a succession regulated by the system of rotation of crops whose vegetative cycle is completed within the year. By means of fallow or, more and more, by crop rotation, most systems of cultivation avoid the exhaustion of the soil, some crops being particularly exhausting. Thus, the field puts on a different dress not only in the course of the year, but also from one year to another. The changes follow a rhythm connected with the constitution of the soil and with sowing, weeding, and reaping.

Plantations of trees and shrubs occupy the soil permanently. The oldest trees so used are the olive, vine, and chestnut. Orchards of fruit and nut trees are more modern, often specialised, and even industrialised. Plantations do not properly belong to the European

10. Water-power site in New England; paper mill on the Androscoggin river, originally established to use water power at a break of gradient, later using steam power

INDUSTRIAL USE OF WATER POWER

11. Hydro-electric power station in the Canadian Shield at Barretts Chute, Ontario

12. Typical spinning-mill architecture at Shaw, Lancashire

TEXTILE INDUSTRIES: COTTON

13. Mechanisation in the cotton industry

system of intensive cultivation, but in more primitive types of rural economy they form areas of great value, in which the most scientific techniques are applied. Groves of date palms require man's constant attention to their irrigation, fertilisation, and the maintenance of their numbers. More scientific still and dependent on advanced technique are plantations of coffee, tea, rubber, or oil palms which all bear great likeness to the big specialised orchards in Florida or California and to the extensive vineyards in Languedoc, La Mancha, and the northwestern Argentine.

Gardens contain in a small space various trees together with crops cultivated according to an annual calendar. Before market vegetables were cultivated on a large scale, various kinds of them were supplied by gardens; but in plots attached to village houses, as in the *dvors* which Russian peasants have even at the present time, there used to be a mixture in varying proportions of grain crops, shrubs, vegetables, melons, cucumbers, and strawberries, aromatic or decorative plants, and sometimes even industrial crops like hemp, which was formerly grown in fresh, well-manured soil near the farms, or like china-grass (*ramie*) which still remains a garden crop in China.

These bits of land, which are sometimes very, very small, too small to be ploughed, with the sum total of human toil expended on them, the mass of fertiliser and manure applied, the frequent watering and making up, the quick rotation of different crops in the same plots, and the presence in the same plot of crops with different periods of growth and maturity, represent one of the most intensive forms of cultivation and use of soil. Horticulture imports into the sphere of European cultivation techniques from the Far East based on a vast expenditure of human toil. The *huertas* in the south of Spain and in Mediterranean France and the Italian countryside in which *coltura promiscua* prevails, afford with their set of different crops examples of districts where the garden predominates.

Grassland, or *pastureland*, is that part of the farm land reserved exclusively for the production of grass and fodder. It is always maintained, if necessary by irrigation. Like the field it needs reaping equipment, which nowadays is mechanised, for cutting, drying, and storing hay. After the hay has been cut, the pasture can be used for grazing. Besides natural grassland which has merely to be maintained, farms include areas of man-made pasture formed and maintained by the same kind of work as is used to make arable fields productive. But man-made grassland, the material symbol of the association of animals with agriculture, demands less frequent attention than does the field. Even when it is included in a system of rotation, it occupies the ground for two consecutive years.

In a region where agriculture is intensive, *forest* is seldom the residue of a natural vegetation-type any more than is the *heath*.

Their inclusion in the region at once entails measures to maintain them, rules for their use, and in the case of the forest especially, a whole science of arboriculture based on the selection of species, plans for felling and clearing, and the protection of the undergrowth. When forest is included in a region, it supplies not only wood for building, for making fences and implements, and for fuel, but also foodstuffs of high cash value and raw materials for modern industry. Mushrooms and fruit from the undergrowth sometimes give rise to a seasonal occupation in collection and canning, and this appeals for labour over a fairly wide radius. Lastly, like the heath, the forest also supplies litter and grazing for the local district.

These various ways of using the land are sometimes clearly separated by fences. But often, too, the fields, meadows, woods, and gardens dovetail into each other. Some areas are both field and grassland, in which there are successive crops of cereals, tubers, vegetables, and winter fodder. Other areas, like the *joualles* in Aquitaine or certain districts in north Italy, are regularly devoted to vines, fruit trees, and grain, or green vegetables. In the most fertile districts the use of fallow, which in some places is bound to last a long time, causes the reappearance of heath dotted with brushwood among the cultivated land. In these areas an increase in green crops at the expense of grain in the arable is accompanied by a change in the farmers' outlook and by a profound alteration in the traditional system of cultivation.

These various combinations and frequent changes in the rural landscape reflect the extraordinary flexibility of intensive agriculture and enable an estimate to be made of the degree of independence of natural conditions won by the farmers. In old agricultural countries crops do not all occupy the ground that their importance would seem to require, and their distribution is explained by causes other than natural factors. Even in new countries, where agriculture has adopted the essential features of European cultivation, the siting of crops has not ceased to vary during the nineteenth and twentieth centuries.

To study the siting of the various products of intensive cultivation one must not consider each product by itself, as if it could choose the best place in which to thrive. One must also consider the siting of rival crops. Thus, in Australia, as formerly in the United States, a struggle for expansion is going on between wheat, barley, and oats, between wheat, maize, and tobacco, between fruit orchards and the vine, and between cotton, maize, and sugarcane.

Besides, some crops have been driven out by others that have become of greater value or are hardier and better able to adapt themselves to natural conditions. Furthermore, the social structure of an agricultural country has a direct influence on the patchwork of crops. Thus in Australia stock-rearing on an extensive system by squatters has retreated before the advance of cultivation, as the large property owner gave way to smallholders who had just a few acres of land. In the Argentine the spread of cultivation in the province of Buenos Aires has, however, been checked by the opposition of large stock-rearing landowners. During the twentieth century there has been in new countries generally a retreat of stock-rearing before the advance of agriculture and a progress of wheat and other cereals from the coast towards the grasslands of the interior. Almost everywhere, too, large-scale grain production has been replaced by dairy produce, sheep have disappeared as horned cattle have advanced, and ordinary cultivation has retreated before irrigation and market gardens. These developments are only adaptations due to new techniques and to the demands of the world market. Hence, since the end of the nineteenth century they have been controlled by the crises and demands of the world market far more than by favourable regional factors.

Up to about 1870, indeed, the European market for agricultural produce had to deal with only a small number of other markets whose productive capacity was small; but about the same time there took place outside the sphere of agriculture a technical revolution in land and sea transport. This lowered the barrier of distance which had isolated Europe from the more distant markets. Within a few years after 1872 the cost of transport was reduced by more than a half for wheat despatched by rail from Chicago to New York, and American wheat brought to Europe across the Atlantic cost less than the European product. In overseas countries railway construction caused an economic upheaval which told wholly in their favour since their almost virgin soil was capable of giving a good yield without being maintained by fertiliser, and since in them land was cheap and still suffered neither the changes nor the handicaps that hamper production in old self-contained agricultural countries. Europe was unable to face the competition of this superabundant, cheap supply without a revolution in her use of land and in her system of cultivation.

In wheat production, for instance, a whole host of countries became producers one after the other as they got the necessary machinery. In the United States the number of cereal farms rose from 2 million in 1860 to 5 million about 1900. The area sown increased from 7·6 to 19·1 million hectares, wheat production jumped from 173 to more than 546 million bushels, and American cereals were sold in Europe as far east as Bohemia. Then from 1880 Canada extended her area sown from 925,000 to 1·8 million hectares. The Argentine increased hers from 1·6 million to 4 million hectares, and Australia from 1·3 million to 2·2 million hectares; and during the same period

Russian exports rose to 4 million tonnes a year. In the face of these gigantic imports the price of wheat continued to fall in Europe. Supplies from the United States had already caused a fall of 25 per cent, and after 1895 imports from Russia and the Argentine provoked a further fall of 18 per cent.

This crisis had an enormous effect on European agriculture, for it accelerated its mechanisation and industrialisation. Whilst the sickle and flail gradually went out of use, applications of chemical fertiliser abolished fallow, and scientific technique came to the help of traditional experience. Crossing improved the breeds of domestic animals, and selection increased the yields of corn, potatoes, and sugarbeet. The farmer gradually gave up his independence and individualism to join in cooperative societies and to pass from an almost closed society to one of open trading. To assist production, the purchase of supplies, and the sale of produce, associations of farmers were quickly formed in Denmark, the Netherlands, and Germany and later, in France and Italy. These changes nearly everywhere involved the introduction of tariffs meant to favour agricultural production in Europe in the local market, and so a precept of economics was formulated by which each country should draw from its own soil the food needed for its people. This theory was not accepted or acted upon in the United Kingdom. The developments were all destined to bring about more or less quickly a change in the appearance of the countryside and a fresh system of crop distribution.

One of the first results was the discontinuance of the traditional crops in favour of new ones. In the first place Europe gave up producing raw materials on her farms, and sheep-rearing was one of the first activities affected. Since the Middle Ages the high market value of wool had caused good returns to European farmers even on the poorest and most infertile soils, but the acclimatisation of wool-sheep in Australia, South Africa, and South America brought on to the market such vast quantities of cheap wool that the price of this raw material fell by more than 34 per cent. Silkworm rearing was similarly destroyed by the competition of Far Eastern countries, which had been brought closer by developments in transport. The sale of oil from cottonseed and groundnuts brought about a general decrease in olive cultivation in Mediterranean Europe, and at the same time the dropping of rapeseed from the traditional rotation of crops in western and central Europe. Of the textiles flax and hemp saw their crops reduced owing to the imports of foreign rivals, the chief of which was cotton. As for very profitable dye plants like madder, they disappeared from 1869 onwards in face of chemical dyes extracted from coal.

On the other hand, some crops benefited by the unprecedented boom. The effects of the crisis were aggravated on viticulture by the ravages of the Phylloxera, but within fifty years the vine gave rise in most of its important areas to a specialised and industrialised form of production. By 1885 it had recovered so greatly that wine production was not long in exceeding demand, and some of the vines were dug up so that the land might be used for other purposes.

Horticulture, that is, the intensive cultivation of green vegetables, fruit, and flowers, developed in proportion as the growth of towns involved modifications in the customary diet by affecting the social structure. In France there came into being a series of districts with market gardens and orchards whose produce was despatched in due season to the home or the export market. Market garden produce from Provence and Rousillon was followed by that from the lower Loire valley, by that from the Channel coast, and, lastly, by that from the Paris region and well watered districts in Picardy and Flanders.

Lastly, the fall in the value of wool, which led European farmers to treat the sheep no longer as a source of that commodity, but of meat, was accompanied by a change in the series of crops. The English breed of mutton-sheep could not in fact be kept on poor pasture and stubble. It dislikes dust, heat, drought, and travel, so fields of clover, lucerne, or roots had to be planted to produce feed for it. In less than fifty years the number of sheep fell off by 75 per cent in Germany and 40 per cent in France. In place of sheep, horned cattle and pigs increased enormously in number, and this caused fallow to be replaced by rich fodder crops that were not seldom added as the last item in the old three-year rotation. The keeping of the animals permanently in stalls, which became possible owing to the abundance of farm-waste and by-products of agricultural industry, ended by making stock-rearing dependent on an increase in agricultural production.

The price of products from stock-rearing having fallen less than that from corn crops and the demand for meat and dairy produce having grown as the population increased, farming in Europe tended towards stock-rearing and dairying. Several regions in which the farmers had used their animals merely to provide food for their families, to give manure, and to work in the fields, now concentrated on the export of meat and dairy produce. By and large rural Britain became a vast grassland in which fodder crops replaced cereals. Gradually, the growing demands of industrial towns attracted butter from Denmark and the Netherlands to the English market. In this way the pull of the market of the United Kingdom had effected a great revolution on farming and agricultural practice beyond the frontiers of England right on to the continent.

In its turn stock-rearing had to adapt itself to the trends introduced into the supply of food by the progress of industrial technique.

About 1870 margarine, a substitute for butter and lard, appeared for the first time on the market. It had been discovered as a result of a competition initiated by Napoleon III. Shortly afterwards stock-rearers began a bitter struggle against the making of fat substitutes which little by little replaced animal fats, vegetable oil, and whale oil. By 1890 the demand for margarine had increased to such a degree that it necessitated a change in direction of intensive cultivation. Until then, in fact, animal fats had been of more value than meat, so that now farmers sent to market animals that were younger and younger and ready for slaughter in a very short time.

Thus, in the nineteenth century the crises that came upon European agriculture greatly modified its structure. During the twentieth century the world depression of 1929–36 merely accentuated developments that had begun previously. The problem was now in what way to struggle against the slump in traditional agricultural produce, and to replace them by new ones in the shape of lean meat, dairy produce, green vegetables, and fruit. Farming gradually became more and more industrialised, and protectionism tended everywhere to be strengthened.

Since the end of the second world war the general economic outlook has greatly changed, but it still continues to move in the direction of increasing the intensive system of cultivation by introducing more and more scientific techniques into underdeveloped regions.

In spite of slumps man's need of foodstuffs has increased faster than harvests have, mainly because of an unprecedented rise in world population. Besides, in overseas lands the agricultural output has not slackened, and these countries have to an appreciable extent followed Europe in giving up cereals in favour of vegetables and dairy produce. In the United States the pioneer age has ended, and, moreover, the demands of the home market have increased to such a degree as to make the exports of meat and wheat insignificant. In Canada and Argentina the best lands have already been cultivated. Lastly, the Soviet Union absorbs in the home market the whole of its agricultural production, both foodstuffs and industrial raw material. Hence, economists are wondering whether world agriculture is capable of modifying its systems of production and the planning of its farm land quickly enough to satisfy the ceaselessly growing demands for foodstuffs. But such fears are groundless, for innumerable agricultural peoples are still using out-of-date methods and have not been touched by the great development that gave European agriculture all its flexibility and all its efficiency. New countries have scarcely begun to practise mixed farming and crop rotation in a reasonable way. The people of the Far East have not yet succeeded in introducing stock-rearing into their plan of work. In fact, the use of techniques can swell agricultural production to astonishing proportions, to such a degree indeed as to render excessive a regular or even periodically slackening production, as was seen in the last century. Geographers must guard against hasty generalisations based on a mere examination of statistics and schedules, and they must not subscribe to the theories of pure economists. In the eighteenth century Malthus calculated that the population of the world would be 20,000 million persons in 1950, and we are still far from that figure. In 1934 demographers foretold that live births in France would not be more in number than a figure which has in fact been exceeded ten times. Lastly, in 1898 Crookes, an English scholar, predicted world famine in 1938, a date on which the world was just recovering from a crisis of general over-production. It may, therefore, be thought that the fears of present-day prophets are without a more serious foundation and that their calculations are no more realistic than those of their predecessors in the dangerous path of forecasting the destiny of the human race and the limitations of its agricultural activities.

CHAPTER 10

RISE OF THE INDUSTRIAL MODE OF LIFE

Industry is to be found everywhere on earth, in every age, and in every degree of technique. It is older than agriculture, older even than pastoralism, for there existed even in prehistoric times places where flint was shaped. Flint implements chipped at Pressigny in France were traded over a wide area. Most primitive men have tools even when they are ignorant of cereal cultivation or the art of domesticating animals. The need for food, clothes, shelter, and defence made various tools, weapons, utensils, and fabrics or dressed skins an absolute necessity.

It is impossible, however, to speak of an industrial mode of life or an economy based on industry so long as the work was carried out in the narrow family circle and its products merely used on the spot, for then the operation formed part of the economic complex which was predominantly pastoral or agricultural according to the influence of conditions in the environment and of the techniques. The industrial mode of life does not really appear until the work is done no longer just for personal use by the individual maker or for the use of members of his narrow community, but for the purpose of trade and with a market in view. It was in the rise of wide intercourse between peoples that the industrial mode of life found the germ of its growth and the basis of its existence. In this intercourse must be sought the motives that inspired technical inventions, discovery of new processes, and the division of labour. In every age and in all countries the industrial mode of life has come into being and grown together with trade.

In early times Greece was a good market for the Phoenicians of the Mycenian era, and in the days described by Homer the Greeks still valued Phoenician goods above all others. Later, in the eighth and seventh centuries, B.C., the Greeks, especially those from Miletus, Chalchis, and Corinth, made persistent efforts to establish outlets in the shape of trading posts for their industrial products and to get markets from which to supply their own workshops. In the sixth and fifth centuries the Athenians began to turn their eyes towards the whole of the Mediterranean, and their industries became vigorous only as their overseas trade increased.

Besides these, many examples can be found in different ages and different countries. China, whose silk cloth and pottery were intended for export as far as to the West, collected around herself a whole host of economic dependants from Japan and India on the one hand to the oases of western Asia on the other. In central Africa and even among the primitive Australian tribes it is possible to find clans that are specialists in the manufacture of tools or weapons and which owe this direction of their rudimentary economy to markets that existed among their neighbours. In the Middle Ages Flemish towns specialised in the cloth industry merely to supply goods to Mediterranean merchants.

In spite of the abundance of her wool, England became a great source of the commodity only when she could work for export and become the rival of the Flemings in Mediterranean and central European markets. Furthermore, she became the home of the great Industrial Revolution at the end of the eighteenth century when her trade spread over the whole world and distant markets became open to her. It is easy to understand the awakening of the spirit of industry in Manchester and Lancashire generally under the influence of trade, first with Ireland in the fourteenth century, then with the Levant through London middlemen, and, lastly, the business complex in Liverpool, which enabled Lancashire and Yorkshire to import wool and cotton cheaply from abroad so as to maintain a great mechanised industry. The same precedence of trade over industry is seen in Glasgow. Examples are no less numerous in France, where the silk industry at Lyon and the textile manufactures in Alsace and at Rouen were created by the demands of trade.

In days nearer to our own the United States did not awake to the industrial mode of life until the end of the nineteenth century. For long years the settlers preferred farm work to any other form of toil, and for more than a hundred years manufactured goods were imported from Europe. The United States did not become a great industrial country until they had a large market. At first such a market was found on their own immense territory, where from 1863 onwards fresh regions called for goods every day. The manufacture of farm machinery and vehicles followed the westward march of centres of grain cultivation. The growth of specialised agriculture was responsible for the manufacture of fertiliser in Georgia, to be used on the cotton and tobacco fields and the market gardens. The growth of towns brought brickfields and cement works to the fore. Near Denver the working of mines started a whole machine industry; and soon all the eastern region and the 'Manufacturing Belt' began to work to supply the vast West with manufactured goods. But though this industry was already huge, it needed the support of the world market, and during the free and widened phase in the two world wars the United States finally became a great industrial country. The new state of their industry is marked by a vast increase in the use of consumer goods, a colossal rush to export machinery, cotton goods, motor cars, aircraft, and machine tools to the whole world.

Thus every widening of geographical horizons and every increase in intercourse carries the formation of industrial centres into most parts of the earth. Under pressure from trade countries most advanced in techniques have had to think out material means of improving and multiplying their manufactures. In particular, because western Europe has become more and more commercial, it has become more and more industrial.

DEVELOPMENT OF THE FORMS OF INDUSTRIAL ECONOMY

The first stage in the development of the industrial mode of life is home and village industry. The family and the village are narrow circles aiming at satisfying their demands without asking anything from others. For long ages at the birth of civilisation and still today in some underdeveloped communities articles in common use are made by the family. By 'family' is meant here not the simple elementary group consisting of parents and children, but a wider whole, an extended family such as existed still a short while ago in western Serbia and included grandparents, collateral relatives, and even the servants. Members of the family are both workers and consumers, an arrangement that demands the development of a great variety of talents in the members of the little community. It was characteristic of Greek society in Mycenian and Homeric times as well as in that of Classical Greece, in which latter, however, several crafts had already emerged from the family circle to operate in specialised workshops. Some particularly isolated districts like the Pyrenees, Norway, and Bulgaria that were poor in surplus goods for use in trading long remained rooted to this elementary economy.

Village economy belongs to the same type of industry, for it is restricted to a closed circle and is a mere extension of family economy. It was characteristic of mediaeval village life in Europe during the feudal ages, and it is still to be found in big villages in India and Southeast Asia. In Europe crafts have gradually disappeared from the villages. First, there developed spinners, weavers, and nailsmiths, then tanners, hatters, tailors, joiners, cartwrights, locksmiths, and even bakers. The tendency to the separation of crafts was encouraged, then more and more increased, by the rise of trade, markets, and intercourse between peoples. Under this influence village economy lost ground. It did so easily in open countries, but was difficult to eradicate in closed countries.

As soon as trade appeared on the horizon, industry tended to escape from the narrow surroundings of the village and to concentrate in towns, where it found more labour, more trade, and greater possibilities for trade. In Europe this form of industrial concentration in the towns was general throughout the Middle Ages. Industry became strongly organised in corporations, which were larger groups than families, but were more specialised. It was characterised by low productivity, constant maintenance of the standard of work, and stability of the supply of labour, raw materials, and conditions of sale. It was due to the fixity of mediaeval society. Its chief aim was to produce goods for regional consumption, for costs of transport over long distances were prohibitive. There were some centres that had a wide trade radius; but they were few, and their activity was often short-lived. Flemish, Italian, and Rhenish towns all had their own times of prosperity.

A day came, however, when wider outlets opened up and towns were led to increase production. Labour had then to be sought in rural districts. In France the development began in the reign of Louis XI, but it took place rather earlier in England and even earlier in Flanders and Italy. The association of towns with rural areas in industry became the rule in western Europe in the seventeenth and eighteenth centuries. The town managed the work, but the looms and work-people were mainly in the country. This arrangement developed owing to the extension of the markets, which necessitated a call for hands from the country to form the labour sufficient to supply the greater demand. Moreover, industry brought in extra cash for the country-folk, who occupied their spare time with it in winter and did not give up working on the land. The combination of loom and field enabled the European countryside to be greatly overpopulated for nearly two hundred years.

The symbiosis lasted for a long time in the Black Forest, Upper Bavaria, the Erzgebirge, the Ardennes, and Bohemia. Today it still constitutes the basis of the silk industry at Lyon, in the region of Milan, and throughout Tosan in Japan. It is also found in some metallurgical industries in the Ardennes, Champagne, and the northern Jura. It might be revived in the modern industrial organisation, which is in course of formation, owing to the systematic decentralisation of some industries and the artificial industrialisation of rural districts. In fact, however, up to the great industrial crisis which preceded the second world war, a progressive disintegration of this association of town and country was evident, as industry became concentrated in large, specialised workshops and factories.

The greatest disadvantage of this industrial system is that its production is seasonal, small, and irregular owing to the instability of the work-people, for whom work in the fields is the spur to home industry. The system could not resist the extension of the markets or the increasing demand, and it already contains the germ of technical contraction, for some employers have acquired the habit of collecting near their residences the hands to whom they supply the articles needed for the work.

The factory system developed in England in the second half of the eighteenth century. It became general in France in the second quarter of the nineteenth century and in Germany twenty-five years later. The system introduced a series of technical changes known as the Industrial Revolution. It took place in countries with the widest and most vigorous foreign trade, that is, in Western Europe and first of all in England. The mechanical inventions that have revolutionised the world were all linked together to meet the need for increased production. In England, for instance, the textile industry was completely changed in twenty-five years. As a result of the improvement of the loom in 1733, the spinners were unable to supply yarn enough for the weavers, and the inventions of Hargreaves, Arkwright, and Crompton, between 1764 and 1779, were needed to give to spinning machinery the ability to supply vast quantities of yarn. The position was, therefore, reversed, and for a time the weavers were unable to use all the yarn supplied by the spinners. A fresh effort was needed to increase the output of the looms. About 1815, after Cartwright's invention of the power-loom, the weavers became able to work at the same pace as the spinners, and the mechanical loom replaced the hand-loom in the industry.

The revolution did not take place simultaneously in the various European countries. The more advanced a country was commercially, the earlier the development was accomplished. It was completed first in England, which was a maritime, commercial, and colonial power in full flight in the nineteenth century. It penetrated into France and then into Germany, but it was slow in reaching the United States, where it afterwards blossomed out, strengthened, and improved in such a way as to attain for man's advantage huge economies of time, labour, and costs.

THE NATURE OF LARGE-SCALE INDUSTRY

One of the chief features of the structure of industry as it was formed in the last century is its geographical concentration. By it a large number of wage earners are assembled in buildings in which powerful and delicate machinery is worked by water-power, steam, electricity, or the internal combustion engine. The machinery is too expensive to be bought by an individual worker, as were the old instruments that were worked by hand or by simple mechanisms, and it is too bulky to be housed in a craftsman's cottage Consequently, it is installed by big capitalists or public companies, or, in some kinds of political organisation, by the state. In any case its operation calls for the building of huge factories employing an ever growing number of skilled and unskilled workers. Factories crowd together and in the end form whole towns concentrating on a single industry. On the continent the oldest of such towns are the iron and steel centres of Le Creusot and Essen: in Great Britain it was the textile industries—cotton in Manchester and wool in Leeds—which gave them birth, and in the United States the engineering industries of New England and the Appalachians

This change in production technique has had incalculable results on the distribution of population. It soon caused the growth of vast industrial districts in which the density of population, artificially influenced by the concentration of industry, has immensely exceeded that of the richest agricultural countries. With a social structure differing profoundly from that of rural districts, the population no longer lives on local resources, as workers used to do in the days of home industry. Its maintenance by means of supplies brought almost wholly from outside demands an enormous increase in trade not only to secure the raw materials for the machinery to turn out vast quantities of manufactures, but also to feed and otherwise supply the swarm of workers. So was set in motion during more than two hundred years a cumulative process that up to the great crises of the twentieth century has built up around great industrial districts huge markets which require a ceaseless growth of trade superimposed on the trade that had initially caused the industries responsible for this hypertrophy.

In each of these modern industries there grew up very quickly a minute division of labour with the aim of increasing production through specialisation in single movements. The classic example is the Lancashire cotton industry, in which merchants bought the raw cotton and sold it to the manufacturers, others carried the raw material over sea or land, and still others, wholesalers, bought the manufactured goods from the mills to sell them again. Some wholesalers sold the goods to retailers in the United Kingdom, whilst others exported them. Some exporters dealt only with China. Furthermore, there were among the manufacturers, who were unskilled in commercial operations, an infinite number of specialisations, including among others spinners, weavers, bleachers, and, dyers. The first of these worked mainly in South Lancashire and were divided into makers of fine and coarse yarn. On the other hand, weavers were concentrated in East Lancashire and were divided according as they made hosiery, quilting, muslin, cotton cloth for export to India, etc.

From this division of labour came technical progress, since it limited a factory or department of a factory to producing a certain uniform type of goods, and this soon led to standardised production at a lower cost by experienced hands. Division of labour came into practice not only in single factories, but also between factories in the same line of production, and indeed between various industrial districts, which introduced it for reasons of economy. In metallurgy, for instance, countries like Great Britain, Germany, and France, which engaged in heavy industry and produced pig iron and steel, were distinguished from those engaged in light industry, like the Netherlands, Switzerland, and Italy.

Yet the division of labour, which commended itself to the technique of production, had great drawbacks for the management and independence of industrial firms. The increasing number of small firms provoked keen competition between factories and led them to lower their prices dangerously in order to sell their products. Besides, it was impossible for a little concern to estimate supply and demand exactly and, consequently, to avoid overproduction, which led to crises of glut, unemployment, and financial straits. The increasing number of producing firms caused a general rise in costs and difficulty in organising advertisement and sales. It also made equally difficult the raising of capital so as to expand production, exploit new inventions, and buy new machinery and equipment. Hence, the individual industries were soon induced to form organic concentrations, and this gave rise to the huge American trusts and more recently to the big Soviet *kombinaty*.

This concentration brought about first of all an integration of firms in the same industries with the object of planning the standardised mass production of a reduced number of lines. The movement led to the German cartels in the coal, steel, and chemical industries; and to the American trusts in steel, electrical apparatus, and oil production. A rapid development of such horizontal integration was seen everywhere: in Great Britain, Italy, and, still very slowly, in Germany.

Vertical integration began first in Germany after 1920 and led to a reduction in the transport of goods by making a continuous chain of production in the same factory between the raw material and the finished product. Instead of passing through several hands in the course of successive processes, the product is wholly made by one and the same firm. In this way the need for intermediate purchases is done away with. For instance, coal and iron mines, blast furnaces, and foundries are united under the control of a single firm. Such was the origin of the great concerns of Hugo Stinnes, Krupp, and Thyssen. This kind of integration gradually became systematic in the steel, oil, and, later, the chemical industries in the United States in spite of the anti-trust laws. In France it was practised by textile firms which controlled *estancias* in the Argentine for the rearing of wool-sheep, by rubber factories which started plantations of *heveas* in Southeast Asia, and by several big producers of chemical products. In Japan trusts combine the exploitation of mines, iron smelting, shipbuilding, shipping business, and colonial enterprise. In the

Soviet Union the creation of a heavy industry concern was entrusted to important state departments which combined the exploitation of ores and coal, the production of electricity, primary metallurgy, and the making of machinery.

These mighty integrations, whose activities affect the economics and foreign policy of whole countries, have all set up a rational organisation of production by controlling the work and the output of the workers and by simplifying the relations between factories, between industry and trade, and between the various sectors of the economy. This development and its cumulative results depends for its success on the capacity of world markets to absorb the production. In fact, several times in the course of the nineteenth and twentieth centuries industrial overproduction has not been avoided. It has caused in European and American industry crises of unemployment and a check on expansion, but it has also led to technical readaptations which have caused wholesale modifications in the structure and localisation of various industries. At the present time industrialisation is tending to spread to underdeveloped countries, but this kind of expansion assumes a constant increase in industrial production and a constant rise in the standard of living of the world's population.

Mechanical equipment has in fact led to an infinity of production, whilst hand work had for hundreds of years checked industrial expansion. In this way mechanisation has revolutionised the textile, boot and shoe, underwear, nail, and paper industries which were formerly worked mainly by craftsmen. The development has had economic and social effects. First of all, it has led to a greater use of manufactured goods by a greater number of persons. Since the last war there has been an extraordinary increase in the production of consumption goods catering for the everyday needs and comforts of the masses. Hence, the most active industries have been those producing motor cars, household equipment, wireless sets, films, and plastic goods. This expansion has been made possible by a certain levelling in the standard of life between the social classes in countries in which an ancient technical civilisation existed. Modern industry tends to bring about this levelling between different countries also, in such a way as to create a market with theoretically unlimited possibilities. But at present it is held up by obstacles due to the technical backwardness of certain sections of humanity, which nevertheless should represent an enormous mass of consumers and producers. At the present time continual industrial expansion assumes not only the development of activity in trade relations, but also the rapid rise of most of the undeveloped peoples to the technical level required for them to be able to become in their turn large consumers of industrial products.

Chapter 11

EVOLUTION AND DISTRIBUTION
OF THE INDUSTRIAL ECONOMY

The industrial mode of life begins and develops in places where the conditions necessary for its expansion are to be found. Such places should, first of all, ensure a supply of raw materials and have a sufficiency of labour. These conditions have been found indispensable everywhere in every age. But there is another requirement which appeared only at a recent period in human history, namely, a form of power capable of multiplying man's strength many times for the working up of raw materials. Coal, which gives steam, and water, which gives electricity, were the two localising factors of mechanised industry, before the discovery of other forms of power, the most recent of which is atomic, enabled industry to be widespread and decentralised.

During the age of steam and electric power it was already clear that local conditions alone did not ensure supplies of raw material, labour, and power; that outside factors intervened to modify distribution; and that the course of trade often brought to less favoured regions raw material, labour, and power which they could not have had from their own resources.

RAW MATERIALS

The presence of raw materials is the fundamental condition of all industry. Among primitive peoples industry naturally comes into being near places where raw materials are to be found. Owing to the fact that primitive man is obliged to use the gifts of nature for all his purposes, articles made by rudimentary peoples evince a deep impress of their place of origin. This is proved by ethnological collections, including central African hide shields, Polynesian grass mats, Amerindian feather cloaks, and primitive Indo-Chinese bamboo gadgets. Even in the most advanced stages of civilisation possession of a raw material favours the rise of industrial activity.

As early as prehistoric times 'workshops' were set up near beds of hard stone. Flint was particularly sought after, and some flint 'workshops' like those at Grand Pressigny supplied tools to distant tribes. The formation of groups of smiths or smelters near beds of ore is clearly shown in every country. The whole district of Laurium was in the time of ancient Greece a centre for working silver-lead ores. In England the centre of metallurgy was for a long time in the

260

Weald near ores in Lower Cretaceous beds. Similarly, in France ancient smithies cluster round easily exploited ores near the surface in Champagne, Burgundy, and Berry. Ores and stone, being heavy materials tend to attract industries to places where they are mined or quarried. But this rule was once far stricter than it is today, because there were formerly less efficient means of transport.

Food preparation has not always been an industrial occupation, but from the day it became so it has been closely linked with the areas in which the raw material was produced, since this was often perishable and needed instant processing. To this type of industry belong fish canneries, which are always on the coast; curing-houses for herring at Great Yarmouth and Fécamp; drying and salting sheds for cod at Norwegian ports and at Bordeaux; packing stations for salmon in New England and British Columbia and for sardines on the Atlantic coasts of Portugal and France; and oyster canneries at Baltimore. Fruit and vegetables are also processed and canned in places where they are grown. Thus, on the coastal plain of New York State and in California canneries are just annexes of orchards and market gardens. In France the districts north of Nantes and Agen, where vegetables and fruit are grown, have large canneries. A regular connexion can also be seen between the great slaughter houses in Chicago or Kansas City and the stock-rearing region of the Great Plains; between big dairy produce factories in Europe and the pastures in Switzerland and Saintonge; sugar-refineries and extensive fields of sugarcane or beet; and potato-starch works and important potato producing districts like Lincolnshire and Groningen.

As wood is heavy and relatively cheap, the work of roughing down tree trunks is done near forests, and sawmills are innumerable in wooded regions like parts of Canada and Scandinavia. Only the later trimming of timber can be done near places where it is sold. Yet many long-standing timber industries, such as clog-making, the minor industries in the Black Forest, and the *kustar* industries in the Russian *tayga* are carried on in forests. And there are other industries connected with forests because of the presence there of raw material. Such, for instance, are the tanneries which still exist near trees that supply tannin in the Appalachians and forests of the northeastern United States. A further example is the paper industry, which since 1867 has been using wood pulp as raw material instead of rags. Before this technical change took place the paper mills in the United States clustered along streams in the neighbourhood of centres of dense population. Since pulp came into use, the paper mills have moved to the forested parts of New York State and New England, where they also find water-power.

It is, however, in textile manufacturing that the dependence of industry on raw material is best seen. Before the Industrial Revolution, cloth-making and the manufacture of articles of clothing from each of the chief textile fibres, cotton, wool, and silk, were more or less tied to the regions where the raw material was naturally produced. The cotton industry first spread through hot countries, where the inhabitants wove from it the soft, flowing garments worn in Turkistan, India, the Sudan, and generally speaking throughout the Islamic world. The woollen industry goes back to prehistoric times, when the sheep was domesticated. Wool was used for making clothes by the peoples of Persia and the Mediterranean, for making tents by nomads, and for the manufacture of clothing by the nations of western Europe, where until the thirteenth century it was the chief raw material of cloth. There it gave rise to a great industry supplied with raw material by countless flocks of sheep kept on the fallow and moorland. The silk industry had its origin in China, where *Bombyx mori*, the silk-worm, was reared on mulberry leaves. Very soon silk gave rise in Chinese villages to a whole nation of weavers, who later adopted cotton as the chief raw material for making cloth for daily use by the lower orders.

Thus, the early textile industries always arose from local raw materials. There has been a suggestion that the geographical distribution of clothing types is a result of climate, and this supports the opinion that geographical conditions influence the beginnings of this very ancient industry. However, in the distribution of raw materials certain influences stem from man and not from nature. For instance, the introduction of domestic animals from Europe into the prairies of North America brought into these plains a plentiful raw material, and the spread of wheat and sugarbeet has in the same way introduced important raw materials into plains naturally without them. The Industrial Revolution and the growth of transport media, especially ocean shipping, helped to free the textile industries from dependence on local raw materials; cotton industries, for example, grew up in Lancashire, in New England, in northern France and at Lodz in Poland, whilst the Yorkshire woollen industry came to depend almost entirely on colonial and foreign sources of wool. Finally, the progress of the chemical industry has still further liberated textile manufacture, for synthetic fibres can now be produced from many different raw materials, throughout the year and whatever the climate.

In fact, industries now exist in places that are naturally without any form of raw material, but into which they can be imported cheaply by easy means of transport. Hence, worldwide trade between countries has stepped in to set industry free and to give it a paradoxical facility of flourishing, though it is far removed from the sources of raw material. Even in the ancient world people had learnt to go afar to seek raw materials. The great Mediterranean cities, Athens, Rome, and Byzantium, got them from every country visited by their ships, which brought them back to the workshops at home. In the Middle Ages English wool reached not only weavers in Flanders, but also the cities of Italy. Yet it is the modern age that has made trade the indispensable creator of industry. Great Britain, the cradle of textiles, still imports all its raw cotton, jute, and silk as well as a great deal of its flax, hemp, and wool. In spite of having plenty of raw silk, China had up to the second world war no industrial production of silk cloth, whilst the United States, though they did not produce raw silk, held one of the leading places in the production of silk cloth. This was because silk from the Far East was imported into the United States through Seattle and other Pacific ports. From there it went by rail to New England and the New York district on the other side of the American continent.

Similarly, heavy materials like certain ores cross the seas in huge quantities to centres where they are worked up. Iron, copper, tin, and zinc reach the United Kingdom by sea. In the United States, iron ore from Lake Superior passes through the Great Lakes to the blast furnaces in Pittsburgh. Thither too comes iron ore from Labrador by way of the St Lawrence Seaway. Iron ore from the Orinoco serves the coastal blast furnaces of Baltimore and Trenton. Copper foundries have been set up at New York, Baltimore, and Norfolk (Virginia) to smelt ores from Labrador, Newfoundland, Spain, Italy, Peru, and Canada. Aluminium factories in the southern United States, the St Lawrence region, and British Columbia get bauxite from Guiana and the West Indies. The potteries at Trenton (New Jersey) have long been getting half their china clay from England. In England itself the pottery towns in north Staffordshire get most of their clay from Cornwall. Large cargoes of grain come from Asia and America to flour mills and distilleries in Europe. The same is true of phosphate and natural rubber, which are sent from their production areas to Europe for working up.

Sometimes the carriage of raw materials in the crude state in which they leave the mine or plantation would be too expensive for distant or badly placed manufacturers to get them. In that case the raw material is given preliminary treatment and dressed so as to be able to bear the high cost of transport, before reaching the place where it is worked up. For instance, Switzerland overcomes the drawbacks of her landlocked position by finishing materials that have already been part manufactured. With the thread she imports she makes lace and embroidery. Some metallurgical centres that are far from the source of ore do not produce cast iron and steel. Getting them in the form of pig iron or ingots, they turn them into more elaborate, lighter, and more expensive articles. This is also what happens in twentieth-century Birmingham, and Italy and Japan similarly import most of their raw material from abroad (though Japan has also a very large import of iron ore from India, Malaya, and Australia to feed its rapidly growing iron and steel industry).

In a technically advanced civilisation in which industry has attained a high degree of skill and motive power under the constant urge of the spirit of invention, it sometimes happens that one branch of industry has at its disposal raw material worked up by other branches. One industry leads to another, and in a highly industrialised district the proliferation of branches of industry has no limit. Science has, indeed, added enormously to the commodities that can be worked up further. By distilling coal man has got from very crude material a whole collection of previously unknown products: gas for light and heat, and all the products extracted from the residual coal-tar: benzine, dyes, disinfectants, and fertilisers. The refining of mineral oil gives a whole set of even more valuable products that are used as raw material for making plastics, varnish, and coating materials, and synthetic rubber and textiles. Similarly, by treating soda, the basis of a host of industrial operations is obtained. Processed articles that have been got without crude raw material to begin with, have been made by combining natural substances that exist everywhere in limitless quantity. For instance, nitrogen from the air can be made to give fertiliser or explosives. Thus, chemical industries have given rise to other previously unknown forms of production, carried on far from the source of, and even without, any 'raw' material. This type of industry now enables one to envisage the industrialisation of new and underdeveloped countries that are poor in raw materials and motive power, ill supplied with means of transport, and off the main currents of trade.

LABOUR

A necessary condition of the industrial mode of life is the existence of persons who are enabled by the environment to neglect the search for food and to devote themselves to industry. The condition is not the direct result of the environment, as is the abundance of raw materials, for there is a touch of human action in the economic state of the region which may afford a plentiful food supply, or in the social condition of the region which may release a considerable proportion of human labour for industry.

In a civilised community there are two fundamental conditions which ensure the availability of labour for industry. First, it must be possible for time to be given, at least for a short while, to industry without compromising the community's supply of food. Secondly, there must be plenty of labour, for in large communities it is easy for some of the people to devote themselves to industry, since the task of providing food can be left to others. In backward communities the first signs of a division of labour are preliminary to the rise of industry. Among some central African tribes there is in families a simple division of labour between the sexes. The men undertake the dangerous or difficult tasks outside the home: hunting, fishing, and tree-felling; whilst the women work at home at spinning, weaving, or pottery-making. In such communities women play a great part in the development of work leading to industrial production.

At a higher stage of civilisation the saving of time and the better work which result from the division of labour are more easily understood. Whole sets of people specialise in producing a certain article; for example, among some Negro tribes the working of iron, boat building, and fishing or hunting are the work of specialists. In the Pacific islands, in Hawaii for instance, besides boat builders there are boat decorators and makers of fishing-nets. Such people form a class that work for the market and have no hand in the actual production of food for their families.

Such a division of labour is possible only in fairly numerous communities, for the short supply of industrial labour appears as a common feature in countries with sparse populations; in regions where the mode of life is pastoral and the people, who are unattached to the soil, travel about with their herds and flocks in search of a poor supply of food; and in new countries where people are too few for any of them to be able to give up working on the land. Hence, though these countries have raw materials, potential motive power, and good harbours, they are backward today in industrial development. This was long the state of things in South America, Australia, central Africa, and the western United States.

Thus, the industrial mode of life may develop in countries that have at their disposal such sources of labour as a peasantry, foreign workers, or surplus local labour. In countries where agriculture feeds crowds of peasants, whose density of population increases faster than the yield from the land, industrialisation finds favourable conditions and may even offer a remedy for rural overpopulation. In China, Japan, and India the dense country population was from early times imbued with traditions of industry. In countries where agriculture affords an off-season with a good deal of leisure, idle hours suggest the wish to add to one's wealth by working at some trade. This is what happened in western Europe when it took to world trade and, to meet the demands of the new markets, called country workers to industry. One of the basic features of the European mode of life is just this interdependence between the industrial and agricultural modes of life. Great Britain, France, and Germany have long had many home industries, not all of which have succumbed to the factory, but have in some cases acted as seeds waiting to germinate in new forms of rural industry amid the development of modern economy.

Home industry existed also in mountain districts with long winters. Many such places, like the Harz Mountains, Black Forest, Erzgebirge, Sudetenland, Jura, Vosges, and, especially, the Alps in France, Switzerland, Austria, Germany, and Italy, have become industrial regions. Similarly, in Tsarist Russia the long winters enabled industry to draw its labour from among the peasants.

In lands where the countryfolk have formed a stock from which factory hands have been drawn, industrialisation has taken from rural districts a more or less considerable fraction of the peasantry. This exodus from country to town has supplied the mass of humanity which in every industrial district forms the population of large towns and causes a distribution of population that is peculiar, artificial, and relatively independent of potential food supplies from the surroundings.

Labour is not always supplied by the industrial district, but often comes from without. Such a supply becomes all the more abundant as communications become easier. Among the instances of labour brought from outside must be placed the slaves of ancient times, who were brought from almost everywhere and collected into workshops in the towns. In Greece a good deal of industry was reserved for the slaves: smiths, makers of trimmings, tanners, and armourers were all slaves. To these must be added mine-workers and domestic servants. The latter did work that has become industrialised today, like making bread and weaving household linen. The Greeks got their slaves mainly from abroad. After the time of Alexander the Great, however, Greece began to export slaves, a practice that led to the establishment abroad, especially in Italy and, later, in Africa, of industrial centres experienced in the tradition of industry in the Hellenic world. Hence the cosmopolitan character of the main industrial centres of Antiquity.

Today easy means of transport carry labour in crowds to places where industry is developing. Italians swarm to the iron mines in Lorraine, Poles to the coal mines in the north of France, and Chinese to the nitrate workings in Chile. Up to the end of the first quarter of the twentieth century the eastern United States owed their great industrial power to the ceaseless flow of European immigrants, whilst the western States, which were still receiving settlers, had only a few scattered industries. This influx of labour sometimes looked like a vast stream of humanity, orderly and controlled, but it often took the form of an invasion, as, for instance, in the gold rushes to California, Australia, and the Klondike.

Such migrations often supplied industry with merely unskilled labour; but in many cases immigration secured for the new country labour that was already experienced in special forms of industry and caused the beginning or resurgence of the industrial mode of life. For instance, workmen from Sidon took industry in the Mycenian period to Tyrins and Mycenae; then there were the Flemish weavers who introduced into England the art of weaving fine cloth. Further examples are seen in the Italian workmen who moved to France in the sixteenth and seventeenth centuries with their secrets of silk manufacture; in the Huguenots who migrated to Prussia; and in the English workmen who in the nineteenth century crossed over to the Continent carrying their mechanical skill and set up lace and tulle industries at Calais. Lastly, there were the European foremen who went over to the United States to start European luxury industries. In these days an industry can be restored or created entirely by the arrival of technicians from abroad. In the United States and in the Soviet Union atomic industry has been greatly advanced by the temporary or final immigration of atomic scientists from Europe.

On the whole, these transfers of labour resulted a century ago in the propagation of inventions and industrial processes, which in this way have come into the common heritage of mankind instead of remaining the property of a closed body jealous of its trade secrets. Gradually these transfers of technique have given rise to countless industrial centres wherever the seed thus sown could germinate on fertile soil.

Labour for new industries may be found on the spot where long experience of work has prepared a favourable social structure. One industry prepares the ground for others, because the human environment is able to adapt itself to new manual tasks. This is why cotton took the place of wool and linen manufactures in Lancashire and of silk in parts of the Lyon district in France. Such local labour is often found in the female population. Whilst the men are employed in heavy work in the mines or in metallurgy, women are available for easier tasks. A combination of the two types of labour has given many varieties of activity to some regions and has added a considerable increase to the income of the working classes. In Belfast, for instance, whilst the men work in the shipyards, the women are employed in weaving; and in Leeds the men make machinery, whilst the women make ready-made clothes.

This is one aspect of the attraction of one industry for others. In a big industrial district there is a constant search for labour. Hence industries that are in want of hands tend to set up in districts where industry has already found a footing. New England, the Ruhr, and the industrial north of France as well as the Paris district and

Greater London illustrate the proliferation and constant diversification of industry near and in the heart of the great centres of industrial activity.

Lastly, it should be said that the distribution and abundance of labour are not solely determined by material factors. They also depend on the environment of the industry, the stage in the development of technique and the conditions in which the work is done. Restriction or prohibition of child labour, regulation of women's work and of the number of working hours in the day and week, method of payment for work by time or piece, and the effectiveness of the social guarantees given to workers have in modern industries a determining influence on the security or abundance of labour as well as on its technical and operational value.

MOTIVE POWER

The discovery of sources of motive power that have ensured the success of industry is a very recent event in the history of man's techniques. His discovery of the control of fire enabled him to work in metals, bake clay, and isolate certain matter necessary for his existence. For thousands of years wood was the only fuel and the only source of heat. Similarly, to handle or move machines invented by him and used to produce raw materials man had for centuries little more than the strength of his arms and fingers. Among the Greeks, for example, workmen did not know how to get from nature the motive power they needed, nor did they know either the water mill, the windmill, or even machinery worked by animals. Later, they learnt to use natural power in wind and water, but these were difficult to control and for a long time they were used only in flour-milling and smithies. It may be said that up to the eighteenth century human strength was the chief motive power in all workshops. About the middle of that century there began, first in England and then in western Europe, a revolution that changed the production of energy by putting into man's hand such power that he became through his industry a real natural factor and shortly after raised him to the position of a cosmic force. Freed from bodily toil, man has lost all affinity with the animal world.

In the past man could produce only a low degree of heat and motive power. Fuel was restricted in its use, and heat and mechanical power were derived from different sources. Today man calls on the same agent to give him both heat and motive power in ever-increasing quantities. Coal was the first agent which he found would be the source of both these forms of energy. Thanks to that mineral, man has made iron into so close a part of civilisation that it has become the symbol of his control of nature. Coal has enabled him to produce a powerful and versatile form of energy in steam and he has used it to help him in all his manufacturing activities.

By means of electricity he has made water another producer of heat and motive power far more flexible and economical. Mineral oil and natural gas have now taken on the work of coal. After that man turned to chemical power and at length made use of nuclear energy, which is now on the way to being mastered. So in less than two hundred years conditions in industry have been completely changed, merely by the appearance of these various sources of energy. They suffice to create the industrial mode of life far from the source of any raw material and even far from any great labour force. With them a new and all-powerful element has broken away from material determinism and penetrated into industry.

Within a few years coal became the symbol of industrial power. It was often said to be the mainspring of industry. That this treasure from under the earth's surface should have been so long in coming into use is indeed astonishing. It was brought to light merely by man's need of it. The part played by it is more than a function of its abundance and is mainly one of the intensity of its use. Now, this use began only when industrial production demanded it. Hence there are countries like India and, even more so, China, with vast deposits of coal that have remained almost untouched because the stir of large-scale industry and world trade had not yet reached them. On the contrary, coal began its wonderful industrial career in Great Britain, a country which had wide international connexions and windows open to the whole world, and which depended on the production of goods for sale abroad.

It was in England that, when used as a source of heat, coal began to change the character of metallurgy when her industry had to expand to keep step with the extension of her trade outlets. For a long time shippers from Liverpool had been carrying Birmingham hardware and Sheffield tools and weapons to the Guinea coast, where they exchanged them for slaves. British iron goods were also sold both in the American colonies and on the continent of Europe. Consequently, production could not keep up with the demand for exports owing to the lack of fuel, for the supply of charcoal was limited by the rapid destruction of the forests. Wood had become so rare and so dear in England that many ironworks closed down. To save the metallurgical industry another fuel with ample resources had to be found, and a method of using coal in the working up of iron had to be tried.

Now, before the eighteenth century coal could not be used to smelt iron ore, because sulphur products due to its combustion made the iron impure, brittle, and not very malleable. It was only in 1709 that Abraham Darby found a way of producing good quality iron with coal at Coalbrookdale in Shropshire. Between 1730 and 1735 his sons made the invention wholly practical by replacing charcoal in the blast furnace by coke, which they got by roasting coal. This invention enabled the country's wealth in coal to be used in ironworks, and it laid the foundation of Great Britain's siderurgical fortunes, at the same time preparing the reign of iron on earth.

The high degree of heat produced by coal, together with the fact that it was available in large, apparently inexhaustible, quantities, made Great Britain for a long time the centre of iron production and of all development in the industry. The first advance was the introduction of puddling (1784), which gave wrought iron. After that there came the Bessemer process (1856), which enabled steel to be produced in large quantities by means of a few simple operations. Thus, between 1860 and 1870 Great Britain was the only country to produce steel on a large scale, and it was at that period that steel became the raw material for making fixed steam engines (1860), then locomotives (1863), railway lines (1856), and ships (1863). Later, the production of steel by the open-hearth Siemens-Martin process required still more fuel, but had the advantage of giving steel of a more uniform quality and in greater quantities. Between 1870 and 1880 Great Britain was still the only country to produce steel by the open-hearth process. In 1879 the Thomas method (basic Bessemer) opened up the use of vast deposits of phosphoric ore and increased the overall consumption of coal even more.

In this way, thanks to coal, the successor to charcoal, Great Britain forged the means of her industrial metallurgical greatness by gradually adapting those means to the needs of her commercial expansion. Coal was, in fact, the basis of metallurgical power and, consequently, the foundation of industrial importance in the sense that cheap production of iron enabled the construction of efficient machinery and the equipment of various countries which followed Great Britain in industrial development. The recent upgrowth of the Soviet Union into a great metallurgical producer took place only after its production of coal had risen from 1·7 million tonnes in 1875 to more than 225 million tonnes in 1957.

As a provider of motive power coal also began its career in Great Britain, where it enabled the best to be made of ingenious spinning and weaving machinery that was too heavy to be worked by hand. The steam engine was an inexhaustible source of energy, which gave great power, was versatile and manageable, able to work heavy, strong machinery, yet capable of being adapted to meet the requirements of delicate machinery. From its first appearance the steam engine was associated with the use of coal, which with a smaller volume gives far more heat than wood does. This use of the steam engine was imposed on Great Britain by the demands of her trade. Water-driven spindles and looms, which were common to all parts of Great Britain up to the beginning of the nineteenth century, had given her the leading place in all forms of textile industry and especially in cotton. This position might have been lost when Germany, France, and Belgium began to use the new machinery, and it was the need to overcome foreign competition that hastened the introduction of the new motive power and the use of the steam engine.

This engine greatly increased the output of both spindles and looms, economised in manpower, and steadied production, which previously had been subject to the seasonal variations of the rainfall. Motive power was no longer controlled in the mills by the volume of streams, but depended on an easy and regular supply of coal. Hence, mills could increase in size and proportionately reduce their overhead costs. They clustered round coalfields, were built close to each other, and specialised within the same group of manufactures. In this way there came about a concentration of industy and a division of labour, which increased Great Britain's capacity for production to such a degree that she was able to overcome the rivalry of other nations in the world market. In 1763 James Watt improved Newcomen's old engine of 1711, and in 1785 the steam engine was used for the first time for spinning at Papplewick (Nottingham-shire). By 1800 eleven of Watt's engines were in use in Birmingham, twenty in Leeds, and twenty-two in Manchester.

Thus, Great Britain's leading position was due to coal as well as to trade-derived capital which was necessary for the construction of heavy machinery. The same causes which connected large-scale industry with coal in Great Britain operated similarly in European countries and later in the United States and the Soviet Union. In all these countries modern large-scale industry has been based on great metallurgical production, which in turn has been supported by a vast extraction of coal. The close interdependence, which up to our own times has controlled the world's industrial structure, is likely to be ended owing to the rise of other forms of energy that are more compact and more easily transported and handled. As the new sources of energy sever the connexion between industry and coal, they are fast redrawing the map showing the distribution of the world's industrial districts. But they have not affected the essential principles of industrial organisation laid down in the coal age. Concentration is the rule in the oil industry, in which refineries always form enormous establishments even exceeding the size of those in the metallurgical industry. The electrical industry with its dams and power-houses also leads to great concentration. Then, again, atomic industry, which calls for the largest concentration and is the best equipped with delicate plant, represents in consequence the greatest concentration of capital on limited areas. So even when freed from its connexion with coal, modern large-scale industry keeps the basic features of structure imposed on it in the last century by the form of energy that gave rise to it and supported it right up to our own times.

The nineteenth century was the age of coal. It created a great metallurgical industry together with the chief means of rapid transport. The first big ships were steamers using large quantities of coal, and the coal trade contributed to the fortunes of ports of call all along the ocean routes, until the first world war. The main coaling stations were all placed in important ports, especially in the Indian and Pacific Oceans. The carriage of the mineral to these distant stations for coaling the world's ships provided the financial basis of the British merchant marine.

The importance of coal gradually lessened during the twentieth century, however, owing to the discovery of a new source of energy in oil. The invention of the internal combustion and compression ignition engines brought about this change. The motor car and the aircraft, which from the earliest stages used great quantities of petrol, were the first extensive users of oil products. Then the invention of sprayers, by which oil fuel derived from the heavy residue after the refinement of crude oil could be burnt, enabled heavy oil to take the place of coal for driving ships, and this caused further consumption of this liquid source of energy. Lastly, the perfection of the diesel engine enabled residual heavy oils to be used to work motors as powerful as the steam engines then in service. From then on, oil products could supply energy directly by combustion in the appropriate engines without the need to use steam as an intermediate factor. This was an immense change, for ships were becoming bigger and bigger and were needing a great deal of motive power. In a short while oil supplied power for transport by land, sea, and air. Even in railways, which fifty years ago were driven exclusively by coal, oil has played an increasing part, even exceeding that played by electrical power in some countries. In the United States, in the late 1950s, there were 24,000 diesel locomotives compared with 3,000 driven by electricity and 8,000 driven by steam. Furthermore, coal has been ousted by heavy oil in stationary engines. Many large spinning mills which drive their spindles by electricity generate their own current in a power plant equipped with a diesel engine. In the Soviet Union several power-houses in the Caucasus and southern Russia are worked by diesels. In Canada and the United States some power-houses are worked by natural gas, the use of which is more recent than that of oil. It is used today for lighting towns and is piped to dwelling-houses, thus gradually taking the place of coal gas. In France gas from Lacq, which is being piped to the whole country, together with gas from the Netherlands, will cause the disappearance of most of the little urban gas works. And in England and Wales the thousand gasworks operating in 1949 were reduced to 100 by 1971, and of these only three made gas from coal, the rest processing North Sea or other imported gas.

During the past fifty years world production of oil has doubled every ten years. About 67,000 tonnes in 1860, it exceeded 2,800 million tonnes in 1974. At the same time the consumption of natural gas rose from 72,000 million cubic metres in 1929 to 1·27 million million cubic metres in 1974. Oil is used as a raw material in chemical industries and as a motive power for transport far more than as a new form of energy for the use of industry in general. It has, however, caused little change in the structure of industry inherited from coal.

A peculiar feature in the geography and economics of oil is that it is used very far from the places in which it is extracted. It is less common than coal, but is dearer, more precious, and far more easily transported. Yet a whole set of specialised transport has to be created for it, whilst coal was satisfied with using the same ships and wagons as other commodities. Oil has given rise to bigger and bigger tankers, some of them designed to carry more than 300,000 tons of the liquid. Then there are pipelines, some of which are transcontinental. Their construction is reckoned among the greatest achievements of modern engineering; they are the equivalents of the great railways built in the last century.

Unlike coal, oil is not immediately used to generate energy, for it has to be refined. Refinement consists of separating the various elements found mingled or combined with natural oil in such a way as to extract a whole series of combustible oils and motor fuels, each of which is suitable for use in one kind of engine. Oil is therefore the basis of a great industry, the greatest in the world after metallurgy, and today it controls whole branches of the chemical industry.

There are now nearly 7,000 large refineries in the world with a capacity that has increased threefold in the last twenty years. Before the second world war and especially before 1925 the refineries were generally placed in the neighbourhood of oilfields. The United States was an exception, for there production had already gone on for some time and the evolution was more advanced. American refineries were placed on the Atlantic coast at Baltimore, Philadelphia, and Jersey City; on the Great Lakes at Erie, Cleveland, and Toledo; and on the Pacific coast at San Francisco and Los Angeles. For a long time neither the Southern States nor Texas had refineries, for the oil was taken by pipe-line or by sea to the

Eastern States. Now, on the contrary, Texas has become a State of refineries with big establishments at Houston and Galveston.

But in the rest of the world development has been in the opposite direction, for refineries were placed near to the oilfields, at ports close to the main seaways. Such were the refineries at Trinidad, Curaçao, and Aruba in the Caribbean, and at Abadan, Kanakin, Kermanshah, Ras Tanura, Mena el Amadhi, and Haifa in the Middle East, Balikpapan, Sungaigerung, and Chopu in Indonesia, and Boela in the Philippines. Since the end of the second world war, however, the refineries have been placed in the chief ports of the main centres of demand for oil. The fact is that the construction of up-to-date refineries in underdeveloped countries is very expensive, for the material required must all be carried thither and highly qualified technicians maintained there. Hence in spite of her relative poverty in oil-bearing strata, Europe has become a great centre of oil refining, and her capacity is eight times what it was before 1940. France was the first European country to effect this geographical revolution, for between 1925 and 1930 she had constructed fifteen refineries near her chief ports. Great Britain came later, with fourteen coastal refineries, mainly constructed since the second world war; and the output rose from $2\frac{1}{2}$ million tonnes in 1947 to 85 million tonnes in 1968. The same tendency is now seen in South America, Australia, and Japan, in the last of which oil from Hokkaido is refined in her southern ports. Even in the Soviet Union a similar movement is taking place. The oldest refineries are at Baku and Grozny on the oilfields, but oil from the Emba field is taken right into the industrial district at Magnitogorsk for refining, and oil from the Caucasus is taken by pipeline for refining at Gorlovka in the Ukraine.

Up-to-date refineries are becoming bigger and bigger and more and more complex, for they are more profitable than little establishments of low output. They are adjacent to factories in which are carried out the working up of coal-tar, the recovery of sulphur, and, recently, the establishment of complete chemical works.

Oil chemistry, which was non-existent thirty years ago, now supplies nearly four-fifths of organic chemical production, that is, 30 million tons of various products extracted from either natural gas or gas from the refineries. These are solvents, detergents, plastics, synthetic rubber, man-made fibres, and anti-freeze. Oil chemistry was started about 1925 in the United States, where it spread rapidly. Now there are three hundred petrochemical works, and these supply more than two-thirds of organic chemical production. Some are in Pennsylvania, others near the big refineries at Philadelphia and Wilmington, a subsidiary of Dupont de Nemours. There are some in Texas, where they form a ring round the refineries from Baton Rouge to Corpus Christi via Dallas, Houston, Baytown, and Galveston. The discovery of natural gas in Europe and the construction of big plants for catalytic cracking in oil refineries have given plenty of raw material for this new branch of chemical industry. Petrochemical works have been built in Great Britain, the Netherlands, France, Germany, and Italy.

The distribution of establishments connected with oil shows that petroleum has not radically changed the world's industrial map, for the refineries and chemical works which it feeds have been built in countries with a high technical standard near the old centres of polymorphous chemical industry. On the whole, the essential characteristic of liquid carburants is that they represent a manageable and compact form of energy. The full use of atomic energy must be awaited before it will be possible to have from a similar weight of matter a concentration of energy greater than that of liquid carburants.

Almost contemporary with oil, hydro-electricity has brought more appreciable modification into the old industrial organisation. Running water has enormous power through its volume and rate of flow. Watermills, which were a common sight in the countryside in the Middle Ages, increased for industrial purposes even more in the seventeenth and eighteenth centuries, but were killed by the steam engine. Now a great change has occurred, for more and more use is being made of hydro-electric power for the production of electricity.

Before the reign of steam, water power became precious as soon as industry began to use machinery. The distribution of mechanical industries then conformed with the hydrography. Most of the valleys with steep gradients developed chains of factories worked by water. For instance, in England industrial populations established themselves on watercourses and abandoned districts with no running water. Wool manufacture increased right along the Tweed valley and along the streams in Yorkshire and the Cotswolds. In America the first industries in New England sprang up near falls in the streams. Towns like Lawrence and Lowell owed their prosperity to their streams. Many names of industrial towns in the eastern United States are significant in this respect; for example, Fall River and Great Falls. The Fall Line in the Southern States marks the position of many industrial towns on the edge of the Atlantic coast plain. In France, too, where the industrial mode of life goes back a long way, there is a swarm of little factories, including nail works, sawmills, forges, papermills, and cloth works along the courses of streams not classed as navigable rivers. In Picardy, for instance, where streams are very regular in flow, there were up to the nineteenth century not only whole strings of mills, but also a crowd of little factories worked by the streams. There water power often remains as a modest ally of steam. There was the same traditional activity along streams in Normandy: at Villedieu and Sourdeval in the *département* of Manche; at Conches, Evreux, Rugles, Laigle, and Bernay in Eure; at Flers and La Ferté Macé in Orne; and at Rouen, which is the centre of a fan-like set of little industrial valleys. This swarm of factories has gradually disappeared before the powerful, concentrating effect of steam. The use of the streams had always been fairly limited. The largest could scarcely be used since they are wanted for water transport. Fierce mountain streams were shunned, and spates involved idleness for machinery and factory, just as did periods of low water.

Hydraulic power entered the circle of industry owing to a series of inventions which connected its use with electricity. These were the turbine, dynamo, and the possibility of transmitting current over long distances. The force of a waterfall, when changed into work, makes the current in a dynamo, and when the current is sent along a metal conductor it runs off to supply power, heat, and light to places near or far. To this water power the term 'white coal' has been commonly applied in France.

This was how hydraulic power first became a source of energy, for an electric motor, like the steam engine, can put into motion various kinds of machinery in factories or even in domestic workshops. It also became a source of heat after the invention of the electric furnace and thus revolutionised certain kinds of metallurgy. The electric furnace has been used for making steel and especially alloys incorporating with steel rare metals like nickel, cobalt, tungsten, and chromium. The electric blast furnace has become a rival of the coke furnace, though it is of much smaller dimensions. Lastly, the use of electricity has completely transformed the production of zinc, copper, and especially aluminium.

Chemical industry has been enriched by a host of manufactures which are essentially based on electrolysis, like caustic soda and chlorine compounds; calcium carbide and cyanamide, and nitric acid formed by the fixation of nitrogen from the atmosphere under an electric arc.

'White coal' is a permanent source of energy. It is never exhausted and regenerates itself naturally. Of course, the catchment works, dams, and head pipes are very expensive; but apart from that the capital required and the running expenses are very small, for not much labour is used in power-houses, where automatic working is carried even further than in oil refining. 'White coal' is very adaptable. It can be split indefinitely to work large electric metallurgical factories as well as workshops with but little machinery. It easily adapts its current to fluctuations in use and enables several

14. Fully integrated iron and steel plant at Port Talbot, South Wales; ore dock, blast furnaces, coke ovens, steel furnaces, strip mills

MODERN LARGE-SCALE INDUSTRY

15. Oil refinery at Llandarcy, near Swansea, South Wales; catalytic cracking plant, power station and water-cooling towers

16. Laden camels in Turkey

TRANSPORT ANCIENT AND MODERN

17. Clover-leaf road junctions on the outskirts of Toronto

types of manufacture to be combined in a single industrial group. In every respect it seems, unlike oil, to be a direct rival of black coal in the complex of industry. First of all, it has enabled countries without coal to become industrial; it has added to the power of countries which used not to produce coal enough for their factories. Sometimes it has even ousted coal. Scandinavia, Switzerland, and Italy have been able to become great industrial countries by its use. A more recent instance is afforded by Canada, which has based its heavy industries on 'white coal', as has also Japan. Today, the Congo, Australia, and Brazil furnish other instances of countries entering the industrial field by calling in the aid of hydraulic power more and more.

Two conditions determine the distribution of water power: an abundant and regular flow of water, and the presence of slopes steep enough to cause natural waterfalls or to allow falls to be artificially made. Several geographical regions afford these conditions. In the first place there are the regions in the northern hemisphere which have been subjected to the action of Quaternary glaciers. They have damp climates with plenty of rain to feed a dense network of streams and they have natural reservoirs in the shape of lakes due to morainic dams or to hollows of glacial origin. A host of such lakes of every size strew the ground in Finland, Scandinavia, and North America. Besides this, the gradients of valleys are constantly broken by obstructions and rock outcrops that give rise to falls or rapids. Hence the part played as producers of motive power by countries lacking coal, such as Scandinavia, Finland, and western Russia.

Other regions that produce hydro-electric power are high mountain areas in which slopes are steep and rainfall great. In regions where the mountains are lower, as in Scotland, the Ardennes, the Appalachians, and the Central Massif of France, the falls are not very high, and the river régime affords less water or a less regular flow. In high mountains like the Alps, the mountains in the west of the United States and Canada, the sierras on the Atlantic coast of Brazil, and the Western Ghats in India, variations in level may amount to several hundred feet and in places exceed 1,000 metres. In some high ranges, like the Alps and the Snowy Mountains in Australia, snowfields and glaciers form natural reservoirs storing up water and letting it flow off in summer. Unfortunately, the harnessing of water in high mountains demands enormous engineering works which can only be undertaken by countries with a very high level of technique.

Another kind of region favourable to the production of hydro-electricity is the great river plain with its low gradient and enormous volume. Here also long dams are needed to raise the water level, make the flow regular, and form an artificial fall. Hence, there has been little harnessing of big rivers in new countries, and, apart from the Kariba dam on the Zambesi, the great rivers of Africa—the Congo in Katanga, and the Niger in western Sudan—still do not yield power to be compared with that of big rivers in temperate lands with a long history of industrialisation. Large constructions undertaken after the second world war have turned the Rhône and Rhine into great producers of hydro-electricity, each of them being now equipped with half a dozen big power-houses. Similar constructions are being made on the Danube in Germany and Austria. In the Soviet Union the Dnepr and Don work huge electric generators, whilst the Russians are busy harnessing the Volga and some of the big rivers in Asia. Lastly, in the United States there is a big dam on the Mississippi at Keokuk, and the Missouri and the right bank feeders are being harnessed; whilst in the plateaux of the west the Hoover Dam on the Colorado and the Coulee Dam on the Columbia are amongst the greatest concrete structures in the world.

Today, rivers are no longer dammed in one place. The high wall with its profile skilfully calculated by engineers is a costly thing, so there is need to ensure its safety and regular working by improving the flow of the feeders and by modifying the régime. Hence the vast constructions undertaken right up in the mountains to dam the headwater streams running down to the main dam, the building of secondary dams to hold in reserve rainwater and meltwater from the rapidly melting snow, the reafforestation of slopes to slow down the run-off of water and to help to feed the springs. The use of hydro-electric power to meet the needs of modern industry is therefore a very scientific business which assumes an advanced state of civilisation. Hence, the countries best equipped industrially are also those that now have the greatest supplies of electricity, that is, countries in Europe and North America. But yet within these countries there still exist districts in which the rivers remain uncontrolled pending the time when they will be harnessed and put to work.

Although hydro-electric power has remained the special possession of a relatively small fraction of the world's population, it has nevertheless introduced into the industrial map two essential modifications. In the first place, it has reawakened industrial life in the mountains, which are naturally hostile to the installation of large-scale industry. It has been said that Bergès[1] through his hydro-electric stations in the Dauphiny Alps, 'freed the mountains

---

[1] Aristide Bergès, born at Lorp in Ariege, was the first French industrialist to use hydro-electric power. In 1868 he set up a wood-pulp factory at Lancey, at the foot of the Belledonne massif.

from the tribute they used to pay to the coalfields in the plains'. It should also be noted that coal reached the main Alpine valleys with difficulty and in small quantities. With the help of hydro-electric power some of the former industries have been revived in Dauphiny, including the making of paper, woollen goods, and gloves. New industries have also been started, the chief of which are electrolysis and the making of machinery. Today, the northern French Alps form a very active polymorphous industrial region based wholly on hydro-electric power.

Secondly, it has checked the tendency to industrial concentration due to coal and seemingly even more emphasised by oil. Owing to the transmission of current along high-tension wires industrial regions have spread out, reviving craftsmanship and home industry. Hydro-electricity does not promise, however, to replace coal for all purposes or wholly to relieve congestion in the great industrial centres inherited from last century.

Since the end of the second world war a new and considerable source of energy has been discovered in nuclear reaction. The potential energy contained in a kilogram of uranium 235 is equal to that of 2,600 tons of coal. Besides, on using up the nuclear fuel in special reactors, or 'breeders', an amount of energy greater than that yielded by the uranium is got from the products of combustion. This is therefore an inexhaustible source of power which seems to grow even greater as it is destroyed in use. It is not accessible, however, like water or coal. The industry which brings it into service depends on three key industries of modern times, metallurgy, electronics, and chemistry. It needs immense capital, the collaboration of all branches of industry in a great country, and the work of a team of scientists. Nuclear energy is therefore not within the reach of underdeveloped countries, of countries with only moderate amounts of capital, and countries that are inadequately equipped with large industries.

It is not astonishing, therefore, that the greatest producer of nuclear power should be the United States, since this country has at its disposal enormous reserves of coal, hydro-electricity, and oil. Nuclear production demands an industry of such a size as few countries can create. The United States produce a thousand times more zirconium than the whole of Europe, ten times more uranium enriched by the separation of isotopes, twenty times more heavy water, which are all essential for atomic industry. Today, the United States have more than 100 of the 130 reactors now existing in the whole world. The submarine *Nautilus* is driven by atomic power, and the well-known aircraft builders, Lockheed, Corvair, and Boeing, are preparing plans for aircraft whose engines will be worked by atomic power. At the present time the Americans have four large electric power-houses worked by reactors at Boston, Columbus, Detroit, and Chicago.

The Soviet Union is another vast country with advanced nuclear equipment. Five large electricity-producing atomic stations are already working, and it is clear that in the years to come Soviet atomic stations will themselves supply twice as much electricity as was formerly supplied by all the power-houses in Russia. The Soviet Union already has an ice-breaker of 16,000 tons driven by atomic power.

Among the great industrial nations other than the United States and the Soviet Union, the first to possess nuclear power stations were the United Kingdom, France, and Germany. During the 1970s, stimulated by the rise in the price of crude oil and the politico-economic crisis brought about by the O.P.E.C. countries (Organisation of Producers and Exporters of Crude), the production of nuclear energy by the great industrial nations has been stepped up in order to reduce the import of expensive oil and so escape the stranglehold of the oil producers. Many plans have been made for the construction of new nuclear power stations, usually in localities away from existing industrial zones and especially on coasts. There are now some 135 atomic power stations in the world, with a total capacity of 5,700 MW; 58 of these came into production within two years in the early 1970s. There are 42 stations within the European Economic Community, the most powerful of which are in Great Britain (nine stations), France (Marcoule, Chinon), and Germany (Biblis, on the Rhine, the most powerful in the world, 1150 MW; Niederreichbach, Wurgassen). To this list may be added those in Sweden (Ringhals), Switzerland (Mühleberg), and outside Europe, in Japan (Fukushima, Shimane), in Canada (Pickering), and several other less important ones in Argentina, India, and Pakistan. The world production of nuclear-generated electricity now reaches 133,000 million kWh, or 1·4 per cent of the total. More than 96 per cent of it comes from the industrial countries of the northern hemisphere, including 45·7 per cent from the U.S.A. and Canada, 43·4 per cent from Europe, 7 per cent from Japan, and under 2 per cent from the U.S.S.R. So nuclear energy still appears to be a replacement rather than something quite new. It is therefore clear that countries with the greatest industrial development and the use of other sources of power now have nearly the whole of the world's atomic energy. Underdeveloped countries which do not possess the former sources of energy or have been unable to exploit them, now find their technical backwardness growing worse in consequence, since chemical industry is the basis of more than a third of all the processes leading to the liberation of atomic energy.

In spite of the enormous increase in motive power due to atomic industry it would seem improbable that the world's industrial map will be changed for a long time to come. The old industrial countries have a growing need of motive power that cannot be satisfied by an increase in the supply of coal, oil, or hydro-electricity. The immense demand for motive power exists mainly in western Europe. The six chief countries on the continent together with the United Kingdom import more than a fourth of the power they use in the shape of either coal or oil. The sources of hydro-electricity which have been used in this region of advanced techniques will be used to the full within twenty years, and nuclear power is counted on, therefore, to make up future deficiency. So in order to strengthen the potential of the world's old industrial regions, the development of the new form of power must be given priority. This is strongly suggested by the present distribution of atomic power outside the boundaries of the United States and the Soviet Union.

LIMITS AND PROSPECTS OF INDUSTRIAL CIVILISATIONS

It may be said, however, that the industrial mode of life, considered in its humblest forms, has in every age been spread universally throughout the world. Traditional crafts which are still flourishing in countries not yet completely changed by the Industrial Revolution, have now almost wholly died out in regions with large-scale industry. The characteristic of these crafts is that they are performed by hand and with tools, not by machinery. They produce in small quantities articles that are not standardised and sell them within a limited radius. Consequently, they directly reflect the conditions of the local environment. In the Soviet Union crafts have survived along with the huge *kombinaty* that concentrate on heavy industry. Their function is to make a few of the articles necessary to ordinary life, but ignored by large-scale industry. One of the characteristic features of this form of industry is the specialisation that takes place within the narrow limits of the guild, the town quarter, or the village. It is found in isolated centres of civilisation. A curious and very significant instance of this is seen in pre-Columbian America, which, being without iron and making fire by the most primitive methods, remained in the Stone and Bronze Ages right up to the arrival of the Europeans; and yet, in spite of its primitive tools, pre-Columbian industry gave proofs of remarkable manual skill in turning out stone and wooden implements, moulding pottery, and, above all, in its practice of weaving and dyeing cloth. Far Eastern civilisations, which are nowadays being greatly affected by the products of large-scale industry, still afford many instances of this kind of local manufacture. On the whole, many centres of traditional industry, which represent the beginnings of civilisation, have attained to an astonishingly high degree of technical skill. In some cases it was to imitate their products that the earliest European machinery strove, and the crafts faded away owing to their inability to use the main sources of natural energy and to their having stuck to man's handiwork.

Unlike the crafts, large-scale industry is marked by two peculiar features in its geographical distribution, namely, its unequal spread over the world and the complexity of the causes that explain its localisation. It is found mainly in Europe and North America on both sides of the Atlantic in a huge area of the temperate belt. It ranges from the heart of the Soviet Union in the east to the shores of the Pacific on the west. Two island groups, the British Isles and Japan, are closely linked with it. In both continents the proportion of the active population engaged in industry is extraordinarily high, reaching from 50 to 60 per cent.

Outside this vast area there are only rather scattered centres of regional or heavy industry which have been started recently, as, for example, in the Far East of Asia. In Africa, South America, and Australia large-scale industry is restricted to a few isolated districts, to some big towns or commercial ports. Much of this unequal distribution is explained by the difficulty of getting an adequate supply of motive power or of certain necessary raw materials; but as a rule it is due to essentially human factors.

Countries with a dense population have a large number of workers for their factories. There is no doubt, for instance, that England has always found manpower without difficulty within her own shores. Similarly, Germany, Italy, and Japan have found in their populations a powerful factor in the development of large-scale industry. But many countries, notably China and India, with large populations have not developed their industry correspondingly. The fact is that the quality of the manpower matters more than its quantity, and long experience in handling machinery is needed to get good outputs from modern industrial equipment. In this way British workers, who gained early experience and got high wages, quickly attained to high outputs. On the other hand, the workers in new countries and those with a rigid out-of-date industrial structure yield poor outputs, since their labour is unskilled, unadaptable, and even hostile to improved machinery. Now, even in basic industries, like coal-mining at great depths, it is necessary nowadays to have very skilled men who are capable of handling complicated machinery safely. The clumsiness of an unskilled labourer and the carelessness of a navvy will not do for a miner at the coal face.

An available market is no less essential. Europe soon had a vast outlet for her industrial commodities, and the United Kingdom was able from the beginning to organise its industry to suit the world market. Similarly, the United States had from the end of the nineteenth century an immense home market for manufactures of all kinds. On the other hand, new, sparsely peopled, and poor countries, whose inhabitants have inadequate purchasing power, cannot set up large factories with a productive capacity greater than the local market can cope with. Hence, little states and underdeveloped countries have long bought manufactured goods from big industrial countries and have not made the goods themselves.

Lastly, the possession of technical and financial capital, due to an accumulated stock of tradition and to the advantage of a long commercial past, is a no less essential factor. In the realm of technical and mechanical civilisation Great Britain has led the world, to which she has been an instructor. Hence she, together with Europe, had a long lead over the other continents. Her technique has of course been transmissible, and there exists a huge world industrial community which works with the same machinery and by the same rules of production. However, a community must be able to assimilate the technique. It must have engineers, scientists, and factory managers; that is, it must have reached a standard of civilisation far surpassing the mere possession of machinery and other material means of production. Now, this stage of general civilisation has not yet been reached in every country in Asia, Africa, or South America, where large factories wholly made abroad are being set up here and there in regions hitherto completely hostile to the industrial mode of life.

Furthermore, a vast outlay of capital is needed to build and equip factories and to provide them with means of transport. Great Britain had acquired reserves of capital by trade, and many European countries had also by the end of the eighteenth century accumulated capital by similar means. In the same way in our own time we have seen countries become industrial because they had attained a high degree of wealth. Among these are the Netherlands, Switzerland, and Sweden, which besides wealth had intelligent workers, technical schools, and—some of them—a merchant fleet. Generally speaking countries that are new and without past experience of trade lack the capital to open up coal mines or harness waterfalls and have to appeal for capital from trading or already fully industrialised nations. Hence in new countries large-scale industry is started not by the initiative of the local people, but by that of business men from Europe or the United States. Oil extraction in Venezuela, copper mining in the Congo, iron mining in Colombia, and the working of bauxite in Guiana or of phosphate in Morocco have been carried out with capital invested by big industrial companies. Many great industrial firms in Europe also have establishments outside their own country. Thus the British firms of J. P. Coates and Courtauld have factories in the United States and in many other countries. French firms like Pechiney and the Compagnie française des pétroles, German chemical firms, Dutch engineering firms (e.g. Philips), and firms from Sweden, also have worldwide interests, to say nothing of the far-flung influence of Swiss and Italian combines (e.g. Montecatini). There are also movements of capital between industrial communities for the purpose of setting up and developing new industries. For instance, since the end of the second world war big American motor car firms have built subsidiary factories in Europe and in Great Britain ; American oil companies have invested capital in many refineries in Europe, notably in those in France. Similarly, trans-Atlantic chemical trusts have supplied money, techniques, and machinery, to many European firms, with a view to widening the area of operations.

On the whole, large-scale industry is not established without much time and effort. That is one of the reasons for the division of industry between countries that supply and those that buy manufactured goods. Probably the industrialisation of new countries will gradually modify the arrangement, for the dispersion of industry brings social advantages, since it gives opportunities for remunerative work to overpopulated countries ; and it also affords economic advantages which have disappeared from countries with a high degree of technique owing to the excessive concentration in the last century, since it enables factories to have the use of large areas of ground of little market value as well as to solve, more easily than the swarming industrial regions, the problems of collecting and storing raw material and of the housing and transport of manpower. Furthermore, this new tendency relative to dispersion is favoured by the ubiquity of electrical or internal combustion engines owing to the ease with which motive power can be transmitted today either in the shape of electricity or in the concentrated form of liquid or atomic fuel.

This industrial decentralisation is bound to modify profoundly the structure and activities of the classical industrial regions of the northern hemisphere that established their world dominance in the age of coal and steam. In modern times, despite the speed and efficiency of their reactions to a world in which they have lost their exclusive political, economic, and even financial control, these industrial civilisations, regarded by some economists as the most complete expression of the technical and intellectual possibilities of mankind at the summit of its evolution, must undergo profound changes, even in the fundamental bases on which they were founded.

Although they had come through, not entirely unscathed but without any changes in their traditional structure, both the economic crisis of the end of the nineteenth century and the Great Depression of 1930–34, which originated in the disequilibrium between production and consumption, the crisis resulting from the political upheavals of the second world war undermined even their means of production. They suffered, in fact, a threefold default—of energy sources, raw materials and capital, which, as we have seen, are the fundamental elements of an industrial economy. And as a backlash of this, even the capital resource represented by labour was compromised by the growth of unemployment, which in 1976 was still rising in Europe, America, and Japan.

The first irreversible decline was in the field of energy. At the beginning of the industrial age, the European industrial regions possessed abundant energy in the form of coal, which provided the motive power for industry and transport alike. Great Britain was thought of as one vast coalfield, and in 1913, Germany produced almost as much—272 million tonnes as against the United Kingdom's 292 millions. Apart from the United States, Europe provided energy—in the form of coal carried as ballast in outgoing ships— for the whole world, as well as satisfying the needs of its own industries. More than half the world's coal—725 million tonnes, more than the output of the United States—came from Europe, and the present E.E.C. countries produced 634 millions, or 48 per cent of the world total. Today, Europe has lost the wealth provided by its role as universal fuel-supplier. Since the end of the first world war, the United States has become the largest producer and exporter of coal, with an annual output varying between 400 and 600 million tonnes according to the general world economy. Further, overseas countries that were formerly purchasers of British and European coal, have opened up their own fields of coal and lignite, such as Canada, Brazil, Australia, India, China, and South Africa. The total output of the Asiatic countries, representing less than 3 per cent of the world in 1913, had already grown to 8 per cent by 1938, and is now more than 25 per cent, whilst Europe can only manage 22 per cent, a proportion that is already almost reached by the Soviet Union (21 per cent).

So coal, the essential European energy source, has seen its markets shrink through the development of coalfields in formerly importing countries and at the same time the growth of exports from the United States. The latter are now even of interest to the Atlantic countries of Europe, and American coal is imported into Great Britain, France, Belgium, Netherlands, Denmark, and Sweden. However, these changes in market orientation, though they have rendered the cost of energy somewhat higher for the European industrial nations, have not jeopardised the security of their supplies.

Distribution and Growth of Coal Production

	1913	1938	1972
World output (million tonnes)	1,342	1,197	2,124
N. America (per cent)	39·6	30·8	26·0
Asia (per cent)	2·5	11·1	25·6
Europe (per cent)	47·8	41·6	21·8
Russia (now U.S.S.R.) (per cent)	3·9	8·4	20·8
Rest of world (per cent)	1·7	2·8	5·6

During the same period (i.e. since the first world war), the European countries had closed many of their low-yield, high-cost collieries, and had sought a cheaper source of energy in petroleum, that could be bought in the crude state at bargain prices from the underdeveloped lands of the Third World, especially in the Middle East, where the fields were exploited by the great capital resources of the United States and international combines.

Of petroleum Europe possesses only insignificant deposits (though the North Sea fields may possibly modify this adjective before the end of the century). In 1973, when world production was more than 2,700 million tonnes, only 40 million tonnes came from Europe. However, during the first half of the present century European countries had constructed great seaport refineries, that consumed 775 million tonnes of crude oil, or 28 per cent of world output, more than half of it coming from the Middle East and North Africa. On the other side of the Atlantic, the United States and Canada, although producing between them 555 million tonnes of crude oil, imported a further 160 million tonnes for their refineries, about half of this from the Middle East and North Africa. Thus, the prodigious development of refining and of maritime transport, to the profit of the great industrial powers, had for a long time been able to conceal a very dangerous disequilibrium produced by the substitution of oil for coal as the major source of energy.

Undoubtedly the exploitation of newly-discovered oilfields on the fringes of Europe and North America (North Sea and Norwegian Sea, Irish Sea and off Baffin Land) and under the neighbouring oceanic floors will give a certain margin of security in terms of oil supplies: between 100 and 150 million tonnes a year may be obtained from the North Sea by 1980, and as much again from the Canadian and Alaskan Arctic; the production of Third World countries outside O.P.E.C. could well reach 60 to 80 million tonnes by the same date. But the energy deficit will remain appreciable.

In assessing the diverse energy resources of the world, and their distribution, in terms of coal equivalent, as is now customary, the position of the great industrial countries is revealed in stark reality.

Distribution and Growth of Petroleum Production

	1913	1938	1972	1974
World output (million tonnes)	90	271·6	2,554·3	2,870·3
N. America (per cent)	64·4	61·0	21·8	18·0
Latin America (per cent)	23·6	15·2	10·1	8·6
East Asia	3·7	3·6	4·7	5·4
Russia (now U.S.S.R.) (per cent)	3·6	11·0	15·4	16·0
Europe (per cent)	1·9	3·0	1·4	1·3
Middle East (per cent) ⎱	1·3	16·0	35·6	37·7
Africa (per cent) ⎰		0·2	10·3	9·1
Rest of world (per cent)	1·5	0·1	0·7	3·9

In 1913, Europe and North America had at their disposal 84 per cent of the world's energy resources, a figure that has fallen in sixty years to 48 per cent. The part now played by the Asiatic countries, and in particular the Middle East, and also by the countries of Africa and Latin America, bear further witness to the importance of petroleum in the strategy of world energy; this position has developed even at the expense of the United States, that formerly exported oil and now finds itself, as an importer, the victim of the politics of the Arab world. The new sources of oil can hardly amount to more than 700 million tonnes of coal equivalent, so that the industrial countries of the northern hemisphere will remain, to the extent of 1,000 million tonnes of coal equivalent, at the mercy of the overseas producers.

Distribution of World Energy Resources
(in millions of tonnes of coal equivalent, 1972; percentages)

	Coal	Oil	Nat. Gas	Hydro-Elect.	Nuclear Elect.
N. America	28·1	21·9	61·0	40·0	38·0
Eastern Asia	21·3	4·7	3·4	11·6	9·4
Middle East	nil	36·0	2·0	nil	nil
U.S.S.R.	20·2	15·6	18·2	11·2	3·6
Europe	32·0	1·5	13·2	29·1	49·0
Rest of world	14·7	20·3	3·2	8·0	nil
World (mn. tonnes coal equivalent)	2,560	3,300	1,580	727	43

Europeans and Americans alike, followed by the Japanese, have responded quickly by the development of an atomic policy involving the construction of nuclear power stations, the energy from which, in the long term, will enable relief from dependence on oil to be obtained; but in the meanwhile the heavy burden of oil imports will remain. France has developed her own long-term plan for 25 nuclear stations. Up to the present, the industrial world has only regained a fraction of its energy independence with 50 million coal-equivalent tonnes from atomic reactors—24 million tonnes in Europe (of which

12·5 millions from Great Britain) and 18·5 millions in the United States. But Europe has no monopoly of nuclear power, for adding the output from Asiatic countries, Japan and India, and several other less important producers, some 9 per cent of the coal equivalent tonnage comes from these half-dozen other countries. Though Europe may lead the way in atomic energy, it has not achieved the supremacy that it had hitherto through coal.

Evolution of Potential Energy

	(*per cent of world*) 1938	1972
N. America	53·0	36·5
Eastern Asia	6·5	10·2
Middle East	6·0	9·0
U.S.S.R.	7·0	14·0
Europe	25·0	25·0
Rest of world	2·5	5·2

It is not impossible, moreover, that in future the nuclear solution might not contain similar hazards to those of oil. Uranium, the modern nuclear fuel, is widespread enough, but the principal deposits that are known and exploited to a greater or less extent are to be found in Canada and the United States, in South Africa, Zaire, Niger, Gabon, in France (Limousin, Vendée, and Forez), in Bohemia, in the Soviet Union, and in Australia. At present North America has 71 per cent and Europe 4 per cent of the output of nuclear fuel—but this means that 25 per cent comes from overseas countries and the Third World. Only North America, the major producer, the African countries and several minor producers have exportable surpluses at the moment, but by 1980 the North American countries will need 25,000 tonnes of 70 per cent uranium oxide, extracted from 16 million tonnes of ore, whilst Europe will need 17,000 tonnes (from 10·6 million tonnes of ore); the needs of the other users of uranium being estimated at 8,000 tonnes (from 600,000 tonnes of ore), it follows that ore extraction will exceed 27 million tonnes, of which an appreciable quantity must come from outside the industrialised countries whose survival depends on the control of energy!

Production and Consumption of Uranium Oxide Nuclear Fuel

	(*tonnes*) Production	Consumption
N. America	39,000	18,100
Europe	2,000	12,250
Africa	11,200	—
Asia	—	2,600
Rest of world	1,500	3,750

It is normal to regard the European countries, amongst the great industrial powers, as being the most directly confronted by the energy crisis; they were earliest in the industrial field, followed much later by the North American countries and the Soviet Union. These latter, comprising huge states that control vast economic spaces, sources of energy and raw materials of all kinds, greater and more varied than those of Europe, have managed to preserve a greater degree of autonomy and initiative in the present crisis. But industries are rare in Europe that have been able to remain free of dependence on other continents and maintain the American ease of manoeuvre in relation to the Third World.

In 1913, Europe produced more than half the world's iron ore. Now the percentage is only 11, and the continent can no longer rely simply on the high-grade ores of Sweden, Spain, and North Africa. It must now import from Liberia and Mauritania, from Brazil and Venezuela—the production of which countries amounts to almost 20 per cent of the world total. Further, Europe must import almost all its manganese, which is indispensable in the manufacture of high-quality steel. Of a world output of a little over 8 million tonnes of manganese, the U.S.S.R. produces 35 per cent, but most of this is used in its own steel industry, so that Europe must seek its supplies in Africa, India and Australia. Some 2·6 million tonnes are produced in Africa, by the South African Republic, Zaire, Gabon, Ghana, and Morocco, 1·5 million tonnes by Brazil and 700,000 by India. But in all these markets Europe encounters competition from the United States, with its hard currency that, within the limits of its own interests, helps to maintain a high price for this raw material.

Production and Distribution of Iron Ore

	1913	1938	1972	1974
World output (million tonnes, iron content)	90	75	417	474
N. America (per cent)	35	20·3	16·5	16·9
U.S.S.R.	6	20·6	27·0	25·6
Europe	53	40·1	12·6	11·3
Africa	—	3·2	7·5	9·7
Latin America	—	1·7	10·8	11·3
Rest of world	6	14·1	25·6	25·2*

* Mainly Australia, India, and China

The situation with regard to other metalliferous ores is not dissimilar. One has only to place side by side a list of the reserve-holders and producers of ore and the states that do the refining and fabrication of the metals, to see the close dependence of Europe on the United States on the one hand and the countries of the Third World on the other.

The case of bauxite is a good example. The European output in 1938 was 1,775,000 tonnes, or 48 per cent of the world; although this had risen to 10,513,000 tonnes in 1972, it only represented 15 per cent of world output. The Caribbean area in the same year produced 27,350,000 tonnes, or 37 per cent of world output. And already certain Third World producers of bauxite, notably Surinam (7·8 million tonnes), and Guinea (2·6 millions) are endeavouring to create an organisation of producers and exporters capable of influencing the world price of the mineral, similar to, though on a smaller scale than, the plan that the Arab countries have succeeded in imposing on the international oil and energy market.

Production and Distribution of Bauxite

	1938	1972	1974
World output (million tonnes)	3·7	68	81
Europe (per cent)	54·0	15·3	14·3
S. America and Caribbean	26·2	37·1	33·6
N. America	9·5	2·8	2·4
Asia	7·4	6·3	5·2
U.S.S.R.	—	8·8	7·4
Australia	—	21·2	24·8
Africa	—	5·1	10·6
Rest of world	2·9	3·4	1·7

The industrial civilisation that was born in Europe, and that still characterises the continent, has ceased to expand. It is a type of structure and civilisation that was created over the centuries and spread overseas in a world that Europe had fashioned. Thanks to the high quality of its technology and the solidity of its structures, which have survived the test of endurance, it may yet retain its effective dynamism, fortified by the wealth of experience of its labour force, the quality of its scientific management, and the strength of its capital resources. It is the combination of these factors that will enable its own basic industries to form the foundations of industrialisation in the new countries, and to act as the starting-point for new developments in pure and applied science.

Chapter 12

DEVELOPMENT AND PERMANENCE
OF THE KEY INDUSTRIES

Some of man's industries have had long and brilliant careers, whilst others have been merely episodic or have passed through the ages without modifying their original humble techniques. The weaving of textiles and the working of metals, which first appeared as modest crafts, have gradually risen to the rank of mankind's chief occupations. Out of them arose large-scale industry which has created an artificial geographical landscape and led vast masses of humanity into hitherto unknown modes of life. It was only later that other kinds of industry began in their time to follow the same course of development and cluster round the centres formed by textile manufacture and metallurgy. By giving to the newcomers machinery and products to finish, while requiring of them various materials that are foreign to their own horizons of work, these pioneer industries continue to play a key part in the great modern industrial complexes. But for them the new industries would fade away or revert to the stage of crafts.

The oldest of these key activities that have shaped the face of industry and built up the great industrial regions are metallurgy and textile manufacture. Large-scale chemical industry, the third key industry of the modern world, arose at a more recent date from the needs of the first two, whilst the older ones took part in man's first efforts to free himself from Nature and her gifts.

THE TEXTILE INDUSTRIES

No industry has followed the upward path of civilisation more closely than the manufacture of textiles. It has risen from the status of a humble craft to that of a great manufacturing industry, mechanised, specialised, and integrated. Day by day it increases the variety of its raw materials and has finally come to use man-made fibres. Except in climates with slight variations of temperature, dress is a human necessity rather than an adornment. In fact, a temperature of from 22° to 25° C is needed to keep the naked human body in health. Below −12° C cold is unbearable whilst above 37° C heat is dangerous. The effect of clothing is to keep near the skin a blanket of air that slows down the diffusion or absorption of heat and prevents the human body from reaching the temperature of the surrounding air too quickly.

Prehistoric man soon took to wearing clothes. Probably, the warm, dry climate of the Chellean period enabled him to go naked. Today, absence of clothing is restricted to a few primitive tribes in central and southern Africa, the Amazon basin, central Australia, and Polynesia. These little groups of peoples wear only very exiguous garments consisting of leaves, bark, or skin in their natural state fastened about the body. Such poverty of dress is found even in very harsh climates. For instance, the Fuegians use nothing but a bit of fur to protect a portion of their bodies against the cutting wind, leaving the rest bare. In spite of this handful of exceptions, the problem of dress was for man a vital one which could only be solved by the use of a high degree of intelligence. Vidal de la Blache insists that, after food, dress is man's most important need and that his social standing is marked by its degree of luxury.

As early as the Mousterian and more markedly in the Magdalenian period man had to clothe himself in the skins of animals so as to cope with the severity of the glacial climate. Among the tools of the Stone Age were many intended for the preparation of skins. They include cutting edges, borers, scrapers, scraping knives for removing flesh, and smoothing tools to soften the pelt. In historical times skin garments still prevailed among backward peoples. Hesiod and the Odyssey describe the countryfolk of Homeric Greece as clad in skins. Herodotus mentions soldiers in Xerxes' army as merely covered with skins. Even later the Germans and Scythians are described by Tacitus as wearing the skins of wild animals. Today, furs and skins of animals are used as a protection against cold in regions with severe winters, even by peoples who have woven garments. Most of the Hyperboreans, and especially the Eskimos, who have no means of procuring fibres to spin and weave, excel in the art of preparing, cutting out, and sewing together the pelts of bears seals, and other fur-bearing animals.

In the course of history man has gradually had to make suitable garments by using first of all the resources of the natural environment, then by making such progress in civilisation as to be able to recognise in its natural state matter suitable for clothing him, to get it in sufficient quantities, and to prepare it for making clothes. Such matter does not exist in plenty, for it must have definite qualities, be a bad conductor of heat, and be waterproof, soft, and durable so as to repay by long service the trouble taken to obtain and fashion it. But it was only in the Neolithic Age that man learnt to make textiles. In peat bogs and the remains of lake dwellings large numbers of bits of rope, string, and even real cloth have been found.

Raw Materials.—The animal kingdom was the first to be laid under contribution, and this happened in various places simultaneously.

In the East goat's hair was used in ancient times, as is evident from the Bible. In the *Georgics* Virgil says that goat's hair gives coarse, but hard-wearing cloth suitable for soldiers and sailors. This fibre, however, is nowadays used only to a slight degree by modern industry. Goats from Tibet and Ankara yield a fine, soft hair which is sought under the name of *mohair* for making luxury goods. Nowadays, mohair is got from South Africa, where Ankara, or 'Angora', goats have been acclimatised and have acquired coats that exceed in quality those of the original Anatolian breed. From earliest times Peruvians have used llama or alpaca wool, but this fibre has spread very little beyond its original home, and, like angora, it is only used by modern industry in the manufacture of luxury goods.

Wool remains the most plentiful and valuable of the fibres derived from animals, and its fortunes are most closely bound up with the history of civilisation. Its use goes back to prehistoric times and was surpassed by that of cotton only in the eighteenth century. As noted above, the sheep was domesticated at a very early period. There is evidence of its being found in Iberia and North Africa in ancient times in association with the goat before the ox or the dog had made its appearance in those countries. It is also found very early in central Europe, where by the Neolithic period it had been domesticated. Wool was the chief fibre throughout ancient times in the Mediterranean and throughout the Middle Ages in Europe, for the use of flax and silk remained very restricted. Wool production spread together with European civilisation from the Old World to the United States, the Argentine, South Africa, Australia, and New Zealand, and today the chief producers are the new countries in the southern hemisphere. Since the beginning of the nineteenth century world production of wool has constantly increased, rising from 200,000 tonnes in 1810 to more than 2,600,000 tonnes in 1973. In spite of this, wool is a relatively scarce raw material, for the market for woollen fabrics has continually expanded, and woollen cloth is coming into use even in the Far East among peoples who hitherto have been loyal to cotton. The recent appearance of Japan as a woollen manufacturer is a new feature in world industry. Furthermore, wool is now only a by-product of mutton, whilst cotton is a main crop. Though an increase in the price of cotton may be at once reflected in increased production, an increase in the price of wool has little effect on production, since this depends on the yield of fully-grown sheep, whose numbers cannot be added to immediately. So great are the demands for wool that the enormous quantity produced in the world is far from being enough. Hence, a process of renovation has come into the industry, by which the fibres from woollen rags ('shoddy') and tailors' clippings ('mungo') are used again after being pulled out and strengthened somewhat with fresh wool. This wool-rag industry began in Great Britain about 1840.

Silk is the most peculiar and costly of all animal fibres. Owing to its insulating properties, its sheen, fineness, and lightness, it would have taken the lead in textile manufacture, had it been cheaper. But the tenuousness of the fibre, the small size of the caterpillar that yields it, and the great care needed to rear this creature, have from the start made silk cloth a luxury. It is not surprising that it was the first fibre to be copied artificially by a product of the chemical industry.

In China, the original home of the silkworm, the process by which the cocoons are used is attributed to mythical personages, and this bears witness to the early age of its discovery. Probably a beginning was made by gathering cocoons from the wild mulberry trees in the woods; then to have more cocoons with greater regularity came the idea of rearing silkworms. The Chinese attribute the putting into effect of the idea to Si Ling Chi (2650 B.C.), the Shu Ching (Book of History) mentions a tribute of silk levied by the Emperor Yu (2200 B.C.), and Chinese documents from the third century B.C. to the thirteenth century A.D. show that taxes were often paid with skeins of silk.

Today, silk is used whenever both strength and fineness are needed. Silk thread and silk cloth are soft, warm, light, and strong. These qualities are not always found together in rayon, nylon, terylene, and other man-made fibres that have been used as substitutes. On the whole, fibres derived from animals have not met all needs and they are costly and difficult to produce. Wool and silk, excellent as insulators, are not cool and do not readily absorb moisture, and, when worn, the cloth allows perspiration to accumulate on the skin. For this reason recourse was soon had to vegetable fibres.

The use of vegetable material to serve as clothes goes back to prehistoric times. It is an easy matter to make pieces of rudimentary clothing from soft leaves and lianas. In New Zealand, where there were no animals to yield skins, the Maoris could only clothe themselves by interweaving leaves and straw. Remains of garments made of esparto grass and dating from the upper Neolithic have been found in caves in Andalucía. In the eighteenth century Captain James Cook described the clothing of the Maoris as made of leaves of a kind of sword-grass, *Phormium tenax*. The plaiting of grass used in these cases was the forerunner of weaving.

Leaves and bark could have only a restricted use, for they lacked fineness and flexibility. In the end experience showed that the inner fibres of certain plants were better endowed with these qualities, and efforts were made to extract them for use. As these experiments went on, various regions were led to take advantage of the resources of the local flora. In Spain the bark of a broom, *Sparteum juncum*, was used; in central Europe the choice fell on the soft bark of certain lime trees; in Mexico the fibres of the *agave* were preferred, and in New Zealand those of the *Phormium tenax*, which were taken from the ribbed leaf that had originally been used whole. However, the demand for fibre led man very soon to increase by cultivation the plants that yielded them. Choice was made of several annuals that were easily propagated and could be included in the series of other crops. One after the other, three plants played an important part in the history of the textile industry. They were flax, hemp, and cotton.

Of course, many other plants must have been able to yield fibre. As early as 1872 a botanist named Bernardin estimated the number of plants yielding fibres used by man at various stages of civilisation as more than 700. Many of them have played no part in world trade. Some like jute, sisal, and china-grass have come into use in European industry, but have been employed only in small quantities and for special manufactures. Their part, therefore, remains subordinate. Altogether, the vegetable fibres now cultivated and used in industry may be placed in two categories. First, there is down, which consists of slender hairs growing on the surface of the organs, seeds, or fruit of a plant. Cotton and kapok belong to this class. Secondly, fibres, or parts that are essentially internal and are found either in the cortex of the stalk, as in hemp, flax, or jute; or in the tissue of the leaves, as in *Phormium*, *agave*, and the banana tree. Before these fibres can be used, they must be removed from the rest of the tissue around them.

A geographical study of all these raw materials brings out two apparently contradictory phenomena. First, the decreasing use of certain traditional fibres and their replacement by others whose production has on the contrary reached enormous quantities. Secondly, the quest for new fibres, which was necessitated by the short supply of raw materials and has led to the introduction of man-made fibres.

Flax and hemp were used at the same time as wool in countries with the most advanced material civilisation. But since the nineteenth century flax has been continually retreating in the face of wool, jute, and cotton; that is to say, in the face of fibres that are cheaper and more easily to be got in large quantities. The struggle was keenest between flax and cotton. The latter's success is partly explained by its arrival on the market as a homogeneous commodity, whilst flax came in batches of various qualities. This advantage is opposed by the greater strength of linen, but is supported by the greater ease with which cotton can be manufactured, as it can be used with lighter and less powerful machinery and requires less motive power and labour. That is why cotton has almost entirely replaced linen for underclothing.

Furthermore, cotton has become the rival of wool in furnishing and the making of ready-made clothing. Before the invention of rayon it even competed with silk. Some cotton fabrics, like sateen, are just like silk, and some mercerised cottons have a silk-like sheen. Cotton has caused a veritable revolution in economic life. Up to the eighteenth century its success had been delayed by the difficulty European manufacturers had in obtaining supplies of raw material, since Mediterranean and West Indian sources furnished it in only moderate quantities. This relative short supply of raw material disappeared at the end of the eighteenth century owing to the expansion of British trade with India and the Far East, while cotton plantations rapidly grew in number in the United States. At the same time the inventions of English engineers enabled hand looms to be replaced by machinery which produced goods cheaply and in large quantities, and to place on the world market a kind of clothing that was moderate in price and thus accessible to the poorer classes in underdeveloped countries.

The present day affords another instance of the struggle between the raw materials used by the textile industry. It has arisen from the invention of artificial and synthetic fibres, which at first competed only with fibres used for luxury goods, but which have been got in greater and greater quantities from less and less expensive raw material, whilst their technical qualities have constantly improved. To begin with there were different varieties of rayon and staple fibre, derived from wood pulp and cotton linters, then there followed a series of fibres got from mineral substances, by-products of the distillation of coal, oil, or other chemicals. From these are manufactured nylon, Terylene, Orlon, Courtelle, Acrilan, and a score of other fabrics. This great new addition of raw material is due to the chemical industry, whose artificial fibres can be used in the same machinery as wool, cotton, and silk. This colossal development has not, however, caused the disappearance of the traditional raw

Production of Textile Fibres
(thousand tonnes)

	1880	1939	1958	1973
Flax	640	647	830	629
Hemp	450	250	320	261
Wool	850	1,100	2,300	2,560
Cotton	2,000	5,510	8,700	13,504
Jute	400	1,580	1,100	4,164
Sisal	*	*	*	1,172
Man-made fibres	nil	1,000	2,700	11,577

materials, for the production of linen, wool, and cotton has not fallen off during the last few years. It could seem rather that the new fibres have come to supplement the traditional ones, since the production of the latter could not keep pace with man's need for cloth and clothing. This is clearly shown by the statistics of production given on page 296.

Industrial Development.—The various fibres soon gave rise to industry based on local resources. Wool, for instance, was originally used in a clearly defined geographical region in the Old World which suited the sheep and in which there existed both pastoralism and the practice of lengthy fallow. Wool was used in Iran, where the usual footwear was for a long time a felt gaiter. It was also used in the Mediterranean, where it is still the material for fishermen's caps and the manufacture of the hooded cloaks of peasants in Corsica and Sardinia ; for the kilts and waistcoats of sailors and peasants in Greece and Macedonia ; for the *burnus* of nomadic Arabs ; and the carpets and felt mats of the nomadic peoples of western and central Asia.

In early times wool also became the raw material for European clothing ; fitting closely to the body it forms quite a different kind of dress from cotton. To this ancient type belong the pantaloons and short-sleeved smocks, the breeches and loose gowns of the Gauls, specimens of which were preserved in peat bogs together with a complete set of Bronze Age tools. The material and shape of these rustic garments have been handed down through the centuries and were still to be seen in the dress of English countryfolk and French peasants right up to the eighteenth century.

Silk became an essential raw material in early times in China, where for long it supplied a domestic industry whose origin mingled in legend with that of agriculture. State control, which has been the economic system of China in nearly all ages, for a long time enabled the Government to keep the monopoly of manufacture of silk cloth and of its sale to the rest of the world. In this way for hundreds of years China was able to support a large number of craftsmen who worked at fixed, time-honoured patterns devoid of elegance and imagination.

At that time there prevailed in this part of the Far East a peculiar type of dress with long-established differences between garments meant for the lower classes and those intended for the governing class. In winter the dress of the former was quilted or lined with fur and consisted of tight-fitting trousers tied with string round the calves, and a sleeved tunic. In summer they were content with a short smock and trousers. But for summer or winter wear these garments were all made of cotton cloth and were quilted with cotton. Silk was reserved for the wealthy classes. It was made into flowing robes embroidered and adorned with buttons of precious metal, the number of which varied with the rank of the official or nobleman. Long, full Chinese gowns and Japanese *kimonos* were the rare and costly garments of a hierarchical system. They were the only Far Eastern costume known to the West and, owing to their luxury, were the only ones to find their way into world trade.

However, the textile industry soon escaped this dependence on local raw material, for fibre is a light commodity easily packed and kept protected from any kind of deterioration. It soon became easy to transport, and today raw material is imported into big centres where the industry had originally been established. This is true of the Lancashire cotton industry, the Lyons silk industry, and the Japanese woollen industry, which is supplied with wool from Australia. Separation of centres of transformation from areas of production is no new phenomenon. It showed itself very early in the textile industry, which has grown up wherever raw material from abroad could easily be had.

If, setting aside problems of raw material and labour, world relations are to be called on in every case to explain the rise of the textile industry and its present distribution, they often show the causes of regional specialisation and division of labour in various branches of manufacture. In particular, they explain the complex relations that exist between the mainly spinning centre at Tourcoing with the mainly weaving centre at Roubaix ; the cotton centre at Manchester and the woollen centre at Rochdale with the centre at Bradford where woollen and cotton goods are finished and dressed. Conversely, non-participation in world trade may be enough to prevent a textile industry from developing into a large integration. There is no better example than the Catalan textile industry, which contents itself with the national market for the disposal of its products. Now, in a country of 35 million people the amount of trade is limited. Besides, the market is not only small, but also rejects standardised goods. Everyone wants to have a different cloth from his neighbour and to show his personality by his shade of dress, thus reflecting the individualistic temperament of a Mediterranean people.

Owing to this, Spanish factories cannot envisage large programmes of manufacture, since they must often change their patterns after a limited output. Hence the small size of the textile businesses in Spain, where every factory works for a small number of customers, whose custom they try to keep by flattering tastes and meeting whims and demands for novelty. Like the markets the firms are split up into small units, most of which remain family concerns with moderate outputs, unless they are foreign companies operating for export. Hence the contrast, especially in organisation, between a textile country like Cataluña, which is restricted to the narrow market of an undeveloped European peninsula and a great centre of world trade like Lancashire, whose blue cotton fabrics for nearly a century dressed the vast crowds in the Far East.

At each widening of its geographical horizon and at each expansion of its trade relations the textile industry has responded with technical progress. Up to the fifteenth century the guild system prevailed in the towns of Western Europe. It depended on the handiwork of families of craftsmen who lived in the towns. Archives kept in Flanders enable us to penetrate deeply into the organisation and life of the guilds, which were more anxious to keep the monopoly of the trade than to increase their output.

As early as the twelfth century the brightly coloured fine cloth made by the guild at Lille was renowned in all the chief fairs in the West. It was a high-class industry using English wool and turning out goods for well-to-do customers. The common people were satisfied with coarse cloth made by village weavers from local wool. Consequently it mattered little to the people of Lille when in 1360 John le Bon, King of France, authorised the bailiff of Lille to issue to the inhabitants of the villages in the district a brand with which to mark the bolts of cloth made by them. But during the Hundred Years War, and at the beginning of the sixteenth century, Lille was unable to get the high quality English wool which was needed for its fine cloth and it had to change its produce to suit the local wool at its disposal. Out of this arose within the town itself the manufacture of *sayette*, or light Flanders serge which was wholly of wool, and *bourgette*, which was a mixture of wool, flax, and silk.

The manufacture of these two kinds of cloth took an important place in the town, and in 1496 the makers of *bourgetterie* obtained from the Chief Magistrate a charter authorising them to manufacture cloth of 'high and low warp', which had originally been reserved for the makers of *sayetterie*. The products of these two kinds of manufacture were very like the village manufactures, and so the new guilds brought an action in the courts against the weavers in the '*plat pays*' of Tourcoing who had never before troubled the old clothmakers' guild. The struggle for the monopoly of producing these goods became particularly bitter in 1534, when the people of Lille obtained from the Emperor Charles V a judgment which forbade the use of the fibre for *sayette* outside the bounds of the town. The judgment raised a storm of protest, following which the people of Tourcoing won the right to have twenty-five looms for making velveteen, those of Roubaix were authorised in 1548 to have '*cinquante outils*'; and those of Leers and Toufflers were granted twenty-eight and twelve respectively. But it was stipulated that the villages were only to make coarse cloth; high quality cloth and fustian were reserved to the guilds in Lille *intra muros*.

Very soon the people of Roubaix and Tourcoing, taking no notice of the cramping regulations, began to manufacture high-quality cloth, and during the whole of the seventeenth century there was a bitter struggle with frequent appeals to the Spanish governors, and after the Treaty of the Pyrenees (1659) to the Court at Versailles. In 1728, when the people of Roubaix started further manufactures, the people of Lille had the looms and cloth confiscated. It was only in 1762 that a decree of the Council recognised the right of the countryfolk to spin all textile fibres without restriction and to manufacture and dress all kinds of textiles. This account shows clearly the tenacity with which French town guilds still defended their monopolies at a time when industrial occupations had long since ceased to be the prerogative of the towns.

The guild system acted as a check on production, for it restricted manufactures to the types recognised by the brand, which had somewhat the same character as our trade marks. It also kept a steady level of employment, maintained supplies of raw materials, and conditions of sale, and, furthermore, imposed a jealous preservation of trade secrets and markets. Such a system fitted well into the narrow, unchanging life of medieval society. It marks an economic state in which craftsmen produce mainly for local use and in which a few specialists devote themselves to manufactures that interest a wider market, to which, however, the flow of goods is limited by difficulties and cost of transport, by the low purchasing power of a society whose masses lack the means to dress in fine cloth.

The system soon changed, and textile manufacture gradually passed nearly everywhere to the countryfolk, as it did in the Lille district. The development began in Flanders, reached England, and was adopted in France in the reign of Louis XI. In the new phase of industry which came over Europe in the seventeenth and eighteenth centuries, towns gradually ceased to manufacture textiles and became commercial centres. The town 'manufacturer' was now merely a merchant whose business was to organise in rural districts the making of the commodities needed by his customers. In fact, he became much more of an entrepreneur than an industrialist.

The association between rural and urban operations, which the guilds so strenuously opposed, could prevail only owing to the pressure of economic facts and the effect of the expansion of the markets. Besides, the possibility of having goods manufactured outside the towns enabled merchants to escape the fussy regulations of the guilds and to meet the demands of the markets. Rural labour, being numerous and able to satisfy all requirements, gave textile industry a previously unknown flexibility. In 1698 the Intendant of Flanders and Artois, Dugué de Bagnole, clearly pointed out the advantages of this type of rural industry.

'The towns of Roubaix and Tourcoing are most important for different kinds of cloth, some of wool and others of silk and wool, which they manufacture and export to almost all parts of the world. The convenience to the inhabitants of adding a little industry to their housework makes them better off than people in closed towns, and this contributes not only to the prosperity of the industry, but would also for that very reason have ruined its town rival, had the manufacture of several kinds of cloth which were forbidden to countryfolk been reserved to the towns.'

In spite of these advantages rural industry had great drawbacks. Though its production was better than that of the guild system, its output was small and, above all, irregular, because it could only yield its full output during the slack seasons in agriculture or when disaster overtook the crops and famine reigned in the land. It could therefore not keep up with the endless expansion of the markets. That explains why it declined so rapidly when machinery was invented in England in the second half of the eighteenth century. The Industrial Revolution was mainly intent on the need to produce quickly. It has been calculated that the old spinning-wheel produced five skeins of yarn in fifty-six working hours. With a mechanised frame a spinner could, with the help of two children, turn out 55,000 skeins in the same time. Modern non-stop spinning machines reach even more impressive figures.

The output of large mechanised textile mills has enabled cloth to be used by a greatly increasing number of persons. It has helped to standardise dress and to abolish local costumes. Jackets and trousers have become essential pieces of clothing in Africa and the Far East. Yet these immense new markets no longer succeed in absorbing an industrial output of textiles which formerly was invariably too little to meet all demands. This is because cotton is the first industry to be established in underdeveloped countries as their standard of living rises. Nowadays, the textile industry, which in the United States and the old countries in Europe has become recognised as a main occupation, is being transplanted into most new countries, including Brazil, India, Egypt, Indonesia, and China, and continues its geographical expansion without on that account abandoning its old traditional centres.

The Manufacture of Textiles.—The textile industry has called for greater intelligence and shrewdness than any other industry. The use of the raw materials indeed requires many delicate operations which have been only slowly brought to perfection. A long series of experiments has made cloth into a valuable commodity due to man's work and intelligence and to his knowledge accumulated from earliest times.

First of all, the raw material must be prepared. Mills can seldom use the fibres just as they have been gathered. Wool must be freed from impurities, scoured, cleaned, and often dyed. These preliminary operations constitute a real industry. Similarly, after cotton has been picked by hand or mechanical picker, it has to be ginned and carded before any further operation. Before being spun flax and hemp have to undergo two processes, both of which have become recognised industries. *Retting* consists of inducing the disintegration of the woody elements in the stems and is nowadays done in an autoclave. *Scutching* separates the fibre, which has remained intact, from the decomposed portions of the stem. Silk is gathered in the form of cocoons from which the thread must be unwound after the chrysalis has been killed. The process is divided into two stages. *Beating* dissolves the outer case of the cocoon in water raised to a temperature of 90° C. Then between four and ten cocoons are taken, and their threads unwound together. This gives raw silk. But it cannot be used directly in silk manufacture, for it must be twisted by *throwing*. This preparation is carried out in little workrooms, some of which in Japan attain the size of small factories.

These preliminary processes are all followed by spinning, which is one of man's oldest inventions. At first it was done by hand with the help of rudimentary implements like the distaff and spindle. Nearly all neolithic settlements have yielded little spindles of baked earth. For a very long time the spinning of yarn was the work of women. Its technique remained unimproved until the eighteenth century, except by the adoption of the spinning-wheel in the sixteenth century. A fundamental change took place in the eighteenth century when warm countries began to supply cotton in plenty. The development due to new mechanical inventions led to the industrial prosperity of Great Britain, and after some delay reached the continent. Mechanical spinning brought a general revival of all the other branches of the industry. Henceforth the heavy and scarcely remunerative task of spinning by hand was over. Mechanisation had been introduced more promptly into spinning than into any other branch of the textile industry, and, consequently, it was the earliest to be held in the firm grip of the capitalist system of industry. Nowadays a concrete idea of the importance of the textile industry of a country is given by quoting the number of spindles working.

Weaving springs from the art of mat-making, an art that still flourishes today in the Far East and the Pacific islands. It consists of interlacing the threads of the *woof* (or *weft*), which run across the cloth, with those of the *warp*, which run lengthways. The warp was stretched on a horizontal frame, and the weft was passed through it by means of a shuttle worked by hand. The same procedure is still followed in Arab, Iranian, and Indian looms. No essential modification was introduced in Europe till the eighteenth century, when a radical change in weaving came with the invention of the flying shuttle (1733) and the replacement of the hand-loom by the power loom (1787). A great change also occurred in the wool and silk industries, but for a long time hand looms were used along with power looms, since weaving kept its craft system longer than spinning. In many districts looms are even in these days not confined to mills, and in old weaving districts hand looms are to be found side by side with the wholly automatic Northrop looms.

The art of dyeing cloth also goes back to very early times, but at first it was used only with high-grade cloth. Before the invention of aniline dyes it was confined to centres of large-scale trade and countries with a high civilisation. An operation then common in trade centres was the purchase of unbleached linen or fulled woollen cloth for dyeing and resale as high-grade cloth according to the richness and beauty of the colouring. This method of increasing the value of poorer quality cloth was practised in ancient times by the Egyptians and Phoenicians. Up to the twelfth century the dyeing of cloth was one of the great Byzantine industries, and later the art was practised in the cloth towns in Italy and Flanders. The Gobelin establishment began its career with the dyeing of wool and other fabrics. Dyes were originally rare and expensive. Purple was got from the *murex* and also from cochineal (a Mexican insect), dyer's moss (a kind of lichen), and madder root. Blues were obtained from the leaves of the woad, or pastel, and later from indigo, a leguminous tropical plant. Other sources of dye were the Central American and West Indian logwood, which gave a black tint, and brazil, the wood that gave its name to the country and yielded a brick-red colour. Modern times have introduced profound changes in the dyeing industry. Already at the end of the eighteenth century the French chemist Berthollet had substituted the use of chlorine for grass-bleaching in the preparation of linen and cotton cloth for dyeing. At the beginning of the nineteenth century there appeared dyes extracted from coal-tar. These gave an infinite number of shades, were very fast, and extremely cheap. Up to the 1914–18 war Germany held a virtual monopoly in the preparation of these dyes and supplied 88 per cent of the world's demand for them.

With dyeing is closely allied the printing of fabrics, by which uniform colouring is replaced by designs in several colours. Printing had also been an ancient art, but its processes had long remained rudimentary and were rather like the batik work in Indonesia. In the eighteenth century Oberkampf, a Bavarian who had a factory at Jouy-en-Josas, near Paris, applied the processes of book-printing to cloth by placing on unbleached cotton fabric a board with designs in relief and coated with colouring matter. Shortly afterwards (1783) James Bell, at Preston in Lancashire, improved the process by placing the designs on a roller which turned continuously after the fashion of the rotary machines used in book-printing; somewhat similar developments were sponsored by Widmer in Switzerland. Next came the process of printing in several colours at once. Owing to this, cloth printing achieved a wonderful expansion in the next century and put within everyone's reach articles that combined artistic quality and practical utility.

The last stage is the making of garments. This was long carried out in the home, where the women cut and sewed the family's clothes from pieces of cloth got from weavers in exchange for raw wool, tow, and yarn from the farms. Even today the clothing industry still employs the greatest number of domestic operatives, who work individually for a steady, but narrow circle of customers. But in this industry too machinery has brought great changes, for the sewing machine, which completes the cycle of ingenious inventions in the textile industry, has led to the concentration of workpeople in workrooms and factories.

The clothing industry belongs essentially to the towns; that is, it is attracted to large industrial centres where there is a sufficiency of female labour. It therefore seems complementary to heavy industries which call for male workers. Concentration in towns is favoured by the presence of big markets formed by great numbers of customers who are reached through large shops. It is significant that all the big shops in Paris that are now department stores (that is, shops offering a large number of different lines of goods) began by selling hats, underwear, and ready-made clothing. The clothing trade is centred particularly in capital cities and great conurbations like London, Paris, Vienna, Berlin, New York, and Los Angeles. New York makes shirts for the whole of the United States, whilst 22 per cent of the 'women's outerwear' industry is concentrated in Los Angeles.

In these big industrial centres the work is seldom wholly done in factories, for the making of a costume needs many details which cannot be carried out by machinery. Finishing touches are often the work of home-workers or little independent groups that take in parcels of goods and trimmings from a factory and prepare them for sale in shops. This is further evidence of the vitality of craftsmanship in the last stages of the textile industry.

Textile manufacture is therefore being executed by the most ingenious inventions and is for this reason one of the most complex achievements of the highest civilisations. It occupies more people and creates greater values than any other industry. Its present form was shaped in Europe, and Europeans are still the world's chief cloth merchants. Although other peoples in Asia and America have built up rival industries, in Europe textile manufacture still occupies the leading place in industrial economy. Europe is the chief focus of the noblest and most scientific form of industry, namely, the making of woollen cloth, in which none of the new countries has been able to equal the skill of experienced European weavers.

Europe, in fact, despite the competition of Asiatic countries, continued to dominate the textile market during the first half of the twentieth century, supplementing its supplies of raw materials, which quickly became insufficient, by imports of fibres from overseas—wool from the southern hemisphere (Australia, Argentina, South Africa), cotton from the United States and from tropical and sub-tropical countries (India, Egypt). Unfortunately, in the latter part of this century most of the natural raw materials are outside the control of the old European manufacturing areas that were the cradle of the industries; cotton is completely lacking, and the wool supply is inadequate, for the trend in agriculture has increased the numbers of beef cattle at the expense of the wool-bearing sheep. The efforts of Europe and the United States to increase the production and use of artificial fibres of chemical origin has lightened this dependence somewhat, but not entirely, for the indispensable raw material of the synthetic fibres is petroleum, so the problem is simply shifted. Europe now produces about 3,730,000 tonnes of man-made fibres, or 32·4 per cent of the world total; but nevertheless its relative position is declining, for in 1938 the percentage was 38. Over the whole range of textile fibres, Europe remains a net importer, dependent on overseas territories. The world output of textile raw materials of all kinds now amounts to about 32 million tonnes a year.

Production and Distribution of Textile Raw Materials

	All fibres 1938	All fibres 1973	Natural fibres 1973
World output (million tonnes)	14·6	31·9	20·8
N. America (per cent)	21·4	20·1	13·8
Europe	5·5	12·7	19·3
U.S.S.R.	10·6	13·5	16·4
Asia	36·8	27·7	29·5
Rest of world	25·7	26	21

The raw cotton market is in fact dominated by the United States, and that of wool, despite the long tradition of London wool sales, is subject to the fluctuation of southern hemisphere production, that periodically places a heavy burden on the European industries.

Distribution and Consumption of Wool in 1973
(thousand tonnes)

Exporters		Importers	
Australia and N.Z.	995	U.S.A. and Canada	92
S. America	140	Japan	320
S. Africa	93	Europe	685
Rest of world	196	Rest of world	371
Total	1,424		1,468

More generally, Europe's share of the world textile market is declining, because of the rise of Third World exporters most of whom are in countries that are in the early stages of industrialisation, possessing, as well as raw materials, an abundant labour supply that a growing textile industry can readily employ without too heavy a capital investment. Such is the case in Brazil, for example, and even more so in certain Asiatic countries. The cotton industries of Japan, India, Taiwan and Hong Kong now represent one quarter of the world's output, and their wares sell as far afield as Europe. The cotton goods exports from Hong Kong were even greater, in 1971, than those from the United Kingdom.

Production and Distribution of Woollen and Cotton Yarn

	1938	1972
World output (thousand tonnes)	6,380	8,520
N. America (per cent)	27·0	20·4
Latin America	1·7	2·4
Asia	20·3	25·0
Africa	2·4	2·0
U.S.S.R.	10·2	22·0
Europe	38·0	28·0
Rest of world	0·4	0·2

METALLURGICAL INDUSTRIES

The search for, extraction, treatment, and use of metals are comparatively recent activities, but they are vital facts in the march of civilisation and in the structure of economic life. Metals are hard and malleable substances that have replaced wood, bone, and stone for making tools and weapons. Man did not suddenly learn how to make full use of these industrial materials, but has mastered them after a long series of discoveries and inventions, the list of which is still far from being closed.

There has always been a time in every part of the world when man was ignorant of the use of metals, but the different peoples have not all advanced from the age of stone to that of iron at the same time. They have all even continued to use old stone implements at the same time as metallic ones, as may still be seen in New Caledonia. For a long time the use of iron was unknown for practical reasons, for industrially it is only a derived product and, unlike copper and tin, cannot be extracted from its ore by a single operation. It was found easier to use bronze, since this was easily cast and recast. Bronze, an alloy of copper and tin, was used in the eastern Mediterranean as early as the fifth and fourth centuries B.C. It was the metal of the Ægeans and Minoans, and is thought to have been first obtained from the Caucasus. It was very slowly replaced by iron, owing rather to the latter's cheapness than to its technical qualities. The first users of iron seem to have been African tribes and probably Caucasian peoples. The use of iron passed through central Europe to become general in the West mainly during the Hallstatt period, when its diffusion was completed between 1300 and 500 B.C. The full use of steel, zinc, platinum, nickel, manganese, aluminium, tungsten, chromium, and molybdenum did not begin, however, until long after, towards the end of the nineteenth century.

The rise of metallurgy was at first partly due to the abundance of ore. But for long this depended on the yield of mines. To extract ore from the ground, miners of old had only pick and hammer and the strength of their arms. Except in a few details, the tools of the medieval German miners were the same as those of their Phoenician and Roman counterparts. Yet these miners of old achieved remarkable success in prospecting for the lodes of metal and in working them deep down. Certain peoples have contributed greatly to the art of mining, especially the medieval Germans, whose mining literature played a great part in promoting the advance of processes in the rest of Europe.

The use of gunpowder caused a revolution in mining in the seventeenth century. It began in the Harz in 1632 and in Staffordshire in 1665. The saving in work due to this enabled subsidiary tasks to be undertaken and tunnels to be dug to drain water from the mines. As this added to their efficiency, the mines at once gave greater yields. The new processes were taken to Mexico and other parts of North America by the Spaniards. A little later machinery was invented to pump out the water, and its use spread during the eighteenth century, especially to mines in flat districts. Progress in equipment enabled greater and greater depths to be reached, to the point of being incommoded by the ever-increasing temperature. Besides, improved and increasingly powerful machinery has been used to win the ore, at first in quarries and then, when electricity came into general use, in the depths of the earth. Machine-drills, which have gradually replaced pneumatic picks, underground trolleys on rails, and lifts to raise the mineral to the surface, have ended by making the bigger mines into real factories needing an immense amount of power for their efficient working.

The progress of mining has been followed by that of metallurgy, which has enabled an increasing variety of ores to be used, and more and more efficient processes to be put into operation for the treatment of ores and metals; and in the end this progress has made ferrous metallurgy the most essential industry in human society. Man's activity in this work is reflected today by a number of modifications in the earth's surface that have utterly changed the scenery and transformed his occupations over vast areas.

Economically and commercially metals may be placed in three groups: precious metals, non-ferrous metals, and iron. These differ not only by their natural properties, which determine the use made of them, but also by the magnitude of their production. Precious metals like gold and silver scarcely reach an annual production of 9,800 tonnes. The production of rare metals which are mainly intended to make special forms of steel, such as molybdenum, tungsten, chromium, and cobalt amount to about 3·5 million tonnes; that of non-ferrous metals to 38 million tonnes. In contrast with these, iron alone exceeds a production of 500 million tonnes. The relative importance of the three groups (in terms only of weight) is clearly shown in the following table:

Iron	91·2 per cent
Non-ferrous metals	8·8 per cent
Precious metals	0·01 per cent

Precious metals are characterised by their resistance to chemical change and by their high density. Their geographical distribution separates them from countries that produce coal and iron, for they occur all along the great mountain ranges bordering the Pacific in the two American continents, in South Africa, Australia, and on the coasts of the Arctic in both the Old and New Worlds. Owing to the part played by gold and silver in coinage, the fact that they are not found in the great trading countries has always been a powerful stimulus to European expansion and trade relations.

Non-ferrous metals have become indispensable to large-scale industry and economic structure of the western type. Their importance does not depend on their total production. Manganese

(9 million tonnes), copper (8 million tonnes), and aluminium (13 million tonnes) are used most. After them come zinc (5 million tonnes) and lead (4 million tonnes). On the other hand, tin production scarcely exceeds 230,000 tonnes and nickel production 700,000 tonnes. In contrast with iron workings, which are nearly always exploited by national capital, copper, lead, and zinc mines and tin deposits most often depend on foreign owners in the shape of big companies that are mainly British for tin and American for copper. On the whole, however, the American continents produce most of the non-ferrous metals with the exception of tin.

The overwhelming preponderance of iron arises from its having been bound up with the whole history of civilisation and mankind's material progress. Its uses have never ceased to grow as its techniques have improved. From its use in the arts of war and agriculture it has become an indispensable raw material in the manufacture of machinery and the means of transport. It has supplanted stone in the building trade, sometimes being used alone, at other times in combination with cement, as reinforced concrete. In spite of the increased use of aluminium in hardware and aeronautical construction, iron is still the emblem of modern civilisation.

Iron in its Natural State.—Iron ore has a strange distribution. It is not found in wide river plains like Egypt, Mesopotamia, northern India, or northeast China, or in the limestone regions around the Mediterranean, and for that reason the great countries in ancient times were without it. On the other hand, its deposits lie thickly in the north of the temperate belt and the Arctic on the very doorstep of the great centres of industry. There are a number of kinds of iron ore that have been utilised in turn as the necessary processes have been discovered. Some, like those from Styria, Ariège, or the Adirondacks, are found in veins and are very pure. Others are residual in character, coming from the weathering of rocks and physico-chemical changes in sediments owing to climatic action. These include lateritic ores (as in Malaya and Guinea) and the ferruginous concretionary masses in solution-hollows in some limestones. Such replacement ores are still developed in Algeria and Tunisia. Other ores are sedimentary in origin, occurring in almost every geological period from the pre-Cambrian to the Tertiary, and including pre-Cambrian ores in South Africa, Ordovician in Newfoundland and Normandy, Silurian in Alabama, Devonian in Algeria, Carboniferous in the British coalfields, Jurassic in Lorraine and in the scarplands of Northamptonshire, Cretaceous in Germany and Tertiary in Colombia and the Crimea. Lastly, and most abundant of all, vast reserves—some of them as yet almost untouched—occur in igneous and metamorphic rocks of pre-Cambrian age, as in India, Brazil, Venezuela, the Lake Superior and Ungava regions of North America, at Krivoi Rog in the U.S.S.R., in several parts of West Africa, and in Australia.

In these ores iron is combined in the form of carbonate, as in those from the English coalfields or Styria; or in the form of oxide, with or without phosphorus. The oxides are by far the most plentiful and varied. The magnetites with a silicious gangue and the hæmatites with an iron content of up to 72 per cent are the best among them.

Ores are found in all geological formations. Magnetites mainly occur, however, in very old rocks like those in central India and Australia; carbonates are particularly plentiful in the Carboniferous series; and brown hæmatites, which are of more recent formation, abound in the Jurassic series, whilst the older red hæmatites occur in Primary rocks, as at Bilbao and in Cumberland.

The extraction of iron ore clearly depends on the presence of good deposits; but abundance of high-quality ore does not of itself lead to mining. The deposits must be accessible, and the country in which they are situated must have an organised transport system. Furthermore, labour must be available, and civilisation should have reached a stage sufficiently high for there to be capital enough to devote to the onerous task of extraction. That is why at the present day the countries that lead in iron-ore production are situated around the North Atlantic and in the west of the Soviet Union.

In America there are large deposits of iron ore on the western and northern shores of Lake Superior, in central Ungava and in Newfoundland. Smaller deposits occur in the Appalachians, as in Alabama, and in several western States. In parts of South America, vast ore-fields in the pre-Cambrian massifs have recently been opened up, usually by foreign companies, in Brazil and Venezuela. In Europe iron ore has been the object of minute prospecting and in some places so vigorously exploited that the oldest deposits are now practically exhausted.

In western Europe the chief producers are France, whose main deposits are in Lorraine, and Great Britain, where there are deposits in several coalfields (no longer worked), in Cumberland, and in the East Midlands. In the last named the ore lies in the Jurassic scarpland stretching from Cleveland through Lincoln and Leicestershire to Northampton and Oxfordshire. In northern Europe Sweden is a very old producer of iron. At one time the ore came mainly from Nórberg, Dannemora, and Grängesberg in central Sweden, but nowadays it comes chiefly from Lapland, where the richness of the ore has justified the construction of a railway across the mountains to the Norwegian port of Narvik.

In central Europe Germany's wealth in coal is in contrast with her poor resources of iron ore. On the other hand, Austria has very rich deposits in Styria, and Bohemia contains some vigorously worked beds. Southern Europe is the only part of the continent that is poor in iron, except for several fields in northern and south-eastern Spain and the hæmatite iron in the island of Elba, which is mined by the Italians for want of something better. The Soviet Union has resources comparable with those in the New World, but more scattered. The three chief iron-ore districts are still the Ukraine with mine-workings at Krivoi Rog, the Urals with deposits at Magnitogorsk and Nijne Taghil, and the Altai with deposits in the Kuznetsk basin.

Iron-ore production has steadily increased, and within the last fifty years new producers have constantly appeared and have supplanted some of the older ones. The rhythm of increase in production has been as follows:

	Million tonnes[1]
1900	92
1913	161
1936	190
1958	207
1962	236
1974	474

The order of producing countries has changed with time, as is shown in the following table:

1900	1913	1936	1958	1962	1973
United States	United States	United States	United States	Soviet Union	Soviet Union
United Kingdom	Germany	France	Soviet Union	United States	United States
Germany	France	Soviet Union	France	France	Australia
Spain	United Kingdom	United Kingdom	Sweden	Canada	Brazil
Russia	Spain	Sweden	Canada	Sweden	Canada
Luxembourg	Russia	Germany	Venezuela	Venezuela	China
France	Sweden	Luxembourg	United Kingdom	India	Liberia

These changes in order of production have led to important trade movements, especially since the first world war. Since iron ore is heavy and of low value in relation to its bulk, it was not generally transported very far, and was formerly used as near as possible to

[1] The figures for 1900, 1913 and 1936 are actual tonnages of ore; those for 1958, 1962 and 1974 are in terms of tonnage of iron contained: the crude tonnage in these cases would be much larger. [*Editor's note*]

the mines. Before 1870 there was no international market for iron ore, which was never carried by sea; but the invention of the acid steel processes in Great Britain, which had but small resources of non-phosphoric ore, led to the importation of hæmatites from central Sweden and northern Spain into Middlesbrough and South Wales, and towards the end of the nineteenth century other trans-oceanic movements began to take place, which have rapidly increased since 1900 as more of the great steel manufacturing countries ran short of iron ore within their own borders, or short of the quality of ore which technical changes required.

Exporters of ore included first of all countries with important metallurgical industries and having large deposits. The first and most important were the United States and France. Then came countries which had a great deal of good quality ore, but did not have a metallurgical industry capable of treating it. The number of this type of exporter has continually increased. The first were Spain and Sweden, which were later joined by Algeria, Tunisia, Newfoundland, Labrador, several West African countries (Liberia, Mauritania, Sierra Leone, Guinea), by Venezuela, Chile and Brazil, and Malaya. Owing to this there are in modern trade a number of iron routes, some overland, others overseas, and others partly one and partly the other. One leads from Sweden to Germany and the United Kingdom, another from North Africa and Spain to the United Kingdom and the Netherlands. A third (overland) runs from France to Belgium and Germany. In America ore moves through the Great Lakes from Duluth to Illinois and Pennsylvania, and from Labrador by the St Lawrence Seaway to the metallurgical centres on the shores of the Great Lakes. Further afield, an important route leads from Venezuela and Brazil to the iron and steel manufacturing district on the Gulf and Atlantic coasts of the United States and to Great Britain, another from West Africa to Great Britain, and others from India, Malaya, and Australia to Japan. Altogether there is an enormous consumption of iron ore, and this is being increased still more at the present time by the efforts of new countries like Colombia, Brazil, Australia, South Africa, India, and China to create or develop heavy industry, which they regard as a mark of industrial independence and the liberation of their economic systems.

The new and essential element in the geography of iron is that the great industrial powers of Europe and the New World must have recourse to more and more distant sources of ore. Formerly, iron ore moved only within narrow limits, and wherever possible with coal as a return freight; thus a two-way mineral traffic existed for a long time between the Pennsylvanian coalfield and the Lake Superior iron ranges, and between Sweden, Spain and France on the one hand and

Great Britain and Germany on the other. Nowadays, the ore routes are considerably lengthened, and the transport, often with no return cargo, is by great ore-carrying ships, between Canada, Venezuela, Brazil and West Africa at the orefields end and the great steel-making centres of North America and north-west Europe at the receiving end.[1] Thus the ore supplies of these great steel industries depend to an increasing extent on long-distance transport, often from countries within the Third World, countries whose output amounts to 164 million tonnes or 37 per cent of the world's total, of which at least 75 per cent is exported. Here is yet another example of the new constraints imposed on the traditional structure of the great key-industries by the politico-economic transformations within the modern world.

Iron and Steel Manufacturing—The iron industry is the work of neither the pioneer nor primitive man, for, in fact, it assumes experience and powerful means of production, the number and efficiency of which have continually grown in the common inheritance of mankind. At the present time when ore and coal are at hand, the treatment of iron has two stages: pig iron and steel (though in a modern integrated works the iron is not cast into pigs but is passed in a molten condition from the blast furnace to the steel furnace). At the first stage there is the absorption by the iron of a certain quantity of carbon, and impurities such as sulphur and phosphorus, which make it brittle, and in the second stage the impurities must be removed and the carbon content reduced in order to give steel suitable for use in industry. Until the fourteenth century iron was produced directly without passing through the pig-iron stage. A hole dug in the ground was filled with wood, charcoal, and ore. Later, as the size of the hearth increased, it had to be made partly above ground, and this led to the invention of the Catalan hearth. The technique of this was like that of forest charcoal burners and resulted in a rough slab of iron known as a bloom. This had to be hammered for a long time to rid it of slag and was then handed over to various craftsmen, including nail makers, blacksmiths, and armourers. Only rich ore could be used in the process, which led to enormous waste, for 40 per cent of the iron sometimes remained in the slag. Hence, modern industry has in some places been able to extract iron from the slag of old ironworks. Such rough treatment of iron is still

---

[1] Since 1964, however, 'OBO' carriers (ore/bulk/oil) have been developed, enabling round voyages to take place, minimising sailing in ballast. Examples of such voyages are: from U.S.A. with coal to Europe, then ballast to Liberia, and iron ore back to U.S.A.; from U.S.A. with grain to India, then ballast to the Persian Gulf, then oil to Japan, then ballast to British Columbia and finally grain to Europe. [*Editor's note*].

practised by African tribes in the Sudan and Uganda, and by the Fans of equatorial Africa.

Fairly pure iron was obtained in this way because the heat applied was not enough to cause the metal to fuse completely. The result was merely a viscous mass forming a bloom at the bottom of the hole. True pig iron was thus obtained by pure accident when the heat was too great, but it was an annoying and irremediable accident. Similarly, chance alone decided whether the bloom contained soft iron or steel, the result often depending on the nature of the ore used. It was a noteworthy invention when a way was found to use pig iron and so escape the drawbacks of the operation by regarding the pig itself as a kind of ore able to give steel. It was achieved by increasing the height of the furnace, a procedure which had been adopted to lessen the quantity of fuel used. Thus, the discovery of pig iron was the result of the use of the blast furnace, that is, of an oven in which with the help of water-driven bellows, a greater quantity of ore could be treated with the same amount of fuel. The invention of the blast furnace goes back, it is believed, to the fifteenth century, and it was first used in Siegerland in the Rhineland.

A revolution of far-reaching importance was occasioned by the substitution, first in Great Britain and later on the European continent and in North America, of coked coal for wood and charcoal in the blast furnace. First successfully developed by Abraham Darby at Coalbrookdale on the Shropshire coalfield, during the first half of the eighteenth century, this use of coke brought about great changes in the location of the smelting industry, and in Great Britain, from being concentrated largely in such forested areas as the Weald and the Forest of Dean, the iron industry began rapidly to develop on those coalfields—as in Staffordshire, Yorkshire, South Wales, and Scotland—where coking coals and iron ores occurred in the Coal Measures. The method of producing pig iron has changed little since the eighteenth century, and the blast furnace remains the chief instrument of primary metallurgy. But its thermal efficiency has been enormously increased, first, in the 1830s, by the substitution of a hot-air blast for the cold blast hitherto employed, and later by many other technical improvements such as the closing of the top and the utilisation of the waste gases. Its dimensions have increased, and modern furnaces sometimes burn continuously for more than ten years. Another feature in its improvement has been that instead of always producing the same quality of pig, it can now be made to produce any quality desired.

For a long time the change from pig to steel was achieved by the lengthy, difficult, and expensive cementation process (developed by Huntsman of Sheffield in 1740), which moreover gave only moderate quantities. The main product of ferrous metallurgy for nearly a century was, however, wrought iron, made in the puddling furnace invented by Henry Cort in 1784. Then another stage was reached when it was discovered how, starting from pig iron, quantities of steel could be made in a single operation with the help of chemical reactions. Steel was not much used in industry until after 1860–65. It was coldly received at first, but it soon became greatly used for making railway rails and ships. By 1882 it had won its way, and the making of steel became the chief branch of ferrous metallurgy.

The new metal had valuable qualities including toughness, ductility, and hardness, which varied mainly with the carbon content. As it could only be made from pig iron, the production of the latter gained new vigour at the end of the century, so much so that the size of blast furnaces increased to the point of becoming veritable workshops within the ironworks. Steel was first made from pig iron by the Bessemer process (1856) and the Siemens-Martin process (1861); and then later by the Thomas process (1879), which permitted the use of pig iron made from phosphoric ores. After that new techniques were developed with the invention of the electric furnace, which was used mainly in making 'special' steel, that is, alloys of steel and rare metals like manganese, chromium, cobalt, nickel, tungsten, and vanadium, or with silicon. Steel comes from the mills in the form of ingots, which are often shipped in that form from the United States, for example, to Denmark, or from the United States to Japan. But as a rule steel undergoes in the works a conditioning that gives it a form which can be used directly, for example, railway lines, girders, plates and sheets of various sizes and thickness, and rods and wire of different gauges.

Distribution of Iron Working.—The location and structure of the main centres of iron-working today depend on economic factors to an even greater extent than on technical exigencies. One of the chief conditions is the possibility of obtaining ore of good quality. The percentage of metal content in the raw ore should be as high as possible. A very rich ore has a content of 60 per cent. But hæmatites from Elba, Cumberland, Krivoi Rog, and the Pyrenees contain more than 50 per cent of iron. On the other hand, Lorraine 'minette' contains only 37 per cent, and the equivalent in Northamptonshire only 32 per cent. An ore with a content of less than 25 per cent is considered to be poor and to need preliminary improvement by calcination, which drives out the carbon dioxide and water in it. Most low-grade ores are nowadays crushed and roasted with coke breeze to form sinter, of much greater iron content than the original ore.

Ore should be easily smelted. The commonest are oxides, which almost always have a gangue of rocky matter. This chemical magma can be disintegrated by the mere action of heat without the necessity for expensive preliminary treatment that exceeds the market value of the raw ore. A silicious gangue, which retains too great a quantity of the iron, gives a poor yield in the blast furnace. It is usually removed by mixing the ore with a limestone flux which acts as a softener and absorbs the silica.

The working of iron has always required huge stocks of fuel. When smelting was done with charcoal, ore was taken into the forest for treatment. In ancient Greece iron-working was located on the wooded mountains in Boeotia, Acarnania, and Laconia, to which ore from Thrace and the Caucasus was taken on the backs of donkeys. The Romans smelted theirs on the wooded slopes of the eastern Alps and carried the iron so extracted to works in Italy. Up to the end of the eighteenth century iron-working remained a rural industry owing to its dependency on forests—as in the Weald of south-eastern England. Even today pig iron is still produced with charcoal in countries with rich and easily smelted ores near to large forests, notably in Sweden, Styria, the Hungarian Carpathians, and southern Chile.

Nowadays coke is the fuel used in iron works. This is artificially produced by roasting certain varieties of coal in a closed vessel. It has the advantage of not sticking to the iron, of giving more heat than charcoal does, and of not containing sulphur or any impurity that might combine with the iron. Hence the preponderant part played by countries that have huge supplies of coking coal. It was to this advantage that Great Britain owed the early and speedy development of her iron industry. It explains furthermore why the control of important iron industries falls to countries or to under-takings that have supplies of coal and why the ore is carried to the coal. Hence, great producers of coal, like the United States and the United Kingdom, are importers of ore, whilst Sweden, Spain, Algeria, Cuba, the West African countries, and Venezuela export their best ore.

Electricity is only used for smelting ores of high content and quality. It has therefore not come into general use except in countries like Scandinavia, where electricity is produced cheaply and in great quantity. But there is no doubt that in the future the iron industry will tend to rely less and less on coal, for new processes using in blast furnaces coal unsuitable for coking are already enabling centres of heavy industry to spring up in regions where formerly there were none.

The working of iron has always been difficult and toilsome, and the worker has generally sought mechanical help. An essential in-vention was the use of hydraulic power to work the bellows. Water-mills appear very early in the history of technology, but do not seem to have been applied to iron forges before the fifteenth century. It was the use of bellows that led to the siting of works on the banks of streams and to the discovery of pig iron. Later on, the blast furnace was itself made into a generator of power. Previously, the gases from the fire escaped freely into the air, burning like huge torches. Today, they are carefully caught and used to raise to a temperature of 800° or 900° C air that is blown through the tuyeres into the blast furnace, or else to produce motive power in steam engines or gas engines for working lifts, gantries, pumps, rolling-mills, and the dynamos that provide electric power for the factory. The gases are also piped out and sold for domestic use. Today, a feeder pipe more than 300 kilometres long leads gas from blast furnaces in Lorraine to the Paris conurbation. Lastly, some of the gases are chemically treated to make disinfectants and fertiliser. These uses of the by-product of blast furnaces make a big modern centre of ironworking into a huge economic unit associated with a swarm of satellite industries, each of which is dependent on the others.

The typical modern blast furnace is capable of producing 1,000 tonnes of pig iron a day; such an output requires 2,000 tonnes of rich iron ore, 800 tonnes of coke, 500 tonnes of limestone, together with over 50,000 tonnes of water and 4,000 tonnes of air!

Transport problems thus loom very large in an industry all of whose raw materials are heavy and bulky. At first, the centres of ironworking grew up in countries where ore and fuel occurred together, such as Great Britain, Pennsylvania, the Ruhr, and the district of Le Creusot in France. But supplies of ore and fuel are not always found together, or else one of them may be exhausted more quickly than the other. Hence, ingenious arrangements have been made to bring the ore and fuel together by means of good and fully used systems of transport. The movement of ore and coal between the north of France and Lorraine inspired the idea of constructing a canal between the Moselle and Schelde and led to the recent electrification of the railway from Valenciennes to Thionville. In the same way the ore and coke trade between Lorraine and Westphalia has led to the canalisation of the Moselle from Nancy to the Rhine. In the United States ore from Mesabi was more than 1,600 kilometres from Pittsburgh coal, but the ore was carried to the coal through the Great Lakes; then gradually heavy industry moved towards the route along which the ore was carried, and important iron works were set up one after another on the south shores of the Lakes at Buffalo, Cleveland, Gary, and at Duluth itself, which was the first port from which the ore was sent. Elsewhere big works have been built on the coast near traffic routes followed by coal and ore. For instance, in France the works on the Adour are close to the seaway taking ore from Bilbao to England

and supplying Spanish ironworks with coal from the United Kingdom; the Dutch works at Ijmuiden lies at the seaward end of the North Sea canal, one of the several points of ingress into the great waterway system that feeds the Ruhr. The largest steelworks in the world is at Sparrows Point, Maryland, near Baltimore; it is supported by Appalachian coal and South American ore.

This shift of blast furnaces and steelworks to the coast is one of the characteristics of the present age. In former times heavy metallurgical industries were located on the coalfields, and it was here, often far from the sea, that the world's great industrial centres were concentrated in the late nineteenth and early twentieth century—the English Midlands, the Ruhr, northern France, the Donetz basin and Pennsylvania. To an ever-increasing extent in modern times the best iron ores are imported by sea, and since in the older industrial regions the space required by a giant integrated steel plant is generally not available, such plants have been systematically located in new industrial zones dependent on large ports. Examples of such developments are the great new steel complexes built during recent years on the coast of Europe, at Europoort at the mouth of the Rhine, near Dunkerque on the coast of northern France, and at Fos to the west of Marseilles. It is likely that both in the older industrial countries in process of modernisation, and in new overseas countries that are in course of development, steel industries will in future be located on sea coasts.

Within the iron industry as a whole there is a division of labour between two branches that differ in the nature of their products and in geographical distribution. *Heavy* or *primary industry* produces mainly pig iron and steel. It is still dependent on coal and is situated where it can get its raw materials cheaply. The *secondary* or *transformatory* branches work up the pig iron and steel into a vast number of articles, both heavy and light, including an infinity of fittings, various gadgets, tools, and instruments. Since it works up articles partly treated and cheaper to transport than coal and ore, it is freer as to locality, less concentrated geographically and at times even fairly scattered, but near towns that supply labour and afford routeways and markets.

Heavy industry is concentrated mainly in three large European, North American, and Soviet groups. To these may be added isolated minor groups in China, India, Japan, and, more recently, South Africa (Pretoria), Australia (Port Kembla), Colombia (Paz del Río), and Brazil (Volta Redonda). The absence of heavy industry in a country is explained by lack of fuel and power as well as by poverty in means of transport. The three main groups are to some extent self-supporting, for each has its own ore and fuel, each forms an economic unity in which each part of the country makes up for the deficiencies by drawing supplies from its neighbours.

On the continent of Europe a cooperative movement has been instituted to pool resources in coal and ore among the six nations: Germany, France, Italy, the Netherlands, Belgium, and Luxembourg. The European Coal and Steel Community (E.C.S.C.) shows by its existence that the steel industry has become so important that countries can no longer rely on their own resources for drawing supplies and finding outlets. This group of States has access to large amounts of Swedish, Algerian, Spanish, and French iron ore and of coal from the United Kingdom, Poland, and Germany. The carriage of these heavy commodities is helped by the deep penetration of the sea into the heart of Europe, and though some European countries have inland centres more or less far from the sea, these are connected with big ports by means of navigable rivers, canals, or railways (e.g. the Ruhr, and Lorraine), whilst there are many coastal centres in Great Britain (Middlesbrough, Cardiff, Dagenham), France (Adour, the lower Loire valley, and Dunkirk), and the Netherlands (Ijmuiden).

The North American industry forms another economic group more productive and homogeneous because it has functioned since its beginning within a single country. Away from the sea (apart from the huge coastal centres at Baltimore and Trenton), but having at its disposal as a means of transport the excellent route through the Great Lakes, together with the St. Lawrence Seaway, it remains today the most important group of metallurgical industries in the world.

The Soviet group contains an older element based on coal from the Donetz and the Moscow region, from which the excellent ore from Krivoi Rog was only 600 kilometres distant. To their western centres have been added *kombinaty* in Asia, the largest of which was for long the Ural–Kuznetsk–Karaganda centre, where ore and coal are gathered into a single industrial integration, though they are brought together over a distance of more than 1,700 kilometres by railways capable of carrying only small loads.

Within each of these large groups there is a clear tendency for ore to move to coal, since until recently two or more tons of coal were needed to smelt one ton of ore. But there are exceptions. Duluth is near the ore from Mesabi and far from Pennsylvanian coal; in Lorraine the blast furnaces and steel works stand on the basin from which the ore is extracted; in England the low-grade ore in north Lincolnshire is smelted on the spot, at Scunthorpe; and the Russians have placed iron works at Magnitogorsk, the source of the ore.

World production of pig iron has steadily increased, as the following table shows:

	Million tonnes
1880	15
1895	26
1913	79
1936	91
1958	205
1962	278
1973	512

In this production the Soviet Union has recently (1973) wrested the lead from the United States, with 96 million tonnes as against 93 millions, and Japan a very close third with 92 millions. The Western European group (including the United Kingdom) produced 129 million tonnes in the same year. Steel production reflects an exactly parallel development:

	Million tonnes
1880	10
1895	19
1913	80
1936	119
1958	292
1962	364
1973	684

In this also, by 1974, the Soviet Union has just topped the United States production, with 136 million tonnes against 132 millions; Japanese output was 117 millions, and Western Europe with the U.K., 177 millions. In world production as in the production of each iron-working country taken separately it is noticeable that the amount of steel produced is far more than that of pig iron, the raw material of steel. The anomaly is explained by the use of an enormous quantity of scrap, which plays an increasing part in the iron industry, as it enables less coal and ore to be used. One-third of it comes from iron and steel articles past use and especially from the hulls of old and obsolete ships, which yield fifteen million tons. The other two-thirds come from factory waste, filings, shavings from lathes, and cut-outs from stamp-presses.

Though Europe retains the lead in steel production, it must not be forgotten that as recently as 1938 the continent was producing 49 per cent of the world's output, while the United States total was only 27 per cent. Since then, the Soviet Union and Japan have risen to the same level as the United States, and all three now produce roughly 20 per cent of the world's steel. Other countries, too, with the aim of founding their economic independence on the possession of a steel industry, have become notable producers. Whilst in recent decades the steel output of Europe has quadrupled, that of Japan has multiplied sixteen times, with a sevenfold increase by the U.S.S.R. and Brazil. It is not surprising that in order to retain its supremacy in the world's steel market, western Europe created the first of the great economic communities in the shape of the E.C.S.C. (European Coal and Steel Community). This, reinforced in 1971 by the entry of the United Kingdom and most of the countries of northern Europe, has an output today of over 160 million tonnes of raw steel a year, about three-quarters of the total European output and more than 23 per cent of world production. This is indeed a solid base for industrial Europe, which is less favoured with other raw materials.

Production and Distribution of Steel

	1913	1938	1973
World output (million tonnes)	76	112	692
N. America (per cent)	42·2	26·7	21·6
Europe (per cent)	56·0	48·6	31·4
U.S.S.R. (per cent)	*	16·0	19·0
Asia (per cent)	*	7·0	22·2
Australia (per cent)	*	1·1	1·1
Latin America (per cent)	*	0·1	1·7
Rest of world (per cent)	0·8	0·5	3·0

As a great steel producer, Europe quite early, and before the United States, developed mechanical engineering industries, and as a result became a large consumer of non-ferrous metals. Amongst these, aluminium, the miracle-metal of the twentieth century, highly desirable for its lightness and physical properties, its resistance to corrosion and its ready association with other metals in alloys of greater hardness, greater ductility or greater conductivity, has rapidly found a place in aircraft and automobile construction, in the fitting-out of ships, and in the building trades and the manufacture of household appliances. From the moment of the chemical discoveries that led to the production of alumina from bauxite, and the smelting of aluminium, Europe became a major producer, having its own abundant supplies of bauxite, notably from Les Baux in Provence. At the beginning of the twentieth century Europe was the world's principal producer of aluminium. But the explosive multiplication of the uses of the metal, and the expansion of the markets, have changed this situation, to the disadvantage of Europe. During the period 1938–1973, world production rose from 630,000 tonnes to 12,700,000 tonnes, an increase of well-nigh 2,000 per cent! At the same time the part played by Europe in aluminium production declined from 51 per cent to 29 per cent, whilst that of North America (U.S. and Canada) increased from 36 to 46 per cent. Japan now figures as third producer, with 13 per cent. Europe has lost its initial advantage of bauxite exploitation; since 1938 its proportion of world output has declined from 48 per cent to 15 per cent. The major producing area is now the Caribbean with 36 per cent, and this has been largely developed by capital from the United States which is itself a large importer of bauxite. South-east Asia and West Africa contribute between them a further 10 per cent.

Production of Aluminium

	1938	1974
World output (million tonnes)	0·63	13·92
N. America (per cent)	36·7	40·0
Europe (per cent)	51·0	26·7
Asia (per cent)	2·5	10·1
U.S.S.R. (per cent)	*	16·0
Rest of world (per cent)	2·9	7·2

To an even greater extent than in the case of iron ore, the industrial countries may view with alarm the fact that 46 per cent of their bauxite requirements come from Third World countries, that may well combine to control the market even as the Arabs have done with petroleum (see above, p. 287).

The same unease is felt regarding supplies of other vital metals. In the case of copper, for example, out of a world production of 7·9 million tonnes (copper content of ore mined), 29 per cent, or almost as much as the combined output of Canada and the United States, comes from the Central African states of Zaire and Zambia and the Andean countries of South America (Peru and Chile). As for tin, 52 per cent of the world's output of a quarter of a million tonnes of concentrates comes from south-east Asia (Malaysia, Indonesia and Thailand), with 12·8 per cent from Brazil and 4·7 per cent from Nigeria and Zaire.

A somewhat similar situation obtains with regard to metals that are indispensable to the steel industry; no less than 42 per cent of the manganese, 40 per cent of the chromium and 76 per cent of the cobalt comes from Third World countries. Hence the great interest aroused in the industrial countries by the discovery of sea-bed minerals, and also the project for the creation, before the end of the century, of an international organisation to regulate the trade between the countries that produce the major raw materials and the countries that must import them (see above, p. 236).

Secondary metallurgy, which finishes the raw or part-worked material of heavy industry, comprises several branches of manufacture. Foundries re-melt pig iron and cast it into various shapes to suit the purposes of shops making boilers, stoves and grates, radiators, and other cast-iron articles. Machine construction, however, forms the greatest branch and calls for the highest degree of skill. It is essentially the key of the iron industry and supplies machinery for other branches. It comprises three groups: the machine-tool group, which produces tools for working metals and manufacturing other machines; the agricultural machinery group, in which tractor making holds first place; and, lastly, the textile machinery group. Today, 85 per cent of the machinery made comes from six great countries: the United States, Great Britain, France, Germany, Japan, and the Soviet Union. The making of machinery occupies nearly three million of the world's industrial workers.

The manufacture of electrical apparatus, including generators, cables, power lines, meters, telephones, radio and television sets, lamps, and electronic devices (which, however, use many other metals and raw materials besides iron and steel), is the most widespread industry and is found even in countries like Japan, Australia, and Canada, where the iron industry is a newcomer. It occupies nearly two million of the world's industrial workers.

More important are the industries which make locomotives, railway carriages, river barges, seagoing ships, various kinds of motor vehicles, and aircraft of all sorts. The motor vehicle, which was invented in Europe, has passed from being a luxury into an object of ordinary use owing to mass-production methods. Every year more than 38 million motor vehicles are produced in various countries.

Growth and Distribution of Automobile Production
(thousands of vehicles)

| | (*Thousands of vehicles*) | | | |
| | 1950 | | 1973 | |
	Number	Per cent	Number	Per cent
World output	11,316	100	30,430	100
U.S.A.	7,200	63·6	12,600	41·4
Japan	—	—	7,000	23·0
Germany (West and East)	1,200	10·6	4,130	13·7
Great Britain	1,500	13·2	2,100	6·9
France	930	8·2	3,000	9·8
U.S.S.R.	486	4·4	1,600	5·2

Europe, however, that formerly supplied the world with machinery, has witnessed the rise not only of the United States, that became a great industrial power between the two world wars, but of numerous other competitors that are now capable of supplying their own national markets and of exporting the products of their engineering industries to the underdeveloped countries of the Third World and even to the manufacturing countries of Europe. This has happened, for example, in the case of the motor vehicle industry.

Thus the output of all the western European countries must now be added together to produce a total that approaches that of the United States and exceeds that of Japan. Japan indeed, which had but an insignificant motor car industry a quarter of a century ago, now exceeds the production of each of the major European producers, the two Germanies, France and Great Britain, and it holds third place in the world production of vehicles of all kinds.

On the whole, it is clear that secondary industries are far less concentrated than primary or heavy industry. There is scarcely one large town without a few engineering factories. In Germany, in addition to the Ruhr, there is a variety of industry in Stuttgart, Nürnberg, Frankfurt, Cologne, and Berlin, ranging from the manufacture of electric light bulbs to that of looms. Switzerland is typical of countries without heavy industry, but with very busy machinery and electrical works at Basle, Zurich, and St Gall. In Great Britain many centres without primary iron and steel industry have important engineering industries, for example, Birmingham, Leeds, Coventry, and Lincoln. In France, in addition to Lorraine and the coalfields, various kinds of machinery are produced in Mulhouse, Strasbourg, Montbéliard, Le Havre, Saint Nazaire, and Boulogne.

It is by the secondary industries that old metallurgical countries keep their lead in the world's markets. In them are concentrated technical skill and the tradition of perfection and finish. On the whole, the enormous industry formed by the innumerable branches of metallurgy continues in control of mankind's industrial development. It is a function of the general economic condition. For this reason it is a good measure of the degree of a country's prosperity. It controls the creation of the means of production, and in socialist and capitalist societies alike it represents the investment and stabilisation of capital. One of the first effects of a great economic crisis is the falling off in the consumption of iron and steel.

THE CHEMICAL INDUSTRIES

Under the name of chemical industries comes the manufacture of products chiefly of mineral origin together with the innumerable industries derived from these manufactures. The chemical industry makes acids, bases like soda and potash, and salts derived from extractive working (rock salt, phosphates, gypsum, limestone, etc.). It is also concerned with organic products such as dyestuffs, paints, fats, and cellulose. But this classification is incomplete, for the meaning of the term 'chemical product' is continually being widened. The iron industry, for instance, depends on chemical processes, since it makes essential use of the power of coal to reduce iron ore; so also is the conversion of iron into steel. However, the subsequent working of the metal consists wholly of mechanical operations in which there is little visible chemical action. The same is true in all metallurgy, though the working of aluminium requires a long chemical preparation of the ore, and though the metal is obtained only from an almost pure chemical compound by an electro-metallurgical process. This process is indeed indistinguishable from electro-chemistry, because the same factories—in the French Alps for example—are engaged in working up the ore, fashioning ferro-alloys, and manufacturing abrasives, calcium carbide, chlorates, and nitrogenous materials.

The raw materials of the chemical industry are manifold, and some of them are found virtually all over the world. The natural or slightly transformed materials are sea or rock salt, calcium phosphate, limestone, clay, coal, mineral oil, and volcanic rocks, not to mention common elements like nitrogen and oxygen from the air, or hydrogen and oxygen from water. Mass production of these key products gives some idea of the importance today of the chemical industry, which has reached a level of equality with the iron industry. Other products from soap to photographic and pharmaceutical chemicals depend on these basic products.

The chemical industry established itself less than a century ago, when it produced cheap heavy chemicals, already in considerable demand, especially sulphuric acid and washing soda (sodium carbonate). Towards the end of the nineteenth century the industry began to produce, in small quantities as yet, a large number of new products derived from organic chemical synthesis, especially dyestuffs. Lastly, beginning from 1930 the industry turned to the manufacture of synthetic products that were in great demand, such as ammonia, which was made from nitrogen from the air; synthetic amines, methanol, man-made fibres, synthetic resins, and plastics.

Today the industry has reached the point of controlling the supply of raw materials to several industries, which up to a short while ago did not depend on them. Thus, the rubber industry formerly required from it only refined sulphur, the rubber being got from plantations in Southeast Asia. Similarly, the textile industry used to depend on the chemical industry only for finishing materials and dyestuffs; but in the nineteenth century it substituted for colours derived from the vegetable and animal worlds dyes derived from minerals and later obtained by synthesis from coal-tar products. It has gone further, for nowadays it supplies the textile industry with fibres. In this way the chemical industry has gradually taken the place of basic operations which at one time supplied material to many secondary industries.

Some chemical products depend fairly closely on certain raw materials, which for that very reason fix the sites of factories on spots where the materials are obtained. Industries producing colouring matter and those using by-products of coal are located on coalfields; for instance, northern France, the Ruhr, the Saar, and Pennsylvania. Similarly, industries using soda and chlorine are tied to deposits of rock salt, as in Cheshire, Lorraine, Thuringia, and Galicia; or to salt marshes, as in Languedoc. The localisation of industries on quarries yielding cheap, heavy material is illustrated by the sulphur works in Sicily, Texas, and New Mexico, by the cement works in the Boulogne district and on the Thames estuary, where there are chalk and clay deposits, and by the great brick-making industry based on the Oxford Clay of the Peterborough and Bedford districts in the English 'Clay Vale'.

On the other hand, some manufactures are independent of geographical environment either because their raw materials (e.g. atmospheric nitrogen) are found everywhere or because they are easy to transport. For instance, some countries have been able in recent times to establish a chemical industry though they have none of the necessary raw materials. Most countries producing super-phosphates have no natural phosphate deposits. Inversely, countries with pyrites are not the greatest producers of sulphuric acid. Spain is the greatest producer of pyrites, whilst the greatest makers of sulphuric acid in Europe are Germany, Great Britain, and France.

The development of new processes continually increases the chemical industry's independence of raw materials and fuel. Indeed, mass producing factories that use a great deal of coal are favoured by a position in a port or on coal-carrying railways. On the contrary, laboratories and workshops that make rare or elaborate articles of high market value show more independence and ubiquity. Labour supply and the presence of industrial traditions usually determine the spots on which they are established.

That is why chemical industries spring up fairly easily in new countries that are poorly equipped with the old traditional in-dustries. Like the cotton industry, the chemical industry can act as a primitive form of a country's industrial equipment. An instance of this appeared in Hungary between the two world wars. Now, Spain, Australia, and the Union of South Africa are setting up

modern industries dependent on chemical factories. It can be foreseen that in the near future many new countries will be able to
satisfy their own demands for synthetic products.

The work of the chemical industry is closely bound up with a
host of dependent industries ; but its flexibility enables it not to
await the demands of the dependants, but to offer them in its own
time new products which answer no demand yet existing, but which
are adopted by the public as soon as they appear on the market.
This was the case with man-made fibres and with the closely related
plastics. Thus, a scientific spirit pervades the whole chemical industry even for the production of bulk products. In fact, the principle of manufacture on an industrial scale was discovered through
scientific experimentation, and it is necessary for chemical industry
to have the constant support of scientific research and laboratories
capable of engaging in long-term experiment and development.

The essential element in chemical production is not the technical
skill of labourers, for the part played in it by machinery is highly developed. The delicacy of some operations requires strict control, and
this is entrusted to automatic regulation by instruments. Labour's
part in the work is restricted to the handling of crude products,
though even this is often effected by mechanical means. Hence, chemical works recruit a good proportion of their workers from among
unskilled labourers. In France, for instance, the small iodine works
on the coast of Brittany employ peasants from near-by villages as seasonal labourers. In Hungary chemical industries used to give seasonal
employment to agricultural labourers available at the end of autumn.
In Germany chemical industry was considered to be an initiation
into industry and a training ground for other branches of it.

In every branch of chemistry the purity of the raw materials and
their good quality are far more important than the skill of the
workers. The chemist is limited to determining the course of
reactions, but once these have been set in motion, they proceed
according to laws beyond human control. The real capital of
chemical industry lies in a collection of formulas. Every big factory
maintains research and experimental departments, from agricultural
research laboratories attached to factories making fertiliser to the
trial grounds in Nevada that are connected with atomic reactors.
That is why, instead of being published and standardised, the processes of chemical industry are as a rule kept secret. By means of
its own experiments each factory arrives at the most profitable
methods of bringing about reactions which are widely known.

In fact, in spite of its potential ubiquity, the chemical industry is
especially developed in countries that have had long industrial
experience, for they have the most highly developed techniques and
the best scientists. Countries rich in coal have an undeniable lead,

for coal has for more than a hundred years determined the industrial conditions from which chemical industry has largely profited. Besides, modern chemical industry uses as its main raw materials products from blast furnaces, coke ovens, and oil refineries. Hence, it encourages the concentration of the industries that supply it and by bringing in new forms of industry it increases the centres that were initially based on the production of iron and textiles.

Technical requirements are more insistent than geographical factors in the concentration of the chemical industry, which demands reserves of capital able to bear enormous losses or, on the other hand, make huge profits when a favourable opportunity occurs. For this reason, it depends on a body of scientists, minute division of labour, and a very strong trade organisation. Merging into great enterprises or trusts is usual in Europe and America, but it holds sway also in Soviet industry. The chemical *kombinat* at Khibini, beginning with apatite, now produces superphosphates and alumina and recovers rare metals from the waste of non-ferrous metals.

The chemical industry has done more than any other to free man from the restrictions of the physical environment, and it supplies new raw materials to various industries. Few of these industries have caused changes comparable to those due to plastics. These are now used for clothing accessories that were formerly of wood or metal, for toilet requisites, electrical equipment, household articles and kitchen utensils, motor-car accessories (including tyres and body work), clothing, and industrial textiles.

The development of plastic substances in number as in tonnage has been so rapid that during the last few years they have formed a characteristic raw material of the modern age just as iron was in the last century. Their industrial success is due to their being able to be used at the same time by a large number of industries, to their fabrication being purely mechanical, and the fact that the processes applied to them are very often allied to those applied to metals. Often the same machinery as is used to work metal has been applied after slight modification to plastics. Like pig iron or copper, plastics can be moulded; like iron and steel, they can be drawn, rolled, and stamped; like wood or metal, they can be turned on a lathe. The machinery used for the work—rollers, dies, hydraulic presses, and lathes—was already available in iron- or wood-based industries. Plastics can also be fabricated by the use of moulding powders or pellets. An important division is into thermoplastic materials (softened by heat) and thermosetting materials (rendered rigid by chemical change on heating).

Most plastic material is formed of large molecules; certain natural substances such as resin and albumin are of this type. Others are obtained by polymerisation, a chemical operation consisting of the linking of small molecules under the action of heat or certain reagents. The synthesis of plastics is effected industrially in several ways, beginning with substances like cellulose (e.g. cotton linters) or from products derived from coal or petroleum, and using also inorganic compounds such as ammonia and chlorine. Countries with the greatest wealth in coal and thermal power hold the lead in the production of plastics: the United States, Great Britain, France, Germany, and the U.S.S.R.

Chemical industries are all relatively young and must therefore often revise their processes. Artificial fibres of the rayon type have been partly replaced by nylon, which is itself threatened by other synthetic fibres. Some plastics have had a very short life, and products of a similar kind are continually ousting one another.

The sophistication of the processes used, and the need for large-scale research and development, require that complex chemical processes be operated by large units. Each of the big international firms has its plastics division and each excels particularly in a certain kind of product. Du Pont specialises in nylon and other fibres as well as Neoprene, which is used in the making of synthetic rubber. Imperial Chemical Industries is concerned with the production of vinylic resins, but also produces fibre-reactive dyes, and various drugs, and terylene. Dow Chemical and Corning Glass specialise in producing silicones. Ciba makes melamine resins and epoxy resins (Araldite) and Rhône-Poulenc cellulose acetate. In these big companies it is not uncommon for the sums devoted to pure research and laboratory experiments to be about 4 per cent of the whole outlay. Besides these big specialist firms, plastics are also made by other chemical firms, like Montecatini in Italy and Pechiney, Kühlmann, and Saint-Gobain in France.

The complicated relations between firms explain why statistics of production are very difficult to obtain on a world scale, but it is agreed that since 1930 the output of plastics and synthetic products has been doubling every three years. This progress is not due only to the steady increase in the manufacture of commodities once they have been discovered, but also to the frequent discovery of new products with improved or novel properties, whose production catches up and surpasses that of older materials.

The appearance of plastics has created a new industrial climate. Though the production of these new and prospering raw materials remains concentrated in the hands of big firms, the users of them are geographically scattered. Many handicrafts have been revived by the new materials which have enabled them to remodel their products and attract another set of customers. The makers of combs, fountain pens, or imitation leather and many other household articles use plastic sheets, rods, or tubes, all of which come from the same chemical works. In this way, the plastics industry together with the manufacture of pharmaceutical products now enters most intimately into daily life and transforms the industrial outlook and the conditions of life in countries that have created it. But it works with wholly artificial raw material on substances that exist nowhere in nature. No industry is a better measure of the degree of freedom man has won by the development of his techniques.

In this way, chemical industry has of itself brought industrial life to regions that were long unfavourable to it. This new activity thrives in the midst of large complex industries which were established long before it and which are based on different techniques. Thus, it helps to stress the diversity of the great modern industrial regions, like the English Midlands, the north and east of France, the Ruhr in Germany, the Borinage in Belgium, Limburg in the Netherlands, the south Muscovite district in Russia, and Pennsylvania. The textile, metallurgical, and chemical industries therefore mark three decisive stages and three fundamental steps in man's enfranchisement and the creation of artificial surroundings fashioned by human intelligence reacting against the laws of nature and the tyranny of the physical world.

Production of Plastics, 1973

World output (tonnes)	33,800,000
N. America (per cent)	30·5
Europe (per cent)	46·0
U.S.S.R. (per cent)	6·0
Asia (per cent)	16·4
Rest of world (per cent)	1·1

CHAPTER 13

TRADE AND ITS ROUTES

Route and trade are two terms closely associated in the vocabulary of geography. It was in order to serve the purposes of trade that the ways and means of travel in the world today came into being, and the desire to quicken its transactions led to technical inventions which equipped trade routes with conveyances capable of even quicker movement. At the present day the greater part of the world's energy is devoted to movement along those routes.

Man probably found travel necessary even before feeling the need for trade, since most modes of life which have an element of nomadism regard trade and commerce as mere accessories to the main business of travel. Some nomadic movements have, however, given rise to real trade routes. American economists point out that the routes from Mexico to the Pacific region, which were established after white settlement in California, followed the trails of Indian hunters who used them to move along paths by which herds of bison migrated. These 'buffalo trails' gave way to real roads and then to railways, for trade quite naturally borrowed the main lines of traffic as the economic development of the country began. To turn to other lands, the heavy carts of the ancient Germans as described by Tacitus and the tilt-waggons of South African Boers in times nearer our own were movable dwellings and not means of trade. Indeed, there are still some peoples whose wanderings are directly meant to satisfy a need for travel. But though nomads have usually discovered the most convenient traffic routes, settled peoples have paradoxically enough created such important constructions as the roads, bridges, quays, wharfs, railways, and runways, that are represented on maps as geographical facts.

Of the vast number of tracks adopted for use by primitive travellers only those that have been used for trade have survived and become human realities as evident as are villages, fields, towns, and factories. Now, trade movements spring essentially from economic inequalities that exist between various human regions. The complex activities denoted by the term 'commerce' result in curtailing distance in time and space between areas of production and consumption, between the producers of tropical commodities and those of 'temperate' commodities, and between countries with a high technique producing industrial goods and the underdeveloped lands that are still unable to manufacture those goods for themselves. Owing to trade the enjoyment of seasonal agricultural produce can be spread

331

over the greater part of the year, thanks to the staggering of the times of harvest from one hemisphere to the other, or from one region to another that differs in altitude or climate. Trade enables the disposal of large surpluses in some regions of monoculture or of stocks of goods manufactured in too great numbers for local needs only. The organisation of traffic routes and means of travel is therefore essential for mankind in exactly the 'same way as the cultivation of land or the construction of factories.

OVERLAND ROUTES

Overland routes were originally established according to the distribution of continents and their relief. There are 'natural routes' through which, before any intervention by man, the relief of the land foreshadowed convenient traffic lines along which trade ultimately passed. The most notable places that have induced traffic to converge in this way are naturally mountain passes, cols, river valleys, and crest lines on tablelands with wide, flat surfaces. These features have been followed by roads used from as early as prehistoric times, and in Europe right into the Middle Ages. But a certain degree of skill is needed to perceive the advantages of these natural routes and the use that can be made of them. However humble it may be, a road is the result of man's work and an unfailing indication of a highly advanced stage of civilisation.

In his *Political Anatomy*, a study of the economic stagnation in seventeenth-century Ireland, Sir William Petty (1623–87) stated his belief that he had discovered the causes of that stagnation in the absence of good roads and ports. Owing to her lack of these Ireland could profit little by her cattle, dairy produce, and wool. Furthermore, economists who have studied changes in European agriculture during the last three centuries agree that the main obstacle to progress was for a long time the impracticability of the roads. A report on the district of Hazebrouck in 1790 emphasised that owing to the bad roads manure could not be taken into the fields until too late in the year, for only then had the muddy ground hardened sufficiently; and there was the further complaint that goods and wood could be carried only at the time when the labourers were needed for work in the fields.

Road improvement enabled a market to be made for agricultural produce; that is, a trade system with a relative uniformity of prices over a wide radius. This fact stands out very clearly when one considers the behaviour of two large internal markets unequally provided with roads and railways. In the United States, on the one hand, starting from the sparsely peopled region of the middle Missouri valley, the price of grain rises in every direction, especially towards the east. This is because until just before the second world war the Middle West was a granary working almost exclusively for sending cereals to the Eastern States and the Atlantic ports. For this a close railway network had been built, and the variation in prices, which moreover was usually small, represented merely the increase in cost of transport with distance. On the other hand, in India centres of population are evenly distributed, and cereals are consumed locally within limited areas between which the price of a given commodity varies enormously. This compartmented structure due to the absence of an adequate railway system is like what must have existed in Europe in the Middle Ages.

Increasingly rapid movement of traffic has made the rise of modern industrial life possible, for industry had previously been subject to the same restrictions in transport as agriculture, when the work of carting logs of wood from the forests to the blast furnaces or of carrying coal from the landing-place on an estuary to the factories was done by labourers between periods of work in the fields. The times of haulage were closely linked to those of sowing, harvesting, grape-picking, and ploughing, and there was no regularity in the work. Consequently, firms had to build up considerable stocks and provide supplies for nearly six months ahead. At the same period the cost of transport represented more than 80 per cent of the price of coal less than 200 kilometres from the pithead.

Railway construction and the development of the internal combustion engine have removed these difficulties. Nowadays, on leaving the chief marshalling yard, and even on leaving the pithead, lorries take to the factories raw material or fuel as these are needed. Consequently, factories in an industrial area can expand by doing without storehouses and stocks, thus lessening the amount of unproductive capital used.

On the whole, road and rail systems faithfully reflect a human community's degree of civilisation and level of technique, for they make traffic possible in places where nature seems to have piled up obstacles and where primitive man would never have tried to pass.

Natural Routes.—For a very long time traffic has followed natural lines that afford a certain number of advantages along their courses. Geographers call them 'natural routes'. Not a few are evident in Europe, including the Danube route from the Burgundy Gate to the Black Sea, and the North German route from Rotterdam to Poland. In America the Hudson valley with the Mohawk Gap and the Erie plain form a similar and obvious natural passage.

In the Old World several of these routes have been followed by trade from very ancient times. The Amber Way connected the shores of the Baltic with those of the Mediterranean from prehistoric ages; the Tin Route passes in the same way from Cornwall and the Channel coast to the Mediterranean. In central Asia too the Jade and Silk Routes were very active even in the distant past, but none of the old ways between China and the West, whether to the north or south of the Tien Shan, were as important as the Tea Route. This connected China with Russia from the seventeenth century onwards. It followed the border of the great Siberian forest through a region in which the break-up of ice on the rivers was earlier and less violent than farther north. It was far from being a carriageway along its whole course. Between Peking and Irkutsk there were roads fit for vehicles and tracks for pack animals. Goods were carried along the Imperial roads from Peking to Kalgan, where the road stopped, but was continued by a track across the desert used by Mongol camel-drivers, who had a monopoly of carriage as far as Kyakta on the frontiers of Siberia.

On both banks of the Argun at Kyakta stood trading stations from which tea was carried to Irkutsk and St Petersburg in a little more than six months. This road, called the Trakt, began to be greatly used in the days when the fairs at Novgorod the Great, which had been very prosperous in the fifteenth century, were abandoned for Nijni Novgorod, which was situated at the gates of Asia on the confluence of the Volga and Oka. From this fair dates the introduction of tea into European Russia. From 1775 until 1903, when the Trans-Siberian Railway ruined the trade of the caravans, the tea trade was of the first importance. All along the track there were big seasonal fairs at Irkutsk, Yenisey, Tobolsk, Tyumen, Irbit, and Perm. The most important tea fair was held in February at Irbit. The same tea was sold again at the great fair in Nijni Novgorod right at the end of July. So, only at the end of six months did the tea delivered at the Chinese frontier travel from stage to stage across the markets of Europe after having been bought on the way in six or seven fairs spaced out along the path of the Trakt, whilst the post completed the journey in six weeks. The Russians had at great expense stationed along the track relays of horses and carriages, many of which were in charge of transported convicts, who were placed at the inns to serve hot drinks at the stages. Most of the traffic passed in winter when the frozen track afforded firm ground for heavily laden sledges.

In seventeenth-century Europe the so-called roads were scarcely better than tracks which crossed streams at fords, were often cut by bogs, were here and there ploughed up for hundreds of yards by farmers who owned the land at the sides, and in other places were blocked with rubbish thrown on them so as to rid the cultivated land of it. In 1706 it still took eighteen days as a rule to go from Madrid to Burgos, a distance of 220 kilometres. Even today in southern India roads that are carefully macadamised as they leave the town fade away sooner or later in a mere track. Most of them cross streams by stone causeways which enable travellers to pass over the water without sinking into the more or less quicksand. The rare occurrence of bridges is explained by the fact that the streams flow during only two or three months in the year.

Overland ways are characterised at this stage of their development by their close dependence on natural conditions. In Mediterranean climates they are impracticable during the autumn rains; the tracks in tropical Africa and many of the highways in tropical colonies, which are merely improved tracks, are impassable in the wet season, and in rainy weather the silty earth on the American prairies or the Argentine pampa turns tracks into quagmires. Soils that dry fairly quickly after rain are better than clayey earth which drains and hardens slowly. Hence the permanence of tracks on sandy or calcareous soil in western Asia, and also the regular choice of loam-covered limestone on which to establish the oldest traffic lines in Western Europe. The vigorous growth of vegetation was another obstacle taken into account by the original layout of these paths. Consequently, most early routes run across bare steppes. When the relief forced them to approach a forest, an effort was made to establish them in clearings or on the edge of the woodland. The road has not been able to free itself from all these difficulties, except by means of highly developed constructional technique, which was the achievement of a very advanced material civilisation.

Carriageways and Motor Roads.—In Europe the main roads were constructed before local requirements were taken into account. Country districts were not provided with good carriageways until after the completion of main roads outside the districts, and it was to these that local roads gave access. Consequently, the carriageway did not in most cases stem from the slowly widened and improved earth road. In France good roads date from before the Revolution and mainly from the eighteenth century.

A carriageway is made of hard material and, being a level platform without the irregularities of the ground, it makes drawing easier for the animals and enables vehicles to be kept in good condition. Roads so made were fairly rare in ancient times and still rarer in the Middle Ages, but have become more and more numerous today, when road construction has kept pace with technique by adapting itself to the requirements of the vehicles in use.

The first Chinese roads were made in very ancient times. In their wide, paved roadways ruts were hollowed out to facilitate the movement of vehicles. This kind of road connected north China with the Yangtse Kiang across the Tsinling Hills. The great routes followed by Ulysses and his companions were artificial roadways along some parts of their courses, notably between Sardis and the sea. The most astonishing of these early man-made roads were those constructed on the Andes by the Incas and those made by the Romans in Europe. Though these two kinds of roads are comparable in construction, they show profound differences due to the civilisations which conceived them. The Inca roads were meant essentially for porterage; hence in steep parts the roadway became a flight of stairs with here and there a landing wide enough for a whole troop to halt on. The existence of these stairways is understandable in a civilisation that was still ignorant of the use of the wheel right up to the sixteenth century A.D. Roman roads, which were constructed to satisfy a more exacting traffic, were planned for use by vehicles drawn by beasts of burden. According to Lefebvre des Noëttes, the ancients were ignorant of the art of harnessing horses conveniently and thus made poor use of the animals' strength. The special care given by Roman engineers to construct a good carriageway so as to spare the horses can therefore be understood. On a base of large blocks they placed a surface of fine material, on top of which they laid a pavement of wide flagstones.

Roman roads ran as straight as possible; they climbed high ground without zigzagging to ease the gradient of the slope. To avoid great differences in level they usually ran like ridge roads along plateaus. The fall of the Roman Empire caused the abandonment and destruction of many of these roads, nor did the revival of trade in the Middle Ages lead at once to road construction. The projects undertaken by towns or some of the big abbeys followed no connected plan, but were restricted to bridge building and to making up the approaches to bridges. Road construction ended after a few miles or even sooner. The facilities thus granted to traders were meant to bring in a profit, for the constructions had no other aim than the imposition of a toll on users. To the lack of good roads must probably be attributed the popularity enjoyed at this time by waterways in Western Europe. The lack of cohesion and planning in the system of overland routes points clearly to the absence of a coordinating power and to the splitting up of authority. a result whose most striking expression was evident in feudalism, A system like that of the old Roman roads did not reappear until the eighteenth century.

Modern roads are made by quite a different method from that employed by Roman engineers, for they are essentially carriageways with irregular profiles and low gradients. Flagstones and 'pavé' (road-setts) gave way to waterbound macadam, which was first used in Great Britain in the nineteenth century by two engineers, Thomas Telford and John London McAdam (1756–1836). Up to the appearance of the motor vehicle macadamised roads were in general use in all European countries.

Whilst the overland route developed in this way from the natural track to the road constructed in a fashion much like that used in building a wall, means of transport developed from porterage to carriage by pack animal, then to wheeled vehicles drawn by animals, and lastly, to motor vehicles. Before the arrival of Europeans in Africa, and even now in some parts where the tsetse fly precludes the use of domestic animals, porterage was the rule even for long distances. This was a slow and expensive method of transport, for the load of a porter was restricted to 25–30 kg, and the day's march was never more than 33 kilometres. Under the direction of a leader the porters formed a caravan whose life was regulated like that of a tribe. It had to carry with it food and necessary utensils. This was the kind of transport used when trade with Europeans began and lines of porters carried rubber, ivory, palm oil, and cotton to the coastal ports. About the year 1900 the rubber trade employed more than 14,000 porters in the Cameroons.

Porterage lasted a long time in the Alps and Mediterranean Europe. In Asia—in Tibet, in the larger East Indian Islands, and in Japan—it lasted even longer. In China brick tea was carried in baskets on the backs of porters right across the country; this method of transport was used especially in the mountain districts. In South America porterage was for long the only means of transport in the Andes, where it very slowly disappeared before the penetration of the European type of trade. In pre-Columbian times long trains of Toltec porters used to go from Mexico to California or else in the opposite direction past Tehuantepec as far as Guatemala. Inca legislation laid down in great detail the maximum load of porters and the maximum length of the day's journey.

The use of pack animals is very ancient, especially in the Old World, where the fauna contained several species of strong, docile animals capable of carrying heavy loads. Some of these animals— reindeer, camel, dog, yak, and elephant—had only a limited range in a restricted geographical region. Others, on the contrary, have been widely distributed and have accompanied man into most of the parts of the earth in which he has firmly settled. These include the horse, ass, mule, and ox.

Important progress was achieved on the day when, not content with making use of animals to carry packs, man harnessed them to a contrivance fixed on wheels. This was another epoch-making invention in the history of human techniques, for it vastly increased the carrying capacity of animals. The wheel is believed to have been invented in regions where the trees yielded very hard wood, that is, somewhere close to the great temperate forest in the Old World. As well as these trees from which wheels could be cut, the use of chariots required flat country and firm ground, since there were no constructed roads; hence, it would seem that the vast steppe region stretching from the Black Sea and Volga to Mongolia and China was the original home of the wheel. Historically, it was between the Karun and Euphrates in Chaldea that, between 3000 and 2500 B.C., the first vehicles were used. Among the Trojans of the Iliad, as among the Assyrians, squadrons of chariots were far better than cavalry. Later, essential improvements were added to carts in lands with favourable soil and relief. The Celts and Scythians rivalled the ingenuity of the Cimbri, whose chariots astonished the Romans.

Although the use of the chariot goes back in this way to a very early age, the vehicle did not become fully efficient until a period relatively close to our own times, that is the tenth or eleventh century A.D. Ancient harness was indeed based on the principle of placing the weight of traction on the throat. The collar, which was a broad strap of soft leather placed on the neck without touching the bones of the shoulders, compressed the throat and hindered the animal's breathing, and, as it had its head drawn backwards, it could not use its whole weight in pulling. The harness which prevailed from the eleventh century onwards, and was always used after the thirteenth century, had a stiff collar resting firmly on the shoulder-blades and thus utilising the whole strength of the beast, which could lay all its weight on the trappings. Owing to this, the size of vehicles and the weight of their loads became greater from the thirteenth century. Swivelling fore-carriages made their appearance in the fifteenth century, and in the sixteenth there appeared in Germany the first carriage with springs. At the end of the eighteenth century selective breeding in Great Britain produced draught horses that were different from riding horses. Lastly, in the middle of the nineteenth century huge coaches weighing from six to nine tonnes were put into service. The horses now drew loads eight times heavier than those in the largest vehicles in the Roman transport system.

The British transport system shows how greatly the progress of vehicular development has always depended on road improvement. Until the first quarter of the nineteenth century transport by pack animal and on horseback remained common for goods as well as for travellers. The first travelling coaches did not appear until the beginning of the sixteenth century and were not much used in the London district until the seventeenth century. In the country and for long distances an express service of 'flying coaches' was organised in 1635. By 1669 these vehicles covered nearly 80 kilometres a day on good roads in summer. Services ran from London to Exeter, Newcastle-upon-Tyne, Edinburgh, Chester, and Wigan. In 1754 the journey from London to Edinburgh took ten days, but in 1776 the same run was covered in only four days. About 1820, owing to the improvement of the roads, the fastest coaches equalled and even surpassed the rate of travel of saddle-horses. In 1836 the journey from London to Edinburgh took forty-six hours.

For carrying goods vehicles with four wheels and a canvas hood increased in number, especially after 1750. Birmingham had services to 168 towns in 1760, and coaches ran from York to Bristol and from Welshpool to Lincoln. By the time the railway age drew near, the number of coach services had increased, and in 1837 weekly services from London included 122 to Birmingham, 119 to Manchester, and 68 to Liverpool. Boats, being more comfortable and less expensive than coaches, were still greatly preferred, especially on the run between London and Newcastle. Furthermore, road transport was not much used. Coaches from London to each of the big towns served carried scarcely a thousand passengers a week. This was a severe handicap to a country which was in the process of becoming industrialised. In Great Britain, as in the rest of Europe, railways were constructed so as to increase overland traffic, for which the roads were no longer adequate, and so to serve industry. From that time on, road traffic fell off, especially over long distances, and it took the invention of the internal combustion engine and the motor vehicle to revive it.

With greater power and speed than vehicles drawn by animals, the motor vehicle has not restricted its operations to made-up roads in countries with an old civilisation. Their pneumatic tyres make their wheels move easily on earth tracks provided that these are relatively level, firm without being stony, compact, and not sandy. Lorries are now found in dry regions where rain seldom falls and the ground is never saturated. Consequently, the motor vehicle was quickly adopted in Syria and the Middle East, where bus services were soon organised between Beirut, Damascus, and Bagdad. Similarly, in Iran (Persia) improvements in a few places have sufficed to make a bus route from Tehran to the frontiers of India. Thanks to the motor vehicle, there have been for more than twenty years regular transport services across the Sahara from the Mediterranean to the Niger.

In the old countries, which were adequately provided with railways, motor vehicles could not put up with macadam roads for very long. To increase their speed they needed roads with a better surface made of fine gravel held together by oil-tar, and at the present time this is the method of road-surfacing in all temperate and rainy countries. It is known as tarmac.

The motor car has led to the modernisation of roads by requiring them to be made fit for travel at great speeds that equal or even exceed those of trains. Roads have had to be widened, excessive curves straightened, and, with experience learnt from the railways, road signs erected. However, the road system, which was inherited from the age before the railways, had not been constructed for traffic as fast and as dense as it is in modern times. Hence the idea of constructing certain roads especially reserved for motor traffic. On these motorways vehicles pay tolls in some countries. The commonly recognised rights of people dwelling beside public roads no longer hold good on the motorway, which in this way is treated like a railway. Furthermore, whilst roads serve the countryside, the motorway ignores it, just as it by-passes the towns to which, on the contrary, the road led during the last century.

The motorway is a world apart, the slave of speed. It has its own restaurants and filling stations outside the towns on the fringe of the outer suburbs, at cross roads and other strategic points. The towns served by motorways are no longer able to cope with the enormous traffic streaming into them. They can neither lodge the travellers who come in vast waves nor garage the excessive number of vehicles. Hence the care taken by the supervisors of motorways in America to build parking-places at intervals with little collections of huts forming 'motels' which make a scene rather like a seaside resort. Thus the motorway, even more than the railway, tends to deprive towns of their function as stopping-places and rests, owing to the modern need for speed and the congestion caused by motor vehicles today.

The motorway is therefore a new form of overland route which does not stem directly from the old carriageway. Some countries like France have not constructed a system of motorways, but have confined themselves to adapting to the new conditions their system of carriageways, since these already had great technical advantages. This solution has been adopted by every country possessing a close, well-built system of roads which was complete when railways were invented. Other countries, on the contrary, have preferred to construct networks of motorways that are quite separate and independent of the old roads. These are usually countries which were ill-provided with roads at the time when railways became general and put a full stop to the expansion of the road system; sometimes they are new countries in which for technical or financial reasons railways were constructed before roads, as happened in most countries in South America; or lastly, they are countries, like Germany, Italy, Belgium, England, and the United States, in which the very density of motor traffic has made necessary the construction of separate fast motorways (*autobahnen, autostrada*).

In old countries in which motor traffic has made use of roads designed for horsedrawn vehicles after they have been improved to meet the new needs, lengths of motorway are restricted to relieving congestion around important places like Paris. In new countries alone do motorways run for long distances. There now exists a great transcontinental road, the Panamerican, 25,000 kilometres long, leading from Alaska to southern Chile. It is not a true motorway from end to end, however, but is merely an adjustment of pre-existing highroads. Thus, in the west of the United States and Canada it follows the interstate or national roads; across Mexico

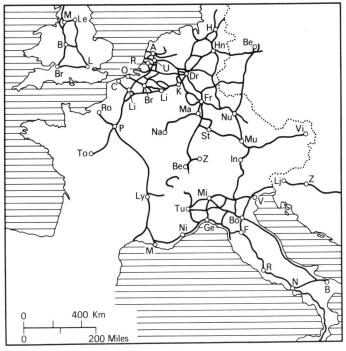

FIG. 6.—PRINCIPAL ROADS OF WESTERN EUROPE.
All the roads shown are 'motorways'.

it coincides with a main national road between Monterey, Mexico City, Tehuantepec, and Cristóbal; but in Guatemala its quality falls off, as it consists merely of lengths of side-roads which, when joined up, afford a passage to South America. In the Old World, should the condition of international affairs allow, it should be possible by means of ways in actual existence in the territories of the Soviet Union to have a long route practicable for motor transport connecting the west coast of Europe with the heart of Siberia and India, thus strengthening one of man's oldest traffic movements.

WATERWAYS

At a certain level of material civilisation the waterway is a profitable means of transport, for it enables heavy goods to be carried easily. In fact, up to the nineteenth century some waterways were main streams of very important traffic. A number of market towns owe the beginning of their prosperity to a waterway; among them are London, Paris, New York, the towns on the Rhine, and several places in European and Asiatic Russia, not to mention Chinese towns in the valley of the Yangtse Kiang. Even nowadays when railways are the greatest and most used form of transport, inland waterways retain an economic function of the highest importance even in industrial districts.

The value of waterways depends far less on the number of streams running through a country than on the physical conditions of the main rivers, on the direction of their feeders, the height of the waterparting between the various streams in the river system, and the general situation of the river mouth. Clearly, running water must be able to collect in permanent courses, that is to say, evaporation must not be greater than the water supply. That explains why most of the rivers flowing near the Tropics, like, for instance, the Niger and Darling, are on long sections of their courses navigable only during the rainy season.

Rivers must also have worn down their beds near enough to the normal profile for obstacles like falls, rapids, and dangerous swirls to have been largely removed. Even in big rivers like the Congo, Nile, and Zambezi the presence of rapids has retarded the penetration of the continent and set difficult problems to modern engineering. Lastly, it is an advantage for the river to have easy contact with the sea, as happens in good, broad estuaries up which the tide can rise into the river valley, as in the case of the big rivers in northwestern Europe. These factors all unite on the world's map to mark off privileged regions in which inland waterways facilitated the passage of men and merchandise from very early times. There are four such regions:

Equatorial regions in Africa and South America, in which the main streams are the Congo and the Amazon.

Tropical monsoon regions, in which rivers are well fed and their volume maintained by melt-water from lofty mountains.

Countries bordering the former Quaternary ice-cap and forming in Eurasia and America alike the broad belts of lakes and big rivers found in north Russia, Finland, Scandinavia, and Canada. Unfortunately, the severity of the winters and the annual freezing-over of the rivers shortens the time during which they can be used for navigation.

The temperate maritime parts of northwestern Europe, where the rivers are fed in all seasons and therefore have a plentiful and constant flow of water.

In the first two regions man has done little more than profit from the natural advantages of the rivers and has used them without making special improvements.   Up to our own times this was the case with China's great rivers, in which the waterway formed the most active and efficient mode of transport owing to the precarious state of the roads and railways.   Ocean-going ships ascend the Yangtse Kiang as far as Hankow, a distance of more than 1,000 kilometres. The town is the home port of more than 25,000 junks and little steamers which serve an enormous economic region of more than 200 million inhabitants, and they are able to do it owing to the network of big feeders running into the Yangtse.   The middle course of this great river is navigable by river boats as far as Ping Chang above the rapids at Ichang, but the point cannot be passed without difficulty by big junks and steamers of any size.   At Ichang, where the Yangtse leaves the Red Basin of Szechwan, the rapids, which are difficult to shoot, attracted a large settlement of boatmen, whose task it was to make up large crews to pull upstream boats that were in difficulty.   Today, the increase of power in boats and, even more, the building on the river of a huge dam equipped with locks are revolutionising the river in its upper courses.

In new and underdeveloped countries efforts have not been made to master the great rivers.   In them sections of railways have usually been built to by-pass stretches with rapids and to connect the navigable reaches.   On the Congo, for instance, there are sections of railway joining Matadi and Kinshasa, Ponthierville and Kisangani, and Kindu and Kongolo.   On the Nile Halfa is so connected with Abu Hamed, and on the Magdalena in Colombia Dorada is joined to Ambalema.

In temperate lands in the northern hemisphere, on the other hand, waterways were improved by man from early times.   Efforts were very soon made to coordinate the naturally navigable parts and to improve the difficult ones.   Many commodities like cereals and iron ore travelled by water in the sixteenth, seventeenth, and eighteenth centuries, especially in districts where streams were regular in profile and slow.   Nowadays, we have little idea how greatly sought after water transport was and to what extent it was preferred, even at the cost of long détours, to spare merchandise the risks of the roads, where bad conditions restricted the loads and the radius of action of carts.

Waterways even carried passengers, for whom boats were more comfortable than coaches.   In this way the Seine, Loire, and Rhône played a great part in communications across France from the sixteenth to the eighteenth century. On a journey from Paris to Lyon the 'water coach' was taken as far as Auxerre; thence the passengers went on by carriage to Châlon-sur-Saône, where another boat was used to go down the Saône to Lyon. The journey along the Loire from Nevers to Nantes lasted only twelve days. This explains why couriers were sent by boat rather than by road.

Today, when the means of fast transport have greatly increased in number, waterways no longer carry passengers or urgent goods. But though their functions have diminished in agricultural countries and transit regions, they have kept a major influence on great industrial centres. There is scarcely an industrial district in the world which does not use waterways. Northern and eastern France, the German Rhineland, and the eastern parts of the United States and Canada are the chief regions of intense inland navigation. Furthermore, it is significant that, as the Soviet Union has become industrialised, it has attached growing importance to its waterways.

To maintain its place in modern times such an old mode of transport necessarily had to change and to introduce specialisation. Like the sea route the inland waterway has benefited by all the technical improvements which scientific progress and machinery have introduced into contemporary civilisation. Its field of activity is henceforth restricted to carrying heavy and bulky goods. For this purpose no other means of transport through a country can be compared with it. Thus on the Rhine the strings of barges, towed or self-propelled, can move a tonnage equal to that of five or six goods trains of the usual type. Coal, wood, building material in the raw or worked up, are the chief commodities transported by water in nearly all the world's industrial countries, whilst liquids and motor fuels go by waterway in self-propelled tankers faster and handier than strings of barges. To carry out this specialised form of transport waterways in temperate countries have had to be equipped with flotillas of tugs, motor vessels, and barges, and with docks and harbours in their banks, with appliances for handling goods, and with railways. They had also to be graded artificially so as to afford navigable water levels from end to end.

The achievement of this grading has moved by stages. The canalisation of natural watercourses so as to serve the purpose expected has proceeded as quickly and perfectly as efficient technical means have become available to the peoples attempting it. Improvement was restricted at first to streams that were slow, of moderate size, and steady volume. The first expedient was the construction across the stream of a number of dams intended to raise the water level upstream and so cover sandbanks and rocky stretches with an adequate depth of water. In this way streams were changed into a series of steps. The passage from one step or reach to another was made at a weir, where the strength of the current necessitated special arrangements for hauling up or lowering boats. On the Seine in the seventeenth century it took seven hours' hauling by forty or fifty horses and 200 to 300 convicts to pass the weir at Pont de l'Arche.

An improvement was introduced in the sixteenth century by the invention of the weir with a lock, which itself was improved in the nineteenth century by the invention of gates. During the eighteenth century great efforts were made in France to canalise most of the big navigable rivers, for instance, the Orne from Caen to the sea and the Moselle from Frouard to Metz. Later, locks with gates were introduced on the Seine, which thus became an excellent continuous waterway from Marcilly to Rouen. Then they were added to the Oise (1840), the Saône (1874), and the Meuse. Canalisation has, however, had little success outside France. In Great Britain the Mersey, Weaver, Aire, Calder, and Don were improved in the early eighteenth century. In Germany the lower Main and some rivers in Brandenburg were canalised, but attention had already been turned to the further improvement of the beds of rivers and to the replacement of natural courses by wholly man-made beds. These are known as canals, whereas canalised rivers are called 'navigations'.

By the nineteenth century the material means at the disposal of engineers had become efficient enough for the complete reconstruction of certain river beds to be envisaged. The term *Strombau* was given by the Germans to these great undertakings, one of the world's most remarkable examples of which is the Rhine. In the course of such reconstruction the line of rivers was straightened by cutting channels directly across meanders that unnecessarily lengthened the streams. Displacements of the beds and formations of sandbanks were corrected either by embankments or by groynes and stakes placed under water athwart the current. The latter device used the force of the current to deepen the bed naturally and scour the navigable channel continuously. The reconstruction of rivers in Europe has had remarkable results during the nineteenth and twentieth centuries, and in fact all the big navigable European rivers have had to undergo it, including the Rhine, Elbe, Oder, Danube (partly), Clyde, Thames, Loire, Garonne, and Rhône.

These engineering methods, however, have had a limited application, for they have been found to be not very effective on rivers of great breadth and poor volume. On rivers in the Soviet Union, and in particular on the Volga, recourse has been had to dredging an opening in alluvial terraces, which the current thus let in sweeps away gradually and so constructs upstream huge reservoirs. This is how the Rybinsk Reservoir was made.

Nowadays the huge improvements undertaken on big rivers are important not for navigation only, but also for the production of hydro-electric power. Dams and sluices on the Volga, Don, Rhine, and Rhône work large powerhouses. As a rule improvement extends to the feeders which bring water into the main stream. Often, too, efforts are made to improve the flow of rivers by constructions right up in the mountains at points where springs occur and all along the slopes of the valleys. After the reconstruction of the bed of the river, that of the basin is attempted; as, for instance, was done by the Tennessee Valley Authority in the United States. The St Lawrence Seaway between the Great Lakes and the estuary and the works on the main feeders of the Mississippi (e.g. the Arkansas) are an extension of the techniques first used in *Strombau*.

The reconstruction of watercourses has been found to be inadequate whenever it has been used with rivers whose volume is poor or whose gradient is so high that groynes have caused too fast a current. The Loire and Rhône are good examples of these cases respectively. Engineers have therefore given up improving the river bed and have restricted themselves to using the water by diverting it into a lateral canal. This is a man-made waterway running alongside the river and is used by boats instead of the natural channel. Instances of this in France are the Garonne Canal between Toulouse and Castels, the Loire Canal between Roanne and Briare, and, lastly, the Tancarville Canal on the right bank of the Seine estuary. On the Rhône successive plans envisaged a simple straightening of the bed, then the construction of a lateral canal along the left bank of the river between Lyon and Arles, and, lastly, the construction, between serviceable reaches, of lengths of canal to be used instead of the natural channel over parts that were difficult for navigation. Each canal feeds a big powerhouse (Donzère-Mondragon, Montélimar) at its exit. The supporters of the two techniques have come face to face on the Rhine, where the improvements in course of construction are very like those on the Rhône in their conception.

Even before it was known how to achieve the perfect continuity of a waterway in one river valley, efforts were made to join separate basins across water-partings. The passage from one slope to the other was made first of all by portage over the low ridge separating two adjacent rivers, especially in regions of former glaciation. Such portages were common in Canada and the eastern United States, as well as in Sweden, Mazuria, and Finland. Sometimes a settlement has been made on these portage ridges by boatmen and ferrymen, as was done in Russia all along the old Varangian route between the Baltic and Black Sea. The idea of replacing an inconvenient track by a short waterway across a ridge goes back a fairly long way in history. Apart from a few canals previously dug to join streams in Lincolnshire (e.g. the Roman Foss Dyke between Witham and Trent), the twelfth and thirteenth centuries in Europe saw these waterway links spread in northern Italy, Holland, and Flanders, that is, in areas of active trade at the time. The first of such canals envisaged in a general plan in France goes back to the seventeenth century. The Briare Canal dates from 1642. As for the great junction systems in European and American industrial districts, the oldest date from the eighteenth century and the most recent from the first half of the nineteenth century. In Canada the Welland Canal dates from 1824, and in the United States the Erie Canal was opened in 1825. In the twentieth century the only countries to have constructed further junction canals are the Netherlands, Belgium, and the Soviet Union. These newer canals are the Juliana Canal, Amsterdam–Rhine Canal, Albert Canal, Stalin Canal, and the Don–Volga Canal. A comparison of these dates shows that the end of the eighteenth century and the beginning of the nineteenth, before the outburst of railway construction, formed the greatest period of achievement. It has been called the age of 'canal fever': in Great Britain between 1791 and 1794 no less than eighty-one Acts were passed authorising canal constructions and river improvements.

These achievements have been successful only in conditions of advanced material civilisation. Whilst in ancient times and in the Middle Ages canals were always dug in flat countries, in modern times they have attacked more accidental terrain, because they have aimed at establishing communication between rivers, and that not near the mouths, but on the contrary in the upper parts of their courses. The paths followed by these canals could not have been determined until engineers had at their disposal good maps that showed heights accurately. In France Cassini's geodetic work was finished only in 1783, and the Ordnance Survey of England and Wales issued its first maps in 1801 (though in fact most of the English canals were already in existence by this time). Often a water-parting could only be crossed through a tunnel. To correct differences in level canals had to be cut up into a large number of level reaches separated by locks. Near the top of the ridge, too, there had to be plenty of water available to supply the wastage at the locks. In some up-to-date canals water is supplied by electric pumps, which raise it from one of the two valleys concerned and put it back into a reservoir constructed near the crest.

The execution of these difficult engineering works in northwestern Europe was possible because this part of the world had from early times to provide for a large volume of traffic. After railways became general and added another more convenient solution of the problem of communication, it was found advantageous—on the Continent at least, if not in Great Britain—to have a system of canals and waterways that was unequalled anywhere else and to maintain it in good working condition so as to be able to serve the most up-to-date and exacting industries.

The age of inland waterway construction is not yet ended, particularly in Europe. After the improvement of the Rhine, creating a long artery from the North Sea to Basle, navigable by barges of between 1,350 and 5,000 tonnes capacity, the joining of the Rhine with the Danube and the Mediterranean has been undertaken. The Germans, by re-excavating and completing some old nineteenth-century canals in southern Germany, have produced a large-dimensioned waterway, using the river Main, between the Rhine and the Upper Danube. But it is across the isthmus of western Europe, between the North Sea and the Mediterranean, that the greatest works are in progress, through France. Already, Franco-German agreements have allowed the improvement of the Moselle from Koblenz to the heart of the Lorraine steel industry. The completion of works to regulate the flow of the Rhône has prompted the decision to link the Rhône to the Rhine by the river Saône and a wide-gauge canal through the Burgundian Gate and southern Alsace. This involves the enlargement to international northwest European dimensions of an old narrow canal, the 'Canal du Rhône au Rhin', constructed during the Second Empire. Thus Marseilles will be linked to Rotterdam by a waterway of large dimensions, capable of carrying heavy industrial traffic between the Mediterranean and the North Sea.

The waterway still has an important part to play in modern industrial transport. The St Lawrence Seaway, which permits ocean-going ships of moderate tonnage to pass from the Atlantic to Chicago, carries over 70 million tonnes of merchandise a year. And the traffic on the Rhine, between Koblenz and the Dutch frontier, amounts to over 130 million tonnes, more than half as much again as that of the Panama Canal!

RAILWAYS

Railways represent a new stage in the history of civilisation, a stage characterised by an increase in speed and power of the means of transport. They have revolutionised geographical conditions on our planet and have brought to man the benefits of the conquest of time and space. Yet they too were the tools of a period and marked the peak of a technique now out of date. In so far as they are a survival of the very near past and the legacy of an economic system in process of dissolution, railways do not answer all the requirements of the economic world of today. Less archaic than the waterway, they none the less suffer the same loss of status in the hierarchy of the means of transport, the leading place having now been taken by the motor vehicle and aircraft.

The original home of the railway and the circumstances of its beginnings make this form of communication a symbol of the type of industrial civilisation which started in Great Britain. Originally, 'iron roads or 'tram roads' were wooden boards on which coal-carts were rolled from the pithead to the riverside at Newcastle-upon-Tyne. The constant passage of the heavily laden carts cut up the ground and caused impracticable ruts. This suggested the notion of protecting the ground by a wooden covering. From 1670 onwards this use of boards became general in nearly all the mines in the country. To check wear and tear, the wood was gradually covered with iron plates. Then metal wheels replaced wooden ones on the carts. After that progress quickened. Boards were replaced by cast-iron rails at Coalbrookdale in 1767, at Sheffield in 1775, and at Durham in 1794. The device was still a part of coalmining and not a general means of transport. The rails were placed on the ground and took on all its irregularities. The vitally decisive step was taken in 1804, when a steam engine was used to draw a train at Merthyr Tydfil in the South Wales coalfield. The locomotive moved at five kilometres an hour.

A wait of twenty-five years and improvements added by George Stephenson (1781–1848) to the locomotive, were needed before the railway came to be regarded as useful for transport in general and as able to compete with the roads and canals. The next step was taken under pressure of economic necessity in Lancashire. Industrial development called for heavy loads of coal and cotton to be carried between Liverpool and Manchester, and the railway constructed between the two towns in 1830 was very successful, for its speed was twice that of the fastest coaches and the cost of transport only half as much. The experience of the Liverpool–Manchester line caused a striking rise in railway construction within a few years, and especially after 1837.

In a fierce struggle with the canal companies the railways were completely successful, for the new mode of transport had a uniform gauge, which enabled goods to be sent long distances without break of bulk. This was impossible on British canals on which there were frequent changes of width, sometimes in distances of less than twelve miles. Furthermore, the speed of carriage, which enabled perishable articles of food to be sent to the towns without fear of the huge losses that had been suffered in the past, contributed to a general fall in the cost of living. Hence, within twenty years the railways seemed destined to oust all other existing means of transport. From Great Britain the revolution spread to the Continent and then after some delay to other parts of the world. As in England, the first railways built outside that country were intended first and foremost as agents of industry and not as general means of transport. Hence, they appeared first in industrial districts and mining centres. Then from 1835 onwards short lengths of line were built in Europe and the United States to connect neighbouring towns, for example, Lyon and Saint-Etienne, Brussels and Malines (Mechlin), Leipzig and Dresden, St Petersburg and Moscow, New York and Trenton.

The railway is a man-made construction that has had to solve the same problems as the road, and some of the problems of the canal. The knowledge accumulated by engineers since the eighteenth century in road and canal construction was all laid under contribution.[1] Rails had to be laid on an even platform which was either horizontal or sloped gently. Consequently, they sometimes had to be laid on a fairly high embankment and at other times to be placed at the bottom of a fairly deep cutting. Besides, considering the great speeds attained by 1850, lines could not be laid with curves of too small a radius. To satisfy the requirements railways had to be constructed with the greatest skill and boldest enterprise that man had up to that time achieved. Tunnels were bored so as to run lines through lofty mountain ranges and under rivers. The Simplon tunnel is nearly twenty kilometres long, and four other tunnels through the Alps are more than ten kilometres long. Crossing wide valleys and arms of the sea has called for the building of huge bridges over the Forth and Tay, across the Danube at Cernavoda, and a great causeway across the Great Salt Lake of Utah.

The construction of these expensive means of transport could be justified only by the effectiveness of the rolling-stock. The motive power and speed of the railway transformed the state of world communications. Already in 1869 the 20,000 locomotives in service in Europe were calculated to represent greater power than that of the 1,300,000,000 persons who then formed the total population. At present, so far as censuses may be regarded as accurate, there are more than 140,000 locomotives in the world, 71,000 of which are in Europe and 45,000 in the United States. This increase in power which mankind owes to the railways can be measured chiefly by the extension of travellers' radius of action. On the Roman roads ninety miles could be covered in a long day's run, and Cæsar went from Rome to Obulco in twenty-seven days (about 2,700 km). In the nineteenth century the express post could do 250 kilometres in twenty-four hours, but commercial rates were usually less than half that. After 1900 runs of 1,200 km a day were easily done along some routes in Western Europe, whilst on the less efficient systems, be-

---

[1] In England the workmen employed in railway construction were known as 'navvies' a name given originally to the builders of the canals and river 'navigations'.

tween Moscow and Irkutsk, for instance, the day's run was more than 600 km. At the present time on electrified lines or by those routes served by fast diesel trains the commercial rate of travel varies between 110 and 140 kilometres an hour over average distances of 1,000 to 1,200 kilometres.

In every country electrification has improved commercial rates of travel by avoiding falls of speed on upgrades and by accelerating starts. Almost everywhere electric traction was first installed on lines in mountains, then on suburban lines in big towns, and, lastly, on main traffic lines. Among the countries in Europe electrification has proceeded most extensively in Italy, Switzerland, the Netherlands, and Scandinavia. This confirms the fact that railways have taken advantage of all the discoveries of science and all the improvements in technique. They have become a typical modern industry. Their workshops are the stations and the permanent way, their driving force coal and electricity, their machinery locomotives and a countless variety of carriages and wagons, and their business is to sell miles to tons of goods. Like all great modern industries railways have continually introduced specialisation into their material, which now ranges from a simple platform on wheels to the tip-truck with an automatic opening for loading and unloading coal and ore, and to the refrigerated van which is kept constantly at a low temperature for the carriage of fish, meat, and fruit. In nearly every country railways form a great national industry. In France, for example, the S.N.C.F. employs 445,000 persons, uses 8 million tonnes of coal, 700,000 tonnes of oil products, and 1,000 million kWh of electricity a year, not to mention the million tonnes of steel used in construction and maintenance.

Railways have enabled the establishment of direct trade relations across great distances owing to the adoption by most countries of a standard rail gauge and nearly the same loading gauge (i.e. maximum size of rolling-stock). They are also characterised by the overwhelming predominance of goods carriage over passenger traffic, a predominance that is especially marked in North America, where goods account for nearly 80 per cent of the total traffic on the railways.

Maps now show railway tracks as close, complex networks in which three kinds of organisation are easily recognised.

First, there are intragressive lines, pushing inland from ports. These are seldom found in Europe, where they occur only in exceptional regions, like Lapland, Murmansk, and from Vorkuta to Salekhard on the Gulf of Ob. A map of the French railway system about 1850 shows that the first lines formed a star radiating from Paris to twelve large towns, whilst there were isolated sections between Metz and Nancy, Dijon and Châlons, Roanne and Lyon,

Alès and Marseille via Avignon. Ten years earlier a map of English railways showed the same arrangement of lines radiating from London, together with other lines in the Midlands and north of England. The explanation is that in these old European lands currents of trade existed before the railway, which simply fixed them on the map. This also explains why railways have often superimposed their lines on other pre-existing routes. There is a striking parallelism between the railway map of Great Britain in the 1840s and the map of canals, especially in respect of the great 'cross' of lines from Mersey to Thames and from Severn to Humber, crossing at Birmingham, and in the trans-Pennine routes between Lancashire and Yorkshire; and also between the railways and the main *routes nationales* as they leave Paris, especially on the journey Paris–Lyon–Marseille, Paris–Tours–Bordeaux–Bayonne, and Paris–Rouen–Le Havre. So it is clear that Europe has never been at the stage of the intragressive railway. The intragressive type is, on the other hand, found all round continents in the tropics, where the railway is a means of both travel and exploitation. In Ethiopia, Nigeria, Cameroon, and Zaire, in Yunnan, Burma, and Thailand, in Chile, Peru, and the coffee region of Brazil the main object of the railway was to link inland centres of production with a port. Thus, intragressive lines answer a very precise economic objective.

Secondly, there are trans-continental lines. These answer another purpose, for they connect distant lands that differ in economic structure and consolidate vast territories by linking centres of population facing two opposite coasts on a single continent. Of this type the Trans-Siberian and the trans-continental lines in Canada and the United States are examples. There are no real trans-continental lines in Europe, for no line has been the result of a single plan of construction with the sole idea of running across the continent from one end to the other. Trans-continental connexions in Europe have come about through the closeness of the railway network, through timetable adjustments, and international agreements. To this kind of trans-continental connexion belong the lines running from the North Sea to the Mediterranean, for whose benefit the great Alpine tunnels have been bored, and the so-called 'Orient Express' routes from the Channel ports to the Balkan capitals.

Although some trans-continental railways have started from intragressive lines which were pushed on farther inland year by year, this is not the normal procedure in which the main lines have been planned to cross the continent from the beginning. As a rule, they have been constructed quickly and hastily laid on a single track, often without ballast, and crossing rivers on wooden bridges. These constructions were all improved afterwards as soon as exploitation became properly organised. For instance, the doubling of the

18. Lock on the St Lawrence Seaway at Montreal, for ocean shipping drawing 9 metres

INLAND WATERWAYS

Pair of locks on Amsterdam–Rhine canal, ⋯therlands. Capacity of each lock about 30 vessels, each 3,000 tonnes capacity

20. Lock on the Oxford Canal, $2\frac{1}{8}$ metres wide; boat capacity 30 tonnes

21. Marshalling yards at Crewe

JUNCTIONS, RAILWAY AND AIRWAY

22. London (Heathrow) airport

track of the Trans-Siberian was not complete until during the second world war.

Thirdly, systems properly so-called form a network of meshes more or less close on the territory of the various countries. In some of them, like Belgium, saturation point seems to have been reached, so that the network is changed only by the construction of direct lines to simplify the plan and shorten rather than lengthen it. Competition with road and aircraft has involved redundancy of lines in most of the old countries in Europe. In France the length of line closed down rose from 2,000 km in 1938 to 15,000 km in 1958. In Great Britain 6,800 km of lines were closed between 1949 and 1961, and the Beeching Plan of 1963 entailed further substantial reductions. In these old countries the railway systems vary greatly from one to the other, for in one it may reflect political and strategic anxiety, in others (as in France) a desire to achieve administrative centralisation, and in others again various economic aims. But in all of them the systems may work as public utilities rather than as means of exploitation and expansion. Hence, the railway system is a faithful indication of commercial activity and the state of civilisation in regions in which it has been established.

INTERCONTINENTAL TRAFFIC

Until the end of the first third of the twentieth century the sea was the only link between the various continents; but now the air shares in that task, and air lines have been superimposed on the old

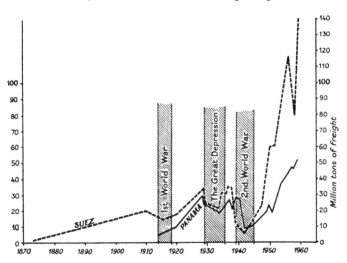

Fig. 7.—The Traffic of the Suez and Panama Canals.

seaways. (See Chapter 8.) Complete mastery of the sea and the establishment of the seaways, marked especially by the great inter-oceanic Suez and Panama Canals, took nearly five hundred years; yet it has taken less than twenty-five years to achieve the mastery of the air, that prelude to the mastery of space, and to establish round the earth a network of airlines whose total length is equal to fifty-five times that of the equator and over which aircraft on regular routes fly every year a total distance of more than 55,000 times the length of the equator. These figures give an idea of the increase in speed attained by modern techniques during the last few decades.

The importance in the modern world economy of the movement of heavy raw materials explains the dominance of maritime transport in international traffic. More than 5,000 million tonnes of merchandise move annually across the oceans and are loaded and unloaded at the various ports; petroleum traffic alone amounts to 1,300 million tonnes. The greatest movement is across the Atlantic Ocean, and the ports on either side deal with more than half the world's tonnage.

Distribution of Maritime Traffic

	Million tonnes	Per cent
World total	5,150	100
Atlantic ports	2,634·1	51·2
Mediterranean ports	753·8	14·6
Indian Ocean ports	725·7	14·1
Pacific ports	1,036·6	20·1

Of the 37 ports than handle over 30 million tonnes of goods a year, nine are on the European Atlantic coast, four on the Mediterranean coast, and nine on the coast of North America between the Gulf of Mexico and the St Lawrence. For a long time New York was the most important, but during the last decade or so its traffic has been exceeded by that of Rotterdam, which now handles twice as much as New York (in 1973, 310 million tonnes against 149 millions; it must be remembered, however, that Rotterdam's total is swelled by considerable quantities of iron ore and oil).

In the Pacific, traffic enters for the most part from the Indian Ocean, but is also concentrated in the northern hemisphere, especially in Japan, where there are three ports each dealing with over 100 million tonnes of cargo, and a total inwards traffic of some 600 million tonnes, more than half that of the entire Pacific Ocean.

As for the traffic of the Indian Ocean, it is dominated by the oil emanating from the Persian Gulf; three ports, Ras Tanura, Kharg Terminal, and Mina el Ahmadi, export between them more than 450 million tonnes of petroleum, or over 60 per cent of the tonnage of cargo handled by all the Indian Ocean ports put together. The Gulf tankers enter the Ocean through the Ormuz Strait, between Iran and Arabia—a passage that is estimated to carry one ship every twenty minutes! Most of the oil traffic formerly went westwards, through the Red Sea and the Suez Canal to the Mediterranean, western Europe and the United States. But even before its closure as a result of the Israel–Arab war, the Canal could not take the super-tankers of over 200,000 dwt fully laden, and the Cape route, abandoned by steamship traffic after the opening of the Canal in 1869, was re-adopted, and an enormous tonnage of tankers took the southward journey down the African coast to the Atlantic. It is fairly certain, however, that even after the re-opening of the Canal and the proposed enlargement of its dimensions, it will never recover all the traffic that made it the world's greatest oil route.

Circumstances have proved more favourable for the Panama Canal, which has doubled its traffic since 1960 and now carries between 110 and 120 million tonnes of cargo annually.

On these great maritime routes, the pattern of which has been so radically modified by the political events of the last two decades and their economic consequences, are deployed the world's merchant fleets, the tonnage of which, swollen by the needs of modern trade, has expanded to over 300 million gross tons. This figure has almost trebled in less than twenty years (cf. Fig. 5, p. 232). However, this world fleet, that by the number and size of its ships and their need for fuel and organised markets, appears to be a most powerful industrial force, is less completely than hitherto at the service of the traditional industrial countries.

No longer does the British merchant fleet sail in every ocean and sea at the service of all nations, and no longer does the size of this fleet dwarf that of Britain's European neighbours. From being by far the most important in the whole world the British merchant navy now has only 10·8 per cent of world shipping; it surrendered first place some time ago to Liberia and Japan.

The United States have never been able to support a merchant navy commensurate with their industrial power and volume of trade. Twice, following the two world wars, they have rapidly lost the temporary maritime supremacy acquired by reason of the partial extinction of the European fleets. But to make up for this loss, since the early 1950s, they have instigated the appearance of the 'flags of convenience' (Liberia, Panama, Honduras, Costa Rica, etc.) that have dealt very serious blows and inflicted irreparable damage on the merchant fleets of the old European countries; for these latter have continued, as in the past, to go their own individual ways, competing in a manner that has become ruinous as a result of the growth of these new fleets that do not bear the heavy financial charges that accompany the economic, social and fiscal systems of present-day Europe. Thus the European flags are now relatively fewer in the world's ports, and even in the ports of Europe itself. Europe's share of the active shipping tonnage has fallen in stages from 67 per cent in 1938, to 49·7 per cent in 1955 and 44·8 per cent in 1973. The flags of western European nations flew in 55 per cent of the world's tonnage in 1938, and only 26 per cent in 1973; whilst the red ensign of the United Kingdom has fallen from 28·7 per cent in 1938 to 10·8 per cent. The 'flags of convenience' ships, which in twenty years have come to represent 20 per cent of the world's tonnage, are supported by wealthy Greek ship-owners or financed in various ways by American capital; their competition has made serious inroads into the European merchant marine. Here, undoubtedly, is a new and uncomfortable situation for the commercial and industrial nations of Europe in particular, in an area where even the first world war did not unduly affect their nineteenth-century dominance.

Evolution and Distribution of Shipping Tonnage

	1938	1955	1974
World tonnage (gross, millions)	63	100	311
N. America (per cent)	20	28	5·4
Latin America (per cent)	1·4	6·0	6·1 (Panama 3·5)
Asia (per cent)	9	4·2	17·4 (Japan 12·4)
U.S.S.R. (per cent)	2·4	2·5	6·0
Africa (per cent)	—	6·0	18·4 (Liberia 18·0)
Europe (of which U.K.) (per cent)	67 (29)	49 (19)	43 (10)
Rest of world (per cent)	0·2	4·3	3·7

The earliest experiments and attempts to fly heavier-than-air machines were made between 1890 and 1897. About then Clement Ader made a series of powered aircraft which he called *avions*. His experiments, which took place just outside Paris, ended in a flight of 300 yards near ground level. His machine crashed and was destroyed; but this began a first period of rapid progress between 1900 and 1914, during which the names of the Wright brothers, Santos Dumont, Voisin, Farman, and Blériot became well known.

A second and decisive period in the rise of commercial aviation began after the 1914–18 war. It was chiefly marked by the establishment of great records and the achievement of famous flights which gradually led to the technical improvement of the machines. By 1935 the record height had been raised to 22,000 metres, and the speed to 700 km/hr. After 1932 specially prepared machines travelled 10,000 kilometres without landing. But the crossing of the North

Atlantic still remained an isolated feat by Alcock and Brown in 1919, and the route followed by mails from Europe to South America and used solely for the carriage of letters still went partly by sea and partly by air.

Though the aircraft was less than six years old when it crossed the Channel, it crossed the Atlantic less than ten years later and went round the world four years later still. In 1919 air routes in service were only 5,000 kilometres in total length, and aircraft covered 160,000 kilometres a year. In 1957 the length of air routes was more than 1,300,000 kilometres, and aircraft flew more than 2,300 million kilometres.

For forty years, however, the general picture of air routes remained very much the same. They follow the seaways fairly closely, giving a preponderance to the Atlantic frontages of the northern hemisphere where three-quarters of the world's air traffic is concentrated. Of this more than 40 per cent concerns the continent of North America alone. For that reason the main commercial airways at the present day are more or less the same as in 1936. Apart from the internal air systems of the various countries, two great clusters of main lines stand out clearly from the maze. In the first cluster are three groups running southwards, namely, those on the American continents, those from Europe through Africa, and those from Europe across the South Atlantic. In the second cluster are lines going round the world. These have sprung from the merging of four original sections : those across the continent of North America, those across the Atlantic, those from Europe to the Far East, and those across the Pacific. In this last cluster the lines crossing the North Pole represent the greatest divergence from sea routes ; but they form a mere short cut of the route from Europe to the Far East. This trans-polar route has been made possible by the high-altitude flights of today.

Just as technical developments in shipbuilding helped to modify the network of seaways, so the modern pattern of airways has been framed to suit the aircraft, and at the present time the pattern is being modified more by technical characteristics of the aircraft than by economic requirements. The rate of development is surprising. For more than four hundred years the sailing ship was the typical instrument of large-scale overseas trade. It was ousted by the steamer only towards the end of the nineteenth century. The abandonment of the sailer took place at the very moment when it had mastered the technique of navigation, had defined the routes it should use, had reached the peak of efficiency, and had completely mastered the ocean. A similar fate is now meeting the aircraft which mastered the Atlantic, Pacific, and the vast continental expanses. However, whilst the reign of the sailer lasted hundreds of years, it will have taken less than twenty years for aircraft with piston engines to be outclassed by those with turbines and jet propulsion. It will have taken less than fifty years for the airscrew, which was the instrument used for mastering the air, to be relegated to the museum for old rubbish and laid aside owing to the arrival of the jet engine.

The influence of engines in aircraft acts more obviously than in the ship and affects the structure and rhythm of activity of the aircraft construction industry, the economic stability of the great international aircraft companies and the terms on which they are formed, and, lastly, on the very objective of the air lines. For instance, now that turbo-jets have become general, trans-polar routes may become normal for all big companies.

Just as the paths followed by seaways are more and more dependent on the positions of big commercial ports, so routes followed by big commercial air lines depend on the positions of airports. There is indeed a great difference between the landing grounds of 1930 and the great modern airports, a difference as great as that between the haven of ancient times, in which boats were beached, and the great port of the present day with its wet docks, dry docks, and powerful cranes for handling cargo. Modern aircraft weighing between 100 and 170 tonnes and reaching the ground at a speed greater than that of a train entering a station cannot land on bare earth. They need concrete runways two or three kilometres long in big international airports. The strips form a pattern on which with the help of a control tower aircraft traffic is moved just as trains are moved in a marshalling yard.

At the airports aircraft ought to be able to renew their stock of petrol, test their engines, and land or take up passengers or freight. These ports contain many workshops in which are carried out not only the minor inspections on landing, but also more important overhauls which are set out in great detail in the companies' regulations and are carried out automatically at the end of a certain number of hours' flying or a certain distance flown. Such workshops sometimes employ 10,000 or 15,000 men. Airports are above all active organs in air traffic and not simple refuges. An aircraft in flight is taken in charge by the technical service at the airport as soon as it comes within range of its instruments and, guided by wireless and radar, it makes its way to the landing-strip and receives permission to land.

Just as there are several kinds of seaports, so there are several kinds of airports distinguished from each other less by the nature of their traffic than by their capacity and the quality of their technical installations. In proportion as air traffic increases in intensity, however, airports tend to specialise. Thus, New York has four specialised airports: one at Idlewild (Kennedy Airport) for overseas traffic, one at La Guardia for short-distance inland traffic, a third at Newark for long-distance domestic traffic, and a fourth at Peterboro for private business aircraft. Commercial aviation now takes a considerable part in carriage overseas and overland. In 1954 its activities ran to 40,000 million passenger-kilometres, which was the equivalent of carrying the whole population of London and Paris across the Atlantic to New York; but in 1961 the world's passenger air traffic amounted to more than 93,000 million passenger-kilometres. Traffic like this assumes vast organisation. At the beginning aircraft companies were fairly numerous, and there were swarms of transport planes. This was because far less capital is needed to form an aircraft company than a shipping company. But, as happened in the last century in sea transport, aircraft transport became concentrated in the hands of a few large enterprises, about 250 in number. Of course, along with these big companies there are private firms whose activities it is difficult to estimate, since like road hauliers they show no regularity in their programmes. To this class belong owners of feeder lines in the United States, their aircraft being the tramps of commercial aviation. In the world's huge total of air traffic the United States hold first place by far, though their air lines developed later than those of Great Britain, France, and the Netherlands. They owe their lead mainly to the need for connecting the Union's big cities, which are separated by long distances.

Since the end of the second world war the big aircraft companies have formed an international association with the object of organising the world's air traffic. The need for such a body was evident when it was realised that the aircraft with its great speed could be used for long journeys. Now, since Europe was partitioned by political frontiers, it was unsuited to enterprises of commercial aviation. None of the countries, except the Soviet Union, could provide sufficiently long runs within its own frontiers. In 1939 the area over which aircraft were forbidden to fly for reasons of military security amounted in Europe to nine-tenths the size of France. Such handicaps were no longer tolerable after the second world war and the extraordinary progress made in the efficiency of aircraft. Hence traffic has now assumed a typically international character, calling for the standardisation of aircraft and installations, harmonisation of the regulations of navigation, and a common discipline. As early as 1919 the Paris Air Convention was officially attended by thirty-three nations which had adopted common regulations for the use of the air. The Soviet Union, the United States, China, and Brazil did not join the agreement. By 1944 it was thought necessary to draw up a form of international law of the air

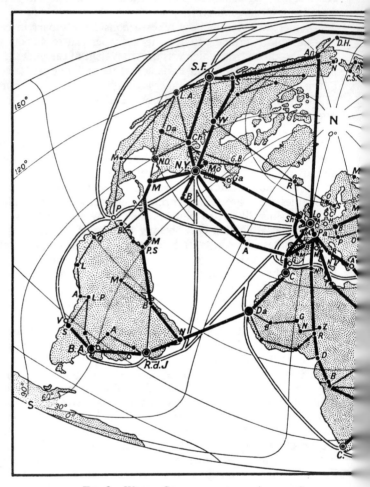

Fig. 8.—World Communications : Air and Sea.

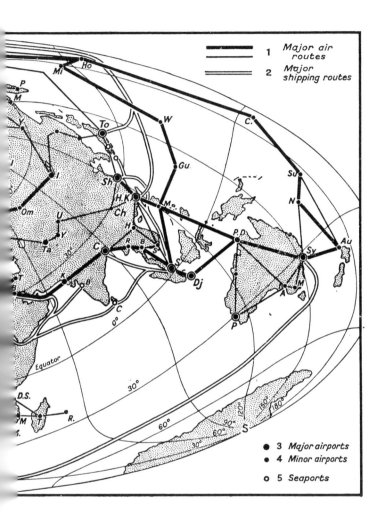

Mi · Ho
P
M
Y
To
W
C.
I
Om
U
Y
Sh
Gu.
Su
Ta
Ch
Me
N
Sc
C
H
P.D.
Au
T
B
B
Sy
C
Dj
A
N
Equator
P
30°
D.S.
M
R.
S
120°
150°
180°
60°
90°
60°
30°

(just as in days gone by a form of international law of the sea had been recognised), and a conference was held at Chicago with that object.

It is worth noting, however, that there has not been equal success in establishing for the air the same juridical system as exists for the sea. Whilst the jurisdiction of states is limited at sea to their territorial waters, it extends boundlessly upwards to include all space above their territory. So much so, in fact, that the right of passage, of merely flying over territory, even at great height, is subject to permission previously obtained from the State over which the aircraft passes. This at once assumes a political appearance. But five freedoms essential to the air have been laid down. Two of them dealing with the right to fly over territory without landing, except in case of damage or danger, have been agreed to by sixty-four nations. The other three freedoms, dealing with trade and in particular the right to take up or land passengers or freight, have been agreed to by only forty-four countries. The fifth freedom, authorising a foreign aircraft to carry passengers, freight, and mails quite freely with the same rights as national aircraft, is least generally accepted. Its rejection forms the chief obstacle to the general use of commercial aviation.

Thus, man's restrictions have continued in space the obstacles overcome by techniques on earth, and mankind have themselves determined the bounds of their own freedom.

However, air traffic has not ceased to grow, to employ ever larger and more powerful aircraft, and to demand more spacious and better equipped airports. The organisation of air space, even more than that of the ocean, becomes more and more constrained by technology and the limitations of the available equipment. During the two decades before the second world war, the aircraft had begun to supplant the ship in the international transport of passengers; by 1950, transatlantic traffic was about equally divided between sea and air; but in 1973, more than 98 per cent of the passengers flew in the large strato-cruising aircraft owned by the airlines of Europe, the United States and numerous other countries.

From passenger traffic, the competition provided by the aircraft has quickly extended to the rapid carriage of light and valuable merchandise, and even, in this age of 'containers', to the mass transport of more ordinary goods. In 1973, the world's airlines carried more than 480 million passengers, equivalent to the combined population of Canada, the United States and the Soviet Union, and representing a total traffic of 600,000 million passenger-kilometres. In the same year, freight traffic, having multiplied six times in ten years, amounted to 75,000 million tonne-kilometres.

The continued growth of air traffic has resulted in bottle-necks at major airports, many of which have had to be enlarged or indeed replaced. Thus in France the great international airport at Orly, south of Paris, despite several extensions, had finally to be duplicated, in 1974, by a new and even vaster airport at Roissy-en-France, northeast of the capital; here, some 250 hectares, over five times as much as at Orly, have been laid out for freight traffic.

PART IV

HUMAN SETTLEMENT

CHAPTER 14

GROWTH AND DISTRIBUTION
OF POPULATION

Man's distribution over the earth's surface is one of the fundamental problems of human geography. By his mere presence and the diffusion of his species as well as by his achievements and the changes he has wrought on nature man is a very powerful geographical factor. Furthermore, the study of the distribution of population assumes a practical character and forms an introduction to economic geography, if it is true that the number of its people is an element of a country's wealth and that the geography of transport systems is itself ordered according to the density and distribution of communities. In the past, even as early as classical times, some writers considered a large population to be an essential element in economic power. In the eighteenth century Moheau, a French economist, wrote that man was the index of all wealth and more precious than mines of gold and silver (*Recherches et considérations sur la population de la France*, Paris, 1778).

The idea is confirmed by the teaching of history in the rise and fall of states. The break-up of great empires has almost always been preceded by a period of demographic stagnation, underpopulation, and a serious want of balance that has imperceptibly come over many of the working class. Greece, for instance, was thickly peopled up to the end of the fifth century, as is testified by the swarming population of her many colonies all over the Mediterranean. In Attica in the days of Pericles there were probably 100 to 140 persons to the square kilometre. Overpopulation is even complained of by writers of the time. Yet from the fourth century Greece was underpopulated. It is thought that birth control was caused by the laws of inheritance, which in Athens imposed the division of the patrimony among the children. Similarly, after the conquest of the Mediterranean lands Rome suffered a decrease in the number of her citizens. The efforts of Augustus to regenerate the aristocracy by laws dealing with the family and favouring large numbers of children were not effective in checking the decline of population. The Barbarians, who had numbers on their side, were for two or three hundred years to supply labour and soldiers. In this way there have always been in demographic problems aspects of an economic and political nature that raise them above pure science and speculation.

367

In 1962 the world's population numbered something like 3,150 million. If estimates of the past are to be regarded as having any value, population seems to have been increasing steadily for many hundreds of years, as the following table shows :

	Million		Million
1650	465	1930	1,833
1750	660	1950	2,370
1800	830	1958	2,873
1850	1,098	1960	2,972
1900	1,550	1962	3,150
		1973	3,860

Distribution of World Population, 1973

	Population (millions)	Per cent of world	Inhabited area (mill. sq. km.)	Density (per sq. km.)
World	3,860	100	140·8	27·4
Africa	374·5	9·7	30·3	12·3
N. America	232	6·0	19·4	11·9
Latin America	300	7·8	22·7	13·2
Asia	2,146	55·6	27·1	79·2
U.S.S.R.	251	6·5	22·2	11·3
Europe	467	12·1	10·5	44·5
Rest of world	89	2·3	8·6	10·3
Antarctica	uninhabited	—	(13·3)	—

These few figures are enough to show that, whilst the world's population has greatly increased, the rate of increase quickened about 1900 and has continued to quicken during the last ten years. In the hundred years before 1750 the increase was mainly among the peoples of Asia. Between the end of the eighteenth century and the first quarter of the twentieth, on the contrary, the highest rate of increase took place in Europe. But at the beginning of the twentieth century Europe's demographic vigour slackened, and from that time the other continents have contributed most to the increase of mankind.

Rate of Increase in Population

	1910–24	1949–58	1964–73 approx.
	%	%	%
World	17	18·14	16·7
Europe	3·9	5	6·1
Americas	26	8·6	15·9
Africa	8·27	13	9·7
Asia	23	21·12	17·7
Australasia	11·3	25	18·0
U.S.S.R.	*	*	9·1

It is only within a comparatively recent period that it has been possible to hold censuses, and a scientific method of counting a population began to be used only in the seventeenth century. In England Graunt (1662) and Petty (1682) followed by Wallace (1752), Adam Smith (1766), and, lastly, Malthus (1798) tried to study the matter systematically, but were too fragmentary in their work. The last two thought that they could draw general conclusions which proved risky and fundamentally wrong. In France the first attempts at demography were no more fortunate, for they were the work of physiocrats and theoretical philosophers. In consequence of incredible aberration and probably misled by his studies of the Roman world Montesquieu thought that he could explain why the world was in his opinion losing population every day. It was necessary to await the coming of Boulainvillers, Deparcieux, and, above all, Moheau (1778) to arrive at proper statistical studies which, though imperfect, showed that demography had ceased to be regarded as mere speculation.

The truth is that everything previous to the nineteenth century has almost no scientific value. No document, whether it contains estimates of antiquity, evidence from the Domesday Book, or the attempts at keeping registers prescribed to parishes in France by Colbert (1670), or in Sweden (1686), was based on an enumeration of the population. Numbers were estimated according to certain facts which have an approximate constant relation to the total population, as, for instance, the number of houses or hearths, or the birth rate. By this procedure Moheau, assuming that one birth would be registered for every twenty-five persons, estimated the population of France in 1778 to be between 23,500,000 and 24,000,000 persons.

The first modern census was held in Sweden in 1749; but it was incomplete, as were also those in Finland, Austria, Norway, and Hungary which took place about the same time. In England a proposal to hold a scientific census was rejected by the House of Lords on the grounds that such a procedure might inform possible enemies of the strength of the country. It was only at the end of the eighteenth century and the beginning of the nineteenth that periodical censuses began to be held. The United States had their first systematic census in 1790, Great Britain and France in 1801. Russia did not have a proper count until 1897, the year in which Egypt held its first census also. India waited for hers till 1869–72, and, lastly, China had its first systematic, complete count only at the end of the second world war. At the present time it may be assumed that 95 per cent of the world's population is scientifically counted at intervals of five or ten years.

An accurate census of all mankind offers a merely abstract idea to geographers. It is essential for anyone who wishes to study the relation of man to the earth to know how the species is distributed over the surface of the globe and in what numerical proportions the different regions are occupied. This suggests the expression of the total number of persons as a function of the area they occupy. But even this idea is purely quantitative, and no really scientific study of population can give an account of man's distribution without considering his occupations, his aptitudes for developing certain techniques and for forming more or less powerful communities so that their members may have moderate facilities for working and living. The mere quotient showing that there exist on earth rather more than fifty persons to the square mile has strictly speaking no meaning, for it is equally silent about the swarms of humanity in regions of advanced civilisation and about the quasi-solitude of those communities that are less advanced technically and socially.

WORLD DISTRIBUTION OF POPULATION

The inequalities in the present distribution of mankind should not make us forget the universal diffusion of the species from earliest times. Man's superior mentality, and especially his mastery of fire, endowed him very early with an ubiquity that characterises his distribution. His widespread diffusion dates from very ancient times. Asia, Australia, and South Africa have yielded almost simultaneously the most ancient traces of primitive man. Since those primordial ages man has gained scarcely any ground, and the bounds of the habitable world have seemed fixed for many thousands of years in the past. Even before Europeans spread abroad only a few islands were uninhabited. The chief of these were the Færoes (sixth century), Iceland (eighth century), Cape Verde Islands (fifteenth century), Bermuda (seventeenth century), St Helena and the Falklands in the Atlantic; the Mascareñas, Seychelles, and Chagos in the Indian Ocean; and the Galápagos Islands in the Pacific.

Today if we stand before a map showing the distribution of man, we see clearly the existence of regions that are underpopulated or overpopulated, and others that are virtually uninhabited; regions that repel men and those that crowd them together in swarms. The first-mentioned, often with fewer than one person to the square kilometre, cover more than 1,000 million square kilometres, which is 75 per cent of the earth's surface; whilst areas with more than 100 persons to the square kilometre cover only three or four million square kilometres.

Sparsely Peopled Regions.—The regions that seem to be shunned by man are arid expanses, the polar caps, lofty mountains, and dense forests. Waterless expanses, the deserts, form the greatest blank spaces in the distribution of population, for without water there can be no vegetation and, consequently, no food for man or beast. Two great series of deserts occur in the trade-wind belt in each hemisphere, but the area of these regions in the northern hemisphere is greater by far than that of those in the south. These deserts are inhabited only at isolated points where there is water. The oasis called Egypt, though stretching along the Nile valley, represents a tiny area swarming with people. Even so, taken as a whole, the density of population in deserts is very slight. In the Libyan desert it is one person in fifteen square kilometres. Yet in some oases the population is too great for local resources. Communities therefore deliberately check the number of births by imposing monogamy or even celibacy on large proportions of their numbers, as is done in Tibet. In some cases this anxiety over population may lead to the rise and long survival of barbarous customs that are deep-rooted obstacles to the material and moral progress of the peoples who practise them; for instance, in some Somali tribes, until very recently, a man might not take a wife until he had killed with his own hands a certain number of men of his tribe.

When dry regions have water enough to support temporary pastures, the pastoral life that begins supports only a small number of persons on vast stretches of country. In Mzab and the Kirghiz steppes beasts often exceed human beings in number. Even on the edge of the central deserts in Australia immense flocks of more than 50,000 sheep require the work of only about fifteen men. Only in exceptional cases, in which the extraction of precious metals has attracted men into the heart of deserts, have true towns been built in such barren surroundings. There miners have to get their whole subsistence and even their drinking-water from outside the region. In this way gold mines right out in the desert have caused the growth of Kalgoorlie in Australia and Cripple Creek in the United States. In the heart of Arabia and the Sahara oil has so far led to the presence of only a few groups of workers and scientists, who do not form a true self-supporting community. Dahran and Hassi-Massaud are only temporary lodgings and technical installations, not towns in the true sense of the word.

Cold imposes less absolute limits on man. During the Ice Ages it probably removed all trace of life from the vast region invaded by the polar ice-caps; but man succeeded in returning to the farthest limit reached by vegetation. Nevertheless, the hunting and fishing peoples of the Arctic are few in number and are like pioneers occupying the outposts of technically more advanced civilisations. Only a few seal-hunting Eskimo tribes have been able to penetrate northwards to lat. 81° 54'. In the southern hemisphere traces of human settlement cease much farther from the Pole. Tierra del Fuego is separated from the uninhabited Antarctic continent by a thousand kilometres of sea, though the fjords of Grahamland, which is in the latitude of Iceland, could possibly shelter a few fishing settlements. Paradoxically enough, settlements connected with mining have been made in cold as in waterless deserts. Iron ore is the true cause of the settlement at Gellivare in Swedish Lapland, gold has founded Dawson City in the Yukon valley in Canada and Fairbanks and Fort Yukon in Alaska, and uranium or other strategic or precious metals have been responsible for settlements at Yellowknife and Norman Wells. In Soviet Siberia gold, oil, coal, salt, apatite, and rare metals have spread a series of towns along the Arctic coast from Murmansk to Ambarchik. Such settlements consist of just so many handfuls of men shut in on all sides by lifeless wastes.

On mountains populations becomes sparser with altitude. Lofty mountains are almost uninhabited. Tibet is empty above the 4,500 metre contour. In Switzerland areas above 1,000 metres contain only 5 per cent of the country's population, and land above 1,500 metres no more than 0·5 per cent. In colder regions sparseness of population descends to much lower levels. In Scotland and Wales sparseness begins only a few score metres above the sea. Yet mountains afford exceptions to this general rule of distribution, and human communities are found in high ranges wherever special advantages appear. First, for example, there are settlements in areas rich in ore. In the Erzgebirge, where the density of population reaches only 43 persons to the square kilometre between the contours for 800 and 900 metres, it goes up to 56 to the square kilometre between 1,000 and 1,100 metres owing to the presence of mining operations for various metals. In spite of the difficult conditions in Peru and Bolivia, due particularly to the rarefaction of the air, the mining of precious metals has given rise to towns at Cerro de Pasco (4,350 m), Potosi (4,070 m), and Oruro (3,764 m). At the headwaters of the Indus the gold mines at Tok Dschalung are the cause of settlements 5,000 metres above the sea.

In lofty tropical regions such as occur in Mexico, Colombia, and Peru conditions of temperature and rainfall induce a concentration of population. In Mexico, for example, Anahuac has more than thirty persons to the square kilometre, whilst the hot coast strip has only eleven. In Ethiopia the big towns in the country are all above the 2,000 metre contour; e.g. Addis Ababa (2,400 m) and Ankober (2,600 m). Mountains in dry regions and in Mediterranean lands similarly attract population. Throughout the interior of western Asia clusters worthy to be called towns are found in the heart of mountain regions; thus, there are Sana (2,130 m) in Arabia, Tehran (1,130 m) in Iran, and Lhasa (3,550 m) in Tibet. Thirdly, there are districts in which mountains have served as refuges for people driven off the lowlands. This explains the abnormally dense populations in Kabylia, Shumadia, and the Transylvanian Alps. But these various advantages that explain the presence of settlements in certain highlands do not prevent such areas from appearing on a globe like so many sparsely peopled regions.

It is difficult to form settlements in forested regions. The forests in the temperate belt were once vast empty spaces. Today the great Amazonian forests have a very scattered population. The lowlands in Colombia, which are covered with tropical forest, are relatively empty compared with the forest-free high tableland with thirty to forty persons to the square kilometre. The same contrast is seen again in the Philippines, where the wooded mountains are uninhabited and the lowlands covered with cultivation and densely peopled.

These sparsely populated regions all have a feature in common, namely, an irregular and sporadic type of settlement. Dispersion of this kind makes nonsense of the idea of density, for large areas remain uninhabited or nearly so, whilst relatively small points swarm with people. The best examples of such islets of dense population are found in the larger oases in the deserts of Africa and Western Asia. These rare spots afford many advantages that compensate for the drought around. They are fertile and have more or less alluvial soil, a warm, sunny climate, and a supply of water, advantages that are found in the lines of oases stretching from the Punjab to Bactriana (northern Afghanistan); in western Asia from Iraq to the coast of Syria and Lebanon (the 'fertile crescent'); and in Egypt, where a large centre of population has persisted. In early times Egypt was acquainted with efficient agricultural methods and the practice of organised, collective irrigation. From the middle of the nineteenth century a prodigious increase in population followed the increase in cultivable land due to permanent irrigation. From 4,400,000 persons in 1846 the population rose to more than 14 million in 1927 and to nearly 36 million today. No other part of the world presents a more impressive contrast between the uninhabited desert and the human swarm living between the scorching cliffs.

Densely Peopled Regions.—On the world map appear four areas of dense population separated from each other by deserts or the sea. They are Europe, the United States, India and China, and Japan. All four are situated in the northern hemisphere and are so placed that more than three-fourths of the world's population are now crowded between the Tropic of Cancer and lat. 69° N. Of these India and China were in existence in earliest times. Europe is less ancient, and the United States has existed for only two hundred years. Except for Japan, they have certain features in common, for they are all countries with extensive lowlands consisting of the valleys of the Hwang Ho and Yangtse Kiang, the Ganges valley, the North and East European plain, and the valleys of the Mississippi and its feeders. They are countries with big rivers and are in easy reach of the sea, and they have all become rich grain-growing lands, whether the crop is wheat, maize, or rice. Europe and the United States are two centres of population separated by the Atlantic Ocean, but in fact closely allied, for their people are derived from the same stock, and they have the same type of civilisation.

How is Europe's dense population to be explained, seeing that the demands of climate are far harsher than in the tropics ? The facts are unique and peculiar in the history of the increase of world population, but they are justified both by the natural conditions and by the triumphs of civilisation. The extraordinary variety of food crops that were able to thrive is explained by the temperate and adequately rainy climate together with a soil that was rich owing especially to the presence of large areas of *loess* and in early times encouraged settlement in glades among the forest cover. Wheat, which was acclimatised from the steppes of western Asia, grew right to lat. 60° N., where oats and barley took its place. Oats is the ordinary cereal crop in Scotland, Sweden, and Norway, where it is associated with rye. Barley is cultivated in Orkney, the Færoes, and thence northwards to the North Cape. Southwards, wheat is grown with maize in the Saône and Tisza valleys, in Romania and Italy. In some districts that are too wet, it can be successfully replaced by potatoes, as in fact is done in Ireland and in the sandy soils of North Germany. To these crops must be added the whole collection of Mediterranean plants around which centres of population gathered in early times.

Throughout the history of agriculture readiness to welcome new crops fairly soon allowed a moderately large increase in population to take place. Overpopulation seems to have occurred at several periods of European history, which were marked by serious famines. Besides, Europe would never have had the swarms of people that it now contains if she had had to feed them with no more than the produce of her own intensive agriculture ; but her capacity was given a tenfold increase by her industry. The rise of large-scale manufacture enabled working people to collect in masses around factories and caused the growth of the monstrous tentacular cities which are the trade mark of the twentieth century. The cumulative improvement of the various kinds of work, and consequently of the workers, which large-scale industry implies, shows clearly that the formation of the European agglomeration is the work of intelligence and method as well as of natural advantages. Trade relations have greatly contributed to building up in Europe a further agglomeration of humanity of like dimensions. They have, for instance, enabled food and raw material to be supplied to the hard-working masses whose ability to produce was no longer restricted by the capacity of the soil. World trade being able to ensure unlimited supplies, this group of mankind was formed in a paradoxical manner, counting only on supplies from abroad and threatened with famine as soon as trade movements happened to slow down. Trade thus appears as the most peculiar feature in European economy, which is a mercantile civilisation whose activity is no longer the exchange of costly goods and spices, but is essentially a vast mart of coal, wheat, cotton, oil, and ores. The whole world is put under contribution for the needs of Europe, whose merchant shipping still monopolises nearly a half of the world tonnage.

This division of mankind, numerically the most considerable, won its pre-eminence only at a comparatively recent date. Excluding the Soviet Union, Europe has more than 460 million inhabitants. Two-thirds of the continent form a nearly compact area of high density. There are no large empty spaces or wide gaps, as there are in India, from Great Britain to the plain of the Po. This swarm of people has been a centre from which emigration has taken place, a seedbed of mankind, which has transformed the world by creating out of nothing new nations in America, Africa, and Australia.

The United States is indeed a European offshoot with a very rapid rate of increase in population, as the following table shows:

	Persons
1800	5,310,000
1850	17,100,000
1900	76,000,000
1930	122,860,000
1950	151,772,000
1958	172,000,000
1960	180,500,000
1962	186,591,000
1974	211,900,000

Like Europe, the United States benefits from having temperate climates which have enabled people and civilisation from Europe to be transplanted easily without being forced to make long and laborious experiments. Three-fourths of the population are clustered between the annual isotherms for 7° C and 16° C, where the rainfall is between 750 and 1,250 mm, and European plants and animals have found their best surroundings. As in Europe, the soil of the lowlands is sometimes of fertile loam and sometimes of equally fertile glacial drift. The treeless prairies, on which a struggle with the forest was unnecessary, quickly became great expanses of cultivation. Lastly, as in Europe, there were below the surface coal, iron, various other ores, and, in addition, oil. Industrial life was able to develop and spread with the advantage of European experience, for a vast capital in the shape of industrial experience was passed on in a few generations. But North America had other advantages that Europe was without. First, lands that could be used spread continuously over vast expanses. Unlike Europe, which is broken by ancient massifs and Alpine ranges, America passes without any obstacle in the relief from the cold climate of Canada to the tropical régime of Louisiana, and in this vast area belts of wheat, maize, and cotton grow one after the other, dovetailing at their borders. Secondly, there is an extension of tropical influence carrying warm, moist air very far north in summer and taking maize cultivation right up to the Great Lakes.

The land was, so to speak, empty, inhabited by weak and scanty tribes, so that increases in population were due to the arrival of swarms of young and adult immigrants. Unlike Europe, whose population has grown merely by natural increase, the population of the United States has been swollen by imports from abroad, for between 1820 and 1920 natural increase accounted for only 73 per cent of the growth. Nowhere else has the phenomenon of immigration appeared so continuous or on so great a scale, supplied as it was from even the most distant stocks of population in Europe. This swarm of people spread over the whole of the Union territory, but in unequal density. In the west where there is a vast arid region hostile to agriculture, the mountains contain hardly as many as three persons to the square mile and the Pacific coast eighteen. There are four areas of fairly dense settlement, namely, Puget Sound and the lower Columbia valley, the district of San Francisco, the district of Los Angeles, and the irrigated land around Denver. In the east, if Maine and Florida are excepted, the mean density is never less than twenty-five persons to the square mile.

Broadly speaking, there is a belt of high density with about 50 persons to the square kilometre running from Boston along the coast of New England and the big estuaries farther south, where are situated Philadelphia, Baltimore, and Washington. It branches through Pennsylvania to the Lakes, whose southern shores it follows through Rochester, Chicago, and Milwaukee. This unusual concentration of population is connected, as in Europe, with great commercial activity. A series of waves of migration from this eastern part of the Union swept across the Mississippi towards the west, the southwest, and the Pacific.

The Far Eastern division, though broken by deserts, mountains, and seas, nevertheless forms a peculiar swarm of mankind, which has in every part achieved an astonishing growth of population in quite a different way from the European. In places they crowd in

	Density of Population per Sq. Km
Agricultural States Minnesota Iowa Missouri Wisconsin Kentucky Tennessee Alabama Mississippi	11–23
Agricultural States with Industrial Centres Michigan Illinois Indiana	24–44
Agricultural States with Great Industrial Development New York Pennsylvania Ohio	54–110
Purely Industrial States Massachusetts Rhode Island New Jersey Connecticut	105–188

hundreds to the square kilometre. Their civilisation is mainly agricultural, the whole of their living being got from the land and its crops. Physical conditions lend themselves to making the most of a highly nourishing plant environment. The monsoon climate ensures regular periodical rains restricted to a single season that is also the hot time of the year. All round its coast eastern Asia has wide plains and deltas with fertile alluvial soil. Throughout the region, too, great skill has been acquired in the control of water and the practice of irrigation. Lastly, the presence of the very prolific rice plant with its hundredfold yield completes the general conditions favourable to a proliferation of mankind. Nevertheless, the human swarms in India, China, and the island fringes differ in certain characteristics.

India is essentially rural and, apart from a few large towns and some recent centres of heavy engineering, industry plays no large part. Agriculture is itself incomplete, for cattle have but a small place in it. Cultivation is absolutely dependent on the monsoon rains, and all food comes from the soil. Human proliferation is due almost wholly to the combined effects of soil, sun, and water.

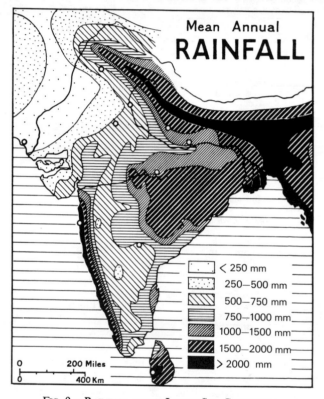

Mean Annual RAINFALL

⟨dotted⟩	< 250 mm
⟨dotted⟩	250—500 mm
⟨cross-hatch⟩	500—750 mm
⟨horizontal lines⟩	750—1000 mm
⟨diagonal⟩	1000—1500 mm
⟨diagonal⟩	1500—2000 mm
⟨black⟩	> 2000 mm

0   200 Miles
0   400 Km

FIG. 9.—RAINFALL IN THE INDIAN SUB-CONTINENT.
Contrast between humid regions with several harvests (in the northeast) and dry or arid regions (central Deccan and the northwest).

Consequently, the vast mass of humanity, depending as it does so closely on the physical surroundings, is distributed strictly according to the physical phenomena, to which it submits, since it has never been able to control them. The distribution of high densities corresponds exactly, therefore, to that of the heavy rainfall that produces

the greatest crops.   The following table shows the relation between
rainfall and density of population :

Place	Mean Annual Rainfall	Density of Population
	Millimetres	*Per sq. km.*
Ganges delta	200	215
East coast plain	120	188
Southeast coast	260	125
The Deccan	75	58
The dry northwest	28	25

The growth of crops and the periodical harvests year by year
depend closely on the regular incidence of the seasonal rains.   This
is particularly striking in Bengal, where usually two, but sometimes

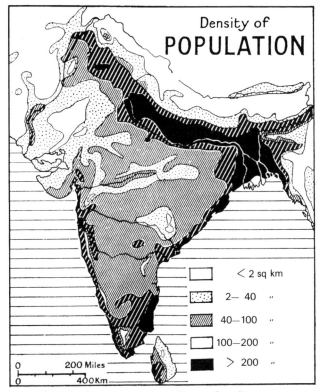

FIG. 10.—POPULATION IN THE INDIAN SUB-CONTINENT.

Compare with map opposite : density varies directly with rainfall, indicating
the close dependence of population on agriculture—a primitive type of rural
civilisation.

three, crops of rice can be grown : one in July–September, a second in November–December, and the third in April–May.

With a mean density of about 120 persons to the square kilometre, the population of India is extremely irregular in its distribution. People swarm in the Ganges valley, which has a greater density than Belgium on an area little less than that of France. It contains 60 per cent of the population of the whole country owing to there being 200 persons to the square kilometre in parts where there are three crops in the year, between 100 and 200 in parts where there are two crops a year, between 40 and 100 in the black earth cotton country, and between 20 and 40 on scrubby uplands or in the mountains. Some districts reach great densities, for in them the profit from industry and commerce is added to the returns from agriculture. The district around New Delhi contains more than 400 persons to the square kilometre, and the Bengal district of Bangladesh more than 650 persons. The vast accumulation of people is explained by the astonishingly small size of the fields whose cultivation succeeds in feeding a family.

China's swarming population has very many of the characteristics of India's. The country is basically rural, but being less tropical than India, it has at its disposal a large collection of plants, which enables more varied combinations of crops to be raised. There are large areas of good soil. The yellow earth in the northwest and deltaic plains of the big rivers act as the supports of an intensive system of cultivation, whose organisation goes back very far into the past. Its technique is that of horticulture and is without improved implements and chemical fertilisers. It depends on an orgy of work and persistent search for all kinds of manure in various sorts of waste and excreta. Human excreta are used more systematically than anywhere else. The soil is dug with spade and hoe, and the plants are manured and watered one by one. Energy is wholly devoted to cultivation. There is no rearing of animals, no grass fields, nothing intended for feeding animals, seeing that man directly needs all the harvest. In the Chinese diet there is neither milk nor meat, except some pork and poultry. Two essential cereals ensure the necessary ingredients of the diet, each in its own area. These are wheat in the north, rice in the south. Yet among his food crops the Chinese peasant readily plants cash crops that give work to all the members of his family, namely, tea, cotton, and the mulberry tree whose leaves feed the silkworm.

The exact figures of the population of China have long been unknown owing to imperfect methods of reckoning, but they used to be estimated to amount to between 450 and 500 million persons. More accurate counts, which have been effected since the accession to power of the Communist Government, have revealed that this huge mass of human beings numbered 827 million persons in 1974. Like the population of India, this great multitude of people is unevenly distributed and does not cover the area uninterruptedly, for high densities occur wherever there are abundant, regular harvests, and this emphasises the close dependence of Chinese cultivators on the physical conditions of their surroundings. Population is sparse in the interior wherever the relief is broken and the climate dry. The Chinaman regards mountains with horror, for good rice will not grow in them, and he does not know how to use the vegetation complex. In the hilly provinces of Yunnan and Kwangsi in the southwest the population scarcely ever exceeds 20 or 30 persons to the square kilometre in spite of the mining operations and important irrigation works now in progress. It is still sparser in Mongolia, where there are six persons to ten square kilometres. Great density occurs mainly in the north, where Shantung contains more than 230 persons to the square kilometre, and in the valley of the Yangtse Kiang. In the latter region from Szechwan to Honan and Kiangsi the density rises from 100 to 200 persons to the square kilometre in the irrigated districts and on the banks of the river, where the swarming population lives in junks on the water. The Chengtu plain has 300 to 350 persons to the square kilometre, the lower Yangtse more than 800, and some of the islands on the delta reach the incredible figure of 1,500.

The same conditions are found also in the inhabitants of the island fringes in east and southeast Asia. Low plains covered with paddy fields and swarming with people contrast everywhere with the hilly parts of the interior which are often still forested and are inhabited by small communities, whose patches of extensive cultivation yield poor returns. In the Philippines, for instance, great densities are found only in the wide central valley of Luzón and in the lowlands in the southern islands. The rest of the group is sparsely peopled.

Two factors alien to the traditional methods of cultivation intervene in the East Indian islands and Japan. Java's enormous density of 400 persons to the square kilometre is explained by the high returns from plantations on rich volcanic soil of economic crops, to which indeed even food crops have been sacrificed in the completely deforested island. In the case of Japan, which now contains a population of nearly 110 million persons and has an enormous mean density of 260 persons per square kilometre, the ability to feed such masses of people on a land two-thirds of which is mountain forest, is due less to the admirable development of its agriculture than to its large-scale industries, whose equipment and organisation are on a par with those in Europe and the United States. The islands show the same demographic contrasts, though slightly more weakly, as do their neighbours on the mainland. Industries have grown up in the heart of centres of dense population, where rice cultivation had previously encouraged crowding. But the hilly districts and northern part of the Japanese archipelago, which are unsuitable to high-yielding rice, have been neglected by polymorphous large-scale industry and even today still appear as sparsely peopled regions.

This quick glance at man's distribution over the globe proves that the distribution is not due simply to the action of natural conditions. Even in the case of communities still subject to changes of climate the degree of civilisation conferred on them by more or less control of nature enables the best-equipped groups to live in great numbers in surroundings that are without special advantages. Improvements in tools and implements, an intelligent division of labour, and the degree of complexity and efficiency of man's work enables advanced communities to afford a comfortable living to a very great number of people on small areas in which underdeveloped peoples would fail to maintain even a few individuals at starvation level.

INTERNAL FACTORS OF DEMOGRAPHIC DEVELOPMENT

Population figures constantly vary owing to changes in the rates of birth and death. Births cause an increase in the number of mankind. The birth-rate is subject to many natural conditions that are often very difficult to analyse. Strict laws cannot be recognised in it, any more than in the other phenomena of life. Yet owing to certain influences it depends partly on the geographical environment. Economic circumstances have the most clearly visible influence. For example, Ireland has long had a low birth-rate not because its marriages prove barren, but because emigration removes the young in the flower of age and since many Irishmen have made homes in the United States by the time they have reached the age of founding a family. In Hungary a direct relation has even been noted between the number of marriages and the size of the year's crops. But the influence of economic facts is limited in application. In Japan, Italy, and some countries in Central America resources are relatively poor, but the birth-rate is very high. Inversely, in Great Britain, France, and the United States, where resources are over-plentiful, the birth-rate is only moderate. In some forms of civilisation the number of marriages and, consequently, the birth-rate is kept very high by social constraint or recent legislative enactments giving privileges to members of numerous families.

Contrary to Malthus's conclusions, a growing tendency to sterility has been generally noticed in communities that have reached a high degree of material civilisation. This kind of decrease in the birth-rate was observed in ancient times. In modern Europe the falling off was noted in Normandy right at the end of the eighteenth century, and it spread slowly in the rest of France until about 1945. It took place similarly in Scandinavia about 1850 and in Great Britain and some countries in central Europe about 1880. In 1885 there were still many European countries with a birth-rate exceeding 30 per thousand. Today only nine out of twenty-six European countries exceed 20 per thousand. The causes of this phenomenon are many, being sometimes moral and at other times economic or social. Children are now regarded as an expense, whilst formerly in the days of the domestic system of industry they were looked on as valuable aids. The love of freedom and the desire not to share out one's wealth among too many children are other factors tending to lower the birth-rate. In addition to this, in very advanced communities marriage takes place at a later age through the exigencies of many callings, and at the same time the emancipation of women often makes them reject marriage and motherhood.

These influences are all found in environments that have sprung from European civilisations. They have taken root in Australia, New Zealand, and the United States, and, consequently, the same decrease is observed in the birth-rate, which does not exceed 25 per thousand. But these influences do not always succeed in bringing about a falling off. Even in Europe the Netherlands with their high standards of living have a birth-rate higher by 4 or 5 per thousand than that in Great Britain, France, or Germany.

Nevertheless, a traditional and old-fashioned type of civilisation certainly has an influence in keeping up a high birth-rate. The peoples of eastern Europe and the Mediterranean, for instance, still have the highest rates in Europe today. In the interior of some countries with a low mean birth-rate there are whole districts in which births are numerous. In France, for example, Brittany and Auvergne have maintained their rate well above the national mean. It is the same in Italy, where a high birth-rate in Calabria and Sicily is in contrast with Piedmont, where the modern way of life has been established. There is the same difference between the Swiss cantons of Schwitz, Uri, and Appenzell on the one hand and Vaux and Geneva on the other; and in the United States it is apparent between the Western States and New England. Lastly, the peoples of the Far East and south Asia all maintain a high birth-rate owing to their fidelity to religious and ancestral traditions. This is always more than 30 per thousand and often even 40 per thousand. A similar rate is also found in Egypt, North Africa, and some small States in Central America.

Yet too backward a civilisation is by no means favourable to a high birth-rate. For a long time the very low birth-rate among the most primitive African negroes as well as among the tribes in the Amazon basin or the Pacific islanders, has been unable to compensate for the ravages of epidemics or abrupt contact with civilisation. In such primitive communities, which are nature's slaves, women are tied down to hard work, suffer great exposure, and so become quickly run down physically into a state of low vitality. This explains the low birth-rate, which is sometimes so noticeable that these primitive folk attribute it to accident or magic.

Unlike birth, natural death is a fact in which human will plays no part. Consequently, the influence of natural causes is greater and more direct on death than on birth. Yet man also has some influence on his own fate. Some stages of civilisation are responsible for high death-rates, whilst others have succeeded in prolonging the average length of life. Thus, there is a striking difference between the death-rate in New Zealand and Australia ($8.5^0/_{00}$), Denmark (10·2), and Canada (7·5) on the one hand and that in Egypt ($13^0/_{00}$), Bolivia (19), or India (17).

Climate exercises a vital influence on man's life. In temperate regions some countries are not very healthy. Malaria has been a scourge in Mediterranean lands. Before the development of modern transport the hazards of climate in causing a crop failure often brought on famines, as they have done, for instance, in Russia, the Balkans, and Ireland, where it was deadly. Natural scourges are, moreover, more strongly armed against man in the tropics. In India, for instance, there are serious diseases, famines, and even wild beasts (tigers, snakes, etc.); terrible mortality is caused among women owing to premature births; and infantile mortality is between 60 and 70 per thousand. In western Europe, on the other hand, the rate is between 10 and 20 per thousand. Famine caused the death of more than 30 million people in India within the space of forty years between 1860 and 1900; between 1897 and 1911 some 8 million Indians died of plague; and in 1918 Asian influenza claimed more than 7 million Indian victims.

Natural calamities are not the only ones. Many people die prematurely owing to their social environment or to dangerous contact with other social groups. The social inferiority of women in some eastern communities certainly explains their higher death-rate. In other countries the want of care bestowed on girls causes abnormally high infant mortality among females. Contact with Europeans has proved fatal to some primitive folk. Institutions like porterage have been the cause of many deaths in Africa, and work in mines had the same effect on the Amerindian peoples in Spanish America. Lastly, in very early times wars ended in the systematic depopulation of conquered countries through both massacre and deportation of survivors, who were reduced to slavery. In spite of the murderous weapons used by modern armies, it has been noticed that the great wars among modern nations in recent years have not had so destructive an effect as did earlier wars on peoples of their time. Wars are not now followed by epidemics, and the increased birth-rate immediately succeeding them almost regularly on the cessation of hostilities prevents the loss of life in battle from having a lasting effect on the course of development of the people as a whole.

Nowadays, most civilised nations value human life greatly and try to lessen the death-rate, first, by saving children in their early years, when they are especially delicate; secondly, by struggling against disease, the most dreadful of which are contagious. That is why the death-rate has steadily fallen in Europe, where the expecta-tion of life has risen in less than a hundred years from forty-eight to sixty-nine years. The same tendency is noticeable today in those non-European peoples who have adopted the same kind of civilisation.

The size of population depends mainly on the relation of the birth-rate to the death-rate. As this relation differs greatly between peoples, there is a large number of demographic types. But human geography can reduce them to two main classes, namely, regions of diminishing and regions of increasing population. In the first class are those regions with an abnormally high death-rate. These are mainly countries inhabited by underdeveloped peoples whose vitality is lowered by widespread diseases like sleeping sickness. Often, too, a high death-rate comes upon weak peoples who suffer violence from stronger peoples. The slave trade was one of the causes of the long stagnation and partial regression of some African peoples. Besides, without any violence, contact between inferior peoples and European civilisation has almost always brought on a crumbling of the old social system of primitive peoples and an upheaval in their way of life, the results of which have been disastrous. There are as many examples among the pastoral peoples of eastern Asia confronted with Russian settlers who took their pastures, as among the tribes in the lower Congo valley and the region of the great lakes of Africa; and also among the Red Indians of North America, who were gradually driven back towards the barren west, as among the natives of the Río Branco. Nowhere was this contact more deadly than in some island groups in the Pacific, where in less than a hundred years the native population was decimated.[1]

[1] Population in the islands has not decreased owing to the clash of culture: in fact, native population has increased since the British and French Govern-ments stopped their tribal wars and cannibalism. Some islands have, however, suffered from European diseases; in 1875 an epidemic of measles broke out in Fiji and swept off a fourth of the natives. The Solomons suffered to a slight extent from the Australian practice of 'blackbirding', or taking Solomon islanders to work on sugar-cane plantations in Queensland. Nowadays, many of the Polynesian islands are overpopulated, Samoa in particular.

Sometimes a district is depopulated because its birth-rate is too low to compensate for the losses caused by even a moderate death-rate. For more than fifty years there was an instance of this in the *départements* in southwestern France, where, however, the soil is fertile and the climate favourable to the cultivation of all sorts of

Growth of Population in Europe (from the Urals to the Atlantic)

Year	Millions
1750	127
1800	175
1914	452
1926	476
1956	570
1960	590
1974	615

food crops. In this way, every demographic type forms a peculiar complex whose factors are the fecundity proper to the community, the state of health and hygiene, and its social characteristics.

Among the regions of increasing population the leading place is taken by Europe, whose total moved between 1850 and 1890 at a rate no statistician would have imagined. This is shown in the table above.

This increase, which is still moving steadily faster, differs from the alternation of periods of increase and decrease which had become common in Europe before the nineteenth century. In some countries the increase is due to a high birth-rate, which gives a surplus every year after the deaths have been taken into account. This is so in several European countries, one of which is Germany, where the birth-rate fell only recently. The same is also true of the Mediterranean countries in Europe and some countries in eastern Europe. This demographic type occurs also in some young countries in America, like the Argentine and the French-speaking part of Canada as well as in some Far Eastern countries like Japan and Indonesia, in independent Near Eastern countries like Egypt, and in India and Pakistan.

In other regions increase in population is due to a low death-rate. Had the death-rate not decreased to a considerable and unexpected degree in most countries in western and central Europe, a slow fall in population would have occurred during the last forty years in at least two-thirds of the continent and particularly in Great Britain, France, Sweden, Austria, and even Germany. It has been due to the excess of births owing to the decrease in the death-rate that the population of these countries has been able to increase still further and that the people of Europe have kept their place as a large and dynamic homogeneous division of mankind. Yet a decrease in the death-rate reaches its limit more quickly than an increase in the birth-rate and only for a time allows a numerical rise in population. Countries belonging to this demographic type usually have a very old civilisation, many resources and complexes, and a great accumulation of wealth. They are characterised by having a large proportion of ageing persons. This ageing of the population induces a peculiar social condition and a structural complexity unknown in young countries, in which the pyramid of age-groups rests on a wider base.

The development of human communities does not, however, depend only on these internal variations which can in fact be aggravated or compensated for by displacements of population. Such displacements have ensured man's ubiquity and are due to his extreme mobility, which has constantly increased in step with technical progress and the creation of important means of travel.

CHAPTER 15

HUMAN MIGRATION AND
OVERPOPULATION

Emigration is a geographical phenomenon that seems to be a human necessity in every age. Just as botany and zoology study the distribution and migration of plants and animals, so human geography studies movements of people. These movements reveal man's tendency to leave areas in which life is difficult for those he believes to be better. This is what impels the highlander towards the lowlands, the pastoralist on poor steppe towards regions of permanent pasture, the wretched peasant towards richer fields, the inhabitants of overpopulated countries towards sparsely peopled lands, and, inversely, countryfolk towards the town. Furthermore, that is what urges seasonal workers to go off peacefully to harvest crops in a neighbouring country; it is what is at the back of aggressive invasions that forcibly establish newcomers on conquered territory; and it is what inspired the gigantic exodus of Europeans to people new continents.

Between all these movements there are great differences in the number of people involved and the distances they travel as well as in the peaceful or violent manner of their settlement. We may perhaps distinguish two major groups:

(a) short-term displacements to no great distance, which do not take men finally from their homes; and

(b) displacements (usually called 'emigration') that go to far distances and take men away for good from their native lands.

It is very difficult to separate the two groups completely, for men who leave their country to go overseas to earn a living are not necessarily lost to their native land. Thanks to the speed and cheapness of modern transport, many emigrants return to their original homes at the end of a few years. Some even go back periodically at the end of a spell of work. Conversely, men who leave their home for another land do not always return, for a short displacement often ends in final expatriation. It is therefore more practical to take account of distance and the numbers involved in relation to the phenomena which accompany or cause emigration rather than to concentrate on their duration.

One of the first motives of emigration seems to be economic. Man's need to have fresh land to till and to rid himself of numbers that are too great for the resources of the country constitutes the most urgent material cause of movement. At different periods of

388

history there have taken place displacements that were destined primarily to people and develop a country rather than to relieve the motherland of surplus population. Thus, there were the migrations of the Israelites by order, first, of Sargon and then of Nebuchadnezzar, for the purpose of supplying labour in Mesopotamia ; those of Roman colonists into Cisalpine Gaul, Spain, and Romania ; and those of the Muslim settlers transplanted into Macedonia and Thessaly by the Turks. It is also possible to regard as organised migrations the transfer of slaves to supply labour in Athens and Rome, and the transportation of African Negroes to plantations in tropical America, a movement which ended in peopling with Negroes parts of the United States and Latin America as well as the West Indies. To the same type belong the appeals issued by landowners in the United States for emigrants from Britain, whose work was to improve the value of the land ; the attractive advertisements published by emigration agents offering a holding of 20 or 40 hectares to wretches who owned nothing acted as an irresistible magnet. As early as 1634 emigration agencies had been opened by William Penn in London and Rotterdam.

Yet immigrants so attracted had not been greatly attached to their original homes. Now any community may find its resources inadequate to support its population, and it may happen in very different kinds of country that there are more people than the land can maintain. Among fishing communities which trooped out of a barren land the best examples are found in the Norsemen who first as pirates and then as colonists settled in Normandy, England, the Canary Islands, and even Sicily. Other examples are afforded by pastoral peoples who had often spread at the expense of sedentary neighbours. Thus, there are Peuls who settled in the Sudan, and the Kurds who settled among the Armenians. In the same way, the Magyars formerly established themselves among the Slav farmers who dwelt on the plains of Hungary.

Strong motives of emigration are seen among working people in countries where there is much unemployment. This was the cause of the emigration of the Scotch-Irish in the seventeenth and eighteenth centuries after the decline of the woollen industry and the slump in linen in consequence of the rise of the cotton industry in Britain ; similarly, with the English village craftsmen after the invention of machinery had ruined home industry. In later times, every step forward in the improvement of machinery caused an exodus to lands overseas, for example, about 1830 after the invention of the spinning machine, and in 1840 after the spread of mechanical looms ; whilst the slump which came over Britain in 1930 ended in an exodus of workers to Canada in spite of efforts to stop it.

Agricultural communities, which are symbolic of stability, are, however, not exempt from the attractions that lure labourers from their native soil. In every age emigration has been rife in islands with restricted areas for cultivation; for example, the Ægean in ancient times, the Pacific in modern times, and more recently Malta and the Azores, have all been emigration centres.

Turning again to modern Europe, it is seen that economic conditions among the peasantry involving poverty and suffering that differed from age to age and country to country have set in motion the greatest migrations. At various times from the thirteenth century onwards, the turning of arable land into sheep walks, the enclosure of commons, and the setting up of large estates at the expense of the holdings of the yeomen in England was followed by the desertion of the countryside and the removal to other, sometimes distant, parts of the kingdom. At the end of the eighteenth and beginning of the nineteenth century the swallowing up of little properties by big sheep farms caused a great exodus from the Highlands of Scotland, Shetland, and the Hebrides. Great economic crises which have aggravated the poverty of the agricultural labourers (the poorest people) in Britain, have at times started a wave of emigration. One took place in 1820 owing to the great fall in the price of corn in the English market and to the new enclosure policy. There was another in 1870 when the competition of new countries completed the ruin of British cereal production within some twenty years.

The largest stream of emigration from Germany, southern Italy, Bohemia, and Galicia always began in districts where there were large estates and where the land was monopolised by a few owners and not worked by and for the peasants, who were reduced to the condition of seasonal labour. But districts with small peasant holdings have also been hit by emigration wherever a difficult and less fertile soil has been unfavourable to the parcelling out of heritages. In consequence, surplus members of families have had to emigrate, as do the Swiss from the most densely peopled cantons. The essentially agricultural nature of European emigration in the nineteenth century explains why an approximate synchronism has been established between the rhythm of good and bad harvests on the one hand and the rhythm of emigration on the other.

But there are also instances of migration being caused merely by overpopulation in a whole community. In such a case emigration may effect all social classes. At the present time this is the most frequent cause at work in Europe, where the proportion of country-folk among the emigrants has steadily decreased and, on the other hand, there has been an increase, first, of domestic servants and unskilled labourers, then of skilled workers, and, lastly, of technicians and intellectuals.

23. The village of Digg in Switzerland; sited on relatively gentle slopes

SETTLEMENTS IN MOUNTAIN ENVIRONMENTS

24. Meyruers, closely packed stone village at foot of steep slope, in the Causse Noir of central France

25. Stone-roofed houses in the upper Engadine, Switzerland

26. (*Left*) Garo houses in India, built on stilts for protection against wild elephants

27. (*Centre, below*) Typical farm in the Cambrésis, northern France; a hollow square with brick-built house on one side, stables and barns on the other sides, and manure heap in the centre

28. (*Bottom*) Roadside farms in Lorraine, with large arched entrances to yards

Among the causes of emigration from Europe an important place must certainly be given simply to human desire, apart from any determining economic motive. Certain persons have for political, religious, or ethnical reasons thought it necessary at least for a time to seek another home owing to the impossibility of their being able to tolerate life with their fellow countrymen. Every period of history furnishes examples of this. In the Middle Ages there was the emigration of Balkan peoples owing to the oppression of the Turks. In modern times there has been the expulsion of the Jews from Spain, the emigration of the Huguenots from France, the emigration of the Pilgrim Fathers to New England, and of the Mormons across the States to Utah, of the Mozabites to North Africa, of the German liberals after 1815, of the Mennonite sects, and, more recently, of German Jews and Communists between 1934 and 1940. Following the great wars of 1914–18 and 1939–45 there were large displacements of people across the new frontiers. Nevertheless, none of the movements induced by political events since 1945 has been as important or as continuous as the migrations due to economic conditions.

Emigration attained its most astonishing figures in modern times. A dense and continuous stream of people has been flowing out of Europe for two hundred years. One of the chief causes of this phenomenon is the enormous increase in the population of the continent during the nineteenth century. Yet, however potent the pressure of population, these displacements would not have been possible but for modern means of large-scale transport and the commercial organisation, in fact, which took charge and guided them.

Emigration did not attain its greatest height until steam navigation became general, for this reduced the length of the voyage from Havre to New York, for instance, from forty-five to ten days and so correspondingly shortened the hardships of the emigrants. The carriage of 'human cargo' was often the foundation of the prosperity of shipping companies, especially of German companies. Between 1871 and 1900 more than 1,180,000 emigrants embarked at Bremen for the United States, and 856,000 from Hamburg. In 1913 alone, German, English, French, and Italian companies landed 870,000 at New York.

Both the country of origin, whose valuable living cargo was seen to be disappearing, and the country that received the immigrants as an aid to prosperity, tried to give these poor folk a guarantee of greater security. At the beginning and for a fairly long time the guarantee did not go very far. In the United States it did no more than ensure for the immigrant who did not just stay in New York or drift to some other town a bit of land to bring under cultivation, but under rather hard conditions. Later came more efficient steps to protect the newcomer. For instance, in the various countries of origin special departments were set up to give information about the countries to which the emigrants were going and to prepare them with a trade. Other organisations advanced the cost of the voyage, and on arrival others advanced a little capital. Finally, welfare services enabled the immigrant to have his family over or to be himself repatriated.

These measures were meant to encourage immigration, but they ceased to be effective as soon as the exodus slackened off. During the second quarter of the twentieth century the receiving country was in fact in the throes of economic crises and tried to restrict immigration instead of encouraging it. The quotas imposed by the United States and shortly after imitated by Canada and Brazil made entrance to new countries more difficult. At the same time certain European countries tried to keep the labour whose emigration they had previously encouraged. With all this regulation the great human phenomenon of emigration, which was as spontaneous as the birth-rate, has become a movement depending on the international situation. It complies less with economic facts than with artificial laws issued by men and directing the despatch of human beings just as if they were merchandise. Yet, these man-made laws cannot altogether check the play of natural laws to which emigration is subject, nor can they utterly deprive it of its innate necessity and spontaneity.

INTRACONTINENTAL MIGRATION

Two kinds of population movement can be determined according to their volume, distance, and means of transport used, namely, intracontinental and transoceanic. The former is the older, commoner, and more limited in volume and duration. It results from a great number and variety of special conditions proper to each region. It includes simple, short movements of little groups of people, but it also comprises movements of large bodies travelling long distances and even across whole continents. It sometimes owes much of its amplitude to the available means of transport, railways in particular, which contributed greatly to migration in America and Asia. The transoceanic kind has been the more important and intense in modern times, affecting mainly the chief centres of population in Europe, India, China, and Japan.

Continents outside Europe.—Outside Europe little is known of the history of the migration of peoples either because documentary evidence is lacking or because the peoples and their civilisations have disappeared under the advance of Europeans. In ancient times many migrations recorded in legends and traditions have aimed at reaching a happy land promised by a divinity. These promised lands were Canaan for the Jews, and the gardens of Sogdiana, Merv, and Bactria for the Persians. In this type of migration are included those that introduced peoples of Mongol stock into Indo-China at various periods. Among these were the Thais, who arrived in Siam from the year 2000 B.C. onwards; the Mans, who entered Tongking four or five centuries ago; and the Meos, who first migrated at the beginning of the nineteenth century. India is a vast world incessantly crossed by eddies of peoples. About the end of the sixteenth century the central provinces were seized and occupied by an agricultural people, and in the nineteenth century there was an exodus of workers from the Deccan to tea plantations in Assam. Migration has enabled the Chinese to colonise Mongolia and Manchuria methodically. Into these *loess* countries Chinese peasants from Kansu, who were always in search of land, poured like a flood. In less than ten years during the first third of the twentieth century more than 30 million Chinese invaded Manchuria and settled there.

Without going back into the past further than the arrival of Europeans in Africa, migration certainly took place in the greater part of the continent at a time not very far past. For instance, the Pahwins still lived around the upper Ubanghi in the middle of the nineteenth century. Driven away by the Muslim Fulani, they moved westwards to the lower and middle Ogowe valley attracted by the sea, that source of wealth. In this trek westwards by the Pahwins the Loangos, Mpongwes, and Bengas were overwhelmed and disappeared. When the French arrived in the north of Banghi a slow migration of Africans was moving towards the south owing to the pressure against each other of tribes along the Ubanghi due to the advance of better organised Muslims from the Sudan. This turned a land of able-bodied men into a source of slaves. Towards the south these displaced peoples came up against a forest barrier in lat. 4° N. and could not cross it, though the Fans succeeded in pushing on farther west and southwest. Many African peoples have been forced to migrate owing to Arab pressure. For instance, the Manyems, who were originally in Uganda, now live between the Congo River and the Mitumba Mountains. The Arabs penetrated into this region and subjugated it, founding the towns of Nyangwe and Kasongo in the midst of the territory.

In southeast Africa the distribution of the Bantus is the result of a series of migrations that have only just ended. Some streams moved from north to south along the belts of savanna, driving back the Bushmen and Hottentots. In their migration they followed the grass-covered plateaus which were fairly well provided with water and were easy for cattle to travel over. The Bantu tribes had had long periods of restlessness, a lengthy history of intestine struggles, and the formation of short-lived empires. At the beginning of the nineteenth century the rise of the Zulus and their appearance as a military power caused many tribal displacements. Finally, the pressure exercised by Europeans started several African peoples on the move. Thus, the Matabele, who had once been settled around the upper Limpopo, retired first to the north of the river and afterwards moved away an appreciable distance from it. Today, black migrations in South Africa have assumed another character owing to the industrialisation of the country. The workers in the Transvaal gold mines come from Basutoland and even Mozambique. Similarly, in North Africa workers migrate from south to north Morocco.

In America it is the same. Both before and since the arrival of the Europeans there has been much migration among the Amerindians, whose memory of the movements is preserved in traditions and legends. The wanderings of the Nahuatlacas towards the 'Land of reeds and gladioli' and the migration of the Tupi Guarani in tropical eastern Brazil began early in the fifteenth century. They are said to have been caused by religious beliefs and the search for the land where no one dies; but these poetic motives conceal more material realities. Many of the movements started from the *sertão*, that is, from an inland scrub region with a well-marked dry season often ending in disaster; and they have led to the wetter regions of the Amazon basin, to the coast of Brazil, and to Paraguay, where good harvests are ensured by almost regular rains, and where human life is less precarious. There was also the fear inspired by Europeans, which made them flee from the latter's violence and traps, and perhaps they feared even more the deadly diseases contracted by mere contact with the whites. Until recently the Amerindian tribes often migrated in United States territory also. The Delawares, for instance, came from the northwest of the Great Lakes, and the Cherokees were driven steadily westwards.

Much internal migration is still observed in the present economic structure of America. In South America there is the movement of *maté* pickers, who start for the forest from southern Brazil, and the *seringueiros* from the northeast to the middle of Amazonia. In Central America and the West Indies gangs of banana pickers go from Jamaica to the main centres of banana production in turn. In Mexico there is a constant stream of workers to the United States. The irrigated crops in California regularly cause large displacements of seasonal workers who in the course of a year travel over the whole country from south to north following work-rounds several hundreds of miles in length. In the rest of the United States a great migration of Negro workers goes on from the Southern

States to the industrial centres in the northeast and by the Great Lakes. For a long time, moreover, the region of the Great Lakes witnessed displacements of lumberjacks who, when summer came, worked at reaping the wheat harvest in the Mississippi valley, and there were also migrations of farmers from Dakota to the wheat belt in the Canadian prairies.

Europe and the Old World.—*Europe.*—For many reasons no other continent holds out so many inducements to travel, so many differences of demographic pressure, or so many contrasting modes of life, owing to the variety of its natural, economic, and human conditions. It has contrasts of mountain and plain, coastal and inland regions, intensive and extensive systems of agriculture, maritime, continental, and Mediterranean climates, agriculture and industrial regions, and areas of high and low densities of population. Consequently, there is much local and regional migration, movements that have always been a peculiar trait in the human geography of Europe. They have occurred in every period of history and they are to be seen today in nearly every country.

The invasions of the barbarians may be considered as one of the most powerful manifestations of the need to migrate, but even now their exact cause is in doubt: was it overpopulation in Germany, or the depopulation of the Romanised districts? In Belgium, for instance, the Salian Franks are found to be settled on the lower Rhine as early as the end of the third century. In the middle of the fourth they had broken out into Toxandria on the left bank of the Rhine. From there they spread afterwards into western Belgium, where they settled slowly in the course of several centuries. Their first settlements were in the valley of the Schelde and Lys (358–450). Slow infiltration took place southwards, where the country was already peopled and cultivated. They avoided the forest in the coal region and in Flanders, settling on sandy areas that were less wooded and more easily tilled. In this way they came into collision with the Saxons, who had already settled in the Boulogne district. Then began the settlement of Brabant between the sixth and eighth centuries. There was a movement of people from the country of the Salian Franks, which had become overpopulated and in consequence was short of cultivable land. Lastly, the Flemish coast was settled in its turn between the seventh and ninth centuries, that is, just as a retreat of the sea allowed Frisian and Saxon settlers to move into it.

Flemish Migration.—From the early Middle Ages Flanders was a great reservoir of people which often overflowed, and for hundreds of years the overpopulated country gave settlers and workers to the neighbouring lands. As early as the twelfth century Flemings settled in the Märschen near Bremen and infiltrated into the country districts of Westphalia, Thuringia, and even Brandenburg. Flemish craftsmen tried eagerly from early times to find work outside their country. They appeared in France, Germany, and Austria, and the English woollen industry owes its inception to the immigration of Flemings in the thirteenth and sixteenth centuries.

At the present time the density of population in Flanders raises afresh the question of overpopulation. The great density in the nineteenth century was due to the crowd of home craftsmen, the number of spinners and weavers amounting to nearly 300,000 in 1840. Home industry has declined throughout the district but the countryside has not been depleted, as might have been feared, for the people simply went to work in the factories that had been built in large numbers in the country. The great density of population was due to the intensive character of the agriculture. The land is cut up into tiny holdings many of which are incapable of supporting a family. Hence the obligation to seek additional resources elsewhere, and these very people who for long were tied to their houses have become the most mobile in Europe. Migration began in the nineteenth century with the decline of home industries. It was further encouraged by crises in agriculture which increased the amount of pasture, developed the use of machinery, and lessened the area devoted to industrial crops. Lastly, it was facilitated by improvement in the means of transport.

Flemish emigrants work by the day or week; that is, they are masons and navvies in the big towns or go as workers to the factories and coal mines. Their movements are often seasonal, as, for instance, the Gossalies brick-makers and the woodcutters from Luxemburg and Entre-Sambre-et-Meuse who go hop-picking at Alost and Poperinghe, or weeding, manuring, harvesting, or working in sugar refineries in districts where there is large-scale agriculture. Some of these seasonal workers go to France. This movement dates from 1845 when sugarbeet began to spread and the population of the French countryside to decrease. Attracted by high wages, the Belgians used to cross the frontier about 15 March every year and, sooner or later according to the work, they gradually reached the *départements* in the centre of the Paris basin. The savings from the trip enabled the migrants to buy land at home, where, during their absence, the women had been working in the fields. But some of these seasonal workers settled in the north of France, whilst others who had rented farms in France stayed there with their families to cultivate the land on their own account.

Irish Emigration.—Ever since the beginning of the eighteenth century working-class Irish have been migrating to Britain. On one side of the Irish Sea the country is poor, rural, and overpopulated, and, on the other there is an industrial country with large towns and intensive agriculture requiring much labour in the thinly peopled rural districts. Unfortunately, the movement was not statistically recorded until after 1840, when it had already begun to slacken and was about to decline, losing more than half its total between 1841 and 1900. Three-fourths of the emigrants came from the poorest part of Ireland, the province of Connaught, nearly half the number coming from the single county of Mayo. County Donegal in Ulster was also a main source of the exodus.

This movement was attended by very serious social and demographic consequences. In some villages there were no able-bodied men left in summer, and the proportion of emigrants in some years represented an enormous fraction of the population: 48 per thousand in Mayo, 15 per thousand in Roscommon, and 13·6 per thousand in Donegal.

The chief cause of Irish emigration was the poverty of the peasants, who were crowded on tiny bits of land too small to feed a family. In Mayo such was the poor quality of the soil that only 7 per cent was cultivable. Most of the emigrants had too small a piece of land with too small a yield. Hence the need for them to go to England to earn a little money. In the northwest this condition of things in country districts went back a good way into the past, for in the eighteenth century Dobbs, Berkeley, and Lecky had described the exodus from Ireland; and in the single year 1787 Manchester received no less than 5,000 Irish immigrants.

A good many of the emigrants took work as agricultural labourers. They set off sometimes in February, but usually in June, so as to return in November. Their work consisted of putting a second dressing on the soil, hay-making, harvesting corn, digging potatoes and other roots, and sometimes of milking the cows. They were content with a frugal diet, so as to take home as much of their wages as possible. Their field of operations lay mainly in the North and Midlands of England, and they rarely went farther south than Cambridgeshire. In Scotland they were numerous in the Lothians and Ayrshire. They also went to the docks and large towns. Manchester and Liverpool, for instance, had large colonies of Irish. Many more were employed in the building of canals, and later on, of railways.

Migration of Central European Peoples.—In spite of differences in physical and ethnical conditions in central Europe, the same economic necessities have imposed on the peoples displacements and migrations, whose nature, destination, and volume have varied enormously from one people to another. The Poles have long included a prolific mass of peasantry, as a rule landless and reduced to the state of jobbing hands on huge farms, but even so they could not find work enough. Before the resurgence of Poland in 1919 between 500,000 and 800,000 emigrated from Polish territories under the rule of Russia, Prussia, and Austria. Many of them went to work on farms in Prussia, central Germany, and Saxony, where intensive cultivation was practised. On sugar-beet farms in Saxony the 'Sachsengänger' played a part like that of the Belgians in Picardy or Beauce. Many Poles also moved to Westphalia and the Rhineland. In 1910 there were already more than 25,000 of them in the latter country. Lastly, between the two wars many Poles went to France either as temporary workers or as permanent immigrants. Numbers of them worked on large farms in the north and in the Paris basin, and they formed an important fraction in the mining population on French coalfields.

Switzerland, too, has sent out many emigrants. Before the development of modern economy there mountain dwellers emigrated in the seventeenth, eighteenth, and nineteenth centuries to all parts of Europe, to Bessarabia, Russia, and Hungary, where they farmed. As early as 1660 they had peopled eight villages in the 'government' of Saratov. During the nineteenth century there was a continuous stream of labourers and little craftsmen (masons and carpenters) from Ticino, of watchmakers from Geneva, pastrycooks from Grisons, and cowmen from Appenzell. Today Swiss migration moves but short distances, making for holiday and winter sports resorts or industrial centres. The economic outlook has in fact changed, for the mountain country, which is most suitable for the tourist trade and possesses a good deal of industry, thanks to hydro-electric power, offers the countryfolk wide outlets in other directions of industry, commerce, and service. The old kind of migration is now represented only by the displacement of a few cowherds towards French communes in the Alps and Jura.

At certain periods Germany was a real reservoir of peoples which fed waves of migration as numerous as they were varied. During the whole of the Middle Ages many streams of German labourers, miners, and craftsmen emigrated to Poland, Hungary, and Transylvania. From the eighteenth century onwards the economic conditions in certain parts of Germany, particularly the Rhineland and the south, made many people ready to emigrate, and some small farmers moved from the Palatinate, Bavaria, and the Salzburg district to settle in Prussian territory. At the end of the eighteenth century Germans were attracted to southern Hungary to occupy frontier districts that had been devastated by war, and between 1768 and 1778 the Banat received 50,000 German settlers. Others were sent in the eighteenth century into parts of Russia that were then being colonised; that is, the lower Volga valley, Livonia, Volhynia, and the Odessa district. These German groups long preserved their racial and economic character in the midst of the Slav population, and it was only as a result of the second world war that the German 'republics' on the Volga were systematically eliminated and dispersed. German settlers went even as far as Spain to work in mines in the Sierra Morena. In the nineteenth century this flood of people turned across the ocean towards America. But right at the end of the century the then industrialised Germany was able to find employment for her labour in the main centres of industry. By 1934 it was in turn to become a centre of attraction of labour and to take in foreign workers, the majority of whom were Slavs and Italians.

Migration of Mediterranean Peoples.—In each of the peninsulas in southern Europe there are mountainous districts that have always been centres of demographic dispersion. A careful study of these local movements escapes statistics, but much of the migration goes to far distances and assumes an international character. In Spain a host of internal migrations have continually gone on round the periphery of the mountain regions. Typical of them are the movements of the Jurdanos of the Sierra de Gata, who earn nearly all their living by work which they do far from their own districts. Emigration occurs in regions of relatively high density of population and those sparsely peopled, for an insufficient standard of living is the basic cause of steady emigration, since it keeps the conditions of life at too precarious a level.

Emigration takes place chiefly from the northwestern provinces of Navarra, Viscaya, and, above all, Galicia. *Gallegos* have always been very numerous in Madrid and the big towns in Portugal, where they work as porters and messengers. They spread into the parts of northern Portugal adjoining Galicia and work in the harvest. There is also emigration from eastern, Pyrenean, Catalan, Levantine, and Mallorcan provinces, from which since 1846 emigrants have been going to Algeria and elsewhere in North Africa, and agricultural labourers and little tradesmen go off for temporary work or else to settle in southwest France, the Rhône valley, and even in the Paris region. The grape-growing districts and irrigated market-garden areas are particularly attractive to them. Nowadays, the development of rice cultivation in the Camargue attracts a good deal of agricultural labour from the *huerta* of Valencia. These intra-continental displacements of Spaniards may be estimated at 30,000 or 40,000 persons a year.

Portuguese emigration is due to the same causes, but it goes mainly overseas, all, that is, except for the portion that goes to France, chiefly to the Paris district, to take work in petty crafts.

In Italy there are countless seasonal movements to and fro between mountain and plain. But besides this, for three-quarters of a century vast numbers of small farmers, workmen, or mere labourers have poured out into neighbouring countries, and these represent today more than half the intracontinental contingents in all Europe, and two-thirds of Italian emigration. The main areas of departure are Venezia, Emilia, and, in the south, Basilicata. At first the emigrants headed for the nearby countries in North Africa, where the climate and general conditions resemble thóse of southern Italy. Many of them went to Algeria, but even more to Tunisia, which is close to Sicily and in which in the first third of the twentieth century there were as many as 40,000 Italians. These were chiefly employed in public works or engaged in handicraft. The greatest number, however, went to France to work in the iron mines in Lorraine, where labour was needed, and towards the sparsely peopled districts in the south of France, where they were engaged as day labourers on farms or else they settled as tenant farmers or landed proprietors. Out of 1,300,000 Italians who left their country and settled elsewhere in Europe more than a million were in France.

One of the characteristics of Italian emigration was that the emigrants kept in touch with their native land. Money earned abroad was often sent or taken back to Italy, where it was used to buy land or to improve a farm. Italian intracontinental emigration was greatly disrupted by the second world war. The Fascist régime showed a tendency to check emigration so as to keep the labour either for improvements in Italy itself in the Pontine Marshes and Emilia or for colonial enterprises in Africa. Nowadays, Italian workmen leave Italy under contracts of work in neighbouring countries, which guarantee to send their savings back to Italy. Italy's adherence to the European Coal and Steel Community has widened the field for Italian workers. Today they are found in Luxemburg, Belgium, Western Germany, and Lorraine in all the mines and factories of the Community.

In the Balkan Peninsula emigration has played an important part owing to economic, political, and religious causes. Most of the big migrations occurred during the Turkish domination, that is, during the four hundred years from the end of the fourteenth century to the beginning of the nineteenth. Immense streams of people, mainly Serbs, constantly headed for Slovenia, Slavonia, Transylvania, Italy, and Russia ; and from the end of the eighteenth century to Moravian Serbia, Croatia, Dalmatia, and southern Hungary. The general direction was north or northeastwards, starting from Herzegovina, Montenegro, Albania, or Bulgaria. The suppression of Serb risings, the Austro-Turkish wars at the end of the seventeenth century, and, later, the attraction of the free Principality of Serbia were also causes of migration. But in addition to these movements there were others of an economic order. Poor countries like the Karst and the

Bosnian mountains were deserted for the fertile lands of the Shumadia and the Banat, whilst districts like those on the Vardar, where Turkish landowners had large estates, were forsaken for Serbia proper. These migrations have profoundly mixed the Balkan peoples and made it difficult to trace the boundaries between the various successor States of the Turkish empire.

Russian Emigration.—The territory at present within the Soviet Union has at all times been very unevenly peopled and cultivated. The efforts of the new political régime during the last forty years to secure a better distribution of population and to make systematic arrangements for streams of migrants and for planting new settlements around artificially created industrial centres have had only partial success. Tsarist Russia had always suffered from the instability of its people, even of the peasants, and in the seventeenth century serfdom had to some degree been meant to keep men on the land. The backward state of agriculture ended in the overpopulation of many areas in which, however, there was fertile soil. Besides, a high birth-rate constantly brought new claimants for land. Another cause of instability was the length of winter unemployment, which for many months made countryfolk who had neither land nor handicraft go without any wages at all. Thus the Black Earth belt, being very fertile, was in a chronic state of overpopulation and had long been a source from which were drawn settlers for the steppes of New Russia and for the country in the southeast, where there were fewer people and where agriculture needed hands. These movements affected more than three million migrants. They went south for the harvest and hay-making after having signed on at the big fairs in Kharkov, Rostov, or Saratov. This exodus lessened as the southeast became peopled, and even before the October Revolution the increasing use of machinery in the big corn-growing estates in the south had dried up these streams.

Large numbers of emigrants from the equally overpopulated districts of Tula and Kursk went to mines in the Donbass, to the rivers during the fishing season or at times of great navigational activity, to work in the forests, and, more and more, to the main centres of public works as more canals, power houses, dams, and railways were built in the Soviet Union. In spite of the artificial character of some of its methods, migration to Siberia was a form of internal or intracontinental migration. It was a mere trickle up to about 1889, but increased enormously after the construction of the Trans-Siberian Railway. Conditions in the country were like those in Russia, for there were the same kinds of soil, the same scenery, climate, and methods of cultivation. Vast areas contained a mere sprinkling of natives, especially in western Siberia. This led to a tremendous flood of migration which has been reinforced by the economic and industrial development of the Soviet Union in the course of the various Five Year Plans. The number of Russian immigrants in Siberia rose from 50,000 in 1889 to 200,000 in 1896 and to more than 500,000 in 1907. Today, of the 44 million Soviet citizens who people Asia more than half are immigrants of recent date or else the descendants of former immigrants. Settlement in this vast continental territory has diverted Russians from transoceanic emigration.

These intracontinental displacements which are found everywhere and at all periods in every country in Europe bear witness to the diversity of economic conditions in regions, many of which are close together. Pockets of alien peoples express geographical contrasts and contacts of different modes of life sometimes at close quarters. Today they have very great numbers in some European countries owing to the progress in the means of transport. When considered on the international plane, these displacements of population reflect the state of the labour market and its fluctuations. In relations between countries the need for labour is reflected by a movement of more than 700,000 workers, and certain centres that attract crowds of people have assumed universal importance.

Of these migration currents, the most important, in Europe and the Old World generally, are those that attract towards the urbanised manufacturing regions of northwest Europe, a labour force emanating from southern Europe and the Mediterranean, from Portugal to Turkey. The migrants are principally workers from Portugal, Spain, Italy, Jugoslavia and Turkey, and they go mainly to France and Germany, and in lesser numbers to other members of the European Community. Mining, metallurgy and chemical industries absorb many of them, and others go into the building trades that have been stimulated by urban expansion, into public works, airport maintenance workshops, ports, motorway construction and other industrial occupations. In France, the call for labour extends beyond the Mediterranean, and large contingents of workers arrive from Algeria and Morocco and from the whole of the Francophone section of Black Africa. Since the decolonisation, most of the old European metropolitan centres have received migrant workers from the newly-established states, the choice depending on the European language that the migrants have learnt. This mobility of labour from abroad is one of the characteristic features of modern industrial civilisation.

TRANSOCEANIC EMIGRATION

Transoceanic emigration began only with the birth of the modern age, in which agricultural production has become subordinate to industry, and the latter to commercial activity. In the course of crisis after crisis it has caused the displacement of tens of millions of human beings. Asia and Europe, or more precisely, the two over-populated frontages of the east and west of the continent of Eurasia, have without apparent loss fed the enormous stream right up to the present day. But the two streams, far distant from each other, seem basically different in continuity, direction, rate, and effects on mankind.

European Emigration.—European emigration is the most tremendous displacement of people ever recorded by history. The numbers involved have never been counted. It began well before the nineteenth century with the discovery of America and its colonisation by the Spaniards; but it has been estimated that between 1821 and 1910 at least 26 million emigrants left Europe for the United States alone. Supan calculates that since the end of the fifteenth century at least 105 million persons have left Europe for the Americas, Asia, Africa, or Australasia. The emigrants issued from different sources according to the period of time, but all European nations have taken part, so that emigration to far countries is an astonishing characteristic shared by the European peoples. In truth, the causes of emigration are found acting together and amplified in Europe, sometimes working simultaneously and at other times separately according to the period and progress of economic conditions.

Europe suffered real overpopulation very early; that is, her resources were insufficient in relation to the number of her population. These resources are not adjusted to needs every year, and a deficit recurs more and more often in a swarm of humanity too numerous to be assured of a sufficient margin of subsistence. In European economy the resources of an agricultural people are uncertain, for the soil has been exhausted by too much cropping and requires a great deal of manure; the traditional crops are threatened by the arrival of cheaper foreign produce; in some places the peasants are too numerous and are consequently landless; many have no ties with the soil because they own no land; and they have often been uprooted because machinery has ruined their home industry. The desire to emigrate became evident at the very moment when vast, almost empty territories were opened in new countries in latitudes favourable to the European way of life and just when new means of transport enabled large numbers of people to cross the seas.

In the sixteenth century three million Spaniards left home for America. If emigration is thought of as a stream that has never ceased to flow, there are certain periods in the nineteenth century when the stream was swollen and swept off greater crowds of people.

These were between 1850 and 1859, between 1880 and 1889, and at the beginning of the twentieth century. On the other hand, on the morrow of the first world war the stream fell off greatly owing to the smaller numbers admitted to the United States, the agrarian reforms in some countries, and to efforts in others to retain their men.

Emigration did not affect all the nations of Europe at the same time. It began very early with the Spaniards and Portuguese; and up to the beginning of the nineteenth century it consisted mainly of English, Scots, Irish, German, and French nationals. When steam navigation facilitated movement various nations succeeded each other in contributing to the vast contingents. They came at first from the countries in the north and northwest, namely, English, Scots, Irish, Scandinavians, and Germans: then came Spaniards and Italians from the south; and after that Slavs from eastern Europe. The lateness of each group depended on the length of time it had remained outside the influence of the modern economic system. Three suitably chosen periods enable one to grasp the changes in racial composition. Thus:

Emigration from Europe (percentages)

	1819–55	1910–12	1920–24
English, Scots, and Irish	55	10	31·5
Germans	28·8	3·2	0·8
French	4·7	0·9	nil
Scandinavians	0·77	3·2	0·46
Italians	0·17	18·7	24·5
Slavs	0·31	40·5	12·3

The destination was mainly the new countries, which were almost uninhabited, but were capable of supporting settlers. Up to 1914 there was a considerable flow to the United States, with times of spate in 1851–60, 1881–90, and 1900–14. In some years more than a million Europeans entered the United States, where two-thirds of this enormous crowd of people settled for good. The three periods of spate correspond fairly closely, the first to high demographic pressure in the European continent, the second to the upsurge of colonisation in the west and industrialisation in the northeast of the United States, the last to the rise of industry in the whole country.

However, a decisive change was caused by the law of 1921 setting up quotas for immigrants. Inspired by the dislike of the American working class to see a fall in their standard of living and by the wish of the nation as a whole to remain homogeneous and basically Anglo-Saxon, this measure produced a profound upheaval in immigration from Europe.

In Commonwealth countries European immigration increased to the extent to which it was shut out from the United States. But it was restricted by legislation meant to limit the number of non-British immigrants and to protect the working class in the receiving countries from the competition even of British workmen. No country in the Commonwealth screens immigrants more carefully than Australia. In Canada an eye is kept on immigration, and, when entry is allowed, preference is always shown to technicians and farmers, workers who are accepted for the human capital they represent.

Most of the countries in South America have tried to attract immigrants from Europe, even when Anglo-Saxon countries restricted their admission. The influx comes naturally from Mediterranean lands, where the climate and forms of civilisation are often similar to those in South America. Thus, between 1820 and 1910 Brazil received about 2,850,000 immigrants, 43 per cent of whom were Italian and 37·9 per cent Portuguese or Spanish. Latin peoples still predominate in immigration today, for the first restrictive measures taken by Brazil during the great world economic crisis were less severe than those in Anglo-Saxon countries and definitely favour Latin immigrants. Between 1857 and 1910 Argentina received nearly 5,700,000 immigrants, three-fifths of whom settled in the country. The large number of those who returned home is explained by the high proportion of seasonal workers among the immigrants. On the average the stream of entrants, whose composition has varied little for fifty years, comprises 50 per cent Spaniards and 25 per cent Italians. Peru, Colombia, Venezuela, and to some extent Mexico remain wide open to European immigration, but seek it mainly from Spain and Mediterranean Europe generally.

This dissemination of Europeans has had long-standing, profound, and far-reaching consequences in every aspect of civilisation. It has given to the new countries European cultivated plants and domestic animals, it has created vast currents of trade over the world, and, lastly, by its example and the material power with which it has begun to endue the coloured races, it has stimulated these peoples, especially those in Asia.

Emigration from the British Isles.—As early as the end of the sixteenth century the first crisis leading to migration occurred in England; it was provoked by the progress of the enclosure movement and the substitution of pasture for ploughland. This in turn was engendered by the rise of the woollen industry; and the enclosure of common land, and the formation of large farms at the expense of the little village holdings, were other aspects of it. The first sparsely peopled territory to receive the uprooted labourers was found in Ireland in the reigns of Elizabeth and the Stuarts, and large settlements were made on the land of the Irish septs. Later, room for settlement was found in the New World. As early as Elizabethan times Francis Bacon and Hakluyt were laying down the principles of colonisation. In the seventeenth century permanent settlement began. In 1606 the London and Plymouth Companies took emigrants not only from religious sects, but also from other groups who were leaving England on account of the economic conditions. By 1643 permanent settlements had been made at Plymouth in Massachusetts and at Newhaven in Connecticut, and by 1688 English settlements on the Atlantic coasts of America contained more than 200,000 inhabitants.

Later, emigration slackened until the middle of the eighteenth century, when the Industrial Revolution began and changed the material conditions of the farm workers. With the decline of the old systems of rotation there appeared a method of intensive cultivation which required more capital. Small holdings became absorbed in large farms, and a number of crises in agriculture, like that in the winter of 1709, finally snapped the bonds that tied the labourers to the soil. The results of the economic revolution all had their chief effects in England. About 1820 an exodus followed the restoration of peace, the consequent fall in the price of corn, and a resumption of the enclosure movement. Another exodus began about 1870 when the competition of new countries ruined the home market for corn and led to unemployment among the labourers. Following on this, every advance in the use of machinery struck at home industry. An enquiry in 1841 reported on the need to help weavers, who were unemployed owing to the increased use of mechanical looms, to emigrate to the Continent or to the New World. English emigrants formed the main body of the exodus from the British Isles and until about 1900 were one-third or one-half of it.

In Scotland the two natural regions of very different economy, the Highlands and Lowlands, have both joined in the stream of emigration. An exodus took place from the barren Highlands as early as the mid-eighteenth century. Its causes acted either one after the other or both simultaneously. Between 1763 and 1775 the ruin of the farmers and the bailiffs of large estates sent more than 30,000 persons to eastern Canada and New England. The farmers, or 'tacksmen', could no longer play the part of recruiting agents for the big landowners and chiefs of clans or endure the raising of farm rents due to the feudatories' growing need of money. They set off for America together with large bodies of labourers who had previously worked on properties managed by them. Such was the case of the Grants, Stewarts, and Macdonalds.

After 1786 emigration drew on a new source. This was the class of wretchedly poor crofters, whose condition had grown steadily worse, owing to the tendency to early marriage leading to a high birth-rate. At the same time the end of inter-clan wars and the gradual disappearance of smallpox caused an astonishing over-population of these barren lands. There were scarcely one or two acres to a family in a damp climate and with uncertain crops. Hence the departure between 1783 and 1820 from Inverness, Ross, and the Hebrides of 25,000 persons who had listened to agents of shipping companies. Between 1790 and 1795 the introduction of the Cheviot breed of sheep and the arrival from the Lowlands of farmers who set up large farms with immense sheepwalks led to the eviction of many little tenants. Some moved to the coast, but the new life was precarious, and they therefore decided to leave their country for good. The exodus became so great as to be frightening, and efforts were made to keep these poor people from going abroad.

Another crisis which occurred between 1820 and 1860 affected people who made a living by coastwise fishing and by gathering seaweed for making soda. The consequent migration almost wholly depopulated the Western Isles and even affected the glens. Argyll, which had had a population of more than 100,000 in 1831, had only 76,000 in 1880. There came a moment at the end of the nineteenth century when Highlanders no longer suffered from the agrarian system or from the extension of large pasture lands. But the poverty of the crofters planted in their minds the hope of better things overseas or in England. So the exodus went on up to our own times because the crofters have had too low a standard of living. Emigra-tion was directed less towards the mines and the industrial firms in Glasgow than towards America, Australia, and New Zealand.

Unlike the Highlands with their pastoral life and barren soil, the Lowlands form a region of fertile cultivation and an industrial mode of life. But they are not free from emigration. From the end of the eighteenth century craftsmen went off, and the exodus grew year by year between 1820 and 1830, when it was swelled by workmen from the Clyde and weavers from the western counties. Then, too, the introduction of spinning and weaving machines had led to frightful poverty among farm workers, and these fled to Glasgow, where efforts were made to organise their emigration and to sub-sidise their voyage. From 1880 onwards the desire to emigrate reached the northeastern districts where agricultural labourers saw their wages threatened by the introduction of machinery and the increase in pasture land. In the same districts the most far-seeing crofters were attracted to Canada, where they were sure of being able to have farms of their own. This led to an exodus of the cream of the farmers from Aberdeenshire, Banffshire, and Morayshire.

The emigration of industrial workers from the Lowlands began to take place by 1912, and this proved most damaging to the country. Unfortunately, the departure of many skilled workers from metallurgical centres on the Clyde, mechanical engineering shops, and shipyards went on until just before the second world war. In 1923 alone 27,000 skilled workers left, three-fourths of them going to the United States. The industries hit hardest by this emigration were those that had suffered most from unemployment. The movement would probably have increased still more after 1934, had not the quota regulations partly shut the gate to entry to the United States. On the whole, Scotland has always been regarded as a nursery of emigrants. About 1851 Australia appealed to the Scots to help in increasing the rearing of wool sheep, and the most dogged squatters were recruited. Later, the Scots furnished the boldest pioneers in northwestern America, and they were largely responsible for the opening up of the Otago region of New Zealand's South Island.

Emigration from Ireland also began well before the nineteenth century. As early as the seventeenth century many Irishmen took refuge in Roman Catholic countries like France and Spain. It was only at the beginning of the nineteenth century, however, that economic conditions led to great emigration. Since early in the seventeenth century there had been a colony of Scottish Presbyterians, all good farmers, who could in addition spin and weave flax. The colony was reinforced year by year with newcomers. Now, during the eighteenth ceutury there was emigration from this colony to America partly because of persecution by the Anglican Church (1728), partly owing to poor harvests, and partly because of the decline of home industry (1771). Irish emigrants across the ocean were therefore neither Roman Catholics nor peasants overwhelmed by rents, but Scotch-Irish, little artisans and farmers, who came from the North and were mainly Protestants. Up to about 1841 emigration carried off hardly more than 30,000 persons. It was after that year that the great emigration of the mid-nineteenth century was launched.

This great exodus was due firstly to an extrordinary increase in the population of Ireland, which rose from 4 million in 1788 to 8 million in 1841. But one-third of the island is barren, a second third is under pasture, and on the third available for cultivation the density of population rose from 83 per square kilometre in 1750 to 165 in 1801, and 250 in 1841, an enormous figure for a rural people practising an extensive system of cultivation. In the face of this increase landlords had been forced to cut up their estates into a great number of farms or holdings. Then from 1820 onwards a change from arable to pasture forced the tenants to crowd together on smaller and smaller holdings. The overpopulation of the countryside was particularly noticeable in the west, where many peasants were landless and even workless. According to the report of the Devon Commission, 585,000 labourers were unemployed for thirty weeks in the year. These indigent millions lived on potatoes, and a bad harvest together with higher prices for their meagre food meant famine for the whole country. Now, there were three almost successive poor harvests in 1845, 1846, and 1848. This was the start of frightful poverty and of a vast exodus, a real flood of emigrants, which in some years carried off more than a third of the population.

Rate of Emigration from Ireland

	Emigrants
1846–51	1,240,000
1851–61	1,150,000
1861–71	770,000
1871–81	620,000
1881–91	770,000

On the whole, between 1850 and 1900 more than four million people left the island. The check on the movement which began in 1885 was due to the depopulation of the island, to a dizzy fall in the birth-rate, and, lastly, to agrarian reforms that relieved the congestion of the countryside and lowered the pressure of population. The reconstitution in the hands of a single owner of property that had been dismembered enabled better holdings to be formed and home industries to be carried on. After 1890 the number of emigrants scarcely ever exceeded 30,000 ot 40,000 persons a year.

By the twentieth century, nevertheless, Ulster had lost 33 per cent of its population, Leinster 41 per cent, Munster 55 per cent, and Connaught 57 per cent. A small fraction of these emigrants went to Glasgow, Liverpool, or Manchester; but 90 per cent went to the United States, mainly to New York or Chicago. By 1900 there were nearly 10 million Irish people in the United States, all very attached to the 'auld counthrie', to which they sent back a great deal of money. In this way emigration has had far-reaching consequences for the Irish people. Unlike many other countries from which there has been much emigration, the empty spaces left in Ireland have not been filled naturally, and real loss of population has resulted. At the present time Northern Ireland and Eire together have a population of only 4,300,000.

Emigration from the British Isles as a whole represents the greatest swarm of mankind that has ever crossed the sea. In round figures more than 17 million persons left the islands between 1815 and 1926, the greatest movements taking place as follows:

Between 1851 and 1860, 2,287,000 emigrants
„ 1851 „ 1890, 2,558,000 „
„ 1901 „ 1910, 2,840,000 „

After 1920 numbers fell off and amounted to scarcely 300,000 persons a year, 40 per cent of whom returned to Britain at the end of a few years or even a few months.

This steady flood of emigration has not diminished the population of Britain, where an excess of births over deaths has constantly kept up the total and even increased it. The population increased from 27,500,000 persons in 1853 to 40,500,000 in 1900 and rose to 55,346,551 in 1971. The occurrence at the same time of great emigration and a steady increase in population demonstrates the wonderful vitality of the British peoples, for whom emigration has never appeared an impoverishment. The advertisements of agencies and the direction of upbringing in the family have created psychological conditions which have ensured the ubiquity of the British and the formation of large overseas colonies by them.

Apart from North America, where in 1760 there were already 2 million British, the temperate lands of the southern hemisphere have become for the most part peopled by British peoples. In addition to liberty these countries offered immigrants facilities for acquiring land and the opportunity of living as in the Mother Country with the same cereals and domestic animals. At certain times the new countries have made a strong appeal owing to their gold mines, as did California in 1848, Australia in 1851, New Zealand in 1861, and South Africa in 1888. Broadly speaking, British settlers have peopled four large areas.

The first of these, the United States, which about 1770 had a total population of only 2,312,000 in all the English colonies, were shut in along the Atlantic coast, being separated from the interior by a barrier of wooded mountains. British immigration brought the energy needed to force open the gates to the west. Between 1820 and 1870 more than half the immigrants had come from Britain, and between 1870 and 1900 more than a third of the newcomers to the United States were from the British Isles. Later, the Anglo-Saxon element tended to lose its purity owing to the infiltration of elements from southern and eastern Europe. But in fact the American nation assimilates foreign elements easily, thanks to the established influence of the Anglo-Saxon element and of the English language.

In Canada settlement was less rapid owing to the colder climate and poorer prospects. The population rose from 582,000 persons in 1825 to 1,840,000 in the mid-nineteenth century, to 8,400,000 in 1920, and to 18,085,000 in 1961. Emigration to Canada did not begin until nearly the end of the nineteenth century after the simultaneous development of steamship lines and railways and after the cultivation of the grain lands of the West and generous offers of concessions of land. In 1881 Canada received 60,000 immigrants, in 1912 it received more than 400,000, and it is estimated that in less than ten years 600,000 British people settled in the Canadian Far West.

Colonists were long kept away from Australia by the existence there of convict settlements. But the transportation system ended in the mid-nineteenth century, and almost at once the discovery of gold caused the first gold rush to the continent. Between 1851 and 1861 no fewer than 510,000 settlers entered Australia, in spite of the distance of the country from Britain. The movement slackened after the coming to power of the Australian Labour Party, which introduced economic Malthusianism, the effects of which were to be felt for a long time. Immigration increased slightly after 1905, but the remoteness of this southern land curtailed its numbers. Today there are 13,340,000 persons in the continent, which according to official accounts would need at least 20 million to reach its optimum. The population is of remarkably pure British origin, for until recently it has not suffered the admixtures which characterise the population of the United States, Canada, and South Africa. The case of New Zealand is even more striking, for here, where settlement only began in 1840, about 90 per cent of the 3 million people are of British origin, the remainder being for the most part the native Maoris and immigrant Polynesians.

In South Africa a twofold obstacle, the presence of Boers and Negroes, has stood in the way of British immigration, which has therefore moved very slowly. At the present time there is one white person to four Negroes and one Boer to every two white colonists in a total of 24 million persons in the Republic of South Africa.

The Boers, who are today known as Afrikaners, consist of the descendants of the earliest settlers. They were in the country before the British and are predominantly Dutch, though they include some elements of Huguenot, Polish, Swiss, and Scandinavian blood. These settled during the period of Dutch colonisation and were subject to harsh conditions, including the renunciation of their mother tongues and the forced learning of Dutch. This old language, enriched with English and Bantu words, now forms the Afrikaans spoken by a large proportion of the population. The interior of the country was settled by a die-hard type of colonist, for it was they who in 1815 after the purchase of the Cape of Good Hope by Britain refused to submit to the change of government and trekked inland to found the two Boer republics of the Orange Free State and Transvaal.

The hard-core of Boers is mainly rural and has taken little part in business or in the mining speculation that brought wealth to British settlers. Being sellers of wool, grain, and other agricultural produce, they have always suffered directly from disasters that killed their flocks or destroyed their crops, and from the great economic crises that brought down the price of wheat or wool. Many of the Boer farmers have had to give up their property and sink to competition with Negroes for low-paid jobs on the farms. Afrikaners form the great majority of 'poor whites', whose fate is tragic in a country where labourers do not get a white man's living wage. It is from among these wretched people that come the fiercest nationalists, antidemocrats, racists, and in some cases Anglophobes.

The British form most of the town population. They hold commercial jobs, manage mining or industrial businesses, and occupy the highly qualified professions. As the extreme racialism of the policy of *apartheid* separates them from Britain, to which they remain deeply attached, British South Africans profess increasing liberalism towards the Negroes, from whom they are economically further removed than are their Afrikaner compatriots.

After the second world war the Union had thought of encouraging an even greater immigration of whites than was accepted by Australia. This would have offered a partial solution to the displaced persons problem in Europe, for South Africa offers land, many mineral resources, and opportunities for modern industrial development owing to the economic changes required by the stagnation of diamond and other mining enterprises. Unfortunately, this immigration policy was curtailed by the amount of financial investment it would have involved, since the establishment of a settler had become far more expensive than formerly.

In general, the outward flow that gave rise to the British stock overseas is moving less vigorously today, but it is still maintained by a continually overpopulated Mother Country that is part of a Commonwealth of nations with the same language and civilisation and still able to offer vast open spaces and mineral wealth so far scarcely touched. One of the chief causes of this mighty transference of population, which is unequalled in man's history, was the way land was to be acquired by the settler. British colonisation was distinguished by a system of land holding that ensured the colonists liberty and independence. Instead of being a concession to them, the land became their freehold property. The basic idea was that the soil was valueless without the man who made it valuable. In return every piece of land should be occupied by a settler, for, if the land were granted to someone who did not work it, colonisation would be merely speculation without human settlement.

In Australia from 1830 onwards the Wakefield regulations laid down that land should be sold publicly at a price high enough to cut out those who for want of capital would have been able to make little use of it. The money from the sales was placed on a special account intended to subsidise immigration, paying for the settler's voyage. The price of £1 per acre was high enough to force new-comers to get the necessary cash only after several years of saving and after having worked for established owners. Between 1830 and 1850 more than 220,000 immigrants reached Australia. Many of them were never able to buy land, but went to work in mines, factories, or sheep farms. In 1851 out of 14·7 million hectares in the then Province of Victoria squatters held more than 12 million. After 1870 laws were passed to break up the enormous sheep farms and forbid their reconstitution.

In Canada the land laws show the same tendencies as in the United States, where the possession of land came easily. The Homestead Act of 1862 laid down the principle of a concession of land to the settler to the extent of a parcel of 160 acres (65 hectares), of which he was to become the owner at the end of three years after having carried out the preparatory work and cultivation. Other Acts ensured loans for carrying out the work. Besides, the big railway companies, the C.P.R. and C.N.R., had acquired vast acres of good wheat-land, which they let at moderate rates. Hence, immigrants were attracted and there developed a class of little landowners which steadily increased. Then, by a system of concessions or else of sales, British policy of land tenure has always aimed at drawing population to a country by guaranteeing freehold ownership of the land to the settler. In these virtually uninhabited countries the most valuable capital was the settler and his family, by whom the land was tilled and made more valuable.

This policy explains why Britain has succeeded in diverting her stream of emigrants from the United States to the countries of the British Commonwealth, where an increase in population was always desirable. As early as the end of the first world war the Overseas Settlement Committee sent many demobilised soldiers to the dominions and colonies, a step aimed at strengthening British trade and at relieving unemployment at home. On their side the overseas lands were glad to have British rather than foreign immigrants, though they wanted farm workers especially, and this class of worker was scarce in Britain and no longer emigrated.

Consequently, in spite of all the favourable factors which might have ensured it a long life, emigration from Britain has gradually lessened owing to other factors that were destined to become more and more important with time. But the rise in the birth-rate, despite full employment and the Welfare State, may yet cause the rate to rise again in the future.

Emigration from Germany.—Germany, too, was a prolific source of teeming population which throughout the Middle Ages was restricted to intracontinental migrations and contributed greatly to the occupation and colonisation of central Europe, but she did not enter on transoceanic emigration till the seventeenth century. The first German colonists, who were recruited by Dutch and Swedish traders, set off to the Hudson River and Delaware regions. But a previous movement involving greater numbers was due to a series of religious causes. About 1677 the preaching of William Penn and other Quakers in the Rhineland produced a few emigrants who founded German settlements at Germantown near Philadelphia and others in Maryland and Pennsylvania. Later came the Mennonites and other non-conformists like the Moravian Brothers. From 1850 onwards a great wave of emigration began owing to the poverty of the countryfolk. Throughout the Rhineland and the Palatinate there was excessive subdivision of land, and the peasants were overwhelmed by taxation. Very soon the movement spread to the neighbouring countries of Swabia, Baden, Wurtemberg, and Switzerland. The emigrants were taken in boats down the Rhine and across the ocean in Dutch and English ships. Between 1727 and 1775 nearly 70,000 Germans landed in America and settled mainly in the county of Lancaster in Pennsylvania, where the Great Valley was wholly colonised by hard-working peasants. About 1766 there were more than 200,000 Germans in the American colonies.

Throughout the nineteenth century and up to about 1900 German emigrants came from among the countryfolk. They went in complete families to seek a new home overseas. At first they consisted of small landowners in Hesse, the Rhenish provinces of Prussia, the Palatinate, and the Neckar valley. These people were unable to make a living from their small properties and so sold their land to big landowners. A disease in the potato crop spread the movement to Munster. Then came the turn of little tenant farmers who could not acquire land of their own and were under the direction of stewards. This movement began in Bavaria, Hanover, and Mecklenburg. Lastly, the exodus spread to landless agricultural labourers such as the *haverlingen* in Hanover and Oldenburg and the *einliger* in the two Lippes. Nearly everywhere these labourers were paid in kind and they could very seldom find work during the whole year on the same farm. Furthermore, in eastern Germany they competed with Slav labourers who worked for lower wages.

Industrial workers scarcely appeared in the stream of emigration before the twentieth century. Immediately after the war of 1914–18 some scientists left the country at a time when the German economic system was in great straits. Later, Hitler's persecution hastened the emigration of liberals, Jews, and communists just when that of peasants and artisans was stopped. The diversity of causes explains why the various German provinces did not all add to the list of emigrants at the same time. Generally speaking, the centre of gravity of emigration moved slowly from the southwest to west, to north, and to east. During the eighteenth century and at the beginning of the twentieth the southwestern province of Swabia and the Palatinate yielded the greatest number. Then after 1820 the Rhineland provinces of Westphalia, Hesse, and Oldenburg lost streams of people until the flow was checked by the rise of the great Rhineland industries. Lastly came the provinces to the east of the Elbe, which were not affected until after 1850, but sent off enormous contingents between 1870 and 1900.

On the whole, the course of emigration was regular up to about 1850, but was not numerous, consisting on an average of 20,000 persons a year. There were three great waves between 1850 and 1854 (654,000), between 1865 and 1869 (580,000), and between 1880 and 1884 (864,000). After 1890, on the contrary, the flow slackened appreciably, for with the attraction of industrial centres emigration became a mere internal displacement, and the emigrants from the eastern provinces went to the Rhineland and Westphalia.

The main body of German emigrants made for the United States to the number of 6 or 7 million people. At the present time more than three-fourths of the emigrants from Germany still go to the United States, and German technicians have played an important

Summary of German Transoceanic Emigration

	Emigrants
1815–70	2,993,000
1871–93	2,292,000
1894–1914	683,900
1914–27	445,000

part in the development of American heavy industry. More recently they have been leaders in atomic industry and in attempts to conquer space.

A large number of Germans also went to settle in Brazil. They showed a preference for the southern states with a more temperate climate, and there they established centres of Germanic society in Santa Catarina and Río Grande do Sul. Unlike British immigrants the Germans only very exceptionally form colonies of settlement, but as a rule are assimilated into the population of the new country, in spite of repeated efforts of German Governments to preserve the original nationality of these immigrants. Though not so numerous as the emigrants from the British Isles, the Germans have nevertheless maintained the prosperity of the ports of Bremen and Hamburg, from which have embarked millions of Germans, and later, owing to the activity of emigration agencies, that still exist, millions of Europeans from the centre and east of the continent.

Emigration from Italy.—Emigrants from Italy have consisted of agricultural labourers from a proletariat that is permanently overpopulated owing to an excessive birth-rate. In many parts of Italy the number of people seems too great for the resources of the country. In the south especially, where the climate restricts food production, overpopulation is a formidable problem. The south devotes a large part of its acreage to wheat, which is the basic food crop and one from which the peasants get their bread directly. But the harvests are uncertain owing to the irregular rainfall. Though the south has taken to cultivating vines and orchard fruit, these crops are very local and restricted in area.

The effects of too great density of population are increased by the agrarian system. In regions where there are small holders, as in the Marches, the land is excessively subdivided. In the north, the Marches, and in Tuscany the land is divided between *métayer* farms worked by tenants. Large farms are divided on the *métayer* system into portions of between only one and 15 hectares and are too small for a numerous family and leased by the owner on too onerous conditions. Lastly, the regions where there are *latifundia* contain many agricultural labourers, *braccianti*, who are numerous in Latium, Basilicata, Calabria, and Sicily. Big estates are worked on extensive systems and by alternating pasture with cereal crops in order to counter drought and allow for fallow. Consequently, there is little work for the *braccianti* on the badly cultivated fields. The peasants are crowded together like factory hands in veritable towns, in which there is often a shortage of water. Yet it was only after the last quarter of the nineteenth century that the volume of emigration increased.

After 1921, owing to legal restrictions on entry into the United

Rate of Italian Emigration

	Emigrants
1876	108,000
1900	352,000
1908	405,000
1914	559,000
1921	450,000

States, Italian overseas emigration greatly diminished. In 1920 there were only 211,000 emigrants and fewer than 135,000 in 1927. Since the end of the second world war the stream of emigration has not recovered its importance. Two parts of Italy were the chief contributors to emigration. In the southern provinces of Abruzzi, Campania, Apulia, Basilicata, and Calabria and in Sicily and Sardinia the movement amounted almost to depopulation. Calabria, Basilicata, and Apulia alone despatched 1,800,000 emigrants between 1876 and 1921, and some parts of Basilicata were deserted. The Reggio district suffered all the more because it lost its strongest and most hard-working men. The northern provinces of Piedmont, Liguria, Lombardy, and Venezia never sent many emigrants overseas, but contributed to intracontinental migration. Italian emigration followed two main directions, to the United States and to South America, but, owing to economic circumstances, the flow was unequally divided. Thus in 1888 12 per cent went to the United States, 33 per cent to Brazil, and 23 per cent to La Plata. In 1927 the proportion was 28 per cent to the United States and 52 per cent to the Argentine.

Between 1880 and 1914 Italians to the number of four million went to the United States, many of them for a time only. They settled mainly in the towns in the east, where they swelled the urban proletariat and the always overcrowded little crafts and petty offices. That explains why since 1921 this immigration was considered undesirable in the United States, and in fact the quota law restricted the number of Italian immigrants to 40,000 or 50,000 a year. Since 1880 more than 2,500,000 Italians have entered Argentina where they engage in cereal cultivation and viticulture. Some 1,500,000 went to Brazil, where they settled in the agricultural States of Minas Geraes, Río de Janeiro, and São Paulo, in which last they number more than 80,000. In Paraná and Santa Catarina they work little farms that carry corn crops and vineyards.

On the whole, overseas emigration has established outside Italy nearly ten million Italians, close on nine million of whom are in America. For many years this swarm has been renewed fairly quickly, for the emigrants seldom set off without meaning to return home. Money earned abroad has been carefully put away or sent to Italy so as in due course to be used for buying land and forming a little family property. In this way, overseas emigration like emigration to nearby countries on the continent, has been a means of re-establishment in the countryside which the emigrants had had to leave under the spur of poverty. This type of emigration has established no nuclei of Europeans in the rest of the world. It is an emigration to seek work and not to colonise and is quite different from the emigration from the British Isles and even from Germany.

Asiatic Emigration.—Three parts of Asia show a high density of population. These are India, China, and Japan, all monsoon lands with intensive cultivation and great rice production. But in spite of their vast agricultural production, great crowds of people exist at starvation level, and are only too anxious to emigrate. For them emigration overseas is not a practice of long standing, but has been facilitated by modern means of transport, as it was in Europe. It must be emphasised, however, that these means of transport were not in the hands of Asiatics, who, with the exception of the Japanese were dependent on European and American shipping companies. Furthermore, emigration became easy for Asiatics only after European colonisation had introduced modes of life that gave work and high yields. Plantations and factories created by Europeans became fields of activity and emigration for Asiatics. These limitations explain why Asiatic emigration had neither the importance nor the effects of European emigration.

Asiatic emigrants naturally went to places that were sparsely peopled or lacked unskilled labour. The emancipation of Negro slaves had created centres of attraction in certain parts of the tropics, especially on sugar plantations. Hence the migration of Indians to some of the Pacific islands (Fiji), Mauritius, the West Indies, and Guiana; and of Chinese and Japanese to Hawaii and a little later of Chinese to the rubber plantations in Malaya. They also made their way to countries settled by whites so as to find work chiefly in mines. The centres of attraction spread round the Pacific have seen Chinese and Japanese arrive in growing numbers in Peru, California, Chile, and elsewhere since the steamship came into general use.

Emigration from India.—The population of India is extraordinarily dense in some parts and exceeds the capacity of the land to feed it even in other parts that are less crowded, but poorer. Undernourishment is traditional and becomes intolerable during the frequent famines. Yet the peasants are attached to their villages often by religious or social ties, so that for a long time emigration was considered to be the worst of misfortunes or even as a sacrilege. It was started by Europeans to suit their own purposes. Sugarcane plantations needed coolies, and some important kinds of work in various parts of the tropics require acclimatised labour. Indians are hard-working, eager to make money, live on little, are satisfied with low wages, and are wretchedly poor in their own country. They are therefore marked out for emigration, and many gangs of them began to be sent to the various sugar islands and to parts of Africa and tropical America.

The first gang of Indian coolies sailed in 1815. It consisted of convicts transported from Calcutta to Mauritius, which became a real training ground for coolie labour on the sugar plantations. After 1834 many free workers were attracted by the climate, which is like that of India. Today, out of a total population of 500,000 persons there are more than 300,000 Indians on the island. A big colony of about 5,000 Indians exists in Réunion, another sugar island.

In Africa where Indians had traded in the train of Arab merchants with the help of the alternating monsoon winds, their immigration began on the day when labour was needed to establish plantations and to construct railways. Then the labourers were soon followed by other social elements such as traders, little shopkeepers, money-lenders, and usurers. What were in the end the largest and most deeply rooted Indian colonies were formed in this way in Natal, Kenya, and Uganda.

Indians in Africa (c. 1950)

Indians		Percentage of Population
Kenya	91,000	2
Uganda	26,000	0·5
Natal	230,000	11
Rest of the Union of South Africa	70,000	0·6

Unfortunately, after the second world war, decolonisation and the creation of separate independent African states in East Africa, have been followed by the expulsion of many of the Indian immigrants, who have suffered, like the white colonists, for being foreigners. Africa is now virtually closed to Indian immigration.

Indians began to reach the West Indies about 1840. Their number was greatest in British Guiana and Trinidad, where there are 180,000 and 200,000 respectively. They have also settled in Jamaica, Martinique, and Guadeloupe in small numbers, but homogeneous groups. In Fiji they first arrived in 1874. Today they number nearly 250,000 and form more than half the population.

At first Indian emigrants were mere coolies engaged by professional recruiting agents, but the Emigration Act of 1922 enabled emigration to be controlled by the Government of India. Then, at the invitation of relatives or friends emigrants freely and voluntarily followed in the track of former indentured labour, and little Indian communities sprang up everywhere with their tradesmen, craftsmen, and in some places their priests and temples.

Altogether emigration has established overseas more than 2½ million Indians. The movement was numerous enough at the end of the nineteenth century for steps to be taken by the colonies to restrict it. This was particularly so in Natal and Kenya. But doors remained wide open to the tea plantations in Ceylon and the rubber plantations in Malaya. In Ceylon, in 1960, there were 1½ million Indians in a total population of 9 million, and there were 650,000 in Malaya out of a total population of 6 million. Most of these overseas emigrants came from the Madras Presidency, where large inland areas are dry and suffer from uncertain harvests, where local industry has had its greatest decline, and where the burden of the land system is made heavier by usury. The overpopulated parts of the Central Provinces sent most of their emigrants to Assam and Burma, where nearly two million have settled.

Emigration from China.—Pressure of population in China has always been great in Shantung, Kiangsi, Kiangsu, and Fokien, where the area of land holdings was too small to support a family. Unlike the Indians, the Chinese are less tied to their land and are more mobile. Owing to the climates in their own country, they have the advantage of being acclimatised in both the temperate and tropical belts. Consequently, Chinese emigration alone achieves ubiquity comparable with that of Europeans and must be regarded as a matter of world importance. Chinese have formed deeply rooted colonies in eastern Siberia, California, South America, and throughout Southeast Asia. They are found in Africa, including Madagascar, and on the whole more than ten million Chinese live out of China.

Not only are the Chinese willing to go abroad, they also adapt themselves very quickly to new surroundings. At first, they may undertake all sorts of jobs, sometimes the rough, unskilled toil of coolies, at other times engaging in trade, whether as humble shop-keepers or as big merchants and shipowners. In this way the Chinese constitute the framework of Far Eastern trade, and none of the peoples of Southeast Asia can do without them.

The Chinese spread first of all to the Pacific lands: the United States (60,000), Canada (12,000), Australia (35,000), Peru (45,000), and Hawaii (25,000). Wherever they went, they undertook the heavy work of mining: nitrate in Chile, guano in the Peruvian islands, and gold (and later railway building) in California. They have also gone to tropical lands in Brazil (20,000), East Africa, the West Indies, and the islands in the Indian Ocean, where they work mainly on sugarcane plantations. But they have always been most numerous in the Philippines and Southeast Asia, where they work as planters, miners, coolies, workers in sugar- or rice-mills, dock labourers, barbers, cooks, gardeners, shopkeepers, and money-changers. Some even go into big business. There are more than 170,000 in the Philippines and at least 1½ million in Indonesia. These adaptable immigrants swarm in Burma (200,000), Thailand (2 million), Malaysia (2,200,000), and in the States of eastern Indo-China,

FIG. 11.—AN EXAMPLE OF EMIGRATION: DISTRIBUTION OF CHINESE EMIGRANTS IN SOUTH-EAST ASIA, ABOUT 1950

where they total nearly 1½ million. Hard-working, honest in trade, with a flair for business, and law-abiding in their new homes, Chinese immigrants have long been regarded as valuable helpers. However, economic crises consequent on the abandonment of gold mines and the competition with which the immigrants faced white workers gradually made the yellow men undesirable, and in 1907 the State of California, followed closely by Canada, Australia, and New Zealand made very severe restrictive laws limiting the entry of the Chinese into White communities in the Pacific. Since 1949 and the proclamation of the People's Republic of China, the flow of Chinese emigration has practically dried up, and the numbers of overseas Chinese now increase only by natural growth, in whatever part of the world they are found. The emigration of Chinese to the new republics of Africa that are politically sympathetic to communism is limited to small contingents of technicians. It may be estimated that at present rather less than six million Chinese live outside China; but to this total must be added the 14 millions living in Taiwan, making 20 millions in all.

Emigration from Japan.—The Japanese islands have always been overpopulated and it is certain that the infanticide of baby girls and the restrictions placed on births before the fourteenth century were primitive ways of countering a too rapid growth of the population. Japan seems to have found temporary equilibrium from the fourteenth to the sixteenth century, when it would appear that the yield from its soil was sufficient for a time. Even in 1638 the Government of the Shogun forbad people to leave the islands on pain of death and prohibited the building of sea-going junks by private persons. This restriction by the authorities was to help to create in the Japanese mind a dislike for emigration that was difficult to overcome in after years.

After 1868, when Japan entered upon relations with other nations, foreign business men tried to engage Japanese labour for their overseas lands. A feeling of hostility had been shown towards the Chinese in the American Pacific States, and it was thought at the time that the Japanese might not arouse the same prejudice. Very soon emigration was monopolised by Japanese steamship companies and regulated by the Government. A special department received both the applications and offers of business men, drew up lists of departures, and intervened in the contracts between employers and emigrants. The latter kept their status as Japanese citizens and on reaching their destination remained under the more or less discreet, but effective supervision of diplomatic representatives from Tokyo. Under such control Japanese emigration remained fairly small, and between 1885 and 1897 only 102,000 emigrants were registered. These rose to 30,000 a year about 1911 and exceeded 43,000 in 1914. After this these figures were seldom reached again, at least in overseas directions.

About 1930, when emigration proceeded at a regular rate, the emigrants went mainly in two directions : northwards to Hokkaido, Karafuto, Korea, and Manchuria ; and southwards to the tropics in Formosa and the Philippines, to Hawaii, and, outside the Pacific, Brazil. Since the beginning of the century indeed the lands of white settlement in the Pacific—the United States, Canada, and Australia —had shut their gates to Japanese as well as to Chinese immigration in consequence of serious politico-racial breaches of the peace in California. What the whites mainly complained about in the Japanese was, besides their competition in the labour market, their settlement in the country as tenants or owners and their resistance to assimilation. Restrictions on the immigration of yellow peoples which began in 1907 were steadily increased until in 1924 they practically reached complete prohibition following the quota laws. At this time there were scarcely more than 110,000 Japanese permanently settled in the United States ; but they were far more numerous in Hawaii, to which they went from 1886 onwards, first as labourers under contract and then after 1900 as free workers. By 1903 they formed two-thirds of the population of the islands, monopolised retail business and petty crafts, and set up as planters of coffee, bananas, and pineapples. In 1939 they numbered 140,000, though entry to the islands had been closed since 1924. Their colony increased slowly by the excess of births over deaths, and in 1970, with 200,000, still represented two-fifths of the population. The restrictions had a strong influence on Japanese policy, but the end of the second world war has not got rid of the obstacles placed in the way of Japanese who wish to emigrate.

Of the two directions taken by the streams of Japanese emigration the one that went southwards to tropical lands proved the more fruitful. Yet officially the Government urged the emigrants mainly towards the north. This was chiefly for political reasons. In spite of big grants of land, few of the colonists stayed in Hokkaido, for its climate was not suitable for the warm country crops familiar to the Japanese. The Government wished to plant large parties of settlers in Korea, but the country was already overpopulated and could hardly receive settlers on its rice plains. To all appearance prospects seemed for a moment to be better in Manchuria, which is a land of grass plains and was still given up to the pastoral mode of life. There well regulated settlement might find vast areas for cereal crops. Up to 1930 the country had no more than seven persons to the square kilometre; but in 1932 the Chinese Government authorised the entry of settlers into Manchuria, and as social troubles had devastated northern China, 32 million Chinese descended on the parts nearest to China, that is, on the most fertile on the Manchurian plain. By doing so they forestalled possible Japanese colonists. Even after Japan had wrested Manchuria politically from China, the country could only take 200,000 Japanese, since it had been settled by millions of Chinese.

Emigration southwards to the tropics was more sustained and spontaneous. In a tropical climate the settlers could cultivate their own familiar crops of rice, tea, sugarcane, and cotton. So more than 350,000 Japanese settled in Pacific islands, nearly 250,000 of them going to Formosa (Taiwan). After the second world war, however, the Japanese Government estimated that the rehabilitation of the country's economy, which had been ruined by the defeat, demanded the immediate emigration of 20 million of its nationals at the rate of two million a year. But many countries which were open to Japanese immigration before 1939 were henceforth closed to it. China, for instance, was absolutely closed after the establishment of the Communist system. In the United States for a time some opinion favoured a revision of the restrictive laws, but although backed by the leading Chicago papers, no alteration of the laws resulted.

Before 1939 Brazil had welcomed Japanese settlers. From 1934 onwards, however, economic difficulties had caused unemployment and restrictive laws had been laid down that, since there were 175,000 Japanese in Brazil, only 3,500 a year would be admitted. After the war Japan asked Brazil to take five million of her nationals over 10 or 15 years ; but Brazil did not go back on her decision in 1934. Her objection was in fact that in the sparsely peopled pioneer regions the Japanese would quickly form a majority and would be concentrated in unassimilable groups. Besides, the country was sought after by many nationals of European countries, whose assimilation would be easier, if merely on account of their language.

Lastly, we turn to the tropical lands of Indonesia and the Pacific islands, which could take many more settlers. Indonesian Borneo (Kalimantan) and New Guinea (West Irian) especially, which are still not cleared of forest, have only five million inhabitants, so that 25 or 30 million Japanese could settle in them without exhausting their capacity to take immigrants. The Japanese dream of colonising these islands as completely as the Indians have done in Fiji. But objections of a political order issue from the centres of white settlement in the south, since the formation in their neighbourhood of large centres of yellow colonisation fully supported by active, politically regulated immigration was clearly a menace. The too recent memories of danger run by various nations in Asia and the Pacific owing to Japanese imperialism continues to confine the Japanese to their islands.

To overcome these prejudices the Japanese Government has given up the old system of control and has left emigration to individual enterprise free from state regulation. Future emigrants are urged to renounce Japanese citizenship and assume that of the country in which they settle, as Japanese in the United States have done. They are also urged to devote themselves to agriculture and forestry so as to avoid arousing economic antagonisms in places where national feelings are strong. But this recommendation, which might effectively contribute to making some countries like Brazil, the Argentine, and the African states more willing to accept Japanese settlers, has the result of increasing the natural repugnance of the Japanese to leaving their native land without hope of return and to giving up all their ties with Old Japan.

Asiatic emigration has therefore nothing in common with European emigration, which is on a larger scale, covers greater distances, and is more varied. Furthermore, the Asiatic version has in the past rather curiously superimposed itself on the whites as if it was incapable of organising independently its fields of expansion and of creating *ex nihilo* the technical conditions of a human settlement. Yet gradually these constraints are being relaxed. , Asiatic emigration has now ceased to be the humble servant of European economy and is being organised according to its own methods; but its effectiveness has never been equal to the great need for room felt by the crowds in Far Eastern Asia.

THE PROBLEMS OF OVERPOPULATION

The world's population increases steadily. In less than three hundred years the increase has been fourfold. Some think this an inescapable fact; others hold that there is a population optimum which varies according to the country, the time, and the general state of civilisation and towards which every group of people tends to blunder. In an ideal state of equilibrium everyone would have an income that would enable him to live comfortably while actively producing wealth for the benefit of others. But the flood of population continues to rise, and estimates already picture the future with numbers that are sometimes astronomical and arouse fears of general overpopulation throughout the world and the ruin of mankind by poverty and hunger. Are such problems correctly stated, and more especially can they be so stated by pure theorists, economists, or sociologists of certain schools without reference to solid geographical foundation? Such a problem is far from admitting the dogmatic solutions that are too often put forward.

Up to the Industrial Revolution a country's desirable population was one that came nearest the supportable maximum. This idea was justifiable so long as the total remained constantly at a fairly low level owing to war, disease, epidemic, and famine. Things became quite different when industrial development, which took place in England first of all, had stimulated an increase in population.

In 1798 in his *Essay on the Principles of Population* Thomas Malthus stated the proposition that all human communities tend to multiply faster than their means of subsistence. This idea was new at the time and was appropriate to the economic background of its age, for the Industrial Revolution had brought Britain unprecedented economic prosperity. The very children earned high wages, and consequently families found the source of their income increased. At the same time vaccination against smallpox (first performed by Jenner in 1796) lowered the death-rate, especially among children. Faced with the rapid growth of human capital Malthus thought that he should formulate a law according to which population would double itself every twenty-five years by geometric progression, whilst the means of subsistence according to him would increase only by arithmetical progression. In such conditions the biological equilibrium of the human race could only be maintained if at intervals mankind suffered massive excisions through war or great epidemics. A less catastrophic remedy was to have fewer marriages and effective birth control. These ideas were adopted later by J. Mill and John Stuart Mill in England and J. B. Say in France. The threat of world overpopulation would have been the result of eternal law or the convergence of eternal laws. It must be admitted that the human mind has seldom conceived such an error in the name of science.

The theory was based on the false hypothesis that the rate of population increase remains invariable during an indefinite series of generations. This is denied by evident and well attested irregularities in the rate of increase seen especially in the United States, France, and, at the present time, Japan, to give but a few examples. Thus, Malthus and his disciples did not and could not have the least idea of the discoveries that technology and science would place at the service of material production. They could not foresee that more rapid transport would enable cheap food to be imported from distant lands and that the importation of that food, the production of which did not exist in their time, would increase enormously owing to the facilities for trade and commerce that had arisen in the nineteenth century. Malthus was wrong again in stating that for mankind there was no natural limit to reproduction and fecundity. The whole of the century just past has shown that the intelligence and foresight of more highly developed communities conflict with the instinct of procreation. In fact, the general rise in intellectual level, the break with traditional social patterns, and the raising of the standard of living have worked together almost everywhere to bring about the lowering of the birth-rate. Charles Fourier (a French philosopher and sociologist, 1772–1837) showed greater perspicacity in pointing this out.

Under the influence of English, German, and Swedish economists a more moderate theory was to prevail from the beginning of the twentieth century. According to this there is an ideal and theoretic state of equilibrium which comes about more or less spontaneously and reaches perfection wherever production as a whole affords the maximum return per head of the population. Now, this optimum is not necessarily found in sparsely peopled countries, where the total return can be shared by a few people, for if the fertility of the soil can be improved, if industrial production can be increased so that food can be had in exchange for manufactured goods, and if the value and volume of production can be raised, the material conditions of the optimum may well be attained. But production is not the only thing to be taken into account. Everywhere, indeed, there exist differences in the amount of wealth consumed by human communities and by individuals separately. Of two equally populated countries one may be overpopulated, if it has a high standard of living with great demands for commodities and comfort, whilst the other may not be overpopulated, if its inhabitants have a lower standard of living. So we reach a flexible definition of the idea of overpopulation in which the number of people is not alone to be considered, for their quality must also be taken into account. This qualitative concept, though it does not simplify the problem, certainly brings out all the difficulties more clearly.

By what signs is a country recognised as being overpopulated in relation to its resources? To answer this, a better conception of density should be envisaged. Simple density per square kilometre, which indicates the mean number of persons living on a standard unit of area, is a poor idea, since it takes into account neither the goodness of the soil nor the social condition of the occupants. Physiological density, which bases population density on the square kilometre of cultivable soil, is a more concrete notion, but it does not reckon on sources of food existing outside the cultivable land. Lastly, there is agricultural density, that is, the number of persons living by agriculture on the area concerned. But this is merely an approximation, for the cultivated area contains bits of land of very different value and quality. Besides, they are used by systems of cultivation which are more or less intensive, more or less speculative, and more or less favourable to high yields. The differences are illustrated by a comparison between Dutch and Roumanian agriculture, or between Indian and Japanese methods. Even when improved, the notion of density remains inadequate, therefore, as a definition of overpopulation. It is very difficult to accept such a notion as an economic sign which would take into account all the activities and conditions indispensable to life.

It should not be thought that a country which suffers from unemployment, as do Europe and the United States, is overpopulated because it confesses itself unable to feed its people. In industrial countries unemployment is not necessarily a proof of overpopulation. For instance, in the days of the great crises before the second world war unemployment in America was attributable to the economic system rather than to an increase in population. Unemployment was indeed not equally great in all parts of the countries. Although as a whole the United States are underpopulated, there were some rural communities which during the crises were at the lowest limit of poverty and distress. Similarly, though France was a centre of attraction for foreigners before the war, some of her industries suffered from unemployment due to an economic system unfavourable to exports and not to an excessive population in the industrial districts. In the same way emigration is not a sure sign of excessive demographic pressure. In fact, the demographic coefficient as defined by natural increase per unit of area is far greater in the Netherlands, where there is less emigration, than in Ireland, where emigration is common.

To define overpopulation it is not enough to estimate the possibilities of subsistence ; account must also be taken of the standard of living, that is, the whole economic system even in its qualitative elements hand in hand with the degree of civilisation and popular psychology. It is possible to try to determine qualitatively the food resources of a country. Van Heek did this for China and came to the conclusion that five Chinese provinces have lean harvests in relation to their population, but that, if rents and taxes were removed, overpopulation would disappear. That explains the policy followed by the Communist Government of Russia after its accession to power, even before collectivisation of the land was complete.

It is also possible to determine quantitatively the amount of food consumed, and this has been done by Reithinger for several European countries. He distinguished countries with a high standard of living, like Britain, Sweden, France, and Belgium from others like Poland and Roumania with a low standard of living. Thus, there are very advanced countries in which consumption is ample because their population increases little and their methods of production are intensive and complicated. On the other hand, there are countries in which the population total and the backward state of their technique lower the standard of living: 'Children have mouths, but no arms.'

By precise calculation of the elements of material life a better definition of the problem of overpopulation is reached. Yet the number of people and the weight of merchandise are still not enough to define the standard of living. Qualitative and psychological factors intervene to bring out the whole value of the relation between production and consumption. A country feels the effects of the pressure of population when its people realise that their standard of living is too low and conceive the hope of improving it by some casual favourable circumstances. That is why migrations start with special ease when there is plainly visible and perceptible difference in the standard of living in two adjacent countries in easy communication with each other. Overpopulation is therefore often relative and subjective. If there are really overpopulated regions in the world, or if only important fractions of mankind realise that they are suffering from overpopulation, what remedies can be applied?

It is certain that production can still be both greatly extended and improved. There are still extensive areas to be brought under a suitable form of cultivation—which may perhaps be quite different from the recognised systems. Such areas exist in Australia, the

Argentine, Canada, the United States, Africa, and eastern Asia. Besides, crops can be changed and yields increased everywhere. The mere adoption of hybrid species enabled the yield from maize to be increased three- and four-fold without any further modification in the system of cultivation. Scientific agriculture has still not paid sufficient attention to food plants like cassava, yam, and taro, whose production depends on primitive techniques and whose uses might be increased. For instance, soya, the cultivation of which has steadily spread, especially in the United States, testifies that agriculture has not yet exhausted all its possibilities of increasing mankind's supplies of food in the most unexpected proportions. Hands, manure, and a good deal of science suffice for this development.

Overpopulation can also be checked by establishing industrial centres or by the industrialisation of country districts that are too exclusively rural. That is how Germany, Italy, and, more recently, Japan reabsorbed part of their emigrants. The remedy may, however, not be lasting. Industrialisation may in fact provoke a further increase in population that will destroy the margin of wellbeing accruing to the masses owing to the increase in industrial resources. This has actually happened in Japan, where the rate of demographic increase has kept in step with the development in industry and the rise in wages. Then, again, Arthur Young's account of the French countryside in the eighteenth century and especially of the Pays de Caux and Picardy show that the industrialisation of the countryside may by the attraction of high wages draw away the countryfolk from tilling the soil and bring about a great deterioration in agriculture and agricultural production in the places industrialised, where excellent land will run to waste. It was noticed in Japan that the yield from cultivated land fell off when industrial centres close by led peasants to seek work in the factories, since this complementary activity gradually took the place of the main function and ended on the whole in decreasing the country's potential food supply. The same result has been observed in industrial districts in France; as, for instance in Lower Alsace or some cantons in Lorraine, where the peasant factory hands form a class of workers insufficiently qualified for industry and having little skill in working the land. Industrialisation is therefore a ticklish and even dangerous remedy if it is to be used systematically wherever overpopulation makes its appearance.

At all events one of the factors favourable to the reabsorption of excess population in any region is the establishment of active relations with the rest of the world. Overpopulation becomes perceptible and intolerable especially at times when international trade is slackened by political events or has suffered from an unfavourable economic contingency. Some countries with a long-standing civilisation no longer live on the produce of their soil. They are no longer regions of subsistence, but merely dwelling places. Their existence depends on world trade, which enables the international division of labour to function. Freedom of markets is a *sine qua non* for the wellbeing of all mankind. The setting up of autarkies and authoritative systems, whatever their origin and forms, fosters—in some cases artificially—the unpalatable features of overpopulation. It is characteristic of economic systems that they start cumulative processes that may end in explosive situations leading to the very great dangers that have at all times threatened mankind.

As emigration ceases more and more to be a practical way of relieving differences of pressure between countries and especially at the present time between the peoples with an old material civilisation and those who are underdeveloped, political views in the second third of the twentieth century have come to advocate a new distribution of the world between the various nations in proportion to their total population and their energetic power. But from this arose the theory of *Lebensraum*, which was one of the causes of the second world war. Others have advocated a better distribution of wealth among the nations so that each may have access to indispensable raw materials and draw from surpluses wasted or destroyed uselessly in areas of overproduction. In this way an idea of the interdependence of nations in dealing with the problem of overpopulation is taking shape within the framework of present-day mercantilist organisation.

At the same time there has appeared to some extent everywhere in really overpopulated countries a tendency to check demographic increase by restricting the number of births. These neo-Malthusian trends and the more or less spontaneous practice of birth control aim at reaching as soon as possible in new countries the equilibrium established in most parts of Europe during the twentieth century, when a decrease in birth-rate accompanied an increase in comfort and a rise in the standard of living. Yet theories claiming that the population must not be allowed to increase are probably only of relative and passing value. Apart from the calculations and generalisations of demographers who are too satisfied with extrapolation, it may be said that the growth of population does not follow as regular a curve as might be believed from the general development which includes compensations hiding the vicissitudes of reality. A population graph shows that a nation's demographic movements work discontinuously and spasmodically. Periods of rest or retrogression follow on others of rapid increase. Probably in times of expansion an increase in population may be rapid and perhaps fairly near the Malthusian geometrical progression; but retrogression can be as rapid and take place as fast. The great depopulation of the empires of antiquity, sapped by 'oliganthropy', the disappearance of the pre-Columbian peoples of North America, of some groups of Pacific islanders, and of some Eskimo tribes in our own times; the depopulation of Ireland in the nineteenth century, the rapid fall in the population of France between 1926 and 1939, all show that the phenomenon can be dangerously reversed. It cannot be denied that some countries cannot safely let their population decrease, because a fall is as difficult to stop or to hold within due limits as is a rise. A falling-off of manpower brings on a decline in the international situation and the spirit of enterprise, too little use of technical capital, and, lastly, the impoverishment of mankind. On this subject the vocal advocacy of some economists of a slackening of demographic increase and their exaggerated anxiety concerning human proliferation are the result of a partial view of the problem and forgetfulness of the teaching of history. The worst danger that can threaten the future of the human species would perhaps be an uncontrollable diminution of population rather than a too exuberant proliferation that is momentarily disordered or uncontrollable. Man constitutes wealth in himself, and mankind must learn to use him.

It is possible now, taking into account the incidence of emigration and immigration, natural growth through the excess of births over deaths, and the increasing precision of modern census methods, to draw up a balance sheet of population for the last eighty years, and the following table is probably accurate to within acceptable limits.

Growth of Population Between 1894 and 1974

	1894	1974	Growth (per cent)	
	(millions)		Overall	Annual
Asia and East Indies	827	2,162	161·5	2·02
Africa	164	378·3	126·5	1·58
N. America	75	232·5	210·0	2·62
Latin America	52	301·5	480·0	6·0
Europe	272	468·4	72·2	0·9
U.S.S.R.	89	249·7	180·5	2·26
Oceania and rest of world	12	32	166·7	2·08
Whole world	1,485	3,860	160·0	2·0

It may be seen that only those countries that have had a massive influx of immigrants, like the U.S.A., Latin America, and Australia, or else a huge territorial expansion with a rapid change from an agricultural to an industrial economy, like the Soviet Union, have recorded a population growth greater than the world average of 2 per cent a year. On the other hand, the countries in which industry is a very recent and highly localised growth, as in Africa, or Europe, which has been the reservoir from which much of the rest of the world has been peopled, have had a growth rate noticeably lower than the world average.

Some precise calculations made about 1895, with the object of forecasting the world population in the year 2000, arrived at a figure of 5,600 millions; but the same calculations gave a world total of 4,200 millions for 1973—a figure 350 millions in excess of the actual population in that year. It is also worth noting that between 1894 and 1914, the annual growth rate did not exceed 0·9 per cent, and it only rose to 2 per cent during the next half-century, a period that proved exceptionally favourable for the numerical growth of the human species.

The fears often currently expressed concerning the possible over-population of the earth thus do not appear to be well founded; they stem from political anxieties and philosophical speculation, as also do the hasty socio-cconomic generalisations that do not take account of the remarkable plasticity of the human race, and the innumerable and unforeseen adaptations and socio-biological reflexes that are quite unpredictable.

CHAPTER 16

SETTLEMENT

Settlement is man's first step towards adapting himself to his environment. Its problems are at the crossroads of several sciences, and the ethnographer, who describes the forms of houses and the materials used in their construction, and who examines the various aspects of social structure and the level of a people's culture, is always faced with geographical problems of settlement. At a higher stage in development, sociologists and economists find that research into problems of settlement come within the scope of their study. Conversely, as soon as human geography aims at studying man's most elementary forms of settlement on the soil, it must direct its investigations into a mass of facts concerning social structure, the development of the law, and religious complexes; and it cannot ignore any of the results got by other sciences in these matters.

The geographer considers first of all whether the material environment has not a paramount influence in the dispositions and forms of man's dwellings. The obvious advantages of a site may of themselves explain its occupation: for instance, strips of dry land or permeable ground in the middle of marshes. Since water is necessary to man, his animals and his crops, attention has often been drawn to the fact that in regions where it is obtained with difficulty, human dwellings have tended to be placed close together round privileged spots where water is easily accessible. On the other hand regions in which human dwellings are scattered are those, where for various reasons determined by the impermeable nature of the soil or by the climate, water can easily be reached everywhere without too much difficulty and too much cost. These facts taken at random show that the physical environment cannot be wholly eliminated from the study of settlement and that certain lodgements and forms of dwelling are very closely connected with the details of relief, geological structure, and other physical features. Anthropological and ethnographical facts are just as closely connected with the forms of settlement. For a theorist like Meitzen, settlements concentrated in large villages must have been first made and spread by the ancient Germans. In eastern Europe, there are big villages wrongly called 'Saxon villages', which are inhabited by Germans, whilst the Slavs and Roumanians dwell in scattered hamlets. Meitzen's theory is obviously a hasty generalisation derived from a few ill-observed facts, but social organisation and institutions exert a direct influence on settlement.

Taboo, or social compulsion in its most primitive form, may intervene to impose on settlements some unusually concentrated form in surroundings where they could scatter without inconvenience. A ban on certain unholy spots, or a recommendation that a certain spot might be beneficial to the community, may bring about a concentration of houses in a certain area.

In the countryside, the agrarian regulations of primitive communal settlements must be taken into account. In the socialistic empire of the Incas, the law strictly determined which land was for cultivation and which was for dwellings. No one could build his house out of the area reserved for housing. When a new household was formed, the village justices assigned to the head of this new family, both a site for his house in the village and an allotment of land in the mountains. This strict separation of dwelling places and cultivated land is found also in the legal codes in medieval Alsace. Various documents describing the lands attached to the Alsatian abbeys mark out distinctly one area for building and another for cultivating, and forbid building outside the former. So, whether they stem from the taboos of a primitive people or from the code of law of a fussy community, social facts have a great influence on the geography of settlement. Although there are many factors involved, theoreticians have a natural tendency to stress the influence of only a few of them. They try to explain the whole phenomenon of settlement with a selected group of factors. None of these theories fully explain the facts. The truth is more complex and is the result of social and physical compulsions as well as of economic and ethnical factors.

UNSTABLE SETTLEMENTS

Human settlements manifest a stability that is in keeping with the resources placed at the disposal of the communities who built them. They may be temporary, semi-permanent or wholly permanent. But it seems probable that permanent human settlements are the result of a long evolution, and that they are related both to an increase of natural resources and to man's ingenuity in multiplying these beyond the natural gifts of the environment. Hunting peoples, pastoralists and even some primitive agriculturalists, have essentially movable dwellings ; nomads almost always pitch their tents within a small perimeter and make very close settlements ; the Arab 'douar' is a form of grouping similar to the Mongol or the Kirghiz camp. In the same way, the Mois of Indo-China and the Fans of West Africa, both itinerant cultivators, build close-set villages which they move, sometimes from season to season.

For all these peoples, the settlement is only one of the aspects of life and the projection on the ground of the community's social structure. Hunters, pastoralists, and itinerant cultivators all have strong social cohesion. Yet the cohesion sometimes gives way temporarily and almost always the form of settlement is changed accordingly. For instance, the Eskimos decide on the site of their dwelling according to the seasonal appearances of game : in winter, the igloos form a stable settlement with grouped dwellings, for this is the period of darkness when all important activity stops and when hunting seals near the igloos can provide extra food. Summer, however, is a time of movement ; the tribe disperses in little nomadic family groups consisting of a few tents. Each group follows a traditional course which will take it back to the winter encampment at the end of the season. This periodical return to the same winter quarters ensures the cohesion of the tribe, for in summer all the moral and religious ties of the little community are relaxed.

The same contrast between life in summer and in winter used to be found among the Red Indian tribes in North America and amongst the people of eastern Siberia. When winter came, the tribes used always to assemble in the same clearings or near the same fords ; in summer they broke up into little bands and followed their herds or their game northwards. Among some pastoralists, there is in the same way, a double form of settlement and dwelling. Reindeer breeders in the Arctic portions of the Soviet Union, and the Lapps in northern Scandinavia, settle in winter on the edge of the forest, where the reindeer find their fodder. They live at that time in a close-set village in partly buried houses. Summer is spent under canvas, and so as to benefit by the greatest possible range of pasture, and to avoid mutual inconvenience between the various groups of animals, the tribe splits into little parties which camp independently.

Even in more advanced stages of civilisation, movement may be necessary in order to feed the animals. Where transhumance is practised, doubling of dwellings for the same purposes is always found. In this case the dwelling itself is not moved. The people occupy two dwellings in turn. These are permanent constructions and each is occupied during a part of the year. On the mountains, the summer chalets are sometimes twenty to fifty kilometres from the permanent villages in the valley below, forming secondary seasonal dwellings. In the Alps, an intermediate resting-place between the valleys and the Alpine pasture settlement is sometimes necessary, and shelters called *granges* are found on the lower slopes of the Alps or, *montagnettes*, which form a third settlement. Now, it is almost always noticed that the valley settlements are very compact, for many factors combine towards this, such as a sunny position on the *adret*, the head of an alluvial fan, or the exit from a gorge through a glacial rock barrier. The summer shelters on the other hand form a scattered type of settlement.

Primitive cultivators, who have constantly to clear new ground, must do an enormous amount of work in common to complete the first clearing of a piece of land. When the soil near the village is exhausted, they prefer to move the village on to a new site rather than clear some distant ground and return to their village at the end of the day's work. The desertion of the first piece of land involves leaving the original settlement as well.

The removals of villages are not carried out at random. Except in the case of very primitive tribes, they recur within a moderate cycle. From time to time it happens that the village is established in a previous site occupied several decades before. This has the advantage of profiting from the previous work, which is never completely lost, since bush, savanna, and forest do not regain in ten years the luxuriance of the primitive vegetation. This kind of life undoubtedly favours close-set villages. Apart from the need to form as homogeneous and disciplined a unit of cultivation as possible, a close-set village is more easily moved than are huts scattered over a large area. Itinerant agricultural tribes are, moreover, forced into strong social cohesion, just as are nomadic pastoralists.

Instances of temporary clearing of land accompanied by displacement of the settlement are frequent among tropical peoples. It is the practice of the Garos of Assam and Jakums of Malaya. It was also the custom amongst the natives of pre-Columbian America, as for example the Iroquois who used to move their villages every ten or twenty years. Nowadays, movements of the Tupis, Mois, and Fans are started sometimes by definite exhaustion of the soil, at other times by an apparent curse on the spot, or perhaps by an accident which is interpreted as a sign of bad luck, or even by the discovery of a band of undesirable neighbours. The migration of the Mois on the plateaux of Annam was often determined by the mere news of a visit from the collector of taxes! The instability of the *ray* villages has always been the despair of officials.

It happens sometimes, however, that this shifting cultivation is adapted to scattered settlement. In the Amazon forest we find shifting cultivators living in close-set villages side by side with others in scattered dwellings. In the upper valley of the Rio Branco, the tribes consist of a few families living separately in little groups of two or three huts. The sites of these are changed every two or three years. In Frontera, between southern and central Chile, the *Araucanos*, who are shifting cultivators, have very scattered settlements. Their homes are made of branches and reeds, so that when they are moved only the framework is taken. Scattered settlement is facilitated by the great number of streams and good sites within a relatively small radius. Very different is the arrangement of settlements in northern Chile, where native villages are compact, like the old Andine villages of Inca times. No mode of life, however primitive it may be, absolutely imposes one kind of settlement rather than another, even if the settlements themselves are impermanent.

STABLE RURAL SETTLEMENTS

To define rural settlement one must consider the occupations of the people who have founded it. In this respect, a rural settlement presents a fundamental difference from urban settlement, for it is not a mere lodging. Even in past centuries when the village craftsman worked at home, his house was distinguished from a town dwelling by its special arrangement and by outhouses for working in. A rural settlement is in fact mainly an agricultural workshop and it cannot be separated from the land whose use it ensures. Its shape and arrangement are often in strict accord with the kind of work, the agricultural techniques, and the way that the soil is used.

As a first approximation, settlements of sedentary cultivators may be divided into grouped and scattered settlements. In its purest form, the grouped settlement is one in which the inhabitants build their houses at the same point within the area of a rural community and in which, as a consequence, the ground occupied by buildings is very clearly distinct from the cultivated land. This type of settlement is seen on a map by the presence at certain points of large agglomerations between which stretch cultivated fields without any other human establishment.

In other areas, dwellings are scattered irregularly and perhaps several dozen may be seen from a point of vantage. These are small groups of dwellings or isolated houses which form a complex of hamlets and farms. Usually such dispersion indicates a very close relationship between the dwelling place and the place of work; each house is found within the group of fields which its owner cultivates.

Between these two extremes, there are many intermediate types. Some regions contain both types; some communes will contain several small groups of settlements, in others one may find, in between the larger agglomerations, an intercalated scattering of smaller units, sometimes in the form of hamlets, sometimes in a swarm of isolated farms and at other times, in complexes of both farms and hamlets. Conversely, amidst areas in which the population is scattered, one can discern a kind of crystallisation, by which the scattered settlement becomes tighter within a well-defined perimeter. Sometimes, too (to use an astronomical metaphor), embryo agglomerations may begin to appear in the centre of these nebulae.

To discover which of these two basic forms of settlement is the primitive one is an essential problem. Is the grouped settlement older than the scattered settlement? Does dispersion stem from the decline of villages, as the existence of an intermediate scattering of smaller units would suggest? Is village grouping the outcome of a concentration of settlement that was originally scattered as the growing density of the 'nebulae' might suggest? Did one form precede the other? Have the two forms always existed side by side? Did they develop separately, to mingle later? Such are the problems which face the geographer who studies the different forms of settlement.

Establishment of the Settlement.—The passage from temporary to permanent settlement has been observed in the past and is still to be seen today. It happens, for instance, when population increases and the available area of land decreases. When this occurs it becomes necessary to produce more food from a smaller area. Extensive cultivation is then replaced by intensive, and at the same time, a reduction in the available area causes the settlement to become permanent.

Many other reasons may cause nomadic life to become sedentary. The Tedas in Tibesti seem to have been originally a nomadic people with no permanent home. It was after losing their herds by Tuareg raids that they became cultivators, so far as cultivation is possible in their barren land. Their settlement then became permanent, though individually the tribe kept its wandering habits.

In some monsoon lands like Assam, which was peopled at a fairly rapid rate and underwent great changes in cultivation, different stages can be seen of the passage from shifting to intensive cultivation. The primitive tribes of cultivators had wide areas of land and could go in for long periods of fallow. That was the time of shifting cultivation, with successive removals of villages following the exhaustion of the soil; but when population increased, the available land became rarer and village-removal more difficult; difficulties were increased by a long period of warfare. Today, there are still tribes that continue to live with the same system of shifting cultivation in the poorest and least populated parts of Assam, but elsewhere the villages have become permanent. The last stage in the permanent establishment of the cultivators on the land is marked, in Monsoon Asia, by the development of rice cultivation. It entails the tying up of manpower to the fields, and the complexity and amount of work which it involves makes rice cultivators most reluctant to leave the land they have fashioned. Rice cultivation, which is the final stage in the development, is also the cement of village communities in the Far East.

Early in prehistoric times, this form of shifting cultivation seems to have been practised in Europe, at least in the Germanic and Slav territories. As the population increased, it was necessary to devise a system of cultivation that used the same soil over and over again, and that arranged its crops so as to feed both people and domestic animals. Hence a firm rooting in the soil of rural settlements in a form probably differing from district to district, since the two types of close-set and scattered settlements, appear together in very ancient times.

The basic features of this ancient form of cultivation in Europe can be described fairly accurately, for they long survived, and have left lasting traces. It is characterised by the parcelling out of holdings. This was due to the wish to give everyone land of equal quality in a district that had areas of unequal fertility. This aim is as evident in one-crop regions like the corn-growing countries, as in regions of polyculture wherever the soil differs greatly in quality, as it does sometimes, within distances of a few yards. When property is to be left to heirs, the desire to maintain this qualitative distribution among the reversioners, led to further parcelling out of land. This carving up of the soil is therefore a very ancient tendency in the European system of tenure, that has been described in Jutland, Great Britain, France, and Italy.

Another characteristic was the existence, up to a very recent time, of 'commons', that is, lands belonging to the community and free to be used by everyone. This land was respected by landowners and smallholders alike, and served for pasturing animals.

A third characteristic was the practice of crop rotation, which seems to have been compulsory at some periods. Usually the rotation was triennal, with one field under a rich cereal crop represented by wheat, another field under a poor spring crop, most usually represented by oats, and a field lying fallow and legally joined to the common for pasturing animals. In this old system of cultivation, which was practised as late as the eighteenth century, the compact village was not placed in the geometrical centre, but near the intersection of the three fields. If plans of medieval English villages and those of old French villages are examined, this arrangement is clearly seen, with the village more or less in the centre of the parish, whilst the paths radiating from it rather like spokes of a wheel, take both the farmhands and the animals to their respective fields and pastures. The obligations of the three-year rotation and of the commons, which, taken together, bound man to the land, materially and socially, brought about the permanent establishment of the settlement. The stability of village communities reflects the systematization of the work on the land in an organisation at once social, technical, and economic. This fixation of settlement has been stressed still more in western Europe, by the gradual disappearance of transhumance under the influence of agricultural organisations, and the general development of the countryside. The draining of valleys has made good meadow-land where there was only swamp; the introduction of fodder crops and roots, together with the giving-up of food crops and industrial crops, such as flax and hemp, has further contributed towards feeding the animals in the winter. This development was only made possible through the breakaway from the isolation and self-sufficiency in which the highlands were forced to live, and by modern means of communication.

In nearly all the mountain regions in Europe, and particularly in the Alps, the population of villages in the valleys has been in process of stabilization for a century or so. This is partly due to the fact that the work on the land, which has become more productive, fills the farmer's calendar more than formerly and so supports a larger number of workers. It is also partly due to the disappearance of the rural proletariat from which the cowmen and shepherds, who went with the herds and flocks up to the mountain pastures, used to be recruited. When these wage earners have not become landowners in their turn, they have found employment in industry down in the valleys. As a result, the upper mountain slopes and the chalet villages have been abandoned.

This more definite establishment of the settlement, this acceptance of the valley as a place for the village which has become the only settlement, with a population of industrial workers as well as farming folk, is certainly progress, considering the efficiency of man's work in one place; but it is a backward move in so far as it ends in the desertion of a source of wealth and symbolises the disappearance of an intensive mode of life.

On the whole, the form of settlement when once fixed, never appears anything but a temporary solution of a complex of economic and social problems pertaining to rural life. Changes tend sometimes to close up the units of a community and at other times to scatter them; sometimes to refuse them independence and at other times to allow them wide relative autonomy; sometimes to impose physical, social or political restrictions and at other times to free them from these restrictions.

Form and Development of the Compact Settlement.—Historical data agree in showing that when agricultural communities have settled firmly on the soil, they have done so by preference, and in most cases, in the form of compact settlements. Prehistoric man, like man in primitive communities today, was incapable of struggling against nature by himself. In the higher forms of civilisation, man may cherish the illusion of acting by himself. In reality he acts with the help of all the cultural and technical inheritance conferred on him by the community's stage of development, with the help of all the tools, seeds, and the mass of material wealth, knowledge, and experience given him by an advanced community. In present-day frontier-lands, man remains dependent on a powerful mechanical civilisation. When primitive man is reduced to poor resources, he has little control over nature : even when it is merely clearing land by fire, he has to act in cooperation with others.

In every country and at all stages of civilisation, the family organisation, whether dependent upon a real or mythical bond, constitutes the earliest community. In the Celtic period in Britain, if tradition is to be believed, such *clans* consisted of several hundred persons ; the passage from the social to a territorial bond is rather obscure and does not take place in the same way in all communities. In many regions and in particular parts of France which have long been left to themselves owing to poor communications, villages consist often of groups of interrelated people. In such conditions, the form of compact settlement is forced on the community which may be satisfied to live under one roof like the common long-house in some Pacific Islands, or among some of the primitive tribes in Amazonia. Later, as numbers increase, the clan scatters them into outhouses built around the ancestral home and within reach of patriarchal authority.

These family ties, however, are not always enough to impose a compact form on the rural settlement. In Eastern Europe family groups live in scattered settlements in small hamlets or groups of hamlets. This is exemplified by the Serbian *Zadruga*, which is a kind of communal society practising mutual help and even holding some goods in common. The community imposes restrictions on all, but ensures in return the enjoyment and use in common, of forest paths, and portions of the woods in which to feed pigs. Festivals are common to all members of the *Zadrugas*, and a private ceremony does in fact unite all the members of the community, however much dispersed. In the Middle Ages, in France, there were communities known as *communautés taisibles* whose members put all their earnings and allowances in common, lent each other help in cases of illness, and sometimes formed a replica of the funerary colleges of antiquity ; they did not develop only in districts with big villages like Laonnais, but also in districts like Limousin, where the settlements are very scattered.

A communal organisation of the people does not necessarily correspond to a compact form of settlement. Conversely also, in communities organised in clans, nucleated villages do not always accurately reflect a close structure in the social body. In Arizona and New Mexico, compact villages inhabited by Moqui and Zuni Indians are lived in by several clans, whose people form a collection of about a hundred huts for about fifteen clans ; there is no segregation of the clans, moreover, in the village architecture and streets, which is just the opposite to what is seen in the Aymara villages in Bolivia.

Primitive men often needed to unite in order to surmount great material difficulties; for instance, to protect themselves from wild beasts who had them at their mercy, and above all to cooperate in tilling the soil. At first sight, the compactness of a settlement seems to be a factor common to all primitive peoples. Neolithic remains always reveal large agglomerations of huts. For example, the Butaraz site in Yugoslavia near Sarajevo has about a hundred huts together; the site at Lengyel on the right bank of the Danube in Hungary contains three hundred huts; at Grimspound in Devon, there is a site with sixty-eight huts in its inner ring; round the ring there are little scattered groups of five or six hamlets built close to the fortress. In Italy, sites of compact settlements are marked by *terramares* or hillocks of fertile land which were once the sites of pile-dwellings and of villages built on artificial mounds.

The needs of security and common defence were not the only causes of nucleation. The position of the neolithic villages was often determined by the situation of land that was fertile and easy to work. For these early pioneers, who had but slight equipment, there was no question of turning up strong, heavy, compact soil. Their preference was for the lighter soil, which modern scientific farmers regard as of lower quality. In western Europe, good, deep alluvial soil was usually avoided by neolithic man, who chose land on a plateau where the soil was pebbly, but more easily worked. Apart from loam on plateaus, which was always their favourite soil, they had a marked preference for limestone soil containing traces of sand. Even soils derived from granite were suitable if they had been deforested and contained little clay. In the central highlands of France, it is always in places now barren or covered with heath, that archaeological sites of neolithic man are to be found, and much the same thing is true of highland Britain.

Thus a curious coincidence has been noticed between the area covered by Campignian civilisation and the area of loam-covered plateaux in the north of France and the Paris basin; archaeological finds occur within an area which on a geological map coincides with *ergeron* which masks the limestone plateaux in Picardy, Lorraine, Champagne, and the Ile-de-France, avoiding Flanders, Woëvre, and the damp Champagne area, where the soil is moist, heavy, and clayey. The Campignians, who had settled in these districts about the fourth of fifth millenium B.C., occupied grassy clearings which had been deforested, and defended these against the encroachment of the forest of the Boreal and Atlantic periods. It was probably owing to their patient toil, that Beauce escaped becoming a wooded area.

Only later, about the third millenium, did the Campignians carry their offensive into the heart of the woodland, choosing the least dense parts, which unfortunately had the shallowest and the least fertile soil. The Campignians were cultivators; they settled on the forest borders and cultivated mainly cereals, as is proved by the flint sickles and millstones which are found in plenty in the presumed sites of their big villagges.

Even in primitive peoples with no knowledge of agriculture, the form of compact settlement is the most often found, since it is forced on them by the very work of the social group. When white settlements were being made in the north of California, the Amerindian hunting and fishing tribes lived in big villages, because compactness was needed for making, maintaining, and handling fishing tackle and boats; the social unit was most often the boat's crew who were under strict discipline; this would have been difficult to maintain in a scattered community. Big villages are still the rule today all along the salmon streams, where fishing requires co-operative management of the weirs and traps on the rivers.

Another example of compactness is found in the same region among the Maitu Amerindians who live by food gathering. They live together in compact villages, each of which has its own area for finding food. To the effects of this division of territory is added the need to remain together so as to maintain and use the tools necessary for making and keeping acorn meal; in addition, every member of the tribe specialises in seeking and gathering a clearly defined article, whether fruit, roots, eggs, or honey. The division and specialisation of labour succeeds in ensuring cohesion in the community and compactness in the settlement.

Throughout the maize belt in the New World, the Amerindian villages were similarly concentrated owing to the communal organisation of cultivating the land : the sites of former native villages have often been adopted by white settlers, whether Spanish, Dutch, or English. But compactness may be imposed by more immediate economic facts : for instance, in Polynesia scarcity of fuel sometimes makes it impossible to build huts for each family; the solution is to build a common oven for use in roasting breadfruit and then to place the men's houses around it, as is done elsewhere round a well or pond.

Compact villages are of different sizes according to the nature and resources of the surrounding country : when the resources are poor and scanty, the villages are small; on the desert borders the groups of *gourbis* often consist of only six or seven huts; on the other hand, in districts well supplied with game and water holes, Hottentot villages, whose inhabitants live almost by hunting and gathering, may consist of a hundred huts. A country's wealth, however, is not static: it depends on the skill of the inhabitants in making use of the resources far more than on the resources themselves. For instance, some Sudanese tribes who are more skilful at cultivating cassava, in planting out banana suckers and looking after crops at the same time as they gather food in the forest, make a practice of living in far larger villages than the other tribes.

Intensive cultivation, which clearly represents the most scientific use of the soil, has given rise to the greatest number of very large villages. The history of settlement very often demonstrates the development of these big villages, in agricultural communities. Faced with increasing population the village, unable to grow further, has, like a swarm of bees, hived off parties to found a village of the same type and similarly organised away from the old home. Such an occurrence has happened again and again throughout the seventeenth century and during part of the eighteenth in south Russia, when villages of Russians from Muscovy stood in regular lines parallel with the edge of the steppes, each village sending out in front of it, at a given moment, a little outpost which grew into a village a little later, on the arrival of fresh settlers. When these second-generation villages had in their turn become too big, they sent out a little offshoot which gradually increased; in this way successive lines of villages appear on the map, running from the interior towards the Black Sea.

In the early days of English settlement in Britain, villages were placed far apart, each having ground enough to enable its folk to keep a few cattle and grow the corn they needed. When the number of people in a village grew too great to be supported by their original allotment, some of the folk moved off a short distance and made a new settlement. The new village often had the same name as the old one with some additional qualifying mark; thus, Great Missenden and Little Missenden, Much Hadham and Little Hadham.

In the Paris region in the twelfth and thirteenth centuries, intermediate villages were founded in the same way, by monks from the abbeys on land dotted with large villages. They were usually placed in forest clearings. In the American West, the Mormons, who were forced to settle in country threatened by hostile Indian tribes, built large villages which later sent out folk to make similar settlements. Other examples are seen in the Sudan, when the Dogons of Bandiagara, starting from defensive sites, increased the number of their compact villages by the migration of family groups; this origin is easily traced by the very names of the new villages, which always keep the root of the name of the old village, modified by suffixes that, as a rule, indicate the founder or the circumstances of their formation. Thus, whenever an organised permanent system of cultivation prevails, the existence of compact villages is borne out.

Settlement in big villages is in fact traditional in Egypt and India, where today 85 per cent of the population still lives in big villages; in China, such villages are counted in thousands.

Usually, concentration has been imposed by the practice of an agricultural mode of life, which is organised on a communal system that calls for a distribution of land and a calendar of work to be observed by everybody. Such a discipline can be observed only in a compact village. Among primitive agricultural peoples who can still be studied by ethnologists, those in the Andes have felt the effects of communal land tenure and communal regulations longest and most heavily. These regulations have prescribed the division even of the Inca villages into quarters inhabited by different clans, who were weighed down with taboos and had obligations forced on them. Many villages on the high plateaux in Bolivia are built around a rectangular square divided into two parts, each of which belongs to one of two *sayas*, or tribes, who usually make up a few dozen village families. The quarter adjoining the part of the square bearing the tribal name is reserved for that tribe; and only members of that *saya* can live there: the houses are built to face the square on each side or in the alleys leading into it. On the square itself, two circles and a series of parallel paths, marked out with bricks or stones embedded vertically in the ground, outline the meeting places that are reserved for each tribe and the paths to them. The parts of the village common to both tribes are built on the other two sides of the square; on the one side the church, to which each *saya* has its own entrance, and on the other the municipal buildings, town hall, police station, and prison.

The cultivated land climbs up the mountain to about 4,000 metres; the *sayas* are the sole owners, and each of them grants its members the usufruct of part of the perimeter of the built-up area and of the cultivated land. When a member of the community founds a family, the village magistrates allot him a spot within the built-up area in which to build his house and grant him a piece of land to cultivate within his *saya's* division, together with pasturage rights on the common. This communal system is therefore less absolute than those of some rural communities in Europe in bygone days, for the Aymara has to comply with no agricultural obligation like that of the three-year rotation of crops: he tills the land in his own way and enjoys the full use of his harvest. On his death, the land returns in principle to the *saya*, but in fact it can be given as a fresh grant to his children. If they are minors, the magistrates appoint a caretaker who is entrusted with the cultivation of the parcel of land for the children's benefit.

Agriculture is the sole occupation of these mountain people, for they have neither herds nor flocks; they grow potatoes, barley,

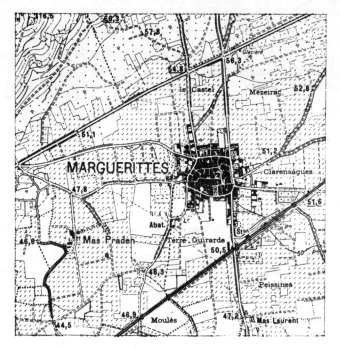

FIG. 12.—VILLAGE-TYPES IN FRANCE.

Compact, nucleated (Marguerittes, Provence).

and a kind of wild sorrel; their only beast of burden is the llama,
which is only used for carrying agricultural implements and for
bringing down the harvests. The villagers leave for the fields in the
morning, and do not return to the village until evening when the
day's work is done.

Before the economic changes in the seventeenth and eighteenth
centuries, big villages were the normal mode of settlement in
medieval England; and France is still a veritable museum of
villages, whose appearance reflects the story of their struggle for
land. Some villages in Picardy and Cambrésis form compact masses;
they are in a regular geometrical pattern as if the only object had
been to save space and to put as many houses as possible on the
smallest possible area. This is the type known in Germany as the
Haufendorf.

Other villages have a linear form; this type is found especially in
the English Midlands and in Lorraine and the borders of the Paris

FIG. 13.—VILLAGE-TYPES IN FRANCE.
Linear (Beaumont-en-Beine, Ile-de-France).

basin in France. The English type favours an arrangement along the 'high street' with houses on either side. The village of Hatfield near Doncaster is typical. Before recent development took place, the village did not cluster in the middle of the land belonging to it, but was in linear formation on one of the boundaries of its land, which instead of being arranged radially, was disposed in a herring-bone pattern. In both English and French types each house occupies the front of a long, narrow strip at right angles to the high street which in this way is bordered by two continuous lines of houses.

If the village runs along a contour and the strips stretch down to the bottom of the valley, the ends of the strips touching the stream form water meadows; higher up towards the village is the arable land, and, lastly, against the houses, is a narrow belt of garden. If there is land above the village reaching to the top of the hill slope, the ends of the strips usually have a fringe of woodland which may still be used according to the regulations affecting commons. Such

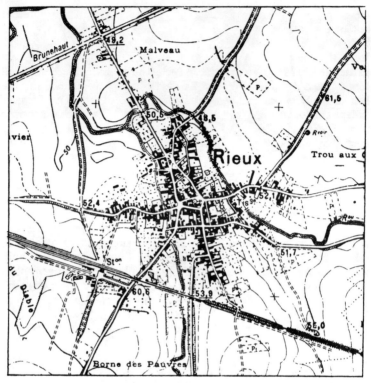

FIG. 14.—VILLAGE-TYPES IN FRANCE.
Star-shaped (Rieux, Nord).

villages are common in England. In many cases, as in the Vale of
Ancholme, the village owns a strip of land running from the river
straight up the slope of the valley to the watershed, thereby securing
water meadows near the stream, ploughland on the rising ground
and woodland and pasture further up the hill. Many of these early
settlements became parishes, and their boundaries have survived to
the present day.

Some of these linear villages are probably old, and their formation
as ancient as that of the 'bunched up' villages in Picardy and
Beauce. But others are comparatively recent and belong to a somewhat different economic stage from that of the primitive communities. In eastern France and western Germany, the villages and
their connected lands were systematically rearranged after the
devastation caused by the Thirty Years War and the villages rebuilt
in linear form. Probably this was the introduction of a form of
village that had grown up elsewhere and in particular, in forest

clearings, into a setting which had previously had quite a different settlement pattern.

It is agreed that at the time of the great increase in population from the eleventh to the thirteenth century, demographic pressure caused migration from the old villages, and clearings were made all along forest paths leading into the depths of the woodland, and the bits of land so won ran at right-angles to the paths. This form of village and its attached land in a herring-bone pattern is characteristic of poor districts which had long been left as forest and only slowly cleared when the need for land made it absolutely necessary. As a rule they can be regarded as a second generation of villages in relation to the older villages of the loamy plateaux. The houses cluster in a small space, but as the square need not be so small in a freshly-occupied area, the front of the strips is wider and the houses do not fill it entirely; hence, each house may be separated from its neighbour by a little garden at its side, or by a path running at right-angles to the high street. This is the arrangement of villages in Aliermont in the north of the district of Caux, which were built following the gradual clearing of woodland; this arrangement is also the forerunner of the Canadian *rang* in the St Lawrence valley and the Province of Quebec, where each house has a long strip of land running back at right-angles to the road or to the river bank.

The compact village was the first form of rural settlement made by settlers in New England; it was necessary for them to remain together in an unknown and hostile land, even if only to profit in common by the tools and foodstuffs imported from the mother country in limited quantities, whilst awaiting the first harvest. Besides, for many of these immigrants, religious faith had caused their leaving their homeland, where they had been persecuted; they had to remain together for worship near the chapel or church built from common funds, and this explains to a great extent the form of the compact villages imposed in the middle of the seventeenth century, on the first settlements of Europeans in the new countries. At this time, moreover, the settlers came from big villages in Europe, which were then overpopulated, and they planned their settlements in a strange land on the model of those they had just left. The parties of settlers often consisted of family groups from the same village, and they gave the village which they built in America the name of their native village in the now abandoned Old World. On the whole the compact village is relatively primitive in form, not only as a settlement of a community close to nature, but also as an establishment, at least temporary, of representatives of more advanced communities in an environment which they have not yet wholly mastered, which therefore put them for a time in conditions not far removed from those of more primitive communities.

However, once the compact settlement is formed, human and social factors suffice to endow it with extraordinary powers of resistance which enable it to survive the disappearance of the economic and technical reasons which give rise to its foundation. Indeed, the village is the focus of social crystallisation. Common interests, and often even common sentiments, unite the villagers from generation to generation. The institutions of the village for promoting help which have an economic, social, moral, and often religious character, are a token of its personality. The most humble of these institutions is the village hall. Among primitive peoples this is the men's house, the meeting-place of the braves, being both their club and their headquarters. But it is also in a sense an inn in which hospitality is dispensed, where travellers are led on to talk and give the latest news. A house of this kind is a fundamental institution in Indonesian villages.

Village cooperation is also shown on the economic plane, by the setting up of equipment for the benefit of all. Often in feudal lands the lord's monopoly of the oven and the mill has cemented the cohesion of the working population. In other forms of civilisation, tradition and experience have also led to the construction of buildings for public use. In North Africa, for instance, there is the *agadir*, a large public market built away from dwelling houses. In it, everyone has his own hut, but the whole place is communal property in charge of a caretaker appointed by the community. Other instances in Negro Africa are the very curious collections of rice and millet granaries, which form a second cluster as compact as the village itself, but some distance from it.

At a stage higher than mere subsistence, when ideas of trade enter the village, there is further cooperation. Whenever there has been set up in the village or its neighbourhood a market in which the cultivators have become accustomed to do business, trade makes the gathering permanent. Even a distant market may have the same enduring effect, for on market days, strings of carts moving as self-contained units are organised and sent to it. These strings of carts, which are familiar sights on roads in India, are in themselves collective institutions. The composition and progress of the strings, the sharing of costs, and the division of the produce of the sales, tighten the interdependence of the villages.

It must not be thought, therefore, that road development has always been a dissolving factor for village communities. The attractions of markets have often enriched the life of countryfolk by starting within the villages an industry of a kind which brings out the personality of the village. In the Far East there are many villages, in which part of the inhabitants, belonging to a definite caste, have specialised in fishing so as to supply with fish those who devote all their time to rice cultivation. Crafts impart to the village a more definite economic self-sufficiency and sometimes ensure that it has wider economic influence. They may even cause such specialisation as to create social segregation. In Tongking, as in China, villages of cultivators without craftsmen are separate from villages of craftsmen without cultivators. Some villages supply pots to a whole district and get foodstuffs in return, whilst others specialise in basketry. In Africa, blacksmiths and tanners often form separate villages and this economic segregation is accompanied by social and religious separation which accentuates the peculiarity of the village.

When, on the other hand, each agricultural village can contain within itself, a certain number of crafts, its economic foundation is much sounder and the compact form of the village is greatly strengthened. Typical of such villages combining agriculture with rural industries in the sixteenth and eighteenth centuries are the old French villages in Normandy and Picardy, where weavers toiled for the foreign markets and craftsmen belonged to as many as thirty different trades. Many similar examples could be found at the same period in East Anglia.

Social cohesion explains the survival of villages even after they have lost some of their functions. A fortified place has often lost all its meaning, industry has disappeared, and rural functions have often been seriously affected by the disappearance of compulsory rotation and of commons. All this crystallisation of ancient

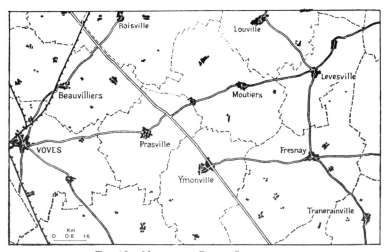

FIG. 15.—NUCLEATED RURAL SETTLEMENT.
Beauce, northeast of Chateaudun (from French *Carte de l'Etat major* 1/80,000). Broken lines are *commune* boundaries.

legislation, in which certain authors have wished to see the origin of nucleation and of village structure, has gone, without the form of the village itself being touched. In Mediterranean Europe and in south Portugal villages have acquired and kept a real personality. Dress differs from village to village, and dances and songs often express the rivalry between them. Even in France today, when traditional costumes have disappeared, village peculiarities still survive in the form of unkind saws used by one village of another. Elsewhere, spiritual independence has sometimes crystallised around the worship of a local saint, who was not always of a very orthodox nature!

DISPERSED SETTLEMENT

Sometimes villages have been so greatly disturbed by the economic development of the countryside that in some regions the old compact arrangement has given place to a scattered order. To grasp this decline of villages, it must be assumed that as the cult of individualism began to spread, newer methods of work more beneficial to the individual appeared, so that the communal institutions which were sometimes tyrannical, became intolerable. A fresh economy, gradually introduced, heralded the desire to break the traditional round of cultivation. This breach with institutions and obligations of the past was accomplished by following the examples of pioneers who had set up on their own account outside the village and who,

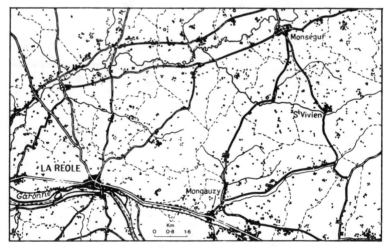

FIG. 16.—DISPERSED RURAL SETTLEMENT.
Guyenne, south of Bordeaux (from French *Carte de l'Etat major*, 1/80,000).

for various reasons, had not been accepted into the privileged class of landholders.

Furthermore, to obtain the higher yield necessary for a growing population, more fodder had to be produced so as to increase the number of cattle and the necessary amount of manure. High yields were only possible through the improvement of the property by draining damp ground, spreading fertilisers, and building walls so as to safeguard these new benefits for those who had undertaken the improvement of the land. Hence, too, the desire of the cultivator to be free on his land ; a parcel of land marked out on the common field was now to be cultivated independently and enclosed, so as not to be spoilt by the communal herds and flocks.

From then on, the traditional structure cracked : the commons gradually disappeared and so did the compulsory rotation of crops ; the partitioning of land decreased, to be replaced by its reunion under one owner, and far more compact farm units were formed. This breaking up of the community and the rearrangement of land-holding have taken many forms ; and the initiative was not always taken by the villagers ; the forms were often imposed by an authority alien to the countryside, and in some districts ended in an artificial and wholesale rearrangement of the land and the settlement pattern.

In western Europe, instances of the scattering of a settlement following upheavals of this kind are legion, particularly in Germany, the Scandinavian countries, and Great Britain.

During the last four centuries in Swabia, the reuniting of parcels of land has been on a grand scale and has effected the reunion of the village's strips into large independent units. At the same time, compact villages have been destroyed, and farms have been rebuilt in isolation, each on its own land. The idea of redistribution of land began with the *Abbey of Kempten*, which broke with the past and applied original conceptions of land utilisation. About the mid-sixteenth century it began to demolish villages and to rearrange the land attached to them ; others followed this example, and the reunion of parcels of land which followed the scattering of the villages increased steadily up to the nineteenth century. This was a revolution which represented a new agricultural mode of life, and which was also aware of the advantage of isolated farms which controlled their own plans of cultivation for the best use of the land.

In Schleswig and the neighbouring districts in Holstein, a similar change took place in the seventeenth and eighteenth centuries. The movement began spontaneously but, from 1766, a law made the reunion of parcels of land compulsory by forcing all landowners to enclose their property, thus scattering the villages.

In Sweden, too, village communities which had been compact since the thirteenth and fourteenth centuries, began to scatter at the beginning of the eighteenth century. In some villages, land belonging to a score of peasants was subdivided into 5,000 or 6,000 parcels. These pieces were so narrow that even a plough could not turn round without overlapping into a neighbour's field. So, for two hundred years a succession of laws brought about the *Storskift* or 'great division' which ended in the formation of large properties easily worked and within easy access. Following this reunion of land, the villages broke up and today the population is scattered in hamlets of six to fifteen houses surrounded by a sprinkling of isolated farms.

From the eighteenth century onwards, many landowners in Denmark succeeded in reuniting parcels of land, either by means of purchase or exchange, thus forming single properties. About 1837 only one per cent of the arable land was still worked under the old system of compulsory rotation and common grazing.

England affords a further instance of the inversion of the settlement pattern through cadastral reconstruction. So long as the 'open-field' system lasted, the houses of the villeins remained grouped together in villages : but when, under the new arrangement of fields, the scattered parcels of land became reunited into compact areas, the farmhouses were built each in the centre of its own property. The enclosure problem was brought up again and again in Parliament, which intervened several times to check the movement in order to save the villeins, and to arrest the destruction of the old medieval boroughs. Enclosures, however, won the day in two particular periods, between the fifteenth and sixteenth centuries and in the late eighteenth and early nineteenth centuries. The most far-reaching transformation of villages seems to have taken place in the first period. Documents dating from the end of the Middle Ages all stress the terrible tragedy of the decay of village life ; and many villages disappeared completely. In the eighteenth century the movement was renewed, but this time in districts that had escaped the first crisis. In one parish in the Midlands, land divided previously amongst sixty cottages and four grazing farms, was joined to form twenty large farms. In Leicestershire, some villages which, whilst the 'open-field' system lasted, had about a hundred houses and families, had at the end of the eighteenth century, only eight or ten houses, that is, forty or fifty people instead of five or six hundred. Hence the problem of *'rotten boroughs'*. As late as 1803, in a parish in Cambridgeshire, forty-three cottages were demolished so as to recover eighty hectares and double the land of an isolated farm.

In France, old villages have seldom disappeared completely. In fact, their dispersion appears as it were, in an intermediate form between the compact villages. In Lower Maine, for instance, in the

29. Lavendon, Buckinghamshire; cross-roads village, with church in centre, in the Ouse valley section of the Great Clay Vale.

ENGLISH VILLAGES

30. Chipping Campden, in the Cotswolds, a one-street village set in a typical English patchwork of arable fields and orchards

31. Assiut, Egypt. Closely packed houses built of mud brick

ANCIENT TOWNS

32. Obidos, Portugal. Walled city with protective castle

eleventh and twelfth centuries, houses were built at short distances between the villages, but the scattered farms did not draw their people from these villages. A new generation of dwellings sprang up between the villages and this prevented their future expansion beyond the boundaries of their former territory. Owing to various economic and social circumstances, such intermediate dispersion also appeared to the west of Paris, and in Puisaye, in the fifteenth century.

Under the 'Ancien Régime' in France, the lord, whatever his rank in the feudal hierarchy, retained the right to try cases of no great importance up to the eighteenth century. Even after the rise of royal authority, questions relating to boundaries and the rights pertaining to the use of water and the exploitation of the woodland, remained in the jurisdiction of the lord. Now these were basic elements of rural organisation, the respect and permanence of which rested on the authority of the lord. Hence, the organisation of tenure rested for several hundred years on feudalism in the widest sense of the term. Owing to differences in skill, in theoretical conceptions, or simply as a result of their own personal whims, these landowners did not always hold the same view of what, in their own interest, was the best form of land use; but from the sixteenth century onward land ceased to be the only source of wealth, for money could be invested in business as well as agriculture; hence the necessity to form units of cultivation giving a high yield and to which the labourer was bound to the landlord by a personal contract free from his management. Thus, at the end of the fourteenth century the Abbeys in Berry and Marche restored the lands ravaged by war and its sequel, not by creating large units of cultivation by villages, but by leasing the land to *métayers* who contracted to settle on it with their families, to cultivate it, and to build on it a barn and a house.

At various times the forming of large estates from parcels of land has increased the scattering of dwellings and the substitution of isolated farms for former villages. In Beauce and Brie, for example, the big farm is a destructive influence on the village community. It often buys up the land for the benefit of an absentee landlord who lives in a town.

In Beauce, the first threats to peasant communities appeared in the eleventh century. In the big collective estates depending on the abbeys, there began at this time the decay of the old communal holdings which eventually became attached to a large domanial farm. These changes have not ended in the complete disappearance of the old villages, as the village tenant-farmers rose to defend their holdings more stubbornly and successfully than did the yeomen in England.

A new attack took place at the end of the seventeenth century and during the eighteenth. The Physiocrats spread the idea through France that there was little profit in small holdings, and that to cultivate land intensively, large capital assets needed to be available; that it was in the interest of the peasants that there should be large estates able to produce more than the mere basic needs and able to struggle effectively against famine. The agricultural changes in England were quoted as a pattern for imitation.

The craze, however, for *fermes champêtres* was rudely checked by the French Revolution, which banned the expansion of large estates, and ordered them to be divided up for the benefit of the peasantry by means of sales of 'national property'. So all these attacks have had but limited effects, merely establishing between the old villages which did survive, three or four large farms which formed an intermediate dispersion.

Today, villages in Beauce are grouped around the church and include, besides craftsmen, small holders who work a '*carcottage*'— a tiny farm consisting of fields; this land grows a little wheat and some fodder, but has no sheep. Its few buildings consist of a farmhouse, stable, and barn. The big farm on the other hand, built some distance from the village, has kept to the main crops of the traditional agricultural system, namely, wheat, oats, secondary corn crops, and artificial fodder. It nearly always has a good flock of sheep and a large sheepfold.

Intermediate dispersion has therefore often occurred, to effect at least a partial disintegration of the villages. In times of crisis the landlords, instead of keeping their tenants grouped in the centre of a single estate, have preferred to distribute their land among several families so as to ensure its best use.

The decline of the compact village in favour of isolated farms and hamlets is not restricted to western Europe, for it has occurred in Tuscany as early as the end of the Middle Ages, and in the Black Forest, Westphalia, the Neckar valley, and in several Swiss cantons. In France, this kind of secondary dispersion is marked by a system of double names: existing villages often bear a name of Latin origin, whilst the hamlets and intermediate farms are named after the forest, for example, *La Chesnaye, La Faye, Le Rouvre, Les Essarts,* etc.; but sometimes they bear the family name of their founders, preceded by an article and followed by the suffix- *ière* or -*erie*; for example, *La Chauvinière, La Miauterie.*

Village decline of the same kind has been observed in far more primitive societies, in which reactions are more spontaneous: for instance, the Lushais in Assam once lived in big villages with 400 or 500 inhabitants, like those in the Far East, compactness being adopted for defence. Later the *pax britannica* made compactness unnecessary, and old villages lost their people, who swarmed instead into scattered hamlets.

Scattered settlement is not always the result of the more or less complete break-up of a compact village. It is often due to the original manner in which settlers occupied the land and it all took place as if scattering belonged to an original kind of rural settlement which seems to have begun very early in western Europe and was preferred at certain times in certain countries to village settlement, such preference depending mainly on a whole set of economic phenomena.

Nowadays, and since the beginning of the nineteenth century, so far as the working of the land and the attaining of yields are concerned, scattered settlements seem to be a superior form of organisation. Modern colonisation has always settled in isolated farms, as if former difficulties that oppressed rural settlement had been overcome, and different problems had influenced the selection of sites. Of greatest importance, apart from subsistence cropping, has been the obtaining of the highest possible yield for the least expense.

Throughout the Tsarist régime, Russian emigrants to Siberia used to build isolated farms arranged in hamlet-groups, the farms often being separated from each other by several hundred yards, or even a mile or two. In the Far East the village has been regarded as an outmoded form of settlement in the colonisation of Hokkaido, and the Japanese authorities have considered that a series of isolated dwellings would be more likely to attract settlers than would the construction of well-ordered and well-administered villages like those in Honshu. Scattered settlement very soon became the habitual way of occupying the land in the United States between the Appalachians and the Mississippi as soon as it was safe to break up the village centres; but settlement in isolated farms developed, as the normal procedure, in occupying land mainly after the Civil War and the promulgation of the Homestead Act. Each settler could establish himself and his family on land of his own choice and from the second half of the nineteenth century, this law resulted in a wholly scattered country population.

In an earlier period, grants of *seigneuries* in French seventeenth- and eighteenth-century colonies in the West Indies, San Domingo and Réunion, carved out long strips running inland from the coasts of the islands; they were from 25 to 30 metres wide and sometimes stretched for 7 to 8 kilometres. On these were built the *habitation*— the house and sugar mill in the centre of its own ground. The same arrangement for settlement existed in the former French Canada, in which the *rangs* in the St Lawrence valley recall the strips on the *seigneuries*. The English part of Canada shows a still more definite scattering, for instead of aligning the houses along the front of the strips, the creation of the 'township'—a square with a length of three miles (5 kilometres) a side and cut up into square divisions of 160 acres (65 hectares) each—has favoured the scattering of the farms. In general, European pioneers of the eighteenth century, limited only by the boundaries of their concessions and often acting according to their own lights, willingly gave up overseas the kind of rural settlement found in their native land. The distribution of concessions and their registrations have merely reflected the settlers' wish to be independent on their own lands. The traditional common property in pasture and forest undoubtedly survived for some time, but in a far more flexible form than existed in Europe at the same period. For the rest, the settlers would have neither the arrangement of the land nor the forms of dwelling which were due in Europe to the parcelling out of the soil, a system inherited from the whole previous history of agriculture.

Scattered settlements also needed to solve for themselves problems of organisation which were not present in the villages. In an old country, as in the basin of Aquitaine in France, the earliest rural community to exist seems to have been the parish. In the seventh century there appeared a host of churches, placed in isolation at key points at crossroads so as to serve the greatest possible number of small scattered farms; the parishes, however, were only a moral framework and had no economic significance. As time went by there appeared rural communities distinct from the parishes in the form of administrative divisions which served as a basis for the collection of taxes. In this way, round the castles and fortified houses rural communities arose in an effort to create centres for the scattered population. Such centres served not only as a safe refuge, but also as a market and a local chief town ; consequently, the Aquitanian village community was formed slowly under the pressure of historical necessity and the centralising influence of a unifying government.

It is different in new countries, and particularly in the rural communities in the centre and west of the United States, which offer a striking contrast to western Pennsylvania and the State of New York. In the Atlantic States indeed, large villages are often found clustering round a church and these, built in the English colonial style, would not be out of place in Europe. Those seen between Harrisburg and Lewistone are formed of little wooden houses built along the roadside. Each house has a lawn in front and is separated from its neighbour either by shrubs or by a piece of empty ground which the owners of the house have bought as a speculative building site : but for these sites, the compact nature of the-villages would be still more obvious. Although farmers are now motorised, most of these old villages have the great disadvantage of being so placed as to necessitate long journeys from the village to the fields. Moreover the very shape of the villages, together with the history of the country, shows them as having been built originally in clearings of land in an age now long past. Though this kind of village is quite tolerable when its land comprises but a hundred or two hectares, it is highly inconvenient when the properties amount to one or two thousand hectares. In Kansas the small density of population on a vast area results in an extraordinary scattering. Within the framework of the impersonal 'townships' are scattered the swarms of 'homesteads'. A township may have only one of its concessions occupied. In such a case, the remaining land cannot be used by that one settler, even as a passageway or as a pasture. A strange regrouping of farmers is therefore in progress round schools and railway stations, which are becoming attraction centres with urban characteristics. In these, the farmers lead the life of a townsman and enjoy all urban comforts. Cultivation is by means of a satellite farm, built a few dozen miles away in the middle of the cultivated land, but this is occupied only seasonally at times of work and harvest. No longer is the place of settlement seen in its agricultural rôle, its rural function has disappeared, there is no longer even a market. This change in living conditions is produced wherever machinery enables the farmer to be transferred easily to and from his land, thus enabling him to live some distance from his fields. This is only possible when no cattle bind him to the soil. Nowadays it is towards development of this kind that rural settlements are tending in many parts of the Soviet Union, where the *Kolkhozy* assume the appearance of country towns or *Agrogrady*. They are merely the residence of a wage-earning population, which works on the land with the help of powerful machinery supplied by the Machine and Tractor Stations.

In countries where the population is scattered, the building of these urban-type villages is due largely to the need for setting up foundations for future centres of attraction. Situated in the midst of their enormous properties, the farmers suffer greatly from isolation. Country towns in the United States build houses of several storeys, similar to town houses together with car parks, filling stations, drive-in cinemas, and laundries, etc. Also, since the neighbouring farms grow nothing but wheat, and have neither dairy cows nor poultry, all supermarkets and drugstores supply their customers with such items as pasteurised milk, fruit, canned vegetables, and even often fresh eggs !

Thus whenever dispersion becomes excessive, social needs, using any existing assets, tend to create artificial groupings, which try to satisfy the material and moral needs of the people. But the completion of such a communal centre is a far slower process than it would be in the case of compact settlements. The results may even end in being foreign to country life as a whole and in extreme cases the centre may even be only a degenerate form of town settlement.

As a general rule, the scattered settlement seems to be less anti-quated than the compact settlement. This has been made obvious by the more recent forms of colonisation. It appears on the other hand to be the final stage of an evolution which passes from the compact towards a looser form of settlement.

In Europe, scattered settlement has more than once appeared to be on the increase, but the trend has not been followed up ; compact settlement has continued to prosper and to consolidate its position until such time as a new movement of decentralisation and dispersion should develop.

Mere pressure of population, too, has caused villages to break up and has made them begin to scatter, this being due to the accepted belief that scattered settlements lead to more intensive production, and that any innovations in agriculture must always be preceded by a breakaway from communal practices of which the compact settlement was the symbol. Often, too, social factors alone could involve a change in the form of settlement, such as, for example, the landowner's view as to the best use of his land. Thus it has come about that the form of rural settlement has at various times and in various places depended on his views and he has acted some-times as a keeper of traditions and an organiser of land, and some-times as a revolutionary reformer.

In Vaucluse and Var, the old villages have been gradually deserted in stages since the sixteenth century ; such villages were usually situated in some high and prominent position for reasons of security, but lacking access to both water and fertile land. As cultivation by irrigation developed the plains below, and the modern means of communication expanded, the population, no longer afraid for their own safety, transferred their living quarters from the hill-tops to the plain, each member building his little farm on the irrigated land he cultivated.

In conclusion, it seems, too, that compact settlement is always due to some constraint : physical constraint when man is ill-equipped to deal with his environment and must needs form a group to succeed ; technical constraint when the equipment demands the formation of a group for maintaining dykes, norias, and appliances for the common use ; and agrarian constraint when the system of rotation demands a set course in the use of the soil. There is also sometimes a social constraint imposed by the landowner, or by rigid social structure of which the *mir* of old Russia and the Soviet *kholkoz* are good examples.

Dispersion on the other hand is a form of freedom. It may

develop when man has mastered nature, and technical development has made possible the extraordinary scattering of human dwellings. Freedom has also come from the progressive mastery of an economic system which taxes the productions rather than the instruments of production; also from the early disappearance of serfdom, of which communal obligations were but one aspect.

It can therefore be seen that the elements of constraint and the factors of enfranchisement have in turn dominated the agricultural system. The development from compactness to dispersion which is very general, and today is still visible, is not irreversible. The Mediterranean part of France went through a period of dispersion in Gallo-Roman times, when the *pax romana* held sway and there was a period of trade and an open economic system. The downfall of the Roman Empire introduced an era of insecurity, which went on after the invasion of the Barbarians owing to the incursions of the Barbary pirates. At the same time, the disappearance of the trade currents precluded the chance of selling harvests. People then withdrew to the hill-tops into big fortified villages and there lived in a closed economic system. Later, the return of security, the beginnings of trade, and the introduction of new techniques encouraged dispersal of settlement once more. It is therefore possible that we are faced with a cyclical phenomenon with subdued oscillations; and this explains why a map showing the distribution of settlements in an old rural area shows the permanence of social and economic stages which have followed one another. These stages have eventually disappeared, but their traces are left in the distribution of settlements; as with old river terraces, the passing of centuries has not obliterated them completely.

CHAPTER 17

TOWNS

The idea of the town is a familiar one; the world's big towns have a personality that is sometimes embodied in a single monument or in some architectural group which is famous all over the globe, thus forming, to some extent, a part of mankind's artistic and scientific heritage. Yet, when smaller and less famous towns are considered, which have played no part in history important enough to make their names familiar, they are by no means easily distinguishable from some of the large rural agglomerations. The truth is that there is no outward criterion that distinguishes with any precision an urban from a rural agglomeration, and to define the word 'town' one should not limit oneself, as do statistics, to counting the number of inhabitants.

In the United States, from 1880 to 1900, a 'town' was defined (for different purposes) as a place with more than either 4,000 or 8,000 population; but since 1900 the censuses have regarded 2,500 as the lower limit for urban classification. In France and Germany, towns have more than 2,000 people. In Britain, there is no suggestion of number. Harrow with a population of 300,000 is an urban district, whilst Wallingford in Berkshire, with a population of only 3,500, is a town. It is rather a matter of history than population. Statistical data are indeed no justification; in Hungary, Southern Italy, and the Spanish province of La Mancha, there are huge agglomerations of peasants and agricultural labourers, which have populations of tens of thousands of persons, but cannot be regarded as towns. On the other hand, in Germany, there are little clusters of townfolk numbering just a few hundreds, right in the middle of surroundings which have remained rural.

There were times when, because of the functions peculiar to them, the towns were clearly distinguished from the open country villages around, and were protected by enclosing walls. Though some villages were also enclosed, they were the exceptions and did not have such strongly fortified walls as did the towns. Another privilege of the towns was the right to hold a market, either within the walls or just outside, and they also possessed the monopoly of certain manufactures, forbidden to the villages in the open country. True, these advantages were of comparatively short duration and as the years passed the towns lost some of their economic prerogatives.

The real criterion should be sought in the essential functions of the towns in normal conditions in their surroundings, by which they are clearly distinguished from the nearby rural clusters. They are usually defined by the preponderance and concentration of the kinds of work connected, not with agriculture, but with trade and industry. The peculiar character of the town as a human institution is therefore due less to the number of its inhabitants than to their occupations, and to the kind of economy resulting from these occupations. A town is thus a form of dwelling-place in which the majority of its residents carry out their work within the built up area. It is also a compact dwelling-place with a varied occupational structure, which omits all the primary occupations, in particular, agriculture. The town thus implies both a concentration of industry and a centre of business, and these two functions are often found together owing to the presence of a road or to a stream of traffic.

THE ORIGIN OF TOWNS

Among the strongest factors of town growth, traffic is the most common, and certainly the oldest. Indeed, trade gives rise to all the advantages conferred by a geographical position on a site in relation to natural routes. In examining the origin of a town, two factors should always be taken into consideration; first the sum total of commercial advantages which have led to the establishment of a permanent, developing dwelling-place in a favourable position on a given route, and, secondly, the human cluster whose work has created and given life to the urban organism.

Now, some historians and economists think that towns are the creation of the routes which are used; there are no towns without roads leading to them, and a purely rural area, whatever its degree of wealth and civilisation, could never give rise to a true town. Others hold that towns are the work of traders, that is, of small parties of people from outside the district, but denizens of the road going through it, who have no connexion with the countryfolk, whose very language they often do not know. At its founding, every town is rather like the Hellenic trading stations on the shores of the 'Barbarian' lands in the Mediterranean, when they set up the only urban settlements of ancient times. Along every route there are numerous sites which have special advantages. First, the actual site itself may be determined by the wear and tear of the material that is used as means of transport; in the days when all carriage was done with either beasts of burden or draught animals, the length of the day's journey was determined by the unavoidable necessity of giving the beasts fodder and water as well as rest before the next day's journey. The stopping places along the main roads were marked by inns and shops, round which sometimes gathered the dwellings of peasants and artisans, such as the farrier, the wheelwright, and the carpenter, who were all indispensable. Such embryo towns, the last of which are seen in the *caravanserai* of the Near East, were placed at stage distance from each other, and their arrangement along the routes followed a certain regularity which reflected the tempo of traffic in those days. Most of these urban centres disappeared when newer techniques modified the length of these stages and the system of traffic. Advantages given by the convergence or the crossing of traffic routes were, however, more lasting. The meeting of two valleys in the mountains has almost always become the site of a growing urban centre: Innsbrück, Trente, and Grenoble are good examples. Larger towns such as Basle, Geneva, Lyon, Milan, and Vienna have developed at points where routes leaving the mountains have come into contact with other converging roads. Since deserts are like mountain ranges in being obstacles to communications, towns have also sprung up at places where tracks converge or leave the desert, e.g. Timbuktu, Sokoto, Kalgan, and Lanchow.

Modern means of communication have, when they converge, the same influence on town growth. Many modern towns have grown up at big railway stations which mark the crossing of main lines. Starting as a collection of hotels and the houses of railway employees, they soon acquired business and residential quarters, and sometimes industrial quarters with factories as well, with workshops and workmen's lodgings: examples are Crewe and Swindon in England; Oberhausen in Germany; Tergnier and Longueau in France, and Novo Sibirsk and Czeliabinsk in the U.S.S.R.

None of the natural routes was more used than were navigable rivers; and it is not surprising that the great river valleys should be favourite places for the sites of towns, especially as the confluence of big rivers always involves convergent trade routes. In Europe, Mainz, Lyon, Mannheim, Ghent, and Belgrade are good examples, whilst in the Americas there are Manaos, Cairo, and St Louis, and in China, Hankow and Chungking.

Seaways also afford sites favourable to town growth, because ships converge and crowd together at certain places along the coasts. In this connexion, straits offer a specially favourable position, and nearly all of them have a large town, sometimes twin towns, facing each other across the river; thus we have Istanbul and Scutari, Messina and Reggio, Gibraltar and Tangiers, Dover and Calais. Along artificial seaways the same advantages and functions have given rise to wholly artificial modern towns such as Port-Said, Ismailia, and Suez, on the Suez Canal, and Cristóbal and Balboa on the Panama Canal.

In the course of history, towns have stood on straits nearly everywhere, and some of them have played important rôles; Troy, the mistress of the Dardanelles, exacted tolls at exorbitant rates from the Greek ships; the Trojan war was an opportunity for the Greeks to destroy a nest of pirates and to set free the route to the corn-lands on the Black Sea.

With its command of the entrance to the Baltic, Copenhagen offers another example of a big capital city founded on the exploitation of a strait. It is situated at the crossing of land and sea routes. Starting from the continent, the land route passes through Jutland and then over the big islands of the Danish archipelago. The narrowness of the straits affords an easy passage to southern Sweden. This is the recognised route from Germany to Scandinavia. The sea route on the other hand passes from the North Sea through the Skagerrak and the Kattegat to the Baltic by the Sund, on which Copenhagen is built. This 'Trader's Haven' has always been the guardian of the gates of the Baltic: tolls at Elsinore were not abolished till 1857. For a time, Copenhagen was the commercial and political capital of a great Baltic state which also included Norway and Skåne, and stretched over the shores of the continent as far as Estonia. The Danish empire, like modern Denmark, is typical of a state wholly founded on a town, whose functions are those of a large seaport.

On seaways, large towns have sometimes grown up on inhospitable coasts at the points of call or where supplies might be taken in; these marked stages on the routes, stages which varied with the sailing techniques used, either sail or steam. The seaway to India was thus laid out by Funchal, Las Palmas, the Cape, and Durban. Another route went through Bombay and Colombo, the two routes converging at Singapore, whose position near the busy straits possesses some of the advantages enjoyed by Copenhagen, although in different economic and political surroundings.

Other favourable places on trade routes are situated at points where transhipment must take place. This means that the geographical conditions of the locality impose a change in the means of transport, and this happens regularly at certain natural obstacles. For a long time, a break in the journey was necessary whenever a river had to be crossed, for bridges were not built in early times, especially over wide rivers. Crossing was made originally either by ferry or ford. As bridges began to be built, very few at first, they became a centre of attraction for the important trade routes and were used as convenient stages. The bridges often stood at a cross-roads between an overland route and a navigable stream, a meeting place that is to say, of trade routes of different kinds from different places. Hence the swarming of towns at bridges, built on both banks where the river is not very wide, but dividing themselves into two separate and often antagonistic towns, facing each other on opposite banks, where the river is fairly wide. Tarascon and Beaucaire, on the Rhône are good instances of this. Most big towns today are bridge towns: for example, London, Paris, Vienna, Budapest, Orléans, Avignon, Frankfurt, and Berne. The function of a town as guardian and user of the bridge is often shown in the name of the town itself, such as Cambridge, Bridgewater, and Bristol in England; Pontoise and Pont-Audemer in France; Innsbrück and Saarbrücken in German-speaking countries, and Mostar in the Balkans.

Mountain crossings too have given rise to stage towns at points where vehicles had formerly to be exchanged for beasts of burden in order to ascend the ridges by mule tracks. Coire, Lucerne, Suse, and Bolzano in Europe; Salta and Santiago in South America, are but a few of the many examples that might be quoted.

Characteristic stage towns are to be found at desert entrances, where vehicles and ordinary beasts of burden must be substituted for camels; at Kiakta and Kalgan on either side of the Mongolian desert for example, where the change of goods from wheeled vehicles to camels, or vice versa, take place.

Other town sites have been determined by points where navigation ends and where cargoes must be transferred from ships to cart or truck. On rivers and canals, the type of boat must sometimes be changed when the water becomes too shallow. At the place where the barges are either lightened or emptied, there is an accumulation of goods and a collection of people, and sooner or later, a town starts up. One of the factors in the growth of the town of Lyon was that navigation on the Saône and on the Rhône required different types of boats, and transhipment was necessary at the confluence of these two rivers. In some areas, the occurrence of rapids necessitates portages; in such cases, the great need for labour to haul the boats across, has given rise to town nuclei developing near the obstacle and near places where long waits are sometimes necessary. A rudimentary collection of sheds and inns, as at Kayes and Itchang, can become a large town which directs busy river traffic, as at Mannheim on the Rhine, and Duluth, Cleveland, and Buffalo on the Great Lakes.

Another site for commercial towns is found where ocean shipping stops on an estuary, and cargoes are transferred from the ships to an overland route or on to rivercraft. This is a common type of town in western Europe and in all countries in which river mouths are entered by the flood tide. The highest point upstream reached by the tide is usually the place where ocean shipping stops, and it often coincides with the site of the lowest bridge across the river. Thus was determined the position of London, Rouen, Bordeaux, Hamburg, Baltimore, and Philadelphia.

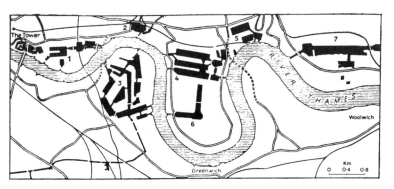

FIG. 17.—A RIVER PORT : LONDON.

1. London Docks. **2.** Limehouse Basin. **3.** Surrey Commercial Docks. **4.** West India Docks. **5.** Millwall Docks. **6.** Victoria Docks. **7.** Royal Victoria Dock. (From British Admiralty Chart.)

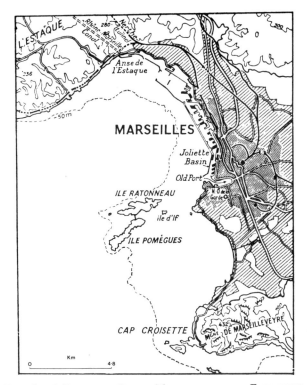

FIG. 18.—A ROADSTEAD PORT : MARSEILLES AND ITS EXTENSIONS.

More generally, the position of harbours where seaways meet overland routes to the interior of the country favours the creation of towns, whose importance increases with the amount of trade they handle. Calcutta, Alexandria, Rio de Janeiro, Melbourne, Santos, Vera Cruz, La Guaira, mark the meeting of the sea with large backlands, thus forming, as it were, both a front door and an exit to the ocean. It may in fact be said that more than one-third of the world's big towns are seaports.

The important part played by trade in the growth of towns explains why human settlements are often found on the borders of regions which differ in their economy. Especially is this the case when the products of such regions are complementary, for then trade begins almost spontaneously like a natural phenomenon.

The need for short-distance trade explains why in France, for instance, many towns line the junction of the plain and of the wooded country (bocage) such as Falaise, Bayeux, and Alençon; of dry cultivated plateaux and damp clayey and sometimes industrialised plains, as at Saint Omer, Aire, Lille, and Douai. The same economic factor also explains the development of towns found at the junction of anciently occupied and newly reclaimed land, that is, between polders and dry land, as at Bruges, Bergues, Groningen; and in Germany, between the Marschen and the Geest.

Apart from the advantages due to traffic, differences in natural product and modes of life often account for the presence of towns at the junction of mountains and plains: Grenoble and Zurich in the Alps; Pau, Tarbes, Foix, and Saint Giron in the Pyrenees; Salta, Tucuman, and Mendoza in the Andes. Similarly, strings of little towns surround the Vosges and the Morvan, while in Scotland they mark the zones of contact between the Highlands and the Lowlands. In other parts of the world, the junction of productive areas as different as the desert and the savanna, cause the rise of urban centres such as Kuka and Zinder.

Thus everywhere, towns mark points of contact between geographical regions engaged in trade with each other. In such a case, the town is essentially a market town, a periodical or seasonal meeting place of traders whose business adds to the transactions of local shopkeepers. Hence the host of little urban centres and market towns, situated on the edge of different little geographical units, not to mention the big towns lining the border of major natural regions, where economic differences cause great trade movements. For instance, the prairies in the United States are encircled by a belt of towns whose functions have remained essentially commercial, such as Kansas City, Omaha, Chicago, and Cincinnati.

Routeways are of such vital importance to the life and growth of towns that some urban centres, situated on important or strategic routes, have been known to develop into states. In this instance, the town has incorporated an accumulation of wealth and such a large population concentrated round a crossroad of trade routes, that it has eventually become strong enough to control its own destinies. Such a town drawing its supplies from a thousand channels is able to live without any territorial support. Historically, there were such towns which had no territory of their own. Ancient times furnished such examples as Tyre and Sidon, Carthage and even Athens. In later times, there were Venice and Genoa, the great trading city of Hamburg which was for a long time an independent republic; even La Rochelle was at one time such a merchant republic.

Today, a capital city like Copenhagen far surpasses in importance that which might have been expected of town growth in the little state of which it is the chief town. Similarly, in the colonies founded by Europeans in America and Australia, the chief town due to the concentration of the commercial life of the whole country is in fact the nucleus of the state. This is true of Rio de Janeiro, Buenos Aires, Montevideo, Sydney, and Melbourne.

On the other hand, when trade falls off, dries up, or moves away, town life declines. The disuse of trade routes has led Ravenna and Pisa into decay; the silting up of the Zwin hastened the decay of Bruges; the closing of the Scheldt by the Netherlands left Antwerp in a state of stagnation for a hundred and fifty years. Towns like Timbuctu and others on the border between the desert and the savanna in Africa, have lost their livelihood since their trade was diverted by the Europeans to the coast of Guinea; and on the fringe of the desert of Syria and western Asia, many cities of the past have died because trade deserted them. There is no doubt that the greatness or the downfall of commercial routes influences the rise or the decline of towns.

Can it be concluded from this that towns are to such an extent alien to their surroundings that they have always owed their foundation to initiative from without, and that their initial population has always comprised a group or even a whole social class completely alien to the country? Pirenne and other historians have upheld the theory that foreign traders must always have brought a kind of revolutionary ferment into rural societies which were unable to escape unaided from their habits of self-sufficiency. But many towns, even in Flanders, appear to belong essentially to their rural surroundings. They by no means look like the artificial creation of traders foreign to the country. They often grew by the slow accretion around a monastery of *villae* in which, beside the cultivators, there were craftsmen working in leather, wool, or parchment; having a little later a *mercatus* or trade centre, where exchanges took place between the compact group, the neighbouring country people, and the itinerant traders who paid dues to the monastery. These first groups often strengthened their cohesion by surrounding themselves with ramparts. From the days of the Norse raids, they therefore became a refuge for the people who lived in the open country. And thus, long before the development of commerce, the combination of *castellum*, of *mercatus*, and of abbey, to which were added the dwellings of the craftsmen and peasants, together formed the core of an agglomeration very different from the country village, and which, even at this stage, deserved the name 'town'.

Many other factors than trade may, moreover, determine the growth of towns. True, they are less strong and universal, they are more localised, but they are none the less able to create towns as imposing, lasting, and dynamic. Among these factors is one which stems from the natural environment and its resources and which creates industrial towns. These are clearly localised and are usually of recent creation. Towns have, however, always been founded on spots where mineral deposits are exploited. The attraction of precious metals is so great that even stark desert—as at Kalgoorlie —and high altitude have not been obstacles to town development when their exploitation was concerned. Cerro de Pasco, for instance, stands 4,352 metres above the sea, and Potosí stands at an altitude of 3,960 metres.

The discovery of gold and silver mines has given rise in many parts of the world to mushroom towns which, within a few weeks, were endowed by bold and enterprising men with streets, hotels, banks, and theatres. The lightning rise of Johannesburg in the Transvaal is well known. It sprang up all of a sudden to cater for the rush of gold prospectors, and has grown to a size justified by the constancy and abundance of the reefs. But it is also characteristic of these mining towns that they die off when the lodes which they work fail. The old towns of Mexico and Peru are instances of this, as are also the towns in Nevada which died with the exhaustion of their mines. Thus the population of Virginia City fell from 11,000 in 1880 to 2,700 in 1900, and that of Eureka was reduced from 4,200 to 800 inhabitants in less than twenty years.

In modern times, towns have grown up through the influence of industrial activity alone. The attraction of industry was very active from the time when mechanical inventions forced machinery to be taken to the streams which supplied motive force. Many mountain villages of rural nature then grew up into little towns in proportion to the amount of energy at their disposal. For instance, large towns were founded and grew up at Manchester, Leeds, and Bradford on the two sides of the Pennines. The same may be observed in the United States along the Fall Line, in New England, and at Saint Paul-Minneapolis.

The modern type of industrial town, a type almost unknown until the end of the nineteenth century, owed its appearance to coal. Within our own time, coalfields with their potential mechanical power have become, nearly everywhere, the support of groups of new towns, often with several kinds of industries. These towns, as they grew, joined with their neighbours, to form enormous multiple towns, to which the name 'conurbation' is sometimes given. The Ruhr coalfield affords the most extraordinary instance of this type, with the towns of Essen, Düsseldorf, Dortmund, Duisburg, Gelsenkirchen, Elberfeld, Barmen, Bochum, Krefeld, Oberhausen, and München-Gladbach. The French coalfields in the *départements* of Pas-de-Calais and Nord and the Belgian Borinage contain similar collections of towns, and the English 'Black Country' is another excellent example. This kind of urbanisation certainly bears the mark of the Industrial Revolution.

The industrial town has not remained the monopoly of coalfields, for it is found wherever coal or other form of energy can be cheaply transported. Then routes, means of transport, and traffic resume their rights in the creation of towns. Ancient cities to which coal could be taken by rail, river, or canal, all acquired a new lease of life. Their factories attracted crowds of workers whose dwellings form an urban cluster. But this cluster depends on traffic for its supplies of raw material, for the despatch of its manufactures, for its supplies of food, and for the movement of its workers. That is why, in modern times, all commercial towns have added an industrial quarter, and there is no large seaport that has not become industrial.

Even in ancient times, as today in some underdeveloped countries, it may be said that the industrial mode of life was concentrated in commercial towns. In these, merchants gather who can direct production, because they are in permanent touch with the markets. This is why, in ancient times, entrepôts like Tyre, Athens, and Rome built huge workshops to house varied crafts, and why African towns like Zinder and Kuka, which were meeting places for caravans from the Sahara, became centres of industry for blacksmiths, goldsmiths, weavers, and dyers.

Human selection, sometimes even the will of a single individual, is enough to found a town that flourishes and grows. Here are some examples. In the first place, there are garrison towns founded with a political or a military object in a conquered country, in order to protect colonists planted by the foreign power. Such are Chester, Colchester, and other towns in England which were founded as Roman *coloniae*. Then there are the many *bastides* in south-western France and the many German towns which were intended to plant colonies of Germans in Slav countries, as well as the English towns established in Wales. Their function was mainly to ensure safety:

hence the concentration on defensive features. To the same type belong all towns founded near castles and monasteries.

Secondly, royal residences have sometimes been due to the whim of a monarch. The constant presence of leading persons in the state has promoted them to the rank of political capital : Versailles, Karlsruhe, Berlin, The Hague, Brussels, and Madrid are instances of this.

Thirdly, there are political capitals which have been deliberately founded to perform this function only. It may even happen that these administrative towns are precluded from certain activities which would like to enter them, but which, if introduced, would harm the special functions of the towns. Thus, industry is not allowed to exist near the administrative centre of Washington. Ottawa and Canberra were also founded to be state capitals. In recent years, Brazil has rejected Rio de Janeiro as its capital, and has created, out of nothing, an artificial town known as Brasilia, in the interior of the country.

Fourthly, strategic capitals have been founded in quite as artificial a fashion, to defend a threatened frontier by means of a firmly planted and strongly defended centre of population. Edinburgh was in turn an Anglian fortress against the Celts, then a stronghold of the Scots against the English. Peking, Delhi, and at one time Petrograd (Leningrad), were also strategic capitals. When strategic conditions change, such capitals often move their position. Thus Moscow has replaced Leningrad as capital of the U.S.S.R.

Fifthly, religious towns are founded around a sanctuary or the tomb of a saint. Olympia and Delphi had such an origin in ancient times. Today there are Mecca, Lourdes, and Lhasa, periodically visited by vast crowds which sometimes travel by the most modern forms of transport.

Lastly, university towns, which are sometimes ancient and live mainly by their intellectual functions, like Oxford (until it became swamped by modern industry), Cambridge, and Louvain. In the United States, some towns have been founded solely to be centres of learning, and in them the function of university takes precedence over all others.

There are also multitudes of special towns that have sprung up in recent times owing to the ease and speed of travel, which enables people who are bent on pleasure or who are seeking a cure, to go— sometimes very far—to find a resort which may give them rest, amusement, or health. To this type belong the hill-stations in hot countries, like Simla or Dalat, where Europeans and wealthy local people can stay high up in the hills to escape the tropical hot season. India, south-east Asia, and Africa have several such towns, which resemble both spas and tourist resorts.

Watering-places, such as Harrogate, Vichy, Carlsbad, Wiesbaden, and Bath; summer stations in the mountains; seaside resorts such as Blackpool, Brighton, Trouville, Biarritz, and Atlantic City, which attract enormous crowds, and winter resorts such as Nice, Monaco, Cannes, and Miami (Florida) all belong to a generation of towns whose development was engendered both by the provision of rapid transport facilities and by the great increase in population in industrial towns. These towns, to which people go for amusement, for holidays, or as tourists, have sprung up in countries already overcrowded with big towns and where the tempo of life forces man to escape periodically from his environment.

These classes of towns being the creation of autocracy, religion, or fashionable whim, cannot grow without the continuance of the psychological factors that created them, or unless civilisation's powerful aid is added to their intrinsic attraction for enticing large numbers of people.

For all these reasons in most European countries nowadays a great number of different types of town may be seen, which fulfilled many functions in the past and still fulfil many today. They sprang up at various periods, and many of them represent the survivals of an economic past that is no more.

THE SITES OF TOWNS

Towns are mainly dependent on their geographical position, which determines their relations with the outside world. Their general situation, however, includes a wide area which may be well placed in relation to natural routes. But within that area lies one unique point, the topographical site that localises the town and gives it its character. In order to fulfil its function, the human grouping which forms a town, however primitive it might be, must assemble particularly valuable forms of wealth and work and thus accumulate a store of resources. So it is not surprising that whenever men have feared for the safety of their towns, they have chosen defensive sites to protect them.

Defensive Sites.—Nature offers a whole range of defensive sites which towns have not failed to use, even though their growth might be hindered. First of all, there are steep-sided hills that are difficult to climb, either completely isolated in the middle of a plain or hollow, or else merely at the tip of a promontory. These are the *acropoles* or *oppida*, naturally strong, but none the less additionally strengthened by ditches and ramparts. In ancient times we find Athens with its Acropolis, Thebes with its Cadmea. In Scotland there are Edinburgh and Stirling perched on volcanic necks; in

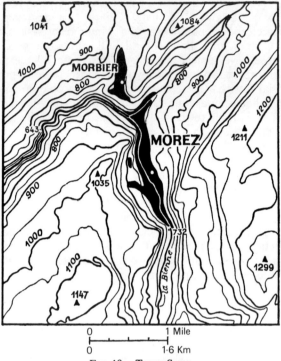

FIG. 19.—TOWN SITES.
Valley-site in mountains—Morez, in the Jura.

Germany, Nürnberg, Tübingen, and Meissen; in Italy, Assisi, Orvieto, and Perugia. In France there is Laon on a hill of sand which stands in front of the Parisian tertiary block, a hill that has resisted erosion owing to its cap of *calcaire grossier* (Eocene limestone). There is also Angoulême on its chalk hill overlooking the valley of the Charente. Very often, considerations of defence have prevailed over all others. Thus, the original position of Athens on the Acropolis is not on the sea. It was only when trading activities developed, and when there was no longer any fear for its safety, that the town spread towards the sea and that the Piraeus was built.

The meander of a river may offer a special kind of isolated high position. Not, of course, meanders that wander over flat country and threaten the town with flood, but incised meanders in dissected terrain. For example, Durham stands on a meander of the Wear and Besançon on a similar bend of the Doubs. Cahors, Toledo, Tirnovo, Berne, and Constantine in Algeria are old towns which make use of similar positions.

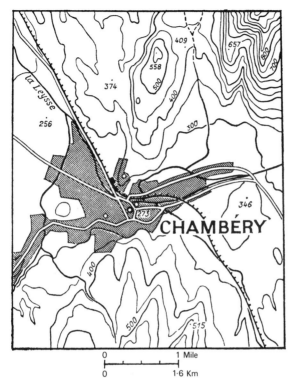

FIG. 20.—TOWN SITES.
In transverse valley—Chambéry, in the Alps.

The belt of water round islands makes defensive positions on which many towns have been built. Seaports like Tyre, Bombay, Singapore, Hong Kong, and New York have thus sprung up on off-shore islands.

Away from the coasts, on important routes, towns have been built on spots where rivers are easiest to approach and to cross. A narrowing of a valley, a ford, or an island are an inducement for routes to cross the river. An island, for instance, reduces the breadth of the stretch of water and so facilitates the construction of a bridge. It also affords a refuge for a settlement which often makes an abusive profit of its position. At Amiens, the Somme divides into some ten narrow channels which flow round islets on which an early town sprang up. The Ile de la Cité, the cradle of Paris, made the crossing of the Seine easy and from the Middle Ages provided a protected site for the town. The earliest settlement in Berlin similarly occupied an island in the middle of the Spree.

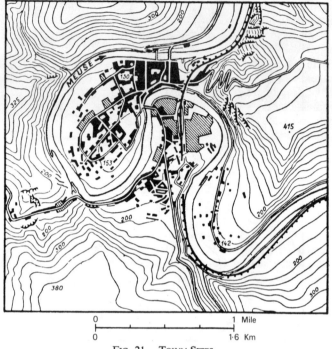

FIG. 21.—TOWN SITES.
In a meander—Revin, in the Ardennes.

Generally speaking, in all its manifestations, whether as swamp, lake, or stream, water affords a multitude of defensive positions. Its proximity sometimes has drawbacks, but in spite of that its help was in the past greatly relied on for defence. Consequently, many towns which were later to deplore its presence, especially in our times when internal peace and continuous traffic are normal conditions of life, sought it out at first as a necessary condition of their existence. Later, they have had to modify their disposition, so as to have an easier approach, as was done in Poznán, Strasbourg, and Mantua. Originally, Hamburg was not built to take advantage of the traffic on the Elbe, or of the tidal estuary, or of the sea approaches near by, but was placed in a defensive position in the swamps of the Alster. The protection of water explains the structure of some aquatic towns in Sumatra and Borneo. These towns are built on the branches of streams where the pile-dwellings are cut off by the flood tide every day.

Economic Sites.—When there is no pressing need for defence, towns are placed directly in useful positions suitable for carrying out their functions. Quite unlike the fortress towns, their site has often to be modified so as to be made more convenient and more accessible.

Some harbours on the banks of a suitable river channel, open yet sheltered, have grown into large towns : Shanghai on the Hwang Pu, Recife (Pernambuco) in an opening in the line of coral reefs which make the coast inaccessible elsewhere, Antwerp on the concave bend of the deep channel of the Scheldt, and Liverpool at the mouth of a small creek on the bottleneck estuary of the Mersey, strongly scoured by the tide.

Economic advantages similarly explain the establishment of towns on rapids or at the lower ends of lakes, as in Zürich, Luzern, Thun, and Geneva.

Other towns have preferred positions in the middle of cultivated plains. The ancient cities of Egypt are an example : they were always threatened by the Nile floods, but were raised on artificial mounds which in turn were held by supports. Others again are situated at the mouths of natural waterways which have had to be closed by dykes to keep out floods, Amsterdam, Rotterdam, and many other towns in the Netherlands are built on such dykes.

It is clear that experience has revealed drawbacks in town sites, which were not noticed by the pioneers. But the force of inertia, as common to human settlements as to other forms of life, has nevertheless kept the towns in their original positions, even where these are recognised as faulty. Hard work has been called for when it has been necessary to modify a position, to strengthen it or to make it healthier. In this way the big town has in many cases become the maker of its own site. Some quarters of Amsterdam are completely built on piles ; parts of Victoria in Hong Kong have been reclaimed from the bay by filling up the shallows with earth.

Changes of Site.—Changes in conditions of safety as well as in general economic conditions have led some towns to rectify their topographical position in order to secure greater comfort or to make them more practical. These towns have therefore had to be moved. Such a removal would be impossible for a large urban agglomeration. But the phenomenon is not unknown in small towns. The borough of Old Sarum, said to be of Celtic origin, was perched up on a waterless chalk hill. It was moved down into the Avon valley to become Salisbury.

In feudal times, the whole population of Déols went off to find shelter at Châteauroux. Sometimes towns have moved twice. For instance, Sancerre began as a Celtic *oppidum*, then it became the Roman town of Saint Satur in the valley of the Loire, and lastly, as a Frankish town it climbed up again on an *oppidum*. Many examples could be given from ancient times, such as Rhodes, and from Gallo-

Roman times, such as Bibracte-Autun. But curious movements of towns have also been seen in modern times. Chicago, for instance, which was founded on ground that was too low, was often flooded during storms on Lake Michigan. It was completely rebuilt on the spot, after its site had been raised by being filled with earth. More recently, Pittsburg has been reconstructed.

The progress of hygiene and town planning nowadays involve the demolition of old quarters in some towns and their reconstruction according to quite new plans which make the old town unrecognisable. Thus, during the Second Empire, Paris was completely transformed as a result of Haussmann's great work. On the other hand, for sentimental reasons, towns destroyed in the second world war have sometimes been rebuilt exactly as they were in 1939 (which means as they had been for several hundred years)—the old centre (Stary Miasto) of Warsaw, for example, and parts of other Polish cities such as Gdańsk and Opole.

The town, which is certainly the most typical form of fixed, stable, and settled dwelling-place, is therefore, like rural settlements and communities of people, also subject to the laws of movement, even if its movement follows a slower rate and is not without resistance.

MAIN PERIODS OF TOWN GROWTH

Consideration of all the factors that have caused towns to spring up leads to the conclusion that, within the course of history, there have been some periods that have been more favourable than others to the rise of this type of human establishment. Brisk town growth is noticed in times of busy trade movements, at times when internal and external colonisation has brought on human displacements and migrations. But it is noticed also in time of insecurity, when some communities have been driven to adopt this manner of uniting for defence. Hence every period of town growth is not one of splendour and prosperous civilisation. A high-pressure commercial life due to intensive movement along the arteries of traffic is needed to make towns into strong, living organisms.

In ancient times the increase in the number of towns occurred at the time of the two great colonising periods, of the Greeks and of the Romans, due to a commercial spirit and to the migration of colonists to form settlements. As early as the seventh century B.C. Greek colonisation started from the cities bordering the Aegean. The colonising movement derived its energy from the expansion of trade. The strongest and more venturesome of these manifestations did not come from the shores of Europe, nor from Megara or Corinth, but from Asia : from Phocaea, from Rhodes, and above all

from Miletus. Thus, there were founded on the shores of the
Mediterranean a whole series of colonies destined to receive Greek
traders and settlers and to establish them right in the midst of a
native environment. These towns were Naupactos, Cyrene, Massilia, Neapolis, Puteoli, Paestum, and later, Alexandria (331 B.C.),
Salonica (316 B.C.), Priene, and Damascus.

Similarly, from the last century of the Republic, numerous Roman
colonists founded a sprinkling of towns over vast territories reaching
to countries far inland, along big rivers and main traffic routes from
the plain of the Po and the Alpine lands as far as Great Britain, the
Rhineland, the East, North Africa, and the Black Sea lands. Among
them were: Aosta, Turin, Ljubljana, Autun, Lyon, Trier, Mainz,
Cologne, Strasbourg, Lincoln, Chester, York, Chichester, Win-
chester, Istambul, Antioch, Antinoe (Sheik Abadeh), Timgad in
Algeria, and Volubilis in Morocco. From the western to the eastern
ends of the ancient world town life bears the mark of Roman
colonisation. It was by this kind of settlement that the Romans
ensured the permanence of their colonies and the security of their
civilisation.

In ancient times, the period of prosperity of the best endowed of
the embryo towns coincides with the time when each civilisation had
control over the main traffic routes and made use of them. Each
period could then bequeath to its successor a number of big towns
which continued to flourish for a long time merely on account of
their permanent advantages. There were Tyre and Carthage, which
were founded by the Phoenicians; Miletus, Athens, Alexandria,
Massilia, and Tarentum which were founded by the Greeks; the
great provincial capitals including Antioch, Damascus, and Lyon
which controlled the eastern and the western routes that the Romans
had created; and above all, Rome, the centre on which all the sea
and overland routes converged.

When the fall of the Roman Empire destroyed the organisation
and security without which towns cannot exist, these were deserted
throughout western Europe, losing their populations to the countryside. In the confusion which ensued, freedom of movement on the
roads disappeared. No more peaceful roads meant no more international trade. Moreover, these roads, which had previously conveyed trade and wealth and whose neighbourhood had been sought
after, became places to be avoided. They brought the barbarian
hosts, and with them death, arson, plunder, and misfortune. Consequently, people shunned them, and communities fled from the
towns exposed to the dangers brought by the roads and settled far
from the ancient highways.

The seeds of town life were able to grow again, however, as soon
as order was restored and maintained by an organised force and

hardy communities were able to re-form. Then defensive towns sprang up in plenty, and gradually towns arising from colonisation followed; but as always, the most powerful towns were those fed and enlarged by trade.

From the moment when castles and monasteries became refuges for defenceless people, a whole swarm of little towns sprang up spontaneously to serve as a centre for everything the communities could wish to protect. Such new towns were usually placed under the protection of a feudal stronghold, but they were independent of the castle. Sometimes, they stood with the castle on top of the hill, as does Castillon in Dordogne. Sometimes they stood on the slopes or at the foot of the hill as do Sévérac-le-Château, Uzerche, Liverdon, Château-Thierry, Châteauroux, Loches, and Niort. At other times, again, town and castle stood on low ground, side by side, as at Chatellerault, Montferrand, and Mirepoix.

Similarly, many towns owe their origin to a monastery near which they found, at first, the same security as near feudal castles. Moissac, Saint Omer, Saint Dié, Saint Emilion, Aurillac, are examples of this. In Italy and Germany, many little towns are found standing in the shade of a castle. They are not so common in England, where after the Norman conquest the king himself undertook to maintain order; but they are not wholly absent, as the following testify: Durham, Kenilworth, Newark, Hexham, Warwick, Norwich.

Some medieval towns were also founded during periods of colonisation. The town was a refuge and protection for the settlers established in a freshly peopled land. To this type of town belong all the *bastides*, the *villeneuves*, or the *sauvetats* in France which were founded mainly from the twelfth century in the south-west by the barons and the kings, in order to protect the rural population in their domains and to defend them against neighbouring barons and kings. In the north and east of France, barons like the counts of Flanders and the dukes of Lorraine also founded such towns, but the greatest town-builders were in the south, the counts of Toulouse, then the kings of France and the kings of England.

All Aquitaine, from the Central Highlands to the Pyrenees, was in this way sprinkled with fortress-towns, which can be counted in hundreds: Sauveterre-de-Béarn, La Salvetat, Castelnau d'Auros, Sauveterre d'Aveyron, Villeneuve-sur-Lot, and many more. Many of these *bastides* have not grown into big towns. Some disappeared very quickly, others are no more than just hamlets; others, however, like Montauban, have kept the appearance and the life of a town.

German settlement went eastwards on the territory then occupied by the Slavs, and is marked by towns founded mainly beyond the Elbe. In this way, hundreds of towns sprang up in Pomerania, the marches of Brandenburg, Silesia, Bohemia, and right into the

Carpathians. They were meant to protect, in occupied country, the chief organs of Germanic life, namely soldiers, leaders, priests, and tradesmen.

In the Saxon period, such towns were especially numerous in the Harz region: Nordhausen, Quellinburg, Goslar. In the twelfth and thirteenth centuries there appeared one after the other: Lippstadt, Hamm, Salzwedel, Brandenburg, Magdeburg, Hamburg, Brunswick, Lübeck, Königgrätz, Budweiss, Pilsen, Frankfurt-an-der-Oder, Berlin, Wismar, Rostock, Stettin, Breslau, Danzig, Königsberg, Thorn, Posen, and many others. Many of these towns were given Slav names again after 1919 and 1945.[1] As with the French *bastides*, many of these German towns disappeared almost at once, or have survived as villages. Others have become large towns, whenever they have been able to use their advantageous position for trading.

In England, the same kind of *bastide* is met with, here and there, especially on the Scottish border and in the Welsh marches, where they were built to check the border raids in the one case, and to serve as English bases in the other: Carlisle, Berwick, Newcastle-upon-Tyne, in the north, and Flint, Conway, Caernarvon in the west.

Whatever the origin or age of these numerous towns founded in the Middle Ages, those which either temporarily or permanently rose above their fellows through wealth, size, or population, owe their success essentially to the currents of trade they have been able to attract and retain. Consequently, there exist several groups of large towns which have not prospered at the same pace, because trade routes have fluctuated between the Middle Ages and our own times.

A first geographical group is formed by the towns of northern Italy: Venice, Genoa, Milan, Florence, and Rome which keeps its leading part as a Christian capital. Secondly, there are the German towns north of the Alps, on routes that issue from the mountain passes, such as Nürnberg, Frankfurt-am-Main, Prague, Munich, Augsburg, all of which are on trade routes towards the north. A third group includes the famous Hansa towns of Cologne, Lübeck, and Hamburg, which were centres of attraction for trade from the

---

[1] Breslau-Wrocław, Stettin-Szczecin, Danzig-Gdańsk, Thorn-Toruń, Posen-Poznan (all in Poland); Konigsberg-Kaliningrad (U.S.S.R.); Budweiss Budejovice, Pilsen-Plzeń (in Czechoslovakia). More recently, many towns all over the world have changed their names, as a result of the re-conquest of territories or of decolonisation. The names given by the former occupants or by the colonists have been replaced by names drawn from the native language, which is now the national language. Thus in Zaire, Leopoldville has become Kinshasa, Elisabethville has become Lubumbashi, Stanleyville, Kisangani; in Algeria, Bône is now Annaba, Bougie is Bejaia, and Philippeville Skikda; in Morocco, Mogador has been renamed Es Saoura, and Fedala, Mohammedia; in Indonesia, Batavia is now Djakarta; in China, Mukden is Shenyang . . . and so on.

south and from the sea. Lastly, there is the group of Flemish towns : Ghent, Bruges, Ypres, Mechelen, and Louvain, which were followed later by Dutch foundations. None of these big towns succeeded even at the time of their zenith, in collecting the colossal masses of population which are characteristic of big contemporary cities.

The modern age forms a third period in this history of urbanisation. Certainly, since the Age of Discovery, the world's economic development has steadily favoured the growth of towns and the strengthening of urban functions. But since the nineteenth century, the introduction of the machine age with its large-scale industry has added to towns in old countries an enormous flood of population, sometimes emptying the countryside to the advantage of the towns, bringing to them vast amounts of energy and a commercial influence which none of the old techniques used in the Middle Ages would have been able to achieve. Moreover, the swarming in all parts of the world of Europeans, imbued with urban civilisation and natural founders of cities, has given birth to large numbers of new towns, first in North America, then throughout the southern hemisphere, and more recently in Soviet Asia and in the frozen regions of the north of Canada and of Siberia. For a long time these new towns have been inhabited mainly by the descendants of their European founders. Like the cities of ancient times and the medieval German tówns, they contained an expatriate population in the midst of a native environment which was sometimes hostile, but which was always far below the standard of civilisation of these newcomers. These new towns have often been the pioneer media and the instructors of less advanced peoples in the higher forms of civilisation and technique. In Brazil, the Argentine, and Australia, the towns have been active agents in increasing the exploitation of the land, in reclaiming it, and even in making it healthier.

Nowadays a great trend towards urban life is observed in many countries that so far had remained unwilling to accept its ways, or in which there have existed only towns founded by foreign immigrants. Following South America, Africa is now the continent where towns multiply and develop at a quicker rate than anywhere else in the world. It looks as though the native African people, who have hitherto been essentially rural, have taken lessons from the town-dwelling and town-building whites.

The enormous growth of all the world's towns and the proliferation of urban centres in countries hitherto containing little town life, form the two characteristic phenomena of modern times where industry has spread everywhere and where the increase in the speed of transport, which would have been inconceivable twenty years ago, has instilled new energy into the flow of trade.

This colossal urge to found towns, which by its strength and distribution over the globe challenges all comparison with the past, began fairly modestly with the vast migrations that followed the Age of Discovery. The migration of a multitude of traders and of European settlers into the new countries involved the creation in each colony of centres of trade which collected the produce of the country and despatched it to Europe. Hence the rise of towns, some of which became enormous later, which specialised in trade. Such was the origin of Sydney, Melbourne, Buenos Aires, Rio de Janeiro, Valparaiso, New York, Cape Town, Algiers, Casablanca, Alexandria, Shanghai, and Vera Cruz.

Later, and particularly in the nineteenth century, in answer to the foundation of new towns overseas, enormous entrepôts grew up in Europe to collect the produce from 'new' continents and distribute it, sometimes even to process it. This movement resulted in the expansion of London, Antwerp, Amsterdam, Hamburg, Liverpool, Marseille, and of many other seaports.

At the same time, town growth was provoked by the development of industry due to machinery and coal. This resulted in the concentration of workers in factories in all the areas most convenient for supplying energy and fuel, and in all towns well placed to get coal easily. Lastly, the improvement brought about by modern means of transport, and the appearance of many new trade routes, have strengthened all trade centres. At the same time they have increased the attraction of towns by ensuring the regular arrival of a constant supply of raw materials and of large numbers of workers.

The town-building trend, general throughout the whole world, has profoundly transformed the structure of various countries, though in various degrees. At the head of the movement, in the nineteenth and still at the beginning of the twentieth century, were Europe, in spite of her long urban tradition, and the American states. From 1866 to 1931, this trend towards urbanisation was especially intense in France, and the proportion of town dwellers with regard to the whole population swelled more rapidly than previously. During this period the number of French towns rose from 102 to 239. But the concentration of population in towns was not accompanied by a change in the geographical distribution of the towns, because this distribution depended on factors which had not been modified, but which, on the contrary, had been strengthened. Consequently, the development had only stressed the fundamental features of geographical distribution that were already in existence.

In France, the districts in which there was an outburst of urbanisation coincide with industrial areas. Thus, the group of towns which sprang up in the Northern Coalfield increased in numbers from seven to twenty-seven in the course of the period under consideration.

A second group of towns owed its existence to the tourist trade, especially on the Côte d'Azur, where Nice grew into one of the largest towns in the country, while alongside it sprang up four towns each with a population of twenty thousand persons. French urban growth, however, is characterised by the increase of existing towns through the development of suburbs. Around all the big cities there spread, at the end of the nineteenth century, little communes with merely conventional administrative independence from the big towns to which they belonged organically. Most of the urbanisation, therefore, comes from the rings of satellites that now encircle the larger places. Lyon and Bordeaux, for instance, have now five communes each attached to their borders. Toulon, Saint Etienne, and Rouen have already absorbed two communes on their periphery while Lille, Roubaix, and Tourcoing, which form a huge 'conurbation', each have annexed a populous suburb stretching as far as the suburbs of the next town.

The most striking instance of the development of such suburbs was Paris, even as long ago as the beginning of the twentieth century. Including the département of Seine and the adjacent communes of Seine-et-Oise, sixty towns there were counted each with a population of more than 15,000 persons, as against five in 1866. This increase in the size of big towns under the threefold influence of the sprawl of suburbs, the rise of industry, and the development of the tourist trade has been the essential mark of towns in Europe for about three-quarters of a century.

During the same period, however, Asia and the U.S.S.R. have, at slightly different times, passed through an extraordinary spell of increase in the number and size of towns. If the count is limited to towns with a population of more than 300,000 persons, a figure which is regarded by some branches of the economy, and especially by air transport concerns, as being the lower limit for a metropolitan centre, one notices both the speed of contemporary town growth as well as the difference of the time of growth between Europe, the new and the underdeveloped continents.

Number of Towns with over 300,000 Population

	1800	1850	1900	1926	1954
Europe (less U.S.S.R.)	4	10	40	60	72
Asia (less U.S.S.R.)	1	5	17	42	61
U.S.S.R.	0	0	1	13	37
America	0	1	16	19	50
Africa	0	1	2	5	12
Australasia	0	0	2	4	5

Africa, the latest arrival in the field of urban development, is now undergoing an extraordinary development of new towns, which grow continually owing to a regular influx of population. And so Africa as a whole, which had towns only on its coasts fifty years ago, already contains some thirty towns with populations exceeding 100,000 persons. These include: Nairobi, Bulawayo, Mombasa, Duala, Ibadan, Lagos, Accra, Leopoldville, and Addis Ababa.

This accelerating urbanisation is resulting, all over the world, in a redistribution of population, for in every country there is an increasing proportion of town-dwellers, a tendency that has become particularly marked in the last two decades. According to the most recent estimates, which include only towns with more than 300,000 inhabitants, there are some 400 million city-dwellers, or a little over 10 per cent of world population; or, to put it another way, as many as the combined populations of the United States, Great Britain, France, and the two Germanies. Other statements are no less arresting: thus, in 1893 there were twelve 'millionaire cities' (with over a million inhabitants) in the world, and 28 with over half a million; in 1973, 127 cities had passed the million mark and 282 were over the half-million. These million-cities contained, in 1893, 15 million inhabitants; in 1973, the total was 230 millions.

The number of very large cities is growing continually, and the oldest of them continue to become distended with new inhabitants. In 1893, the cities with more than half a million contained but 18 human beings out of every thousand—but by 1973 this figure had swollen to 98.

Distribution of Large Cities in 1973

City Size	World	Europe	U.S.S.R.	Americas	Asia	Africa	Oceania
Over 5 million	17	2	1	7	6	1	0
5–1 million	110	31	11	31	30	5	2
1–½ million	155	32	28	34	44	14	3
Total	282	65	40	72	80	20	5

GROWTH OF TOWNS AND ORGANISATION OF SPACE

Modern town growth, which goes on under our very eyes, has thrown up monster cities of a colossal type, veritable provinces covered with houses, continuous groups of towns forming conurbations, which is a massive kind of human settlement hitherto unknown and capable of existing only by its ability to attract people and commodities from without through a close and prolonged network of traffic lines.

These gigantic cities have, like living organisms, a complex rhythm of life, the functioning of which may be jeopardised by the very size of the urban entity. Many of these towns of the industrial era or of the present age have sprung up spontaneously and have produced a disordered outcrop of suburbs and surrounding built-up areas with no development plan. Others have grown so quickly that their increase could not be kept under any sort of supervision or control. In too many cases, therefore, and notably in Asiatic towns, the result has been an accumulation of houses around tortuous streets and in too narrow a space. Many of the European towns are encircled by well-populated but ill-regulated suburban areas, which act as a stranglehold on traffic and gradually stifle the ancient city centre. These suburbs which have arisen too quickly and consist of houses without comfort which soon fall into a state of disrepair, have created dangerous agglomerations of hovels: the slums of English towns or the *corons* or *courées*, i.e. miners' quarters, of certain industrial towns in France. At the beginning of the twentieth century, there was scarcely a town in Europe or America which had not its swarms of wretched and insalubrious quarters. In the new countries, the same defects appeared in the neighbourhood of the colonial towns, built by Europeans, which had already acquired an adhesion of wretched living-quarters composed often of sheds, sordid little huts, and even tents. Such, for instance, were the shanty-towns (*bidonvilles*) of the African cities, and the *favellas* of Rio de Janeiro. The old city centres simultaneously suffered considerable changes, for most of the old residential areas deteriorated. Sometimes the former middle-class occupants went out to new districts, leaving their old homes to petty tradesmen, who were not in a position to maintain the properties. Sometimes there was an exodus of the inhabitants from the central area, which was turned over to offices, government departments, and business houses.

Confronted with the spontaneous transformation of towns, many economists have wondered whether their evolution could not be foreseen and regulated and whether the town could not be constructed on technical lines, like a block of flats or a factory, according to plans which would ensure the proper accomplishment of its various functions, while allowing for a logical and ordered development. The modern age would thus become an age of 'neo-technical' town planning. Various town planners have therefore applied themselves to the problems of reconstructing ancient towns and adapting them to the demands of modern life, in which the requirements of hygiene for great masses of humanity are paramount, as are also the requirements of traffic. While differing in their conceptions, all are agreed on the necessity of organising the planning of the town, the distribution of its activities, of its network of traffic and on the allocation of specific areas or sectors to specific urban functions. As a general rule, they seek to define one or several residential areas, provided with amenities and green open spaces, an industrial area, generally on the outskirts or situated near the town, a commercial and administrative area in the centre of the town.

Other designs aim at shaping a very large town into an aggregate of relatively autonomous districts, each one containing its own industries, blocks of flats, commercial centres, and cultural amenities. This island structure has the advantage of alleviating the internal traffic by placing shopping centres and jobs within easy reach of each group of persons.

Almost everywhere in the New World, then somewhat later in Europe, and in our own time in Africa, urban architecture has developed in height. Typical of this urban construction is the sky-scraper, conceived originally in New York but reproduced increasingly often, particularly during the last twenty years, throughout the entire world. The skyscrapers of America are enormous structures of thirty to sixty storeys and are as a rule commercial centres rather than residential buildings. Centrally heated and air-conditioned on all floors, provided with restaurant rooms and all amenities, supplied by direct, express or intermediate elevator services with communication between the different sectors of each floor, each of these constitutes what is in fact a city containing more inhabitants than an urban district and even than many a small European town.

However, the American town planners of today are critical of this pattern of excessive vertical concentration. Its major defect is that it discharges into the street at one time enormous masses of pedestrians. Some of these buildings contain five or six thousand persons, who pour into the street from the lifts in the few moments of closing time and artificially create a mass eruption, assembling in a single street, which has suddenly become too narrow, the population of a small provincial town, thus blocking all traffic. The city architects of the New World consider that concentration in a vertical direction should be limited to eighteen to twenty-five storeys, under threat of causing the total collapse of the traffic and transport system of a metropolitan city.

One of the greatest problems of neo-technical town planning is, in fact, that of traffic and parking in modern towns. No town in the world more than New York, which has $11\frac{1}{2}$ million inhabitants, can offer a more striking example of this.

The transport system consists, first of all, of a network of metropolitan railways and buses; the 'metro' running sometimes underground (subway) and sometimes overhead, carried by viaducts on a level with the second storeys of the houses. For the crossing of the sea-arms (River Hudson and East River), ferry-boats have been introduced, and twelve of these cross the Hudson. There is also a collection of road and rail bridges, seven across the East River of which two are motorway viaducts, and fifteen across the Harlem River, of which two are similarly reserved for the motorway. Finally, the George Washington suspension bridge spans the Hudson, and, in addition, three road and rail tunnels pass underneath, whilst there are two more under the East River and one under the narrows between Richmond and Brooklyn.

Further, the motor traffic requires the provision around the town of bypass motorways. A network of 'parkways' and 'express parkways' reserved for fast-moving vehicles, surrounds Brooklyn and Manhattan. To the north of Manhattan five motorways leave the peninsula in the direction of New England or of Pennsylvania. On the other bank, a motorway emerges from Lincoln tunnel, crosses Newark, and continues towards Philadelphia. There is thus a whole network of fast traffic lines, and this saves considerable time and speeds up all transport.

On the other hand, in the towns of Europe, which were built in a period when traffic was less dense and less swift, it has often not been possible to make provision for roads sufficiently wide to cater for the requirements of modern transport, although these are essential to a large metropolis.

Many town planners advocate for old towns a new system of planning, which would parcel out the areas into blocks of buildings of twenty or thirty storeys, each of which would have on the ground floor all the shops that are indispensable to the daily life of the community. In this way a great part of the internal traffic of the towns would be limited to traffic in a vertical direction inside the residential blocks, and the street traffic would be alleviated and reduced either to periodic restocking of the retail shops in the block, or to communication between the residential quarters and the centres of work. This would be easy along the wide avenues separating the residential blocks.

Other proposals are to divert underground the motor transport, by adapting to its requirements the design for underground railways. Unfortunately, the diversion of traffic underground or overhead presents serious aesthetic problems, as well as problems of hygiene and finance, besides which there is the added disadvantage of severing all easy contact between the pedestrian and the means of transport which solicit his patronage.

On the whole, our town planners set the problem on a wrong basis by trying to make the streets of a town too much like interurban highways. The character of the latter alters as soon as they come into contact with the towns. They cease to be high-speed traffic channels and turn into areas of contact between those who

33. Petersburg, Virginia, a loosely-knit city of detached houses, devoid of tall buildings, and with grid-iron road pattern only moderately developed

CONTRASTS IN AMERICAN CITIES

34. Dallas, Texas. Rapidly expanding and wealthy city, built on grid-iron plan with many skyscrapers and modern road approaches

35. (*Above*) Outside Nairobi, Kenya

THE SHANTY-TOWNS
OF THE
MID-TWENTIETH
CENTURY

36. On the outskirts of Barcelona, Spain

37. Outside Casablanca, Morocco

pass through the towns and those who live in them. In a town, streets and public squares are not entirely devoted to transit but have definite commercial purposes. These are to attract prospective customers so that they will stop and look at the shop-windows, to store the goods that these customers may want, and to hold them ready for sale, as well as to make movement within the town possible. It must be kept in mind that towns owe their creation to traffic only in so far as obstacles to this existed. Most of the time these obstacles have been an asset to the towns, which have artificially prolonged them in order to keep their functions as stage halts. A sensible town planner would not draw plans making traffic so easy as to be completely useless to the town through which it passes. Each town poses its own special problems; those of the old towns of Europe are not the same as those of the great metropolitan cities of the New World, which are free from the fetters of an historic past. They differ too from those of the new African towns and those which are rising equally rapidly in other underdeveloped territories of the world.

The enormous growth of towns and cities, and the extension throughout the world of urbanised areas built at the expense of other forms of human occupation and land-use, poses problems, towards the end of the twentieth century, that can no longer be resolved within the context of urban geography alone but demand planning on a regional or even a national scale. Often the older towns, constructed to serve other needs than those of the present day, can no longer be reconstructed and re-oriented on their original sites. In Great Britain, which was the first country to suffer from the decay and congestion of its old industrial conurbations, that grew in the nineteenth century, one solution has been found in the construction, during the last few decades, of 'New Towns'. In France, similarly, new towns have been created in the Paris region, as at Evry, Cergy-Pontoise and St Quentin-en-Yvelines, in order to reduce the congestion of the older suburbs that were encircling the capital too closely. In these days the town planners have not only to resolve the physical problems of the expansion of existing towns *versus* the creation of new towns, but also the hitherto neglected or little-understood problems of urban functioning in the light of modern activities and needs: socio-economic problems of housing, work-places and commuting, leisure and the well-being of the future citizens, whether in old towns rebuilt or new towns started from scratch.

Urban renewal implies slum-clearance, whether in the centre or on the periphery, the restoration of the historic centres that, with their monuments of the past give character to the town, and the replacement of congested quarters by high-rise blocks with open spaces. In Paris, for example, the reconstruction of the Marais district and neighbouring areas has involved the destruction of the slums and shanty-towns of the old suburbs of the northwest.

In the development of suburbs, the two solutions most commonly employed are individual detached houses, each with its surrounding garden, and blocks of flats that house more people on less space. However, the high-rise solution, of which the Sarcelles district, northeast of Paris, offers a typical example, creates serious social problems. Devoted exclusively to residence, the blocks provide their inhabitants, often more numerous than those of a small country town, with none of the normal urban services, some of which, like shopping centres, may have to be specially created. Often they are purely residential; the people work in the city or in neighbouring industrial or commercial areas during the day, returning to their 'dormitory town' at night.

These difficulties have given birth to new ideas in town development, which involve, instead of unlimited concentric suburban expansion, self-contained suburban units with urban functions, residential and including secondary and tertiary sector employment opportunities; this is the principle underlying the 'satellite towns' around London and Paris.

It is very difficult to determine the optimum population for a town, beyond which the human agglomeration creates almost insuperable problems of food supply, traffic and safety. The growth of giant cities often results from an excessive centralisation, political, industrial or economic, within a region or country; New York, with $11\frac{1}{2}$ million inhabitants, has for long been the main entry port and the economic driving force of the whole North American continent. Paris, which forms an agglomeration of 8·2 million people, or 16 per cent of the French total, owes its hypertrophy to the undue political and administrative centralisation of France, as well as to the convergence upon it of all the routes that cross the French isthmus, and to the concentration of great industries. Examples can readily be multiplied, and if one Frenchman in six lives in Paris, it is also true that one Mexican in six lives in Mexico City, and one Australian in five lives in Sydney!

To counteract the gigantism of these huge cities in countries with an old and well-developed urban civilisation, the expansion of regional centres is generally favoured. In France the current urban policy is to encourage the growth of 'regional metropolitan centres'. Thus Lyon and Marseille have already passed the million mark, and seven others of 200,000 or so will expand to 300,000–400,000, whilst twenty smaller centres, each having over 100,000, will grow to

250,000–300,000. In this way an urban population of 3½ millions could be accommodated outside the Paris region.

In all countries with a high urban density another urgent problem arises: the great cities, with their built-up areas and lines of communication, are massive consumers of space. For a long time the desire to retain, in the proximity of towns, areas of woodland and farmland has prompted the limitation and disciplining of urban expansion. In Great Britain a 'green belt' is created around old agglomerations and new urban areas, or between two adjacent urban agglomerations, in which no new building is allowed, and no felling of woodland, at least in principle and with only rare exceptions. Much the same thing is true in France, where certain woods and rural areas near to towns are protected against urban encroachment; but it is often difficult to enforce these restrictions, and in both countries there are complaints of development permits being obtained through pressure from financially powerful real-estate companies and the building industry. The relation between urban space and the environment creates problems of increasing severity. In the United States, where the immensity of the territory had hitherto discouraged any such fears of disequilibrium between urbanisation and its environment —a danger already well appreciated in several European countries— contemporary economists are now alarmed at the proliferation of urban areas at the expense of the countryside, at a time when, since about 1970, some of the greatest cities have ceased to grow. New York has actually lost 300,000 citizens, or 2·5 per cent of its population, whilst Detroit has lost 2·4 per cent and Philadelphia 1·3 per cent. The situation at the moment in the United States is that 64 million people live in old city centres, 70 millions in suburbs and 64 millions in smaller towns of over 50,000 inhabitants. It is these smaller towns that are now absorbing the overflow from the great cities and the newcomers to urban life; thus their number is increasing, and always at the expense of the rural surroundings. This small-town urbanisation is happening all along the Atlantic coastlands from Maine to Florida, along the shores of the Gulf of Mexico from Alabama to Texas, and over the whole of the great manufacturing belt from Pennsylvania to Minneapolis. The exodus is impoverishing the great cities, and the growth of the small towns is reducing the area of agricultural land and spoiling the American environment. Indeed it has been estimated that this new form of urbanisation could destroy, by the end of the century, more forest and agricultural land than that taken by the old cities in the last three hundred years.

In sum, then, if it is apparent that the end of the twentieth century is one of those periods in human history that have witnessed the proliferation of towns, it is no less certain that this cannot be allowed to go on uncontrolled; its destructive effects on the environment are such as to demand more and more careful overall planning and organisation of geographical space, the inevitable consequence of man's total occupation of the earth.

CHAPTER 18

STATES AND NATIONS

Of all human institutions, the state is the most complex and highly organised, and geography has the same bearing upon it as upon the elementary groups of individual human beings which make up villages and townships. The state presupposes dominion over a territory, and the political life of any society is to some extent determined by the environment in which it develops. But the state does not simply define territorial bounds; it is a social reality, independent of the race relationships of the human groups which make it up: political geography studies the nature and geographical form of states, their ties with the natural landscape and human environment; it is the science of those phenomena which mark the variations between the political communities of mankind.

The science of the state lies basically in three separate sciences: economics, sociology, and geography; but in so far as it is a geographical phenomenon, i.e. an organism sprung from a synthesis of a human group with its fragment of the earth's surface, the state depends essentially upon geographical sciences for the study of its organisation and its evolution.

GEOGRAPHICAL FOUNDATION OF STATES

Aristotle, when he wrote of man as a political animal, foreshadowed one essential discovery in human geography, which teaches us that even the most backward races already possess an elementary social organisation, often more complex than the low level of their living standards could have allowed one to suppose possible.

From prehistoric times, men have lived in organised clans: among predatory peoples, gleaners, hunters, and fishermen, often too among pastoral groups, the social unit is the clan, linking the members of the same family with several generations recognising a common ancestor, real or mythical. The ancestor is sometimes deified, or symbolised by a totem chosen from the animal world (wolf, crocodile, antelope, and so on). Each member of the same clan scrupulously observes certain rules of life. Thus the Banyoros in Central Africa forbid the drinking of milk for two days when their members have been eating potatoes or beans; often men of the same clan are obliged to wear traditional marks on their faces or bodies, painted or tattooed.

These small political cells do not always live in isolation. Among shepherd peoples especially, clans often group themselves into tribes, of whom the ones best known to us are the great nomadic peoples of Western Asia or North Africa. Some of these big tribes possess a feudal structure: they acknowledge a chieftain (among Arabs, the Sheik), who owns flocks and reigns over the tribe as an autocrat; others form little republics, governed by an assembly of heads of families.

The first form of political organisation among agricultural peoples is the village. Like the tribe, a village may be governed by a chief, the ruler of the territory, or by a village council made up of elders. All these elementary forms of political life offer certain features in common: to every member is assigned his own position and work to do; rules for working and living are imposed on each member of the community; everyone has the pledge of a share in the profits of the community.

States present more highly developed forms of political organisation: during the course of history, their numbers have always increased, and the ambition of all peoples, on reaching a certain level of civilisation and power, has ever been to found a new state. If we count as single states such federations as the United States, the Soviet Union, Brazil, Australia or Malaysia, we may distinguish, at the end of 1975, no less than 153 sovereign states, of which 143 are members of the United Nations Organisation. Of these states, about 75, underdeveloped or in course of development, have come into existence within the last thirty years; for the most part they belong to the 'Third World'.

The greater the number of peoples grouped together and the more widely various their activities, the greater becomes the need for complex organisation. One would have thought that the smaller groups would be formed into clans and tribes, while those people showing kinship of race, language, and religion would form themselves into states as soon as they reached the strength and level of higher civilisation. In practice, it has not been found that the existence of states depends upon any such factors. Norway constitutes a state with a population less than half that of the Parisian urban cluster. On the other hand, with over forty million inhabitants, neither the Ukraine nor Manchuria make up sovereign states. Ethnic unity may encourage the birth of a state, as was the case for Hungary, Bulgaria, and Thailand. But many other states include men belonging to very diverse races: in America, the United States and Brazil are nations whose citizens belong to practically every race on earth. It is most usually found that a state once formed, tries artificially to achieve a racial entity: Germany tried to do this between 1934 and 1944, that is after more than half a century of existence as a unified and centralised dominion. Unity of language does not specially promote the formation of states; it is rare that one common language is used throughout the whole area as may be seen in Sweden, Norway, Spain, and Portugal; on the other hand, Catalan is spoken on French soil in the Department of Pyrénées orientales, French is the language of the Val d'Aosta, on the Italian slopes of the Alps; Flemish is spoken in the north of France beyond the Belgian frontier. Today, particularly in Europe, there may be found well-entrenched polyglot states like Belgium, which has two official languages, French and Flemish; or like Switzerland which has four, French, German, Italian, and Romansch.

Even at the start of political history, language has evidently not been a basic element in the making of a state. On the contrary, it has more often been a consolidation of political unity which has brought with it the strengthening and extending of certain tongues. The expansion of Greek towards the eastern Mediterranean followed the setting up of the empire of Alexander and the Succession states. In the same way, Latin followed the expansion of the Roman world, for pre-Roman Italy was a mosaic of Aryan and non-Aryan languages; at the time of the Punic wars, the various contingents facing Hannibal did not all speak Latin. Equally there were Pontic influences which shaped the speech forms of Central and Eastern Europe, driving back the Roman dialects towards south and west Germany, under Germanic pressure.

Then again a shift of tongues may be noted, which corresponds to the shifting of frontiers. The use of the French language surged eastwards as the strength of that state grew ever greater. At the end of the Carolingian era the frontiers of the two languages, French and German, were still to be found west of the Meuse and south of the Somme. But in the sixteenth century and later, after the Thirty Years War, French advanced strongly towards the east and northeast. At the time of the Carolingian Empire, German ceased to be spoken on the line of the Elbe–Saale; a few centuries later, it had advanced eastward to the detriment of the Slav languages.

The Chinese state imposed its language and at the same time its civilisation upon very mixed races, and in the same way the Arab tongue spread with Arab domination over the greater part of western Asia and over northern Africa as far as the Sudan. In Egypt, the language has altered following the various political changes; during the first centuries of the Christian era, Greek had almost taken the place of Egyptian; with the spread of Christianity, Egyptian or Coptic supplanted the Greek, and finally the Arab conquest made Arabic the official language of Egypt.

In general, the area of a language does not increase as fast as the area of the state which promotes it. Great nations, whose growth has been very rapid, often had several languages in their early stages, for example, the Persian, Roman, and Arabian Empires. Often the vanquished adopted the tongue of their conquerors, but the contrary has also been seen, when one such language, not necessarily the conqueror's own, possessed a technical superiority, a richer vocabulary, and lent itself more easily to cultural exchanges. Frequently too, by adopting a language of its own, a nation sub-consciously becomes more separated from others; never have there been more written languages than since the start of the twentieth century. Since 1919, each Central European state has adopted a national language. Each of these new tongues is far more erudite than popular, created by educated patriots, writers, and journalists whose talent has changed local speech forms into nationalistic literary languages. The majority of these tongues copy the abstract elements of the great civilised languages, and keep only the common vocabulary of everyday life belonging to their national speech. Exactly the same thing as happened in Europe after the first world war has now occurred in the new states that were born after de-colonisation.

Neither does religious unity create a state. The Turkish state, a Muslim power whose sovereign held the title of 'Commander of the Faithful', extended its rule over Christians and Jews. Attempts at religious consolidation have been tried in already integrated states, anxious perhaps to establish conformity amongst their subjects. In the sixteenth century, faced with the advancing tide of the Reforma-tion, certain statesmen had the idea of systematically enforcing a religious uniformity within their different countries, to stop inter-necine quarrels and religious wars; but it was never possible to apply their principle *cujus regio, ejus religio* in the larger states; even Switzerland was obliged to accept a religious dualism which was super-imposed upon the several languages in the country. On the whole the grand political units of history—the empire of Alexander, the Roman, Turkish, and Austro-Hungarian empires, and in our own time, the U.S.S.R.—have always united under one authority peoples of varying races, languages, and religions.

States are not predetermined in single territorial units. Some natural regions may spontaneously have provided a framework for countries which later overran others of closer similarity. Certain peninsulas have often been endowed with their own political life, especially when protected by mountain systems which have cut them off from the continental land mass; thus, Spain, Italy, and India were early able to become unifying national frameworks. Sometimes men have artificially strengthened the natural barriers by building earthworks such as the 'Danewerk' and the Wall of the Picts. One notices too, that the four most ancient states on earth were all developed in great plains, directly on the banks of a great river, which rose in high mountains and thus ensured a regular supply of water. This was certainly the case for Egypt, Mesopotamia, the India of the Punjab, and the Honan and Shensi provinces in Central China. These states were situated in very dry areas, bounded or encircled by deserts and made habitable by the water supply and silt of their great rivers, the Nile, Euphrates, Indus, and Hoang Ho. Well protected, too, from continental invasions, these countries filled their entire natural framework and built up a firm political entity. Egypt, encompassed south and east by the desert, in the north by a sea which became navigable only in the fifth millennium B.C., in the south by the cataracts of the Nile, formed a perfectly sealed-off enclosure, inside which the floods of the Nile created a particular social organism and a unique economy.

Nevertheless, the existence of a well-marked natural environment developing similar ways of life will not of itself bring forth a state ; nowhere, either in the Ancient or in the New World, is there to be found a Hyperborean state which embodies the Arctic regions ; even inside the U.S.S.R., these polar territories come within the jurisdiction of five administrative or political authorities ; the low density of settlement and the isolation of the inhabitants who belong to various ethnic groups, yet are conditioned to the same way of life, explain this lack of political unity in reasonably uniform surroundings.

Conversely one may note that certain clearly defined territories have been shared out between different states. The large island of Hispanolia is shared by two countries, Haiti and the Dominican Republic; Ireland does not belong wholly to the Irish Republic; the Scandinavian Peninsula is divided between Sweden and Norway; the Iberian Peninsula between Spain and Portugal. On the other hand, Italy spreads widely beyond the Mediterranean Peninsula, over the plain of the Po and into the Alps which, geographically, belong to central Europe. Thus a state no more requires racial unity for its building than an individual territory. Most nations rise on the frontiers of different civilisations or in areas which favour the grouping of dissimilar territories with complementary resources. Zones of friction are to be found between mountain dwellers and peoples of the plains ; between nomadic pastoralists and settled populations ; between trading groups established on the banks of a river or sea and the landowners of the interior ; between the man of the forest and the man of the steppes ; between the highland shepherd and the tree-grower of the well-watered valleys. According to Plutarch, the Athenian state came into being after the disturbances of 612 B.C., thanks to a politico-social compromise, in accord with the geographical division of Attica. This allowed a grouping together of the highland shepherds (poor men who wanted to see established a great democracy), the agricultural people of the plain (who included most of the rich families and tended to want an oligarchy), and the sailors of the coast, fishermen and traders who were anxious for some intermediate though still democratic pattern of government. The question was, how to associate politically the inhabitants of three geographical areas, each with its own way of life and its original social structure.

Other states like Russia and China came into being at the boundaries of agricultural and stock-farming regions ; the centre of the Chinese state has always been near lines of contact between the world of the steppes and the world of the cultivator. There, the masters of China have always placed their capital and their armies, to confront the barbarians from the west and north, and protect the toiling masses of peasants and traders who laboured in the hinterland. The Chinese capital was either at Si-Ngan or at Lo-Yang, or Peking. In this vital zone, the Great Wall was built between 214 and 204 B.C. Finally, other states have arisen at the junction of travellers' routes marked out between countries exporting different products. In Asia, the Mongol empire was founded in the twelfth century, upon the caravan routes linking China with Europe, either via the ancient highroad of the Gate of Zungaria, or along the tracks followed by caravans from Peking to Urga, Chita, and Irkutsk ; there the empire of Genghis Khan developed, spreading later southeast and southwest towards China and Europe. Its capital, Karakorum, built near the upper course of the Orkhon river, became an important centre of political life in the thirteenth century. In Europe, during the fifteenth century, the Burgundian state came into being along the great crossroads of the Saône valley, at the junction of routes to the Mediterranean, Flanders, the Channel, and southern Germany.

The more capably a nation can integrate and combine the various operations of mankind, the more likely it is to endure, grow, and evolve. Confined within a small sphere of activity, it runs the risk of becoming weak and breaking up. In this connection, it is noteworthy that the great empires created by nomadic peoples have never endured as long as those founded by settled agriculturalists. Shepherd tribes, forced to move from one pasturage to another according to seasonal changes, could never attach the same importance to territorial boundaries as peasants tied to the soil ; thus they must always have lacked the idea of territorial prescriptive rights, foundation stone of the state which is to endure. The great nomadic empires have simply been sovereign states with fluctuating boundaries, constantly in dispute and upheld only by a powerful military machine. Whereas settled states have survived heavy defeats in battle and suffered the amputation of part of their possessions without losing their identity, a few disastrous battles and a weakening of military potential have been enough to bring down the great empires of the shepherd rulers. One sees that agriculture, which is the symbol of union between man and the soil, is a powerful factor in the formation of states. All forms of agriculture, it is true, are not equally favourable to the building up of great political units; the extensive farming economy of hot countries, which takes no account of saving or stock-piling, and allows men to live from day to day at the mercy of famine or surfeit, has been unpropitious to the creation of substantial permanent political groups. Thus the state must organise and look ahead, gathering reserves in times of abundance against the day of famine. Only such men as understand the use and sharing out of resources, or at least know how to concentrate their energies on development, can create a state. Each member must agree to forfeit a certain measure of sovereignty and wealth in exchange for greater advantages, in the shape of personal security and quiet enjoyment of the rest of their possessions. On the technical plane, the state reveals a basic human tendency to rationalise every activity as the level of civilisation grows in complexity.

THE ORGANISATION OF STATES

When we come to consider our modern states we notice two elements which are closely linked: (a) a group of human beings, of varying ethnic relationships yet claiming an overall high level of civilisation; (b) a territory, independent of the features of its physical geography. The human group is responsible for the constitution of the country, which depends upon the organising abilities of the group and on its moral qualities. A hard-working and capable nation will found a state on territory where lesser men might have continued as anarchic tribes; thus Europeans were able to build modern states in South Africa, Australia, and New Zealand, where native peoples had succeeded only in setting up wretched clans, living in a constant state of warfare.

Territory is an indispensable element in the founding of a state. A group of human beings without land to dispose of has never brought a nation into being: for example, the Gypsies live in a 'diaspora', that is, dispersed among several states but keeping faithfully to their racial purity, language, and religion. When the Jews wished to build a state, their first act after 1919 was to demand the allocation of a territory, patiently re-colonising Palestine to make the state of Israel. Similarly, at the present time, faced with the existence of the state of Israel, the Palestinians wish to acquire their independence and the political status of a state recognised by the

United Nations, and distinct from their neighbours in Egypt, Jordan, Syria, and Lebanon. They lay claim to the liberation of a 'national' territory as the indispensable territorial basis of statehood. Thus it is necessary for a group of men founding a state to occupy an area and set up homesteads, harnessing its resources, and developing its wealth on behalf of a community. The state thus coordinates a number of regions, the economic and spiritual forces of which are able to achieve the common good in the face of private interest and as justice best dictates.

The unifying work of a state finds practical expression in the creation of a political centre or capital, in laying down lines of communications (linking the various outlying regions), and in setting up frontiers which define, characterise, and protect the national territory. Contrary to what we might suppose, the first duty of a state is not to mark out the extent of its area, nor to define its frontiers; these matters are most frequently attended to after the nation has been constituted. Frontiers, indeed are not simply boundaries which one might compare with the demarcation of a private estate. Some geographers have described them as 'peripheric' systems, fulfilling the rôle of boundaries but having as well a strategic and connectional function, by ensuring exchanges of men and exports between neighbouring countries.

Capitals.—The choice of a capital often reveals very clearly the political thinking behind the making of a state, for the function of a capital is to ensure the smooth running of all parts of the national body. In a compactly shaped state, the capital usually occupies a central position: examples of this abound, with Moscow, Prague, Budapest, Warsaw, and Bogotá; or in former times Stuttgart and Hanover; and Berlin at the centre of the old Prussian possessions. Madrid was chosen by Philip II as his capital simply because of its geometrically central position in the Iberian peninsula; until then, kings of Spain had used either Toledo or Valladolid. We note, too, that Washington, which today appears remote as a capital in relation to the whole United States, was roughly at the centre of the area occupied in 1790 by the thirteen federated colonies. In a coastal state, the capital occupies a central position accessible to the sea: for example, Lisbon, Rome, Athens, Lima, and Sydney. The eccentric position of some capitals can always be explained by the prejudices of the founding state. When the area spreads over zones which vary in climate and general economy, a government will site its capital in the most favourable district. Thus it is noteworthy that every provincial capital in Canada is to be found in the south, be it Quebec, Ottawa, Winnipeg, Regina, or Edmonton. The position of Helsinki, Stockholm, Oslo, and Edinburgh is explained by the greater wealth of those districts of the national territory. The capitals of Iran have always been placed in the best irrigated regions : Suse, Persepolis, or Teheran. Certain capital cities like Berlin, Vienna, or Peking, placed near the frontiers administered by these governments, were originally fortresses where the sovereign found it prudent to live, close to the boundaries most threatened by the Slavs (Berlin), by the Turks (Vienna), by Mongols or Manchus (Peking). The political thought behind the making of Peking may be studied in the regular plan of the city, in the heights of its ancient ramparts, and in the triple enclosure which marked out three cities each defended by a fortified wall. A further good example of non-central capitals is found in the 'capital-ports', built on the coasts where all the strands of distant communications vital to the country may be caught together ; such a position underlines the importance of sea communications in the economy of these nations : for example, London, Oslo, and Lisbon in Europe and Rio de Janeiro and Buenos Aires in South America.

Moreover the location of the capital may change whenever the political or economic concerns of the country themselves alter. The resiting of capitals is quite a normal process amongst states whose means of communications are rudimentary. Iran moved its capital from Ispahan to Teheran, Morocco transferred its own from Marrakech to Fez, Abyssinia has in turn had Ankober, Entotto, and Addis Ababa as its capital, the latter being confirmed in this rôle after the building of the railway from Djibouti. Sometimes, in the past, a transfer of capital has shown a shift of internal equilibrium and a change in the national centre of gravity. The Russians have thus, in succession, had Kiev, Suzdal, Vladimir, Moscow, and St Petersburg as their capital city ; the Swedes had Uppsala, Sigtuna, and Stockholm ; the Norwegians, Trondheim, Kongehalle, and Oslo.

Often the growth or contraction of an area has led to an alteration in the site of the capital. Thus in Spain it was moved from Burgos to Valladolid and Toledo before being fixed at Madrid. In Egypt the northeast capitals grew in importance as trade developed with the Mediterranean countries ; and the centre of gravity in Egypt shifted from Memphis to Bubastis and then to Sais. After the conquest of China, Kubla Khan brought forward his capital from Karakorum to Khambalik (Peking) at the heart of the newly conquered territory.

The same displacements may follow a contraction of boundaries, thus the capital of the Turkish empire which transferred from Konya to Brousse, then to Adrianople and later to Istanbul during successive stages of Turkish expansion, withdrew to Ankara after the loss of the Balkan territories.

Sometimes a shift of capital is due more to economic than to political reasons : thus the growing ascendancy of maritime interests in Japan's economy brought about successive moves from Kamakura to Kyoto and from there to Tokyo in 1868. In the same way, Oslo replaced Trondheim as the Norwegian capital, as soon as that country became interested in Baltic and trans-Baltic commerce. Peter the Great transferred his capital from Moscow to St Petersburg when he decided to make his state into a Baltic power ; since 1917, the Russians have wished to turn the U.S.S.R. into a continental Federation and their capital has duly been moved from St Petersburg (renamed Leningrad) to Moscow, as being more easily accessible to the Asiatic areas which require to be colonised.

Even today we may see states duplicating their capitals, or seeking new locations for them. Thus since the end of the second world war, the Dutch royal residence has remained at The Hague, whereas the ministries and seat of government have been moved to Amsterdam, which is a former capital of the country. When Brazil developed the inland states of São Paulo and Minas Geraes and began the systematic exploitation of Amazonia, the capital of Rio de Janeiro seemed too remote ; an entirely new capital city, Brasilia, has been built in a federal area at the centre; inaugurated in 1960, it already had half a million inhabitants by 1972. The moving of capitals from place to place is a sign of instability, pointing to the need for political modifications or basic changes in the economy of the country.

Communications.—The building of a network of communications has always been a sign of unifying activity; a good system is essential to link the complementary regions of a nation. Without a rational system of arterial roads, it is impossible to turn every resource to good account or maintain friendly relations with other states. Even in ancient times, no great nation lacked its network of highways. In the Persian empire, the route from Suse to Sardes bound the capital to the Aegean and Pontic provinces, which were the most far-flung of the empire. The Roman road system was both strategic and economic, and gave cohesion to the empire over a period of four centuries, allowing the spread of Latin over the whole area. At the time of the Inca empire, a network of roads linked Cuzco, the capital, to the northern and southern extremities of the territory, opening communications between the high mountainous regions and the plains bordering the Pacific ocean.

In France itself, national cohesion and the spread of French over the whole country were greatly helped by the building of arterial roads linking Paris and Versailles to every frontier in the kingdom from the eighteenth century onwards.

More recently this rôle of political consolidation has devolved upon the railways. It was as a means to national unity that the first trans-Canadian railway was thought of, British Columbia's terms for her entry into the dominion being that she should have access by railroad to the capital Ottawa. In the United States too, the Union Pacific, significantly so called, was built in 1869 after the annexation of California, connecting to the eastern states this newly conquered region far away at the other end of the continent.

In Asia, the building of four great railway systems: Trans-Siberian, Trans-Caucasian, Trans-Caspian, and Trans-Aralian was undertaken for a double purpose, strategic and economic, to link Russia with distant territories deprived of lines of communication. At a later date, these railways made easier the unification of the U.S.S.R. and the absorption of colonial regions into the federal Soviet system.

In other parts of the globe, it was by building communications that the European powers sought to strengthen the interdependence of their colonial possessions. By such means the integration of certain Asiatic and African countries gave the inhabitants the feeling of belonging to one and the same nation. It is not in doubt that the Union of South Africa, India, Vietnam, and more recently the Mali Federation have all become more aware of their nationhood as a result of railway lines and roads, and now of air communications.

So long as the work of integration and coordination is unfinished, separatist tendencies may subsist between the members of a group, and sooner or later, these will bring about the disintegration of the whole country. The falling apart of the Austro-Hungarian empire after 1919 was helped by a lack of cohesion between member states, and by the bad condition of the central European and Danubian communications which paralysed the flow of traffic. More recently, the splitting of Pakistan and the secession of East Pakistan to become the independent state of Bangladesh, resulted from the difficulty of communications and of commercial and cultural exchanges of all kinds between western Pakistan and the eastern province, separated from the capital, Rawalpindi, by two political frontiers and 2,000 kilometres of Indian territory, or, alternatively, a sea passage of 2,600 nautical miles from Chittagong to Karachi round the periphery of India; under such circumstances no national solidarity could possibly develop between the two Pakistans.

When cohesion has been fully achieved, strong ties are felt between the parts of the body politic; loyalties to a common heritage and its traditions; the wish to make sacrifices that brotherhood may endure, will become a strong influence; and in this way the idea is created of a 'motherland', the cornerstone of a nation in its territorial setting.

Frontiers.—One might be tempted to think that the limits of a nation's territory are defined by physical obstacles marking the frontiers; thus we find the Pyrenees standing between France and Spain, and the Danube, flowing over a great distance between Bulgaria and Roumania. But just as often huge obstacles are found which define no frontier: the boundary line between Turkey and the U.S.S.R. comes well south of the Caucasus, a range so hard to cross that it could form the finest natural frontier imaginable between the two countries. The Alps never seem to have served as a boundary to the Romans; standing first on the line of the Po, they came later north of the Alps, to the Rhine and the Danube; and later again, their frontiers (*limes*) were marked by entrenchments, built beyond the Rhine and the Danube.

The idea of a 'natural frontier' was an illusion on the part of the eighteenth-century political thinkers who wrongly attributed it to Richelieu. This idea would be a complete anachronism, for under the *Ancien Régime*, neither kings nor statesmen thought along those lines: the 'natural frontier' grew in the minds of a few isolated thinkers, and did not influence official policies. Later on a few revolutionary statesmen, of whom Danton was one, declared the frontiers of France to be in accordance with the natural setting, four-square between the Ocean, the Rhine, the Alps, and the Pyrenees. In 1792, defending the first annexation of Savoy, the Abbé Grégoire held that France was a self-sufficient whole: 'Upon every side, Nature has provided her with boundaries which she is not obliged to widen. Thus her interests are at one with her principles.' As a matter of fact, it is unusual to find a group of mountains which separate unequivocally two neighbouring nations. The dwellers in many a mountain village lead their flocks to pasture on opposing slopes, and thus it is that, on both sides of a mountain, the inhabitants often share a common race and language as, for instance, the Basques in the western Pyrenees, and the Catalans in the east of that range. At the time when the Roman empire stretched to its widest extent, mountain masses such as the Alps and the Pyrenees were contained within the state boundaries.

Nowadays the Franco-Spanish frontier does not follow precisely the ridge-line of the Pyrenees: the treaty of 1659 did not lay down an exact plan, and successive misunderstandings led to lengthy negotiations between France and Spain from 1853 to 1868. Spain soon abandoned the principle of the 'ridge' frontier, preferring to claim the common rights over pasturage and forest land of the French and Spanish mountain villages. In many places, these rights had been agreed as far back as the thirteenth century, and rather therefore than claiming the Pyrenees as a natural frontier, it is more correct to say, that France and Spain, acting together, have adapted their frontier to the line of the Pyrenees.

However conveniently it may flow, a river does not always make an acceptable natural boundary. To begin with, many great rivers change their course, so that the towns through which they flow appear first on one bank and then on the other: Vieux Brisach, which, up to the sixteenth century, was to be found on the left bank of the Rhine, now stands in German territory on the right bank where an intersecting branch of the river has formed a natural loop. Then, from the time of the Congress of Vienna (1815), people were apt to reckon the line of demarcation as following the thalweg, in the case of a frontier river, but at that time nobody knew how a thalweg might change and thus a source of disputes and difficulties became apparent; a special agreement had therefore to be negotiated between Switzerland and Austria after the regulating of the Rhine in 1892, to re-establish the frontier between the two countries, along the old course of the river.

In the case of small rivers, a frontier follows either the line of midstream or one of the banks; and long ago, when exact frontiers were hard to define, river courses were considered useful guides. When Charlemagne's empire was carved up, the Rhine and the Meuse served as frontiers for France; the Rhine for Lotharingia and the Elbe for Germany. In practice, however, rivers only make good natural frontiers in a region of plains, where a wide stretch of water between the two banks makes crossing difficult and where perhaps swamps add to the hazards of approach. The Congo river, for example, provides an excellent frontier, and from one bank to the other, neighbouring settlers know little of each other. It is very different when the river forms a link and a natural means of communication, rather than an obstacle. In the case of the great navigable waterways, the greatest riparian power will tend to monopolise traffic, by including both banks within its national territory and bringing forward its own frontier beyond the river line; Germany acted in this way over the Elbe, and in part over the Rhine, between the Lauter and the frontier of the Low Countries. Poland did the same thing over the Oder, pushing back the German–Polish frontier towards the left bank in Silesia and at the river-mouth; the Netherlands occupied both banks of the Meuse in the region of Maastricht; Yugoslavia occupied both banks of the Danube, from which she thrust back Hungary and Rumania, between Batina and Vrska Gradiste.

Now and then dense forests have been used as boundaries between peoples, at least as often as mountain ranges or rivers. In Gaul, forests became virtual frontiers between the city territories; the boundary of the ancient region of the Tricasses (Troyes) was formed originally of a wide and lengthy forestal zone, whose vestiges are known to us as the forests of Othe, Rumilly, Chaource, and Chappes. North of Orleans, as far as the limits of Lutetia, from the regions of the Carnutes (Chartres) to the Viliocasses (Vexin) lay another frontier march, and the last traces of it are to be found in the forests of Orléans, Montargis, Fontainebleau, Rambouillet, and Laye.

We may note that among primitive civilisations the settled areas frequently denote lines of demarcation between human groups, so that the earliest frontiers coincided with depopulated zones lying between two states. The states of antiquity and of the Middle Ages did not themselves consider frontiers as precise limiting demarcations ; wherever settlement ceased, the realm was understood to end. Barth and other German travellers told how in the nineteenth century in Africa frontiers between human groups were formed by depopulated and partly wooded zones, which served as battlefields. During the tribal wars, these security zones might widen out of all proportion, up to sixty or a hundred miles. They were to be found between the Hausa and Fulani districts, between the tribes of Wandala and Bornu ; in the region of the Welle, these empty tracts might be found twenty to three hundred miles wide ; Azande and Bongo on one side, Azande and Banza on the other, were separated by deserted regions. In ancient times in Scandinavia, Celtic, Germanic, and Slav civilisations also had frontier zones not unlike those in Africa.

The great icefields of Scandinavia formed a desert zone of considerable width between Norway and Sweden ; to the north of Trondheim, this great empty territory was regarded as common ground between Sweden, Norway, and Russia ; nomadic groups of Lapps living with their reindeer paid a small tribute to each of the three states. These empty spaces remained without inhabitants until about 1600 when the Finns settled there sporadically. Thus a foreign element of Lapps and Finns was introduced between Sweden and Norway, the marking of a precise boundary not being accomplished until 1751, and between Norway and Russia in 1826.

Such desert spaces were for a long time regarded as the best protection for states, as an enemy had first to make a journey across them before any attack ; some were maintained with care and even built up in the common cause, as a safety measure by neighbouring states. Caesar tells us that an unpopulated forest march was to be found between the Sueves and Cherusci. In 448, Attila asked Byzantium to leave a strip of territory 200 kilometres wide, south of the Danube, to be kept wild and uncultivated. Later again, on the frontiers of England and Scotland, the kings of Scotland entrusted the Scottish barons, who were landlords near the Border, with the safeguarding of the frontier. Unable to cultivate such exposed lands, the Border clans left the fields untilled and merely kept up constant raids over the boundary wilderness between Scotland and England. Empty forest spaces, where husbandry was impractical, were also to be found between Celtic peoples in Great Britain, and between Scandinavian groups in Westgotland and Bohusland. On the borders of Lithuania, the territories of the Teutonic Order were edged by forests some sixty to a hundred and twenty miles wide, along the Memel, through which passed three routes lined with fortified outposts, leading respectively to Grodno, Kovno, and Ontelsburg. More than half the area conquered from the Slavs by this Order was filled by this frontier zone, which began to be colonised only towards 1550.

The oddest example of these frontier deserts is that established by agreement between the Chinese and the Koreans : over a sixty-mile stretch between the two countries they drove away the population, destroyed villages and agriculture, threatening with the death penalty any person found in the forbidden zone. Trade between the two countries was carried along a single track, open three times a year to allow the caravans through.

In the New World similar frontier deserts existed before the Europeans arrived : a neutral zone, unpopulated, merely a hunting ground, separated the territories of the Cherokees and the Creeks. The latter, whose most westerly villages were built on the banks of the Coosa and the Alabama at the end of the eighteenth century, were separated from the Chikasaws by over five hundred kilometres of wilderness, and from the Choctaws by another vacant space, three hundred kilometres wide: the most northerly Choctaw village was three hundred kilometres distant from the Chikasaws, who had withdrawn in a compact group, north of the watershed between the Tombigbee and the Yazoo.

After their protective rôle had ceased, these frontier deserts often became a refuge for criminals pursued with a price on their heads by one or other of the two states. Forty years ago, the boundary between the United States and Mexico had become so notorious a hideout for criminals that the United States police force was obliged to use what were virtually military tactics against them.

With the spread of civilisation, frontier deserts were replaced by exactly defined lines of demarcation, and in Europe the increase of population and the general progress of civilisation soon resulted in their disappearance altogether. States were brought to a halt, just like arable fields or village domains, by frontier lines staked out by posts or milestones. The placing of these exact boundaries has always created serious political problems ; and the majority of interstate wars since the end of medieval times has been concerned with the shifting of frontier lines. At every peace treaty, the principal objective of diplomatists was to settle these lines anew.

Rarely has a frontier line been agreed by simple geometrical drawing. The earliest example of this kind of boundary-making is given us by Pope Alexander VI's arbitration, when he chose the meridian drawn a hundred leagues west of the Azores, to divide the Portuguese colonial possessions to the east, from those of the Spaniards to the west : later, another arbitration determined a new dividing-line, 297½ leagues east of the Moluccas. It was chiefly during the nineteenth century that, owing to the advances in the mathematical sciences and in surveying, limits of this kind could be laid down so exactly; the boundaries between the different states in the commonwealth of Australia are good examples. In 1818, the London agreement fixed the frontier between Canada and the United States, from the Great Lakes to the Pacific, along the forty-ninth parallel. In 1825, the meridian of 141° W. longitude was adopted as the frontier line between Canada and Alaska.

Amongst the long-civilised countries, where changes in the frontiers have been frequent, and topographical knowledge is more complete, states have tended to let their boundaries follow the natural features which were prominent on the landscape, such as mountain ranges, and the banks of lakes or rivers. These barriers were in bygone days sufficient to stop troops, either on foot or on horseback, and they were frequently strengthened or completed by lines of trenches which improved their strategic value.

Among strategic frontiers, the longest was the Great Wall of China, set up in the third century B.C., 2,500 kilometres in length, between the Sungari and Lanchow. In Europe, the oldest fortified frontiers date from the time of the Roman Empire: the *limes germanicus*, built between Neuwied on the Rhine, and Kelheim on the Danube, divided the Roman world from Germania. Hadrian's Wall between Newcastle and Carlisle, built from A.D. 122 onward, defined the northernmost limit of the Roman Empire. It included eighty forts and three hundred and twenty watch-towers ; and for three centuries it repelled the assaults of the Picts. Later again, the *Dänewerk*, built in A.D. 808 by the Danish king Götrik, became Denmark's first frontier.

If natural obstacles have lost all strategic value owing to the modern weapons of war, they retain at least a certain interest as convenient landmarks. In following their outline, however, it is easy to encircle minorities within a state—small human groups which on account of their ethnic, linguistic or religious affinities, consider themselves as belonging to adjacent countries. In our time, owing to the tangle of different nationalities, skilful handling has been required in the drawing of frontier lines between the countries of the Balkan Peninsula, and later between the central European nations. In setting up the boundaries of Roumania, two possible solutions were debated: in 1919, the favoured outline followed the rivers, the dividing lines between water-courses and peaks; in 1941, on the contrary, the allies of wartime Germany undertook a temporary rectification in the shape of a new frontier which followed the contours of non-Roumanian racial groups. The formation of an ethnic frontier as against a strategic one presents difficulties no less acute. It may indeed happen that cities include a racial majority differing in composition from the neighbouring countryside: the Germans and Czechs in Bohemia, or the Italians and Yugoslavs in Venezia Giulia, before 1939. In such cases the establishment of a racial frontier would lead to the ruin of the country's economy by separating the town from the country districts which feed it and are given work in return. Thus, after the second world war, plans were made for the suppression of minorities and the unification of these racial groups within the old, and now restored, strategic frontiers of Central Europe. This was achieved by means of a systematic transfer of population, and when the constitution of the new Asian states, together with the defining of their boundaries was taken in hand, this same solution was agreed upon, particularly between India and Pakistan, between North and South Korea, and until 1975 between the communist state of North Vietnam and the anti-communist South Vietnam.

Nevertheless it does happen that some frontiers seem to follow the natural features of the landscape of their own accord without pressure from ethnic considerations: such is the case with the Franco-Belgian boundary, which disregards rivers, hills, and forest-belts in many places in order to follow simple communal demarcations such as ditches, or the borders of private estates; such frontiers are merely lines of contact between two states which profess no mutual antagonism and have indeed many common interests.

One might almost say that each frontier line is virtually an intentionally arbitrary creation, an abstraction which separates two living organisms and thereby modifies their pulse or life rhythm; by the simple fact of their existence some frontiers provide geographical contrasts between adjacent countries, whilst others seem to create small new geographical units across the border of two countries.

Frontiers also form economic barriers, which sometimes provide curious contrasts between the divided regions. On either side of the Franco-Belgian frontier wheatfields have long been more in evidence in France than in Belgium, although the soil is no more fertile; this is explained by the fact that wheat enjoys customs protection on the French side and so gives the peasant a better cash return. So, too, on either side of the Franco-Spanish border,

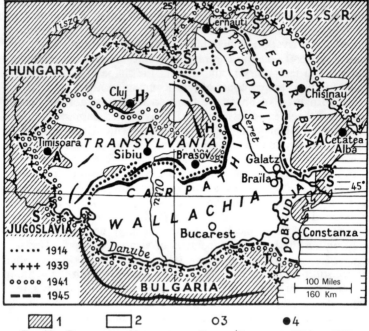

FIG. 22.—ROUMANIA : NATURAL AND RACIAL FRONTIERS, 1914 TO 1945.

1. Non-Roumanian population (A. Germans, H. Hungarians, S. Slavs, T J. Turks and Jews). **2.** Roumanian population. **3.** Roumanian towns. **4.** Towns with non-Roumanian majority.

Roussillon and Ampurdan although geographically similar, today produce quite different crops. This is because Roussillon was incorporated into the French southern market when the railways were built and remains a source of wines and early vegetables; Ampurdan, on the other hand, produces mostly cereals and vegetables for the local markets of the Barcelona industrial area.

In present times, several frontiers, far from being deserted land, have become densely populated zones where constant trading is carried on, and where contraband also plays a part. The inhabitants of one region often find that it pays them to work in the factories across the border where employment may be easier and the wages higher. In this case they may settle quite near the boundary line which separates them from their work. An example of this is seen in the Belgians who travel daily to the textile mills and coal mines in northern France.

Thus it comes about that some frontier areas eventually feel closer economic ties with the border region of the neighbouring state than with the central area of the country to which they belong politically, for example, the city of Geneva, closely surrounded by the French frontier on the banks of the lake, gets its food more cheaply from the French hinterland than from Swiss territory; the same is true of Basle whose markets are supplied in part with vegetables from adjacent Alsace. Many French boundary communes, too, were for long regarded as free zones, for although politically part of France, they remained independent of the French customs and traded more freely with Switzerland than with France.

In modern times, however, the frontiers of most states are little more than limits of sovereignty. In the great federations of relatively recent date, like the United States and the Soviet Union, as well as to an increasing extent in states with very old political or territorial structures, they have lost all military and strategic significance. In the United States, the boundaries of the fifty states of the Union have only an administrative and juridical function, comparable to the provincial or regional boundaries of the old countries of Europe. In the Soviet Union, the autonomy of the federated republics is within linguistic and cultural limits only, and is confined to local administration—an arrangement which ensures that the laws and decisions of the central authority are carried out.

For a long time, in Europe, frontiers have retained an important economic role, thanks to the establishment of customs barriers, the object of which is to tax imported goods and so protect national industries. But more and more they are losing this protectionist function as states become aware of their economic solidarity in the modern world. One of the first effects of the great European 'Communities' has been to remove or diminish the customs barriers between the member states and to permit the free movement of people and goods across their frontiers. This economic solidarity, limited at first to the six continental states of northwest Europe, and extended later to include nine neighbouring states, is moving progressively, thanks to the improvement of international motorways, railways and airways, towards unifying and harmonising the economic structures and gradually reducing the partitioning effect of frontiers. From this it happens that frontier zones, far from being, as in former times, zones of sparse population and slow economic development, are becoming zones of great activity and dense population, with a work force that daily crosses the frontier in both directions. Thus, as has for some time been the case with the Franco-Belgian frontier, state boundaries are gradually losing their administrative and customs function, as they have already lost their military function, retaining only their fundamental and essentially political role of defining territorial areas and the limits of action of two neighbouring sovereignties, in the sphere of spatial organisation and social structure as well as of neighbourly relations and international collaboration. In other words, frontier zones become new geographical environments, living regional realities, at the contact of two political sovereignties.

THE LIFE OF STATES

In the same way as any living organism, states must develop and be fed in order to exist. In the past it can be seen how increasing power and maturity have gone hand in hand with increasing annexations of territory, whilst conversely, all loss of material and spiritual power seems to have coincided with their amputation sooner or later. In our day, the extent and ease of our communications have made states interdependent, and it is rare to find any country so vast that it can supply every need of a great industrialised human group. Hence the tendency among civilised states to merge into unions and federations, both political and economic, with some abrogation of national sovereignty, particularly in the sphere of customs.

Growth in Space.—The territorial expansion of a state, whether warlike or pacific, depends upon the attainment of two objectives, pursued either separately or together. (a) *Free areas* must be acquired, sufficiently sparsely settled to be able to receive an overflow of population. (b) *Trade routes* or sources of essential wealth must be available to supplement the national resources. These ambitions may be satisfied by two different methods, giving rise to two kinds of political structure: (1) Adjacent territories may be annexed to such an extent that a whole continent is involved. The great continental empires of antiquity and of medieval times—the Persian, Roman, and Mongol empires—were built up in this way, as were the great modern continental unions of the U.S.A. and the U.S.S.R. (2) Overseas colonies may be founded, either by settling emigrants from the mother country in empty territories, or by setting up the political and economic framework necessary to exploit a populated but poorly developed overseas country in a way profitable to the expanding power. By such methods were founded the mighty colonial empires both of antiquity and of modern times, the Athenian, the Portuguese, the Spanish empires, and, until the last quarter of the twentieth century, the great political unions born of recent changes within the former colonial empires of Great Britain (the Commonwealth) and France (the *Communauté*).

Generally speaking, the great states have usually developed from small beginnings: the birthplace of the Assyrian empire was to be found between the Tigris and the Zagros; the Babylonian empire sprang from a town, the Roman from Latium, and the Chinese from the Khotan oasis. O. Maull compares the newly born state to a living cell, of which the nucleus corresponds to centres of population set amidst the cultivated land; the membranes are the forests, pasture-lands, and mountainous rocks.

The high valley of the Aa was the domain of the monastic state of Engelberg. It was surrounded by high mountains. Upstream, at a high altitude, was a pass, while downstream the valley could easily be blocked. In the Alps this kind of political development may be seen in most of the valley groups.

The laws governing the decadence of states are less well known, although one can study the process of their disintegration in history. The Roman empire achieved its widest territorial scope early in the second century A.D. with the annexation of Dacia, the fringes of Syria, Arabia, Armenia, and Mesopotamia. Soon after this apogee, its dismemberment began in Asia Minor, and two hundred years later the whole edifice had crumbled. Long before the Barbarian invasion internal dissolution had started; towards A.D. 235 under soldier emperors, the provinces were struggling to seize political power, and the periphery threatened government at the centre. This trend had its ups and downs. The division of the empire under Diocletian while maintaining imperial supremacy was not enough to reverse the trend. In 395, a decisive step was taken towards partition, with the separation of the Hellenised east from the Romanised west, at the very moment when the enemy was crossing the frontiers both from the north and the east.

In the same way, the Arabian empire was destroyed piecemeal, starting with the loss of its more distant possessions—Spain in 755, Morocco in 790, the remnants of the Maghreb in 800, Egypt and Cyrenaica in 872–91 together with eastern Arabia and southern Persia, Kurdistan in 934, and so on.

In every age, states have believed that in order to endure, a substantial trading position and a strong, powerful economy was essential. Most of them have attempted to dominate politically the whole field of their commerce as well as of their trade routes, and many states have in the course of history devoted their political aims to achieving access to the sea. One cause of the wars of the Medes and Persians was the Persian desire to seize maritime trading positions held in the Aegean Sea by the Greeks. During the 'share-out' of Charlemagne's empire, each of the three dividing powers (Charles, Lothaire, and Louis) obtained an outlet to the sea. Later, Prussia struggled repeatedly to reach the coast: in the mid-seventeenth century, the Grand Elector acquired Emden; during the eighteenth century, Frederick-William I obtained Stettin and part of Pomerania with the Oder; in mid-nineteenth century she annexed Schleswig-Holstein and got a foothold on the North Sea. The Austro-Hungarian empire relentlessly pursued its object of lengthening its coast-line, first by the annexing of Bosnia-Herzegovina (1907), then by attempting the seizure of the port of Salonica

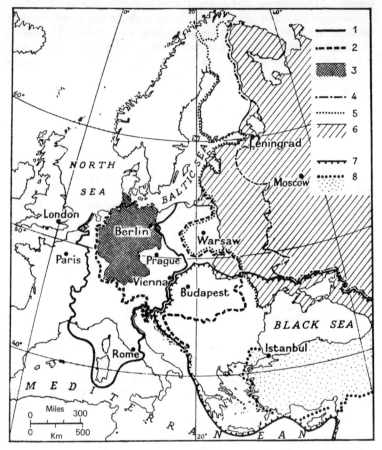

FIG. 23.—EXAMPLES OF THE EXPANSION OF EUROPEAN STATES.
1. Limits of Holy Roman Empire. **2.** Frontiers (1914) of the Central Powers (Germany and Austria-Hungary). **3.** Present-day Germany. **4.** Russian frontier in seventeenth century. **5.** Frontier of Russian empire at its maximum extent. **6.** Present-day U.S.S.R. **7.** Frontier of Ottoman Empire at its maximum extent. **8.** Present-day Turkey.

through the tutelage or annexation of Serbia and Macedonia. Poland and Bulgaria in Europe, Bolivia in South America provide other examples of states whose policy was governed at one time or another by the need to obtain or extend a sea outlet. As for Russia, this country has constantly sought an outlet to the open sea bearing some relation to her continental size, first on the Black Sea by pushing back the Turks, then on the Baltic by sweeping aside the claims of Sweden, Germany, and Finland; later, on the Pacific ocean, by obtaining from China the bordering zone of the Japanese Sea and building Vladivostok, finally by enlarging her arctic outlet west of Murmansk at the expense of Finland.

An outlet to the sea is often the first step towards the enlargement of a state. A powerful state living on the borders of a well-defined maritime basin, feels an urge to strengthen its hold upon the whole coast-line. Thus, the Athenian empire spread over all the islands and almost over the entire coastline of the Aegean Sea. The Romans also conquered all the Mediterranean basin before stretching out across the Rhine and the Danube. In the eleventh century, Danish kings reigned over most of the North Sea coast, and in the thirteenth century, they extended their hold all round the Baltic. In the middle of the seventeenth century, on the other hand, the kings of Sweden had succeeded in turning the Baltic into a Swedish lake.

A strong state is often inclined to regard with a proprietary eye any sea navigated by its own sailors; the Aegean Sea, for example, during the twelfth century was thought of as byzantine; the Romans called the Mediterranean *mare nostrum*, and English sovereigns from the sixteenth century affected to call the sea separating Great Britain from the continent, 'our channel'; and what Frenchmen call the Pas-de-Calais is known to the English as the Straits of Dover.

These claims gave rise to serious international conflicts from the sixteenth century onward, when Portuguese and Spaniards made an attempt to monopolise sea trade. Francis I jokingly objected that he knew of no clause in Adam's will which might prevent him from sharing the 'common sea'. As a matter of fact, the political mastery of the seas often started from land-locked seas like the Mediterranean, to be extended to wider oceans. Islands have frequently served as a starting point, such as Cyprus for the Phoenicians and the Ptolemies; Salamis for the Athenians; Sicily, Corsica, and Sardinia for Rome and Italy; the Estonian islands Oesel and Dagoe for the Teutonic Orders.

Usually the decisive step was the conquest and consolidation on the opposite shore, such as the south coast of Asia Minor by the Phoenicians, the coasts of the western Mediterranean by Carthage, the coasts of Spain, Istria, Dalmatia, Epirus, Albania, and North Africa by Rome. As a further stage often came settlement on a very remote coast, such as the colonisation of Brazil by Portugal and the rest of South America by Spain. Usually, a substantial grip on the intermediate stages has been necessary in order to buttress these infiltrations, and to ensure mastery over the routes linking the overseas trading posts; thus the Phoenicians progressed from island to island, from Tyre to Cyprus, and on to Rhodes, Crete, Thera, Malos, and Paros; to Malta and Pantelleria, to Sicily, Sardinia, and the Balearic Islands. Later the Normans conquered the Faroes and the Shetland Islands, Iceland and Greenland, the Hebrides and Ireland; the Portuguese occupied the Azores, Madeira, the Cape Verde islands on the Atlantic trade-routes, and further afield too, Ceylon, Malacca, and the Moluccas.

The Dutch followed the same trend, setting up posts at São Thome, St Helena, Mauritius, and then in Ceylon, Sumatra, Java, Timor, and Formosa. Later on Great Britain, inheriting the Spanish and Dutch naval power, took over their island positions and set up British posts all through the Mediterranean and the Indian Ocean.

More recently, the expansion of the United States as a sea power is shown on the political map by the occupation of Puerto Rico, Panama, Hawaii, Guam, and the Philippines. In this sphere, however, the political growth of great states has always been checked by international law which has laid down the principle of neutrality over vast ocean spaces and has defined the exact and precise limits of national territorial waters (cf. p. 234).

Economic Factors.—It is often difficult for a densely populated state to live as an autarky, that is by using only such native resources as it may possess. The need for a wider economic foundation was felt even by the great nations of antiquity. Two thousand five hundred years B.C., Egypt, lacking trees for her shipbuilding, undertook the conquest of Lebanon, which was rich in forests, and in order to get copper, malachite, and turquoise the Egyptians likewise mastered the Sinai region about 2900 B.C. The Treaty of Verdun, which divided Charlemagne's empire between his three grandsons in A.D. 843, laid down the boundaries of France, Lotharingia, and Germania so as to ensure to each of the three, horse-grazing in the clay plains of the north, wheatfields in the loamy districts of the interior, and vineyards in the Rhine valley and the Mediterranean areas.

In the seventeenth century, Switzerland had to insist upon the cultivation of cereal crops by farmers in the mountain districts as well as in the plains, so that production might be sufficient for the needs of the population and any likelihood of famine averted. When a region is completely lacking in certain products, the state will sometimes try to acquire them by annexing neighbouring regions which are better supplied. Thus the expansion of the

Venetian state on the Adriatic aimed at the fulfilment of well-defined needs. Bosnia provided wood for shipbuilding, Dalmatia supplied horses, the alpine districts cattle, and the Ionian islands wines and fruits.

Europeans in the sixteenth century founded the first colonial empires, to keep the countries producing sugar, spices, and precious metals under their control. It was with the economic aim of securing a cheap labour force of slaves, for opening up the tropical regions of America, that these early colonial powers founded slave-trading posts along the African coastline. Later on, the discovery of gold, silver, and copper in the Rocky Mountains encouraged the expansion of the United States towards the west, while their need for tropical products (cotton, sugar, rice, and oil) drew them towards the south, as far as the Gulf of Mexico, from the shores of which they ousted successively France, Spain, and Mexico.

The need to obtain complementary products has become still more urgent since the nineteenth century. As modern states have progressed in setting up great mechanical industries, so have they required ever greater supplies of increasingly diversified raw materials. As soon as the textile industry began to use more wool than the sheep in Europe could supply, the English were the first to go in quest of great empty spaces overseas for the intensive breeding of wool-bearing sheep. This explains the importance of South Africa and Australia to them. In European countries today, where the greater part of the population no longer live off the land, not only must raw materials be imported but basic commodities of every kind must also be brought in from outside.

Industrial nations have other reasons for wishing to extend their political influence; they need customers to buy their factory products, and of course the most faithful customers are to be found living in their political dependencies. In times past, in the mercantilist organisation of the first colonial empires, the Europeans assigned to their overseas territories the simple rôle of suppliers of raw materials, jealously guarding for themselves the rôle of manufacturers. William Pitt, one of the greatest of British statesmen, is credited with saying, 'if the American colonies took upon themselves to manufacture so much as a stocking or a horse-shoe, I should let them feel the whole weight of British power.' The need for customers drove Japan to annex Korea in 1907; although very few emigrants could be sent there, and few surplus products obtained, as the country was seriously overpopulated already. Nevertheless, as time went on, certain powers gradually relaxed the leading-strings of their colonies: before independence, India had already become industrialised, setting up blast-furnaces, steelworks, and textile mills where the cotton cloths, previously bought from Manchester, were now manufactured from the native cotton crop. But even today we find that the strongest bonds between great world federations are created by economies which supplement each other.

Different Types of States—Their Evolution.—The humblest form of state is that which German geographers have termed the 'cell-state' of primitive man, forming, according to their district, the horde, the tribe, or the village. Among Australian primitives the political unit did not include tribes bearing the same name, or having a common language and way of life, but rather localised groups of men, possibly living in fifties, who monopolised a given hunting area.

Among the sedentary tribes of New Guinea and Melanesia, the political unit was the village community, built on a patriarchal basis. In southern India, forest and jungle tribes are divided into village communities, which also form the political unit. Other similar communities have been found in Amazonia, and among the natives of Sonora and California. This form of 'cell-state' follows the pattern of the little cities of antiquity. It has survived throughout the Middle Ages in some principalities and is still to be found vestigially in Andorra, Monaco, and San Marino, as tiny autonomous states bound by close political ties to the great powers which surround them.

Beyond the cell-state we find political groupings created, as it were, by a fusion of several similar cells developing in a relatively restricted area. The Athenian state evolved out of three initial cells of Attica; Sparta came from the amalgamation of seven small principalities; the Roman state was only constituted at the end of the Samnite wars. Other similar states were founded in Polynesia and Micronesia, uniting the Caroline, Marshall, and Gilbert Islands, or again the Hawaii group. In Africa, the kingdoms of the Congo, Lunda, Makololo, Uganda, and Monomotapa were built up in the same way. In America, too, we note the Iroquois, Huron, and Natchez confederations, and in the same way in Europe, the primitive barbarian kingdoms of the Franks, Alamans, Saxons, and Frisians.

The great states of antiquity were at once more complex and more typical and already showed signs of sophisticated political organisation. We do not know a great deal about their origins, whence came their strength, or how they developed in their characteristic setting. In general they seem to have been linked with very ancient centres of civilized life, such as Egypt, Mesopotamia, India, or China, all of them poor in natural vegetation, but thanks to their favourable climate able to develop the oases by irrigation. Otto Maull distinguishes several different types of these ancient empires, in the course of whose history the basic structure remained unaltered despite changing contours; and we may perhaps attribute their disintegration at a later date to this static condition and lack of sustained evolution.

An *oriental type* of state arose in the setting of three great river oases of the Nile, Mesopotamia, and the Indus, providing three focal centres of highly civilised life, all three shut in by mountains or deserts.

The Tigris–Euphrates basin lies at the centre of this little world, between the Punjab and Egypt. At the dawn of history, early in the third millennium B.C., Babylonia was already a focal point of irrigated cultivation, a centre of industry which exported its manufactures and an urbanised region possessing great cities, seats of small principalities which for a long time strove one against the other. One of these small overlordships managed little by little to extend its conquests from the Persian Gulf to the Mediterranean. The Babylonian states encountered many ups and downs, but the lower courses of the Tigris and Euphrates remained throughout the cradle of political groups which dominated the entire region from one sea to the other. Thus, by reason of her dominion over the oldest routes between the East and the West, Babylonia played an intermediary rôle during the dynasties which succeeded each other over 2,500 years. After her incorporation into larger empires, such as the Persian, Macedonian, and later the Arabian, she still continued to do this, and it was probably owing to her great commercial strength that the Babylonians were able to preserve a social structure founded on great feudal and ecclesiastical possessions. She could draw upon a massive labour force which she held under conditions of slavery and often recruited by the displacement of people from the periphery towards the centre of the empire. Some of these deportations were the starting point of migratory movements which the Babylonians were unable to control, and, several times during the course of centuries, Arabs coming from the poorer countries in the south penetrated to the heart of the ancient state in successive waves, and for a time injected it with new strength.

Assyria furnishes an example of another type of oriental empire. It was born in the mountain foothills of Mesopotamia, and was obliged from the start to struggle incessantly against the mountain-dwellers, brigands, and nomads who came through the cols of Armenia and Media to lay waste the crops. It is here that we have the reason for Assyria's unrelenting warfare against Elam and the Armenian region of Urarthu.

Unlike the Babylonian state, it would seem that the Assyrians built up their social structure from an association of small freeholders, forming a solid army of peasant-proprietors. The struggle against Babylon which was to culminate in the creation of the great Assyrian empire was not inspired by the need for territorial expansion, but rather by the wish to take over Babylon's monopoly of vast trade channels in the east. Sargon II completed this empire which spread over nearly 400,000 square miles, from Babylon to the Mediterranean, taking in Syria, Palestine, Armenia, the outer Persian foothills, northern Arabia, and even Cyprus. Assarhaddon added Egypt to his possessions. It would seem that, as in the case of the Roman Republic later on, these acquisitions profoundly changed the social structure which made up Assyria's strength; the army of mercenaries replaced the peasant army, just when the fringe provinces (Egypt, Medea, and Babylon) were beginning to claim an autonomy perilous to the cohesion of the great state.

The empire of the Medes and Persians which inherited the Assyrian power was content at first to displace the political centre of gravity. This moved from the foothills to the highlands of Iran, while retaining political mastery over all the territory which had made up the Assyrian empire. The Persians, moreover, quickly overflowed the boundaries of the older state, and pushed forward their frontiers to the Danube in the west, and to Turan and the Indus in the east. At the date of its greatest expansion, the state spread from the Indus to the Danube, and from the Jaxartes to Cyrenaica, covering more than five million square kilometres, or barely 30 per cent less than the U.S.A. today. For the first time it incorporated two contrasting worlds under one sovereignty; the oriental, east of the Euphrates, and the Mediterranean. Egypt played only a supernumerary role in this combination. Founded in a centre of irrigated agriculture which was exceptionally fertile, and placed between the Red Sea and the Mediterranean, on the trade routes between India, Arabia, and the Mediterranean, she was able to take advantage of temporary weaknesses within the Mesopotamian states, and to extend her frontiers with Syria and even, under Thothmes III, to reach the Euphrates. But, owing to the peculiar 'off-centre' position of Egypt in the western horn of fertile lands of the Middle East, somewhat on the edge of the great continental trade routes, her expansion remained slight.

At the other extreme of this 'fertile crescent', Punjabi India developed another centre of civilisation destined to turn alternately first towards the western and then the far-eastern spheres of influence. Dominated in general by religious considerations and based on princely states or sacerdotal caste systems, the framework of the Indian states rarely attained great size under one sovereignty. Like Egypt, India was contained, in whole or in part, within the great continental empires of the Middle Ages. Nevertheless, Indian civilisation gave birth to a succession of temporary states in the world of southeast Asia and these formed fairly widespread and

STATES AND NATIONS 521

politically influential units which advanced Indian cultural and
religious trends up to the threshold of Chinese power. In the first
century A.D., the kingdom of Funan, built along the lower course of
the Mekong, became a flourishing branch of Indian culture; somewhat later, the kingdom of *Champa* held its own between the second
and the fifteenth centuries, with varying degrees of fortune, until
it yielded to the Annamites; over the same period, the kingdom
of Burma and Pegu developed, whose rulers and ways of life were
of Indian origin. This political colonisation, which recalls that of
the Mediterranean Greeks in a different form, became linked in the
first century with the creation of the kingdom of *Majapahit*, sub-
jugating Sumatra, Java, and nearly the whole of the Indonesian
archipelago. In Indo-China itself, the Indian element was, however,
submerged during the thirteenth century by the Thai invasion,
which brought political domination to the whole western area of
the peninsula, while Annamites colonised the eastern region.

A Mediterranean state is typified by two **empires**, the Greek and
the Roman.

The empire of Alexander recalled, by its form, the great oriental
states, but its structure was new and original: colonisation by city
building replaced the forcible mass movements of population of
earlier days, and such urban development greatly helped in the
mingling of the different civilisations and diffused the spirit of
hellenic culture.

For nearly a thousand years, until the coming of the Arabs,
Syria, Asia Minor, and Egypt remained part of the Mediterranean
political system; Antioch and Alexandria became far more flourishing centres of Greek culture than Corinth or Athens; and even
after the political break-up, all parts of the region long retained a
deep cultural identity, both social and economic, which is a characteristic of Mediterranean empires.

The Roman empire brought together in one great political synthesis all the distinctive attributes which had sustained the old
oriental empire states, coupled with the dynamic civilising influence
which had ensured political sovereignty to the Greek empire. Italy
occupied a central position in the world which was to become the
empire; and she brought with her not only numerous economic
advantages but also an already dense population. Above all, from
the time of her conquest of Sicily and the elimination of Carthage,
she held undisputed sway over Mediterranean sea routes.

Within two and a half centuries, Rome had subjugated the Mediterranean world with an army made up of 'free-citizen' farmers and
through the building of cities and of strategic roads across her
dominions, she not only symbolised the unifying vocation of the
Roman empire but stamped her political dominion upon the whole

Mediterranean basin. Only slightly less vast than Alexander's empire, Rome, at the height of her power, spread over five million square kilometres; in Gaul, Great Britain, and Germania, she went beyond the geographical limits of the Mediterranean world. The germs of dissolution were similar to those which had earlier destroyed the Persian state ; the shift of power from the centre to the provinces on the periphery; the rapid disappearance of the citizen-soldiers and their replacement, in control of the army, by mercenaries or by newly created citizens coming from the outlying areas. Thus the political strength and cohesion of the empire was sapped, even before inroads were made by the people living outside the 'Roman World'.

American States in the pre-Columbian Period.—These old empires, whose technical development was in no way related to their huge size, may be regarded as abortive prototypes of the great modern states and as linking up with the pre-Columbian states of the New World. There existed indeed, in the two Americas, several highly organised states in the midst of more rudimentary political forms, which showed some likeness to those of the Old World in antiquity.

The highlands of the tropical zone were their cradle ; climate was favourable owing to the altitude, and a moderate vegetative cover was easily subdued by agriculture. In this framework the Aztec empire rose and flourished from Mexico to the Tehuantepec isthmus, and that of the Incas in the Peruvian Andes. Possessing an essentially military and theocratic structure, they typified an early very rigid kind of social and political life. Possibly, too, for the first time on earth, they evolved a form of totalitarian state in which the individual was wholly sacrificed to the social body. He was merely a cog in the wheel, and his right to life was measured by the contribution he could make to the organic, functional life of the community. This perfect type of state communism, including in its orbit whole peoples of differing race and language, made lasting political groupings which were nevertheless founded on a very narrow basis both geographically and economically.

The great pre-Columbian states were provided with a redoubtable military machine and a network of fortresses perfectly adapted to shield the vast conglomeration of cells which made up the empire. These units were disciplined and upheld by a class structure reminiscent of the hive or the ant hill ; a network of wide roads, like those built by the Romans, symbolises for us the coordinating vocation of the Inca state, so too does their adoption of Quechua as the official language through the entire territory. The rigid, monolithic structure of these states, however, gave them a deceptive appearance of strength and cohesion ; no cultural unity, no national tradition or spiritual energy issued from it, and the moral strength which welds together great civilising communities was wholly absent. It is possible that the internal cohesion of such massive units would never have been threatened had they only been capable of withstanding outside pressure, or had they known how to link up with other civilisations. They perished for lack of any evolutionary principle, which alone could have injected new life into a decrepit and outmoded structure while there was still time.

Medieval Empires of the Old World.—After the great empires of antiquity, we see in the Old World a new type of state, arising in the main from important migratory movements among peoples settling in the newly unified territories. The history of these states varied widely between Europe and Asia.

In Europe, several insecure ephemeral kingdoms arose, such as those of the Visigoths who moved from France (Toulouse) into Spain, and the Ostrogoths who came down towards Italy from the Danubian area. These states were unable either to evolve or to secure a firm base upon which to build. The same was true of the Burgundian and of the Anglo-Saxon kingdoms, each one of these states drawing upon the vestigial remains of Roman administration in the civil and ecclesiastical fields. They made up so many parasite cells which were incapable of either absorbing or of organising their only viable economic support, the native population, through lack of an adequate army. Such states only achieved stability on the furthest fringe of the old Mediterranean empires.

All the Germanic powers founded in the Mediterranean sphere at the time of the great invasions disappeared like so many artificial limbs grafted on to an ageing body incapable of integrating them, and in due course they were destroyed, so were those states set up in the Holy Land at a later date by the Crusaders. Asia, on the other hand, saw the rise of two more durable powers, as though the tradition of great states had been preserved among them through the long survival of the 'Romanitas' of Byzantium. Behind the Byzantine frontiers, indeed, the Moslem world succeeded in rebuilding an oriental conception of the state, which diffused the Islamic spirit from the Malay archipelago to central Africa, and from the Indian Ocean to central Asia. This new political structure, whose foundations are still with us, was held together by a religious ethos, and owed its rapid spread to a powerful fanatical force. The cradle of Islam was the ancient land of Arabia, where the dynamic cell of Medina quickly triumphed over the exhausted Mecca. From this point, the Arabs surged in two directions, embracing the trading system of the eastern Mediterranean; one tentacle reached out towards Persia, Mesopotamia, and Syria, the other towards North Africa, Spain, and southern France.

This conquest was pioneered by Bedouin, but the empire really took shape when the ancient cities were reoccupied, and when settled military depots appeared. Agriculture was also put in hand once more, and irrigation developed, which gave new impetus to trade relations and navigation.

Altogether, the *Khalif* state followed the ancient pattern of empire, and in particular that of Persia and Macedonia, but it contributed, nevertheless, a new political factor. Its strength was drawn from its physical situation on the borders of the steppes and a Mediterranean coastline fringing the desert. From this circumstance, the nomadic peoples who had constantly attacked and harassed the empires of antiquity, now found themselves the natural supporters and spreaders of the Arab state, earliest synthesis of two hostile and disparate human groups. This integration was nevertheless fragile, and the vast Arab empire was subject to the same crumbling on its periphery which had undermined its predecessors. Localised dynasties (Edrisites in Morocco, Aglabites in Tunisia and Tripolitania, Tulunides in Egypt and western Arabia, Tahirides and Sassanides in Persia) detached the fringe provinces, and in time the political centre moved from Damascus to Baghdad.

Outside the Khalif empire, Islam originated a multiplicity of temporary states in Africa and Asia. Along with religious faith, it had disseminated the principles of a feudal structure and a type of city life built on trade and craft industries. Many Sudanese states came into being in Ghana, Mossi, and Mandingo, in Bornu and Kanem, Baghirmi and Wadai, Darfur, Ashanti, Dahomey, and Benin. In Asia, the creation of Sultanates went on long after the disappearance of the Baghdad Khalifate. Such were the sultanates of Macassar and Gowa (Sulawesi) (which spread over Lombok, Sumbawa, and Flores) and Ternate and Tidore, during the sixteenth and seventeenth centuries.

The Baghdad Khalifate succumbed to the attacks of Mongols, who achieved the last great political structure of a continental type in the Ancient World. Its disappearance gave place to the Turkish empire, in western Asia, which finally embraced all the new young nations which arose from Islam, or from the ruins of the Byzantine empire. As with the Mongol power, however, it was a system of political expediency resting on military control, taking root neither in the soil nor among peoples who were brought temporarily together and exploited by their conquerors, without a thought for the economic good or the principles of civilisation.

The Turks became merely administrators of tribal life, without seeking to impose their own religious beliefs. They allowed provincial idiosyncrasies and nonconformism to be perpetuated, and in less than five centuries this toleration undermined and destroyed their empire.

Political evolution in Europe, apart from the Mediterranean areas, was very different. Here, upon the ruins of the Roman empire, the rebuilding of states proceeded swiftly on a national basis, offering a cultural and psychological heritage on traditional soil, together with a whole system of economic interests. In spite of its peninsular character and clearly drawn frontiers, Italy remained for a long time fragmented. The northern areas became part of the Germanic empire, whereas the south was in the hands of Byzantium; for many centuries Italy continued to be a pawn of power politics outside Rome and the peninsula.

Spain also was still partly under the influence of Islam, though secluded mountain regions like the Asturias, Navarre, Aragon, Castile, and Leon, provided bases for small Christian states. It took them several centuries to drive back the Moors and achieve political unity in the peninsula, although the division was perpetuated between Portugal and Spain, as indeed it is today.

It was in France that the building of a national state proceeded in the swiftest and most orderly way. Contrary to the case of other barbarian foundations, the Frankish state always preserved strong ties with its place of origin; the Pepin dynasty itself stemmed from the regions of the Meuse, round Heristal. In addition, the Franks had kept close links with the Gallic Roman culture and the urban economy of the Roman world. Their political expansion, far from being the result of crude military raids, had been carefully prepared beforehand, by the building up of individual units in Gaul and by Merovingian settlement. This also explains the swift conversion of the Franks to Christianity, which brought together the conquerors and the conquered. It was possible early to discern the marks of the novel social evolution in the Frankish state. At the start of the Merovingian power, government was assured by a class of peasant freemen; under the Carolingians, the ruling class developed into a temporal or spiritual aristocracy, which had also the character of a landowning middle class. During the slow evolution of the Franks, a rift early became apparent, between the re-romanised area of Neustria and Burgundy on the one side, and those parts which remained germanised, Austrasia, on the other. This racial division emerged in political matters, which swiftly took control of boundary-making in these districts, whereas in the eastern region, ephemeral groups of states rose and fell. A political variant was being strengthened in the west, preparing to set apart France, Germany, and Italy for the future rôles they were to play. Between these powers, too, buffer states were lodged temporarily (e.g. the kingdoms of Burgundy and Arles) at periods when differences in national characteristics became acute.

To sum up, political geography needs to be studied in the light of history. We only gain an over-simplified abstract view by comparing a state to a living organism which is born, exists, and dies, and has imperative needs to satisfy. Conditions of life in great states vary according to the material and moral levels of humanity, and the general organisation of our planet at a given time. It is the *whole* of humanity which is comparable to one living creature; states are only temporary instruments, which change with changing circumstances, whose function is sometimes to ensure the safeguarding of a common inheritance, sometimes to assist the spread of material or spiritual advantages which are destined to enrich this inheritance.

THE MODERN STATE

In the political and economic complexity of our modern world, we find a climate already entirely different from that which prevailed in antiquity, and in the Middle Ages; new states have other needs and the means of satisfying them are not always those which succeeded in times past.

Some modern states include whole continental blocks under one sovereignty, embracing great spaces within their frontiers, together with all the resources necessary for great nations; this is the case with China, U.S.A. and the U.S.S.R.

China began to build a strongly unified state in the third century B.C. when the Han emperors had brought under their control the regions of Hoang-Ho, the Yang-tse-kiang, and the Su-Kiang, thus associating crops of temperate agriculture (wheat) with the tropical products (rice, silk, sugar). All round primitive China, whose frontiers were defined by the Great Wall, the Chinese people multiplied, and the continual increase in their population demanded ever more land to cultivate. This was easily acquired on the fringe areas of the central Asiatic steppes, out of which the Chinese dug their fields, piece by piece, particularly in Inner Mongolia and Manchuria. Over 55 million Chinese immigrants have settled in the plains of Manchuria during the last forty-five years. Threatened several times by disruption, like the huge empires of Western Asia, China has managed to preserve the whole extent of her territory (nearly ten million square kilometres) under one sovereignty to the present day.

The life of this state presents an extraordinary phenomenon. It spreads over temperate and tropical regions, wet and very dry; it includes plateaux of the steppes, wide river valleys, which indeed form internal marshy deltas, and wooded hills. It embraces many peoples of yellow races who speak such different languages that from one province to another they cannot understand each other. The

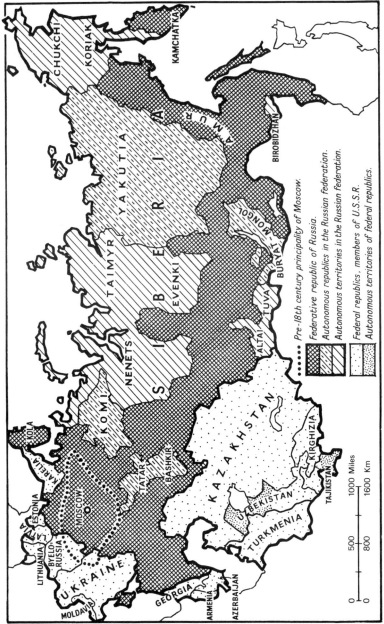

FIG. 24.—POLITICAL DIVISIONS OF THE U.S.S.R.

.... Pre-18th century principality of Moscow.

Federative republic of Russia.

Autonomous republics in the Russian federation.

Autonomous territories in the Russian federation.

Federal republics, members of U.S.S.R.

Autonomous territories of federal republics.

Chinese state is based essentially upon the idea of cultural unity. It has remained up to the present day a vast rural community of toiling peasants with the same way of life, the same desires and traditions. Chinese writing, moreover, symbolising as it does objects and not words, has helped these yellow peoples to exchange the deepest, most subtle ideas in writing, and to read the same books, whilst unable to understand each other's speech.

This amazing cohesion was strengthened in 1949 by the rise of the Communist party to power, whose dream was to create a totalitarian China, in which every activity could be directed and controlled by the central power. To execute this programme, the party's first concern was to acquire those great industries by which the country may turn out the machinery and other manufactured products that she needs, and provide work for a great labour force. China already draws very large amounts of agricultural produce from her huge territory. She is the world's largest producer of rice, and the second or third largest producer of wheat, yet these crops barely suffice to feed her 825 million inhabitants. As well as a high production of cotton and silk, China owns some of the elements necessary to big industry, in particular, her coal deposits, which supplied 400 million tonnes in 1974, and in the same year, 50 million tonnes of crude oil.

The Soviet Union, created from a number of little principalities in the forest zone of central Russia, has become in our time an immense continental state, spreading from the Baltic to the Pacific Ocean, from the Black Sea to the Arctic. It covers nearly 22 million sq. km. of which, however, 15 million are made up of tundras and forests. It contains 250 million inhabitants of all races, at every stage of civilisation, speaking over 120 officially recognised languages. Russians make up only 58 per cent of the population. Politically, the U.S.S.R. is a federation of more or less autonomous republics, in which the different peoples are free to retain their own languages, way of life, and traditions. The link uniting them, is the representative of the 'national' Communist party, which heads each local government, and is a member of the Moscow central body.

Since 1925 the U.S.S.R. has taken in hand the reconnaissance and exploitation of its vast continental territory; in Siberia and central Asia have been found suitable soil for growing cereals and cotton, steppes for breeding cattle, and deposits of gold, iron, coal, and oil. The U.S.S.R. is by far the largest producer of wheat in the world; it leads the production of sugar beet; it rivals the United States in coal production and ferrous metallurgy, and takes third place for aluminium, and a leading place for petroleum. Thus endowed the Soviet Union has resources which would enable her, if she so wished, to live apart from other nations. She does in fact keep her trade exchanges to a minimum, consuming her own wheat, which had been the chief export under the Czars, and manufacturing cloth from her own cotton or flax. For long an importer of manufactured goods, today she has achieved a powerful metallurgical industry. She can supply her own needs for tractors, railway rolling stock, cars, and planes, and has scarcely yet begun to find foreign market outlets. We notice, too, that the U.S.S.R. relies less upon her economic power to improve her international trade, than to further the expansion of her political systems.

The setting up of Communist governments under the name of 'people's republics' in East Germany, Poland, Czechoslovakia, Hungary, Bulgaria, Roumania, and later in China, has facilitated trade exchanges with these countries where Russia may get coal (Poland), petrol (Roumania and Hungary), and manufactured products (Czechoslovakia); others are good customers for steel and tractors (China). If Russia had been able to bring China into a closer federation of Communist states, we should have witnessed the creation of the greatest and most powerful continental state known to history. The example of Yugoslavia, however, has shown that a state may adopt the Communist ethos while declining to become absorbed into the U.S.S.R. economic sphere. Between Russia and her satellites, economic ties have been loosened during the last few years. China is pressing towards her industrial target, and her first objective is to outstrip Russia in every field of industrial production. During the last twenty years she has become a formidable rival to the Soviet Union, both economically in the Asiatic market, and ideologically, not only in Asiatic countries like North Korea, Cambodia, and Vietnam, but also in Indian Ocean lands such as Yemen, Tanzania, and Mozambique and in other recently-formed African states, of which 25 out of 47 have set up a communist régime that has attached itself, economically and ideologically, to China rather than to the Soviet Union. In this way China may be limiting the politico-ideological expansion of the Soviet world.

Another example of a great federation is furnished by the United States. In 1790, they extended between the Appalachians and the Ohio, and gradually spread to the Mississippi (1790–1820), and from thence to the Pacific (1830–90). This increase was brought about by the creation of thirty-five new states, each delimited by geometrical boundaries; seven of them were carved out of lands taken from Mexico.

Fixed at forty-eight states until 1945, the federation was later enriched by the addition of Hawaii and Alaska. Thus the Union occupies 9,300,000 square kilometres, of which 7,835,000 belong to

Fig. 25.—Territorial Expansion of the United States of America.
1. The thirteen colonies (1783). **2.** Expansion up to 1820. **3.** Expansion from 1820 to 1860. **4.** Expansion from 1860 to 1890. **5.** Expansion after 1890 **6.** Former Mexican frontier. **7.** Present Mexican frontier. W=Washington.

one territorial block. To exploit this vast dominion, the U.S.A. can call upon a population of 210 million, who belong racially to the most developed countries of Europe. Arriving in great numbers between 1880 and 1914, these immigrants cleared steppes and forest, prospected for inexhaustible mineral deposits, and set up the most powerful factory plant in the world. Thanks to this feverish activity, the United States today ranks as the top producer of nearly every world commodity. Coal, iron, steel, oil, copper and lesser metals, cotton, and cereals abound, as well as huge quantities of meat and dairy products, sugar, and fruit of all kinds. These resources have long permitted the United States to be self-reliant without a thought of economising wealth. Up to 1890, the U.S.A. took little notice of world affairs, and only saw to it that European powers were prevented from acquiring further colonies or from extending their possessions on the continent.

In the last fifty years, however, the United States has become a great manufacturing power and has been on the look-out for customers. They have also needed to look outside their own country, for certain raw materials like rubber and tin. These needs have prompted the wish to cultivate trade relations with the far more densely populated countries of the Far East, and even more so with the Southern American states which are industrially weak but whose standard of life and buying potential are higher than in China.

This policy has created a desire to achieve good trading positions on the sea routes to South America. The U.S.A. purchased from Denmark islands which the Danes had owned in the Antilles; and their greatest achievement was the building of the Panama Canal, on land conceded to them by the Republic of Panama. This canal has made it possible for them to capture most of the trade previously carried on by Great Britain with Colombia, Ecuador, Peru, and Chile. Trade between the U.S.A. and the South American states has increased fivefold during the last twenty years, and American financiers have invested large amounts of capital in plantations, mines, factories, and railways. United States airlines today weave a dense network of communications all round South America, and North American universities attract numbers of students from Brazil, Venezuela, and Chile.

The United States has more than once suggested the merging of all nations of the New World into one great economic federation. This would create a vast Pan-American union, constituting a viable autonomous world in which the South, essentially tropical and pastoral, would complement the temperate, industrialised North in a satisfactory way.

Alongside—or perhaps opposite to—these essentially continental giants there were created, during the late nineteenth and the first half of the twentieth century, great political associations of states, of which the most important, and the most typical, were the British Commonwealth, and later the French *Communauté*; these replaced with modernised political structures the former colonial empires of the western European nations. Until the end of the nineteenth century, the colonial possessions (with their home countries) accounted for 57 million square kilometres, or 42 per cent of the earth's surface. They contained over 850 million people, or 39 per cent of the world's total.

These dominions differed from the great continental states in that they included lands of every size, scattered over five continents and sometimes placed at the maximum distance possible from the mother country (e.g. New Caledonia and New Zealand). These possessions were divided into two categories:

1. Those settled by white peoples of European origin, wholly as in Canada and Australia, or very largely as in South Africa and Algeria. These were termed 'settler's colonies'.

2. Those with indigenous peoples who were very often coloured folk, amongst whom the white people were a minority, (e.g. India, the East Indies). These were termed 'colonies for exploitation'.

Among these colonial possessions, the ones owned by Great

Britain, France, and the Netherlands were the largest, the most highly populated, and the richest. They had many points in common; first, that their extent and the number of their inhabitants greatly exceeded that of the ruling power; secondly, that they were made up of scattered territories, though the French empire was mainly in Africa whilst the Dutch colonies were principally in Asia; finally, that their cohesion was ensured by commercial links both by sea and by air with the metropolitan territory.

These empires have become disrupted, many of their territories having attained sovereignty and others constituting associated territories of the parent state. This evolution was the inevitable result of the efforts of the colonisers themselves, whose self-appointed task was the raising of indigenous peoples to the level of their own civilisation. The territories peopled with whites, particularly numerous in the British Empire, were placed on an equal footing with the mother country by attaining dominion status. Such were Canada, South Africa, Australia, and Southern Rhodesia. Subsequently India and other former colonies, such as Ghana and Nigeria in Africa, have gained independence.

The Commonwealth which has evolved from these transformations embraced at that time territories of the widest diversity imaginable; arctic lands and tropical virgin forests, cornlands and ricelands, wool-producing and cotton-producing regions. To connect them, maritime routes were established, demarcated by strategic island positions where telegraph cables converged, bunker-coal was stock-piled, and vast tanks later erected for fuel-oil.

Politically these territories were divided into the five former dominions which had become sovereign states, autonomous states such as Ceylon or the Federation of Malaysia, and Colonies, which remained provisionally under British administration. The sovereigns of the United Kingdom, who had relinquished the title of 'Emperor of India', were not recognised as king (or queen) in all the countries of the Commonwealth, which formed, nevertheless, a free association of sovereign states. Sometimes in London, sometimes in another large city of the Commonwealth, there took place periodically a conference at which the Prime Minister of one of the associated states presided and the problems connected with the preservation and the defence of the common heritage were studied.

Gradually, however, during the last 25 years, the political links between these diverse associated countries have loosened and finally broken; following India, Pakistan, and Burma, the peninsular and island territories of south-east Asia, and tropical African lands on both sides of the equator—like Ghana, Nigeria, Kenya and Tanzania —have acquired total political independence and have become members in their own right of the United Nations Organisation.

Since 1958 the old *Union française* has become a *Communauté* comparable to the British Commonwealth. Even before the second world war the French Empire contained several protectorates, that is native states that had retained their own rulers, assisted by a French Resident, and the essence of their own administrative system. Such were Morocco, Algeria, Tunisia, Annam, Cambodia, and Laos. These protectorates graduated very easily to independence, while conserving their economic and cultural links with the former controlling power. Other territories had developed a variety of status: some achieved a considerable measure of autonomy, others were already virtually independent, like the Malagasy Republic, Togo, Dahomey, Cameroon, Senegal, Ivory Coast and other territories of west and central Africa that were once French colonies; these last had been given the status of French overseas *départements*, the inhabitants having the same rights and the same form of administration as those of metropolitan France. Some, like the Antilles islanders, indeed, were proud to proclaim that they were 'French before the Corsicans, the Savoyards, and the inhabitants of Nice'!

Under these various forms of relationship, the state had freely chosen to form part of the French *Communauté*—with one exception, Guinea, which opted for complete separation and independence. The President of the French Republic was at the same time President of the *Communauté*, with a permanent elected Council located in the old metropolis, and a Congress, consisting of the prime ministers of the various states or their deputies, rather like the British Commonwealth Conference, which met in one of the various state capitals. Here also, however, the ties have slackened, and now all the states of the former *Communauté* have become politically independent, the most recent being the Comoro Islands. The only territories remaining politically united with France are those with overseas *département* status, such as Guadeloupe, Martinique, French Guiana, and Réunion.

The break-up of the old empires was made more inevitable by the fact that in their international relations the democracies of western Europe had always favoured the principle of the freedom of peoples to decide for themselves whether to accept tutelage under one of the Great Powers or to reject it. The desire for emancipation and autonomy had itself developed as a result of the material and cultural progress of the former colonies. But there often remain, between the new sovereign states and the metropolitan country, many material, spiritual, and moral links; frequently, indeed, the élite from which the rulers of the new states have been drawn, has lived for long periods in the metropolitan country and has been trained in its schools and universities. It may be noted also that most of the new

African states have retained the language of their former colonial rulers for administrative purposes or even as their 'national' language; thus English is used in Nigeria, Ghana, and several East African states, French in Senegal, Mali, Ivory Coast, Cameroon, Upper Volta and the states of central Africa (Gabon, Congo, Central African Republic)—together with the three North African states (Morocco, Algeria and Tunisia) in which French is still the language of government. Furthermore, all these states have preserved the administrative structures and the essence of the legal system implanted by the colonial power; they have retained the old regional divisions, and usually also the international frontiers that the diplomats of the various colonial powers had established amongst themselves years ago as the limits of their respective spheres of influence.

At the beginning of the twentieth century there were 58 sovereign states in the world, of which 25 were in Europe. After the first world war the number had risen to 66 (32 in Europe), an increase due to the collapse of the Turkish and Austro-Hungarian Empires and alterations to the eastern frontier of Germany and the western frontier of Russia. In 1975, there were 153 sovereign states in the world, a great increase resulting from the successive waves of de-colonisation—British, French, Dutch, Portuguese—the last in the line being Angola, that ceased to be a Portuguese colony in 1975. Thus 23 new states have appeared in Asia and 44 in Africa.

This multiplication of states, arising from the principle of self-determination, is quite contradictory to the modern tendency for the creation of economic empires that require a reduction of national individuality and a closer solidarity between nations, with the consequent voluntary restriction of sovereign rights. Rather than a proliferation of small independent states, what is now advocated is the economic and political integration of vast areas, comparable with the United States, the Soviet Union, and China. Already, there have been efforts amongst the Asiatic and African states to create politico-economic federations or *ententes*, though most of them have had but a short life (e.g. between Mali and the United Arab Republic). The new states, lacking political and diplomatic traditions, are tending rather to seek cultural and economic links with the great industrial powers of the northern hemisphere, on whom they are dependent for technical aid and equipment, and also financial assistance for the construction of the public works that are required for the development of their territories, and military aid to protect their frontiers and their independence. The type of relationship chosen usually depends on the political régime and form of government that the new states have adopted: thus, of the 47 new African states, six have a political régime modelled on that of the free democratic countries of the northern hemisphere, 25 have adopted, under the title of 'people's democracy', a one-party régime resembling those of Cuba, the Soviet Union and China (and similar régimes are installed in Asia in the Democratic Republic of Yemen, in Vietnam, in North Korea, and in the Khmer Republic that was formerly Cambodia); whilst 16 are military dictatorships, sympathetic to either China or the Soviet Union. Over the world as a whole, most of the new states are oriented towards one or other of the West, China and the Soviet Union.

The sphere of economic expansion of the great modern states extends far beyond their political dependencies, whatever their character. In our own time, indeed, economic interests together with social problems dominate the whole political life of the states. Furthermore, it is no longer necessary to annex territories in order to extract their wealth, since economic expansion procures as many advantages as does political conquest. This expansion is facilitated by a tendency common to all great modern industrial enterprises to extend a monopoly over certain manufactures whilst continuing to control the basic materials, the means of production, and the markets. Thus are created the trusts and the cartels which concentrate in their hands the control and the capital that are often superior to those of the state. Thus, one of the world's largest trusts, the United States Steel Corporation, combines all the means of production of steel; the coal mines, the iron mines, coking plants, blast furnaces, rolling mills, manufacture of pipes, together with railways, canals, and ports. It extracts 46 per cent of the iron-ore, manufactures 38 per cent of the cast iron, and 40 per cent of the steel of the United States. One finds other big trusts in all economic spheres. The oil companies, for example, the Royal Dutch Shell (Anglo-Dutch) and the Standard Oil (American), possess oil wells in all regions of the world, with a network of pipelines and fleets of oil tankers. In the world production of petroleum, the American groups have a 70 per cent share and the British and Anglo-Dutch companies an 18 per cent share. Ford's, the car manufacturing company, owns factories in numerous countries beyond the United States, together with rubber plantations in South America and West Africa. The United Fruit Company has plantations of pineapple, citrus fruit, and bananas in Peru, Ecuador, the West Indies, and Venezuela, and through its fleet of ships and its telegraph lines it dominates the whole of Central America.

There is today no part of the world which is not within reach of a nation's commercial enterprises ; the manufacturing countries which are provided with materials and capital have all the facilities for constructing factories, ports, and railways on the territory of less well-equipped regions, and everywhere they can manufacture and sell their products under advantageous conditions. Thus the Standard Oil Company has installed several large oil refineries in France, whilst the Ford Company has constructed car factories on the out-skirts of London and Paris.

Until the first world war, the great powers used to compete for the construction of railways in Turkey (England, Germany, and France), in China (Japan, England, France, and the United States), and in Manchuria (Russia and Japan). Nowadays, it is the great banks of the United States who finance the air companies of the South American States.

All these enterprises have contributed towards linking the interests of the various countries. Instead of competition there has often been collaboration between them in the exploiting of certain resources and they are now so interdependent that a war is more ruinous to the victor than the vanquished.

However, at the present time the pooling of resources does not extend to the entire world. It is restricted to the formation of a

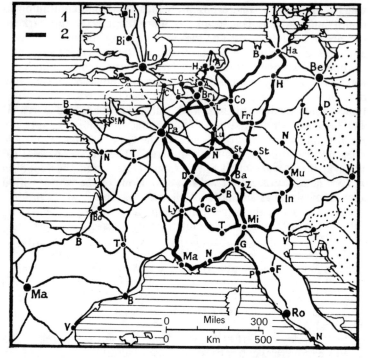

FIG. 26.—PRINCIPAL RAILWAYS OF WESTERN EUROPE.
1. Main lines. 2. Routes of T.E.E. (Trans-European Express).

limited number of economic blocs, more or less endowed with political powers within a certain international domain. That of Western Europe is in the process of being organised through the drawing up of regional pacts like that of Benelux, which links Belgium, the Netherlands, and Luxembourg, through the formation of such groups as, for example, O.E.E.C. (Organisation for European Economic Cooperation), E.C.S.C. (European Coal and Steel Community), Euratom, for the common study and exploitation of nuclear energy. The six countries of Europe which were the original members of E.C.S.C. (Italy, France, Germany, Luxembourg, Belgium, and the Netherlands) have sought to extend economic collaboration beyond the metal industries, to transport and general trade, through the medium of a Common Market; this would gradually do away with customs barriers and other restrictive legislation that exists between them at present. In 1973, this 'Europe of the Six' became 'Europe of the Nine' by the inclusion of the United Kingdom, Denmark, and Eire.

In our time international economic collaboration extends more widely still in other spheres. Thus, for the development and operation of railroads, the International Railway Union groups together forty-eight railway systems belonging to thirty-seven different countries in Europe, Asia, and North Africa. The T.E.E. (Trans-European Express) organises the rapid transit of express trains across the frontiers of eight different countries, from Oslo in the north to Genoa and Rome in the south. International collaboration extends further still in the air, in which the International Air Traffic Association and the International Organisation of Civil Aviation have their essential rulings accepted by sixty-four countries.

Numerous other international organisations, some of them developed since the second world war, because of the multiplication of sovereign states, extend their activities over the whole world. Such are:

(a) The World Meteorological Organisation (W.M.O.) with its headquarters at Geneva; it disseminates meteorological information throughout the world, much of it now obtained from satellites.

(b) The Universal Postal Union (U.P.U.), located at Berne, controls international postal rates throughout the world; it celebrated its centenary in 1974.

(c) The Food and Agricultural Organisation (F.A.O.), with headquarters in Rome, is directed towards the better world distribution of food products, particularly to the benefit of the overpopulated and under-developed countries that form the Third World.

(*d*) U.N.E.S.C.O., that facilitates cultural exchanges of all kinds between the various nations.

(*e*) O.E.C.D. (Organisation for Economic Cooperation and Development), located in Paris, studies, for the benefit of all countries, the incidence of politico-economic phenomena, with a view to preventing crises of overproduction or scarcity that result in under-consumption and unemployment.

(*f*) The International Monetary Fund (I.M.F.), also located in Paris, that upholds rates of exchange and offers financial aid to states whose economy is temporarily or seriously out of balance.

The same fostering of economic collaboration is found between the Soviet Union and other socialist countries, notably those of eastern Europe, and a politico-economic organisation—COMECON —exists, comparable with the Common Market in the west; its headquarters is in Moscow.

Elsewhere in the world, groupings to foster economic solidarity have been created on a regional basis between neighbouring states, with the object of integrating the economic resources and coordinating trade over wider areas. Such is the Organisation of Central American States, designed to encourage reciprocal exchanges and prevent undue competition between the members in the sale of their exportable produce on the international market. In Africa, an Equatorial African Customs Union links Gabon, the Central African Republic, and Chad in a kind of common market covering territories totalling 2½ million square kilometres, with a population of 5 million consumers.

All these groupings linking states of greater or lesser extent are a response to the need to reduce the hindrance of frontiers and the crumbling of economies that results from the proliferation of national territories. And as for the great international organisations, they are a response to the profound feelings of human solidarity on a planet, the resources of which are not all renewable after exploitation.

All told, there are now more than 60 'world' organisations, apart from those of military character; 44 are based in Europe, and 35 of these in western Europe, where the most important centres are Geneva, Paris, Brussels, London, Rome, Strasbourg, and Luxembourg. The organisations within the Soviet bloc are located in Moscow, Warsaw, Prague, and Budapest. Another eight have their centres in America, mostly in Washington and Montreal; and the remainder are based in Asia.

All these international organisations display at an economic level the efforts for coordination which are being expressed elsewhere on a political plane by U.N.O. (United Nations Organisation), an effort being made towards a supranational parliament which sits in New

York and intervenes to settle differences between nations in such a way as to avoid wars, or at least to localise the conflicts and reduce their duration by imposing a cease-fire followed by negotiations.

At present time 143 states are members of the U.N.O.; 29 are European, 35 Asian, 48 African, 29 American, and four from Oceania.

Whilst economists and statesmen alike seem to emphasise that countries adhering to such agreements may well lose at least part of their sovereign rights, no fears are expressed that such limitations could undermine the independence or autonomy of the various countries, or impair their national unity. A British geographer has indeed remarked with humour that towns can have the same system of lighting, the same means of transport, and analogous statistical services, but it does not follow that their inhabitants must wear the same clothes, eat the same food, and enjoy the same entertainments.

CHAPTER 19

CONCLUSION: THE EARTH AND HUMAN ENVIRONMENTS

SPACE AND HUMAN POTENTIAL

In 1975 there were at least 3,860 million people on the earth, belonging to 153 independent states, each controlling its own future. Setting aside Antarctica (an area of 13,320,000 square kilometres), where a few hundred men live temporarily and under entirely artificial conditions in stations equipped with all the latest appliances for survival and for the observation of meteorological, seismological, geomagnetic, and astronomical phenomena, this population is spread over about 135,300,000 square kilometres, of which about 130 million are part of continental land-masses and 5 million made up of islands and archipelagoes.

Contrary to popular belief, the human race really takes up only a very small part of the earth. This was first noted by the French geographer Elisée Reclus, in his book *L'homme et la terre*. He estimated that in 1905, if one were to allow each individual, from the newborn to the most aged, one square metre of space, the entire human race could be encompassed within the limits of the London Police District—roughly equal to a circle with a radius of 23 kilometres, centred on Charing Cross, and a circumference passing through Cheshunt, Romford, Dartford, Epsom, and just south of Watford; thus, 1,700 million people could have stood comfortably in an area normally inhabited by 8 million of the English. A hundred years earlier, in 1801, the 680 million inhabitants of the world would have filled, on the same basis, a circle of only 14·6 kilometres radius. At the present time, the 3,800 millions would need a circle with 35 km radius, or 12 km more than in 1905. If, however, as Reclus also suggested, the population was mustered shoulder-to-shoulder, as indeed they are frequently nowadays in city streets and squares on the occasion of political rallies, or twice a day in public transport during the rush hours, the circle around Charing Cross needed by the 1801 population would be of only 6·5 km radius, with a circumference passing through Fulham, Surrey Docks, and the southern end of Victoria Park; at the beginning of the twentieth century, the radius required would have been 10·7 km, and at the present time 15·7 km (Fig. 27). Thus for nearly two centuries the entire world

540

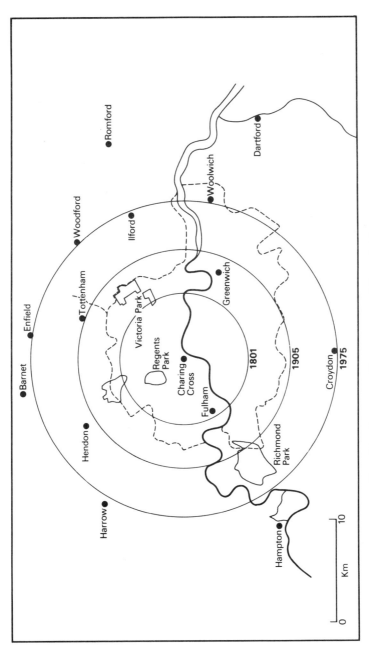

Fig. 27.—Standing Room for the World's Population.

population, which meantime has multiplied sixfold, would not have spread beyond the limits of suburban London, and the growth to 8,000 millions that some rather imprudent statisticians have forecast for the twenty-first century would only enlarge the circle to a radius of 22·5 km from Charing Cross!

Such figures make obvious nonsense, but by their very absurdity they show on the one hand the quite small importance of mankind in the mass of the biosphere, and on the other hand the enormous space requirements resulting from the proliferation of the human species. Since the days when their remote ancestors left the tropical forests for the steppes, men have always been great consumers of space, even before they started consciously to organise their geographical environment. Viewed in this light, it seems that the over-population that is feared, and that is already apparent in many parts of the world, is not so much due to the physical increase in human numbers as to the growing potential energy that they represent, which cannot be developed in too restricted a geographical space. Whilst early geographers rightly emphasised the fundamental importance of environment—mainly at first the physical environment—regional studies, gradually extended over a wide range of lands, soon showed that physically homogeneous geographic spaces could serve as the framework for very different and even opposed ways of life, and more generally for quite different types of civilisation.

Here lies the basis of the fundamental concept, developed in the preceding chapters, of a symbiosis between the natural environment and the social, political, and cultural structures of the people who have occupied it and organised it within the framework of a legal and political system. The essential problem of modern human geography is to be found in the study of the convergence of all the factors which, in one part of the world or another, have led to the creation, maintenance, and development of differentiated geographical spaces, analysing the past, the current changes and the possibilities for the future. The geographer is no longer content merely to define an environment in terms of its geographic coordinates, its physical controls, and the number and ethnicity of its people. New ideas are brought in: one is the standard of living, an essentially quantitative measurement, expressed in part by the degree to which the population can obtain adequate food and the wherewithal of domestic comfort; another is the quality of life, rather more qualitative and subjective, and expressed in terms of the conservation of a natural environment in which there can be some escape from the constraints of daily life and work and a flowering of the arts. The 'development of civilisation' would thus lie in the harmonisation of these two objectives within the spatial framework provided by the actual distribution of mankind. This requires analyses of geographic space, deeper and more numerous than those made by the regional geographers of the early twentieth century; the goal is now to determine how space is organised and what factors influenced that organisation, as well as how it is managed, that is, how and by what means the organisation is maintained or transformed; for man and his spiritual energy remain, in the last analysis, responsible for the form and appearance of geographic space.

THE UNEQUAL DYNAMISM OF HUMAN REGIONS

As a first broad generalisation, we can nowadays distinguish, on the one hand, countries that are underdeveloped or in course of development, sometimes known collectively as the 'Third World', and on the other hand, the highly developed countries. Between these two groups the standard and quality of life differ profoundly, to the detriment of the Third World. Despite liberal-minded affirmations of the unity of the human race, and notwithstanding the material and cultural assistance given by the developed countries to further the progress of the Third World, it is agreed that almost everywhere the divergence between these two sections of humanity continues to widen, and that progress towards a better quality of life only seems to benefit the developed countries; this seems to reveal an inadequacy in the analyses and a fundamental error in the conclusions, that are contrary to what was sought and hoped for.

What we have witnessed in the modern world, in fact, is the rich nations rapidly increasing their standard of living and their purchasing power, squandering both their own natural resources and those that the poorer countries sell them cheaply, so cheaply as to provide an income that is insufficient to combat the malnutrition of their people, whose standard of living, instead of gradually approaching that of the rich countries, continues to lag behind and even to deteriorate in face of the too rapid development of activity and consumption in the growth-poles and the developed countries.

These phenomena of disequilibrium are also present within the developed countries themselves, not all parts of which experience the same rhythm of growth, and some indeed suffer a decline relative to the thriving economy of the whole. Thus in Italy, which is one of the 'developed' countries, twenty economic regions are recognised, of which some have a total income less than the national average. It has been noticed that in the five years between 1965 and 1970, these less favoured regions found themselves even further depressed in relation to the others, because of the latter's more dynamic expansion, which they could not match. On a large scale, it is apparent that the countries of southern Europe as a whole have seen the gap widen between themselves and the highly developed countries of northwest Europe, though this gap should really have been progressively closing. What are the mechanisms that control these phenomena of disequilibrium that we wish to alleviate but only succeed in aggravating?

The struggle to reverse this tendency, which can only end in the accumulation of wealth in certain parts of the globe and the impoverishment or even de-population of other areas where life still goes on, albeit at a slower pace, must involve a reorganisation of geographic space and concerted action to avoid starting these apparently irreversible trends.

At first the highly developed nations undertook to assist the Third World countries through the agency of international organisations, and at the same time to re-activate the 'depressed areas' within their own territories. Within the European Community, for example, the Regional Economic Commission provided capital to improve the Italian 'Mezzogiorno', which was suffering from over-population, under-employment, and malnutrition. This assistance, however, had but a limited effectiveness, and often no useful effect at all on the dynamism and activity of the beneficiaries. The partial failure was due to many causes, some local, others more general.

In fact it is the sheer necessity of giving aid in the form of money, the only convenient vehicle of exchange that permits the purchase of goods for immediate consumption and equipment for future development, and is negotiable in the currency market, that introduces a fatal element into the aid and reciprocal exchange agreements between the givers and the beneficiaries. Though occasionally barter arrangements can be made without monetary transactions, it is certain that in the absence of an international currency of fixed value, an important part of external aid is diverted and sterilised through currency manipulations, of less and less advantage as they increase the foreign debt of the assisted country without solving its adverse trade balance.

Then, too, the structure of the Third World states is often characterised by social inequalities by which wealth and profits are concentrated in the hands of a small oligarchy, whilst the vast majority of the population exist on low incomes and constitute an enormous proletarian mass with a low standard of living. Under these circumstances, external aid merely provides more profit for the rich and hardly benefits the masses at all, who are too poor to derive real benefit from the investments and often too uneducated to fill the employment created. Thus the rich get richer and the poor get poorer, and the disequilibrium that it is desired to reduce is in fact aggravated.

The financial help designed to reduce the gap between the developed and underdeveloped countries thus only ends by enlarging further the gap that already exists within the assisted countries between rich and poor. All in all, the Third World countries get less profit from the aid than the developed countries that are providing it, because of the bankruptcy of their own social structures. This failure may result in a backlash that may actually hinder the growth of the developed countries: as a sign of the times it may be noted that today it is the rulers of the underdeveloped countries of the Middle East, source of much of the world's petroleum, who are investing their capital in the old industrial countries of Europe and even in America, for the construction of steel or chemical works or for new port developments, whilst devoting what are proportionately only insignificant amounts to the equipment of their own states. They demonstrate in this way that investments in countries that are already well developed, capable of quickly modernising their means of production, always seeking new developments, and already possessing enormous invested capital resources, are more fruitful than any that they might place in the stagnating countries, which are the very ones that must be rescued from their state of depression. In the long run, however, this search for the maximum return by the investment of capital outside, and often at the expense of, its place of origin, may, by still further widening the gulf that separates them, prove dangerous for both the underdeveloped and the rich countries that appear to be benefiting; for many examples prove that growth cannot be maintained for long if foreign investment exceeds that arising from within the country itself, the internal dynamism of which has attracted the foreign capital.

Modern analyses by numerous schools of economists, sociologists, and geographers have shed light on the complicated mechanisms that now, largely owing to the greater ease of space-relationships between human groups and geographical environments, interfere with the normal functioning of socio-economic phenomena. The organisers of this research are rendering valuable service by introducing a great number of new factors into their analyses of the spontaneous or controlled evolution of a given situation. In France, for example, some 1,600 parameters, each with ten levels of intensity, have been introduced into analyses of the environments that are present in modern industrial countries. The analysis of less complex geographic spaces would obviously need fewer parameters, but the amplitude of their reciprocal influence differentiates them, less by reason of their physical characteristics, which are relatively homogeneous, than through the incidence of human factors. Thus the attempt has been made to specify the nature and potentialities of the arctic polar regions (cf. Chapter 4). Here, the notion of 'nordicity' or 'northern-ness' is obviously dominated by cold, that appears in about half the parameters used in the analysis: latitude, level of summer warmth and winter cold, thickness and evolution of ice-cover and frozen soil, the form and significance of precipitation, etc. All these data help to define 'polar values', and to them are added other parameters defined by the nature and form of the flora and fauna, the density and arrangement of the human population, and its ethnic character. Other 'polar values' express the influence of accessibility, particu-larly the frequency of air services, and the level of economic activity, in relation especially to mineral resources and industrial possibilities. The combination of all these values makes it possible, amongst all the northern lands, to identify areas that have a 'polar value' greater than 200. On this basis, Canadian geographers have affirmed that the limits of 'nordicity' are around 50° N. latitude in eastern Canada and 55° in British Columbia. At Schefferville, in Quebec Province, the 'polar value' is 295, at Fairbanks, Alaska, it is 337, and at Keewatin (N.W.T.) 812. Outside North America, it is 737 in Spitz-bergen and 631 at Verkhoyansk in eastern Siberia. These parameters lead to the definition, in the Canadian North, of three 'northern' environments of different quality, separated not by lines but by transitional zones several dozen kilometres wide; each of these northern belts constitutes a recognisably different environment that depends not only on physical factors but also on human factors, the intensity level of which is unstable and liable to change.

Transposed into other geographical contexts, such as the semi-arid tropics, coastal zones or mountain massifs, these methods of analysis can help to explain the global distribution of human phenomena and lead to more prudent and more effective intervention in their develop-ment, within the present global framework.

THEORETICAL MODELS AND ACTUAL CASES

Confining ourselves to the rate of growth of gross income, which is a much simplified economic notion, it is possible to draw up a very rough balance sheet of the dynamism of the major groups of states or geographical regions. This single parameter gives an empirical integration of the physical and material factors, and a number of human elements, often somewhat abstract and difficult to measure, such as density of population, social structure, the general economic disequilibrium, even the geographical situation itself with regard to the main currents of trade, and so on.

This table conceals one very important fact: the unequal distri-bution of incomes within each group. Thus the relatively important growth in the Middle East is based largely on the increase in oil revenues, that are of interest to a tiny fraction only of the population; in contrast, a similar growth rate in North America affects a much larger proportion of the population of the United States and Canada. But it does bring to light another equally important fact, namely that while the average growth for the world as a whole was roughly 8·3 per cent, the countries that have had the most rapid growth are those in which the income level was already high.

Average Growth of Gross Income, Between 1965 and 1975

	%		%
Europe, North Atlantic	13·2	North America	7·3
Europe, continental and		Oceania	7·3
Mediterranean	11·5	Africa	5·4
Japan	10·8	S. and S.E. Asia	4·5
Middle East	7·6		
Latin America and			
Caribbean	7·5		

The evolution, that it would be preferable to steer in the direction of harmonisation and a régime of complementarity rather than towards a utopian unification, tends more frequently, at the present time, by reason of the insufficiency of the original analyses and unjustified extrapolations, to increase the tensions and reinforce the antagonisms that we would rather allay. Within the existing mosaic of geographic spaces, we can nevertheless distinguish several types, in which the convergence and interference of groups of parameters direct the course of the evolution. Everywhere, indeed, natural regions, economic zones, ethnic, socio-political or national groupings tend to cluster in the heart of the great geographic entities in which, on top of the internal forces and tensions, are superimposed powerful constraints coming from other humanised spaces, or simply from old socio-political or politico-economic ideologies that, with a new spiritual force, may remodel the structures and re-orient the lines of evolution hitherto followed. A careful analysis of the great groups of geographical environments will produce a patchwork of many shades.

We may distinguish in the first place the highly developed regions, corresponding to those parts of the globe that for centuries have embraced industrial capitalism, which had its origin in the mercantilist system. They combine a high standard of living and a high quality of life, shared by a large proportion of the population, with a tendency for the beneficial effects to grow and diversify. Such is the case in the continental surroundings of the North Atlantic, in which the standard of living has attained a high level, reached in several phases of vigorous growth, the main motive force of which has been the mercantile and industrial economy.

On the American side of the Atlantic, the installation of a vast array of material equipment and the huge accumulation of capital have ensured such a growth that the American dollar became an international currency, that in many and sometimes obscure ways has influenced developments the world over. The very high standard of living does not, however, prevent the existence of social inequalities within the Union, that are becoming less and less acceptable as the quality of life declines and pollution, even of rural areas, increases.

On the European side, the relative importance of the various parameters is inverted. It is not a question of a geographic space, the power and economic influence of which are of recent origin, but on the contrary a region of very old social development, that found itself until the first world war politically and economically dominant, even as North America now is. However, unlike the latter, it had undergone several centuries of consolidation. Suffering the backlash, since the second world war, of American economic expansion, capitalist Europe has sought, through energy economies and full employment, to maintain a standard of living, lower than that of America, but with less inequality between classes. The evolution of this part of the developed world is thus directed towards a better quality of life, though starting from a lower income level.

It is worth emphasising that the same objective is pursued, in a different political context and from a lower and less diversified economic base-level, by the socialist countries of central and eastern Europe. The result is a more equal distribution of incomes, and the quality of life is maintained at a higher level than would be expected from the mere rise in gross incomes.

Another type of spatial organisation is illustrated by groups of countries that have not themselves generated industrial capitalism; but the latter, through the medium of trade, sometimes reinforced by cultural contributions, has catalysed them from without. This is the case with most of the Third World countries. In most of them, decolonisation has not broken the subordination sufficiently to allow a new local dynamism to flourish, even in the cases where the political links with the old colonising power have been broken and the means of production established by foreign companies have been nationalised, the capital frozen and their foreign workers and management expelled. Everywhere there is a low standard of living, the internal inequalities in the distribution of wealth have not disappeared—quite the contrary—and indeed there has been a deterioration in the quality of life, evidenced by the unplanned growth of towns and their *bidonville* fringes, chronic unemployment, the abandonment of agricultural land and the uprooting of families.

Sometimes there is a positive balance, and certain countries, by equipping themselves, developing their exports and judiciously investing the foreign aid, have made obvious progress, without however reducing the gap, in standard and quality of life, that still separates them from the developed countries. Fashioned by industrial capitalism, they are still tributary to it. In other cases, where decolonisation, by breaking the ties with industrial capitalism, has led to a socialist structure, anxious to even out the internal economic levels, albeit at the expense of the quality of life, the standard of living remains low and rises even more slowly. Economic opinion is that these are examples of a recessive development, that is based, for better or worse, on the more or less positive balance sheet of decolonisation, and can only lag far behind the general world progress.

Other things being equal, the mode of life is a matter of choice: it conditions the quality of life and comfort within a human group or territory. Certain peoples, even today, by all accounts, are more sensitive to the constraints produced by the rise in the standard of living than to the greater enjoyment that it produces. The voluntary restriction of the growth-rate, already perceptible in the peoples' democracies of Europe, has become a veritable politico-economic doctrine in modern China and in the other socialist countries of the world that are furthest removed from industrial and mercantile capitalism.

Thus, geographical realms, physically homogeneous, have been able to effect the integration of several ecosystems, none of which, taken alone, could have led to the establishment of a stable and balanced regional unity. To at least as great an extent as the Scandinavian countries, for example, the African Sahel offers physical constraints, precise and readily characterised: it is physically wedged in between other major environments, it is arid, and has no large sources of underground water. However, within this relatively homogeneous environment, the sparse population is still fragmented and dissociated by human factors such as ethnic and cultural traditions and politico-economic organisations. The life of the region hinges between nomadism and a settled existence, each at different levels and constituting a separate ecosystem. On the one hand there is the true pastoral nomadism of the Tuaregs, characterised by far-ranging seasonal migrations, and on the other, in areas of more accidented relief, notably in the Hombori massif, the coexistence of small groups of cattle-raising nomads, with small herds and short wanderings, and cultivators, with varied but always limited resources, living in symbiosis with the pastoralists, whom they appear to dominate economically. Further afield, southwestern Gourma is the domain of the sedentary Dogons, cultivators and colonisers. This brief analysis shows that these three ecosystems, by their coexistence, define a type of spatial organisation that makes the Sahel a recognisable entity. Whilst complete agricultural settlement would be an ecologically dangerous solution, given the climatic uncertainties, the fragility of the soils and the low yields, so likewise the extension of pastoral nomadism would be fatal, for the same reasons, and would also entail de-population through the simultaneous disappearance of both the small pastoralists and the sedentary cultivators who help to support them. Many other types of geographical environments similarly lend themselves, not to a narrowly directed specialisation but to the formation of symbiotic relationships that allow a better use to be made of all the environmental advantages, and not merely of one of them, and take advantage of the resilience of human intelligence and activity.

Similar conclusions, however, can be reached in more complex cases and in more diverse environments. Historically, the geographical regions that have witnessed the greatest human accomplishments, and the greatest changes, are those that have always allowed such symbiotic relationships and have known how to vary the expression thereof during the ages. No realm shows this better than that of the Mediterranean countries of the Old World, on which climate, relief and the presence of a sea that was apt for human enterprises by its dimensions and its articulation, have at all times impressed a character, an originality, that has not however hindered the profound modifications that have taken place throughout history—modifications that are still in progress at the present time under the impact of changes in world economy, and are revealed even in the rural landscapes, that usually conserve their inherited structures most closely. Thus, in Italy, Umbria has abandoned the *coltura promiscua* that was traditional from the fifteenth century, a form of agriculture that combined, on the same plot of ground and in the hands of small peasant farmers, cereal-growing, horticulture, and aboriculture; its place has been taken by specialised monocultures extending over vast, mechanically cultivated areas, run by rich landowners who are often strangers to the area and for whom the vine is but one of a number of essentially commercial crops. At the same time, the less fertile cereal lands, increasingly abandoned since the start of the rural exodus to the north Italian industrial cities, have been taken over by sheep-rearing immigrants from Sardinia. This is a transformation of the rural landscape and of rural society, that is also found in Friuli, where the stony soils have been transformed by irrigation into vineyards, orchards and meadows for cattle grazing, and a whole army of Venetian landowners has repopulated the countryside that had been abandoned by the old peasantry, who were too poor to purchase the abandoned lands, even at a very low price, or to buy the equipment necessary for the new style of land use. The Adriatic Abruzzi, the northern Peloponnese, Thrace, and Thessaly have also seen their rural landscapes and economy transformed; their production henceforth is to be dominated by the demands of foreign markets, and particularly those of the industrial cities of northwest Europe, rather than by the physical advantages of the Mediterranean environment or the needs of the local rural and urban populations. Such a resilience, however, is only possible at present in the case of geographical regions accustomed by the vicissitudes of a long history to changes in their way of life, their economic structures, and even their political fortunes.

Here lies the explanation of the development of internal stresses within the well-developed states. Even in the countries of the North Atlantic, that are usually regarded as the opposite of the Third World, one can note the existence, in between the areas of dense population, characterised by dynamism, rich opportunities and a high standard of living, gaps where the population is sparser, where towns are decaying, and where opportunities and the standard of living are both declining. This is the opposition of the 'growth poles', active and prosperous, and the *régions déprimées* of France, the 'depressed areas' of Great Britain, or the *zone depresse* of Italy. Even within the 'growth poles' themselves, it is easy to detect a lack of complete equilibrium, for the standards of living do not always correspond to a quality of life in keeping with the economic affluence engendered by the high level of development. The distortion is most apparent in the great urban agglomerations, the rehabilitation problems of which we have discussed in Chapter 17. Thus the general opposition between the developed countries and those of the Third World does not take account of all the many evidences of ill-balance that hinder the smooth progress of human society.

Two very important results, however, can be clearly seen from these detailed analyses, the multiplication of which in the many and diverse earthly environments may one day lead to a better management of terrestrial space, just at a time when the exploitation of the seas is adding to the thousand and one spatial problems posed by the organisation of the continents.

The first is undoubtedly the preponderant role of human factors in spatial management, in the light of population growth and the very survival of the species. These factors will become more and more efficient and compelling as man's technology reduces the power and the tyranny of physical controls; man will become ever more uniquely responsible for his life and destiny.

The second is the recognition that at various times in the history of mankind, disequilibria between man and the land have been created and have grown progressively in inescapable fashion, just like those between human groups and even within such groups. These tensions, ignored, misunderstood or recognised too late, have always ended in upsets of greater or less depth and extent within the global environments, that it is now our business to understand and control.

BIBLIOGRAPHY

The literature covering the aspects of human geography considered in this book is enormous. The following bibliography is but a skeleton, covering the major recent books in English, French, and German, with a few classics of earlier date. Articles in periodicals have been almost completely excluded; but most of the books quoted have themselves extensive bibliographies.

Place of publication London unless otherwise indicated.

(Chapters 1 to 3) General Reading

BEAUJEU-GARNIER, J. *Methods and perspectives in geography.* Longman, 1976.

BROEK, J. O. M. and WEBB, J. W. *A geography of mankind.* 2nd edn. New York, McGraw-Hill, 1973.

BRUNHES, J. *La Géographie humaine.* New edn. Paris, Presses Universitaires de France, 1956.

BRYAN, P. W. *Man's adaptation of nature.* University of London Press, 1933.

CARTER, G. F. *Man and the land: a cultural geography.* 3rd edn. New York, Holt, Reinhart and Winston 1975.

DEFFONTAINES, P. *L'Homme et la forêt.* Paris, N.R.F., 1933.

DEMANGEON, A. *Problèmes de géographie humaine.* Paris, A. Colin, 1942.

DENIS, J. *Les Grands Problèmes de la géographie humaine.* Leverville, 1957.

DERRUAU, M. *Nouveau Précis de Géographie humaine.* Paris, A. Colin, 1971.

DICKINSON, R. E. and HOWARTH, O. J. R. *The making of geography.* Oxford University Press, 1933.

ELHAI, H. *Biogéographie.* Paris, A. Colin, 1968.

ERICKSTEDT, E. *Rassenkunde und Rassengeschichte der Menschheit.* Stuttgart, Enke, 1942.

FAUCHER, D. *Le Paysan et la machine.* Paris, Éditions de Minuit, 1954.

FEBVRE, L. *La Terre et l'évolution humaine.* Paris, La Renaissance du Livre, 1923.

FORDE, C. D. *Habitat, economy and society.* Methuen, 1934.

FREEMAN, T. W. *One hundred years of geography.* Duckworth, 1961.

GOUROU, P. *Pour une géographie humaine.* Paris, Flammarion, 1973.

HAGGETT, P. *Geography: a modern synthesis.* 2nd edn. Harper and Row, 1975.

HARTSHORNE, R. *The nature of geography.* New York, Association of American Geographers, 1939.

— *Perspective on the nature of geography.* Murray, 1960.

HARVEY, D. *Explanation in geography.* Arnold, 1973.

HOUSTON, J. M. *Social geography of Europe.* Duckworth, 1953.

KENDREW, W. G. *The climates of the continents.* Oxford University Press, 1961.

LEBON, J. H. G. *An introduction to human geography.* 5th edn. Hutchinson, 1963.

LOCKWOOD, J. G. *World climatology: an environmental approach.* Arnold, 1974.

NOUGIER, L. R. *Géographie humaine préhistorique.* Paris, Gallimard, 1959.

— *Les Civilisations campigniennes.* Paris, 1950.

PHLIPPONNEAU, M. *Géographie et action: Introduction à la géographie appliquée.* Paris, A. Colin, 1960.

PRENANT, M. *Géographie des animaux.* Paris, A. Colin, 1960.

RATZEL, F. *Anthropogeographie.* Stuttgart, 1899.

RIVET, P. *Les Origines de l'homme américain.* Paris, Gallimard, 1957.

RUSSELL, SIR E. J. *World population and world food supplies.* Allen & Unwin, 1954.

SEMPLE, E. *Influences of geographic environment.* Constable, 1935.

SORRE, M. *Les Fondements de la géographie humaine.* Paris, A. Colin, 1943–52. (Vol. 1, *Fondements biologiques*; Vol. 2, *Les techniques*; Vol. 3, *L'habitat.*)

— *L'Homme sur la terre.* Paris, Hachette, 1961.

SPENCER, J. E. and THOMAS, W. L. *Introducing cultural geography.* Wiley, 1973.

STAMP, L. D. *Our developing world.* Faber, 1963.

— *The geography of life and death.* Collins, 1964.

TAYLOR, G. (ed.). *Geography in the twentieth century.* 3rd edn. Methuen, 1957.

TIVY, J. *Biogeography.* Oliver and Boyd, 1971.

VALLAUX, C. *Les Sciences géographiques.* Paris, Alcan, 1923.

VIDAL DE LA BLACHE, P. *Principes de géographie humaine.* Paris, A. Colin, 1925.

WAGNER, P. *Human use of the earth.* New York, Free Press of Glencoe, 1960.

WOOLDRIDGE, S. W. and EAST, W. G. *The spirit and purpose of geography.* Hutchinson, 1951.

Climate and man. Washington, 1941. (1941 *Year-book of Agriculture.*)

PART II

(Chapters 4 and 5) Cold and Temperate Regions

ARMSTRONG, T. *Russian settlement in the North.* Cambridge Univ. Press, 1965.

BAIRD, P. D. *The polar world.* Longman, 1964.

CAMERON, I. *Antarctic: the last continent.* Cassell, 1974.

GEORGE, P. *Les Régions polaires.* Paris, A. Colin, 1946.

GOULD, L. M. *The polar regions in their relation to human affairs.* New York, American Geog. Soc., 1958.

HAMELIN, L. E. *Nordicité canadienne.* Montréal, Hurtubise, 1975.

HRDLICKA, A. *The Aleutian and Commander Islands and their inhabitants.* Philadelphia, The Wistar Institute of Biology, 1945.

KIMBLE, G. H. T. and GOOD, D. (eds.). *Geography of the Northlands.* New York, American Geog. Soc., 1955. (Spec. Publ. No. 32.)

KING, H. G. R. *The Antarctic.* Blandford Press, 1969.

KRYPTON, C. *The northern sea route and the economy of the Soviet North.* New York, A. Praeger, 1956.

PHARLAND, O. *The law of the sea and of the Arctic.* Ottawa, 1974.

ROGGE, J. (ed.). *Developing the subarctic.* Winnipeg, 1973.

ROMANOVSKY, V. *Le Spitzberg et la Sibérie du Nord.* Paris, Payot, 1943.

THIEL, E. *The Soviet Far East, a survey of its physical and economic geography.* Methuen, 1957.

WELZL, J. *La Vie des Esquimaux.* Paris, N.R.F., 1934.

*   *   *

BEAUJEU-GARNIER, J. *Les régions des Etats-Unis.* Paris, A. Colin, 1969.

HAYSTEAD, L. and FITE, G. C. *The agricultural regions of the United States.* Methuen, 1955.

HOUSTON, J. W. *The Western Mediterranean World.* Longman, 1964.

JAMES, P. E. *Latin America.* New York, The Odyssey Press, 1942.

JORRÉ, G. *The Soviet Union.* 3rd edn. Longman, 1967.

KLATZMANN, J. *La Localisation des cultures et des productions animales en France.* Paris, I.N.S.E.E., 1955.

MEYNIER, A. *Les Paysages agraires.* Paris, A. Colin, 1958.

MUTTON, A. F. A. *Central Europe; a regional and human geography.* 2nd edn. Longman, 1968.

SCHWARZ, G. *Siedlungsgeographie.* Berlin, Walter de Gruyter, 1961.

WATSON, J. W. *North America.* 2nd edn. Longman, 1968.

(Chapters 6 and 7) Warm and Dry Regions

BUCHANAN, K. *The transformation of the Chinese earth.* Bell, 1970.

CANTOR, L. *A world geography of irrigation.* 2nd edn. Oliver and Boyd, 1970.

CRESSEY, G. B. *Asia's lands and peoples.* 3rd edn. New York, McGraw-Hill, 1963.

— *Land of the 500 million, a geography of China.* New York, McGraw-Hill, 1955.

DAVEAU, S. and RIBEIRO, O. *La zone intertropicale humide.* Paris, A. Colin, 1973.

DUMONT, R. *Révolution dans les campagnes chinoises.* Paris, 1957.

DWYER, D. J. *China now.* Longman, 1975.

FARMER, B. H. *Pioneer peasant colonization in Ceylon.* Oxford University Press, 1957.

FISHER, C. A. *South-east Asia.* Methuen, 1964.

FISHER, W. B. *The Middle East.* 5th edn. Methuen, 1963.

FRYER, D. W. *Emerging southeast Asia.* Philip, 1970.

GALAIS, J. *La condition sahélienne: pasteurs et paysans du Gourma.* Paris, C.N.R.S, 1975.

GOUROU, P. *The tropical world.* 4th edn. Longman, 1966.

GRENFELL PRICE, A. *White settlers in the tropics.* New York, American Geographical Society, 1939. (Special Publ. No. 23.)

LEFÉVRE, M. A. *La Vie dans la brousse du Haut-Katanga.* Louvain, M. et L. Symons, 1955.

LE LANNOU, M. *Le Brésil.* Paris, A. Colin, 1955.

MANSHARD, W. *Tropical agriculture.* Longman, 1974.

MONTAGNE, R. *La Civilisation du désert.* Paris, Hachette, 1947.

MORGAN, W. T. W. *East Africa.* Longman, 1973.

NIR, D. *The semi-arid world: man on the fringe of the desert.* Longman, 1974.

OOI JIN BEE. *Peninsular Malaysia.* Longman, 1976.

PELZER, K. J. *Pioneer settlement in the Asiatic tropics.* New York, American Geographical Society, 1945. (Special Publ. No. 29.)

PLANHOL, X. DE and ROGNON, P. *Les zones tropicales arides et subtropicales.* Paris, A. Colin, 1970.

ROBEQUAIN, C. *Malaya, Indonesia, Borneo and the Philippines.* 2nd edn. Longman, 1958.

SPATE, O. H. K. and LEARMONTH, A. T. A. *India and Pakistan.* 3rd edn. Methuen, 1972.

STAMP, L. D. *Africa: a study in tropical development.* 3rd edn. Wiley, 1972.

WALTON, K. *The arid zones.* Hutchinson, 1969.

WHITE, G. F. (ed.). *The future of arid lands.* Washington, 1956.

(Chapter 8) Mountain Regions and the Sea

BLACHE, J. *L'Homme et la montagne*. Paris, Gallimard, 1934.

PEATTIE, R. *Mountain geography*. Cambridge, Mass., Harvard U.P.; London, O.U.P., 1936.

* * *

ALEXANDERSSON, G., and NORSTROM, G. *World Shipping*. New York, Wiley, 1963.

ARMSTRONG, T. *The Northern sea route, Soviet exploitation of the North East passage*. Cambridge Univ. Press, 1952.

BARTZ, F. *Die grossen Fischereiräume der Welt*. 2 vols. Wiesbaden, Franz Steiner, 1965.

COULL, J. R. *The fisheries of Europe*. Bell, 1972.

CUSHING, D. H. *Marine ecology and Fisheries*. Cambridge Univ. Press, 1975.

GRUVEL, J. *La Pêche dans la préhistoire, dans l'antiquité et chez les peuples primitifs*. Paris, Société d'éditions géographiques et coloniales, 1928.

HERUBEL, M. *L'Homme et la côte*. Paris, N.R.F., 1937.

HYDE, W. W. *Ancient greek mariners*. New York, 1947.

KING, C. A. M. *Introduction to marine geology and geomorphology*. Arnold, 1974.

— *Introduction to physical and biological oceanography*. Arnold, 1974.

LEGENDRE, R. *La Découverte des mers*. Paris, Presses Universitaires de France, 1948.

LORY, M. J. *L'Europe et la mer*. Bruges, 1955.

LOTURE, R. DE. *Histoire de la grande pêche à Terre-Neuve*. Paris, N.R.F., 1949.

LUARD, E. *The control of the sea-bed: a new international issue*. Heinemann, 1974.

MARGUET, C. *Petite Histoire de la navigation*. Paris, Societe d'éditions maritimes et coloniales, 1934.

MORGAN, R. *World fisheries*. Methuen, 1956.

PRESCOTT, J. R. V. *The political geography of the oceans*. Newton Abbot, David and Charles, 1975.

ROBERT-MULLER, CH. *Pêche et pêcheurs de la Bretagne atlantique*. Paris, A. Colin, 1944.

SIEWERT, W. *Der Atlantik, Geopolitik eines Weltmeeres*. Leipzig, 1940.

WATER, D. W. *The art of navigation in England in Elizabethan and early Stuart times*. Hollis & Carter, 1958.

PART III

(Chapters 9 to 13) Industry and Transport

ALLIX, A. and GIBERT, A. *Géographie des textiles.* Paris, Génin, 1956.

ASHTON, T. S. *The industrial revolution 1760–1830.* Oxford University Press, 1948.

BOESCH, H. *A Geography of World Economy.* 2nd edn. Princeton and London, Van Nostrand, 1974.

DUNHAM, A. L. *The industrial revolution in France, 1815–1848.* New York, Exposition Press, 1955.

ESTALL, R. C. and BUCHANAN, R. O. *Industrial activity and economic geography.* 3rd edn. Hutchinson, 1973.

LEFEBVRE DES NOETTES. *La Force motrice animale à travers les âges.* Paris, Berger-Levrault, 1924.

MANNERS, G. *The geography of energy.* Hutchinson, 1964.

MOUNTJOY, A. B. *Industrialisation and the developing countries.* Hutchinson, 1975.

OBST, E. *Allgemeine Wirtschafts- und Verkehrsgeographie.* Berlin, 1964.

ODELL, P. R. *An economic geography of oil.* Bell, 1963.

ROUSIERS, P. DE. *Les Grandes industries modernes.* Paris, A. Colin, 1928.

VOSKUIL, W. H. *Minerals in world industry.* New York, McGraw-Hill, 1955.

WARREN, K. *World steel: an economic geography.* Newton Abbot. David and Charles, 1975.

*   *   *

BARKER, T. C. and SAVAGE, C. I. *Economic history of transport in Britain.* Hutchinson, 1974.

BLANCHARD, M. *Géographie des chemins de fer.* Paris, Gallimard, 1942.

CAPOT-REY, R. *Géographie de la circulation sur les continents.* Paris, Gallimard, 1946.

CLOZIER, R. *Géographie de la circulation.* Paris, Génin, 1963.

COUPER, A. D. *Geography of sea transport.* Hutchinson, 1972.

DACHARRY, M. *Géographie des transports aériens.* Paris, 1959.

DEMANGEON, A. and FEBVRE, L. *Le Rhin, problèmes d'histoire et d'économie.* Paris, A. Colin, 1935.

DURAND, P. M. F. *Les Transports internationaux.* Paris, Sirey, 1956.

GREGORY, J. W. *The story of the road.* 2nd edn. Maclehose, 1938.

HILLS, T. L. *The St. Lawrence Seaway.* Methuen, 1959.

HURST, M. E. E. (ed.). *Transportation geography.* New York, McGraw Hill, 1974.

MORGAN, F. W. *Ports and harbours.* Hutchinson, 1952.
O'DELL, A. C. and RICHARDS, P. S. *Railways and geography.* 2nd edn. Hutchinson, 1971.
PEPIN, R. *Géographie de la circulation aérienne.* Paris, Gallimard, 1956.
SEALY, K. R. *The geography of air transport.* Hutchinson, 1957.
SIEGFRIED, A. *Suez and Panama.* Cape, 1940.
ULLMAN, E. *American commodity flow.* Seattle, University of Washington Press, 1957.
VIGARIÈ, A. *Les Grands Ports de commerce, de la Seine au Rhin.* Paris, S.A.B.R.I., 1963.
— *Géographie de la Circulation. La circulation maritime.* Paris, Génin, 1968.
WOLKHOWITSCH, M. *Géographie des transports.* Paris, A. Colin, 1973.

PART IV

(Chapters 14 and 15) Population studies

BEAUJEU-GARNIER, J. *Géographie de la population.* 2 vols. Paris, Librairie de Medicis, 1956–58.
— *Geography of population.* Longman, 1966.
CIPOLLA, C. M. *Economic history of world population.* 6th edn., Penguin, 1974.
CLARKE, J. I. *Population geography.* Pergamon, 1972.
COX, P. R. *Demography.* 4th edn. Cambridge Univ. Press, 1970.
DEMANGEON, A. *Problèmes de géographie humaine.* Paris, A. Colin, 1941.
HAWLEY, A. *Human ecology.* Ronald Press Co., New York, 1950.
HUBER, M., BUNLE, H. and BOVERAT, F. *La population de la France, son évolution et ses perspectives.* Paris, Hachette, 1965.
KELSALL, R. K. *Population.* Longman, 1967.
KOSINKI, L. *The population of Europe: a geographical perspective.* Longman, 1970.
— and PROTHERO, R. M. (eds.). *People on the move: studies on internal migration.* Methuen, 1975.
LEBRET, L. J., PIETTRE, A., SAUVY, A. and DELPRAT, R. *Économie et civilisation.* Paris, Les Editions ouvrières, 1956.
PARK, R. E. and BURGESS, E. W. *Human communities.* Glencoe, Illinois, 1952.
Royal Commission on population. Report. London, H.M.S.O., 1949.
SORRE, M. *Les Fondements de la géographie humaine.* Paris, A. Colin, 1943.
— *Les Migrations des peuples.* Paris, Flammarion, 1955.
THEODORSON, G. A., ed. *Studies in Human Ecology.* Evanston, 1961.

TREWARTHA, G. T. *A geography of population: world patterns.* Wiley, 1969.

VIDAL DE LABLACHE, P. *Principes de géographie humaine.* Paris, A. Colin, 1905.

WITTHAUER, K. *Die Bevolkerung der Erde.* Gotha, Hermann Haack, 1958.

(Chapters 16 and 17) Rural and Urban Economies

BERTRAND, A. L. and CORTY, F. *Rural land tenure in the United States.* Baton Rouge, 1962.

BRACEY, H. E. *English rural life.* Routledge, 1959.

— *People and the countryside.* Routledge, 1970.

CAVAILLÈS, H. 'Comment définir l'habitat rural', *Annales de géographie,* 1936.

CHISHOLM, M. *Rural settlement and land use.* Hutchinson, 1962.

CLOUT, H. *Rural geography.* Pergamon, 1972.

DAVIES, E. and REES, A. D. *Welsh rural communities.* Cardiff, University of Wales Press, 1960.

FLATRÈS, P. *Géographie rurale de quatre contrées celtiques: Islande, Galles, Cornwall et Man.* Rennes, 1957.

LEBEAU, R. *Les grands types de structures agraires dans le monde.* Paris, Masson, 1972.

LE COZ, J. *Les réformes agraires.* Paris, P.U.F., 1974.

PATMORE, J. A. *Land and leisure.* Newton Abbott, David and Charles, 1970.

REES, A. D. *Life in a Welsh countryside.* Cardiff, University of Wales Press, 1950.

SAVILLE, JOHN. *Rural depopulation in England and Wales 1851–1951.* Routledge, 1957.

SIMMONS, I. G. *Rural recreation in the industrial world.* Wiley, 1975.

WILLIAMS, W. M. *The country craftsman.* Routledge, 1958.

— *West country village: Ashworthy.* Routledge, 1963.

* * *

ASHWORTH, W. *The genesis of modern British town planning.* Routledge, 1954.

BEAUJEU-GARNIER, J. and CHABOT, G. *Urban geography.* Longman, 1967.

BERRY, B. J. L. *The human consequence of urbanisation: divergent paths in the urban experience of the Twentieth Century.* Macmillan, 1973.

— *Growth centers in the American Urban system.* 2 vols. Cambridge, Mass., Ballinger Pub. Co. (Wiley), 1974.

BONNOMME, C. *et al.* *L'Urbanisation français.* Paris, 1964.

BOURNE, L. *Urban systems: strategies for regulation.* Oxford, 1975.

BREESE, G. *Urbanisation in newly developing countries.* Englewood Cliffs, N. J., Prentice Hall, 1966.

BRIGGS, A. *Victorian cities.* Odhams Press, 1963.

CARTER, H. *The study of urban geography.* Arnold, 1972.

CHALINE, C. *L'urbanisme en Grande Bretagne*, Paris, A. Colin, 1970.

CLAWSON, M. and HALL, P. *Planning and urban growth: an Anglo-American comparison.* Baltimore, Johns Hopkins, 1973.

CORNISH, V. *The great capitals.* Methuen, 1923.

CULLINGWORTH, J. B. *Problems of an urban society.* 3 vols. Allen and Unwin, 1972–3.

DICKINSON, R. E. *City, region and regionalism.* Routledge, 1947.

— *The West European city.* Routledge, 1951.

DUNCAN, O. D., *et al.* *Metropolis and region.* Baltimore, Johns Hopkins Press, 1960.

DWYER, D. J. *People and housing in Third World cities.* Longman, 1975.

EVANS, H. (ed.). *New Towns, the British experience.* Knight, 1972.

FOLEY, D. L. *Controlling London's growth: planning the great wen,* 1940–60. Berkeley, Calif., U.P., 1963.

FREEMAN, T. W. *Geography and planning.* Hutchinson, 1958.

— *The conurbations of Great Britain.* Manchester University Press, 1959.

GLASS, D. *The town and a changing civilization.* Lane, 1935.

GOTTMANN, J. *Megalopolis: the urbanized northeastern seaboard of the United States.* New York, Twentieth Century Fund, 1961.

HALL, P. *The world cities.* Weidenfeld and Nicholson, 1966.

HERBERT, D. T. *Urban geography: a social perspective.* Newton Abbot, David and Charles, 1973.

I.G.U. *Symposium of Urban Geography.* Lund, 1960.

JOHNSON, J. H. (ed.). *Suburban growth.* Wiley, 1974.

JOHNSTON, R. J. *Urban residential patterns.* Bell, 1971.

LEIBBRAND, K. *Transportation in town planning*, Leonard Hill, 1970.

MAYER, H. M. and KOHN, C. F. (eds.). *Readings in urban geography.* University of Chicago Press, 1959.

MOINDROT C. *Villes et campagnes britanniques.* Paris, A. Colin, 1973.

MOLS, R. *Introduction à la démographie historique des villes d'Europe du 14ᵉ au 18ᵉ siècle.* Louvain, 1954–56.

MUMFORD, L. *The city in history.* Secker & Warburg, 1961.

— *The culture of cities.* Secker & Warburg, 1938.

PARK, R. E. and BURGESS, E. W. *The city.* Chicago, 1925.

PIRENNE, N. *Mediaeval cities.* New York, 1925.

QUEEN, S. A. and CARPENTER, D. B. *The American city.* New York. McGraw-Hill, 1953.

QUEEN, S. A. and THOMAS, L. P. *The city.* New York, McGraw-Hill, 1939.

RIMBERT, S. *Les paysages urbains.* Paris, A. Colin, 1973.

SANTOS, M. *Les villes du Tiers Monde.* Paris, Génin, 1971.

SELF, P. *Cities in flood.* Faber, 1961.

SJÖBERG, G. *The pre-industrial city.* New York, Free Press of Glencoe, 1960.

SMAILES, A. E. *The geography of towns.* Hutchinson, 1953.

WEST MIDLAND GROUP. *Conurbation.* Architectural Press, 1949.

WYCHERLEY, R. E. *How the Greeks built cities.* 2nd edn. Macmillan, 1962.

(Chapters 18 and 19) Political Geography and Organisation of Space

ANCEL, J. *Géographie des frontières.* Paris, Gallimard, 1936.

BLUNDEN, J., BROCK, C., EDGE, G. and HAY, A. *Regional analysis and development.* Harper and Row, 1973.

BROOKFIELD, H. C. (ed.). *The Pacific in transition.* Arnold, 1973.

— and HART, D. *Melanesia: a geographical interpretation of an island world.* Methuen, 1974.

CLAVAL, P. *Régions, nations, grands espaces.* Paris, Génin, 1968.

COHEN, S. B. *Geography and politics in a world divided.* 2nd edn. Oxford Univ. Press, 1974.

DAVEAU, S. *Les régions frontalières de la montagne jurassienne.* Lyon, 1959.

DE BLIJ, H. J. *Systematic political geography.* Wiley, 1973.

DEMANGEON, A. *Le déclin de l'Europe.* Réédition par A. Perpillou, Paris, 1975.

DION, R. *Les frontières de la France.* Paris, Hachette, 1947.

DORION, H. *La frontière Québec–Terre Neuve.* Quebec, 1963.

EAST, W. G. and MOODIE, A. E. (eds.). *The Changing World.* London, Harrap, 1956.

— and PRESCOTT, J. R. V. *Our fragmented world: introduction to political geography.* Macmillan, 1975.

GOBLET, Y. M. *Political geography and the world map.* Philip, 1955.

GOTTMANN, J. *La Politique des Etats et leur géographie.* Paris, A. Colin, 1952.

HAGGETT, J., ORD, K., BASSETT, K. and DAVIES, R. B. *Elements in spatial structure: a quantitative approach.* Cambridge, 1975.

HERMITTE, J. *Analyse, organisation et gestion de l'espace.* Nice, 1975.

HOYLE, B. S. (ed.). *Spatial aspects of development.* Wiley, 1974.

JOHNSTON, R. J. *Spatial structures; introducing the study of spatial systems in human geography.* Methuen, 1973.

KOSSMANN, E. O. *Warum ist Europa so?* Stuttgart, 1950.

LABASSE, J. *L'espace financier.* Paris, A. Colin, 1974.

LENTACKER, F., *La frontière franco-belge.* Lille, 1974.

MOODIE, A. E. *Geography behind politics.* Hutchinson, 1948.

MORRILL, R. L. *Spatial organisation of society.* 2nd edn. Duxbury, 1974.

MUIR, R. *Modern political geography.* New York, Halstead Press, 1975.

PARKER, W. H. *The super powers: the U.S. and the Soviet Union compared.* Macmillan, 1972.

POUNDS, N. J. G. *An historical and political geography of Europe.* Harrap, 1947.

RECLUS, E. *L'homme et la Terre.* Réédit. par P. Reclus Paris, 3 vols. 1930.

SPORCK, J. A. *Mélanges de géographie physique, humaine, économique et appliquée.* 2 vols. Gembloux, 1967.

INDEX

The more important references are set in bold type.